W9-BKQ-966

TWELFTH EDITION

PSYCHOLOGICAL TESTING AND ASSESSMENT

LEWIS R. AIKEN

Pepperdine University

GARY GROTH-MARNAT

Pacifica Graduate Institute
Fielding Graduate University
Private Practice

PEARSON

Boston   New York   San Francisco
Mexico City   Montreal   Toronto   London   Madrid   Munich   Paris
Hong Kong   Singapore   Tokyo   Cape Town   Sydney

Executive Editor: *Karon Bowers*
Editorial Assistant: *Deb Hanlon*
Executive Marketing Manager: *Pam Laskey*
Editorial Production Service: *Tom Conville Publishing Services, LLC*
Manufacturing Buyer: *JoAnne Sweeney*
Electronic Composition: *Omegatype Typography, Inc.*
Cover Administrator: *Kristina Mose-Libon*

For related titles and support materials, visit our online catalog at www.ablongman.com.

Between the time Web site information is gathered and then published, it is not unusual for some sites to have closed. Also, the transcription of URLs can result in typographical errors. The publisher would appreciate notification where these occur so that they can be corrected in subsequent editions.

Library of Congress Cataloging-in-Publication Data

Aiken, Lewis R.
     Psychological testing and assessment / Lewis R. Aiken, Gary Groth-Marnat. —12th ed.
          p.   cm.
     Includes bibliographical references (p.   ) and indexes.
     ISBN 0-205-45742-8
     1. Psychological tests.   I. Groth-Marnat, Gary.   II. Title.

   BF176.A48   2006
   150'.28'7—dc22

                                                                                    2005045343

Printed in the United States of America

10   9   8   7   6   15 14 13 12 11 10

Whatever exists at all exists in some amount. (Thorndike, 1918)

Anything that exists in amount can be measured. (McCall, 1939)

CONTENTS

CHAPTER FOUR

Item Analysis and Test Standardization   64

CHAPTER FIVE

Reliability and Validity   87

PART II   ASSESSMENT OF COGNITIVE ABILITIES

CHAPTER SIX

Intelligence Testing   111

CHAPTER SEVEN

Individual and Group Differences in Cognitive Abilities   146

CHAPTER EIGHT

Neuropsychological Assessment   176

CHAPTER NINE

Standardized Achievement Tests   200

CHAPTER TEN

Applications and Issues in Ability Testing   225

PART III   VOCATIONAL ASSESSMENT

CHAPTER ELEVEN

Testing Special Abilities   247

CHAPTER FIFTEEN

Observations and Interviews   349

CHAPTER SIXTEEN

Checklists and Rating Scales   372

PREFACE

Welcome to *Psychological Testing and Assessment,* Twelfth Edition. I hope you find it rewarding, engaging, and enjoyable. Lewis Aiken and I, Gary Groth-Marnat, have worked to give you an introduction to assessment that balances breadth with depth and is both accessible and scholarly. Lewis Aiken has given the field well over 30 years and eleven editions of *Psychological Testing and Assessment.* It has clearly passed the test of time and, as a result, can now be considered a classic. As a result, I was pleased to be given the offer of revising a twelfth edition. I only regret that this happened as a result of Dr. Aiken's demise in early 2004.

I look forward to carrying on Dr. Aiken's tradition. In particular, I will rely on his expertise in educational and achievement testing that he has included in previous editions. My background is somewhat different in that I was trained and have practiced and taught in the area of clinical psychology and clinical neuropsychology. This has primarily included teaching undergraduate and graduate students for the past 25 years. I have also published several graduate-level books and continuously practiced as a clinical psychologist. My clinical work has required me to use many of the tests discussed in *Psychological Testing and Assessment* to assist with client evaluation in medical, forensic, and psychological contexts. It is this combined practical and academic clinical experience that I hope I have successfully infused into this revised twelfth edition.

The major objective of the twelfth edition of *Psychological Testing and Assessment* is, as it has been since the first edition was published over 30 years ago, to improve the knowledge, understanding, and practices of persons who construct, administer, and take tests, as well as those who score and interpret the results and make decisions based on them. Like its predecessors, the twelfth edition is designed primarily as a textbook for college students. It is appropriate for a one-semester course in testing and assessment at the undergraduate or beginning graduate level in psychology, education, and related fields. The book should also serve as a useful reference and review source for psychologists and other professionals who conduct evaluations and assessments and interpret and implement the results.

The basic structure of the twelfth edition of *Psychological Testing and Assessment* is similar to that included in the previous eleven editions. Instructors who are acquainted with any of the earlier editions will find themselves in familiar territory. For convenience, the 18 chapters may be grouped into the following four parts: Introduction and Methodology of Assessment, Assessment of Cognitive Abilities, Vocational Assessment, and Assessment of Personality. The structure of the five chapters in Part One is much the same as that of earlier editions, but the material in Parts Two to Four has been rearranged. I hope this rearrangement will facilitate study and understanding of the material on cognitive abilities in section two and on personality, interests, attitudes, and related constructs in Part Four.

The educational emphasis given by Lewis Aiken in his previous editions has been maintained. However, I have tried to include and balance this with somewhat more of an applied, clinical "feel." One strategy has been the inclusion of brief psychological reports in a number of the chapters. In the process of making these reports concise, I have had to greatly simplify the cases. However, I hope I have achieved my goal of extracting those aspects of assessment that demonstrate how testing data can be used to make significant decisions related to clients. In many other sections of the book I have also tried to provide further insights into an "inside" view of how professional psychologists actually work with assessment data. In particular, this has included fairly extensive revisions to the chapters on neuropsychology, objective personality tests, and projective testing. At the same time, I have included the most relevant and up to date research on the many issues that confront the field.

An important goal has been to increase the ease with which students learn and integrate the material. This can be seen in structural changes to each chapter. They begin with a clear statement of chapter objectives. At the end of the chapters each objective is summarized. A further section, Mastering the Chapter Objectives, is included. It provides questions related to each chapter objective. Some of these emphasize rote learning (e.g., "Define what is meant by . . . "), whereas others focus on applying the information. Integration between the three sections is facilitated by maintaining numbered points. Thus number 1 in the Chapter Objectives is also number 1 in both the Summary and Mastering the Chapter Objectives sections. Finally, and in keeping with the greater emphasis on applications, each chapter has a section entitled Experiencing Psychological Assessment. This section has activities such as designing portions of a test, performing a statistical analysis, interviewing participants, or taking a psychological test. This is a reflection of my belief that students learn best when they are actively engaged with practical activities.

A further new feature has been the inclusion of Web sites embedded in the text. These can be used to increase the depth of the material. They include links providing such things as in-depth descriptions of tests, discussions of controversial issues, or new developments in the field. One warning is that these Web sites change over time. Some close down, material is deleted, or they are moved to new locations. I would estimate that as many as a quarter of the Web sites, or at least material on these Web sites, will not be able to be located a year or two after this book is published. However, with each new edition I will work on updating them.

Several notable, if not revolutionary, changes in psychological and educational testing have taken place in recent years, and they have been given adequate attention in this book. Included among these changes are revisions in the content and format of college entrance examinations, new editions of various tests, increased interest in the politics of ability testing, and computer-based assessment. Greater attention has also been given to psychometric theory, neuropsychological and developmental testing, testing on the Internet, positive psychological testing, virtual reality testing, and the use of testing in noneducational contexts such as health, medical practice, and law enforcement. This is consistent with the assumption that many students reading this book are likely to be interested in entering educational–school, industrial–organizational, clinical–counseling, or legal–forensic settings.

A Web site of study material is available for students at www.ablongman.com/aiken12e. An Instructor's Manual/Test Bank and a computerized version of the Test Bank are also available. The Test Bank portion includes several hundred multiple-choice and true/false test items. Please contact your Allyn & Bacon representative for details and to obtain these supplements. I hope these resources will be valuable supplements to the learning process.

I am grateful to the many students and colleagues who worked their way through the preceding eleven editions of this book. They provided valuable suggestions and criticisms, many of which have been incorporated. Special thanks goes to Crister Brady, who was my research assistant during the final phases of manuscript preparation. In addition, I would like to thank Karon Bowers, executive editor at Allyn and Bacon, and her assistants, Lara Torsky and Deborah Hanlon. They were superb at answering my many questions and otherwise facilitating production. They also arranged for and supplied me with helpful reviews of both the eleventh edition and drafts of selected chapters of the twelfth edition. My thanks to Dr. Jacqueline Cuevas, Midwestern State University, and to Jacqueline Remondet Wall, University of Indianapolis, reviewers who made many helpful comments.

Finally, I would like to thank the copy editor, William O. Thomas, for his tireless efforts and expertise. I sincerely hope that the results of those efforts are revealed in the finished product.

Gary Groth-Marnat
Hollister Ranch, Gaviota, California

CHAPTER ONE

HISTORICAL AND PROFESSIONAL MATTERS

CHAPTER OBJECTIVES

1. Describe the contributions made by the early founders of testing.
2. Describe sources of information about psychological tests.
3. Explain the major ways tests can be classified.
4. Describe the possible uses of tests.
5. Explain and describe the qualifications of test users.
6. Describe the ethical guidelines for using tests.

Anyone who has enrolled in an educational institution, joined a military organization, or applied for a job during the past several decades has probably taken one or more psychological tests. Testing and other psychological assessment procedures have important influences on the lives and careers of people throughout the world. The materials used in such assessments may include not only published and unpublished tests, but also questionnaires, inventories, rating scales, checklists, and projective techniques.

Whenever information is needed to help make decisions about people or to assist them in making choices pertaining to their future educational, occupational, or other status, some form of psychological assessment instrument may be used (available online at www.psychologymatters.org/testing.html). Such instruments are used extensively in schools, clinics, business and industry, and the civil and military services. They are administered for diagnostic evaluation, selection, placement, and promotion purposes. In addition to their applications in practical decision making, tests are used extensively in research.

Considering its many functions, it is not surprising that psychological testing has become a big business. According to the Association of American Publishers, in 2003 the total sales figure in the United States for standardized tests administered in grades K–12 alone was an estimated $234.1 million, a figure that increases around 7% each year. Professional organizations such as those in Appendix C specialize in the publication and distribution of tests and other psychometric instruments for assessing the abilities, personality, interests, and other characteristics of individuals of all ages and in various circumstances. The organizations in Appendix D are concerned with the appropriate use of tests for various applied and research purposes.

Psychological testing and assessment will be introduced by discussing its history, the use of assessment by the profession of psychology, and the ethical standards that users and developers of tests must adhere to. Understanding these crucial areas will provide a good grounding to enable students to explore additional areas in the field.

HISTORICAL OVERVIEW

The fact that people differ in cognitive abilities, perceptual–motor skills, and personality and that these differences can be evaluated in some way has been recognized since the dawn of human history. Plato and Aristotle wrote about individual differences in abilities and temperament nearly 2,500 years ago, but even these sages were preceded by the system of examinations practiced in ancient China (Bowman, 1989; Doyle, 1974). As early as the 2200 B.C., a civil-service examination system was instituted by the Chinese emperor to determine if government officials were fit to perform their duties. This system, in which officials were examined every 3 years for their proficiency in music, archery, horsemanship, writing, arithmetic, and public and private rites and ceremonies, was continued by later Chinese rulers to include knowledge of civil law, military affairs, agriculture, revenue, geography, composition, and poetry (Green, 1991). These were oral rather than written examinations, in which not only the answers given by examinees, but also the manner in which they were given, were evaluated. During the 19th century, the British, French, and German governments patterned their civil service examinations after the early Chinese system.

Concern with individuality, at least from a scientific viewpoint, was almost nonexistent in Europe during the Middle Ages. In the social structure of medieval European society, the activities of people were determined in large measure by the social class into which they were born. Little freedom was permitted for individual expression or development. By the 16th century, however, European society had become more progressive and less doctrinaire; the idea that people are unique and entitled to assert their natural gifts and improve their position in life was growing. This Renaissance era and the subsequent period of Enlightenment represented not only a reawakening and fostering of interest in learning and creativity, but also a rebirth of individualism. The spirit of individual freedom and worth, which flourished with the political and economic stimulation provided by capitalism and democracy, found expression in art, science, philosophy, and government. Not until the late 19th century, however, did the scientific study of individual differences in abilities and personality based on a scientific approach begin.

Mental Measurement in the 19th Century

Scientists during the early 19th century generally viewed individual differences in sensori-motor and mental abilities as a nuisance or source of error more than anything else. Before the invention of precise, automatic instruments for measuring and recording physical events, the accuracy of scientific measurements of time, distance, and other physical variables depended to a great extent on the perceptual and motoric abilities of human observers. Most of these observers were highly trained and very careful in making such measurements, but those made by different people and by the same person on different occasions still varied appreciably. Because the search for general laws of nature is difficult when measurements of natural phenomena are imprecise and unreliable, physical scientists directed their attention to the construction of instruments that would be more accurate and consistent than unaided human observation.

The growth of interest in the study of individual differences during the latter part of the 19th century was stimulated by the writings of the naturalist Charles Darwin on the origin of species and the emergence of scientific psychology. Darwin was an Englishman, but the science of psychology was formally begun in Germany during the late 19th century, where Gustav Fechner, Wilhelm Wundt, Hermann Ebbinghaus, and other researchers demonstrated that psychological phenomena could be described in quantitative, rational terms.

Events occurring in France and the United States were also important to the growth of scientific psychology and psychological testing in particular. The research of French psychiatrists and psychologists on mental disorders influenced the development of clinical assessment techniques and tests. Furthermore, the increased attention given to written examinations in U.S. schools resulted in the development of standardized measures of scholastic achievement.

Many psychologists in Europe and North America played significant roles in the pioneering phase of mental measurement. Especially important during the late 1800s were Francis Galton, J. McKeen Cattell, and Alfred Binet. Francis Galton (Figure 1.1), a cousin of Charles Darwin, was an English gentleman who became interested in the hereditary basis of intelligence and the measurement of human abilities. Galton was particularly concerned with investigating the inheritance of genius, and for this and other purposes he devised a number of tests and other procedures for measuring individual differences in abilities and temperament. Using a set of fairly simple tests, Galton made measurements on over 9,000 people who ranged in age from 5 to 80 years. Among Galton's many methodological contributions was the technique of *co-relations,* which has continued to be a popular technique for analyzing test scores.

James McKeen Cattell was an American who, after earning a doctorate in experimental psychology from a German university, stopped over in England and became acquainted with Galton's methods and tests. Later, at Columbia University, Cattell tried relating scores on these measures of reaction time and sensory discrimination to school marks. The relationships, or correlations, between performance on the tests and scholastic achievement were found by Clark Wissler (1901) and other researchers to be very low. It remained for a French psychologist, Alfred Binet, to construct the first mental test that made a significant contribution to the prediction of scholastic achievement.

FIGURE 1.1   Francis Galton. The designated
"father of individual psychology," Galton
pioneered the study of intelligence and its origins.

Testing in the Early 20th Century

In 1904 the minister of public instruction in Paris, France, commissioned Alfred Binet
(Figure 1.2) and his associate Theodore Simon to develop a procedure for identifying chil-
dren who could not benefit sufficiently from instruction in regular school classrooms (see
Binet's original early article at psychclassics.yorku.ca/Binet/binet1.htm). For this purpose,
Binet and Simon constructed an individually administered test consisting of 30 problems
arranged in order of ascending difficulty. The problems on this first practical *intelligence
test,* which was published in 1905, emphasized the ability to judge, understand, and reason.
A revision of the test, containing a large number of subtests grouped by age levels from 3
to 13 years, was published in 1908. In scoring the 1908 revision of the Binet–Simon Intelligence Scale, the concept of *mental age* was introduced as a way of quantifying a person's
overall performance on the test. A further revision of the Binet–Simon scale, published after
Binet's death in 1911, extended the test to the adult level.

Among other pioneers in psychological testing and assessment were Charles Spearman in test theory, Edward Thorndike in achievement testing, Lewis Terman in intelligence
testing, Robert Woodworth and Hermann Rorschach in personality testing, and E. K.
Strong, Jr., in interest measurement. The work of Arthur Otis on group-administered tests
of intelligence led directly to the construction of the Army Examinations Alpha and Beta by
a committee of psychologists during World War I. Each of these tests, the Army Alpha for
literates and the Army Beta for illiterates, was administered on a group basis to measure the
mental abilities of thousands of U.S. soldiers during and after the war.

FIGURE 1.2 Alfred Binet. With Theodore Simon, in 1905 Binet constructed the first practical intelligence test.

(Reprinted by permission of Culver Pictures, Inc.)

Current Developments

Many individuals have contributed to the theory and practice of psychological and educational testing since World War I. The names of some of these people are listed in Table 1.1 and are still to be found in the titles of tests and in references to techniques, procedures, and other developments to which they contributed. One major development has been innovative methods of test development. In particular, *item-response theory* (IRT) has allowed test developers to understand the relation between responses to individual items and anticipated levels of difficulty based on test theory (see detailed description in Chapter 4). Much of this and other techniques have been dependent on computers. Computer technology has also enabled ease of scoring, innovative means of presentation, online assessment, and narrative interpretations of the meanings of individual scores (*computer-based test interpretation*).

Other major issues have been multiple challenges directed at testing. Legal challenges have resulted in legislation on tests for such purposes as employment, graduation, and use with various ethnic groups. Part of this has been fueled by the accountability movement in education, as well as the civil rights movement in the 1960s. There has also been widespread public criticism of testing, such as Hoffman's (1962) *The Tyranny of Testing*. Test developers as well as practitioners have responded to these challenges by extensive research on such areas as test bias, development of culture-fair tests, legal defenses, and the development of ethical and practice guidelines.

TABLE 1.1   Selected Events in the History of Psychological and Educational Assessment

1845	Printed examinations first used by Boston School Committee under the guidance of the educator Horace Mann.
1864	George Fisher, an English schoolmaster, constructs a series of scales consisting of sample questions and answers as guides for evaluating students' answers to essay test questions.
1869	Scientific study of individual differences begins with the publication of Francis Galton's *Classification of Men According to Their Natural Gifts.*
1882	Emil Kraepelin uses word-association techniques to study schizophrenia.
1884	Francis Galton opens the Anthropometric Laboratory for International Health Exhibition in London.
1888	J. M. Cattell opens a testing laboratory at the University of Pennsylvania.
1893	Joseph Jastrow displays sensorimotor tests at the Columbian Exhibition in Chicago.
1897	J. M. Rice publishes his research findings on the spelling abilities of U.S. schoolchildren.
1904	Charles Spearman describes his two-factor theory of mental abilities. First major textbook on educational measurement, E. L. Thorndike's *Introduction to the Theory of Mental and Social Measurement,* published.
1905	First edition of Binet–Simon Intelligence Scale published.
1908	Revision of Binet–Simon Intelligence Scale published.
1908–1909	Objective arithmetic tests published by J. C. Stone and S. A. Courtis.
1910	Carl Jung develops standardized list of word-association stimuli and collects associated norms for analyzing mental complexes.
1908–1914	E. L. Thorndike develops standardized tests of arithmetic, handwriting, language, and spelling, including the *Scale for Handwriting of Children* (1910).
1914	Arthur Otis develops the first group test of intelligence, based on Terman's Stanford Revision of the Binet–Simon Scales.
1916	Stanford–Binet Intelligence Scale published by Lewis Terman.
1917	Army Examinations Alpha and Beta, the first group intelligence tests, constructed and administered to U.S. Army recruits.
1921	Herman Rorschach publishes *Psychodiagnostik.*
1926	Scholastic Aptitude Test (SAT) first used to screen applicants for admission to college.
1927	First edition of Strong Vocational Interest Blank for Men published. Kuhlmann–Anderson Intelligence Tests first published.
1936	Graduate Record Examinations (GRE) first used to screen applicants for admission to graduate school.
1937	Revision of Stanford–Binet Intelligence Scale published.
1938	Henry Murray publishes *Explorations in Personality.* O. K. Buros publishes first *Mental Measurements Yearbook.*
1939	Wechsler–Bellevue Intelligence Scale published.
1942	Minnesota Multiphasic Personality Inventory published.
1949	Wechsler Intelligence Scale for Children published.

TABLE 1.1   Continued

1960	Form L–M of Stanford–Binet Intelligence Scale published.
1970	Increasing use of computers in designing, administering, scoring, analyzing, and interpreting tests.
1971	Federal court decision requiring tests used for personnel selection purposes to be job related (*Griggs* v. *Duke Power*).
1980–2002	Development of item-response theory.
1981	Wechsler Adult Intelligence Scale-Revised published.
1985	Standards for Educational and Psychological Testing published.
1989	MMPI-2 published. Wechsler Preschool and Primary Scale of Intelligence-Revised published.
1990	Wechsler Intelligence Scale for Children-III published.
1997	Third edition of the Wechsler Adult Intelligence Scale (WAIS-III) published.
1999	Revision of *Standards for Educational and Psychological Testing* published.
2003	American Psychological Association puts revision of *Ethical Principles of Psychologists and Code of Conduct* into effect; *Fifteenth Mental Measurements Yearbook published*, fourth edition of the Wechsler Intelligence Scale for Children (WISC-IV) published.
2005	New SAT administered for the first time.

TESTING AS A PROFESSION

The field of psychological testing has grown rapidly since the 1920s, and thousands of tests are now commercially produced and distributed. After World War II, standardized testing spread throughout the world. Many American- and British-made tests of ability and personality were translated from English into other languages. In addition to published standardized tests, hundreds of unpublished test materials became available. These tests, which are cited in professional journals and books, have been used in countries throughout the world.

Sources of Information

Information concerning psychological tests and other assessment instruments can be found at the Web sites and in the catalogs of companies that distribute tests (see Appendixes C and D). Various strategies for using this information can be found through the following American Psychological Association Web site: www.apa.org/science/faq-findtests.html. Many of the companies that distribute tests also publish multiple testing catalogs. For example, The Psychological Corporation has separate catalogs in the areas of Psychological Assessment Intervention Products, Speech & Language Assessment and Essential Resources, Therapy Skill Builders and Products, and Human Resource Assessment. Pro.ed has separate catalogs for: Psychological Products; Special Education, Rehabilitation,

Gifted & Developmental Disorders; Early Childhood; and Speech, Language, & Hearing. More details concerning specific tests are given in the manuals accompanying the tests.

Two important reference sources that provide descriptive information on thousands of commercially available tests are *Tests in Print VI* (Murphy, Plake, Impara, & Spies, 2002) and *Tests-Fifth Edition* (Maddox, 2003). Another important source is *The Fifteenth Mental Measurements Yearbook* (Plake, Impara, & Spies, 2003) and previous editions. The 15 editions of the *Mental Measurements Yearbook* contain descriptions and reviews of tests. Test reviews are also given in the 11 volumes of *Test Critiques* (Keyser & Sweetland, 1984–2003) and online at Web site www.unl.edu/buros. Also available at the same Web site is a computer search engine for locating information on over 4,000 commercially available tests.

In addition to standardized tests, many questionnaires and rating scales are administered in applied psychology contexts (see Aiken, 1996, 1997). *Measures for Clinical Practice: A Sourcebook* (3rd ed.) (Corcoran & Fischer, 2000) contains descriptive information on dozens of instruments of this kind that are used in clinical and counseling situations.

Details on unpublished tests and scales may also be found in the *Directory of Unpublished Experimental Mental Measures* (Goldman, Mitchell, & Egelson, 1997, and earlier volumes), *A Consumer's Guide to Tests in Print* (Hammill, Brown, & Bryant, 1992), and *Index to Tests Used in Educational Dissertations* (Fabiano, 1989). For information on unpublished measures of attitudes, the series of volumes produced at the University of Michigan's Institute for Social Research (Robinson, Shaver, & Wrightsman, 1991, 1999, and earlier volumes) is recommended. The HAPI (*Health and Psychosocial Instruments*) database, which contains descriptions of over 15,000 psychometric instruments, is available at many college libraries. Other useful databases for information on unpublished scales and other psychometric instruments are PsycINFO and PsycLIT, which are accessible in many libraries or at Web site www.apa.org.

Reviews of selected tests are published in a number of professional journals, for example, the *American Educational Research Journal, Journal of Educational Measurement, Measurement and Evaluation in Counseling and Development, Personnel Psychology,* and *Psychoeducational Assessment.* Articles on the development and evaluation of psychological tests and measures are included in professional journals such as those listed in Table 1.2. Citations of sources of information on specific tests may also be found in *Psychological Ab-*

TABLE 1.2   Representative Journals Publishing Articles on Psychological and Educational Tests

Advances in Personality Assessment	*Journal of Learning Disabilities*
Applied Neuropsychology Assessment	*Journal of Personality Assessment*
Applied Psychological Measurement	*Journal of Psychoeducational Assessment*
Educational and Psychological Measurement	*Journal of School Psychology*
European Journal of Psychological Assessment	*Journal of Vocational Behavior*
Journal of Clinical Psychology	*Psychological Assessment*
Journal of Counseling Psychology	*Psychology in the Schools*

stracts, Education Index, and *Current Index to Journals in Education.* Entire books have been written on single tests, such as the Minnesota Multiphasic Personality Inventory (MMPI), the Rorschach Inkblot Test, and the Wechsler intelligence scales.

Test Classification

As is true of other professions, psychological testing has its own special vocabulary. The glossary at the back of this book contains definitions of dozens of psychometric terms, many of which refer to types of tests or methods of classifying tests. Tests may be classified according to their content, how they were constructed, what they were designed to measure or be used for, and even how they are administered, scored, and interpreted. One simple way of classifying tests is by the dichotomy *standardized* versus *nonstandardized.* A *standardized test* is constructed by professional test makers and administered to a representative sample of people from the population for which the test is intended. It has fixed procedures for administration and scoring that are constant across examinees, thus providing all examinees with an equal opportunity to respond to the questions or items according to their abilities or inclinations.

Standardized tests usually have *norms.* These consist of various types of converted scores computed from the raw scores obtained by a *test standardization group,* a sample of people like those for whom the test is intended. Norms serve as a basis for interpreting the scores of people who subsequently take the test. Even more common than published standardized tests are nonstandardized classroom tests that are typically constructed in an informal manner by teachers.

Another way of classifying tests is *individual* versus *group.* An *individual test,* such as the Wechsler Intelligence Scale for Children, is administered to one examinee at a time. A *group test,* such as the Cognitive Abilities Test, can be administered simultaneously to many examinees.

Whereas the dichotomy individual versus group is related to the efficiency of administration, the dichotomy *speed* versus *power* pertains to the time limits of a test. A pure *speed test* consists of many easy items, but the time limits are very strict and almost no one finishes in the allotted time. The time limits on a *power test* are ample for most examinees, but it contains more difficult items than those found on a speed test.

A third test classification dichotomy, *objective* versus *nonobjective,* is concerned with the method of scoring. An *objective test* has fixed, precise scoring standards and can be scored by a clerk. On the other hand, scoring essay tests and certain types of personality tests is very subjective, and different scorers may obtain different results.

Tests may also be classified according to the kind of material or the type of task presented to examinees. Some tests contain only *verbal* or *language* items (e.g., vocabulary, reading passages), whereas other tests consist of diagrams, puzzles, or other *nonverbal* or *nonlanguage* materials. The distinction between verbal and nonverbal tests also pertains to the form of response required. Tests that require oral or written responses are often referred to as *verbal* tests, whereas those that require examinees to point to the correct answers, construct something, or otherwise manipulate the test materials (putting puzzles together, placing blocks into holes, etc.) are called *nonverbal* tests or *performance* tests.

Another broad classification of tests according to their content or process is *cognitive* versus *affective*. *Cognitive tests* attempt to quantify the processes and products of mental activity and may be classified as measures of achievement and aptitude. An *achievement test,* which assesses knowledge of some academic subject or occupation, focuses on the examinee's past behavior (what he or she has already learned or accomplished). An *aptitude test* focuses on future behavior, what a person is capable of learning with appropriate training. Thus, tests of mechanical aptitude and clerical aptitude are designed to assess the ability to profit from further training in mechanical and clerical tasks. Achievement and aptitude, however, are not separate entities; what a person has accomplished in the past (achievement) is usually a fairly good indicator of how he or she can be expected to perform in the future (aptitude). Some psychologists prefer not to use the terms *achievement* and *aptitude* as ways of classifying tests; rather, they refer to both kinds of tests as measures of ability.

Affective tests are designed to assess interests, attitudes, values, motives, symptoms, temperament traits, and other noncognitive characteristics of personality. Various techniques, such as behavioral observation, paper-and-pencil inventories, and projective pictures, have been designed for this purpose.

Certain institutions and organizations that maintain collections of psychological and educational tests have formal systems for classifying these instruments. One of the most comprehensive classification systems is that of *The Mental Measurements Yearbook.* In this system, tests are classified into the 18 broad content categories listed in Table 1.3.

Purposes and Uses of Tests

Psychological tests and other assessment instruments are administered in a wide range of settings: academic, clinical–counseling, business–industrial, criminal justice–forensic, government, and military. Personnel psychologists, clinical psychologists, counseling psychologists, social psychologists, and many other applied and research-oriented specialists in human behavior spend a substantial amount of their work time administering, scoring, and interpreting psychological tests. The Web sites of some of the more important professional organizations concerned with psychological testing and assessment are listed in Appendix D.

The main purpose of psychological testing today is the same as it was throughout the 20th century: to evaluate behavior, cognitive abilities, personality traits, and other individ-

TABLE 1.3   Categories of Tests Listed in *The Fifteenth Mental Measurements Yearbook*

Achievement	Foreign Languages	Reading
Behavior Assessment	Intelligence and General Aptitude	Science
Developmental	Mathematics	Sensory–Motor
Education	Miscellaneous	Social Studies
English and Language	Neuropsychological	Speech and Hearing
Fine Arts	Personality	Vocations

ual and group characteristics to assist in making judgments, predictions, and decisions about people. More specifically, tests are used as follows:

1. Screen applicants for jobs and educational and training programs
2. Classify and place people in educational and employment contexts
3. Counsel and guide individuals for educational, vocational, and personal counseling purposes
4. Retain or dismiss, promote, and rotate students or employees in educational and training programs and in on-the-job situations
5. Diagnose and prescribe psychological and physical treatments in clinics and hospitals
6. Evaluate cognitive, intrapersonal, and interpersonal changes due to educational, psychotherapeutic, and other behavior intervention programs
7. Conduct research on changes in behavior over time and evaluate the effectiveness of new programs or techniques

In addition to describing and analyzing individual characteristics, tests may be used to assess psychological environments, social movements, and other psychosocial events.

No one knows exactly how many of each kind of commercially and noncommercially available tests are administered and in what situations, for what purposes, and by whom they are given during a given year. A rough indication of the most frequently used tests can be found in the results of various surveys (Camara, Nathan, & Puente, 2000; Piotrowski & Keller, 1992; Watkins, Campbell, & Nieberding, 1994; Watkins, Campbell, Nieberding, & Hallmark, 1995). Understandably, the findings of these surveys depend on the kinds of practitioners and/or researchers included in and responding to the survey questions, their theoretical orientations, and the goals of the assessment process. The first two sections of Table 1.4 list the tests, in rank order, reportedly used most often by clinical psychologists and neuropsychologists who responded to the Camara et al. (2000) survey. As seen in this table and the results of other surveys of test usage, the most popular intelligence tests are those in the set of tests in the Wechsler series, and the most popular personality tests are those in the MMPI series. This pattern has remained mostly unchanged for the past 30 years.

Reporting Assessment Results

Whatever the reasons for a psychological examination, some kind of written report of the results is usually required. The outline and length of a report of a clinical case study vary with the purposes of the study and the readers for whom the report is intended, but Form 1.1 provides details on the kinds of information included in most reports. At various places throughout the text you will see examples of condensed reports. These will illustrate the manner in which assessment can be used to answer referral questions and help people make important decisions.

When preparing a formal report of a psychological examination, the writer should keep clearly in mind the referral questions or principal complaint(s) (why the person was referred for psychological assessment or sought it) and how the assessment findings bear on answers to these questions or solutions to these problems. Information on current mental

**TABLE 1.4   Tests Used Most Often by Clinical
Psychologists and Neuropsychologists**

TESTS USED BY CLINICAL PSYCHOLOGISTS[a]

1. Wechsler Adult Intelligence Scale-Revised (WAIS-R)
2. Minnesota Multiphasic Personality Inventory (MMPI) I and II
3. Wechsler Intelligence Scale for Children-Revised (WISC-R and III)
4. Rorschach Inkblot Test
5. Bender Visual Motor Gestalt Test
6. Thematic Apperception Test (TAT)
7. Wide Range Achievement Test-R & III
8. House–Tree–Person Projective Technique
9. Wechsler Memory Scale-Revised
10. Beck Depression Inventory, Millon Clinical Multiaxial Inventory

TESTS USED BY NEUROPSYCHOLOGISTS[a]

1. Minnesota Multiphasic Personality Inventory (MMPI) I and II
2. Wechsler Adult Intelligence Scale-Revised (WAIS-R)
3. Wechsler Memory Scale-Revised
4. Trail Making Test A and B
5. FAS Word Fluency Test
6. Halstead–Reitan Neuropsychological Test Battery
7. Boston Memory Test
8. Category Test
9. Wide Range Achievement Test-R & III

[a]Based on data reported by Camara, Nathan, & Puente, 2000.

status and emotional stability should also be considered, as well as the probable outcomes (prognosis) of the patient's condition. The examinee's characteristics and their interrelationships should be described as fully and as specifically as possible, avoiding vague generalizations, stereotypes, and banalities. Finally, the report should be written in a succinct, clear style that is comprehensible to the reader. A psychological report is of little value if it is not understood or not read by those who are in a position to use the information to help to make decisions bearing on the life and well-being of the examinee (see Groth-Marnat, 2003, in press; Groth-Marnat & Horvath, in press).

TESTING STANDARDS AND ETHICS

The increased use of standardized tests of all kinds has brought with it a recognition of the need for greater public awareness of the advantages and limitations of psychological and educational assessments and the motivations and practices of those who market and use

FORM 1.1 Format for a Psychological Evaluation (from Groth-Marnat, 2003)

Name _____ Birth Date _____ Education _____

Examiner_____

Date(s) of Examination _____ Referred by _____

Referral Question. Briefly describe client along with short description of the presenting problem. Specify the rationale for assessment and the specific questions that need to be answered.

Evelution Procedures. List names of tests (with abbreviations), type of interview, all persons interviewed, and any recorde reviewed (medical, educational, occupational, psychiatric, legal, etc.).

Behavioral Observations. Describe the appearance and behavior of the examinee during the examination. What behaviors on the part of the examinee were symptomatic of physical, cognitive, or affective conditions or characteristics? Describe the examinee's characteristics, his or her approach to the tasks, level of motivation, emotionality, ability to focus on the task, and any other factors that might have influenced the results of the examination. State the extent to which the results are a valid assessment.

Background Information. Describe background information relevant to the case. This should include a history of the problem (onset, duration, frequency, severity), family background, personal history (infancy, early childhood, etc.), academic history, legal problems, and occupational background. Give the examinee's own story, as well as those of other observers if available. In the case of children in particular, information on the home and family (social status, characteristics of parents, siblings, and so forth) is important.

Test Results. A simple listing of test scores. Note that this section is often ommitted.

Interpretation and Impressions. This is the main body of the report. It can be organized around many topics depending on the referral question. The most frequent topics (domains) relate to intellectual level, emotional functioning, interpersonal patterns, and client strengths. Be as specific as possible in interpreting the results, describe the person (not merely test scores), use everyday language, give examples, avoid technical jargon. All information should be carefully integrated, rather than presented test by test.

Summary and Recommendations. Briefly summarize the main conclusions. Briefly answer each referral question. This is sometimes done by numbering or bulleting the major points or answers to the referral questions. What recommendations are warranted by the assessment? These may include additional psychological assessment (be specific), neurological or other medical examinations, counseling or psychotherapy, special class placement and training, vocational rehabilitation, and institutionalization.

_____

Signature of Examiner

tests and other assessment instruments. A continuing concern of professional organizations of psychologists and educators is that commercially available tests should measure what the test authors, publishers, and distributors claim they do. Contributing to this goal is a booklet of technical standards, the *Standards for Educational and Psychological Testing* (AERA, APA, & NCME, 1999), prepared by representatives of the American Educational Research Association (AERA), the American Psychological Association (APA), and the National Council on Measurement in Education (NCME). Like its 1985 predecessor, the 1999 edition contains recommended standards for test development and applications. Criteria for evaluating tests, the practice of testing, and the effects of test usage are all dealt with in some detail.

Also concerned with the proper use of psychological and educational tests are the *Guidelines for Computer-based Tests and Interpretations* (American Psychological Association, 1986) and the *Principles for the Validation and Use of Personnel Selection Procedures* (Society for Industrial and Organizational Psychology, 2003). The latter document contains a set of principles concerned with the conducting of selection and validation research on personnel selection, principles regarding the application and use of selection procedures, detailed information for individuals who are responsible for authorizing or implementing validation efforts, and information for those who evaluate the adequacy and appropriateness of personnel selection procedures.

Qualifications of Test Users

Qualifications for administering, scoring, and interpreting tests vary to some extent with the particular type of test. Qualification standards are more stringent for users of individual tests than for group tests and for tests of intelligence and personality than for tests of achievement and special abilities.

Whoever the users may be and whatever their qualifications, ethical responsibility for ensuring that tests are sold only to qualified persons rests squarely on the shoulders of test publishers and distributors. The qualifications required to administer and interpret specific tests must be spelled out and enforced by these organizations.

Reputable commercial test publishers require test purchasers to meet certain requirements, depending on the nature of the test and/or the degree of training needed to administer it. A three-level (A, B, and C) test-user qualification policy is followed by The Psychological Corporation, American Guidance Systems (AGS), and certain other commercial organizations. AGS defines these three levels as follows:

Level A: User has completed at least one course in measurement, guidance, or an appropriate related discipline or has equivalent supervised experience in test administration and interpretation.

Level B: User has completed graduate training in measurement, guidance, individual psychological assessment, or special appraisal methods appropriate for a particular test.

Level C: User has completed a recognized graduate training program in psychology with appropriate coursework and supervised practical experience in the administration and interpretation of clinical assessment instruments.

These user qualifications are rated by test distributors to decide who they can sell their products to (for an example of such a form, look at www.agsnet.com/site7/appform.asp). Such ratings should result in users adhering to the following set of guidelines (Moreland, Eyde, Robertson, Primoff, & Most, 1995):

1. Maintain the security of testing materials before and after testing.
2. Avoid labeling individuals based on a single test score.
3. Adhere strictly to the copyright law and under no circumstances photocopy or otherwise reproduce answer forms, test books, or manuals.
4. Administer and score tests exactly as specified in the manual.
5. Release results only to authorized persons and in a form in keeping with accepted principles of test interpretation. (Moreland et al., p. 23)

More recently, a set of guidelines considered by a committee of the American Psychological Association to be important for the competent and responsible user of psychological tests has been described by Turner, DeMers, Fox, and Reed (2001). As discussed in this source, the knowledge and skills required to use tests have some cross-situational generality, but they also vary with the specific context in which testing occurs (employment, educational, career and vocational counseling, health care, forensic) as well as its purposes.

The ethical use of tests can be controlled to some extent by a code of ethics to which professional testers and publishers subscribe. The American Psychological Association (APA), the American Personnel and Guidance Association (APGA), and the National Council on Measurement in Education (NCME) have ethical codes pertaining to test administration and the provision of other psychological services. The APA, APGA, and NCME ethical codes cover many of the same matters of test administration, standardization, reliability, and validity as the *Standards for Educational and Psychological Testing* (AERA, APA, & NCME, 1999). All three codes stress the importance of considering the welfare of the examinee or client and guarding against the misuse of assessment instruments.

With respect to evaluation and diagnosis, Section 9 of the "Ethical Principles of Psychologists and Code of Conduct" (American Psychological Association, 2002), like the previous edition of the code (American Psychological Association, 1992) stresses that scientific procedures are employed in designing and selecting tests and techniques that are appropriate for specified populations; that evaluation and diagnosis should be conducted only in a professional context by trained, competent administrators of appropriate tests; that test scoring and interpretation services should be used carefully; that the results of testing and assessment should be interpreted judiciously and explained carefully by qualified persons; and that test security must be maintained at all times.

The mere existence of high-quality tests and a set of standards or principles for test publishers, test distributors, and test consumers does not guarantee that tests will be administered and interpreted properly. Responsibility for the proper use of tests rests with the test administrators and interpreters themselves, a responsibility that has been increasingly recognized by professional psychologists. Unfortunately, the skills and knowledge possessed by many counselors, clinicians, and other professionals are inadequate for administering certain tests. Therefore, psychological and educational examiners must be made aware of the limitations of their professional qualifications, the need for further training, and the necessity of obtaining assistance from other professionals and up to date sources of information. Examiners must also be able to make sound ethical judgments by being sensitive to the needs of examinees as well as those of the organizations in which they practice and of society as a whole.

Informed Consent and Confidentiality

Improper disclosure of test data, especially data identified by the name of the examinee, is a matter of continuing concern to professionals in psychological assessment. The expanding use of computers and associated data banks has increased the need for vigilance in ensuring that test scores maintained in electronic files in particular are adequately protected against improper disclosure. Except when (1) mandated by law or government regulations, (2) implied because testing is conducted as a routine educational, institutional, or organizational activity, or (3) when one purpose of the testing is to evaluate decision-making capacity (American Psychological Association, 2002), the *informed consent* of examinees or their legal representatives is required to release test results identified by the examinee's name to any other person or institution. The stipulation of informed consent implies that an individual who has agreed to have personal information released knows what the information consists of and with whom it will be shared. Details regarding the need for informed consent are presented in language that the examinee can understand and may involve the services of an interpreter.

Form 1.2 is an informed consent form that should be read and signed by the examinee or another responsible party before a psychological examination is conducted. As stated on this form, before any tests or other psychometric procedures are administered, the examinee must be told the nature and purposes of the assessment, why he or she is being tested, who will have access to the information, and how it will be used. Information regarding fees for assessment services, the limits of confidentiality, and the involvement of third parties should also be given.

In addition to the rights of informed consent and confidentiality, the least stigmatizing label should be applied in reporting the presence of certain psychological symptoms, disorders, or other conditions. For example, "mentally impaired" is clearly less personally and socially stigmatizing that "feebleminded," "idiotic," or "moronic," and "adolescent adjustment reaction" is less stigmatizing than "psychopathic personality."

From a legal standpoint, psychological test data are *privileged communications* to be shared with other people only on a need to know basis. Examinees should be told at testing time why they are being tested, who will have access to the information, and how it will be used. After being tested, examinees have a right to know the results of the assessment in language that they can easily understand. Except under unusual circumstances, as when a person is dangerous to himself or other people, test information is confidential and should not be released to third parties without the necessary informed consent. Even with informed consent, the information may be *privileged*. This means that, with the exception

FORM 1.2   Informed Consent Form for Conducting a Psychological Examination

I, _____ voluntarily give my consent to serve as a participant in a psychological examination conducted by _____. I have received a clear and complete explanation of the general nature and purpose(s) of the examination and the specific reason(s) why I am being examined and of any fees connected with the procedures. I have also been informed of the kinds of tests and other procedures to be administered and how the results will be used.

I realize that it may not be possible for the examiner to explain all aspects of the examination to me until it has been completed. I also understand that I may terminate my participation in the examination at any time without penalty. I further understand that I will be informed of the results and that they will be reported to no one else without my permission. At this time, I request that a copy of the results of this examination be sent to:

_____   _____
Signature of Examinee   Examiner Prints Name Here

_____   _____
Date   Signature of Examiner

of the examinee and, in the case of a minor or legally incompetent person, the parent(s) or guardian, only the examinee's attorney, physician, or psychologist can obtain a copy of the information.

Not only do legally responsible persons have the right of access to the findings in their own test reports, but they can also arrange for transmittal of their scores to educational, clinical, or counseling agencies for any appropriate use. At the same time, every effort should be made to maintain confidentiality of test scores and other personal information. The Family Educational Rights and Privacy Act of 1974 specifies, for example, that test results and other student records maintained by educational institutions that receive federal funds can be made available in a personally identifiable manner to other people only with the written consent of the student or his or her parents or guardian. However, this act permits parents and school personnel with a "legitimate educational interest" to review student records, as does Public Law 94-142 in the case of handicapped children.

In 1998 the Joint Committee on Testing Practices published a set of rights and responsibilities designed "to enumerate and clarify the expectations that test takers may reasonably have about the testing process, and the expectations of those who develop, administer, and use tests may have of test takers." The "rights" portion of the list is given in Table 1.5. The fundamental responsibility of test takers is to make certain that they understand the rights listed in this table and to act on this information in an appropriate manner (see rights and responsibilities of test takers at www.apa.org/science/ttrr.html).

TABLE 1.5   Rights of Test Takers

As a test taker, you have the right to:

1. Be informed of your rights and responsibilities as a test taker.
2. Be treated with courtesy, respect, and impartiality, regardless of your age, disability, ethnicity, gender, national origin, religion, sexual orientation, or other personal characteristics.
3. Be tested with measures that meet professional standards and that are appropriate, given the manner in which the test results will be used.
4. Receive a brief oral or written explanation prior to testing about the purpose(s) for testing, the kind(s) of tests to be used, if the results will be reported to you or to others, and the planned use(s) of the results. If you have a disability, you have the right to inquire and receive information about testing accommodations. If you have difficulty in comprehending the language of the test, you have a right to know in advance of testing whether any accommodations may be available to you.
5. Know in advance of testing when the test will be administered, if and when test results will be available to you, and if there is a fee for testing services that you are expected to pay.
6. Have your test administered and your test results interpreted by appropriately trained individuals who follow professional codes of ethics.
7. Know if a test is optional and learn of the consequences of taking or not taking the test, fully completing the test, or canceling the scores. You may need to ask questions to learn these consequences.
8. Receive a written or oral explanation of your test results within a reasonable amount of time after testing and in commonly understood terms.
9. Have your test results kept confidential to the extent allowed by law.
10. Present concerns about the testing process or your results and receive information about procedures that will be used to address such concerns.

(*Rights and responsibilities of test takers: Guidelines and expectations.* American Psychological Association. Copyright 2000 by the Joint Committee on Testing Practices. www.apa.org/science/ttrr.html?CFID=2655584& CFTOKEN=99958212. Reprinted with permission.)

SUMMARY

1. The roots of psychological testing and assessment can be traced to ancient Greece and China. A scientific approach began in the late 19th century with Galton and Cattell and continued into the 20th century with Binet and Simon, Rorschach, Strong, Spearman, Otis, and Murray. Psychometric instruments of various kinds were employed extensively in educational, clinical, business, government, and military situations.
2. Descriptions of tests can be obtained (usually available online) from test publishers (see Appendix A) and evaluations can be found in *The Mental Measurements Yearbook, Test Critiques,* and books such as *Measures for Clinical Practice: A Sourcebook* and in many journals on assessment.
3. The following describes the way tests can be classified:
   a. Standardized versus nonstandardized
   b. Individual versus group

      c. Speed versus power

      d. Objective versus nonobjective

      e. Verbal–language versus nonverbal–nonlanguage

      f. Cognitive–ability (achievement and aptitude) versus affective

4. Tests can be used for screening job applicants, educational (and other) classifications, counseling–growth, personnel decisions, diagnosis, evaluation for interventions, or research.

5. Test-user qualifications have been developed to ensure users have appropriate training (supervised experience, relevant coursework) and will adhere to ethical and legal codes of conduct.

6. The American Psychological Association, American Educational Research Association, American Personnel and Guidance Association, and National Council on Measurement in Education have published standards and codes of ethical and fair testing practices. These include guidelines for informed consent and confidentiality as well as test security, confidentiality, appropriate test design, scientific test selection, judicious interpretation of results, and appropriate feedback to examinees.

MASTERING THE CHAPTER OBJECTIVES

1. *Roots and history*

    a. What procedures or instruments were used in ancient times to assess the abilities and personalities of people, and how were the results of the assessments used?

    b. Identify the contributions made by each of the following men to psychological and educational assessment: Alfred Binet, J. McKeen Cattell, Francis Galton, Hermann Rorschach, Charles Spearman, Lewis Terman, Edward Thorndike, Robert Woodworth, and E. K. Strong, Jr.

    c. Consult articles or book chapters on the history of psychological and educational testing (e.g., Anastasi and Urbina, 1997; Geisinger, 2000; Groth-Marnat, 2000a; Hogan, 2003) and the Internet for detailed information (see psychclassics.yorku.ca/author.htm for full text listings of classic articles).

2. *Sources of information*

    a. A friend informs you he will be administered a psychological test. Describe how you could obtain both a description and an evaluation of the test.

    b. Select an actual psychological test (i.e., Wechsler Adult Intelligence Scale-III) and find both a description and an evaluation of it.

3. *Test classification*

    a. Using the classification test in the chapter, classify the following three tests: Scholastic Aptitude Test, Beck Depression Inventory, and the Armed Services Vocational Aptitude Battery.

    b. Consider three tests you have taken and decide which classifications best describe them.

4. *Test uses*

    a. Consider three tests you have taken and, using the information from the chapter, elaborate on their actual and potential uses.

    b. Consider the following three clients: one is being assessed due to a crime and is pleading insanity, a second wants to know the best type of psychotherapy for him- or herself, and a third is being evaluated for special education classes. Using the terms in the chapter, describe how the tests are likely to be used.

   c. Log on to the Psychology Matters Web site (www.psychologymatters.org/testing.html) (APA online) and read about ways in which psychological testing and assessment have improved our lives.

5. *Test user qualification*
   a. Develop four reasons why it's important to ensure that test users are properly qualified.
   b. You would like to purchase a copy of the Wechsler Adult Intelligence Scale-III. Describe what you would need to do to be properly qualified.

6. *Ethics*
   a. Why is it necessary to have an explicit code of ethics governing the practice of psychology in general and psychological tests in particular?
   b. If you were a professional psychologist, what things would you need to tell your client before giving them a psychological test?

EXPERIENCING PSYCHOLOGICAL ASSESSMENT

1. Examine the yellow pages of a large city telephone directory and note the types of psychological and educational testing and assessment services that are offered. You should look under various headings—psychologist, counseling, testing, examinations, for example.

2. a. Log on to Web site www.apa.org.
   b. Click on "Students."
   c. Under "Topics," click on "Testing."
   d. Explore the "Testing and Assessment" page by clicking on the various highlighted topics.

3. Consider one of the many Internet tests that offer to evaluate your IQ, personality, or level of compatibility. What ethical issues are raised by these services (think of test security, validity, informed consent, feedback, client welfare)?

CHAPTER TWO

TEST DESIGN AND CONSTRUCTION

CHAPTER OBJECTIVES

1. Describe issues to consider when planning a test.
2. Describe the types of educational objectives relevant for organizing test items (taxonomy of cognitive objectives).
3. Describe behavioral and content considerations for preparing test items (table of specifications).
4. Know the advantages and disadvantages of selected versus constructed response items and be familiar with the following types of test items: true–false, matching, multiple choice, Likert, short answer, essay, storytelling.
5. Know what to consider when assembling and reproducing a test.
6. Describe the advantages and disadvantages of oral testing.
7. Understand the strategies of performance testing.

The amount of effort involved in constructing a psychological or educational test varies with the type of test and the purposes for which it is intended. Most classroom teachers probably spend relatively little time preparing essay or short-answer tests for evaluating pupil progress in a unit of instruction. On the other hand, the tests of ability and personality designed by specialists in psychological assessment usually require the efforts of many individuals working for extended periods of time.

The procedures employed in constructing a test also vary with the type of test and the aims of the users. Preparing a paper-and-pencil inventory of interests or personality characteristics involves different problems than constructing a test of achievement or aptitude. Similarly, the complex procedures followed by professional test designers are unfamiliar to the majority of teachers. Whatever the kind of test or the goals of the users, some degree of content planning is necessary before the items comprising the test are written. Test planning should include clear definitions of the variables or constructs to be measured, descriptions of the persons to be examined, the conditions under which the test will be administered, and information concerning the scoring, interpretation of scores, and how the results will be used.

PLANNING A TEST

Constructing a test demands careful consideration of its specific purposes. Tests serve many different functions, and the construction process varies to some extent with the purpose of a test. For example, different procedures are followed in constructing tests for achievement, intelligence, special aptitude, or a personality inventory. Ideally, however, the construction of a test or other psychometric device begins by defining the variables or constructs to be measured and outlining the proposed content.

Screening Tests

Constructing an aptitude test to screen applicants for a particular job starts with a detailed analysis of the activities comprising the job. A task analysis, or *job analysis,* consists of determining the components of the job so that test situations or items can be devised to predict employee performance. These specifications may include *critical incidents*—behaviors that are critical to successful or unsuccessful performance—and other information describing job activities. Because the description of a particular job is usually long and involved, the finished test will not measure all aspects of employee performance. It will deal with only a sample of behaviors important to the job; this sample should, at best, represent all tasks comprising the job.

Intelligence Tests

Procedures employed in designing intelligence tests are described in detail in Chapter 6, so only a brief description will be given here. As in constructing any other test, a pool of items that presumably measures some aspect of the construct "intelligence" is assembled. These items may be constructed according to a specific theory of intelligent behavior or simply with reference to the kinds of tasks that highly intelligent people presumably perform more effectively than people of lower intelligence. The selection of items for the final test may be made on the basis of the relationships of item responses to criteria, such as chronological age, and the relationships among the test items themselves.

Personality Inventories and Scales

Various approaches, some based on common (or educated) sense, others on personality theories, and still others on statistical procedures, are employed in constructing personality inventories and rating scales. As described in Chapters 16 and 17, many recently published personality assessment instruments have been constructed by combining theoretical, rational, and empirical approaches. One or more of these approaches may be employed at different stages of instrument development.

Achievement Tests

More attention has been devoted to procedures for constructing tests of scholastic achievement than other kinds of tests. This is understandable when one realizes that more achievement tests are administered than all other types of tests combined. Despite the widespread use of achievement tests, most classroom teachers, who presumably are well acquainted with their subject matter, do not devote enough time to the evaluation of student achievement. Often teachers view testing as a somewhat disagreeable adjunct to instruction, rather than as an integral, formative part of the educational process. Frequent testing, however, is essential to effective instruction. Students learn and remember more when they are tested fairly often.

The results of testing are not limited to evaluating and motivating students. They also provide information to teachers, school administrators, and parents concerning the extent to which specific educational objectives have been attained. By yielding data related to the effectiveness of the school curriculum and teaching procedures, test scores can contribute to the planning of instruction for individual students or for entire classes and school districts.

Questions for Test Planners

Planners of classroom achievement tests should begin by giving careful attention to the following questions:

1. What are the topics and materials on which students are to be tested?
2. What kinds of questions should be constructed?
3. What item and test formats or layouts should be used?
4. When, where, and how should the test be administered?
5. How should the completed test papers be scored and evaluated?

Questions 1, 2, and 3 are discussed in this chapter, and questions 4 and 5 in Chapter 3.

Taxonomy of Cognitive Objectives

The preparation of a test to measure specific instructional objectives is most effective when the behaviors to be assessed are clearly defined at the outset. Since the mid-1950s, a number of formal, standard systems or taxonomies for classifying the cognitive, affective, and psychomotor objectives of instruction have been proposed. The purpose of these taxonomies is to go beyond merely constructing items for measuring simple rote memory and to devise items to assess the attainment of higher-order educational objectives that require more in-depth working with the material. Table 2.1 is an example of the possible types of learning that may be incorporated into test construction. The following items, which may be presented in either essay or objective test format, illustrate the taxonomies described in Table 2.1:

What is the formula for computing the standard error of measurement?   (*Knowledge*)

Examine the following graph and determine how many items must be added to a 50-item test to increase its reliability from .60 to .80.   (*Comprehension*)

Compute the standard error of estimate for a test having a correlation of .70 with a criterion having a standard deviation of 10.   (*Application*)

Differentiate between a classroom achievement test and a standardized achievement test in terms of what each test measures and how it is used.   (*Analysis*)

Formulate a theory relating interests to personality, and cite appropriate supporting research evidence.   (*Synthesis*)

Evaluate criticisms concerning the content and uses of the SAT.   (*Evaluation*)

Table of Specifications

Most test designers do not adhere rigidly to a formal taxonomy in specifying the objectives to be measured. Nevertheless, it is helpful in planning a test to construct a two-way table of specifications. In preparing such a table, the behavioral objectives (i.e., knowledge of terminology) to be assessed are listed as row headings and the content (topical) objectives as column headings (i.e., preparation, construction). Then the descriptions of specific items

---

TABLE 2.1   Categories from the *Taxonomy of Educational Objectives: The Cognitive Domain*

  I. *Knowledge* involves the recall of previously learned facts. Sample verbs in knowledge items are *define, identify, list,* and *name.* A sample knowledge item is "List the six major categories of *The Taxonomy of Educational Objectives: The Cognitive Domain.*"

 II. *Comprehension* means understanding the meaning or purpose of something. Sample verbs in comprehension items are *convert, explain,* and *summarize.* A sample comprehension item is "Explain what the test reviewer means when he says that the test is unreliable."

III. *Application* involves using information and ideas in specific situations. Sample verbs in application items are *compute, determine,* and *solve.* A sample application item is "Compute the mean and standard deviation of the following group of scores."

IV. *Analysis* is breaking down something to reveal its structure and the interrelationships among its parts. Sample verbs in analysis items are *analyze, differentiate,* and *relate.* A sample analysis item is "Analyze this instructional unit into its several behavioral and content categories."

 V. *Synthesis* is combining various elements or parts into a structural whole. Sample verbs in synthesis items are *design, devise, formulate,* and *plan.* A sample synthesis item is "Design a table of specifications for a test on elementary statistics."

VI. *Evaluation* is making a judgment based on reasoning. Sample verbs in evaluation items are *compare, critique, evaluate,* and *judge.* A sample evaluation item is "Evaluate the procedure used in standardizing this test."

(*Source:* From *Taxonomy of Educational Objectives: The Classification of Educational Goals: Handbook I: The Cognitive Domain* by Benjamin S. Bloom et al. Copyright © 1956, 1984 by Longman Publishing Group.)

falling under the appropriate row and column headings are written in the body (cells) of the table. Such a table (or grid) allows test designers to determine if they are assessing a sufficiently wide range of areas.

A table of specifications should be fairly detailed in terms of the knowledge and skills that examinees are expected to demonstrate, but it is important not to overemphasize a particular objective. It may be easier to construct items that assess knowledge of terms and facts than items that measure the ability to analyze and evaluate, but items in the last two categories should also be included on the test.

Table 2.2 is an example of a table of specifications relevant for the material covered in the first few chapters of this book. It relates to the test preparation, administration, and item analysis of tests. Note that the total number of items to be devoted to each topic is

TABLE 2.2 Specifications for a Test on Preparing and Administering Tests

Behavioral Objective	CONTENT (TOPIC)				
	Preparation	*Construction*	*Administration*	*Scoring*	*Item Analysis*
Knowledge of terminology	Job analysis; critical incidents; representative sample (3 items)	Matching item; spiral omnibus; response set (5 items)	Rapport; halo effect (2 items)	Strip key; composite score; machine scoring (3 items)	Criterion; internal consistency; test homogeneity (3 items)
Knowledge of specific facts	Categories in *Taxonomy of Educational Objectives* (2 items)	Advantages and disadvantages of essay items and objective items (4 items)	Factors affecting testing performance (3 items)	Rules for scoring essay and objective tests (3 items)	Methods of determining item validity; purposes of item analysis (3 items)
Comprehension	Explanation of purposes of making a test plan (2 items)	(0 items)	(0 items)	Effects of item weighting on total score (1 item)	Explanation of relationship between *p* and *D* (1 item)
Application	Specifications for a unit on testing (1 item)	Examples of multiple-choice items to measure comprehension, application, analysis, synthesis, and evaluation (4 items)	Directions for a test (2 items)	Correction for guessing; confidence weighting; use of nomograph for scoring rearrangement item (4 items)	Computation of difficulty and discrimination indexes; distribution of responses to distracters (4 items)
Total	8 items	13 items	7 items	11 items	11 items

given in parentheses below the topic. Once a set of objectives for a course or unit of instruction has been determined and a topical outline prepared, test items can be constructed to measure the extent to which students have attained the objectives listed for each topic.

Certain types of test items are more appropriate than others for measuring the attainment of specific objectives. Short-answer and completion items are suitable for assessing knowledge of terminology, but they are inadequate for assessing higher-order cognitive abilities. For this reason, the table of specifications for a test should be carefully inspected before deciding what types of items and how many of each are appropriate. Practical considerations such as cost, time available for administration, item arrangement, and testing conditions must also be considered in planning a test.

PREPARING TEST ITEMS

The primary goal of test planning is preparation of a detailed outline, such as a table of specifications, to serve as a guide in constructing items to assess or predict certain objectives. Once a table of specifications or a detailed content outline of the test has been prepared, the next step is to construct the items. For objective tests, it is generally recommended that about 20% more items than actually needed should be prepared initially so that an adequate quantity of good items will be available for the final version of the test. Commercial testing organizations such as Educational Testing Service employ as item writers persons who possess both a thorough knowledge of the subject matter of the test and skill in constructing test items. Anyone who wants to learn how to construct good test items can profit from inspecting a sample of those contained on published tests, because they are among the best available.

All test items represent procedures for obtaining information about individuals, but the amount and kinds of information vary with the nature of the tasks posed by different types of items. Asking examinees to compare the Battle of the Bulge with the Battle of Hastings requires a different kind of response than that required when students are told to indicate which of a series of listed events occurred in each battle. Complex integrating and organizing abilities are demanded by the first item, whereas only recognitive memory is needed to answer the second item.

Various methods of classifying items according to the form of the response required have been suggested. The two major categories are *selected-response format* and *constructed-response formats*. As the title indicates, a selected response format requires examinees to *select* their response from a variety of responses *that have been given*. These are also referred to as *forced-choice* formats and include multiple-choice and true–false items. In achievement tests, examinees must identify or recognize the correct answer. In personality tests, they usually answer the item according to which alternative most describes themselves. In contrast, constructed-response items require the examinee to create and organize a response (also called *free-response* items). Examples include personality tests that request the participant to tell a story for a picture or respond to an inkblot. Within classroom achievement testing, this distinction often occurs between *objective tests* (selected-response items) and *essay tests* (constructed-response items). Examples of various kinds of test items are provided in Table 2.3.

TABLE 2.3   Examples of Various Types of Test Items

I. Selected-response items
   A. *True–false*
      Directions: Circle T if the statement is true; circle F if the statement is false.
      T   F   1. The most comprehensive test classification system is that of *The Mental Measurements Yearbooks.*

   B. *Matching*
      Directions: Write the letter corresponding to the correct name in the second column in the appropriate marginal dash of the first column.
      ___ 1. individual intelligence test   A. Pearson
      ___ 2. inkblot personality test   B. Binet
      ___ 3. product–moment correlation   C. Rorschach

   C. *Multiple choice*
      Directions: Write the letter of the correct option in the marginal dash opposite the item.
      1. Jimmy, who is 8 years, 4 months old, obtains a mental age score of 9 years, 5 months. What is his ratio IQ on the test?
      (a) 88   **(c)** 113
      (b) 90   **(d)** 120

   D. *Likert format*
      Directions: Place a check by the item that most reflects your feelings.
      1. I am interested in becoming a psychologist.

      Strongly agree   Agree   Neutral   Disagree   Strongly disagree

II. Constructed-response items
   A. *Short answer*
      Directions: Write the appropriate word(s) in each blank.
      1. The only thing that is objective about an objective test is_____.

   B. *Essay*
      Directions: Write a half-page answer to the following item.
      1. Contrast the advantages and disadvantages of essay versus multiple-choice tests.

   C. *Storytelling technique*
      Directions: Look at this picture (examiner shows examinee a picture of a person playing a musical instrument) and tell me what the person is doing.

One distinction is that an *objective* item may be of either the selection or constructed type, depending on whether examinees are required to construct a response or select the best answer from a list of alternatives. The crucial feature of objective items is not the form of the response, but rather how objectively the items can be scored. Barring clerical errors, different scorers of an objective test will assign the same score to a given test paper. Scoring for a multiple-choice exam is typically objective. In contrast, scoring for an essay test is typically not objective since two or more scorers may disagree on the correctness of a given answer and how many points it should receive. If, however, an objective scoring system can be designed for an essay question, then it is possible to convert it to an objective item. This might be done, for example, by only scoring points if predesignated phrases occur in the essay responses.

Selected-Response Formats

Achievement tests typically score a response that has been given by the examinee as either right or wrong. In some cases, bonus points might be added for superior responses. This sometimes happens with individually administered intelligence tests for which a participant might be given extra points for a more rapid response. In contrast, personality tests do not have right or wrong answers. However, higher scoring might be given for particularly strong attitudes (see example of a Likert scale item in Table 2.3).

Objective items are not limited to the traditional four formats (true–false, matching, multiple choice, and Likert), but these are the most popular. One advantage claimed for objective tests is that they can be scored easily and objectively. Because each item takes less time to answer than a corresponding essay test, a broader sampling of content is permitted on an objective test. In preparing objective tests, care should be taken to make the items clear, precise, and grammatically correct. They should be written in language suitable to the reading level of the persons for whom the test is intended. All information and qualifications for selecting a reasonable answer should be included in the item, omitting nonfunctional or stereotyped words and phrases.

It is tempting to construct selected-response items by lifting statements verbatim from textbooks or other sources, but this practice emphasizes rote memory while neglecting comprehension. Item writers should also be careful not to include clues to the correct answers and to avoid interrelated or interlocking items. Two items are *interrelated* when the wording of one item provides a clue to the answer to the other item. Two items are *interlocked* when it is necessary to know the answer to one of them to get the other one right.

True–False Items.   One of the simplest types of test item to construct, but probably the most criticized by professional testers, is the true–false item. True–false items can be written and read quickly and thereby permit a broad sampling of subject content. A notorious shortcoming of true–false items is that they are often concerned with trivial information or are constructed by lifting statements verbatim from textbooks. Consequently, they are said to encourage rote memorization and thereby misdirect efforts to learn. Other criticisms of true–false items are that they are often ambiguous and cannot be used to measure more complex instructional objectives. Also, because the total score on a true–false test can be affected by the tendency of an examinee to guess when in doubt or to agree (or disagree), the accuracy of the score may be questionable.[1]

On average, examinees will get 50% of the items on a true–false test right simply by guessing. Scores may be inflated even more when items contain *specific determiners*: words such as *all, always, never,* and *only* that indicate the statement is probably false, or words such as *often, sometimes,* and *usually* that suggest the statement is true.

---

[1]The tendency to agree when in doubt (*acquiescence*) is a response set. *Response sets* are tendencies on the part of examinees to answer test items on the basis of their form, that is, on the way the items are worded, rather than on their content.

Despite these shortcomings, true–false items do not have to be trivial or ambiguous and to consequently misdirect learning. In defense of true–false items, Ebel (1979) maintained that "the extent of students' command of a particular area of knowledge is indicated by their success in judging the truth or falsity of propositions related to it" (p. 112). He considered such propositions to be expressions of verbal knowledge, which is viewed as the essence of educational achievement.

Ebel's defense of true–false items can be questioned, but there is no questioning the fact that well-designed true–false items can measure more than rote memory. For example, by including two concepts, conditions, or events in a true–false item, the examiner can ask if it is true that they are moderately to strongly related (Diekhoff, 1984). Other possibilities are to ask if (1) one concept, condition, or event implies or is a consequence of another event; (2) one concept, condition, or event is a subset, example, or category of another event; (3) both concepts, conditions, or events are true. Such items can measure understanding, as well as significant knowledge of concepts and events.

Whatever the objectives of a true–false test, in constructing items of this type, it is advisable to attend to the following suggestions:

1. Make certain that the statements deal with important (nontrivial) matters.
2. Make the statements relatively short and unqualifiedly true or false.
3. Avoid negatively stated items, especially those containing double negatives.
4. Avoid ambiguous and tricky items.
5. As a rule, avoid specific determiners. If specific determiners are used to trip up unknowledgeable but testwise examinees, they should be included in true statements as often as in false ones.
6. On opinion statements, cite the source or authority.
7. Make true and false statements about the same length, and make the number of true statements approximately equal to the number of false statements. Because false items tend to be more discriminating than true items, it can be argued that the number of false statements should be greater than the number of true statements. However, if the teacher follows this practice on successive tests, students may become aware of it and begin to answer "false" when in doubt about the answer.
8. Make wrong answers more attractive by wording items in such a way that superficial logic, popular misconceptions, or specific determiners suggest that wrong answers are correct. False statements having the ring of truth may also trip up unknowledgeable examinees.

Matching Items.   In a sense, both true–false and multiple-choice items are varieties of the matching item. On all three types of items, a set of response options is matched to a set of stimulus options (premises). The distinction is that true–false and multiple-choice items have only one premise (the *stem* of the item) and two or more response options, whereas matching items have multiple premises and multiple response options. The examinee's task on a matching item is to pair the response options with the correct premise. Matching is usually one-to-one (one response per premise), but it may well be one-to-many, many-to-one, or many-to-many. Examinees should, of course, be told which of these procedures applies on a particular item.

Matching items are easier to construct, and they cover the material more efficiently than many other types of items; unfortunately, they usually measure only rote memory for facts.[2] Also, the necessity of making the options homogeneous (all response options of the same kind, such as dates, places, or names) limits the type of material that can be fitted into a matching framework. Some guidelines for constructing matching items are these:

1. Arrange the premise and response options in a clear, logical column format, with the premises in the left column and the response options in the right column.
2. Use between six and fifteen premises, with two or three more response options than premises.
3. Number the premises successively, and place letters (a, b, c, etc.) before the response options.
4. Clearly specify the basis for matching.
5. Place the entire item on a single page.

A special type of matching item is the *rearrangement item,* on which examinees are required to sort a group of options into a fixed number of predetermined categories. On a particular type of rearrangement known as a *ranking item,* respondents rearrange a set of options in order from first to last (or highest to lowest).

Multiple-Choice Items.   No one knows for certain who constructed the first multiple-choice test item, but from the viewpoint of psychological assessment it was a fortunate event.[3] Multiple-choice items are the most versatile of all objective test items in that they can be used to measure both simple and complex learning objectives at all grade levels and in all subject-matter areas. Although answering essay items demands greater organizational ability than selecting answers to multiple-choice items, responding correctly to a well-prepared multiple-choice item requires good discriminating ability and not merely skill in recognizing or recalling the correct answer. Scores on multiple-choice items are also less affected by guessing and other response sets than are scores on other objective items. Useful diagnostic information may be obtained from an analysis of the incorrect options (*distracters*) selected by examinees.

Among the shortcomings of multiple-choice items are that (1) good ones are difficult to construct, especially items on which all options are equally attractive to examinees who do not know the correct answer; (2) they emphasize recognition, rather than the recall and organization of information; and (3) they require more time to answer and may sample the subject-matter domain less adequately than true–false items. They also encourage rote learning of details, rather than understanding of the material in a more in-depth, meaningful manner (Schmidt, 1983).

Guidelines for facilitating the construction of high-quality multiple-choice items are given in Box 2.1 (see also www.uleth.ca/edu/runte/tests/testtaking.html). These guidelines

---

[2]Shaha (1984) found that that it is possible to construct matching items that are equal to or even superior to multiple-choice items as measures of the content domain of interest and in the attitudes of test takers toward them.

[3]Arthur Otis is credited with pioneering the use of the multiple-choice item format on group intelligence tests. The first published test to employ this format was the Otis Self-Administering Tests of Mental Ability (1916–1917).

■ ■ ■ ■ ■

BOX 2.1

GUIDELINES FOR CONSTRUCTING MULTIPLE-CHOICE ITEMS

1. Either a question or an incomplete statement may be used as the stem, but the question format is preferred. If the stem is an incomplete statement, place the blank at the end of the statement.

2. State the specific problem of the question or incomplete statement clearly in the stem and at a reading level appropriate for the examinees, but avoid taking questions or statements verbatim from textbooks.

3. Place as much of the item as possible in the stem. It is inefficient to repeat the same words in every option, and examinees have less difficulty scanning shorter options.

4. Employ opinion questions sparingly; when they are used, cite the authority or source of the opinion.

5. Four or five options are typical, but good items having only two or three options can also be written. With students in the lower grades, three options are preferable to four or five. Haladyna and Downing (1993) concluded that three options are probably suitable for most ability and achievement tests.

6. If the options have a natural order, such as dates or ages, it is advisable to arrange them in that order. Otherwise, arrange the options in random or alphabetical order (if alphabetizing does not provide clues to the correct answer).

7. Make all options approximately equal in length, grammatically correct, and appropriate in relation to the stem. However, don't let the stem "give away" the correct option by means of verbal associations or other clues.

8. Make all options plausible to examinees who don't know the right answer, but make only one option correct or "best." Popular misconceptions or statements that are only partially correct make good distracters.

9. In constructing each distracter, formulate a reason why examinees who don't know the correct answer might select that distracter.

10. Avoid, or at least minimize, the use of negative expressions such as "not" in either the stem or options.

11. Although a certain amount of novelty and even humor is appropriate and may serve to interest and motivate examinees, don't use ambiguous or tricky items and options.

12. Use "none of the above," "all of the above," or "more than one of the above" sparingly. Also, avoid specific determiners such as "always" or "never."

13. Place the options in stacked (paragraph) format, rather than in tandem (back to back); use numbers to designate items and letters for options.

14. Prepare the right number of items for the grade or age level to be tested, making each item independent of other items (not interlocking or interrelated).

15. Make the difficulty levels of items such that the percentage of examinees who answer an item correctly is approximately halfway between the chance (random guessing) percentage and 100%: correct = $50(k + 1)/k$, where k is the number of distracters per item.

are primarily the products of logic and experience, rather than research, and following them will not guarantee the construction of good multiple-choice tests. Constructing good items depends on knowledge of the subject matter of the test, understanding what students should know and are unlikely to know about the subject matter, and the art or skill of asking questions. Even when the guidelines are not followed precisely, multiple-choice items tend to be fairly robust in their ability to measure knowledge and understanding.

A critical factor in determining the effectiveness of multiple-choice items is the selection or construction of *distracters* (incorrect options). Either a rational or an empirical approach to item selection may be employed. The *rational* approach requires the test constructor to make personal judgments concerning which distracters are appropriate. In contrast, the *empirical* approach consists of selecting distracters from the most popular incorrect responses to the stems of items administered as open-ended statements. There is no consensus as to which method yields better distracters, but examiner judgment appears to be at least as effective as the empirical approach.

Test designers usually have more difficulty constructing items to measure understanding and thinking than items that measure straightforward knowledge of the subject matter. Various ways of composing objective items to assess more complex instructional objectives have been proposed. Options such as "all of the above," "none of the above," "two of the above," and "all but one of the above" can make an examinee's choice more difficult. The task can also be complicated by making all options correct (or incorrect) and requiring examinees to select the best or most nearly correct option for each item. Other ways of making an examinee's decision more demanding are to (1) include multiple-answer items in which variable numbers of options are correct and the examinee must indicate which (if any) options are correct or incorrect, (2) have examinees select an answer and improve on it or write a brief justification of it, and (3) ask examinees to identify the correct setup (such as an equation or method of solution) on problem-solving tasks. Additional procedures for increasing the complexity of multiple-choice items are illustrated in Box 2.2. All these techniques are designed to make the process of selecting correct options a thoughtful, analytical process in which various cognitive abilities, rather than just rote memory, come into play. Finally, the use of a problem sets format, in which two or more multiple-choice items are related to the same illustration, graph, passage, or scenario, has been a popular format on credentialing examinations (Hambleton, 1996).

Likert Format.   A Likert format typically consists of a 5-point set of items ranging on a continuum from strongly agree to strongly disagree (see Chapter 13). However, it can also have only three or four choices or can have more than five. A variation of this is a *visual analogue* or *graphic rating scale,* which is simply a line in which an examinee marks their level of agreement or disagreement (i.e., Hostile _____ Friendly). This format is clearly more appropriate for measures of attitudes and personality, rather than achievement.

Constructed-Response Formats

The core feature of response formats is that they request an examinee to create or construct a response. A relatively structured variation is the fill-in-the-blank technique used for short-answer items. Far less structured methods are requesting an examinee to submit a portfolio of one's work or asking a family or a work applicant to solve a simulated problem. The most common constructed-response formats are short-answer items, essays, and storytelling techniques.

■ ■ ■ ■ ■

BOX 2.2

SOME COMPLEX FORMS OF MULTIPLE-CHOICE ITEMS

1. *Classification.* The examinee classifies a person, object, or condition into one of several categories designated in the stem.

   Jean Piaget is best characterized as a _____ psychologist.
   a. clinical   c. psychometric
   b. developmental   d. social

2. *If–Then Conditions.* The examinee must determine the correct consequence of one or more conditions being present.

   If the true variance of a test increases, but the error variance remains the same, which of the following will occur?
   a. Reliability will increase.   c. Observed variance will decrease.
   b. Reliability will decrease.   d. Neither reliability nor observed variance will change.

3. *Multiple Conditions.* The examinee uses the conditions or statements listed in the stem to draw a conclusion.

   If the mean of a test is 59 and its standard deviation is 2, what is Mary's z score if her raw score is 60?
   a. −2.00   c. .50
   b. −.50   d. 2.00

4. *Multiple True–False.* The examinee decides whether one, all, or none of the two or more conditions or statements listed in the stem is (are) correct.

   Is it true that (1) Alfred Binet was the father of intelligence testing, and (2) his first intelligence test was published in 1916?
   a. both 1 and 2   c. not 1 but 2
   b. 1 but not 2   d. neither 1 nor 2

5. *Oddity.* The examinee indicates which option does not belong with the others.

   Which of the following names does not belong with the others?
   a. Alfred Adler   c. Carl Jung
   b. Sigmund Freud   d. Carl Rogers

6. *Relations and Correlates.* The examinee determines the relationship between two concepts and indicates which of them (a, b, c, d, etc.) is related to a third concept in the same way as the first two concepts are related to each other.

   Mean is to standard deviation as median is to:
   a. average deviation   c. semi-interquartile range
   b. inclusive range   d. variance

Short-Answer Items.   A short-answer or completion item is the simplest form of a constructed-response format. An examinee is required to complete or fill in one or more blanks of a statement with the correct word or phrase or to give a brief answer to a question. In terms of the length of the constructed response, short-answer items fall somewhere between essay and recognition items. Short-answer items are among the easiest to construct, requiring examinees to supply the correct answer, rather than simply recognize it. Some short-answer formats can be used to assess personality. The examinee is requested to complete a sentence that reveals something about his or her personality (e.g., "The thing that most worries me about relationships is _____"). They are also often used for the assessment of knowledge (e.g., "The definition of the Standard Error of Measure is_____"). Although they can certainly be useful for assessing knowledge or terminology, short-answer items have serious limitations: they are inappropriate for measuring complex instructional objectives, and, because there may be more than one correct answer, scoring is not always entirely objective.[4]

These guidelines should be followed in constructing short-answer items:

1. Direct questions are preferable to incomplete statements.
2. Phrase items in such a way that the answers are brief and unambiguous.
3. If an incomplete statement is used, place the blank at the end of the statement.
4. Make all blanks the same length.
5. Avoid multiple blanks in the same item, especially if they make the meaning of the task unclear.
6. Indicate the units in which numerical answers should be expressed.

Essay Test Items

The most important advantage of essay items is that they can measure the ability to organize, relate, and communicate. These behaviors are not so easily assessed by objective items. They also encourage students to learn material in relatively meaningful and holistic ways. Essay tests have the additional advantages of requiring less time to construct and of reducing the likelihood that examinees will get items right simply by guessing. However, essay questions may be so general that different test takers may interpret the questions very differently. Scoring the answers may also result in differing interpretations of what the best answer is. Also, only six or so essay questions can be answered in a typical 50-minute class period. This may not be sufficient to determine the full range of a person's knowledge of the subject matter. Other shortcomings of essay tests are that they are susceptible to bluffing by verbally skilled but uninformed examinees and scoring them is subjective and time consuming.

A history teacher reportedly administered an essay test that included the question, "What were the causes and consequences of the Battle of Hastings?" One unmotivated student whose preparation in English history had failed to include events prior to the 14th century began his answer to the question with the statement, "Far be it for me to comment on the

---

[4]A type of completion item designed to evaluate reading ability is the *cloze technique.* In this procedure, respondents are directed to replace the missing words that have been deleted at random in written passages. A measure of the respondent's reading ability is the extent to which he or she fills in the blanks correctly and thus makes sense of the passages.

Battle of Hastings, but let's turn our attention to the Hundred Years War." This is a rather extreme example of the tendency of uninformed examinees to answer a slightly different question from the one being asked to emphasize what they know, rather than what they don't know. This is similar to politicians who answer the question they *wish* they had been asked, rather than the one they were *actually* asked. One way to cope with this problem, though laborious to both test takers and scorers, is the famous Chinese examination procedure of asking students to write down everything they know about a specified topic. It is possible that what would be measured by such a test is susceptibility to fatigue, rather than general knowledge!

In designing essay questions, the item writer should try to make the questions as objective as possible. This can be done by (1) defining the task and wording the items clearly, for example, asking examinees to "contrast" and "explain" rather than "discuss"; (2) using a small number of items, all of which should be attempted by all examinees; (3) structuring the items so that subject-matter experts agree that one answer is demonstrably better than another; and (4) having examinees answer each item on a separate sheet of paper.

Storytelling Techniques.   One method that claims to detect patterns of personality is to ask a person to narrate a story. Typically, the examinee is shown a picture and requested to say what the people are doing in the picture, what they are thinking and feeling, what events led up to it, and what the outcome will be (see Chapter 18). The various themes that emerge are considered to reflect such things as the examinees' central needs, how they perceive their environment, and typical problem-solving styles.

Using Computers in Test Construction.   Gone are the days when test constructors had to rely on paper and pencil or hunt-and-peck to compose and copy their tests. Now high-speed computers and associated equipment do much of the work. The most common application of computers in test construction consists of word-processing programs to assist in typing the items, formatting, checking for errors in spelling and syntax, and so forth. Test construction is facilitated even more by a combination of word-processing and graphics programs that support the preparation of tests comprised of words and drawings. These program packages contain banks or pools of test items that can be accessed by entering certain keywords indicating the content and psychometric characteristics desired in the test. Item banks, from which items can be selected and retrieved in designing tests, are available from textbook publishers as supplements for certain books.

Computer-based test-item writers, domain specification algorithms for generating test items, and linguistic-based or concept-learning approaches to item writing may provide more efficient and accurate procedures for constructing test items (Herman, 1994). Be that as it may, at present the preparation of good test items remains as much an art as a science.

ASSEMBLING AND REPRODUCING TESTS

Once the items for a test have been prepared, it is advisable to have them reviewed and edited by other knowledgeable persons. Even the most painstaking efforts do not necessarily produce a good test. In-class, self-made achievement tests might be improved by a friend or associate who can frequently spot errors and make valuable suggestions for improving items. Item content for more formal tests requires review by a panel of professionals.

Assuming that the test designer has constructed a sufficient number of satisfactory items, final decisions concerning several matters must be made before assembling a test:

1. Is the length of the test appropriate for the time limits?
2. How should the items be grouped or arranged on the pages of the test booklet?
3. Are answers to be marked in the test booklet, or will a special answer sheet be used?
4. How will the test booklet and answer sheet be reproduced?
5. What information should be included in the test directions?

Test Length

How many items to include on a test depends on time limits, reading level of the examinees, and the length and difficulty of the items. Shorter items and/or those necessitating only rote memory of facts can be answered in less time than longer items requiring laborious computations and/or abstract reasoning. Prior experience with items of the same general type as those included on a test will help in determining if the time limits are appropriate. On tests of moderate difficulty administered at the secondary school level and beyond, a good rule of thumb is to allow 1 minute for each multiple-choice or short-answer item and 1 minute for every two true–false items. Thus, a 50-item multiple-choice or short-answer test and a 100-item true–false test are usually appropriate for a typical 50-minute class period at the junior or senior high school level. Five or six essay questions requiring half-page answers can be prepared in this same time. Unless the items are very long or extremely difficult, at least 90% of the students in a typical secondary school class will be able to finish the test in the allotted time. The test length and time limits must be adjusted downward or upward when testing elementary school pupils or college students, respectively.

There are, of course, differences among examinees in the time required to finish a test. It might be expected that students who are most knowledgeable or skilled in the subject matter of the test would finish first, but this is not always the case. Less informed students may simply guess or "give up" and leave early when permitted to do so. Furthermore, the test-taking habits of high-scoring examinees may lead them to review the test items several times to make certain that they did not overlook or misconstrue something. Certain students, both high and low scoring, may also have heard that their initial answers are more likely to be correct and therefore that it is generally not a good idea to reconsider one's first choice. All these factors make it difficult to predict how long a given student will take to complete a test. It depends on a complex interaction between the preparedness, personality, and emotional and physical state of the examinee; the nature and difficulty of the test material; and the testing environment (noise and other distractions, behavior of the examiner or proctor, etc.). The examiner can probably make actual time on task more uniform by requiring the examinees to remain in their seats after finishing the test, but there may still be substantial differences among examinees in the time needed to complete the test.

Arrangement of Items

With respect to the arrangement of the options on multiple-choice items, it has been alleged that examinees show position preferences in that they are more likely to select certain options (say *b* and *c*) than others (*a* and *d*) when they are uncertain of the answers. Though research has failed to demonstrate that such position preferences have a significant effect on test scores (Jessell & Sullins, 1975; Wilbur, 1970), it is advisable to arrange multiple-choice and true–false items so that the answers follow no set pattern. Arranging the options for multiple-choice items in alphabetical order may be satisfactory, but a better strategy is to randomize the order of options within items. This will ensure that at least the test constructor was unbiased in positioning the correct options. Of course, "all of the above" or "none of the above," when used as options, should be placed in the last position.

On matching or rearrangement items, examinees find it more convenient and that scoring is easier if all premises and response options are placed on the same page. Placing short-answer items in groups of five or so can also reduce errors in taking and scoring a test. Whether the answers are written in the test booklet or on a separate answer sheet, sufficient space should be provided for answering short-answer and essay items.

Concerning the layout of the test as a whole, it might be expected that the examinee's task will be easier if items of the same type (multiple choice, true–false, etc.) and items dealing with the same topic are grouped together. It is true that arranging items in groups according to type or topic may make test preparation, administration, and scoring simpler, but there is no evidence that this practice improves scores. Be that as it may, on tests containing both objective and essay items, the latter, which typically require more time and different thought processes than the former, are usually placed last.

Another reasonable supposition is that test scores will be higher if subsets of items are arranged in order from easiest to hardest. Success in answering easier items presumably creates positive anticipations of success, thereby encouraging examinees to exert more effort on more difficult items. However, this supposition has not always been confirmed by research (Allison, 1984; Gerow, 1980; Klimko, 1984). An occasional easy item may improve performance on subsequent items, but, in general, arranging items in order of difficulty appears to have little effect on overall scores. Exceptions to this conclusion are tests that are speeded (Plake, Ansorge, Parker, & Lowry, 1982) or very difficult (Green, 1984; Savitz, 1985). On either a speeded test or one that is very difficult, placing the hardest items at the end of the test seems to improve overall scores somewhat.

A logical conclusion from research findings on the effects of ordering items according to difficulty level is that, in constructing nonspeeded tests of easy to moderate difficulty, test designers should be less concerned with item arrangement and more with making certain that the items are well written and measure what they are supposed to measure. When a test is very difficult or speeded, arranging items in order from easiest to most difficult may ensure more efficient use of the examinee's time and improve motivation, thereby resulting in higher test scores.

Answer Sheets

For most classroom tests, especially in the lower grades, it is advisable to have students mark or write their answers in the test booklet (Airasian & Terrasi, 1994). This results in fewer errors in responding. On objective items, requiring examinees to write the appropriate letters or answers in marginal spaces on the left of the questions also facilitates scoring.

Separate answer sheets, which are easy to score, can be used at the upper elementary school level and beyond. Commercially distributed answer sheets will have to be used if the test is to be machine scored. On these answer sheets, examinees respond by filling in the cor-responding numbered or lettered circle or space next to the item number. If the test is to be scored by hand, the classroom teacher can easily make up an answer sheet and have it dupli-cated. An answer sheet for a 75-item multiple-choice test might have the following format:

1. a b c d e	26. a b c d e	51. a b c d e
2. a b c d e	27. a b c d e	52. a b c d e
. . .	. . .	. . .
25. a b c d e	50. a b c d e	75. a b c d e

Examinees are instructed to mark the letter corresponding to the correct answer to each item. SCANTRON answer sheets that can be scored either by machine or hand are also available.

Every educational institution has facilities for reproducing written or printed materi-als for classroom use. Photocopy machines can be used to duplicate test booklets in one- or two-sided printing format, sometimes in color. If the same type of answer sheet is used for different tests, a large quantity can be printed in a single run of the machine and stored for other test administrations.

Test Directions

The general directions for an essay or objective test administered simultaneously to a group of people are placed at the front of the test, and the specific directions for each part of a mul-tipart test are placed before the respective part. It is usually wise to type the directions in bold type so examinees are less likely to skip or overlook them. Because the wording of the directions can have an effect on the obtained scores, they should be precise, rather than gen-eral (Joncas & Standig, 1998). It is also advisable for the overall directions to be read aloud by the examiner if they are unusual or unfamiliar to the examinees. On an individual test, where the examiner presents each task and continuously interacts with the examinee, the di-rections are given orally. Whether they are presented orally, in printed form, or both, the di-rections should inform the examinees of the purpose of the test (or item), how their responses should be indicated,[5] what sort of help examinees can expect if they do not un-derstand something, how long they have to complete the test, how responses will be scored, whether it is advisable to guess when in doubt, and how to correct a response if they make a mistake. The following general directions for a group-administered achievement test are representative:

> Write your name in the upper-right corner of the answer sheet, but do not write on the test booklet. This test is designed to evaluate your knowledge and understanding of developing a psychological test. There are 60 items, and you will have exactly 90 minutes to complete the test. Indicate your response to each item by filling in the appropriate space on the answer sheet below the letter corresponding to the correct answer. Your raw score on the test will be

---

[5]Because the method of responding on computer-administered tests may be unfamiliar to some examinees, suffi-cient instructional time should be allocated to show them how to operate the equipment. In addition, they should be monitored during the test to make certain that they are using the equipment properly.

the number of items you answered correctly. Although wild guessing will not add to your score, if you can eliminate at least one option on an item, it is wise to make an informed guess from the remaining options. You should have enough time to answer all items and to review your answers. If you finish before time is up, please sit quietly until everyone has finished.

When the test directions are given orally, they should be read slowly, clearly, and exactly as they appear. After the directions have been read, examinees should be permitted to ask questions and, regardless of their seeming triviality or redundancy, to have them answered in a patient, informative manner.

On multipart tests consisting of a variety of topics and/or types of items, specific instructions may be necessary for each part. Directions regarding many of the same matters—how to mark responses, how to correct mistakes, whether to omit answers or guess when in doubt—may vary with the type of objective items. Instructions for answering essay items may include suggestions for structuring answers (outlining, formatting, and the like); how long answers should be; how much scoring weight will be given to content, form, grammar, penmanship, and other features of answers; and whether all or a selected number of questions should be attempted or whether some questions are mandatory and others optional.

ORAL TESTING

An *oral test* is an evaluation situation in which examinees respond to questions orally; the questions may be presented orally, in writing, or both. Oral achievement testing is more common in European educational institutions than in the United States, where the practice of oral testing declined during the 20th century and is less common in higher than in lower grades.

Many students do not like oral tests and feel that they are unfair measures of knowledge and understanding. However, teachers of speech, dramatics, English, and foreign languages often deplore inattention to the assessment of spoken language skills and feel that the consequence of such neglect is a citizenry that cannot speak correctly, comprehensibly, or comfortably. While many teachers of languages and other subjects in which the development of speaking skills is important admit the desirability of oral exercises and evaluations, they also realize that oral tests are not only very subjective, but often inefficient.

Advantages of Oral Tests

Since the early part of this century, oral achievement tests have tended to be perceived as lacking in efficiency and psychometric rigor. They have also been criticized as being too time consuming, providing a limited sample of responses, and being poorly planned in most instances.

Despite the shortcomings of oral tests, even their critics admit that such tests possess some advantages over written tests. One advantage is the interactive social situation provided by oral examinations, permitting the evaluation of personal qualities such as appearance, style, and manner of speaking. The face to face situation also makes cheating and perhaps bluffing less likely. Other advantages of oral tests are that they frequently require responses at a higher intellectual level than written tests and provide practice in oral communication and social interaction. They also encourage more careful review of the test material and can be completed in less time than comparable written examinations. Oral examiners may be better able to follow the thought processes of examinees and locate the boundaries of their knowledge and understanding of the subject matter more readily. These boundaries can be determined by asking examinees to explain, defend, or elaborate on their answers. Finally, the time needed to prepare and evaluate oral answers may be less than that on a comparable written test.

Oral tests are especially appropriate for primary school pupils and others who experience difficulties in reading or writing. Even at higher grade levels, the administration of an occasional oral test is justified when time and/or facilities for duplicating test materials are in short supply. In subjects such as speech, foreign languages, and dramatics, oral examinations are crucial.

Structural interviews consisting of oral questions and answers are often conducted with applicants for positions in governmental and industrial organizations. These interviews often take place over the telephone when applicants cannot travel to the examination site. A certain amount of standardization and control can be introduced into such oral examinations by asking all examinees the same questions, limiting the time they have to answer them, and electronically recording their answers for later playback and evaluation.

Oral Versus Written Examinations

The fact that scores on oral achievement tests have only moderate correlations with scores on comparable written tests suggests that they measure different aspects of achievement. In general, knowledge of specific facts can be determined more quickly with objective written tests, so oral examinations should not contain large numbers of these kinds of questions. As with essay tests, oral tests are more appropriate when the questions call for extended responses.

Because the achievements or behaviors assessed by oral tests are arguably just as important as those measured by written tests, more attention should be paid to the major source of error in oral testing: the examiners or evaluators themselves. A thorough knowledge of the subject matter and a keen awareness of the appropriate responses are needed by oral examiners. Also, the categories used by the examiners in describing or rating examinees' responses should cite specific, observable behaviors, rather than nebulous concepts such as *creative potential, character, general ability,* or *interpersonal effectiveness.* These undefined, and perhaps undefinable, concepts are no more easily measured by oral tests than by written ones.

PERFORMANCE TESTING

Paper-and-pencil tests are the most efficient and objective of all types of tests, but they usually provide only indirect information about a person's ability to do or make something. Knowledge of the subject matter can be demonstrated fairly thoroughly in a short period of time by means of an essay, multiple-choice, or other written test. Possessing a body of information about a topic or being able to explain how to do something is not, however, the same as using the information or skill in practical situations. The first author (L. A.) once conducted a human relationships workshop with a group of assembly-line supervisors. Although all the supervisors did well on written tests of the material presented in the workshop and agreed that a democratic approach to supervision was superior to an authoritarian one, the majority resumed their authoritarian approach to supervision on returning to the assembly line. There are many other examples of situation-specific behaviors in which students learn to give the correct answer in class or on a paper-and-pencil test, but abandon it when confronted with a real-life situation where it might be applicable.

Much learning that goes on in classrooms is related to behavior in nonacademic contexts, but the relationship is far from perfect. Generalization of knowledge and skills from the classroom to real-life situations is particularly tenuous in the case of verbal knowledge. Teachers realize that if schooling is to prepare students for life then skills as well as knowledge must be taught in such a way that they will transfer to job situations and other nonschool contexts. Teachers of science, athletics, dramatics, music, industrial arts, speech, foreign languages, penmanship, agriculture, and many other subject-matter areas recognize the need for students to engage in repeated practice and to have practical experience if the skills are to be well learned and transferable. Science labs and projects, psychomotor skills learned in games and sports, playing musical instruments and singing, acting in plays, constructing or applying useful objects in shop, practicing public speaking and conversation in English and other languages—all provide opportunities to learn and practice skills that are potentially useful outside class and serve as a foundation for later practical experiential learning.

Because of its greater realism than written tests, performance testing is sometimes referred to as *authentic assessment* or, to emphasize that it is an option to written testing, *alternative assessment.* The emphasis in alternative assessment is placed not only on what a person knows, but also on what he or she can do. The assessment activities are generally realistic and, in keeping with their simulated realism, they may have more than one correct answer.

In recent years, advances in computer-based technology have led to the development of simulators that provide for the *virtual reality testing* of real-life skills. These devices, which require examinees to wear a head-mounted display that provides them with a realistic impression of moving through an environment, are being used not only in teaching and testing perceptual–motor skills, such as driving or piloting skills, but also in situations calling for the exercise of judgment, problem-solving skills, and therapeutic interventions (Wiederhold & Wiederhold, 2005).

Though it may not be necessary to follow a taxonomy of psychomotor objectives in planning a test to measure how well a person has learned a particular skill, it is useful to construct a detailed list of the behaviors that are indicative of a range of proficiency in this skill. Decisions should be made beforehand as to how much (numerical) weight will be given to each aspect of the performance and what deductions (if any) will be made for mistakes, slowness, or sloppiness.

A performance test should focus mainly on the product or end result of performing a skill, but the process by which it is performed is also important (Wechsler et al., 2004). For example, two clients might have received the same low score on a memory test. One client might have done so due to trying to purposefully fake bad in the hopes of receiving compensation for a personal injury case. A second client might have done poorly due to having an acquired brain injury. On performance tests involving a tangible finished product, not only the quantity and quality of a product, but also how efficiently it was made, should be noted.

Both the products and processes of performance are typically evaluated subjectively, primarily by observation, combined with a written or electronic record and a checklist or rating scale. Entire *portfolios,* or collections of a person's performances and products over a period of time, may be scrutinized and evaluated. Careful observation that is as free as possible from bias is critical to the accurate evaluation of performance. Structured performance tests, in which every examinee is tested under the same conditions, are usually more objective than unstructured ones, in which students are observed and evaluated unobtrusively during class, in the hall, or on the school grounds. But even when the utmost care is exercised, by their very nature performance tests are less objective and consequently less reliable than written tests. In addition, performance tests take more time than written tests and often involve expensive equipment and other time-consuming arrangements. For these reasons, whenever the cost and inefficiency of a performance test is not offset by its real-world character, a written test is preferable.

SUMMARY

1. A crucial initial issue when constructing a test is whether it will be a test for screening, intelligence, personality, or achievement.

2. Another important step is to specify the test objectives. A table of specifications giving the number of items needed in each content (topical) category for each behavioral objective should then be constructed. For example, Bloom and Krathwohl's *Taxonomy of Educational Objectives: Cognitive Domain* (1956) organizes learning objectives into the following categories: knowledge, comprehension, application, analysis, synthesis, and evaluation.

3. A further strategy is to form a grid with the behavioral objectives in the left column and the content areas as a row on the top. Areas to include on the test are identified in the boxes where the behavioral objectives and content areas intersect.

4. Selected-response items include true–false, multiple-choice, matching, and Likert formats and are varieties of objective test items. Of these, multiple-choice items are the most versatile and popular. Selected-response tests are typically time efficient and cover a broad range of areas, and the scoring is usually more consistent between scorers. Constructed-response tests such as essay items are easier to construct, but scoring them objectively is more difficult. Whereas selected-response achievement tests encourage a rote learning style, constructed-response tests (primarily essays) are more likely to result in a more holistic, meaningful way of learning.

5. In assembling a test, attention should be given to factors such as test length and format, the method of recording responses, facilities for reproducing the test, and the directions for administration. Directions for administering a test include the purpose(s), time limits, scoring procedure, and advisability of guessing when in doubt.

6. Oral tests are not used as often as written tests but, when carefully planned, administered, and evaluated, they can have advantages over written testing. These include observations of the examinee's personal appearance, manner of speaking, and ability to organize information; examinee's thought processes; flexible questioning to locate boundaries of knowledge; and minimization of cheating.

7. In a sense, both written and oral tests are measures of performance, but performance testing has typically focused on nonverbal behavior. Because it is more realistic than verbal testing, performance testing is sometimes referred to as authentic assessment. Rather than simply describing how to do something or what was done, performance tests require examinees to demonstrate a process. Such tests are used extensively for evaluating learned abilities in both laboratory and field situations, ranging from the science laboratory to the sports arena and other applied contexts. Portfolios of performance and products are often kept and evaluated as a means of assessment.

MASTERING THE CHAPTER OBJECTIVES

1. *Types of tests*
   a. Describe screening, intelligence, personality, and achievement tests.
   b. What considerations for test construction might arise with each of the above types of tests?

2. *Educational objectives for test construction*
   a. Explain the importance of conceptualizing educational objectives prior to developing items for a test.
   b. Consider a course you are taking (possibly this one) and develop one question for each category in Table 2.1 (one question for knowledge, one for comprehension, etc.).

3. *Behavioral and content considerations*
   a. Explain why it might be important to organize relevant behaviors and contents before developing test items.
   b. Using Table 2.2 as an example, construct your own taxonomy of objectives for a course you are currently taking. Form a grid with knowledge, comprehension, and application (as per Table 2.1) on the left column and at least three topics on the top row. Develop four examples of items that correspond to the boxes in the grid.

4. *Types of test items*
   a. List three reasons why multiple-choice items are generally considered superior to other types of objective test items.
   b. Can you think of any situation in which true–false, completion, or matching items would be better than multiple-choice items.
   c. Based on the topics covered in this chapter, write five true–false items, five multiple-choice items, and five essay questions. Have a fellow classmate critique your items.
   d. Describe the relative strengths and weaknesses of selected-response and constructed-response tests. For what purposes and under what conditions is each type of test most appropriate?

5. *Assembling and reproducing a test*
   a. List the considerations you need to have when assembling and reproducing a test.
   b. How would you decide if the length of a test is appropriate?

6. *Advantages and disadvantages of oral testing*

   a. What are the advantages and disadvantages of oral tests compared with written tests?

   b. How should an oral test be designed, administered, and scored?

7. *Performance testing*

   a. What do performance tests measure that cannot be measured by means of paper-and-pencil (written) tests or oral tests?

   b. Describe two or three performance tests that you have taken.

EXPERIENCING PSYCHOLOGICAL ASSESSMENT

1. Select a public figure (politician, actor, etc.). Create five Likert format questions to assess people's attitudes toward this person (i.e., "[Person X] has a high level of integrity." Strongly agree, agree, etc.) and administer your test to five people.

2. Choose an area you feel competent in. How would you develop a portfolio (e.g., performance "test") to document your level of competence?

CHAPTER THREE

TEST ADMINISTRATION AND SCORING

CHAPTER OBJECTIVES

1. Describe the examiners' duties before and during testing.
2. Understand strategies for improving test scores, what is meant by "testwiseness," and how to counter it.
3. Understand the rationale and strategies for adaptive testing.
4. Understand the following considerations in test scoring: strategies for minimizing error in essay tests, strategies for scoring objective tests, scoring weights for multiple-choice tests, correction for guessing, strategies for scoring oral tests, and weighting final scores.

No matter how carefully a test is constructed, the results are worthless unless it is administered and scored properly. The necessity of having established procedures or guidelines for administering and scoring psychological and educational tests is recognized by all professional organizations concerned with the assessment of people. One relevant source is the *Standards for Educational and Psychological Testing* (American Educational Research Association, American Psychological Association, & National Council on Measurement in Education, 1999), a set of 264 standards for constructing, evaluating, administering, and scoring tests and other psychometric instruments and interpreting and using the results. The 16 standards pertaining specifically to test administration, scoring, and reporting emphasize the importance of having clear directions for administration and scoring that are followed carefully. The standards also emphasize that test materials must be kept secure, cheating must be detected and controlled, and interpretations of scores must be understandable to those who read them.

TEST ADMINISTRATION

The procedure to be followed in administering a test or other psychometric instrument depends on the type of instrument (individual or group, timed or nontimed, cognitive or affective), as well as the chronological age, education, cultural background, and physical and mental status of the examinees. Whatever the type of test and the characteristics of the people who take it, factors such as the examinee's preparedness and motivation, amount of sleep the previous night, physical discomfort, anxiety pertaining to the test, other emotional problems, and any drugs they were taken can affect a person's performance.

Not only the preparedness, testwiseness, and motivation of test takers, but also the examiner's appearance and behavior and the testing situation can influence test performance. The skill and personality of the examiner are particularly important in the case of individual tests. Those who administer most individual tests must be formally licensed or certified by an appropriate state agency or supervised by a licensed examiner. Such requirements help ensure that examiners have the knowledge and skills to administer, score, and interpret psychometric instruments of various kinds.

Situational variables, including the time and place of testing, and environmental conditions, such as illumination, temperature, noise level, ventilation, and other distractions, can also contribute to the motivation, concentration, and performance of test takers. For this reason, one must make certain before administering a test that the physical environment is appropriate.

Examiner's Duties before a Test

Scheduling.   When scheduling a test, the examiner should take into account the likely condition of the examinee. For example, a legal evaluation should not be conducted too close to a court appearance since the likelihood of increased anxiety may affect the results. It might also be unwise to test schoolchildren during lunchtime, playtime, when other pleasurable activities typically occur or are being anticipated, or even when enjoyable or exciting events have just taken place (such as immediately after a holiday). The testing period should seldom be longer than an hour when testing elementary schoolchildren or an hour and a half when testing secondary school students. Because 30 minutes is about as long as preschool and primary schoolchildren can remain attentive to test tasks, more than one session may be required for administering longer tests to young children.

With respect to classroom tests, students should be informed well in advance when and where the test will be given, what subject content will be included, what kind of test (objective, essay, oral) will be administered, and how much time will be permitted. Students deserve an opportunity to prepare intellectually, emotionally, and physically for a test. For this reason, it is usually inadvisable to give pop quizzes or other unannounced tests. If the teacher feels that occasional pop quizzes help ensure that students keep up with the course material, such quizzes should not carry the same weight as regular examinations.

Informed Consent.   In many states, administration of an intelligence test or other psychodiagnostic instrument to a child requires the informed consent of a parent, guardian, or someone else who is legally responsible for the child. *Informed consent,* which was discussed at some length in Chapter 1, consists of an agreement between an agency or individual and a particular person or his or her legal representative. Under the terms of the agreement, permission is given to administer psychological tests to the person and/or to obtain other information for evaluative or diagnostic purposes (see Form 1.2 on page 17).

Becoming Familiar with the Test. There should be no question regarding the examiner's familiarity with the test material and administration procedure when he or she is the same person. Because the person who administers a standardized test is seldom the one who constructed it, the accompanying manual should be studied carefully before the testing process. It is particularly important to become familiar with the directions for administration and the content of the test. To acquire this familiarity, it is recommended that the examiner take the test before administering it to anyone else. Finally, it is advisable to review the directions and other procedural matters just prior to administration. Test booklets, answer sheets, and other materials should also be checked and counted beforehand. *Secure tests* bearing serial numbers, such as the Scholastic Assessment Test and the Graduate Record Examinations, must be inspected closely and arranged in numerical order.

When a child or an adult is referred for an individual psychological examination by an outside agency or by a person such as a physician or court judge, the tests and other psychodiagnostic procedures will depend on the kinds of information requested by the referral source and the purposes for which the information will be used. Consequently, it is important for the referring person to specify precisely what information is needed and what will be done with it. In any event, the examiner should be thoroughly familiar with the tests or other psychometric instruments and the kinds of individuals and conditions for which they are appropriate.

Ensuring Satisfactory Testing Conditions. Examiners should make certain that seating, lighting, ventilation, temperature, noise level, and other physical conditions in the testing environment are satisfactory. A room that is familiar to the examinees and relatively free from distractions is preferred. A "Testing—Do Not Disturb" sign on the closed door of the examination room may help to eliminate interruptions and other distractions. Exits and rest room facilities should also be easily accessible.

It is best to administer an individual test in a private room, with only the examiner, the examinee, and if necessary the latter's parent, guardian, or other responsible person present. In administering either an individual or a group test, special provisions may need to be made for physically handicapped or physically different (for example, left-handed) examinees.

Minimizing Cheating. Trained examiners are well aware of the importance of test security, both before, during, and after a test is administered, and for accepting the responsibility of making certain that it is maintained. Before the test, comfortable seating that minimizes cheating should be arranged. Though preferable, it is not always possible for examinees to sit one seat apart so that cheating is difficult. Preparing multiple forms (different items or different item arrangements) of the test and distributing different forms to adjacent examinees can reduce cheating on group-administered tests. Another possibility is to use multiple answer sheets, that is, answer sheets having different layouts. Several roving proctors should also be employed whenever a large group of people is tested. Proctors can assist in distributing and collecting test materials and answering procedural questions, and their presence tends to discourage cheating and unruliness. Proctoring and other procedures designed to guard against cheating are viewed seriously in administering secure standardized tests such as the Scholastic Assessment Test and the Graduate Record Examinations. These tests, the booklets and answer sheets for which are carefully counted before and after administration, are closely supervised. Persons who take these tests are required to show proper identification before being admitting to the examination room.[1]

Minimizing Faking Good or Faking Bad.   In certain legal or employment contexts, examinees may attempt to distort test responses. For example, a person might fake memory problems in the hope that they might receive compensation in a personal injury case. In contrast, a job applicant might exaggerate his or her positive qualities to increase the chances of being hired. To reduce these types of distortions, examinees need to be told that it is important to present themselves as accurately as possible. They might also be informed that inaccurate responding can usually be detected and, when it does occur, it invalidates the results and works against them.

Examiner's Duties during a Test

Following Test Directions.   Carefully prepared test directions, which are read slowly and clearly when presented orally, inform examinees of the purposes of the test and how to indicate their answers. Examiners of standardized tests are required to follow the directions for administration carefully, even when further explanation might clarify the task for examinees. Departure from standard directions may result in a different task from the one the test designers had in mind. If the instructions are not identical to those given to the sample of people on whom the test was standardized, the scores will not have the same meaning as those of the standardization group. Consequently, a useful frame of reference for interpreting scores will have been lost.

Examiners in clinical and educational contexts sometimes go beyond the test directions, and attempt to "test the limits" of an examinee's abilities or personal characteristics. This may be done by employing *dynamic* or *authentic* testing procedures to obtain additional cues for purposes of interpretation or diagnosis. Illustrative of dynamic assessment is Feuerstein's *learning potential assessment* (Feuerstein, Feuerstein, & Gross, 1997). Learning potential assessment involves a test–teach–test format in which the examinee is tested, given practice on the test materials, and then retested. The change in performance level from test to retest is calculated as a measure of the examinee's learning potential (also see Tombari & Borich, 1999).

[1]There is, of course, a difference between cheating and legally sharing information. In most testing situations, examinees are not permitted to cooperate in determining their answers, but this is permitted in *team testing,* in which two or more students work together and hand in a single answer sheet or essay. Although there are arguments pro and con for the practice of team testing, it is true that on the job and in many other walks of life people need to cooperate with each other to perform effectively. The results of studies with undergraduates have shown that students scored higher when tested in cooperating pairs than when tested alone (Nowak et al., 1996; Zimbardo, Butler, & Wolfe, 2002).

Remaining Alert.   When administering a group test, whether standardized or nonstandardized, the examiner should be alert to cheating, as well as talking and other unnecessary noise. It is also a wise precaution to have a messenger available in case of medical emergencies or other problems. On teacher-made tests or even on standardized tests, if the directions permit, students may be told periodically how much time is remaining by writing the time on a chalkboard or other visible surface.

Establishing Rapport.   On both individual and group tests, the behavior of the examiner can have a significant effect on the motivation and behavior of examinees. Sometimes even a friendly smile may provide enough encouragement to anxious or inadequately prepared examinees so that they remain calm and perform optimally. Because individual administration provides a better opportunity to observe examinees than group administration, low motivation, distractibility, and stress are more likely to be detected in an individual testing context. Efforts can then be made to cope with these problems or at least to take them into account in interpreting scores. In a group testing situation, where personal interaction with every examinee is usually impossible, the examiner is more limited in sensing how well each person is feeling and doing. On both individual and group tests, a good rule to follow is to be friendly but objective, authoritative but not authoritarian, appropriate in manner and dress, and in charge of the testing situation. Such behavior on the part of the examiner tends to create a condition of *rapport*—a cordial, accepting relationship that encourages examinees to respond honestly and accurately.

Preparing for Special Problems.   In some circumstances, examiners need to be especially active and encouraging. A test in a traditionally difficult subject such as science or mathematics in particular can create a certain amount of tension in almost anyone, and sometimes a person becomes very anxious. Testing very young or very old, mentally disturbed or mentally retarded, and physically handicapped or culturally disadvantaged persons presents special problems. In certain situations, questions and answers may have to be given orally, rather than in print, or in a language other than English. The examiner must not only be familiar with the test material, but also alert, flexible, warm, and objective. These qualities are not easily taught, but experience in a variety of testing situations plays an important role in acquiring them.

Flexibility.   Some flexibility is usually permitted in administering nonstandardized tests and even certain standardized instruments, but too much flexibility may render the test norms useless for interpretive purposes. In testing with these measures, sensitivity and patience on the part of the examiner provide a better opportunity for handicapped individuals and those with other special problems to demonstrate their capabilities. Other recommended procedures, which have been adapted from well-known instructional techniques, are as follows:

1. Provide ample time for examinees to respond to the test material.
2. Allow sufficient practice on sample items.
3. Use relatively short testing periods.
4. Watch for fatigue and anxiety and take them into account.

5. Be aware of and make provisions for visual, auditory, and other sensory of perceptual–motor defects.
6. Employ a generous amount of encouragement and positive reinforcement.
7. Don't try to force examinees to respond when they repeatedly decline to do so.

Oral Testing.   Students frequently regard oral examinations with mixed feelings and often considerable apprehension. Consequently, efforts to calm their fears and provide alternative testing methods for those who become emotionally upset in oral testing situations can improve the effectiveness of these kinds of tests. Examiners who make special efforts to establish rapport with examinees discover that the latter may even come to enjoy oral tests.

Taking a Test

In general, pop quizzes are not considered fair. Students deserve a chance to prepare for a test. They should be informed in advance not only when and where a test will be given, but also what it will cover and what sort of test it will be. With respect to the format of a test, the results of both classroom and laboratory studies reveal that people tend to make higher scores on recall (essay, short answer) tests when they are told that an essay test will be given (e.g., May & Thompson, 1989).

The results of classroom studies indicate that announcing in advance that an objective test will be given tends to yield higher scores on multiple-choice, true–false, and other recognition tests (for strategies on taking multiple-choice tests, see www.uleth.ca/edu/runte/tests/testtaking.html). However, the results of laboratory studies are more complex (Lundeberg & Fox, 1991). Furthermore, other factors, such as mental ability, testwiseness, guessing, and careful reading and consideration of items, appear to have as much effect on test scores as knowing what type of test will be administered. In any event, when administering an achievement test, it is only fair to provide information beforehand on its form and coverage.

Testwiseness.   When answering objective test items, people often employ different strategies than those intended by the item writer. Not all examinees read the items carefully, and they often fail to use all the information given. Higher scores may be earned by attending to the format and characteristics of the test material. Sometimes it is possible to recognize correct answers to multiple-choice items without having read the material on which the questions are based. For example, the length, technicality, and exoticness of options may provide cues to the correct answers. Wrong options may be eliminated by noting that certain options are worded incorrectly or are too broad or too narrow. The correct answers to multiple-choice items may also be revealed by alliterative associations, grossly unrelated or irrelevant options, inclusionary language, keyed options that are more precise than other options, specific determiners ("all, none, everyone"), and giveaways that are answered in other items.

Observations of students taking multiple-choice tests and posttest interviews reveal that, although items are often answered merely by eliminating obviously incorrect choices, a more common practice is to make comparative judgments among options. The results of research by Rogers and Yang (1997) indicate that one must first have some knowledge of the content of the stem and/or item options to be able to eliminate incorrect options and take advantage of item cues.

Another aspect of testwiseness is knowledge of the teacher's idiosyncrasies. *Test-wiseness* appears to be a nongeneral, cue-specific ability that develops as students mature and share information on test-taking skills. Also of interest is the fact that the influence of testwiseness is generally greater for four-option than for three-option items (Rogers & Harley, 1999). Boys appear to be more testwise than girls, and verbal items tend to be more susceptible than numerical items to testwiseness (Rowley, 1974). Finally, some aspects of testwiseness or test sophistication can be taught (Johns & VanLeirsburgb, 1992; Roznowski & Bassett, 1992). Box 3.1 is a list of 15 suggestions that, when practiced before and during a test, can increase testwiseness and improve scores.

Changing Answers.   Examinees are often faced with the question of whether to change their initial responses to test items. Because first answers tend to be right, it is sometimes maintained that going over a test and changing answers that have already been thought about is counterproductive. The results of a number of investigations indicate, however, that examinees tend to make higher scores when they reconsider their answers and change those about which they have second thoughts (e.g., Geiger, 1991a, 1991b; Kruger, Wirtz, & Miller, 2005; Vispoel, 1998). Answers are more likely to be changed from wrong to right than vice versa, although the actual number of changed answers tends to be relatively small.

Guessing.   Directions for objective tests often include advice concerning whether to omit an item or to guess when in doubt about the correct answer. Guessing, which is more likely to occur when items are difficult or wordy, results in greater score inflation on true–false than on multiple-choice tests. In general, it is advisable for test takers to guess only when they can eliminate one or more options or they have some idea about which option is correct. Because it is usually possible to eliminate at least one option on an item, guessing rather than omitting items typically results in higher scores. This is true whether or not scores are "corrected" for guessing.

Understandably, examinees guess less when they are informed that a penalty for guessing will be subtracted from their scores than when no directions concerning guessing are given or they are told to guess when in doubt. Unfortunately, examinees do not always read or follow test directions carefully. Even those who read every word of the directions do not always interpret them in the same way. Regardless of what the test directions do or do not advise, some people are low–risk takers who are reluctant to guess when they are uncertain of the correct answer.

Examiner's Duties after a Test

After administering an individual test, the examiner should collect and secure all test materials. Examinees should be reassured concerning their performance, perhaps given a small reward in the case of children, and returned or directed to the appropriate place. In clinical testing, it is usually important to ask the person if she or he has any questions. Also after the test, information on what will be done with the results can be given to examinees and/or

■ ■ ■ ■ ■ ▬

BOX 3.1

SUGGESTIONS FOR IMPROVING YOUR TEST SCORES

Before the Test
1. Ask the instructor for old copies of tests that you can legitimately inspect.
2. Ask other students what kinds of tests the instructor usually gives.
3. Don't wait until the day before to begin studying when the test has been announced well in advance.
4. Study for the type of test (multiple choice, true–false, essay) that has been announced.
5. If the type of test to be administered is not announced, it is probably best to study for a recall (essay) test.
6. Don't make studying for the test a social occasion; it is usually better to isolate yourself when preparing for a test.
7. Don't get too comfortable when studying. Your body assumes that you want to sleep when you lie down or get too comfortable.
8. Try to form the material that you are studying into test items, for example, into multiple-choice items if a multiple-choice test is to be given or into essay items if an essay test is scheduled.
9. Apply the Survey Q3R (survey, questions, reading, recitation, review) when studying for a test. Survey the material, ask yourself questions about it, read it attentively with an intent to remember, recite the material to yourself after reading it, and review it just prior to the test.

During the Test
1. Read the directions carefully before reading the test questions. If certain information, such as time limits, correction for guessing, item weighting, or the like, has been omitted, don't hesitate to ask the test administrator about it.
2. On essay tests, think about the questions and formulate answers in your mind and/or on scratch paper before you begin writing.
3. Pace yourself in taking a test. For example, on a multiple-choice test you should have answered $1/n$th of the items when $1/n$th of the time has elapsed.
4. Whether or not a correction for guessing is used in scoring the test, don't leave an item unanswered if you can eliminate even one option.
5. Skip more difficult items and return to them later. Don't panic if you can't answer an item; circle it and come back to it after you have answered other items. Then, if you still aren't certain of the answer, make an educated guess.
6. Don't be overly eager to hand in your test paper before time has expired; when time permits, review your answers.

persons accompanying them. The examiner reassures those who are concerned, promising to communicate the results and interpretations to the proper individual(s) or agency and to recommend any further action.

Following administration of a group test, the examiner should collect the test materials (booklets, answer sheets, scratch paper, pencils, etc.). In the case of a standardized test, the test booklets and answer sheets should be counted and collated and all other collected materials checked to make certain that nothing is missing. Only then are examinees dismissed or prepared for the next activity and the answer sheets arranged for scoring.

Adaptive Testing

Historically, a test-administration procedure in which the same items are presented to all examinees was not followed precisely on all tests. In general, however, little flexibility was permitted in determining which items to present. This traditional approach to test administration is particularly inefficient with achievement tests, because examinees are given many items that are either too easy or too difficult for them. Adapting the content of the test to the ability level of the examinee eliminates the necessity for administering many very easy or very difficult items, thereby saving time and effort.

In *adaptive* or *tailored* testing, the specific items administered to a particular person depend on the person's responses to previous items. Because a test is most precise in measuring a person's ability if the difficulties of the administered items correspond to the person's ability level, reestimates of ability as an examinee proceeds through the test permit the selection and presentation of items that are closer in their difficulty level to the examinee's actual ability (see Meijer & Nering, 1999; Wainer, 2000).

Item banks or pools for adaptive tests can be assembled by computers programmed to follow one of the item-response methodologies (see Chapters 4 and 5). Certain assumptions of item response theory (IRT) must be met in adaptive testing, including (1) all items in a pool measure a single aptitude or achievement dimension and (2) the items are independent; that is, a person's response to one item does not depend on his or her response to any other item. Satisfaction of the first assumption, that of unidimensionality, is more likely to be met by item pools or tests derived by factor analysis (see Appendix A). The second assumption is met if the items are not interlocked or interrelated in some way.

The adaptive procedure for administering an achievement or aptitude test works in the following way. Applying an appropriate statistical model and item-response methodology, a pool of test items varying in difficulty and perhaps other characteristics is assembled for administration by computer. An estimate of the examinee's ability level dictates which items are administered first. Alternatively, items of medium difficulty may be administered initially. The selection of items to be administered subsequently depends on the examinee's responses to previous items. Testing continues until the estimate of error or level of accuracy of the responses reaches a specified level.

Unlike the traditional testing procedure, on adaptive tests examinees are usually not allowed to skip items or to review or change their responses.[2] But because not all items in a pool are administered to every examinee, adaptive testing is more efficient than conventional testing. Only about half as many items are administered to a given examinee as in

---

[2]Rocklin, O'Donnell, and Holst (1995) proposed a variant of computerized adaptive testing called *self-adaptive testing* that provides examinees with the opportunity to dynamically tailor the difficulty of items and thereby enhance their affective and motivational states. In this procedure, prior to presentation, items on a *self-adaptive test* are grouped by difficulty level on the basis of normative data. The examinee is allowed to specify the difficulty category from which each successive item should be drawn. In this way, an examinee who is seeking challenge can specify that the next item should be difficult, whereas an examinee who is trying to avoid failure may specify that the next item should be fairly easy.

the traditional testing practice, with no loss of information and equivalent reliability and validity.

A person's score on most adaptively administered tests is not determined by the traditional procedure of counting the number of items answered correctly, but by taking into account the statistical characteristics of the items. In any event, research has shown that scores on computerized adaptive tests are highly comparable to scores on equivalent paper-and-pencil tests (Kapes & Vansickle, 1992; Mead & Drasgow, 1992). Also, by administering items that are most appropriate to the examinee's ability level, an adaptive test may be more reliable than a longer test designed to measure the same ability.

Test security is easier to maintain in the case of computer-assisted adaptive tests. But security is of particular concern in the case of Internet-enabled assessment systems (Naglieri et al., 2004). Other advantages of computer-assisted adaptive tests include more accurate and immediate scoring and reporting, less error due to guessing, and the possibility of recording response times as well as responses. A disadvantage, at least when testing individuals or small groups, is the initial investment cost and the expense of maintaining the computer hardware and updating the software.

Adaptive testing of general intelligence and special abilities is now a fairly common practice. A number of organizations offer computerized, adaptive versions of the Scholastic Assessment Test (SAT), the Armed Services Vocational Aptitude Battery (ASVAB), the Graduate Record Examination (GRE), and certain other tests of cognitive abilities (see Bergstrom & Lunz, 1999; Mills, 1999; Segall & Moreno, 1999) and personality (e.g., Forbey, Handel, & Ben-Porath, 2000; Reise & Henson, 2000).

TEST SCORING

Professional test designers do not wait until a test has been constructed and administered before deciding what scoring procedure to use. On a teacher-made test consisting of several parts dealing with different content or different types of items, the teacher may wish to obtain both separate scores on the various parts and a composite score on the test as a whole. Also to be decided are whether to subtract a correction for guessing, to assign different scoring weights to different items or sections, or to report the results in raw-score form or to convert them to other numerical scales. For standardized tests, the classroom teacher does not need to make all these decisions. Answer sheets can be scored by machine, and even when they are hand scored, scoring stencils provided by the test publisher can be used according to the directions given in the manual.

Scoring Essay Tests

Essay questions are more effective when the task is structured clearly so that the interpretation of a question does not vary widely from person to person. Scoring can then be based on the quality of the answer. Similarly, the scoring procedure for essay items should be as structured and objective as possible so that the scores will depend less on noncontent, impressionistic factors and more on the level of knowledge and understanding demonstrated. Scoring on the basis of penmanship rather than quality of the answers, being overly general (*leniency error*), and giving a high score to an answer simply because the examinee scored high on other items (*halo effect*) are among the errors that can affect scores on essay items.

A number of steps can be taken to make scores on essay tests more objective and reliable. To begin, the scorer must decide whether to score the question as a whole or to assign separate weights to different components. Whole (*global* or *holistic*) scoring is common, but it is perhaps more meaningful to use an *analytic* scoring procedure in which points are given for each item of information or skill included in the answer. On the essay item (II.B) on page 27 (Table 2.3), for example, 1 point may be awarded for each correct advantage or disadvantage listed and a maximum of 5 points for the manner in which the answer is organized. The maximum number of points allotted to an item should be determined not only by the examiner's judgment of the importance of the item, but also by the assigned length of the answer. When the directions specify a half-page answer, the item should be weighted less than when a whole-page answer is specified.

Whatever the scoring weights assigned to specific questions and answers, it is advisable for the test designer to prepare ideal answers to the questions beforehand. It is also recommended that the names of examinees be blocked out before inspecting the test papers so that they can be scored anonymously. Other recommendations are as follows:

1. Score all answers to one question before going on to the next question.
2. Score all answers to a specific question during the same scoring period.
3. If both style (mechanics, quality of writing) and content are to be scored, evaluate them separately.
4. Have a second person rescore each paper, and make the final score the average of the number of points assigned by the two scorers.[3]
5. Write comments next to the examinee's responses, and mark corrections on the papers.

Corrections and comments written on classroom test papers are a valuable supplement to the number of points or the grade assigned. A student is more likely to learn something if the responses to a test are corrected and commented on, rather than merely being assigned a number or letter grade.

Computer software for scoring certain types of essay items is now available for use on the Web in a write–evaluate–rewrite format. Two examples are the Intelligent Essay Assessor, which is based on latent semantic analysis (Landauer, 1999; see description on www.knowledge-technologies.com/IEA.shtml) and ETS's e-rater software. Current computer-based essay scoring and grading procedures begin by having the software learn about the assigned topic by reading hundreds of thousands of words from online texts. Essays written by experts on the topic and student essays already graded by instructors are digested by the software to set up its evaluative procedures. The programs go beyond merely checking word lengths and mechanics and evaluate topic- and question-specific learning. The inclusion of key concepts and the semantic structure and direction of the writer's arguments are determined and evaluated. Essay-grading software does not determine the extent to which writing is creative or sophisticated; rather, it is oriented toward expository essays on factual topics (Murray, 1998).

---

[3]When every test paper is scored by two or more people, periodic recalibration of the scorers to ensure that they consistently use the same criteria in evaluating answers is advisable.

Scoring Objective Tests

A unique advantage of objective tests is the efficiency and accuracy with which they can be scored. Whereas scorers of essay tests typically spend hours reading answers and evaluating their correctness, a clerk can score an objective test quickly and accurately with a scoring stencil or machine. Then the test papers can be returned to the respondents while the material is fresh in their minds.

A strip key or stencil for hand scoring test booklets or answer sheets can be easily prepared. A strip of cardboard containing the correct answers at positions corresponding to the spaces in the test booklet where answers are to be written makes a satisfactory strip key. A scoring stencil for use with a special answer sheet can be prepared from a blank sheet of paper or cardboard by punching out the spaces where the correct answers should be.

Machine Scoring.   Although the majority of answer sheets for commercially distributed tests can be scored either by hand or machine, those distributed by certain organizations can be scored only by machine. After a test is administered, the answer sheets are mailed to a special scoring service or returned to the distributor for machine scoring.

Test-scoring machines have been available since the first half of the 20th century. The machines of yesteryear were sensitive only to magnetic marks on paper, so special magnetic pencils were required for marking answer sheets. Contemporary machines for scoring large batches of test answer sheets are optical scanners that are sensitive to marks made with ordinary pencils.

A computer is not needed for rapid and efficient scoring of tests, but it provides flexibility and further statistical analysis, interpretation, and storage of test scores and other personal data. In addition to local scoring by an optical scanner, answer sheets can either be mailed or transmitted by a modem to a central scoring service.

The amount of programming required to use a desktop optical scanner is fairly simple and includes a wide range of features, such as item weighting, part scoring, item analysis and flagging, and a printout of various kinds of data, statistics, and graphs. In addition to raw and converted scores, frequency distributions and histograms, test statistics (arithmetic means, standard deviations, internal consistency reliabilities), and item statistics (difficulty and discrimination indexes, distributions of responses to options, etc.) are reported.

Test scoring, score analysis, and score reporting may all be accomplished by using an optical scanner connected to a microcomputer containing appropriate assessment system software. However, software packages that construct tests according to certain specifications, score them, and analyze and report the results are complex and expensive. An example of such a general-purpose system is MicroCAT (from Assessment Systems Corporation), which makes possible the construction, administration, scoring, and analysis of tests designed from item-response or classical testing perspectives and administered by adaptive or conventional procedures. MicroCAT creates and maintains item banks consisting of text, graphics, and digitized images; develops and creates printed test forms; constructs and administers computerized tests, ranging from single conventional tests to sophisticated adaptive tests; and performs conventional item analysis, item-response analysis, and item calibrations. Certain test construction and administration features of MicroCAT are made available online by means of computer software such as the C-Quest and FastTEST Pro systems provided by Assessment Systems Corporation.

Human Scoring Errors.   Computer scoring of tests is not completely error free, and it is recommended that test scoring services should monitor their error frequencies and issue corrected score reports when errors are found in test scores (American Educational Research Association et al., 1999). Compared with hand scoring, however, the error rates of computer scoring are small.

Considering the fact that the directions for scoring many individual tests of intelligence and personality are not always clear and objective, it is not surprising that sometimes different scores may be assigned to the same response. Though the variability of scores is probably greater with less experienced scorers, even highly experienced scorers make errors. In administering an intelligence test, the errors may be of sufficient magnitude to result in assigning individuals to the wrong intelligence level. Trained clinical personnel also make mistakes in hand scoring personality inventories, some being serious enough to alter clinical diagnoses (Allard & Faust, 2000; Simons, Goddard, & Patton, 2002). Other studies have found that scoring is affected by the examiner's or scorer's liking for the examinee. Perception of the examinee as a warm person or as bright or dull can also affect the scoring of an individual test. Errors in converting raw scores to standard or scaled scores may occur when the examinee's exact chronological age is unknown or computed incorrectly.

Scoring Weights for Multiple-Choice and True–False Items.   It might seem that on objective tests, as on essay items, the number of points assigned to an answer should vary with the kind of item and the quality of the response. Many studies of the effects of a priori weighting of responses to conventional objective test items, that is, allocating different numbers of points to different item types and different responses, have been conducted. Although a priori weighting may be more discriminating and reliable than conventional scoring, the advantages of differential weighting of item responses do not seem to be justified by the increased scoring time and cost. On tests of 20 or more items, simply assigning a score of 1 to each correct response and 0 to each incorrect response is as satisfactory as using differential weights. Thus, possible scores on a conventionally scored 50-item multiple-choice or true–false test scored by this procedure range from 0 to 50.

Scoring Ranking Items.   As with true–false and multiple-choice items, short-answer and matching items may be scored by assigning 1 point to correct responses and 0 points to incorrect responses or omissions. Because of the large number of different orders in which a group of items can be arranged, the scoring of ranking items presents a special problem. For example, the error of assigning to second place an item that actually belongs in first place is not as serious as placing the same item in fourth place.

Two formulas that can be used for scoring ranking items are

$$S_1 = c \left[1 - \frac{2\Sigma |d|}{c^2 - j} \right], \tag{3.1a}$$

$$S_2 = c \left[1 - \frac{3\Sigma (d)^2}{c(c^2 - 1)} \right]. \tag{3.1b}$$

In these formulas, c is the number of things ranked, the d's are absolute values of the differences between the ranks assigned by the examinee and the keyed ranks, and $j = 0$ if c is even and 1 if c is odd. To illustrate the use of these formulas, assume that five cities are to be arranged in rank order according to population by assigning a rank of 1 to the city with the largest population, 2 to the next largest city, and so on. The names of the five cities are given in the first column of Table 3.1, the keyed ranks in the second column, and the ranks assigned by a hypothetical examinee in the third column. The fourth column contains the absolute values of the differences between the correct rank for each city and the keyed rank, and the fifth column contains the squares of these differences. The sum of the absolute values of the differences between the examinee's ranks and the keyed ranks is 10 and the sum of the squared differences is 28. Substituting $c = 5, d = 10$, and $j = 1$ in formula 3.1a yields $5[1 - 2(10)/(5^2 - 1)] - .83 \approx 1$. Substituting $c - 5$ and $d^2 = 28$ in formula 3.1b yields $5\{1 - 3(28)/[5(5^2 - 1)]\} = 1.5 \approx 2$. The results of applying these two formulas do not agree because, compared with formula 3.1a, formula 3.1b gives more weight to larger than to smaller differences in ranks. Either formula is satisfactory, depending on whether the scorer chooses to assign an extra penalty to responses that are very different from the keyed ones. In any event, no single method of scoring test items is best in all respects: it depends on the evaluator's philosophy and goals.

Correction for Guessing.   After the total raw score on an objective test has been determined, the question arises as to whether the score is an accurate indicator of the examinee's true knowledge of the area or whether it has been inflated by successful guessing. The chances of improving scores in this way, especially on items having few options, can be high. If, for example, an examinee randomly guesses on a four-option, multiple-choice test, he or she would be expected to get 25% of the answers correct. To put this in statistical terminology, if all options are equally attractive, the chances of selecting the correct option by guessing are $100/k$ out of 100, where k is the number of options per item (in this case, 4). Thus, the chances of guessing the correct answer on a four-option, multiple-choice test are 25 out of 100. The chances of guessing correctly on a true–false test are 50 out of 100. Obviously, guessing the answer to a large number of items can have a more serious effect on scores on a true–false test than on a multiple-choice test.

Correcting for the effects of guessing on certain standardized tests entails subtracting a portion of the number of wrong answers from the number of right answers. The reasoning behind correction-for-guessing formulas need not concern us here, except for the question-

TABLE 3.1   Scoring an Illustrative Rearrangement Item

CITY	CORRECT RANK	RANKING BY EXAMINEE	ABSOLUTE VALUE OF DIFFERENCE	SQUARE OF DIFFERENCE
Houston	4	1	3	9
Chicago	3	2	1	1
Los Angeles	2	3	1	1
Philadelphia	5	4	1	1
New York	1	5	4	16
Sums			10	28

able assumption that examinees guess blindly when in doubt. The most popular correction-for-guessing formula is

$$S = R - \frac{W}{k-1},$$ (3.2)

where R is the number of items the examinee gets right, W is the number of items the examinee gets wrong, k is the number of options per item, and S is the corrected score. This formula has been criticized for yielding scores that are too low when examinees are less familiar with the test material and too high when they are more familiar with the material. An alternative formula proposed by Little (1962) is

$$S = R - \frac{W}{2(k-1)},$$ (3.3)

Professional testers generally agree that correction-for-guessing formulas do not really correct for guessing and typically have little effect on the rank order of scores. Exceptions occur when the number of unanswered items varies greatly from person to person and when certain items are more likely to be guessed at than others. These formulas, which involve procedures similar to assigning differential weights to different items, are not generally recommended in scoring classroom tests. The formulas are probably most helpful in scoring true–false and speeded tests, where guessing is more of a factor, than on other types of tests. Negative scores, which occasionally occur when formula 3.2 is applied to true–false tests ($S = R - W$), are usually changed to zeros. In any event, examinees have a right to know if their scores will be corrected for guessing. Information on how a test is scored, including whether a correction for guessing is employed, should be included in the directions accompanying the test.

Converted Scores.   It is usually not worthwhile to alter raw scores on objective tests by differential item weighting or correction-for-guessing formulas, but the scores are often changed in other ways to make them more meaningful. As described in the section on norms in Chapter 4, the process of interpreting test scores is facilitated by transforming them to percentile ranks or standard scores.

Detection and Scoring for Cheating

As documented in numerous sources (Cizak, 1999), cheating on tests occurs throughout the school grades, college, and graduate and professional schools. It occurs in all countries, both sexes, and all ethnic groups. Students who are determined to cheat often discover or invent ingenious but illegitimate ways of doing so, such as writing answers in small letters on Kleenex tissues or on the inside of a label pasted to a water bottle.

Methods of deterring cheating, such as special seating arrangements during tests, alternate test forms or answer sheets, using a sufficient number of roving proctors during exams, and keeping test questions secure both before and after a test are fairly effective in reducing widespread cheating. Special statistical procedures are sometimes applied with in-class objective tests, and computer-based strategies for cribbing (copying) have been employed to detect cheating (Cizak, 1999; Harris, 2002).

Scoring Oral Tests

Although errors are more likely to occur in scoring responses to oral questions than to written ones, special forms for rating performance can improve the objectivity of scoring oral tests (see Form 3.1). Careful attention to the design of questions, construction of model answers to questions before administering the test, use of multiple raters or scorers, and training examiners to avoid favoritism and other rater biases can also reduce errors in scoring oral tests. If the time allotted to scoring is not critical, the accuracy with which oral tests are scored can be improved by electronically recording examinees' responses for later playback and (re)evaluation (see Aiken, 1983).

Score Evaluation and Grading

After a test has been administered and scored, the scores need to be evaluated in some way. In the case of teacher-made achievement tests, score evaluation usually implies the assign-

---

FORM 3.1   Form for Evaluating Oral Reports

Directions: For each question listed below, rate the student's performance on a scale of 1 to 10: 1 is very poor and 10 is excellent. Write the appropriate number (1 to 10) in the marginal dash.

____ 1. How well does the student know the subject matter of the report?

____ 2. How well organized was the report?

____ 3. How effective was the introduction to the report in capturing your attention?

____ 4. How clearly and distinctly did the student speak?

____ 5. How interesting was the topic?

____ 6. How effective were the audiovisual materials (films, posters, chalkboard, etc.) if any were used?

____ 7. To what extent did the student look at the class during the report, rather than spending most of the time looking at his or her notes?

____ 8. How effectively did the student use gestures, body postures, and other nonverbal messages to communicate?

____ 9. To what extent did the student refer to research or other primary sources in presenting the report?

____ 10. How would you rate the closing (summary of major points, presentation of thought questions, etc.) of the report?

Comments:

---

ment of letter grades or marks. Grade assignment is a fairly subjective process, depending not only on the test itself, but also on the expectations of the evaluator and the scores obtained by other students. Some teachers grade strictly on the curve, whereas others grade in terms of a fixed performance standard or criterion. The majority, however, probably employ a combination of curve and fixed-standard grading. In one curve-grading procedure, the *Cajori method,* As are assigned to the top 7% of test papers, Bs to the next 24%, Cs to the next 38%, Ds to the next 24%, and Fs to the lowest 7%. A disadvantage of this method is its failure to consider that tests vary in difficulty and the average ability level is not the same for students in different classes. An alternative curve-grading procedure establishes letter-grade boundaries on classroom tests when the ability level of the class, the class's test performance relative to that of other classes, and the test scores themselves are all taken into account (Aiken, 2000).

The traditional grading system, in which A is considered excellent or superior, B is above average or good, C is average, D is below average or poor, and F is failing, is a type of score or performance evaluation. Every public or private organization has standards that its students, employees, or members are expected to meet. The standards may be flexible, but at some time the proficiency or participation of members of the organization is evaluated. The penalty for receiving a negative evaluation may consist of remedial work, demotion, suspension, or even dismissal. The rewards for a good evaluation include prizes, privileges, and promotions.

Letter grading implies evaluation of scholastic performance by administering various kinds of achievement tests to students. Scores on other tests of ability and personality also require interpretation if they are to be used for certain purposes: for placement in special classes or jobs, for psychodiagnosis, or for psychological treatment or other interventions. Interpreting scores on such tests can be a very complex process, depending on the type of test and the purposes(s) for which it is administered. Score interpretation involves both objective and subjective factors, including the use of norms as discussed in the next chapter.

SUMMARY

1. Prior to giving a test, examiners should help test takers to be prepared, motivated, and relatively free from stress and other disruptive conditions. Test administrators should be trained, familiar with the particular test, and confident that everything is in order before giving a test, and they should try to establish rapport with the test takers. Examinees should be informed of the purpose(s) of a test, where and when it will be administered, the format of the test, and the material with which it deals. Examiners should follow the test directions carefully, take precautions to minimize cheating, and be prepared to handle emergencies and other special problems. Some flexibility is usually permitted in administering both teacher-made and standardized tests, but radical deviations from the directions for administration will invalidate the use of norms on the latter type of test.

2. Test scores can be improved by such things as reviewing previous tests, tailoring study to the type of test, and using the Survey Q3R method. Testwiseness, successful guessing, changing answers, and cheating are some of the factors that can inflate

scores on objective tests; bluffing, a sophisticated writing style, and good penmanship can do the same on essay tests. The effects of testwiseness are minimized by constructing items carefully and avoiding cues such as item length, specific determiners, grammatical errors, stylistic giveaways, and heterogeneous (nonparallel) options.

3. Adaptive testing, in which the sequence of questions presented to an examinee varies with his or her estimated standing on the specified variable and responses to previous items, substantially reduces the time to administer a test. Using computers for presenting test items and evaluating answers makes adaptive testing an efficient, albeit more expensive, alternative to the traditional approach of presenting the same items to all examinees.

4. The following considerations are important when scoring tests:

   ■ Essay tests may be scored holistically or analytically, but in either case examinees should be told how the test will be scored. Scoring the responses of all examinees to a specific essay question before going on to the next one is recommended, as is scoring responses separately for content and style. In addition to a numerical score, written comments, corrections, and explanations are often helpful in providing feedback on essay test performance.

   ■ Many objective tests are scored by computers or other special machines. Machine scoring is generally superior in terms of speed and accuracy, but less flexible than hand scoring.

   ■ Correction-for-guessing formulas are sometimes applied to reduce the effects of guessing but, with the possible exception of true–false items, are usually not worth the time or effort for classroom testing.

   ■ The scoring of portions of many individual tests of intelligence and personality is not completely objective and may result in errors on the part of professionals and trainees alike.

   ■ In general, a priori scoring weights are not recommended on tests consisting of 20 items or more. Scores on classroom tests are often converted to grades, either by using a fixed set of percentages, such as those specified by the Cajori method, or in a more subjective manner.

MASTERING THE CHAPTER OBJECTIVES

1. *Examiners' duties before and during testing*
   a. List the things an examiner should do before giving a test.
   b. Observe the administration of a test in one of your classes. Did the test administrator follow the guidelines described in this chapter? If not, what mistakes did he or she make, and what were the actual or possible consequences of these mistakes?

2. *Strategies for improving test scores*
   a. List four things test takers might do to improve their test scores when preparing for a test and four things they might do when actually taking the test.
   b. Define *testwiseness,* and describe test-taking behaviors that are indicative of testwiseness.
   c. What can a test designer do to minimize the effects of testwiseness on scores?

3. *Adaptive testing*
   a. What is adaptive testing?
   b. In what ways is adaptive testing superior to conventional objective testing procedures? In what ways is it inferior?

4. *Test scoring*
   a. What can be done to minimize error when scoring essay tests?
   b. What are some advantages and disadvantages of constructing, administering, and scoring tests by computer as compared with performing the same procedures in the traditional manner?
   c. What are the advantages and disadvantages of computer- and machine-scoring tests?
   d. John takes a 50-item, four-option multiple-choice test. He gets 30 items right, 16 items wrong, and leaves 4 items blank. What is his total score on the test, both corrected and uncorrected for guessing? If all items are true–false and he gives the same number of correct and incorrect answers as those listed above, what is his total score, both corrected and uncorrected for guessing? (See Answers to Quantitative Questions, p. 485.)
   e. What are three strategies for scoring oral tests?

EXPERIENCING PSYCHOLOGICAL ASSESSMENT

1. Question a group of your fellow students about the techniques they use in selecting answers to items on multiple-choice tests when they have not studied the material adequately. What techniques are most popular, and how effective are they?

2. Consider the last test you took. Evaluate which strategies you used and list at least three additional ones you might have used (but didn't) to improve your score.

CHAPTER FOUR

ITEM ANALYSIS AND TEST STANDARDIZATION

CHAPTER OBJECTIVES

1. Understand the concept and strategy for selecting test items based on external criteria.

2. Understand the concept and strategy for selecting items based on internal consistency, including item difficulty (item difficulty index or p) and the ability to discriminate between groups (item discrimination index or D).

3. Understand the concept and strategy for selecting multiple-choice item distractors.

4. Understand the concept and strategy for selecting items based on item-response curves and item-response theory (IRT).

5. Describe strategies for developing a standardization sample.

6. Describe percentiles as well as the following standard scores: z scores, Z scores, CEEB scores, and normalized standard scores.

This chapter deals with somewhat technical but important topics: item analysis and test standardization. Both topics involve the computation of certain statistics that must be examined closely to determine if all items on a test are functioning as they should and how the test scores may be interpreted. Item analysis focuses on the functioning of individual items, whereas test standardization is concerned with the normative interpretation of scores on the test as a whole or on the several parts or subtests comprising it. The topics in this chapter and the next are discussed primarily from the perspective of classical (traditional) test theory, but more recently developed approaches from item-response theory are not neglected. Classical test theory (CTT) and item-response theory (IRT) are useful in test development, analysis, and applications and, depending on the specific task, both have adherents.

ITEM ANALYSIS

Even after a test has been administered and scored, it is not always certain that it has done its job well. When a test is tried out initially, it is likely that a number of problems will be encountered. This is one reason why commercially distributed tests are administered first to a sample of people who are representative of the group for whom the test is ultimately intended. The responses of this pilot sample can then be analyzed to determine if the items are functioning properly.

Whatever the type of test—standardized or teacher-made, ability or personality—a post-mortem or post hoc analysis of results is just as necessary as in medicine or any other human enterprise. Among the questions that need to be answered are these: Were the time limits adequate? Did the examinees understand the directions? Were the testing conditions appropriate? Were emergencies handled properly? Were the items clear? Was the test fair? A simple feedback questionnaire incorporating these and other relevant questions can often help refine the test. Rarely is every problem or contingency that arises during a test anticipated, but a post hoc analysis can provide information and motivation for anticipating and coping with similar situations in future administrations.

An analysis of responses given by a group of people to the individual items on a test serves several functions. The major aim of such an *item analysis* is to help improve the test by revising or discarding ineffective items. Another important function of an item analysis, especially of an achievement test, is to provide diagnostic information on what examinees know and don't know.

Criterion-Referenced Tests and Mastery

The procedure employed in evaluating the effectiveness of test items depends to some extent on the purposes of the test. For example, a test developer may want to design a test that predicts relevant clinical phenomena, such as outcome to psychotherapy or psychiatric diagnosis. Thus, items on the test will be selected based on how well they predict these events. Another test developer may be concerned with determining how much an examinee knows about the content of an academic area. In this case, performance is measured against a criterion or standard established by the classroom teacher or by institutional policy. The purpose of such *criterion-referenced* (or domain-referenced) testing is not to discover how each person scores in relation to other people, but rather to determine where he or she stands with respect to certain course objectives or clinical phenomena. A particular type of criterion-referenced test designed to measure the attainment of a limited range of cognitive skills is known as a *mastery test*. A person's score on a mastery test is expressed as a percentage of the total number of items answered correctly; a perfect score indicates 100% mastery of the material.

Individual Differences and Item Validity

Because it is often difficult to obtain agreement on how much someone should know about a particular subject or what constitutes mastery of it, scores on psychological or educational tests have traditionally been interpreted by comparing them with the scores obtained by other people. Psychological tests have been devised primarily to assess differences among individuals in cognitive and affective characteristics. People differ in their abilities and personalities, and psychologists attempt to evaluate these differences with various kinds of tests. The more carefully this is accomplished, the more precisely behavior can be predicted from test scores. Consequently, professional test constructors try to devise items that differentiate among people in terms of whatever is to be measured. By so doing, the variability of total test scores is increased, and a given score becomes a more accurate index of a person's standing in relation to the standings of other people.

To assess the usefulness of an item as a measure of individual differences in ability or personality characteristics, testers need some external criterion measure of the characteristic. If the test is being constructed to predict performance on a job or in school, then an appropriate criterion is a measure of job performance (e.g., supervisor's ratings) or of school achievement (e.g., teacher-assigned marks). The *validity* of an item for predicting standings on an external criterion may be determined by correlating scores on the item (0's for wrongs and 1's for rights) with scores on the criterion measure. Different types of correlation coefficients have been used for this purpose, the most common being the *point-biserial coefficient*. This coefficient can be computed with the formula

$$r_{pb} = \frac{(\overline{Y}_p - \overline{Y}_t)\sqrt{n_t n_p/[(n_t - n_p)(n_t - 1)]}}{s_t}, \tag{4.1}$$

where n_t is the total number of examinees, n_p is the number of examinees who get the item right, $\overline{Y}_p$ is the mean criterion scores of examinees who pass the item, $\overline{Y}_t$ is the mean of all criterion scores, and s_t = the standard deviation of all criterion scores. The criterion may be an external one (job productivity, course grades, etc.) or even an internal criterion such as total scores on the test.

To illustrate the computation of the point-biserial coefficient, assume that the mean and standard deviation of the total test scores of a group of 30 people are 75 and 10, respectively. Now, if the mean score of 17 examinees who get a certain item right is 80, substitution in formula 4.1 yields

$$r_{pb} = \frac{(80 - 75)\sqrt{30(17)/[13(29)]}}{10} = .58.$$

The higher the item–criterion correlation, the more accurate are the item scores as a predictor of the criterion. Whether an item is retained or discarded depends on the size of this coefficient. Items having correlations as low as .20 with the criterion may contribute to predicting it, though higher coefficients are preferred. An item having a correlation close to or less than .00 with the criterion should certainly be revised or discarded. The usefulness of an item for predicting a specified criterion depends, however, not only on the item–criterion correlation, but also on the correlation of the item with other items on the test. Items having high correlations with the criterion but low correlations with other items are best because they make a more independent contribution to the prediction of criterion scores.

Item Difficulty and Discrimination Indexes

There is usually no readily available external criterion against which to validate items. As a result a different procedure, *internal consistency,* is often used. As with any other test, an item analysis entails determining the percentage of examinees who respond in a certain way on the items and the correlation of the item with a criterion measure. In the case of a classroom achievement test, the items are correlated with the total scores on the test itself. Assuming that the set of items as a whole is an adequate measure of achievement in the subject, total scores are used as the criterion in determining the internal consistency of the test.

A shortcut procedure is to sort the examinees into three groups according to their scores on the test as a whole: an upper group consisting of the 27% who made the highest scores, a lower group composed of the 27% who made the lowest scores, and the remaining 46% in a middle group. When the number of respondents is small, upper and lower 50% groups on total test scores are sometimes used for item analysis purposes. In any event, the following statistical indexes are computed from scores on the upper and lower groups:

$$p = \frac{U_p + L_p}{U + L} \qquad\qquad (4.2)$$

and

$$D = \frac{U_p - L_p}{U}. \qquad\qquad (4.3)$$

U_p and L_p are the numbers of people in the upper and lower groups, respectively, who get the item right; U and L are the total number of people in the upper and lower groups (note that $U = L$). The value of p is referred to as an *item difficulty index* and D as an *item discrimination index.* To illustrate the computation of these indexes, assume that 50 people take a test. Then the upper and lower groups can be formed from the top $.27 \times 50 \approx 14$ and the bottom 14 on total test score. If 12 of the people in the upper group and 7 of those in the lower group pass item A, then $p = (12 + 7)/28 = .68$ and $D = (12 - 7)/14 = .36$.

The item difficulty index has a range of .00 to 1.00. An item with $p = .00$ is one that no one answered correctly, and an item with $p = 1.00$ was answered correctly by everyone. The optimum p value for an item depends on a number of factors, including the purposes of the test and the number of response options. If the purpose of a test is to identify or select only a small percentage of the best applicants, then the test should be fairly difficult, as reflected in a lower mean value of p. If the test is designed to screen out only a few very poor applicants, then a high mean value of p is best.

The optimum value of p depends on the purposes of the test. For example, the optimum p should be fairly low for items on a test designed to assign scholarships or for advanced placement, but fairly high on a test designed to identify students for remedial programs. On a test designed to measure a broad range of ability, the optimum p value is closer to .50. As shown in Table 4.1, the optimum mean value of p for such a test also varies inversely with the number of response options (k). The p's for acceptable items fall within

TABLE 4.1   Optimum Mean Item Difficulty Indexes for Test Items Having Various Numbers of Options

NUMBER OF OPTIONS (*k*)	OPTIMUM MEAN DIFFICULTY INDEX (*p*)
2	.85
3	.77
4	.74
5	.69
Open ended (essay, short answer)	.50

(*Source:* Constructed from data provided by F. M. Lord, *Psychometrika, 17* (1952), 181–194.)

a fairly narrow range, approximately .20, around these tabled values.[1] Although several very easy and several very difficult items are often included on a broad-range test, they actually add very little to the overall effectiveness of a test in distinguishing among students who possess different amounts of knowledge, skill, or understanding of the test material.

The item discrimination index (*D*) is a measure of the effectiveness of an item in discriminating between high and low scorers on a test. The higher the value of *D,* the more effective the item is in discriminating between examinees with high scores and those with low scores on the test as a whole. When *D* is 1.00, all examinees in the upper group and none of those in the lower group on total test scores answered the item right. Rarely, however, is *D* equal to 1.00, and an item is usually considered acceptable if it has a *D* index of .30 or higher. But *D* and *p* are not independent indexes, and the minimum acceptable value of *D* varies with the value of *p*. A *D* value somewhat less than .30 is acceptable as *p* becomes increasingly higher or lower than the optimum value, particularly when the sizes of the upper and lower comparison groups are large. Also, an item having a low *D* index is not automatically discarded: it may be possible to salvage the item by modifying it. Constructing good test items is a time-consuming process, so defective items should be revised and retained whenever possible.

Factors Affecting Item Functioning

The results of an item analysis often vary substantially with the specific group tested, especially when the number of examinees is small. Certain items may be answered differently by males than by females or by one ethnic, age, or socioeconomic group than another. In constructing a standardized test, it is now common practice to examine each item and its associated statistics for indications of group discrimination or bias. Statistical indexes of *differential item functioning* (*DIF*) are often computed to facilitate this process. Many approaches to obtaining information on the differential functioning of test items have been

---

[1]The range of *p* should be less than .20 in a *peaked test* designed to measure efficiently within a fairly narrow range of ability. This is the case, for example, with a test designed to select or identify a relatively small group of persons of very low or very high ability or any other characteristic with a low occurrence rate (base rate) in the population of interest.

proposed, including item delta plots and various chi-square procedures (see Camilli & Shepard, 1994).

Simply because the way in which an item is answered varies from group to group does not necessarily mean that the item is biased against one of the groups. Technically, an item is biased only when it measures something different—a different characteristic or trait—in one group than in another. If item scores reflect true differences in ability or whatever characteristic the item was designed to measure, the item is technically unbiased. Conducting a separate item analysis for each group should reveal the presence of item bias, that is, whether the item discriminates well between high and low scorers in both groups.

Problems also occur in the item analysis of speeded tests, for which the time limits are short and not all examinees have time to finish. On a speeded test, items near the end of the test are attempted by relatively few people. If those who reach and therefore attempt an item are the most capable examinees, the discrimination index (D) will probably be greater than it would be if the time limits were more generous. On the other hand, if the most careless responders are more likely to reach and attempt items toward the end of the test, the D values of those items will tend to be smaller than the D values of items near the beginning. Various procedures have been proposed for coping with problems encountered in analyzing items toward the end of speeded tests, but none of them is completely satisfactory.

Despite their shortcomings, the item difficulty and discrimination indexes provide useful information on the functioning of individual items. In general, it has been found that item analyses produce significant improvements in test effectiveness. The item discrimination index in particular is a fairly good measure of item quality. Along with the difficulty index (p), D can serve as a warning that something is wrong with an item.

Test constructors were traditionally advised to record the statistical results of item analyses, along with the item itself, on index cards and file the cards for later use. With the advent of high-speed computers, test items can now be coded by topic, difficulty, and discrimination levels, and perhaps even the cognitive processes involved in answering them and then stored in an item bank. Such item banks are used not only by professional test constructors but are also provided as supplements with many textbooks, to be used as practice tests or to serve as a pool of items for constructing classroom tests. Computers can be used to select items from a bank dealing with different content and assembled as a unit test or examination. Specialized computer programs are also available to facilitate selection of items dealing not only with a specified topic, but also with certain desired statistical characteristics.

Internal Consistency versus Validity

The concept of item validity usually refers to the relationship of an item to an external criterion. In contrast, D is a measure of the relationship of item scores to an internal criterion—total test scores—rather than to an external criterion. Selecting items having high D values will result in an internally consistent test on which the correlations among items are highly positive. Scores on an internally consistent test, however, are not necessarily highly correlated with scores on an external criterion. To construct a test having a high correlation with an external criterion, items having low correlations with each other but high correlations with the criterion measure should be selected. Selecting items on the basis of the D statistic yields a different kind of test than one composed of items selected for their high correlations with an external criterion. Which of these strategies—internal or external—is superior depends on the purposes of the test. If an internally consistent measure of a characteristic is desired (e.g., scores on an achievement test), the discrimination index (D) should be used in selecting items. If the most valid predictor of a particular external criterion is needed (e.g., suicide risk), item–criterion correlations should be used. Sometimes a combination of the two strategies is appropriate: a composite test is constructed from subtests having low correlations with each other and substantial correlations with an external criterion, but the items within each subtest are highly intercorrelated.

Criterion-Referenced Test Items

Difficulty and discrimination indexes may also be computed on criterion-referenced test items that are designed to determine examinees' standings on specified educational objectives. In this case, the examinees are divided into two groups: an upper group consisting of the U examinees whose total test scores meet the designated criterion of acceptable performance and a lower group consisting of the L examinees whose total scores fail to meet the criterion. For a particular item, U_p is the number in the upper group (above criterion level) who get the item right, and L_p is the number in the lower group (below criterion level) who get the item right. Then the item difficulty index is defined by formula 4.2. Because U and L are not necessarily equal, the item discrimination index is defined as

$$D = \frac{U_p}{U} - \frac{L_p}{L}. \qquad \textbf{(4.4)}$$

An external criterion may also be used in forming the upper and lower groups. In the case of a criterion-referenced achievement test, for example, respondents may be sorted into two groups: those who received instruction in the subject matter associated with the test (U) and those who did not receive such instruction (L). The U and L groups may also consist of the same individuals, both before (L) and after (U) instruction. In either case, formula 4.4 can be used to determine an item discrimination index.

Analysis of Distracters

The analysis of multiple-choice items has traditionally begun with the computation of difficulty and discrimination indexes for each item. A secondary analysis is concerned with the functioning of the $k - 1$ incorrect options (distracters) for each item. The item discrimination index (D) provides some information on the functioning of the distracters as a whole. A positive D means that examinees in the upper group (on total test score) tended to select the correct answer, whereas those in the lower group tended to select one of the distracters; the magnitude of D indicates the extent of this tendency. On the other hand, a negative D indicates that the distracters were chosen more frequently by examinees in the upper group than by those in the lower group and that the item needs revising. However, the sign and magnitude of D do not reveal whether all distracters functioned properly.

The simplest method of determining whether all distracters are working as they should is to count the number of times each distracter is selected as the right answer by examinees in the upper group and by those in the lower group. If, on an otherwise satisfactory item, too many examinees in the upper group or too few of those in the lower group selected a given distracter, the distracter should be edited or replaced. Ideally, all $k - 1$ distracters should be equally plausible to examinees who don't know the correct answer to an item; consequently, every distracter should be selected by approximately the same number of people.

Item Characteristic Curves

Even acceptable values of p and D do not guarantee that an item is functioning properly across all levels of performance on the test. To be most effective, the proportion of people who answer a test item correctly should increase fairly steadily with increases in total scores on the test or subtest. Whether a test item functions in this manner can be determined from the *item characteristic curve* (*ICC*). In constructing an ICC, the proportion of respondents who gave the keyed answer is plotted against their scores on an internal criterion (e.g., total test scores) or an external criterion such as scholastic achievement or occupational performance. Once the characteristic curve for a particular item has been constructed, the difficulty level and discrimination index for the item can be determined. The *difficulty level* (*b*) is the criterion score at which 50% of the examinees gave the correct (keyed) answer; the *discrimination index* (*a*) is the slope of the item-response curve at the 50% point. For example, of the two ICCs plotted in Figure 4.1, a value of .50 on the vertical axis corresponds to total test score of 68 in the case of item 1 and 77 in the case of item 2. Consequently, item 2 is more difficult than Item 1. However, the ICC of item 1 has a steeper slope than that of item 2, so item 1 discriminates better than item 2 between high and low scorers on the test as a whole. These two measures (location and slope on the ICC) are similar to the p and D indexes of traditional item analysis, but an ICC goes further in providing a detailed picture of item functioning across the entire range of internal or external criterion scores. In addition to plotting the proportion of correct responses corresponding to total scores on an internal or external criterion measure, the proportion of individuals with each score who selected a particular distracter may be plotted in analyzing the effectiveness of item distracters.

Item-Response Theory

Item-response theory (*IRT*) is a sophisticated, in-depth method for analyzing items (Baker, 2001; Embretson, 2000). At its simplest, it first develops a theory on how items should function based on knowledge of an ability or trait. It then compares actual responses to items to determine how well the items function. Thus, the actual items are compared to how they should theoretically function (see edres.org/irt/). The computations involved are very complex and generally must be made by means of a computer package (LOGIST, BILOG, ASCAL, BIGSTEPS) (see Hambleton & Pitoniak, 2002; Henard, 2000).

The usual IRT model is a logistic function having one, two, or three parameters. The formula for generating probability estimates in the *three-parameter model* is

$$P(\theta) = c + (1 - c)\frac{1}{1 + e^{-a(\theta-b)}}. \tag{4.5}$$

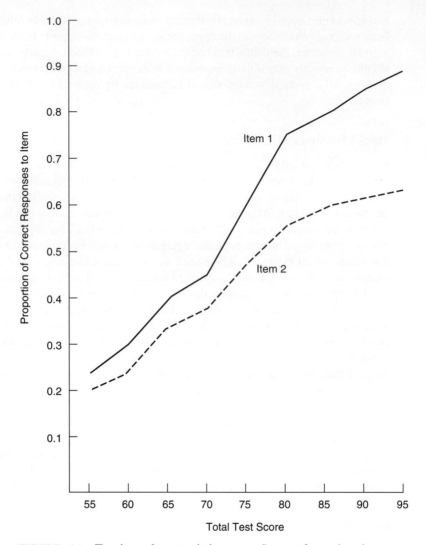

FIGURE 4.1   Two item characteristic curves. See text for explanation.

In this formula, *e* is the base of natural logarithms (2.718282), *a* is an item slope (discrimination) parameter, *b* is an item location (difficulty) parameter, *c* is a pseudo-guessing parameter, θ is the respondent's ability level on a standard score scale, and $P(\theta)$ is the probability that a person with ability level $P(\theta)$ will answer the item correctly. Assuming that $c = 0$, formula 4.5 reduces to the equation for the *two-parameter model:*

$$P(\theta) = \frac{1}{1 + e^{-a(\theta - b)}}. \tag{4.6}$$

An additional assumption that all items are equally discriminating yields the equation for the *one-parameter,* or *Rasch, model:*

$$P(\theta) = \frac{1}{1 + e^{-1(\theta-b)}}. \tag{4.7}$$

Although the Rasch model has generated a great deal of psychometric research, the two-parameter model is at least as popular.

As illustrated in Figure 4.2, the shape of an item-response curve varies with the values of the *a* and *b* parameters. Both of the curves in this figure were constructed by the

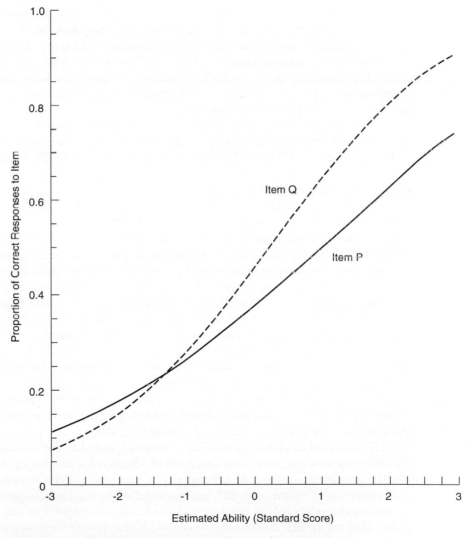

FIGURE 4.2 Two item-response curves. See text for explanation.

two-parameter function in formula 4.5. In curve P, the difficulty parameter (b) is 1.00 and the discrimination parameter (a) is .5; in curve Q, $b = .25$ and $a = .75$. Note that b is the value of (the point on the horizontal axis) corresponding to $P(\theta) = .5$, and a is the slope of the curve at $P(\theta) - .5$. In the three-parameter model, b is the value of $P(\theta)$ corresponding to $.5(c + 1)$, where c is the point at which the item-response curve crosses the vertical axis. An informative exercise is to plot several one-, two-, and three-parameter item-response curves using various values of the appropriate parameters. The scores on the latent ability continuum are expressed in standard (z) score units, but in most educational applications the z scores are transformed to a scale having a mean of 300 and a standard deviation of 50.

In actual practice, neither the item parameters nor the latent ability scores (θ's) of the examinees are known. The problem is to find the item-response curve that best fits the responses to individual items. This involves an iterative, maximum-likelihood procedure of assuming certain initial values for the item parameters, computing the $P(\theta)$'s corresponding to the various values of θ, comparing the predicted with the actual item responses, and continuing the process until a best-fit solution is achieved. The process of estimating item parameters requires the responses of a large number of examinees who are representative of the population of potential test takers—approximately 2,000 for the three-parameter model and 500 for the one-parameter (Rasch) model.

An important feature of the computed item parameters is that they are relatively independent of the ability level of the particular sample of people on which they are based. Unlike traditional testing methodology, which confounds test difficulty and discrimination with the particular sample of people who are tested, in IRT these parameters are, at least in theory, independent of the tested sample.

In addition to providing estimates of item parameters, IRT can be used to estimate the scores of examinees on the latent ability continuum. Actually, this is the principal purpose of administering a test constructed by IRT principles. As in estimating item parameters from ability levels, the estimation of individual scores on the latent ability continuum is an iterative process that begins by substituting certain trial values for the examinee's ability and the assumed item parameters into the appropriate logistic equation. The resulting $P(\theta)$'s are then compared with the actual $P(\theta)$'s, and the process continues until a best-fit equation is obtained. The standard errors of the estimated θ's, a measure of the variability of the estimated θ's around the actual but unknown θ's, can also be computed.

Another interesting property of IRT, the invariance of the examinee's ability with response to the items used to estimate it, stems from the process of estimating the θ's. This feature of IRT means that a test of any level of difficulty can be administered to determine a person's standing on the latent ability continuum. However, the most accurate estimate is obtained when the items comprising the test, and hence the test itself, are most appropriate, that is, at the same level of difficulty as the examinee's ability.

IRT has been employed for a variety of purposes, including the construction of tests, the calibration of test scores to provide a frame of reference for interpreting them, test standardization, the determination of differential item functioning (DIF), and adaptive testing. With regard to test construction, IRT regions on the ability continuum where more precise measurements are needed can be targeted so that items are not wasted on less important regions. Thus, using IRT, it is possible to develop highly precise screening tests, selection tests, and criterion-referenced tests, as well as more traditional tests having a broader spectrum across the ability continuum. The IRT approach to DIF is to plot the item-response curves separately for the two or more salient demographic groups of people (Whites vs. Blacks, men vs. women, etc.). Item-response curves having significantly different shapes for the comparison groups provide evidence of differential item functioning.

One shortcoming of most IRT models is the assumption that only a single latent trait underlies test performance, but progress on multidimensional models has been made. Most IRT models are also limited to 0–1 scoring, though more complex models involving multi-point scoring have been developed (Thissen, Nelson, Rosa, & McLeod, 2001). Thus, these newer techniques can be used for rating scales and multidimensional analysis (see McDonald, 2000).

TEST STANDARDIZATION AND NORMS

A core feature of most psychological tests is that an individual's score must be compared with some normative group. This allows us to interpret the meaning of the score. For example, we know that a person scored high on introversion since other people responding to the same items endorsed a fewer number of items related to introversion. To accomplish this task, the test, inventory, rating scale, or other psychometric device must be standardized.

Any standardized test has standard directions for administration and scoring that should be followed closely, leaving little room for personal interpretation or bias. Standardization also involves administering the test to a large sample of people (the *standardization sample*) selected as representative of the *target population* of persons for whom the test is intended.

The major purpose of standardizing a test is to determine the distribution of raw scores in the standardization sample (*norm group*). The obtained raw scores are then converted to some form of derived scores, or *norms*. The major types of norms are age equivalents, grade equivalents, percentile ranks, and standard scores. Most test manuals contain tables of norms listing raw scores and some type of converted scores corresponding to them. Then a person's standing on a test can be evaluated by referring to the appropriate norms table and finding the converted score equivalents of his or her raw scores(s). In this norm-referenced interpretive approach, the obtained norms do not serve as standards of desirable performance, but simply as a frame of reference for interpreting scores. Norms indicate a person's standing on the test relative to the distribution of scores obtained by people of the same chronological age, grade, sex, or other demographic characteristics.

In evaluating handicapped children, it is sometimes necessary to administer an *out-of-level test* designed for an age or grade level below that of the person being tested. Special out-of-level norms are then needed to assist in interpreting the scores. A number of standardized tests provide for out-of-level testing and corresponding norms.

In terms of sample size and representativeness, group tests, and achievement tests in particular, are often standardized more adequately than individual tests. Norms for group tests may be based on as many as 100,000 people, whereas the size of the norm group for a carefully standardized individual test is more likely to be between 2,000 and 4,000. A large standardization sample, however, does not guarantee that the sample is representative of the population of interest. The sample must be carefully selected in order to be representative of this *target population.*

Selecting a Standardization Sample

To serve effectively in the interpretation of test scores, norms must be appropriate for the group or individual to be evaluated. For example, a particular fourth-grader's score may surpass that of 80% of fourth-grade children and 60% of sixth-graders. Though it may be of some interest to compare a fourth-grader's score with the scores of third- and sixth-graders, the student's standing in his or her own (fourth grade) group is of primary concern. Whenever a test score is converted by referring to a table of norms, it is important to make note of the characteristics of the sample (age, sex, ethnicity, education, socioeconomic status, geographical region) of the particular norm group and to include this information in all communications regarding the person's performance. Another important consideration is when (on what date) the norms were obtained. Norms on certain tests can become outdated during times of rapid social and educational change or when the test has been used repeatedly in preceding years. Changes in school curricula, for example, may necessitate restandardizing and perhaps modifying or reconstructing an achievement test every few years.

The manner in which a standardization sample is selected from a population varies from simple random sampling to more complex sampling strategies, such as stratified random sampling and cluster sampling. In *simple random sampling,* every person in the target population has an equal chance of being selected. However, randomness does not ensure representativeness. Consequently, a more appropriate way to standardize a test is to begin by categorizing, or *stratifying,* the population on a series of demographic variables (sex, age, socioeconomic status, geographical region, etc.) that are presumably related to scores on the test. Then the number of individuals selected at random from each category or stratum is proportional to the total number of people in the population who fall in that stratum. When this *stratified random sampling* procedure is employed, the likelihood of selecting an atypical, or biased, sample is minimized. The obtained norms provide a better basis for interpreting scores on the test than norms determined on a simple random sample.

Cluster sampling is more economical than stratified random sampling and more likely than simple random sampling to yield a representative sample of the target population. The process begins by dividing a designated geographical region or other relevant entity into blocks or clusters. Then a specified percentage of the clusters is chosen at random, and within each cluster a certain number of subunits (schools, residences, etc.) are randomly selected. The final step is to administer the test to everyone in each subunit or at least a random sample of people having the designated characteristics.

Administering all items on a test to a stratified random sample or a cluster sample of individuals is tedious and time consuming, so less costly strategies for obtaining norms have been proposed. One such strategy is to sample items as well as individuals. In *item sampling,* different samples of items are administered to different, randomly selected samples of people. One group answers one set of items, and other groups answer other sets. The process is efficient, in that more items can be administered to a large number of persons in a fairly short period of time. Item analyses can then be conducted and norms based on the scores of representative samples can be determined for a wide range of test content. Norms derived from item sampling are very similar to those obtained by the traditional but more laborious procedure of administering the entire test to a large representative sample.

The norms published in test manuals are useful for comparing an examinee's score with the scores of a sample of people from various localities, sometimes a cross section of the entire nation. But teachers are typically more interested in knowing how well students perform in comparison with other students in a specific school, school system, state, or region, rather than with those in a nationwide sample. When interest is restricted to the test scores of a particular school, the test administrator will want to convert raw test scores to *local norms* by the procedures discussed in the following sections. Local norms are often used for selection and placement purposes in schools and colleges.

Age and Grade Norms

Among the most popular types of norms, primarily because they are fairly easy for test users to understand, are age norms and grade norms. An *age norm* (age equivalent, educational age) is the median score on a test obtained by persons of a given chronological age; a *grade norm* (grade equivalent) is the median score obtained by students at a given grade level. Age norms are expressed in 12 one-month intervals, ranging for the tenth year, for example, from 10 years, 0 months to 10 years, 11 months. Grade norms are expressed in 10 one-month intervals, based on the assumption that growth in the characteristic of interest during the summer months is inconsequential. For example, the range of grade norms for the fifth grade is 5–0 to 5–9, in one-month intervals from the first to the last month of the school year.

Despite their popularity, age and grade norms have serious shortcomings. The main problem is that growth in cognitive, psychomotor, or affective characteristics is not uniform over the entire range of ages or grades. Because age and grade units become progressively smaller with increasing age or grade level, a difference of 2 months' growth in achievement at grade 4 (say, from 4–2 to 4–4) is not educationally equivalent to 2 months' growth in achievement at a later grade level (say, from 8–2 to 8–4). Age and grade norms incorrectly imply that the rate of increase in tested abilities is constant from year to year, so their use is frequently discouraged by specialists in educational measurement. Norms in which the unit of measurement is less variable across the score range are preferred.

Because of their convenience, age and grade norms continue to be used at the elementary school level, where the growth units are more nearly constant across time. Even at this level, however, age and grade norms should be supplemented with percentile norms or standard score norms for a particular age or grade.

Typically, students in a given grade on whom grade norms are determined have a rather wide range of ages; the scores of certain students who are actually much older (or younger) than the average student in that grade are included in the norms. To provide a more accurate index of the average score of students at a given grade level, the scores of students who are significantly older or younger than the modal age are sometimes omitted, and the median score is computed only on students who are of the appropriate age for that grade. These restricted norms are referred to as *modal age norms*. Modal age norms, which are rarely found in contemporary achievement test manuals, are mentioned here primarily for their historical interest.

The term *mental age* will be recalled from the brief discussion in Chapter 1 of the history of mental measurement. This concept, which was introduced by Alfred Binet, is a type of age norm employed on various intelligence tests. The mental age score of a particular examinee corresponds to the chronological age of the subgroup of children (all of the same chronological age) in the standardization group whose median score is the same as the examinee's score. The practice in many schools for the mentally retarded has been to group such children according to mental age, rather than chronological age, for instructional purposes.

An older practice in testing, which has virtually disappeared, is to convert age norms to quotients by dividing the age scores of each examinee by his or her chronological age (in months) and multiplying the resulting quotient by 100. The *intelligence quotient (ratio IQ)* on the older Stanford–Binet Intelligence Scale, for example, was defined as

$$IQ = 100 \frac{MA}{CA},\qquad\qquad(4.8)$$

where MA and CA are the examinee's mental and chronological ages in months. Similarly, an *educational quotient* on certain achievement tests was computed as the ratio of educational age (age norm on an educational achievement test) to chronological age in months. By comparing the results of an intelligence test with those of an educational achievement test, an *accomplishment quotient* could be computed as the ratio of educational age to mental age. Some of these quotients are still calculated in evaluating test scores, but the practice is discouraged by psychological measurement specialists.

Percentile Norms

Percentile norms consist of a table of percentages corresponding to particular raw scores. The raw scores are referred to as *percentiles,* and the percentage of the norm group falling below a particular score is the *percentile rank* of this score. Columns 2 and 5 of the distribution in Table 4.2 show that, for this group of scores, the percentile rank of a score of 625 is approximately 82 and the percentile rank of a score of 475 is approximately 23. Alternatively, it can be said that the 82nd percentile is 625 and the 23rd percentile is 475.

Percentile norms are often used for selection and placement purposes in a given school or grade group, so the procedure for computing them will be described in some detail. Columns 1 and 3 of Table 4.2 are a frequency distribution of 250 scores obtained on a scholastic ability test, and column 2 gives the midpoints of the score intervals. To compute the entry in column 4 (cumulative frequency below midpoint) for a particular interval, the frequencies on all intervals up to that interval are summed. To this sum is added one-half of the frequency on that interval. For example, the entry 227.0 for the interval 650–699 is computed as $1 + 13 + 25 + 38 + 65 + 49 + 27 + \frac{1}{2}(18) = 227.0$. Since the entry for a particular interval in column 4 is the cumulative frequency below the midpoint of that interval, the percentile rank of a given interval midpoint may be computed by dividing the corresponding cumulative frequency in column 4 by the total number of scores (n) and multiplying the resulting quotient by 100. For the data in Table 4.2, $n = 250$, so each percentile rank in column 5 is equal to 100 times the corresponding cumulative frequency in column 4 divided by 250. For example, the percentile rank of the midpoint 674.5 is $100(227/250) = 90.8 \approx 91$.

TABLE 4.2   Percentile Ranks and Standard Scores Corresponding to Midpoints of a Frequency Distribution of Test Scores

(1)	(2)	(3)	(4)	(5)	(6)	(7)	(8)	(9)	(10)
SCORE INTERVAL	MIDPOINT	FREQUENCY	CUMULATIVE FREQUENCY	PERCENTILE RANK OF MIDPOINT	z	Z	z_n	T	NCE
750–799	774.5	3	248.5	99.4 (99)	2.59	76	2.51	75	103
700–749	724.5	11	241.5	96.6 (97)	2.03	70	1.82	68	88
650–699	674.5	18	227.0	90.8 (91)	1.48	65	1.33	63	78
600–649	624.5	27	204.5	81.8 (82)	.92	59	.91	59	69
550–599	574.5	49	166.5	66.6 (67)	.37	54	.43	54	59
500–549	524.5	65	109.5	43.8 (44)	−.19	48	−.16	48	47
450–499	474.5	38	58.0	23.2 (23)	−.74	43	−.73	43	35
400–449	424.5	25	26.5	10.6 (11)	−1.30	37	−1.25	38	24
350–399	374.5	13	7.5	3.0 (3)	−1.85	31	−1.88	31	11
300–349	324.5	1	.5	.2 (0)	−2.41	26	−2.88	21	−10

Percentile ranks are fairly easy to compute and understand and therefore are more popular than standard score norms. Thus, a psychological report that is striving toward clarity might say something like "John scored in the high average range or 85th percentile. This means that he scored higher than 85% of his age-related peers." Tables of percentile norms within grades, chronological ages, gender, occupations, and other demographic groups are listed in the manuals accompanying many psychometric instruments. Unfortunately, the problem of unequal score units, which was referred to earlier in the discussion of age and grade norms, is not solved by percentile norms. Percentile ranks are ordinal-level rather than interval-level measures (see Appendix A), and hence the units are not equal on all parts of the scale. With respect to the attribute being measured, the difference between two percentile ranks on either the high or low end of the percentile equivalents scale (see Figure 4.3) is greater from that between two percentile ranks with an equal numerical difference but closer to the center of the scale.

The fact that percentile rank units bunch up in the middle and spread out at the extremes of the scale causes difficulty in the interpretation of changes and differences in these transformed scores. Thus, the difference in ability between a person with a percentile rank of 5 and one with a percentile rank of 10 on an achievement test is not equal to the difference in ability between a person with a percentile rank of 40 and one with a percentile rank of 45. In terms of the attribute (ability) being measured, the difference between percentile ranks of 5 and 10, for example, is greater than that between 45 and 50; this is so because the unit of measurement for the first difference is larger than that for the second difference. To interpret percentile norms accurately, one must remember to give greater weight to percentile rank differences at the extremes than to the same differences nearer the middle of the scale.

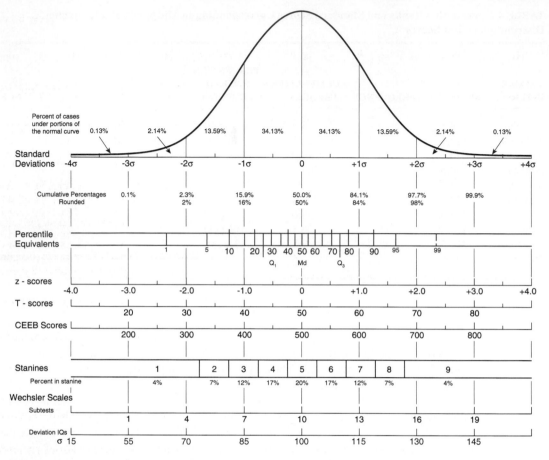

FIGURE 4.3   Percentile ranks and standard scores corresponding to various points on the baseline of a normal distribution of scores.

(H. G. Seashore, *Methods of expressing test scores,* The Psychological Corporation Test Service Bulletin, No. 48, 1955.)

Standard-Score Norms

Unlike percentile ranks, standard scores represent measurement on an interval scale. *Standard-score norms* are converted scores having any desired mean and standard deviation. There are many different types of standard scores, including *z* scores, *Z* scores, CEEB scores, deviation IQ scores, stanine scores, *T* scores, and *NCE* scores.

***z* Scores.**   *z* score equivalents of a particular distribution of raw scores may be determined as

$$z = \frac{X - \overline{X}}{s},\tag{4.9}$$

where *X* is a given raw score, $\overline{X}$ is the arithmetic mean, and *s* is the standard deviation of the raw scores. Transforming raw scores to *z* scores yields a score distribution having the same shape, but a different mean and standard deviation than the raw score (X) distribution. The mean of the z scores is 0, and the standard deviation is 1.

The z scores corresponding to the interval midpoints listed in column 2 are given in column 6 of Table 4.2. The mean and standard deviation of the distribution of scores in Table 4.2 are 541.5 and 90.3, respectively. Therefore, the z score corresponding to the midpoint 774.5 is $(774.5 - 541.5)/90.3 = 2.58$. The z scores corresponding to the midpoints of the other intervals may be found in the same way. The z scores of various points along the base line of the normal curve are given in Figure 4.3.

Z Scores.   The fact that z scores can be negative or positive decimal numbers creates some difficulty in manipulating them. The problem can be solved by multiplying the z scores by a constant and adding another constant to the products. Multiplying z by 10, adding 50 to the product, and rounding the result to the nearest whole number yields a Z score. The mean of a set of Z scores is 50 and their standard deviation is 10, but the frequency distribution of the Z scores has the same shape as the original raw-score distribution (see column 7 of Table 4.2).

CEEB Scores.   At one time standard scores (CEEB scores) on tests published by the College Entrance Examination Board were determined by multiplying the corresponding z scores by 100 and adding 500 to the products. For example, this was done to the raw scores on the Scholastic Aptitude Test (SAT) administered in 1941, yielding a new distribution having a mean of 500 and a standard deviation of 100. Subsequently, however, the scores obtained by students taking the SAT were not transformed in this manner. Rather, to ensure a constant score unit for comparing test results from year to year, beginning in 1941 scores on the SAT scale were based on the results of the test administered in that year.

Wechsler Scores.   Raw scores on the subtests of the Wechsler intelligence scales were transformed to have a mean of 10 and a standard deviation of 3. However, Verbal, Performance, and Full Scale scores (deviation IQs) on the Wechsler tests were converted to a distribution having a mean of 100 and a standard deviation of 15 (see last two lines of Figure 4.3).

Normalized Standard Scores.   The standard-score norms described above are simple linear transformations of raw scores. The mean and standard deviation of the transformed scores are different from those of the raw-score distribution, but the shapes of the raw- and standard-score distributions are identical. If the raw-score distribution is symmetrical, the distribution of transformed scores will also be symmetrical; if the former is skewed, the latter will also be skewed.

To make the scores from different tests more directly comparable, a transformation procedure is used that not only affects the mean and standard deviation, but also changes the shape of the distribution of raw scores to that of a normal distribution. Transforming a group of raw scores to *normalized standard scores* begins by computing the percentile ranks corresponding to the raw scores. Then, from a table of areas under the normal curve (Appendix B), the z score corresponding to each percentile rank is found. For example, assume that the midpoints (column 2) of the distribution in Table 4.2 are to be converted to normalized standard scores. Because the percentile ranks of these midpoints have already been found (column 5), we begin by converting the percentile ranks to proportions (e.g., 99.4 becomes

.994). Then, from the table in Appendix B, the z scores below which the given proportions of the area lie are determined. Thus, the z score (z_n) below which .994 of the area under the curve lies is 2.51. The other normalized z scores in column 8 of Table 4.2 were determined similarly. To eliminate decimal points and negative numbers, these z_n scores were transformed to T scores by the formula $T = 10z_n + 50$ (column 9) and to NCE (normal curve equivalent) scores by the formula $NCE = 21z_n + 50$. T scores range from approximately 20 to 80 and NCE scores from approximately 0 to 100.

The z_n scores may be transformed to normalized scores having any desired mean and standard deviation. Another score scale is the *stanine* (standard nine) scale illustrated by the third scale from the bottom in Figure 4.3. On this normalized standard scale, which has a mean of 5 and a standard deviation of approximately 2, there are nine different ranges, or stanines. These ranges are designated by the numbers 1 through 9 and, as shown in the figure, a certain percentage of a normal distribution of scores falls within the interval represented by a given stanine. The stanine scale, however, is not a true standard-score scale because the first and ninth stanines are open-ended. Notice in Figure 4.3 that the widths of stanines 2 through 8 are equal, indicating equal standard-score units, but that stanines 1 and 9 span a much wider distance.

One advantage of stanine scores is that they represent ranges rather than specific points. This helps counter the tendency to view test scores as precise, unvarying measures of individual differences. Another procedure having the same effect is to report not only the percentile rank or standard score corresponding to a given raw score, but also a percentile rank or standard score interval within which the examinee's true standing on the test might reasonably be expected to fall. This practice is a recognition of the fact that scores on psychological and educational tests are not exact, but are subject to errors of measurement.

EQUATING TESTS

In many situations involving applications and research with psychological tests, more than one form of a test is needed. *Parallel forms* of a test are equivalent in the sense that they contain the same kinds of items of equal difficulty and are highly correlated. Therefore, the scores made on one form are very similar to the scores of the same examinees on a second form at the same age or grade levels as the first form. Constructing parallel tests is, unfortunately, a rather expensive and time-consuming process. It begins with the preparation of two tests having the same number and kinds of items and yielding the same means and standard deviations when standardized on the same group of people. The resulting parallel forms are then *equated* by converting scores on one form to the same units as those on the other form. This may be done, for example, by the *equipercentile method* of changing the scores on each form to percentile ranks. Then a table of equivalent scores on the two forms is prepared by equating the pth percentile on the first form to the score at the pth percentile on the second form.

The process of equating, or rather making comparable, two tests of the same difficulty level (e.g., the same grade) is referred to as *horizontal equating*. Equating may also be done *vertically*, as when scores on two tests having different levels of difficulty (viz., different grades) are equated. In general, the process of equating involves anchoring the tests to a common test or pool of items, as was done every year with the older Scholastic Aptitude Test (SAT). By using a set of common anchor items that were the same as a subset of items on at least one earlier form of the test, scores on each new form of the SAT administered each year were statistically equated to scores on previous forms on the test.

The previous discussion of *item-response theory* indicated that it calibrates a set of test items based on how items should theoretically perform. It then compares actual responses to items to see the extent to which they approximate the theoretical performance (usually represented by standard scores on the horizontal axis of an item-response curve). This method has also been applied to the task of equating tests. The IRT approach to equating involves finding a linear equation that transforms the item parameters (difficulty and discrimination indexes) of one form of a test to those of a second form. This process is referred to as *linking*. Linking procedures require that the two tests share some common (anchor) items or that a subset of examinees take both tests or a third test measuring the same trait. The equating procedures of item-response theory are economical in that item sampling, in which randomly selected subsets of items are administered to different randomly selected groups of people, is also involved.

Whatever the method employed in attempting to equate two tests—equipercentile, item response, linear or nonlinear score transformations, tests that either measure different psychological characteristics or have different reliabilities cannot, strictly speaking, be equated. In almost every case, about the best that can be done is to make the two tests or other psychometric instruments comparable.

SUMMARY

1. Test items may be analyzed by comparing item responses with scores on an external criterion, such as outcome to psychotherapy, grade point average, ratings by supervisors, or scores of other examinees. If the goal is to construct a test that is most predictive of scores on an external criterion, then the items should be validated against that criterion. The point biserial coefficient is the most common statistic used for this.

2. Items can also be analyzed with an internal criterion such as total test score. Formulas can be used to determine an item difficulty index (p) (how easy or difficult the item is) and a discrimination index (D) (how well it discriminates high versus low scorers). These indexes are also applicable to both norm- and criterion-referenced items. The optimum value of p depends on the purposes of the test and the number of options per item. In most situations, a D value of .30 or higher is required for an item to be acceptable.

3. Distractors on a multiple-choice test should be chosen equally as often by those who do not know the material (missed the item). Marked variations from uniformity in the frequency distribution of responses to the distracters are a sign of a poorly functioning item and it should therefore be replaced by another item.

4. In constructing an item characteristic curve, the proportion of examinees who give the keyed response to an item is plotted against scores on an internal (total test scores) or external criterion. An extension of the item characteristic curve approach known as item-response theory involves inserting theoretically based levels of difficulty, discrimination, and guessing into an equation. The equation compares the examinees'

actual responses with what their responses should have looked liked based on an understanding of an ability or another unidimensional characteristic.

5. Standardization consists of administering a test to a representative sample of people under standard (uniform) conditions and scoring it by a standard procedure. Norms computed from the obtained test scores provide a frame of reference for interpreting scores made by people who subsequently take the test. Test norms have traditionally been determined by testing a sample (random, stratified random, cluster) of the population of people for whom the test is intended. Less expensive and more efficient than traditional test-standardization procedures are item-sampling techniques in which not only people but also test items are sampled, with different groups of examinees answering different sets of items. Age and grade norms, which are determined most often for tests of achievement, permit comparisons of individual test scores with the average scores of people from a certain age or grade. The main shortcoming of age and grade norms is that growth in achievement or ability is not uniform over age or grade levels. Percentile norms, in which raw test scores are converted to the percentages of people in the standardization group who made those scores or lower, also suffer from the problem of unequal score units. Age, grade, and percentile norms are fairly easy to understand and convenient to use, so they will undoubtedly continue to be popular.

6. Standard-score norms are converted scores having a designated mean and standard deviation. Unlike the ordinal measures represented by age, grade, and percentile norms, standard scores (z, T, CEEB, and others) are interval-level measures. Not all standard scores are normally distributed, but they can easily be converted to normalized standard scores.

MASTERING THE CHAPTER OBJECTIVES

1. *Selecting test items based on external criterion*
   a. When would you want to use an internal item selection strategy versus an external item selection strategy?
   b. Name five examples of external criterion.

2. *Selecting items based on internal consistency*
   a. Describe the conceptual strategy behind selecting test items based on internal consistency.
   b. What are the difficulty (p) and discrimination (D) indexes of a test item administered to 75 people if 18 of those in the upper group (upper 27% on total test score) and 12 of those in the lower group (lower 27% on total test score) get the item right? Note that rounding yields 20 people in the upper group and 20 people in the lower group (see Answers to Quantitative Questions, p. 485).
   c. Compute the difficulty (p) and discrimination (D) indexes of an item on a criterion-referenced test taken by 50 people, 30 of whom scored at or above the criterion level and 20 of whom scored below the criterion level. Of those who scored at or above the criterion level, 20 got the item right; of those who scored below the criterion level, 10 got the item right (see Answers to Quantitative Questions, p. 485).
   d. The following two-way table indicates whether each of 20 people got each of the 10 items on a four-option, multiple-choice test right (r) or wrong (w). Classifying examinees A through J in the upper group and examinees K through T in the lower group on total

test score (see last line of table), compute the difficulty and discrimination indexes for each item. Write these values in the last two columns of the table. By inspecting the p and D indexes, decide which items are acceptable and which need revising or discarding (see Answers to Quantitative Questions, p. 485).

Examinee

Item	A	B	C	D	E	F	G	H	I	J	K	L	M	N	O	P	Q	R	S	T	p	D
1	r	r	r	w	w	w	r	r	r	r	w	r	r	w	w	w	r	w	w	w		
2	r	r	w	r	w	r	w	r	w	r	r	w	w	r	w	w	w	w	r	w		
3	r	w	r	r	r	w	r	w	r	w	w	r	r	w	w	r	w	w	w	w		
4	r	r	r	r	r	r	w	r	w	r	r	w	w	r	r	w	w	w	w	w		
5	r	r	w	r	r	r	r	r	w	w	w	r	w	w	w	w	w	w	w	w		
6	r	r	r	r	r	r	w	r	r	r	r	w	r	r	w	r	w	r	w	r		
7	r	w	w	w	r	r	r	r	w	r	w	w	r	w	r	w	w	r	r	w		
8	r	r	r	r	r	w	w	w	r	w	r	r	w	w	w	r	r	w	w	w		
9	r	r	r	r	w	r	r	w	r	r	r	r	w	r	r	w	w	w	w	w		
10	r	r	r	w	r	r	r	w	r	w	w	w	w	w	w	w	r	w	w	w		
Score	10	8	7	7	7	7	6	6	6	6	5	5	4	4	3	3	3	2	2	1		

3. *Multiple-choice item distractors*
   a. Describe an ideal distractor on a multiple-choice question.
   b. How would you detect a poor distractor on a multiple-choice question?

4. *Item-response curves and item-response theory*
   a. Describe the underlying concepts behind item-response theory.
   b. Describe the step by step process involved in using item-response theory.

5. *Standardization*
   a. Define simple random sampling, stratified sampling, cluster sampling, and item sampling.
   b. Describe the advantages and disadvantages of age and grade norms.

6. *Standard scores*
   a. Suppose that George makes a raw score of 65 on an arithmetic test having a mean of 50 and a standard deviation of 10, but makes a raw score of 80 on a reading test having a mean of 75 and a standard deviation of 15. What are George's z scores and Z scores on the tests? Is he better in arithmetic or reading? (See Answers to Quantitative Questions, p. 485.)
   b. By referring to a table of areas under the normal curve (Appendix B), find the z scores corresponding to the 10th, 20th, 30th, 40th, 50th, 60th, 70th, 80th, and 90th percentile ranks. Then convert the z scores to T scores, z scores, NCE scores, CEEB scores, and stanines (see Answers to Quantitative Questions, p. 486).
   c. Construct a frequency distribution of the 30 scores listed below, using an interval width of 3. Then compute the percentile rank, z, Z, z_n, and T scores corresponding to the interval midpoints.

82	85	70	91	75	88	78	82	95	79
86	90	87	77	87	73	80	96	86	81
85	93	83	89	92	89	84	83	79	74

(See Answers to Quantitative Questions, p. 486.)

d. Why are standard-score norms viewed as superior to age norms, grade norms, and percentile norms?

e. The following is a list of scores on an eight-item Similarities Test on which the possible scores ranged from 0 to 16. Compute the percentile rank, z score, and T score corresponding to each raw score. Refer to Appendix A for help.

RAW SCORE	FREQUENCY	PERCENTILE RANK	z	Z	T
16	8				
15	26				
14	71				
13	140				
12	171				
11	223				
10	272				
9	250				
8	257				
7	209				
6	183				
5	124				
4	89				
3	79				
2	51				
1	23				
0	25				

EXPERIENCING PSYCHOLOGICAL ASSESSMENT

1. Write five multiple-choice items for a course you are taking. Have three classmates evaluate how "good" they feel the items are (i.e., too hard/easy, good representation of the content). Translate as many of the comments as possible into their relation to the following terms: external criterion, internal consistency, item-difficulty index, item-discrimination index, item characteristics, item-response theory.

2. To get a feel for the size and nature of standardization samples, read through the test descriptions for five or six personality or intelligence tests provided in the catalog or on a Web site for a major test publisher such as Psychological Corporation (PsychCorp.com) or Psychological Assessment Resources (parinc.com).

■ ■ ■ ■ ■

CHAPTER FIVE

RELIABILITY AND VALIDITY

CHAPTER OBJECTIVES

1. Describe the concept of reliability, including major sources of unreliability in test scores.
2. Be able to define and calculate test–retest, parallel forms, split-half, Kuder–Richardson, coefficient alpha, and interscorer reliabilities.
3. Describe when each type of reliability would be most appropriate.
4. Describe the relationship between reliability and test length, item difficulty, and heterogeneity of items.
5. Define and be able to calculate the standard error of measurement.
6. Describe generalizability theory and explain what it tries to accomplish.
7. Define content, criterion (concurrent and predictive), incremental, and construct validity (including convergent and divergent).
8. Define the standard error of estimate.
9. Describe the use of tests in personnel decision making, including factors that affect predictive accuracy and the use of multiple cutoffs and multiple regression.

Standardization is an important step in designing and evaluating tests and other psychological assessment devices, but it is not the last step. Before a test can be used with some assurance, information concerning the reliability and validity of the test for its specific purposes must be obtained.

RELIABILITY

No psychometric instrument can be of value unless it is a consistent, or *reliable,* measure. Consequently, one of the first things that needs to be determined about a newly constructed test is whether it is sufficiently reliable to measure what it was designed to measure. If, in the absence of any permanent change in a person due to growth, learning, disease, or injury, scores on a test vary markedly with the occasion or situation, it is probably not sufficiently reliable to be used for describing and evaluating people and making predictions about their behavior. Strictly speaking, rather than being an aspect of a test, reliability is a property of the scores when the test is administered to a specified group of people on a particular occasion and under designated conditions.

Note that *reliability* is not the same thing as *stability:* in determining reliability, it is assumed that the test is measuring a relatively stable characteristic. Unlike instability, unreliability is the result of measurement errors produced by temporary internal states, such as low motivation, indisposition, or external conditions such as a distracting or an uncomfortable testing environment.

Classical Reliability Theory

In classical test theory, it is assumed that a person's observed score on a test is composed of a true score plus some unsystematic error of measurement. A person's *true score* on a particular test is defined as the average of the scores the person would obtain if he or she took the test an infinite number of times. Obviously, a true score can never be measured exactly; it must be estimated from the examinee's observed score on the test. It is also assumed in classical test theory that the variance of the observed scores (s_{obs}^2) of a group of people is equal to the variance of their true scores (s_{tre}^2) plus the variance due to unsystematic errors of measurement (s_{err}^2):

$$s_{obs}^2 = s_{tru}^2 + s_{err}^2 \tag{5.1}$$

Then the reliability (r_{11}) of the scores is defined as the ratio of true score variance to observed score variance, or the proportion of observed variance that is accounted for by true variance:

$$r_{11} = \frac{s_{tru}^2}{s_{obs}^2} \tag{5.2}$$

The proportion of observed variance accounted for by error variance or unaccounted for by true variance can be determined from formulas 5.1 and 5.2 as

$$\frac{s_{err}^2}{s_{obs}^2} = 1 - r_{11}. \tag{5.3}$$

The reliability of a set of test scores is expressed as a positive decimal number ranging from .00 to 1.00. An r_{11} of 1.00 indicates perfect reliability, and an r_{11} of .00 indicates complete unreliability of measurement. Because the variance of true scores cannot be computed directly, reliability is estimated by analyzing the effects of variations in conditions of administration and test content on observed scores. As noted previously, reliability is not influenced by systematic changes in scores that have a similar effect on all examinees, but only by unsystematic changes that have different effects on different people. Such unsystematic factors influence error variance and hence the reliability of test scores. Each of the several methods of estimating reliability (test–retest, parallel forms, internal consistency) takes into account the effects of somewhat different circumstances that can produce unsystematic changes in scores and thereby affect the error variance and reliability coefficient.

Test–Retest Coefficient

A *test–retest* coefficient is computed to determine whether a test measures consistently from one time to another. This coefficient, also known as a *coefficient of stability,* is found by correlating the scores obtained by a group of people on one administration with their scores on a second administration of a test. The test–retest procedure takes into account errors of measurement resulting from differences in conditions (environmental, personal) associated with the two occasions on which the test is administered. Because the same test is administered on both occasions, errors due to different samples of test items are not reflected in a test–retest coefficient. Also, differences between conditions of administration are likely to be greater after a long time interval than a short one. As a result, test–retest reliability tends to be higher (less error) when the interval between initial test and retest is short (days or a few weeks). In contrast, test–retest reliability tends to be lower (more error) when the interval is longer (months or years).

Parallel-Forms Coefficient

When the time interval between initial test and retest is short, examinees usually remember many of the questions and the responses on the initial test. This obviously affects their responses on the second administration, a fact that by itself would not alter the reliability coefficient if everyone remembered the same amount. Typically, however, some people remember more of the test material than others, causing the correlation between test and retest to be less than perfect. This is the major shortcoming of test–retest reliability. What seems to be needed to overcome this source of error is a parallel form of the test, one consisting of similar items but not the same items. Then a *parallel-forms coefficient,* also referred to as a *coefficient of equivalence,* can be computed as an index of reliability.

The parallel forms idea is reasonable in principle: by administering a parallel form after a suitable interval following administration of the first form, a reliability coefficient reflecting errors of measurement due to different items and different times of administration can be determined. To control for the confounding effect of test form with administration time, Form A should be administered first to half the group and Form B to the other half; then, on the second administration, the first group is given Form B and the second group is given Form A. The resulting correlation between scores on the two forms, referred to as a *coefficient of stability and equivalence,* takes into account errors due to different administration times or different items. The problem, however, is that it is often very difficult to develop two versions of a test that are truly parallel.

Internal Consistency Coefficients

Parallel forms are available for a number of tests, particularly tests of ability (achievement, intelligence, special aptitudes). A parallel form of a test is, however, often expensive and difficult to construct. For this reason, a less direct method of taking into account the effects on reliability of different samples of test items was devised. This is the *method of internal consistency,* including Spearman's split-half method, the Kuder–Richardson formulas, and Cronbach's coefficient alpha. Errors of measurement, caused by different conditions or times of administration, are, however, not reflected in an internal consistency coefficient. Consequently, internal consistency coefficients cannot be viewed as truly equivalent to either test–retest or parallel-forms coefficients.

Split-Half Method.   In this simplest of internal consistency approaches, a single test is viewed as composed of two parts (parallel forms) measuring the same thing. Thus, a test can be administered and separate scores assigned on two arbitrarily selected halves of the test. For example, the odd-numbered items may be scored separately from the even-numbered items. Then the correlation (r_{oe}) between the two sets of scores obtained by a group of people is a parallel forms reliability coefficient for a test half as long as the original. Assuming that the two equivalent halves have equal means and variances, the reliability of the test as a whole may be estimated by the *Spearman–Brown formula:*

$$r_{11} = \frac{2r_{oe}}{1 + r_{oe}} \tag{5.4}$$

To demonstrate the use of formula 5.4, assume that the correlation between total scores on the odd-numbered items and total scores on the even-numbered items of a test is .80. Then the estimated reliability of the entire test is $r_{11} = 2(.80)/(1 + .80) = .89$.

Kuder–Richardson Method.   A test can be divided in many different ways into two halves containing equal numbers of items. Because each way may result in a somewhat different value of r_{11}, it is not clear which halving strategy will yield the best estimate of reliability. One solution to the problem is to take the average of the reliability coefficients obtained from all half-splits as the overall reliability estimate. This can be done, but the following short-cut procedure was devised by Kuder and Richardson (1937).
    Under certain conditions, the mean of all split-half coefficients can be estimated by one of the following formulas:

$$r_{11} = \frac{k[1 - p_i(1 - p_i)/s^2]}{k - 1}, \tag{5.5}$$

$$r_{11} = \frac{k - \overline{X}(k - \overline{X})/s^2}{k - 1}. \tag{5.6}$$

In these formulas, k is the number of items on the test, $\overline{X}$ is the mean of total test scores, s^2 is the variance of total test scores (computed with n instead of $n - 1$ in the denominator), and p_i is the proportion of examinees giving the keyed response to item i. The p_i's are summed over all k items. Formulas 5.5 and 5.6 are known as Kuder–Richardson (K–R) formulas 20 and 21, respectively. Unlike formula 5.5, formula 5.6 is based on the assumption that all items are of equal difficulty; it also yields a more conservative estimate of reliability and is easier to compute than formula 5.5.

To demonstrate the application of formula 5.6, assume that a test containing 75 items has a mean of 50 and a variance of 100. Then, $r_{11} = [75 - 50(75 - 50)/100]/74 = .84$.

Coefficient Alpha. Formulas 5.5 and 5.6 are special cases of the more general coefficient alpha, defined as

$$\alpha = \frac{k\left(1 - \Sigma\, s_i^2/s_t^2\right)}{k - 1}, \tag{5.7}$$

where k is the number of items, s_i^2 is the variance of scores on item i, and s_t^2 is the variance of total test scores. The Kuder–Richardson formulas are applicable only when test items are scored 0 or 1, but coefficient alpha is a general formula for estimating the reliability of a test consisting of items on which different scoring weights may be assigned to different responses.

All internal consistency procedures (split-half, Kuder–Richardson, coefficient alpha) overestimate the reliability of speeded tests. Consequently, internal consistency procedures must be modified to provide reasonable estimates of reliability when most examinees do not complete the test in the allotted time. One possibility is to administer two split halves of the test at different times, but with equal time limits. The correlation between scores on the two separately timed halves are then computed, and the resulting coefficient is corrected by formula 5.4. The test–retest and parallel-forms procedures may also be used to estimate the reliabilities of speeded tests.

Interscorer Reliability

Barring clerical errors, the scores calculated by two different scorers of an objective test taken by a certain individual will be identical. Scoring essay and oral tests, in addition to certain other evaluative measures (personality ratings, projective test scoring) can often be a more subjective process. In evaluating scores involving subjective scorer judgment, it is important to know the extent to which different scorers agree on the ratings or other numerical values given to the responses of different examinees and items. The most common approach for determining this *interscorer or interrater reliability* is to have two persons score the responses of a sizable number of examinees and then compute the correlation between the two sets of scores. Another approach is to have many persons score the test responses of one examinee or, better still, have many persons score the responses of a number of examinees. The last approach yields an *intraclass coefficient* or *coefficient of concordance,* which is a generalized interscorer or interrater reliability coefficient. Procedures for computing these coefficients are described in many statistics books.

Oral tests are not known for their high reliabilities, but special forms are available that can improve the objectivity, and hence the reliability, with which oral performance is judged (see Form 3.1 on page 60). Though oral examinations typically have lower reliabilities than comparable written tests, careful attention to the design of oral questions, the construction of model answers to questions, and the use of multiple raters or scorers can enhance the reliability of scores on oral tests. Such procedures have resulted in interscorer reliability coefficients in the .60's and .70's for oral tests administered in certain undergraduate, graduate, and professional school courses. Other suggestions for improving the reliability of oral performance evaluations include encouraging examinees to delay answering until they have thought about the question for a while and electronically recording responses for later playback and reevaluation by scorers.

Interpreting Reliability Coefficients

The reliability coefficients of affective instruments such as checklists, rating scales, and inventories of personality, interests, or attitudes are typically lower than those of cognitive tests of achievement, intelligence, or special abilities. However, the reliability coefficients obtained with such affective instruments can be very respectable, and those obtained with cognitive instruments are sometimes fairly low.

How high should a reliability coefficient be for a test or other psychometric instrument to be useful? The answer depends on how one plans to use the test scores. If a test is to be used for determining whether the mean scores of two groups of people are significantly different, a reliability coefficient of .60 to .70 may be satisfactory. On the other hand, when the test is used to compare one person's score with the scores of other people or the former's score on one test with his or her score on another test, a reliability coefficient of at least .85 is needed to determine whether small differences in scores are significant.

Variability and Test Length

As with other measures of relationship, reliability coefficients tend to be higher when the variance of the test scores, item scores, ratings, or other variables being assessed is large than when it is small. Because test score variance is related to test length, one method of increasing reliability is to make the test longer. However, simply including more items on a test will not necessarily increase its reliability. The new items must be of the same general type and measure the same thing as the items already on the test. In fact, adding items that measure something different from whatever the original items measure can lead to a reduction in reliability.

The general Spearman–Brown formula is an expression of the effect on reliability of lengthening a test by including more items of the same general type. This formula, a generalization of formula 5.4, is

$$r_{mm} = \frac{mr_{11}}{1 + (m - 1)r_{11}} \qquad (5.8)$$

where m is the factor by which the test is lengthened, r_{11} is the reliability of the original, unlengthened test, and r_{mm} is the estimated reliability of the lengthened test. For example, if a 20-item test having a reliability coefficient of .70 is made three times as long by adding 40 more items, the estimated reliability of the lengthened test will be $3(.70)/[1 + 2(.70)] = .875$. Figure 5.1 illustrates the effects on reliability of increasing the number of items on a test by a factor of 1 ½, 2, 3, 4, or 5. Note that the incremental increase in reliability is less when initial reliability is high and with successively greater increases in test length.

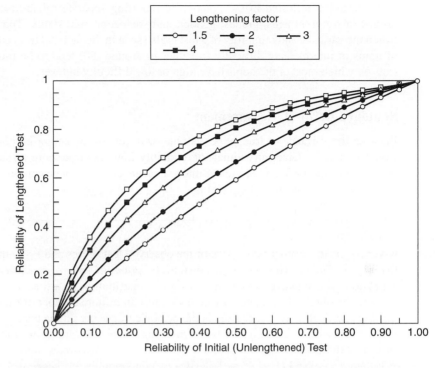

FIGURE 5.1 Reliability of a lengthened test as a function of initial reliability and lengthening factor. Reliability increases as more items of the same general type are added to a test, but the amount of increase is greater when the initial reliability is low. In addition, the reliability of the lengthened test gradually levels off as the test is made increasingly longer.

Solving formula 5.8 for m yields the following formula for determining how many times longer a test of reliability r_{11} must be to obtain a desired reliability (r_{11}):

$$m = \frac{r_{mm}(1 - r_{11})}{r_{11}(1 - r_{mm})} \tag{5.9}$$

This formula may be used to determine the necessary increase in test length and consequently the number of items to be added to a test to increase its reliability from a value of r_{11} to r_{mm}.

In addition to being dependent on the number of items, the variance and reliability of a test are affected by the heterogeneity of the sample of people who take it. The greater the range of individual differences on a certain characteristic, the larger will be the variance of the scores on a measure of this characteristic. Consequently, the reliability coefficient of a test or other assessment instrument will be higher in a more heterogeneous group with a larger test score variance. The fact that the reliability of a test varies with the nature of the group tested is reflected in the practice of reporting separate reliability coefficients for groups of different ages, grades, gender, and socioeconomic status. The association between the variance and reliability of a test is also seen in the fact that tests comprised mostly of items of intermediate difficulty (p values of around .50) tend to be more reliable than tests on which most of the items have high or low difficulty indexes.

Standard Error of Measurement

Because the variance of true scores is unknown, reliability cannot be computed directly from formula 5.2. Given an estimate of reliability, however, true score variance can be computed from formula 5.2 or, of greater interest, error variance can be computed from formula 5.3. Solving formula 5.3 for s_{err} yields

$$s_{err} = s_{obs}\sqrt{1 - r_{11}} \qquad\qquad (5.10)$$

where s_{obs} is the standard deviation of the observed test scores and r_{11} is the test–retest reliability coefficient. This statistic, known as the *standard error of measurement* (s_{err}), is an estimate of the standard deviation of a normal distribution of test scores that would presumably be obtained by a person who took a test an infinite number of times. The mean of this hypothetical score distribution is the person's true score on the test.

To illustrate the computation and meaning of the standard error of measurement, assume that the standard deviation of a test is 6.63 and the test–retest reliability coefficient is .85; then $s_{err} = 6.63\sqrt{1 - .85} = 2.57$. If a certain person's test score is 40, it can be concluded with 68% confidence that he or she is one of a group of people having observed scores of 40 whose true scores on the test fall between $40 - 2.57 = 37.43$ and $40 + 2.57 = 42.57$. To obtain the 95% confidence interval for a true score, s_{err} must be multiplied by 1.96 and the resulting product added to and subtracted from the observed score: observed score $\pm 1.96 s_{err}$.

Figure 5.2 is a profile or *psychograph* of the scores obtained by an 11th-grade female on the 10 tests and three composites of the Armed Services Vocational Aptitude Battery (ASVAB). The student's score on a particular test or composite is indicated by the short vertical lines projecting from the middle of the corresponding horizontal bar. The width of the horizontal bar is equal to 1.96 times the standard error of measurement of the particular test or composite. Consequently, we can say that the probability is .95 that the student's true score on the test falls within the numerical range represented by the horizontal bar extending from observed score $-1.96 s_{err}$ to observed score $+1.96 s_{err}$.

As a rule of thumb, the difference between the scores of two persons on the same test should not be viewed as significant unless it is at least twice the standard error of measurement of the test. On the other hand, the difference between the scores of the same person on two tests should be greater than twice the larger standard error of measurement for the difference to be interpreted as significant. This is so because the standard error of the difference between scores on two tests is larger than the standard error of measurement of either test.

As seen from formula 5.10, the standard error of measurement is inversely related to the reliability coefficient. When $r_{11} = 1.00$, there is no error at all in estimating a person's

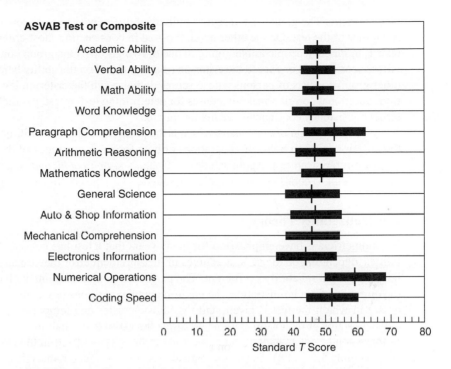

FIGURE 5.2 **Plot of a student's *T* scores (short vertical lines projecting from middle of horizontal bars) and bars representing the 95% confidence intervals for the student's true *T* scores on the 10 tests and three composites on the Armed Services Vocational Aptitude Battery (ASVAB).**
See text for details.

true score from his or her observed score; when $r_{11} = .00$, the error of measurement attains its maximum value (s). Of course, a test having a reliability coefficient close to .00 is useless because the accuracy of any decisions made on the basis of the scores will be at a chance level.

Unlike classical test theory, in which the standard error of measurement applies to all scores in a particular population, in item-response theory (IRT) it differs from score to score. In IRT, the standard error of measurement of the scores corresponding to a particular ability level is equal to the reciprocal of the amount of information conveyed by a score at that level. The amount of information provided by responses to a particular item is determined from the item information function, and the information provided by the test as a whole at a particular ability level is the sum of the item information values at that ability level.

Reliability of Criterion-Referenced Tests

The traditional concept of reliability pertains to norm-referenced tests, which are designed primarily to differentiate among individuals who possess various amounts of a specific characteristic. The greater the range of individual differences in test scores, the higher the reliability of the test. On the other hand, the goal in constructing most criterion-referenced tests is to identify people as belonging in one of two groups. One group consists of persons whose scores equal or exceed the criterion (mastery) level on the ability being assessed; the other group consists of persons whose scores do not reach the criterion level. In this situation, traditional correlational procedures for determining test–retest, parallel-forms, and internal consistency coefficients are inappropriate.

The *coefficient of agreement,* which is the proportion of scores falling above or below the criterion level on both administrations or both forms, is one index of the reliability of a criterion-referenced test. Another index is Cohen's *kappa coefficient,* which is somewhat more difficult to compute, but statistically sounder than the coefficient of agreement.

Generalizability Theory

Psychometricians have emphasized for many years that a test has not one, but many reliabilities, depending on the various sources of measurement error that are taken into account in computing a reliability coefficient. The particular sample of items included on the test, the directions for administration, the environmental conditions (e.g., temperature, lighting, noise) in which the test is given, and the idiosyncrasies and temporary psychological or physical states of the examinees can all affect the estimated reliability of a test. Any or all of these conditions may contribute to error variance, symbolized in the classical test variance formula 5.1 (p. 88). The mathematical procedures of factor analysis (see Appendix A) provide a way of partitioning the true score variance in formula 5.1 into common and specific-factor variances, but the formula does not differentiate among various sources of error contributing to error variance.

The notion that a test may have many reliabilities, depending on the effects of various sources of error variance, or *facets,* has been incorporated into other approaches to test theory. One of these approaches, *generalizability theory* (see Brennan, 2001), begins by conceptualizing an observed test score as an estimate of a corresponding *universe score.* The degree of accuracy with which the test score estimates the universe score depends on the nature of the universe, that is, the particular facets that define it.

A test score may be generalizable to many different universes, each defined according to a certain combination of facets. The facets characterizing a given universe, such as conditions of test administration and the composition of items or test forms, may be very different from those defining other universes. Some of these facets may have no effect whatsoever on the generalizability of the test scores, whereas the effects of other facets may be significant.

The computations of generalizability theory involve the application of analysis of variance statistical techniques to determine the generalizability of test scores as a function of changes or differences in the persons taking the test, different samples of items comprising the test, the situations or conditions under which the test is taken, and the methods or people involved in scoring it. A *generalizability coefficient,* which is similar to a traditional reliability coefficient, may then be computed as the ratio of the expected variance of scores in the universe to the variance of scores in the sample. Finally, a universe value of the score, similar to the true score of classical reliability theory, can be estimated.

By emphasizing the importance of the conditions under which a test is administered and the purposes for which it is designed, generalizability theory shifted the focus of test users beyond preoccupation with the test itself as a good or poor psychometric instrument in general to the question of "Good or poor for what purpose?"

Generalizability theory, item-response theory, structural analysis, and other modern statistical methods are certainly more technically sophisticated than classical test theory. Be that as it may, test development and applications still rely greatly on the traditional concepts of reliability and validity and the procedures derived from them.

VALIDITY

Traditionally, *validity* has been defined as the extent to which a test measures what it was designed to measure (see www.socialresearchmethods.net/tutorial/Rymarchk/rymar2.htm). A shortcoming of this definition is the implication that a test has only one validity, which is presumably established by a single study. Actually, a test may have many different validities, depending on the specific purposes for which it was designed, the target population, the conditions under which it is administered, and the method of determining validity.

The methods by which validity may be determined include (1) analyzing the content of the test, (2) computing the correlation between scores on the test and those on the criterion of interest, and (3) investigating the particular psychological characteristics or constructs measured by the test (see www.uic.edu/classes/socw/socw560/MEASURE/sld002.htm). All these procedures are useful to the extent that they improve understanding of what a test measures and provide information for making decisions about people. It may also be of interest to evaluate a test's *incremental validity,* that is, how much the test adds to the prediction and understanding of criteria that are already being predicted to some extent.

Unlike reliability, which is influenced only by unsystematic errors of measurement, the validity of a test is affected by both unsystematic and systematic (constant) errors. For this reason, a test may be reliable without being valid, but it cannot be valid without being reliable. Reliability is a necessary but not a sufficient condition for validity.

Content Validity

The physical appearance of a test with regard to its particular purposes (*face validity*) is certainly an important consideration in marketing the test. The concept of *content validity,* however, refers to more than just appearance. Content validity is concerned with whether the content of a test elicits a range of responses that are representative of the entire domain or universe of skills, understandings, and other behaviors that a test is designed to measure. Responses to the sample of items on a well-designed test are presumably indicative of what the responses would be to the entire universe of behaviors of interest.

An analysis of content validity occurs most often in connection with achievement tests, for which there is usually no specified external criterion. Content validity is also of concern on measures of aptitude, interest, and personality, though perhaps less so than criterion-related or construct validity. The content validity of an achievement test is evaluated by analyzing the composition of the test to determine the extent to which it represents the objectives of instruction. One way of accomplishing this is to compare the test's content with an outline or table of specifications concerning the subject matter to be covered by the test. If subject-matter experts agree that a test looks and acts like an instrument that was designed to measure whatever it is supposed to, then it is said to possess content validity. Such judgments involve not only the appearance of the test items, but also the cognitive processes involved in answering them. Obviously, the process of evaluating content validity should not wait until the test has been constructed. Expert judgment concerning what items to include is necessary from the very beginning of the test-construction process. By defining the universe of the content of the test and the sample of this universe to be included, test designers are setting the stage for a content valid instrument.

Criterion-Related Validity

Validation of any test of ability consists of relating scores on the test to performance on criterion measures or standards with which the scores can be compared. Traditionally, however, the term *criterion-related validity* has referred to procedures in which the test scores of a group of people are compared with ratings, classifications, or other measures of performance. Examples of criteria against which tests are validated are school marks, supervisors' ratings, and number or dollar amount of sales. Whenever a criterion measure is available at the time of testing, the *concurrent validity* of the test can be determined. When scores on the criterion do not become available until some time after the test has been administered, the focus is on the *predictive validity* of the test.

Concurrent Validity.   Concurrent validation procedures are employed whenever a test is administered to people in various categories, such as clinical diagnostic groups or socioeconomic levels, for the purpose of determining whether the test scores of people in one category are significantly different from those of people in other categories. If the average score varies substantially from category to category, then the test might be used as another, perhaps more efficient, way of assigning people to these categories. Scores on the Minnesota Multiphasic Personality Inventory (MMPI), for example, have been useful in identifying specific mental disorders, because it has been found that patients who are diagnosed by psychiatrists as having particular disorders tend to make different scores on certain groups of items (*scales*) than do people in general.

Predictive Validity.   Predictive validity is concerned with how accurately test scores predict criterion scores, as indicated by the correlation between the test score (the predictor) and a criterion of future performance (what the test predicts). Predictive validity is of concern primarily with respect to aptitude or intelligence tests, since scores on these kinds of instruments are often correlated with ratings, course grades, achievement test scores, and other performance criteria.

The magnitude of a predictive validity coefficient is limited by the reliabilities of both the predictor and criterion variables; it cannot be greater than the square root of the product of these two reliabilities. For this and other reasons, the correlation between a predictor and a criterion variable, computed by procedures described in Appendix A, varies with the specific criterion, but is seldom greater than .60. Because the proportion of variance in the criterion variable that can be accounted for by variation in the predictor variable is equal to the square of the correlation between predictor and criterion variables, typically not more than 36% of the variation in criterion scores is predictable from scores on a test or other psychometric device. This leaves 64% of the criterion variance unaccounted for or unpredicted. Considering that the predictive validity of most tests is less than .60, it is understandable why claims concerning the predictability of performance criteria from scores on psychological tests must be made cautiously.

Standard Error of Estimate.   The section on regression and prediction in Appendix A describes the procedure for determining a regression equation (prediction equation) for forecasting the criterion scores of a group of people from their scores on tests or other variables. However, entering a person's test score into a regression equation yields only an estimate of the score that the person will actually make on the criterion variable. If the predicted criterion score of a certain person is viewed as the mean of a normal distribution of the obtained criterion scores of a group of people who make the same score on the predictor variable as that person, then the standard deviation of this distribution is an index of the average error in those predictions. This statistic, known as the *standard error of estimate* (s_{est}), is approximately equal to

$$s_{est} = s\sqrt{1 - r^2}, \tag{5.11}$$

where s is the standard deviation of the criterion scores and r is the product–moment correlation between predictor (test) and criterion scores.

Assume, for example, that the standard deviation of a certain criterion measure is 15 and the correlation between test and criterion scores is .50; then $s_{est} = 15\sqrt{1 - .50^2} = 13$. If a person's predicted criterion score is 50, the chances are 68 out of 100 that the person will obtain a criterion score between 37 and 63 ($Y_{pre} \pm s_{est}$) and approximately 95 out of 100 that he or she will obtain a criterion score between 25 and 75 ($Y_{pre} \pm 1.96s_{est}$). More precisely, the chances are 68 out of 100 that the person is one of a group of individuals with a predicted criterion score of 50 whose obtained criterion scores actually fall between 37 and 63. Similarly, the chances are approximately 95 out of 100 that the individual is one of a group of people with a predicted criterion score of 50 whose obtained criterion scores fall between 25 and 75. As illustrated by this example, when the correlation between the test and criterion scores is low, a person's obtained criterion score may be very different from his or her predicted score. For this reason, caution must be exercised in interpreting predicted scores when the correlation between the test and the criterion measure is modest. The smaller the correlation coefficient, the larger the standard error of estimate will be and the less accurate the prediction from test to criterion.

Factors Affecting Criterion-Related Validity

The criterion-related validity of a test can be influenced by a number of factors, including group differences, test length, criterion contamination, and base rate. The incremental validity of a test, that is, the contribution of the test above and beyond that of other variables, should also be considered in deciding whether to use the test for purposes of selection and placement.

Group Differences.   The characteristics of a group of people on whom a test is validated include such variables as sex, age, and personality traits. These factors, which are referred to in this context as *moderator variables,* can affect the correlation between a test and a criterion measure. The magnitude of a validity coefficient, like that of a reliability coefficient, is also influenced by the degree of heterogeneity of the validation group on whatever the test measures. Validity coefficients tend to be smaller in more homogeneous groups, that is, groups having a narrower range of test scores. The size of a correlation coefficient is a function of both the predictor and criterion variables, so narrowing the range of scores on either variable tends to lower the predictive validity coefficient.

Because the magnitude of a validity coefficient varies with the nature of the group tested, a newly constructed test that is found to be a valid predictor of a particular criterion variable in one group of people should be cross-validated on a second group. In *cross-validation,* a test is administered to a second sample of people to determine whether it retains its validity across different samples. Due to the operation of chance factors, the magnitude of a validity coefficient usually shrinks somewhat on cross-validation. Consequently, the correlation between predictor and criterion scores on cross-validation is considered in most instances to be a better index of predictive validity than the original test–criterion correlation. Cross-validation, which is one way of determining the *validity generalization* of a test, that is, whether the test remains valid in different situations, may also involve a different (parallel) sample of test items. With different samples of examinees, different samples of test items, or both, there is typically some shrinkage of the validity coefficient on cross-validation. Formulas for correcting for such shrinkage have been proposed, but they involve certain assumptions that are not always met.

Test Length.   Like reliability, validity varies directly with the length of the test and the heterogeneity of the group of people who are tested. Up to a point, scores on a longer test and scores on a test administered to a group of individuals who vary greatly in the characteristics being measured have larger variances and, consequently, higher predictive validities than shorter tests or tests administered to more homogeneous groups of people. Formulas that correct for the effects on validity of restricted score ranges and curtailed test length have been proposed, but they are appropriate only under certain special circumstances.

Criterion Contamination.   The validity of a test is limited not only by the reliabilities of the test and criterion, but also by the validity of the criterion itself as a measure of the variable of interest. Sometimes the criterion is made less valid, or becomes contaminated, by the particular method of measuring the criterion scores. For example, a clinical psychologist who knows that a group of patients has already been diagnosed as psychotic may misperceive psychotic signs in the personality test responses of these patients. Then the *method of contrasting groups,* in which the test scores of the psychotics are compared with those of normals, will yield false evidence for the validity of the test. Such contamination of the criterion (psychotic versus normal) can be controlled by *blind analysis,* that is, by making available to the diagnostician no information about the examinees other than their test scores. Many clinical psychologists maintain, however, that blind analysis is unnatural in that it is not the way in which tests are actually employed in clinical settings (see www.psych.umn.edu/faculty/grove/112meehlscontributiontoclinical.pdf).

Incremental Validity. When trying to decide whether administering a particular assessment instrument for predictive or diagnostic purposes is justified by the cost, *incremental validity* should also be considered. Incremental validity is concerned with the question of how much more accurate predictions and diagnoses are when a particular test is included in a battery of assessment procedures. It is possible that other, less expensive methods of assessment (observation, interview, biographical inventory) can fulfill the purposes of assessment just as well without administering another test. Incremental validity is related to the concept of utility, as applied in employment selection contexts. The *utility* of a test is defined as a measured increase in the quality of employees who are hired or promoted when a test or other assessment procedure is used compared with the quality of employees hired or promoted when the procedure is not used.

Construct Validity

Predictive validity is of greatest concern in occupational or educational selection and placement. Ability tests of various kinds, and sometimes personality and interest tests, are used for selection and placement purposes. Of even greater concern with respect to personality tests is construct validity. The *construct validity* of a psychological assessment instrument refers to the extent to which the instrument measures a particular *construct* or psychological concept, such as anxiety, achievement motivation, extroversion–introversion, or neuroticism. Construct validity, the most general type of validity, is not determined in a single way or by one investigation. Rather, it involves a network of investigations and other procedures designed to determine whether an assessment instrument that presumably measures a certain personality variable is actually doing so.

Evidence for Construct Validity. Among the sources of evidence for the construct validity of a test are these:

1. Experts' judgments that the content of the test pertains to the construct of interest
2. Analysis of the internal consistency of the test
3. Studies, in both experimentally contrived and naturally occurring groups, of the relationships between test scores and other variables on which the groups differ
4. Correlations of scores on the test with scores on other tests and variables with which it is expected to have a certain relationship, followed by factor analyses of these correlations
5. Questioning examinees or raters in detail about their responses to a test or rating scale to reveal the specific mental processes involved in responding to the items

As revealed by this list, various kinds of information contribute to the establishment of the construct validity of a psychometric instrument. The information may be obtained from rational or statistical analyses of the variables assessed by the instrument and studies of its ability to predict behavior in situations where the construct is operating. What may be somewhat confusing about the above list is that some of the sources of evidence may sound like content or criterion validity. This is true in that any other type of validity can be used to help create an understanding of its construct validity. It is also possible to provide measures of the relative strength of test validity (Westen & Rosenthal, 2003; see www.psychsystems .net/lab/type4.cfm?id=400&section=4&source=200&source2=1).

Experimental demonstrations such as those used in the construct validation of the Taylor Manifest Anxiety Scale (TMAS) (Taylor, 1953) are particularly important in establishing construct validity. According to Hullian learning theory, anxiety is a drive, and hence highly anxious people should condition more easily than less anxious people. Assuming that this theory is correct, individuals who have a high anxiety level should acquire a conditioned eyeblink in a light airpuff–eyeblink classical conditioning situation more quickly than those who have a low anxiety level. So if it is a valid measure of the construct *anxiety,* high scorers on the TMAS should condition more readily in this situation than low scorers. Verification of this prediction contributed significantly to acceptance of the construct validity of the TMAS.

Convergent and Discriminant Validation.   A construct-validated instrument should have high correlations with other measures or methods of measuring the same construct (*convergent validity*), but low correlations with measures of different constructs (*discriminant validity*). Evidence for the convergent and discriminant validity of a psychometric instrument can be obtained by comparing correlations between measures of the following:

1. The same construct using the same method
2. Different constructs using the same method
3. The same construct using different methods
4. Different constructs using different methods

The construct validity of a psychometric instrument is confirmed by this *multitrait–multimethod approach* (Campbell & Fiske, 1959) when correlations between the same construct measured by the same and different methods are significantly higher than correlations between different constructs measured by the same or different methods. Unfortunately, the results of such comparisons do not always turn out this way. Sometimes correlations between different constructs measured by the same method are higher than correlations between the same construct measured by different methods. This means that the method (paper-and-pencil inventory, projective technique, rating scale, interview, etc.) is more important than the particular construct or trait in determining whatever is being measured than the construct or trait that was presumably being assessed.

USING TESTS IN PERSONNEL DECISION MAKING

Since antiquity, people have been selected, classified, and placed in positions to perform various duties. Often, however, the procedures followed in personnel selection, classification, and placement have been haphazard and unsystematic. A variety of procedures for personnel selection and appraisal, many of which were based on casual observation and intuition, has been employed. For example, at one time great importance was attached to physical features such as head shape, eye movements, and overall body appearance. Ethnicity, social status, and social connections were also factors in determining who was appointed to a position, hired for a specific job, or accepted for a certain educational program.

Screening

Traditionally, personnel selection has been concerned with identifying, from a pool of applicants, those who are most able to perform designated tasks. In this approach, psychological tests are used, together with nontest information (personal history, physical characteristics, recommendations, etc.) to assist in selecting applicants who can perform particular jobs either immediately or following appropriate training.

A personnel selection procedure may be fairly simple or very complex, depending on the nature of the organization and the task for which applicants are being selected. The most straightforward approach is the sink-or-swim strategy in which all applicants are selected or admitted, but only those who perform effectively are retained. In some ways this is an ideal selection strategy, but it is also expensive to both the organization and the applicants. Consequently, almost all sizable organizations now use some kind of *screening* procedure by which applicants who are clearly unsuitable for the task (job, program, or other activity) are rejected immediately. When the screening procedure involves a test of some kind, applicants who make a specified minimum score (*cutoff score*) or higher on the test are accepted, and those who score below the cutoff score are rejected. This procedure is fairly impersonal, and it may occasionally seem unkind from the applicant's perspective. However, the goal of this and other procedures is to increase the chances that those who are eventually selected will be the best qualified.

Classification and Placement

Initial screening is usually followed by *classification* and the assignment of selected applicants to one of several occupational categories. Classification decisions may involve grouping employees on the basis of their scores on more than one psychological test. Screening and classification are frequently followed by *placement* of those who have been selected at a particular level of a certain job or program.

The process of personnel selection usually consists of a sequence of stages entailing a series of yes–no (pass–fail) decisions based on information obtained from application blanks, letters of reference, telephone calls, personal interviews, observations, and psychological tests. The purpose of collecting such information is identical to that of any other application of psychology: to make better predictions of future behavior on the basis of past and present behavior. The more reliable and valid the information is, the greater the likelihood of making accurate predictions of on-the-job or in-the-program behavior and hence the sounder the selection decisions. Of course, the reliability and validity of psychological assessment instruments and procedures for making selection decisions cannot be determined merely by inspecting the assessment materials. Reliability and validity must be evaluated empirically, which is one of the tasks of personnel psychologists.

An Expectancy Table

When tests are used for selection purposes, it is not essential to determine the test–criterion correlation and the regression equation linking performance on the criterion variable to scores on the test. Correlational methods are applicable to the construction of theoretical expectancy tables, but an empirical expectancy table can be constructed without computing a correlation coefficient or any other statistic except frequencies and percentages. Assume, for example, that Table 5.1 was constructed from a joint frequency distribution of the scores of 250 job applicants on an Occupational Selection Test (OST) and the ratings given to the applicants by their work supervisors 6 months after being hired. The OST score intervals are listed on the left side of the table, and the performance ratings (on a scale of 1 to 8) across the top. The unitalicized frequencies in the cells of the table are the numbers of employees who obtained OST scores within a specified 5-point range and the performance ratings indicated at the top of the column. For example, 10 employees whose OST scores were between 81 and 85 were given a performance rating of 5 by their supervisors, whereas 14 employees whose OST scores fell between 66 and 70 were given a performance rating of 4.

The italic numbers in parentheses in Table 5.1 are the percentages of people having OST scores in a given interval whose performance ratings were equal to the corresponding

TABLE 5.1   An Empirical Expectancy Table

OCCUPATIONAL SELECTION	PERFORMANCE RATING							
TEST SCORE	1	2	3	4	5	6	7	8
96–100					(100) 1			(67) 2
91–95					(100) 2		(82) 5	(36) 4
86–90				(100) 1	(94) 8	(50) 3	(33) 4	(11) 2
81–85				(100) 4	(85) 10	(48) 7	(22) 5	(4) 1
76–80			(100) 6	(88) 12	(63) 16	(31) 13	(4) 2	
71–75		(100) 4	(94) 7	(83) 25	(45) 21	(12) 5	(5) 3	
66–70		(100) 5	(87) 10	(61) 14	(24) 7	(5) 2		
61–65	(100) 1	(96) 6	(72) 8	(40) 5	(20) 4	(4) 1		
56–60	(100) 2	(85) 5	(46) 4	(15) 2				
51–55	(100) 1							

value in the given cells or higher. For example, 85% of employees whose OST scores fell in the interval 81–85 received performance ratings of 5 or higher, and 61% of those having OST scores between 66 and 70 had performance ratings of 4 or higher.

To illustrate how this kind of information is applied to the process of employee selection, assume that John, a potential employee from a group similar to that on which Table 5.1 was constructed, makes a score of 68 on the Occupational Selection Test. Then it can be estimated that John's chances are 61 out of 100 of receiving a rating of 4 or higher on job performance by his supervisor 6 months after beginning the job, but his chances of obtaining a performance rating of 6 or higher are only 5 out of 100. If a rating of 4 or higher is acceptable, then John will probably be hired.

Factors Affecting Predictive Accuracy

The accuracy with which an applicant's criterion score can be predicted depends not only on the size of the correlation between the predictor and criterion variables, but also on the number of false-positive and false-negative errors, the selection ratio, and the base rate. If the cutoff score on a test is set very low, there will be many incorrect acceptances, or *false positives*. These are applicants who were selected but do not succeed on the job or in the program. On the other hand, if the cutoff score is set very high, there will be many incorrect rejections or *false negatives*. These are applicants who were not selected, but who would have succeeded if they had been. Since the purpose of personnel selection is to obtain as many "hits" as possible—to select those who will succeed and reject those who will fail to perform well on the job—the cutoff score must be set carefully.

To illustrate these concepts, refer again to Table 5.1. Suppose that the cutoff score on the OST is set at 66 and that 4 is considered a minimum acceptable job performance rating. Then $4 + 5 + 6 + 7 + 10 = 32$ of the employees represented in Table 5.1 will be classified as false positives: they scored at least 66 on the OST, but had performance ratings of less than 4. On the other hand, $5 + 2 + 4 + 1 = 12$ employees will be false negatives: they scored below 66 on the OST, but received performance ratings of 4 or higher. Observe that raising the cutoff score on the OST decreases the number of false positives, but increases the number of false negatives. The opposite effect—an increase in false positives and a decrease in false negatives—occurs when the cutoff score on the OST is lowered.

When setting a cutoff score on a test or test composite, it is also important to consider the proportion of applicants to be selected, the *selection ratio*. The lower the selection ratio, the higher the cutoff score is, and vice versa. Because the number of false-positive and false-negative errors is affected by where the cutoff score is set, one might argue that the selection ratio should be determined by the relative seriousness of these two types of errors. Is the error made in accepting an applicant who fails to perform the task satisfactorily (false positive) more or less serious than rejecting an applicant who could have performed the task successfully if he or she had been selected (false negative)? Such errors should be taken into account, but at least as important in determining the selection ratio is the total number of applicants. For example, when the labor market is tight, the number of applicants will be small. Then the selection ratio will need to be high and, consequently, the cutoff score on the test must be fairly low to obtain the desired number of people. On the other hand, in a free, or open, labor market, the number of applicants is large, so the selection ratio will generally be low. A low selection ratio means that the cutoff score on the test will need to be set fairly high, leading to a smaller number of accepted applicants. It also means there will be a smaller number of false positives but there will (unfortunately) be a larger number of rejected applicants who would have done well on the job if given a chance (false negatives). The percentage of successful applicants varies inversely with the selection ratio, but it also varies directly with the validity of the test or other selection device. In general, a more valid test leads to a greater percentage of "hits" (true positives and true negatives) and a smaller percentage of false positives and false negatives.

Another factor that affects the accuracy with which a test can identify people who will behave in a certain way is the *base rate,* the proportion of applicants expected to perform satisfactorily on a job even if no selection instrument or procedure is employed. As with the selection ratio, a test designed to predict a particular type of behavior is most effective when the base rate is 50% and least effective when the base rate is either very high or very low. For this reason, a test designed to select people for a highly complex job on which relatively few applicants can do well will not be as effective as a test designed to select people for a job that half the applicant population can perform satisfactorily. The concept of base rate is not limited to personnel selection; it is also important in clinical diagnosis. For example, because the incidence of suicide in the general population is very low (low base rate), a test designed to identify suicidal persons will not be very accurate. A test designed to identify people who fulfilled the criteria for depression will be much higher since the percentage of people with a depression in the general population is higher (2% to 9% of the population) than that of potential suicides.

The amount of information contributed by a test beyond the base rate can be determined by consulting the *Taylor–Russell table* for the specified base rate (Taylor & Russell, 1939). The table lists the percentage of selected applicants who would be expected to succeed on a job or in another selection situation as a function of the validity coefficient of the test, the base rate, and the selection ratio. Inspection of several Taylor–Russell tables for specific base rates shows that the percentage of applicants who are expected to succeed varies directly with the validity coefficient, but inversely with the selection ratio. In general, at an intermediate base rate and with a low selection ratio, scores on a test having a very modest validity coefficient can produce a substantial increase in the number of hits in a selection situation.

Use of the Taylor–Russell tables assumes a clear, discrete, dichotomous definition of success (versus failure) in a selection situation. Additional approaches involve integrating several sources of information (Jeanneret, D'Egidio, & Hanson, 2004), connecting selection with job satisfaction (Dawis, 2004), and the economic utility of personnel decisions (Raju, Normand, & Burke, 1990).

Multiple Cutoff and Multiple Regression

Setting the cutoff score on a selection or placement test is a complex judgmental process. In addition to the factors discussed above, the cutoff score and the usefulness of a test in general are affected by other applicant information.

Frequently, a set of test scores and other measures are combined in making selection and classification decisions. One procedure for combining scores, referred to as *successive hurdles* or *multiple cutoff*, is to set separate cutoff scores on each of several measures. Then an applicant must score at the cutoff point or above on each separate measure in situations where a high score on one measure does not compensate for a low score on another measure. For example, the ability to differentiate between tones of different pitches is essential to effective performance as an orchestra conductor. Regardless of how high their scores on tests of cognitive abilities, people who are tone deaf would not be expected to be good orchestra conductors.

A more mathematical approach to combining the scores of a large sample of people on several measures is to determine a *multiple-regression equation* in which different statistically assigned weights are applied to scores on different tests. A procedure for computing these regression weights is described in Appendix A. Once the regression weights have been determined, a single predicted criterion score for each applicant can be computed by multiplying the applicant's score on each variable by the appropriate weight, adding the products, and subtracting a constant. For example, a multiple-regression equation employed for admission purposes at one college was $GPA_{pre} = .002(SAT-V) + .001(SAT-M) + .030(HSR) - 2.00$, where SAT-V and SAT-M are the applicant's scores on the Verbal and Mathematical sections of the Scholastic Assessment Test, HSR is a T score measure of the applicant's rank in his or her high school graduating class, and GPA_{pre} is the predicted college freshman year grade-point average of the applicant. If a particular applicant's scores on the two sections of the SAT are 600 and 500 and his or her high school rank is 70, then the applicant's predicted grade-point average is $GPA_{pre} = .002(600) + .001(500) + .030(70) - 2.00 = 1.8$, which is equivalent to a low C.

In the multiple-regression approach, a high score on one predictor variable can compensate for a low score on another predictor variable. Consequently, this approach should not be used when a minimum score on any of the predictors is essential for effective performance on the criterion. When the multiple-regression approach is used, a *multiple correlation coefficient* (R), which is an index of the relationship of a weighted combination of the predictor variables to the criterion variable, should be computed. The procedure for computing R, which ranges from .00 to 1.00 and is interpreted in a manner similar to that for the product–moment coefficient, is described in Appendix A.

SUMMARY

1. Reliability refers to the relative freedom of test scores from errors of measurement. In classical test score theory, reliability is defined as the ratio of a test's true score variance to its observed score variance. Because true score variance cannot be computed directly, reliability must be estimated by one of several procedures that take into account various sources of measurement error.

2. Three traditional methods for estimating the reliability of a test or other assessment instrument are test–retest, parallel forms, and internal consistency. Test–retest is a measure of the tests temporal stability and is the correlation between two administrations of the test at two different times. Parallel forms reliability, which considers errors due to different administration times and to different samples of test items, is the most satisfactory, but tends to be expensive. Internal consistency approaches, which

are less appropriate for speeded tests, include split half, Kuder–Richardson, and co-efficient alpha. Interscorer reliability is simply the level of agreement among scorers.

3. Different types of reliability are appropriate for different purposes. Test–retest is important when the test will be used to make a prediction, parallel forms is important in reducing practice effects (and for predictions), internal consistency is important for concurrent measures, and interscorer reliability is crucial when there may be some variability between different scorers.

4. Longer tests tend to be more reliable. The Spearman–Brown formula can be used to calculate the effect that lengthening a test will have on its reliability. Reliability also varies with the difficulty level of the items comprising the test and is highest with items of intermediate difficulty. Reliability is also higher when there are more heterogeneous items.

5. The standard error of measurement, which varies inversely with the magnitude of the reliability coefficient, is used to compute confidence intervals for true scores on a test. The larger the standard error of measurement, the wider is the range of scores that can be said, within a specified degree of confidence, to contain an examinee's true score on the test.

6. Generalizability theory conceptualizes a test score as being a sample derived from a population. Theorectically it is an estimate of a true score or universe value. Its reliability is not set, but is rather dependent on different conditions and the purposes the test will be used for.

7. Information on the validity of a test may be obtained in various ways: by analyzing the test's content (content validity), by correlating test scores with scores on a criterion measure obtained at the same time (concurrent validity), by correlating test scores with scores on a criterion measured at a later time (predictive validity), and by systematic study of the adequacy of the test in appraising a specified psychological construct (construct validity). Information on the construct validity of a test as a measure of a particular psychological variable or characteristic can be obtained in a variety of ways. Especially helpful is an analysis of correlations between the test and other measures of the same construct obtained by the same or different methods and measures of different constructs obtained by the same or different methods (multi-trait–multimethod matrix). Finally, incremental validity is the extent to which a test increases information above existing forms of assessment. It should be noted that achievement tests are usually content validated, predictive validity is of greater concern with regard to aptitude tests, and concurrent and construct validity are important for personality tests.

8. The amount of error made in predicting a person's criterion score from his or her score on a test is estimated by the standard error of estimate, which varies inversely with the size of the criterion-related validity coefficient. Both the criterion-related validity coefficient and the standard error of estimate are affected by a number of factors, including group differences, test length, and criterion contamination. Because the magnitude of a validity coefficient can be affected by chance factors, tests used for predictive purposes should be cross-validated on separate samples of people.

9. Psychological tests are administered in occupational settings for purposes of employee selection, classification, promotion, and periodic appraisal. Some statistical

procedures used for these purposes are expectancy tables, selection ratios, multiple-cutoffs and multiple-regression methods.

MASTERING THE CHAPTER OBJECTIVES

1. *Concept of reliability*
   a. Define what is meant by reliability.
   b. Why might a test have high or low reliability?

2. *Types of reliability*
   a. Define the following types of reliability: test–retest, parallel forms, internal consistency (split half, Kuder–Richardson, and coefficient alpha), and interscorer.
   b. Calculate both split-half (odd–even) and Kuder–Richardson reliability (formulas 20 and 21) coefficients on the following scores of 10 examinees to the 10 items on an achievement test, where 1 indicates a right answer and 0 a wrong answer

EXAMINEE

ITEM	A	B	C	D	E	F	G	H	I	J
1	1	1	0	1	1	0	1	0	1	0
2	1	0	0	0	0	1	0	0	0	1
3	1	1	1	1	1	0	1	0	0	0
4	1	1	1	0	0	1	0	1	0	0
5	1	0	1	1	0	0	0	0	0	0
6	1	1	1	0	1	1	1	0	0	0
7	1	0	1	1	0	0	1	1	0	1
8	1	1	1	0	1	1	0	0	1	0
9	1	1	0	1	1	1	0	1	0	0
10	1	1	1	1	1	0	0	0	1	0
Totals	10	7	7	6	6	5	4	3	3	2

The mean $(\overline{X})$ of the total scores is 5.30, and the variance (s^2) is 5.21. (See Answers to Quantitative Questions, p. 486.)

3. *Appropriateness of different types of reliability*
   a. Describe when it would be appropriate to use the different types of reliability.
   b. Determine which types of reliability would be best for the following types of tests: a test to determine suicide risk, an achievement test for a history class, and an essay test in which there may be ambiguous scoring criteria.

4. *Variables affecting test reliability:*
   a. Describe the three variables that affect test reliability.
   b. A test consisting of 40 items has a reliability coefficient of .80. Approximately how many more items of the same general type must be added to the test to increase its reliability to .90? (See Answers to Quantitative Questions, p. 486.)

5. *Standard error of measure*
    a. Define what is meant by the standard error of measure.
    b. Compute the standard error of measurement (s_{err}) of a test having a standard deviation of 10 and a parallel-forms reliability coefficient of .84. Then use the obtained value of s_{err} to find the 95% confidence interval for the true scores corresponding to obtained scores of 40, 50, and 60. (See Answers to Quantitative Questions, p. 486.)

6. *Generalizability theory*
    a. What is generalizability theory trying to accomplish?
    b. Why is generalizability theory potentially an improvement on classical views of reliability?

7. *Types of validity*
    a. Define what is meant by the following types of validity: content, criterion (predictive and concurrent), construct (include convergent–divergent), and incremental.
    b. For what kinds of tests and situations is each type of validity most appropriate?

8. *Standard error of estimate*
    a. What is the difference between the standard error of measurement and the standard error of estimate?
    b. How are these two statistics related to the reliability and validity coefficients for a test?
    c. What is the standard error made in estimating grade-point averages from scores on an aptitude test if the standard deviation of the criterion is .50 and the correlation between test and criterion is .60? If a student's predicted grade-point average is 2.5, what is the probability that the student's obtained grade-point average will fall between 2.1 and 2.9? Between 1.72 and 3.28? (See Answers to Quantitative Questions, p. 486.)

9. *Personnel decision making*
    a. What are three strategies for using tests in personnel decision making?
    b. Construct an empirical expectancy table for the paired *X, Y* scores in Table A.2 of Appendix A. Let *X* be the predictor (row) variable and *Y* the criterion (column) variable. Use an interval width of 7 for both variables in setting up the score intervals for *X* and *Y*. (See Answers to Quantitative Questions, p. 487.)

EXPERIENCING PSYCHOLOGICAL ASSESSMENT

1. Look through the Web site of an online dating service that offers psychological testing, such as eharmony.com. What type of validity measures will be most appropriate? What type of criterion measures do you think will be most appropriate?

2. Consider your SAT scores. Do you believe they had good predictive validity in your case? Why or why not?

CHAPTER SIX

INTELLIGENCE TESTING

CHAPTER OBJECTIVES

1. Provide definitions of intelligence.
2. Describe the three major categories related to the theories of intelligence.
3. Understand the applications of intelligence testing.
4. Describe the history, format, and purpose of the Stanford–Binet.
5. Describe the format, IQs, indexes, and subtests of the Wechsler intelligence scales.
6. Describe additional wide-range individual intelligence tests.
7. Describe special-purpose, nonverbal intelligence tests.
8. Describe the major group intelligence tests.
9. Describe the major academic ability and admissions tests.

By administering intelligence tests, many psychologists during the early 20th century discovered they could make a living in their profession by doing something other than teaching and research. For this reason, intelligence testing has sometimes been referred to as "the bread and butter of psychology." Today, assessing cognitive abilities still forms a core activity of many professional psychologists, particularly in clinical, legal, educational, and organizational settings.

HISTORY, DEFINITIONS, AND THEORIES

Intelligence, a common term in the vocabulary of most people today, was almost unknown in everyday speech a century or so ago. During the latter part of the 19th century, many scholars and scientists were attracted to Charles Darwin's theory that differences among species evolved by natural selection. Two of these individuals, the philosopher Herbert Spencer and Darwin's gentleman–scientist cousin Francis Galton, were interested in

intraspecies differences in mental characteristics and behavior. These men and their follow-
ers maintained that there exists in human beings an innate degree of general mental ability,
which they referred to as *intelligence.*

Unlike Spencer, Galton was not content merely to speculate and argue about the nature
of intelligence. He attempted to demonstrate a hereditary basis for intelligence by studies
of family trees and devised a number of tests of sensory discrimination and reaction time to
measure its components (see Galton's original articles at psychclassics.yorku.ca/author.htm).
These and other sensorimotor tests (of movement speed, muscular strength, pain sensitivity,
weight discrimination, etc.) were studied extensively by the American psychologist J. McKeen
Cattell. Unfortunately, the tests proved to be relatively useless as predictors of accomplishment in schoolwork and other tasks that presumably require intelligence.

Radically different from the analytic procedure of trying to measure the components
of intelligence was the approach of the French psychologist Alfred Binet. Binet maintained
that intelligence is manifested in performance on a variety of tasks and that it could be measured by responses to a sample of these tasks. Because Binet's work in designing the first
successful intelligence tests was motivated by the problem of identifying mentally retarded
children in the Paris school system, it is natural that the sample of tests selected by him was
heavily loaded with school-type tasks.

In 1905, Binet and his physician associate, Théodore Simon, published their first set
of intelligence tests, 30 short tests arranged in order from easiest to most difficult (Binet &
Simon, 1905). Further work led to the publication in 1908 of a revised Binet–Simon scale
consisting of 58 tasks arranged at age levels from 3 to 13 years. The tasks were grouped by
chronological age according to what research had indicated normal children of a given age
could do. A child's mental age (MA) was determined by the number of subtests passed at
each level, and a mental age strikingly lower than the child's chronological age was considered indicative of mental retardation. A final revision of the scale was published in 1911
(Table 6.1), but after Binet's untimely death during that same year, the scene of later developments in intelligence testing shifted to the United States and Great Britain.

Definitions of Intelligence

Ever since Binet and Simon produced the first practical intelligence tests, psychologists
have tried to formulate a workable definition of the concept. Binet's definition emphasized
judgment, understanding, and reasoning. Other definitions described intelligence as the
ability to think abstractly, the ability to learn, or the ability to adapt to new situations. All of
these definitions were criticized, however, for one reason or another. Adaptability is obviously necessary for survival, but it is too broad as a definition of intelligence. On the other
hand, Lewis Terman's definition of intelligence as the ability to do abstract thinking is too
narrow. Abstract thinking ability is an important aspect of intelligence, but certainly not the
only one. Finally, the popular conception of intelligence as the ability to learn is inadequate
if intelligence tests are accepted as measures of intelligence. Intelligence is also often associated with motivation and planning. Thus, it is sometimes conceptualized as the ability to
focus and sustain one's ability to achieve a desired goal. Sometimes the speed of learning is
also associated with intelligence, although speed is often not associated with the amount or
complexity of learning.

TABLE 6.1   The 54 Subtests on the 1911 Binet–Simon Scale

Age 3
Points to nose, eyes, and mouth.
Repeats two digits.
Enumerates objects in a picture.
Gives family name.
Repeats a sentence of six syllables.

Age 4
Gives own sex.
Names key, knife, and penny.
Repeats three digits.
Compares two lines.

Age 5
Compares two weights.
Copies a square.
Repeats a sentence of 10 syllables.
Counts four pennies.
Unites the halves of a divided rectangle.

Age 6
Distinguishes between morning and afternoon.
Defines familiar words in terms of use.
Copies a diamond.
Counts 13 pennies.
Distinguishes pictures of ugly and pretty faces.

Age 7
Shows right hand and left ear.
Describes a picture.
Executes three commands given simultaneously.
Counts the value of six sous, three of which
   are double.
Names four cardinal colors.

Age 8
Compares two objects from memory.
Counts from 20 to zero.
Notes omissions from pictures.
Gives day and date.
Repeats five digits.

Age 9
Gives change from 20 sous.
Defines familiar words in terms superior to use.
Recognizes all the (nine) pieces of money.
Names the months of the year in order.
Answers or comprehends "easy questions."

Age 10
Arranges five blocks in order of weight.
Copies two drawings from memory.
Criticizes absurd statements.
Answers or comprehends "difficult questions."
Uses three given words in not more than
   two sentences.

Age 12
Resists suggestion as to length of lines.
Composes one sentence containing three given words.
Names 60 words in 3 minutes.
Defines three abstract words.
Discovers the sense of a disarranged sentence.

Age 15
Repeats seven digits.
Finds three rhymes for a given word in 1 minute.
Repeats a sentence of 26 syllables.
Interprets pictures.
Interprets given facts.

Adult
Solves the paper-cutting test.
Rearranges a triangle in imagination.
Gives differences between pairs of abstract terms.
Gives three differences between a president and
   a king.
Gives the main thought of a selection that he
   has read.

Rather than attempting to formulate a universally acceptable definition of intelligence, certain psychologists have suggested that it might be better to abandon the term altogether. If an alternative term is needed, perhaps *general mental ability, scholastic aptitude,* or *academic ability* would be preferable. The last two terms are a recognition of the fact that traditional intelligence tests are primarily predictors of success in schoolwork.

No matter how strong opposition to the term *intelligence* may be, it is certainly less intense than dislike of the term *IQ.* Because of the controversy surrounding IQ and the implication that it is a fixed measure of cognitive ability, certain psychologists who have devoted much of their professional lives to the study of intelligence have expressed an interest in abandoning the term *IQ* altogether (Vernon, 1979).

Not all instruments discussed in this chapter are specifically labeled *intelligence tests;* rather, they have been proposed as measures of *general* mental ability. In this sense, they are to be distinguished from the measures of *special abilities* considered in Chapter 11. The distinction between tests of general mental ability (intelligence) and tests of special abilities is, however, not clear-cut, and certain tests of scholastic ability discussed in the present chapter might fit equally well in Chapter 9.

Theories of Intelligence

Theories of intelligence, or rather theories of intelligent behavior, have been based on psychometric, developmental, and information-processing models (see Flanagan & Harrison, 2005). The first two types of theories represent traditional approaches, and the third is more recent in origin.

Psychometric Theories.   The psychometric approach, which has resulted in many tests of intelligence and a variety of statistical methods for analyzing scores on these tests, focuses on individual differences in cognitive abilities and the search for the causes of these differences. Among theories or models of cognitive abilities based on the psychometric approach and stemming in particular from the results of factor analyses (see Appendix A) are Spearman's (1927) two-factor theory (consisting of a general factor plus several specific factors for each test), Thurstone's (1938) multifactor theory of seven primary mental abilities, Guilford's (1967, 1988) structure-of-intellect model, and Vernon's (1960) hierarchical model. Vernon's model consists of a general factor at the first level, verbal–educational and practical–mechanical–spatial factors at a second level, and a number of minor group factors at a third level. Cattell's (1963) theory of two kinds of intelligence, fluid and crystallized, is also based on the results of factor analysis and is related to Hebb's (1949) distinction between Intelligence A and Intelligence B.

The best supported and most influential current theory of intelligence is the Cattell–Horn–Carrol (CHC). It is an extension of Cattell's earlier distinction between fluid and crystallized intelligence, but was expanded in 1993 through extensive factor analyses. It is very complex, contains numerous components, and, as a result, has been described as being analogous to the table of periodic elements in chemistry (Kaufman & Lichtenberger, 2002, p. 566). The theory is based on a hierarchy that begins with narrow aspects (or *stratums*) of intelligence and works its way up to far broader aspects. The first (narrow) stratum comprises factors that measure fairly discrete abilities, such as simple reaction time, visual memory, spatial scanning, and speech sound discrimination. The second and broader stratum of the theory consists of combinations of the abilities in the first stratum. Examples are general fluid intelligence (*Gf*), general crystallized intelligence (Gc), and general visual–spatial thinking (Gv). The third, or highest, stratum of Carroll's theory is general intelligence or *g* and is a combination of abilities in the second stratum.

Developmental Theories.   Developmental theories of cognitive abilities, which stem from research on human developmental psychology, emphasize uniformities or interindividual similarities in cognitive growth, rather than individual differences. A prime example is Piaget's (1972) conception of cognition as developing from the actions of assimilation and accommodation on the external world. *Assimilation* consists of fitting new experiences into preexisting cognitive structures (*schemata*), while *accommodation* is the modification of these schemata as a result of experience. By interacting with the environment, a growing child creates schemata to serve as explanatory maps and guides to behavior. According to Piaget, children normally develop intellectually through a series of progressive stages: sensorimotor (birth–age 2), preoperational (ages 2–7), concrete operational (ages 7–11), and formal operational (ages 11–15). Piaget believed that the growth of intelligence ceases at around age 15, but a number of researchers have taken issue with this assertion.

Information-Processing Theories.   Information-processing theories or models of problem solving and thinking are concerned with identifying the cognitive processes or operations by which the brain deals with information. Research on attention and processing speed has received particular emphasis from an information-processing perspective. Illustrative of theories falling within this framework are Sternberg's (1982, 1986) component process and triarchic theories and Gardner's (1983, 1993) theory of multiple intelligences.

Sternberg (1982) initially hypothesized five classes of *component processes* by which the brain operates on information and solves problems: metacomponents, performance components, acquisition components, retention components, and transfer components. Among the various components in these five classes, encoding and comparing are especially critical for effective problem solving. In an extension of his component process theory, Sternberg (1986, 1994) proposed a *triarchic theory* that includes three subtheories: a componential subtheory, an experiential subtheory, and a contextual subtheory. The componential subtheory consists of metacomponents, performance components, and knowledge-acquisition components. The experiential subtheory is concerned with the ability to formulate new ideas by combining seemingly unrelated factors or information. The contextual subtheory is concerned with the ability to adapt to changing environmental conditions and to shape the environment in such a way that one's strengths are maximized and one's weaknesses are compensated for. In a further modification of his theory, Sternberg (1988) proposed the concept of *mental self-government,* which represents an attempt to combine the concept of intelligence with that of personality. The manner in which the three types of intelligence delineated by the triarchic theory—componential, experiential, and contextual—are brought to bear in solving everyday problems is characterized as *intellectual style.* The effectiveness of a particular intellectual style depends on the extent to which it matches the person's intellectual ability, his or her preferred style, and the immediate problem to be solved (Sternberg, 2003).[1]

According to Gardner's (1983, 1993) theory of multiple intelligences, human cognition and information processing involve the deployment of various symbol systems that are characteristic forms of perception, memory, and learning. Gardner proposed that there are

---

[1]A recent entry in the intelligence-testing sweepstakes is the Sternberg Triarchic Abilities Test (STAT), a battery of multiple-choice items designed to measure the analytic, practical, and creative aspects of intelligence.

seven forms of intelligence: linguistic, logical–mathematical, spatial, musical, bodily kinesthetic, and two forms of personal intelligence (intrapersonal and interpersonal). He maintained that only the first three forms are measured by conventional intelligence tests and that Western culture has overemphasized the first two of these. Gardner notes, however, that the other forms of intelligence are more valued in many societies and circumstances. He has more recently proposed a nature-oriented form of intelligence and an existential intelligence (Gardner, 1999).

Despite these and other efforts, no theoretical approach has succeeded in providing a completely satisfactory explanation of how intelligence develops and changes, the causes of individual differences in intelligence, or the specific cognitive and physiological processes that are responsible for intellectual activity. Presumably, all current theories are correct to some extent, but certainly none of them provides a comprehensive, empirically verified explanation of cognitive structure and functioning (see a summary of the areas experts do or do not agree on at www.apa.org/releases/intell.html).

For the present, it appears that information-processing theories offer the best chance for a logical and empirically based conception of cognitive abilities, but the situation could change as research progresses. In any event, one thing is certain: other theories of intelligence will be forthcoming, and their value will be determined by their effectiveness in predicting and explaining human learning and thinking.

Applications of Intelligence Testing

In contrast to more theoretical definitions, operational definitions of intelligence focus on its measurement and associated applications. The most operational of such definitions was suggested by Boring (1923), who proposed to define intelligence as "whatever is measured by an intelligence test." Whatever it is that intelligence tests measure, these tests have been used for a number of practical purposes, including the following:

1. Diagnosis of the presence and nature of brain damage; evaluating low and high mental ability and the assignment of mentally retarded and mentally gifted children to special programs or classes
2. Selection (screening), placement, and classification of students in institutions of higher education, employees in business and industrial organizations, and personnel in military and governmental departments
3. Determination and diagnosis of job-connected disabilities for insurance claims
4. Vocational and educational counseling and rehabilitation
5. Psychodiagnosis of children and adults in clinical or psychiatric contexts
6. Evaluation of the effectiveness of psychological treatments and environmental interventions
7. Research on cognitive abilities and personality

Individual and Group Tests

The formats of tests of general intelligence are not identical. On some tests, items of different types are mixed or alternated, increasing in difficulty throughout the test. The items on other intelligence tests are grouped as sets of separately timed subtests.

The most common way of classifying intelligence tests is by the dichotomy *individual* versus *group*. Individual intelligence tests, which are administered to one person at a time, have a somewhat different focus than group intelligence tests, which can be administered to many people simultaneously. The emphasis of individual tests is to understand an individual's cognitive strengths and weaknesses. This information can then be used to assist with a wide number of possible decisions. These might include academic placement, competency to make legal decisions, developing an optimal treatment plan, or ability to perform complex jobs. The focus of group tests, on the other hand, tends to be narrower: to predict academic or occupational performance (see Schmidt & Hunter, 2004). Also, administering an individual intelligence test is usually more time consuming than administering a group test. An advantage of individual tests is that examiners can pay more attention to the examinees. This might include an examinee's level of anxiety, confidence, problem-solving strategies, level of frustration, distractibility, and motivation. In addition, performance can be encouraged and rewarded more effectively. Also, scores on individual tests are not as dependent on reading ability as scores on group tests.

The greater economy of administering a group test in certain situations results in many more group than individual tests being given. Also, in spite of what advocates of individual tests have sometimes maintained, certain group tests of intelligence may have even higher validity coefficients than individual tests.

Group intelligence tests are more often used for initial screening in educational and employment situations, to be followed by individual testing when an examinee makes a low score on a group test and/or more information on his or her cognitive strengths and weaknesses is needed. Individual intelligence tests are also more likely to be used in clinics, hospitals, and other settings, in which clinical diagnoses are made. In these settings, such tests serve not only as measures of general mental ability, but also as a means of obtaining insight into personality functioning and specific cognitive disabilities.

INDIVIDUAL INTELLIGENCE TESTS

The tests stemming from the work of Lewis Terman and David Wechsler have been the most popular individually administered measures of intelligence (see history in Boake, 2002). Over the years, these tests have been used to evaluate the intellectual abilities of children and adults in many different countries and contexts. Other individual tests, some representing variations or extensions of those devised by Terman and Wechsler, have been designed specifically to assess the mental abilities of young children and persons with linguistic or physical handicaps.

Older Editions of the Stanford–Binet

There have been three English translations and adaptations of the Binet–Simon scale in the United States. One was prepared by H. H. Goddard of the Vineland Training School, another by Frederic Kuhlmann of the University of Minnesota, and a third by Lewis Terman of Stanford University. The most popular of these revisions, the Stanford–Binet Intelligence Scale, was published by Terman in 1916.

The 1916 Scale.   Like the earlier Binet–Simon scales, the 1916 Stanford–Binet was an age scale on which the subtests were grouped into chronological age levels. Terman selected items from the Binet–Simon scales, as well as new items representing a broad sample of tasks that presumably tapped intellectual abilities. Efforts were also made to include tasks that were not so dependent on specific school learning experiences.

One criterion for including an item on the Stanford–Binet was that an increasing percentage of children at each successive age level should be able to answer the item correctly. For certain statistical reasons having to do with maintaining a fairly stable intelligence quotient (IQ) scale across age levels, the percentage-passing requirement was set lower for items included in subtests at higher-year levels than for items at lower-year levels. In any event, the percentage-passing criterion served as an objective means of making certain that every item on the test was placed at an appropriate age level.

An examinee's *mental age* (MA) and *intelligence quotient* on the Stanford–Binet depended on the number of subtests passed at successive age levels. IQ was determined by dividing the examinee's mental age (MA), the total number of months credit earned on the test, by his or her chronological age (CA) in months, and multiplying the resulting quotient by 100. In symbols, this *ratio IQ* was computed as

$$IQ = 100\,\frac{MA}{CA} \tag{6.1}$$

For many years, the Stanford–Binet Intelligence Scale served as a standard against which other intelligence tests were evaluated. Nevertheless, it had a number of shortcomings. For example, the 1916 version was standardized on only 1,000 children and 400 adults. The sample was, by present-day standards, not selected carefully and not representative of the U.S. population at the time. Two other shortcomings were inadequacies in testing adults and very young children and the lack of a second form to permit retesting. Therefore, in 1937, Terman and his associate, Maud Merrill, published a revised, updated, and restandardized version of the scale (Terman & Merrill, 1937).

The 1937 Scale.   The 1937 version of the Stanford–Binet Intelligence Scale had a lower *floor* and a higher *ceiling* than the 1916 scale, two parallel forms (L and M), and better standardization. The 1937 scale was standardized in stratified fashion on 100 children at each half-year interval from ages 1½ through 5½ years, 200 children at each year age interval from 6 through 14 years, and 100 children at each year age interval from ages 15 through 18. Equal numbers of boys and girls were tested in 17 communities of 11 states, but the sampling was limited to native-born Whites who, as a group, were somewhat above average in socioeconomic status. Consequently, the sample was not truly representative of the entire U.S. population.

Three criteria were used for including an item on the scale: (1) the item was judged to be a measure of intelligent behavior, (2) the percentage of children passing the item accelerated with chronological age, and (3) children who passed the item had a significantly higher mean mental age than those who failed the item. Items were grouped at half-year intervals (levels) from Year II through Year V and at yearly intervals from Year VI through Year XIV; there was also an Average Adult level and three Superior Adult levels (Superior Adult I, II, and III). The six subtests at each level from Year II through Year V were given

1-month credit each; from Year VI through Year XIV, the subtests were given 2-months' credit each; and the six subtests at Superior Adult levels I, II, and III were given 4-, 5-, and 6-months' credit each, respectively.

In testing a child with the Stanford–Binet, the examiner first established the child's basal age. The *basal age* was the highest year level at which the child passed all subtests. Testing then continued until the *ceiling age,* the lowest year level at which the child failed all subtests, was reached. Mental age was computed by adding to the basal age the number of months' credit received for passing each subtest up to the ceiling age. Then the IQ was computed by formula 7.1.

The 1960 Scale.   The third edition of the Stanford–Binet Intelligence Scale, published in 1960, consisted of an updating of the best items from Forms L and M (Terman & Merrill, 1960). Like its predecessors, the third edition was used to measure the intelligence of individuals from age 2 to adulthood. The procedure for administering the test was similar to that for the 1937 scale, but certain changes were introduced. One of these consisted of an alternative subtest at each age level for use when a particular subtest was either not administered or administered incorrectly. Testing time could also be shortened in certain instances by administering only four selected subtests instead of six at each year level. One issue was that the ratio IQ, like any other age norm, did not satisfy the requirement of equality of age units. For example, a 5-year-old child who is performing 1 year ahead of his age peers will have an IQ of 120. In contrast, an adolescent of 15 would need to be performing a full 3 years ahead of his peers to have an IQ of 120. Furthermore, it was meaningless when applied to adults because there was no satisfactory answer to the question of what chronological age should be used as the denominator of the MA/CA ratio when testing adults. Fourteen years, 16 years, and 18 years had all been claimed as the age at which mental growth stops, and hence any one of these ages might be a suitable denominator in computing the IQ. Because of such problems in determining the ratio IQ, a decision was made to change from a ratio IQ to a *deviation IQ* scale having a mean of 100 and a standard deviation of 16. The means and standard deviations were based on the performance of various age groups. Despite this, the older ratio IQ was still reported on occasion, and tables for computing it were supplied in the 1960 Stanford–Binet manual.

The standardization group for the 1960 Form L–M of the Stanford–Binet consisted of 4,500 children ages 2½ through 18 years who had taken either Form L or M of the 1937 scale between 1950 and 1954. Realizing the need for updated norms, the publisher arranged for the test to be administered in 1972 to a stratified national sample of 2,100 children (100 children at each half-year interval from 2 through 5½ years and at each year interval from 6 through 18 years). The sample was more representative than earlier normative samples of the general U.S. population. Based on the 1972 standardization, a revised manual for the third edition was published (Terman & Merrill, 1973). The manual listed test–retest reliability coefficients of over .90. As with the first two editions, there were moderate correlations with school grades and achievement test scores (.40 to .75).

Newer Editions of the Stanford–Binet

SB-IV.   The fourth edition of the Stanford–Binet Intelligence Scale (SB-IV), which was published in 1986, was constructed with attention to the needs of clinical, school, and other psychologists who use intelligence test information (Thorndike, Hagen, & Sattler, 1986). SB-IV maintained historical continuity with the older versions of the Stanford–Binet, but it represented a distinct departure from its predecessors in terms of its theoretical and psychometric bases, content, and administration procedure. Like many modern tests, SB-IV was constructed by using sophisticated psychometric procedures, such as item-response theory (Rasch scaling) and ethnic-bias analysis. In addition, it was designed not only to assist in identifying mentally retarded and mentally gifted individuals, but also to provide diagnostic information concerning specific learning disabilities. With respect to sex and ethnic bias, items judged to be unfair or that showed atypical statistical differences between the sexes or ethnic groups were omitted.

Theoretical Model and Tests.   The model on which SB-IV was based consists of a three-level hierarchy with a general intelligence factor (*g*) at the first level, three broad factors (crystallized abilities, fluid-analytic abilities, and short-term memory) at the second level, and three factors (verbal reasoning, quantitative reasoning, and abstract–visual reasoning) at the third level. The verbal and quantitative reasoning factors at the third level comprise the crystallized abilities factor at the second level, and the abstract–visual factor at the third level comprises the fluid-analytic abilities factor at the second level.

Like its predecessors, SB-IV was designed to measure intelligence from age 2 years to adulthood. There are 15 tests: three or four tests in each of the three broader categories of Level 3 (Verbal Reasoning, Quantitative Reasoning, Abstract–Visual Reasoning), plus four Short-Term Memory tests. Each test is arranged in a series of levels consisting of two items each. Almost all tests include sample items for familiarizing examinees with the nature of the specific task.

Administration.   Administration time for the entire SB-IV scale is approximately 75 minutes, varying with the age of the examinee and the number of tests taken. The adaptive or multistage nature of the scale calls for giving the Routing (Vocabulary) Test first to determine the entry level on the other tests. The entry level on the Routing Test is determined by the examinee's chronological age (CA). Administration of the Routing Test continues until the examinee fails three or four items at two consecutive levels, the higher of which is the *critical level*. The entry level for the remaining 14 tests is determined from a table by a combination of the critical level on the Routing Test and the examinee's CA. Administration of each test begins at the entry level and continues downward until the examinee passes both items at two consecutive levels (*basal level*) and upward until he or she fails three or four items at two consecutive levels. The higher of these levels is the examinee's *ceiling age* for that test.

Scoring.   An examinee's raw score on each of the 15 tests is equal to the number of items he or she passes. Raw scores are converted, within each age group, to *standard age scale (SAS) scores* having a mean of 50 and a standard deviation of 8. Raw scores on each of the four areas (Verbal Reasoning, Abstract–Visual Reasoning, Quantitative Reasoning, Short-Term Memory) are equal to the sum of the raw scores on the three or four tests comprising that area. These area scores are converted to *standard area scores (SAS scores)* having a mean of 100 and a standard deviation of 16. Finally, an overall *composite score* consisting of the sum of the four area scores is converted to a standard age score scale having a mean of 100 and a standard deviation of 16. The range of the overall composite scores is 36 to 164, which is equivalent to a z score range of –4 to +4.

Standardization. SB-IV was standardized on over 5,000 individuals between the ages of 2 years and 23 years, 11 months in 47 states and the District of Columbia. The standardization sample was stratified by gender and race–ethnicity, and student examinees were also stratified according to relative standing in their school class. Despite efforts to select a standardization sample that was truly representative of the U.S. population, the sample contained disproportionate numbers of individuals in the upper socioeconomic and higher educational levels. An attempt was made to correct for this problem in scoring the test, but it was not completely successful. Other problems are that the factors measured by the scale are not uniform across age levels and that the reliability information in the Technical Manual is inadequate. However, split-half and test–retest coefficients, computed on measures obtained over a time interval of 2 to 8 months, indicate that the reliabilities of the 15 tests, the four areas, and the composite are satisfactory. Reported reliability coefficients for the subtests are mostly in the .80's and .90's; the median reliability of the composite score is .97.

SB-V

Advances in psychometric and cognitive theory since 1986 prompted a further revision of the Stanford Binet in 2003. This fifth edition (Roid, 2003) can be administered to individuals from age 2 to 85 or older. It combines features of earlier editions with item-response theory and the findings of research and practice with the SB-IV. In addition to testing individuals within the normal range of cognitive abilities, SB-V was designed to assess clinical and neuropsychological disabilities and exceptionalities and to be useful in special-education placements, workers-compensation evaluations, career planning, employee selection, forensic contexts, and other applied settings. The design of the SB-V relies extensively on the Cattell–Horn–Carrol theory of intelligence. It includes general intelligence factor (*g*) at the top, five composite factors at a second level, and 10 subtests with various degrees of difficulty at a third level (see Table 6.2).

Testing on SB-V begins with the administration of one verbal (Vocabulary) test and one nonverbal (Object Series–Matrices) Routing Test. Scores on the Routing Tests are used to estimate the examinee's ability level and to select additional verbal and nonverbal subtests for administration. Each subtest takes approximately 5 minutes, for a total administration time of around an hour.

Raw scores on the 10 subtests are converted to standard scores having a mean of 10 and a standard deviation of 3. Scores on the five factors, each consisting of one verbal and one nonverbal subtest, are converted to composite indexes having a mean of 100 and a standard deviation of 15. Scores on the five verbal subtests are combined to yield a Verbal IQ (VIQ), scores on the five nonverbal subtests to yield a Nonverbal IQ (NVIQ), and scores on all 10 subtests to yield a Full Scale IQ (FSIQ). These are deviation IQs having a mean of 100, a standard deviation of 15, and a range of 40 to 160. Raw scores on the composite (factor) scales can also be combined to yield Change-Sensitive Scores (CSSs). The conversion

TABLE 6.2   Factors, Domains, and Subtests of the Stanford-Binet, Fifth Edition

	DOMAINS	
FACTORS	**NONVERBAL (NV)**	**VERBAL (V)**
Fluid Reasoning (FR)	*Nonverbal Fluid Reasoning** Activities: Object Series/Matrices (Routing)	*Verbal Fluid Reasoning* Activities: Early Reasoning (2–3), Verbal Absurdities (4), Verbal Analogies (5–6)
Knowledge (KN)	*Nonverbal Knowledge* Activities: Procedural Knowlege (2–3), Picture Absurdities (4–6)	*Verbal Knowledge** Activities: Vocabulary (Routing)
Quantitative Reasoning (QR)	*Nonverbal Quantitative Reasoning* Activities: Quantitative Reasoning (2–6)	*Verbal Quantitative Reasoning* Activities: Quantitative Reasoning (2–6)
Visual-Spatial Processing (VS)	*Nonverbal Visual-Spatial Processing* Activites: Form Board (1–2), Form Patterns (3–6)	*Verbal Visual-Spatial Processing* Activities: Position and Direction (2–6)
Working Memory (WM)	*Nonverbal Working Memory* Activities: Delayed Response (1), Block Span (2–6)	*Verbal Working Memory* Activities: Memory for Sentences (2–3), Last Word (4–6)

Note: Names of the 10 Subtests are in ***bold italic***. Activities are shown with the levels at which they appear.
*Routing Subtests

(Copyright © 2003 by the Riverside Publishing Company, 425 Spring Lake Drive, Itasca, IL 60143-2079.)

to CSSs is based on item-response theory scaling and is useful in comparing changes in a person's measured abilities over time.

SB-V was standardized on a national sample of 4,800 individuals between the ages of 2 and 85+ years selected to match the 2000 U.S. Census data. Test items were checked for gender, ethnic, cultural, religious, regional, and socioeconomic bias. SB-V was also co-normed with the Bender Visual–Motor Gestalt Test, Second Edition, and a measure of test-taking behavior. Reliabilities range from .84 to .89 for the subtests, from .90 to .92 for the composite indexes, and from .95 to .98 for the Verbal, Nonverbal, and Full Scale IQs (Roid, 2003).

Wechsler Intelligence Tests

Although subtests at the adult level have been included on the Stanford–Binet since the 1937 revision, it has often not been considered to be a satisfactory measure of adult intelligence. Consequently, in 1939, David Wechsler, a psychologist at Bellevue Hospital in New York, published an individual intelligence test designed specifically for adults (Wechsler, 1939). To this test, the Wechsler–Bellevue Scale Form I, Wechsler added a second form in 1947, the Wechsler–Bellevue Scale Form II. A complete revision and restandardization of Form I was published in 1955 as the Wechsler Adult Intelligence Scale (WAIS) (Wechsler, 1955). The WAIS was revised, restandardized, and republished in 1981 (WAIS-R) and 1997 (WAIS-III), and another revision is scheduled for 2008. A downward extension of the Wechsler Bellevue Form I was published in 1949 as the Wechsler Intelligence Scale for Children (WISC). It was revised in 1974 (WISC-R), 1991 (WISC-III), and 2003 (WISC-IV).

WAIS-III. As with other tests of cognitive abilities, the content and norms on intelligence tests become somewhat out of date over the years. For this reason, a new edition of the WAIS-R, the WAIS-III, was constructed and standardized in the mid-1990s and published in 1997 (Wechsler, 1997). It was standardized on a sample of 2,450 adults aged 16 to 89 years. The sample was stratified by race–ethnicity (White, African American, Hispanic, Other), sex, educational level, and geographical region within each age group. In constructing the WAIS-III, particular attention was paid to verbal subtests such as Information, Vocabulary, and Comprehension, which, because they are more subject to cultural changes, become outdated more quickly than other subtests.

Average split-half reliability for the WAIS-III IQs were very high (.94 to .97) as were test–retest reliabilities. This indicates it is one of the most reliable tests published. Correlations with scores on other tests within the Wechsler family, as well as the Stanford Binet–Fourth Edition and Raven's Progressive Matrices, have been supportive of the validity of the WAIS-III. Patterns of scores among various clinical groups (e.g., head injured, learning disabled) were in the expected direction (i.e., head injured patients had poor attention and slow processing speed). The WAIS-III has also been co-normed with the third edition of the Wechsler Memory Scale (WMS-III), permitting an examination of the relationship between a person's intellectual functioning and his or her memory (see Groth-Marnat, 2003).

One feature of the WAIS-III is that administration time for the standardization sample was between 60 and 75 minutes. In contrast, clinical populations often require 1.5 hours or longer. Another feature is that, when compared to previous versions, the floor for most subtests has been lowered to provide a better estimate of the cognitive functioning of individuals in the low and extremely low ranges of intelligence.

The WAIS-III is comprised of verbal and performance (or nonverbal) subtests (see Table 6.3). The subtests are further clustered into four index scores that measure four major cognitive abilities. These include verbal reasoning–comprehension (Verbal Comprehension), attention (Working Memory), how fast the person can perform (Processing Speed), and ability to solve nonverbal information (Perceptual Organization). These four factors (or indexes) provide a model for the major components of intelligence. They have also proved to be useful for interpreting various patterns of strengths and weaknesses (see Groth-Marnat, 2000, 2003b).

One issue in interpreting any of the Wechsler intelligence scales is that some caution needs to be used in understanding the meanings of individual subtests and various patterns among the subtests. Originally, Wechsler planned to obtain more than an estimate of a person's overall mental ability. He hoped that patterns of subtests could be useful in identifying such characteristics as schizophrenia, juvenile delinquency, and personality disorders. Unfortunately, research has provided little support for Wechsler's hypotheses regarding the diagnostic significance of many of the patterns of subtests.

TABLE 6.3   Subtests on the Wechsler Adult Intelligence Scale-III

VERBAL SUBTESTS

Vocabulary: 37 words to be defined are presented in order of increasing difficulty.

Similarities: 14 items of the type "In what way are A and B alike?"

Information: 33 general information questions to be answered in a few words or numbers.

Comprehension: 18 questions requiring detailed answers are presented in order of ascending difficulty.

Arithmetic: 15 arithmetic problems are presented in order of increasing difficulty.

Digit Span: 7 series of digits to be recited forward and 7 series to be recited backward.

Letter–Number Sequencing: series of letters and numbers presented orally in mixed-up order, examinees reorder and repeat the list by saying the numbers in ascending order and then repeating the letters in alphabetical order.

PERFORMANCE (NONVERBAL) SUBTESTS

Picture Completion (P): 27 pictures on cards, each having a missing part; the examinee has 20 seconds to indicate what part is missing.

Block Design (P): 10 red and white geometric designs on cards and 9 red-and-white blocks; the examinee is instructed to duplicate each design with 4 or 9 blocks.

Picture Arrangement (P): 10 sets of cards, each containing a small picture; the examinee is told to arrange the pictures in each set of cards to make a sensible story.

Matrix Reasoning: series of pictures of five geometric shapes; examinees are required to name or point to the correct shape.

Digit Symbol (Coding): 93 boxes to be filled in with the appropriate coded symbol corresponding to the number appearing above the box.

Symbol Search: series of paired groups, each pair consisting of a target group and a search group; examinees mark the appropriate box to indicate whether either target symbol appears in the search group.

Object Assembly: 4 cardboard picture puzzles presented to the examinee in a prearranged format; the examinee is told to put the pieces together to make something.

Problems in attempting to analyze patterns of high and low subtests ("subtest scatter") on the Wechsler tests are that subtest-scaled scores are not highly reliable and some subtests have substantial correlations with each other. Consequently, the difference between a person's scaled scores on two given subtests must be very large before it can be viewed as significant or meaningful. Large differences between subtest-scaled scores and Verbal and Performance IQs, however, are of some value in the diagnosis of organic brain damage and psychopathology and in differentiating between intelligence and the resources or opportunities available to the person. A significantly lower Performance than Verbal IQ, for example, may be consistent with brain damage to the right hemisphere (since this hemisphere mediates nonverbal, or performance, information; see Groth-Marnat, 2003). Interpretation of index scores has also been fairly successful. For example, a low score on the Processing

Speed Index is likely to be not only consistent with a person who has had a head injury, but the low score is also likely to reflect slow problem solving in everyday situations as well.

WISC-IV. The WISC-IV is the latest update (2003) of the Wechsler intelligence scales and was designed for children between the ages of 6 and 16 years 11 months. It consists of 10 core and 5 supplementary (or optional) subtests grouped into four index scores (see Table 6.4). The four index scores are Verbal Comprehension, Perceptual Reasoning, Working Memory, and Processing Speed. Part of the rationale for the WISC-IV was based on recent research findings that speed and working memory–attention are the optimal means of measuring intelligence (Sattler & Dumont, 2004; Wechsler, 2003). As a result, these have been emphasized in the development of the WISC-IV and are reflected in the Working Memory and Processing Speed indexes. They are also helpful indicators of learning disabilities and attention disorders and are sensitive to cognitive impairment resulting from such factors as substance abuse and head injuries. For example, Psychological Report 6.1 indicates a client who had been misdiagnosed as being mentally retarded when in reality he had a pattern of abilities that were much more consistent with learning disabilities. One main feature of the WISC-IV is that verbal and performance IQs have been eliminated. Instead, interpretation relics mainly on the Full Scale IQ and the four index scores listed above (and included in Table 6.4 see also WISC-IV description harcourtassessment.com/haiweb/Cultures/en-US/dotCom/WISC-IV.com.htm).

One feature of the WISC-IV is that it consists of downward extensions and revisions of subtests found on the WISC-III and WAIS-III (see Table 6.4). However, Picture Concepts, Word Reasoning, and Cancellation are three new subtests unique to the WISC-IV. On Picture Concepts, the examinee is presented with multiple rows of objects and asked to select the objects that are similar with respect to an underlying concept. It measures the ability to categorize. On the Cancellation subtest, the examinee is presented with a page

TABLE 6.4   WISC-IV MODEL

FULL-SCALE IQ (FSIQ)			
Composite Indexes			
Verbal Comprehension	Perceptual Reasoning	Working Memory	Processing Speed
Core Subtests			
Similarities	Matrix Reasoning	Letter–Number	
Vocabulary	Block Design	Sequencing	Symbol Search
Comprehension	Picture Concepts	Digit Span	Coding
Supplemental Subtests			
Information Word Reasoning	Picture Completion	Arithmetic	Cancellation

PSYCHOLOGICAL REPORT 6.1   WISC-IV Assessment of Learning Disabilities

Name of Examinee: Fred   Sex: Male
Age: 16   Education: 10th grade
Date of Testing: 3/10/04

Test Administered: Wechsler Intelligence Scale for Children-IV

REFERRAL QUESTION

Fred is a 16-year-old, left-handed European American male in his tenth year of high school who was referred by his pediatrician because he was doing poorly in school. He wanted an explanation for these difficulties, with recommendations for an optimal educational placement.

BACKGROUND INFORMATION

Four years prior to the current evaluation, Fred had been placed in classes for mentally retarded students. His parents could not recall if previous formal testing had been done. However, they were confused by his diagnosis since he seemed quite competent at practical tasks such as disassembling and reassembling his bicycle.

WISC-IV RESULTS

Full Scale IQ = 83
Index Scores: Verbal Comprehension = 84   Processing Speed = 75
                   Perceptual Reasoning = 120   Working Memory = 72

INTERPRETATION AND IMPRESSIONS

The WISC-IV results indicate a Full Scale IQ of 83. This places him in the Low Average range or lower 13% of the population when compared with his age-related peers.

His clear and noteworthy strength is his ability to organize and solve nonverbal problems. His ability is so pronounced that he scored in the Superior range or top 9% of the population. This means that when working with nonverbal material that involves simultaneous processing he can work efficiently and accurately. His ability to understand commonsense situations and knowledge of vocabulary words was in the Low Average range.

Pronounced weaknesses were found in his ability to work quickly and concentrate effectively. This suggests he is distractible and would have difficulty organizing information in an orderly sequence (numbers, reading, following verbal instructions).

SUMMARY AND RECOMMENDATIONS

Clearly, the diagnosis of mentally retarded was incorrect. In contrast, Fred seems to have considerable strengths working with practical, nonverbal information, but has pronounced weaknesses related to being able to pay attention, work quickly, and sequence material in an orderly manner. This seems to be much more consistent with a diagnosis of a learning disability. Accordingly, his educational program should address these difficulties as well as emphasize his strengths. Vocational guidance and training should similarly focus on capitalizing on his strengths and minimizing his weaknesses.

covered with pictures of animals and other common objects, arranged randomly or in rows and columns, and asked to mark through, or cancel, the animals as quickly as possible. This subtest is a measure of attention and processing speed. Finally, Verbal Reasoning requires the examinee to identify underlying verbal concepts from successive clues. It measures the ability to reason with verbal materials.

The standardization group was based on 2,200 children that were stratified based on age, sex, race–ethnicity, geographical region, and parental education. The sample closely paralleled the 2,000 U.S. Census data. They were divided into 11 age groups, with 100 boys and 100 girls in each group.

As with previous versions of the Wechsler intelligence scales, reliability and validity were excellent. Internal consistency for the Full Scale and Index scores ranged from .91 to .97 (Wechsler, 2003). Test–retest for the same measures ranged from .79 to .89. Measures of validity indicate it correlates with relevant criterion measures. It also reflects the patterns of cognitive abilities expected among various clinical populations. Finally, the index scores are supported by factor analysis (Sattler & Dumont, 2004; Wechsler 2003).

Wechsler Preschool and Primary Scale of Intelligence

The third member of the Wechsler intelligence tests, the Wechsler Preschool and Primary Scale of Intelligence (WPPSI), was first published in 1967 and a revision, the WPPSI-R, in 1989 (Wechsler, 1989). The six verbal subtests are Information, Comprehension, Similarities, Arithmetic, Vocabulary, and Sentences. The six performance subtests are Object Assembly, Geometric Design, Block Design, Mazes, Picture Completion, and Animal Pegs. Designed for children aged 3 to 7 years, the WPPSI-R was standardized in the late 1980s on a national sample of U.S. children aged 3 to 7 years. Stratifying the sample by gender, ethnicity, and parental educational and occupational level made it more representative of the U.S. population in this age range. WPPSI-R yields separate Verbal, Performance, and Full-Scale IQs based on a standard score scale having a mean of 100 and a standard deviation of 15.

The WPPSI-R was revised and published in 2002 (WPPSI-III; Wechsler, 2002). It was designed to be administered to children between the ages of 2:6 and 3:11 years in 30 to 45 minutes and to children between 4:0 and 7:3 years in 45 to 60 minutes. Similar in design to WISC-IV, the WPPSI-III consists of 15 subtests. Six of the subtests (Picture Naming, Receptive Vocabulary, Matrix Reasoning, Picture Concepts, Symbol Search, and Coding) are new. They were designed to measure verbal and nonverbal fluid reasoning, receptive versus expressive vocabulary, and processing speed (see Sattler & Dumont, 2004).

Wechsler Abbreviated Scale of Intelligence

The need in educational and clinical contexts for a reliable measure of intelligence that could be administered more quickly than the WAIS-III and WISC-III led to the development of the Wechsler Abbreviated Scale of Intelligence (WASI). The subtests on the WASI were constructed independently from but parallel to the corresponding subtests on the WAIS-III and WISC-III. The four-subtest form of the WASI consists of Vocabulary, Similarities, Block

Design, and Matrix Reasoning subtests. The first two of these subtests constitute the Verbal Scale, and the last two the Performance Scale of the WASI. The two-subtest form of the WASI consists of Vocabulary and Matrix Reasoning. The four-subtest form takes about 30 minutes and the two-subtest form takes about 15 minutes to administer. As with the WISC-III and WAIS-III, the WASI yields separate Verbal, Performance, and Full Scale IQs.

OTHER BROAD-RANGE INDIVIDUAL INTELLIGENCE TESTS

Although the Stanford–Binet and Wechsler tests are the most popular individual tests of intelligence in the United States, they are by no means the only wide-range batteries for assessing general mental ability. Nor are they the most popular tests of mental ability in other countries. Especially noteworthy in the United Kingdom are the British Ability Scales (BAS), which was revised by The Psychological Corporation and restandardized in the United States as the Differential Ability Scales (DAS).

Differential Ability Scales

The basic purpose of the Differential Ability Scales (DAS) (Elliott, 1990) is to provide ability profiles for analyzing and diagnosing children's learning difficulties, to assess changes in abilities over time, and to identify, select, and classify children with learning disabilities. The DAS consists of 20 subtests, including 12 core subtests, 5 diagnostic subtests, and 3 achievement subtests. The three achievement subtests (Number Skills, Spelling, Word Reading) are useful in assessing basic academic skills, but the core and diagnostic subtests provide the principal means of assessing cognitive abilities. Four to six core subtests, from age 2 years 6 months through 17 years 11 months, are administered to each examinee. Scores on various core subtests are combined to yield overall indexes of Verbal Ability and Nonverbal Ability for preschool children; Verbal, Nonverbal Reasoning, and Spatial Ability for school-aged children; and General Conceptual Ability on a scale having a mean of 100 and a standard deviation of 15 for preschool and school-aged children. Although the diagnostic subtests are not used in computing the ability indexes, they provide useful information for understanding a child's cognitive strengths and weaknesses.

The DAS norms are based on a sample of 3,475 U.S. children, stratified by age, sex, race–ethnicity, parent education, geographical region, and educational preschool enrollment. Exceptional children (learning disabled, speech and language impaired, educable mentally retarded, mentally gifted, emotionally disturbed, sensory or motor impaired) were included in the sample.

Detroit Test of Learning Aptitude

Another noteworthy individually administered intelligence test battery is the Detroit Test of Learning Aptitude. Administration of the primary edition of this battery (DTLA-P-2), which was designed for children aged 3 to 9 years 11 months, takes 15 to 45 minutes. The subtests include Articulation, Conceptual Matching, Design Reproduction, Digit Sequences, Draw-a-Person, Letter Sequences, Motor Directions, Object Sequences, Oral Directions, Picture Fragments, Picture Identification, Sentence Imitation, and Symbolic Relations.

The fourth edition of the Detroit Tests of Learning Aptitude (DTLA-4) (Hammill, 1999) was designed for children aged 6 to 17 years and takes 50 to 90 minutes to administer. The DTLA-4 subtests include Word Opposites, Design Sequences, Sentence Imitation, Reversed Letters, Story Construction, Design Reproduction, Basic Information, Symbolic Relations, Word Sequences, and Story Sequences. Standard scores, percentile ranks, and age equivalents for the 10 subtests and the composites (Overall, Optimal Level, Domain, Theoretical) can be determined. The Domain composites are Verbal, Nonverbal, Attention-enhanced, Attention-reduced, Motor-enhanced, and Motor-reduced. The theoretical composites are Fluid and Crystallized, Association and Cognitive, Simultaneous and Successive, and Verbal and Performance. DTLA-4 is an improvement over its predecessors with respect to clarity, ease of administration, standardization, reliability, validity, and other statistical characteristics.

At the upper end (ages 16 to 79 years) of the DTLA series is the Detroit Test of Learning Aptitude—Adult (DTLA-A). The 12 subtests on the DTLA-A can be combined into 16 composites to measure specific ability areas, based on various theories of intelligence and general intelligence. Total testing time on the DTLA-A ranges from 1½ to 2 hours.

Kaufman's Intelligence Tests

The Kaufman Assessment Battery for Children (K-ABC) was designed by A. S. and N. L. Kaufman to assess the abilities of 2½- to 12½-year-old children to solve problems requiring simultaneous and sequential mental processing (Kaufman & Kaufman, 1983). The K-ABC also includes an Achievement Scale to measure acquired skills in reading and arithmetic. Based on extensive research in neuropsychology and cognitive psychology, the K-ABC was designed especially for preschool, minority, and exceptional children. Thirteen of the 16 gamelike subtests comprising the K-ABC can be administered in 35 to 85 minutes. Scores are obtained in four global areas: Sequential Processing, Simultaneous Processing, Mental Processing Composite (Sequential plus Simultaneous), and Achievement.

A revision of the K-ABC, the KABC-II, appropriate for ages 3 to 18 years, was published in 2004 (Kaufman & Kaufman, 2004). The KABC-II was constructed from a dual theoretical framework: Luria's (1973) neuropsychological model of simultaneous and successive reasoning processes and the Cattell–Horn–Carroll (CHC) model of fluid and crystallized abilities (Carroll, 1993; Horn & Cattell, 1966). The subtests comprising each of the four scales (Simultaneous Processing, Sequential Processing, Planning Ability, Learning Ability) of the KABC-II core battery, following Luria's model, require a total of 25 to 55 minutes to administer. The subtests comprising the five scales (Visual Processing, Short-term Memory, Fluid Reasoning, Long-term Storage & Retrieval, Crystallized Ability) of the core battery, following the CHC model, take a total of 35 to 70 minutes. Overall composite scores obtained from the four to five scales are a Mental Processing Index and a Nonverbal Index, following the Luria model, and a Fluid-Crystallized Index and a Nonverbal Index, following the CHC model.

As was the K-ABC, the KABC-II was designed to be fair to children with diverse backgrounds or disabilities. In particular, the nonverbal subtests are useful in assessing children whose verbal skills are severely limited. In addition to the core subtests, a number of supplemental subtests can be administered for further exploration of hypotheses concerning an examinee's cognitive abilities. Both the K-ABC and the KABC-II were standardized on representative samples of children. Scores on the various scales and overall composites may be converted to age-based standard scores, age-equivalent scores, and percentile ranks.

Two other noteworthy intelligence tests designed by Alan Kaufman and Nadeen Kaufman are the Kaufman Adolescent and Adult Intelligence Test (KAIT) (Kaufman & Kaufman, 1993) and the Kaufman Brief Intelligence Test (K-BIT) (Kaufman & Kaufman, 1990). Both tests are based on the theory of fluid and crystallized intelligence. The KAIT is designed for ages 11 to 85+ years and takes 60 to 90 minutes; the K-BIT is designed for ages 4 to 90 years and takes 15 to 20 minutes.

Woodcock–Johnson III Tests of Cognitive Abilities

The Woodcock–Johnson III (WJ-III) is made up of two co-normed batteries for measuring general intellectual ability, specific cognitive abilities, and academic achievement (Woodcock, McGrew, & Mather, 2001). One of these batteries, the Woodcock–Johnson III (WJ-III) Test of Cognitive Abilities, is based on the Cattell–Horn–Carroll (CHC) theory of cognitive abilities (see Woodcock, 1998). This battery consists, in turn, of a Standard Battery of 10 tests and an Extended Battery of 10 additional tests. These tests have a broad age–grade range (2 to 90+ years, kindergarten to graduate school) and a relatively short testing time (approximately 5 minutes per test).

Scores on six clusters (Verbal Ability-Standard, Thinking Ability-Standard, Cognitive Efficiency-Standard, Phonemic Awareness, Working Memory, Delayed Recall) are determined from the Standard Battery. Scores on 14 additional clusters are obtained when the Extended Battery is administered. In addition to scores on the separate clusters, a General Intellectual Ability (GIA) score is computed by combining the scores on the first seven tests or a GIA (Extended) score by administering 14 cognitive tests. A Brief Intellectual Ability (BIA) score may be computed by combining scores on the Verbal Comprehension, Concept Formation, and Visual Matching tests. Scores may also be determined on seven broad CHC factors: Comprehension–Knowledge (Gc), Long-term Retrieval (Glr), Visual–Spatial Thinking (Gv), Auditory Processing (Ga), Fluid Reasoning (Gf), Processing Speed (Gs), and Short-term Memory (Gsm).

Das–Naglieri Cognitive Assessment System

Another recent entry in the intelligence test sweepstakes is the Das–Naglieri Cognitive Assessment System (CAS) (Naglieri & Das, 1997). The CAS is similar to the Woodcock–Johnson III in that it is based on a cognitive theory and published by the same company (Riverside Publishing). Reflecting its orientation toward school-aged children and adolescents, the age range of the CAS (5 to 17 years 11 months) is narrower than that of the WJ-III.

The CAS was designed "to provide a cognitive processing measure of ability that is fair to minority children, effective for differential diagnosis, and related to intervention." It is based on the Luria/Das–Naglieri PASS (Planning, Attention, Simultaneous, Successive) theory of cognition (see page 185) and is appropriate for school-aged children and adolescents. Testing time is 40 minutes for the Basic Battery of eight subtests and 60 minutes for the Standard Battery. The subtests are grouped under the four cognitive processes of the PASS model:

PLANNING
Matching Numbers
Planned Codes
Planned Connections

ATTENTION
Expressive Attention
Number Detection
Receptive Attention

SIMULTANEOUS
Nonverbal Matrices
Verbal–Spatial Relations
Figure Memory

SUCCESSIVE
Word Series
Sentence Repetition
Speech Rate (ages 5 to 7 years)
Sentence Questions (ages 8 to 17 years)

The Basic Battery consists of two subtests from each of these four categories.

In addition to scores on the separate tests, standard scores having a mean of 100 and a standard deviation of 15 are obtained on each of the four CAS scales. A Full Scale standard score is also obtained by combining scores on the all scales. The CAS was carefully standardized and has acceptable reliabilities. Research evidence concerning various types of validity (construct, concurrent, predictive, discriminant) is reported in the test manual (Naglieri & Das, 1997).

Individual Nonverbal Ability Tests

Psychometric assessments that require pointing, manipulating objects, or other nonverbal responses, rather than speaking or writing, are referred to as *nonverbal tests*. Performance on certain tasks on these tests may be facilitated by verbal language, but its use is minimized. Such tests are often used with people with certain types of handicaps or ones from divergent cultural backgrounds.

The fact that the Wechsler scales contain separate verbal and performance measures makes them more suitable than older versions of the Stanford–Binet for examining persons with physical, linguistic, and cultural differences. The Wechsler performance subtests tend to be more accurate measures of mental ability in hearing-handicapped and culturally different children, whereas the verbal subtests are more valid measures for the blind and partially sighted. In testing blind persons, a series of six specially designed performance tests known as the Haptic Intelligence Scale for Adult Blind (Shurrager & Shurrager, 1964) has sometimes been administered in conjunction with the WAIS-Verbal Scale as a measure of the intelligence of blind and partially sighted adults.

Single-Task Tests

One of the oldest nonverbal tests, the Seguin Form Board, was introduced in 1866. It was not until the early part of the 20th century, however, before Knox, Kohs, Porteus, and other psychologists made serious efforts to standardize such tests. In addition to many types of form boards, nonverbal tasks such as puzzles of various kinds, sequential tapping of cubes, matching problems, block designs, mazes, person drawings, and picture pointing have been used to measure mental abilities.

Mazes have been used extensively in psychological laboratories and clinics and included on a number of standardized tests. The Porteus Mazes (Porteus, 1915), described by their designer as a measure of foresight and planning ability, consists of a series of mazes arranged in order of increasing difficulty. On each maze the examinee is directed to draw the shortest path between the starting and finishing points without lifting the pencil or entering a blind alley. The Porteus is particularly suitable as a brief test (25 minutes) for the verbally handicapped and has been employed in a number of anthropological investigations and studies of the effects of drugs and neurosurgery.

Another nonverbal performance test for the handicapped consists of block designs such as those on the Wechsler scales and the Differential Ability Scales. One of the oldest tests of this type is the Kohs Block Design (Kohs, 1920). The materials on this test consist of 16 colored cubes and 17 cards with colored designs to be duplicated by the examinee. The Kohs Block Design was considered especially appropriate for language- and hearing-handicapped children, but it is seldom administered today.

Another single-task test, which requires only picture pointing, is the Columbia Mental Maturity Scale (CMMS) (Burgemeister, Blum, & Lorge, 1972). The CMMS was designed originally for testing the general reasoning ability of cerebral-palsied children, but it can be administered to other children having impaired verbal or motor functioning (visually handicapped, speech impaired, hearing handicapped, mentally retarded), as well as to hyperactive children. The test materials consist of 92 pictoral and figural classification items, each printed on 6- by 19-inch cards. The examinee (ages 3½ to 10 years) is asked to select from the series of drawings on each of 51 to 65 cards appropriate for his or her chronological age group the drawing that does not belong with the others. Testing time is 15 to 20 minutes; directions are given in English or Spanish. Performance is expressed in terms of age deviation scores ranging from 50 to 150, as well as percentile ranks, stanines, and maturity indexes.

Performance Test Batteries

The first battery of standardized performance tests to be distributed commercially was the Pintner–Paterson Scale of Performance Tests (Pintner & Paterson, 1917). Equally well known is the Arthur Point Scale of Performance Tests, which was published initially by Grace Arthur in 1925 and subsequently revised (Arthur, 1947). Two performance test batteries that have been used fairly extensively with speech- and hearing-handicapped children and are still available are the Leiter International Performance Scale (Leiter & Arthur, 1979) and the Hiskey–Nebraska Tests of Learning Aptitude (Hiskey, 1966). Also of interest are more recently published batteries, such as the Comprehensive Test of Nonverbal Intelligence, the Naglieri Nonverbal Ability Test, and the Universal Nonverbal Intelligence Test (see McCallum, Bracken, & Wasserman, 2001).

Hiskey–Nebraska and CID-PPS. The Hiskey–Nebraska Test of Learning Aptitude was designed specifically to assess the cognitive abilities of children (ages 3 to 17 years) with hearing impairments. It consists of 12 nonverbal subtests administered with pantomimic directions to deaf children or verbal directions to normal children. The test is unspeeded and yields a mental age and an intelligence quotient. Another multiple-subtest, nonverbal test of intelligence for hearing-impaired children, the Central Institute for the Deaf Preschool Performance Scale (CID-PPS), has a narrower age range (2 to 6 years) than the Hiskey–Nebraska, but likewise does not require spoken words from either examiner or examinee.

Leiter-R. The revised version of the Leiter International Performance Scale (Leiter-R) is promoted as a culture-fair measure of cognitive skills appropriate for people in various cultural contexts (Roid & Miller, 1997). It has an age range of 2 to 21 years and can be administered without verbal language to children with hearing disorders or other receptive or expressive language problems and culturally different, motor-impaired, autistic, and even mentally gifted children. Examinees are required to match a series of colored response cards with corresponding illustrations on an easel display. The four Reasoning subtests and the six Visualization subtests of the Visualization & Reasoning battery require a total of 40 minutes to administer. The eight Memory subtests and the two Attention subtests on the Attention & Memory Battery take 35 minutes. Screening for IQ or LD/ADHD can be accomplished in 25 minutes by administering an incomplete battery; Gifted Screening Assessment requires 35 minutes. The Leiter-R was standardized in the mid-1990s on 1,719 typical and 692 atypical children aged 2 to 21 years. Evidence for the reliability and validity reported in the manual indicates that the Leiter-R is a fairly psychometrically sound instrument (McCallum et al., 2001; Roid & Miller, 1997).

Comprehensive Test of Nonverbal Intelligence. The Comprehensive Test of Nonverbal Intelligence (CTONI) is one of the newest nonverbal tests for the handicapped. It has a wide age range (6 through 90 years) and can be administered in about an hour. CTONI is particularly appropriate for estimating the intelligence of children and adults who have problems with language or fine-motor skills. They may be persons who speak a language other than English, are socioeconomically disadvantaged or deaf, or have a language disorder, a motor disability, or a neurological impairment.

The six subtests on CTONI are Pictorial Analogies, Geometric Analogies, Pictorial Categories, Geometric Categories, Pictorial Sequences, and Geometric Sequences. These subtests were designed to measure analogical reasoning, categorical classifications, and sequential reasoning abilities, as revealed in responses to pictures of familiar objects (animals, people, toys, etc.) and geometric designs (drawings, unfamiliar sketches, etc.). As on the Leiter-R, examinees taking the CTONI indicate their responses by pointing to alternative choices. The responses are then scored and the scores combined to provide three composite quotients: Nonverbal Intelligence Quotient (NIQ), Pictorial Nonverbal Intelligence Quotient (PNIQ), and Geometric Nonverbal Intelligence Quotient (GNIQ).

CTONI was standardized in 25 U.S. states, Canada, and Panama. Though fairly small, the samples were stratified by gender, geographical regions, ethnicity, race, urban–rural residence, and disability. Reliability coefficients of .80 or greater are reported, and some evidence for content, criterion-related, and construct validity is also given in the manual (Hammill, Pearson, & Wiederholt, 1996). Especially noteworthy are the efforts that the designers of the test made to detect and eliminate cultural, gender, racial, and linguistic bias in the items.

Universal Nonverbal Intelligence Test (UNIT). As with other tests described in this section, the UNIT was designed to provide a measure of intelligence in individuals with speech, language, or hearing impairments and in persons who are verbally uncommunicative or have different cultural or language backgrounds. To ensure fairness regardless of culture, ethnicity, gender, or hearing, the UNIT was developed with both nonverbal administration and response formats. Administration of this test battery also involves multiple response modes, including the use of manipulatives, paper and pencil, and pointing. Eight universal hand and body gestures are used to explain the test tasks to the examinee. In addition to these gestures, administration of the test includes demonstrations by the examiner, sample items, corrective responses, transitional checkpoint items, and items not permitting examiner feedback.

There are six subtests on the Extended Battery of the UNIT: Symbolic Memory, Object Memory, Spatial Memory, Analogic Reasoning, Cube Design, and Mazes. Raw scores on these subtests are converted to scaled scores having a mean of 10 and a standard deviation of 3. The following five quotients are also determined from combinations of scores on the six subtests of the Expanded Battery or the four subtests of the Standard Battery: Full Scale Intelligence Quotient (FSIQ), Memory Quotient (MQ), Reasoning Quotient (RQ), Symbolic Quotient (SQ), and Nonsymbolic Quotient (NSQ). The Expanded Battery takes 45 minutes to administer, whereas the Standard Battery takes 30 minutes. A two-subtest Abbreviated Battery, which may be used as a screener, takes 10 to 15 minutes to complete.

UNIT was standardized during the mid-1990s on a national sample of 2,100 children and adolescents (ages 5 to 17:11 years). Reliability data are satisfactory, and research evidence pertaining to the concurrent, predictive, and discriminative validity of the instrument is given in the manual (Bracken & McCallum, 1998; McCallum et al., 2001).

GROUP INTELLIGENCE TESTS

During the second decade of the 20th century, Lewis Terman regularly taught a course at Stanford University on the Stanford–Binet Intelligence Scale. It was in a section of this course that a student, Arthur Otis, reportedly had the idea of adapting selected Stanford–Binet tasks to paper-and-pencil format. Shortly thereafter, many of Otis's adapted tasks and others were combined as the first group intelligence test, the Army Examination Alpha.

The Army Alpha and the Army Beta, a nonlanguage test for non-English speakers and illiterates, were administered to nearly 2 million U.S. Army recruits during and after World War I for purposes of military selection and job classification. The Army Alpha consisted of items involving analogies, arithmetic problems, number series completions, synonyms and antonyms, cube analysis, digit symbols, information, and practical judgment. The Army Alpha prompted and served as a model for the development of other group tests of intelligence and academic aptitude after the war. Arthur Otis and other psychologists began publishing their own group tests of intelligence, and by the 1930s several such instruments were commercially available.

A typical group intelligence test consists of a series of multiple-choice questions arranged in a spiral-omnibus format or as a series of separately timed subtests. In the *spiral-omnibus format,* several types of items comprising the test are mixed together and arranged in order of increasing difficulty; items with the same degree of difficulty are grouped together.

Administration, Scoring, and Reporting

Group intelligence tests can be administered to small groups of children as young as 5 or 6 years or to larger groups of adults. When testing young children, care must be taken to ensure that the examinees understand the directions, turn to the right page, start and stop on time, and so forth. In scoring group intelligence tests, raw scores, whether part or global, can be converted to percentile ranks, standard scores, or other numerical units.

Scores on group tests, even more than on individual tests, should be interpreted cautiously and against a background of other information (school grades and interview–observational data) about the examinee. Interpretative profiles of scores can also be prepared by a test-scoring service. Examinees with very low scores should be given additional tests, preferably individual, before diagnostic or placement decisions are made.

Illustrative Group Tests of Intelligence

Four of the most popular group tests of intelligence are the Otis–Lennon School Ability Test, the Wonderlic Personnel Test, the Cognitive Abilities Test, and the Test of Cognitive Skills.

Otis–Lennon School Ability Test.   This test (by A. S. Otis and R. T. Lennon) is a revision of earlier tests in the Otis series: the Otis Self-Administering Tests of Mental Ability (OLSAT), the Otis–Lennon Mental Ability Test, and the Otis Quick-Scoring Mental Ability Tests. Like its predecessors, the eighth edition of the OLSAT consists of a variety of pictorial, verbal, figural, and quantitative items to measure Verbal Comprehension, Verbal Reasoning, Pictorial Reasoning, Figural Reasoning, and Quantitative Reasoning from kindergarten through grade 12. There are seven levels of the OLSAT-8 (Kindergarten, Grade 1, Grade 2, Grade 3, Grades 4–5, Grades 6–8, and Grades 9–12), each of which can be administered in 60 to 75 minutes. Scores include School Ability Indexes (SAIs), percentile ranks and stanines based on age and grade level, scaled scores, and normal curve equivalents (NCEs). The SAIs have a mean of 100 and a standard deviation of 16. The norms, which are based on a large national sample, are expressed as percentile ranks, stanines, and NCEs by grade. Comparisons between ability and achievement can also be made when the OLSAT is administered with the Stanford Achievement Test Series, Ninth Edition.

Wonderlic Personnel Test.   The Wonderlic Personnel Test (by E. F. Wonderlic) is a brief (2 to 3 minutes for reading directions, 12 minutes for taking the test), 50-item instrument based originally on the Otis Self-Administering Test of Mental Ability. Questions on the Wonderlic, examples of which are given in Figure 6.1, consist of analogies, definitions, logic, arithmetic problems, spatial relations, word comparisons, and direction finding. This test has been used extensively as a screening device in employment situations for many years, and research indicates that it is a fair and valid selection device for a wide range of

---

Look at the row of numbers below. What number should come next?

8   4   2   1   1/2   1/4   ?

Assume the first 2 statements are true. Is the final one: (1) true, (2) false, (3) not certain?

The boy plays baseball. All baseball players wear hats. The boy wears a hat.

One of the numbered figures in the following drawing is most different from the others. What is the number in that figure?

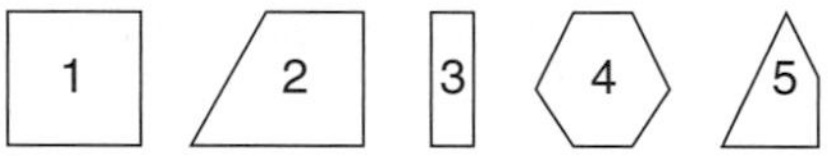

A train travels 20 feet in 1/5 second. At the same speed, how many feet will it travel in three seconds?
How many of the six pairs of items listed below are exact duplicates?

3421	1243
21212	21212
558956	558956
10120210	10120210
612986896	612986896
356471201	356571201

The hours of daylight and darkness in SEPTEMBER are nearest equal to the hours of daylight and darkness in

(1) June   (2) March   (3) May   (4) November

FIGURE 6.1   Sample items from the Wonderlic Personnel Test.

(Reprinted by permission of Wonderlic Personnel Test, Inc., Libertyville, IL)

jobs. Despite the brevity of the Wonderlic, its reliability coefficients and correlations with scores on other measures of intelligence reportedly extend into the .90s (see Belcher, 1992).

Cognitive Abilities Test. The sixth edition of the Cognitive Abilities Test (CogAT) (by D. F. Lohman and E. P. Hagen) is a successor to the Lorge–Thorndike Intelligence Tests. It is designed to assess the abilities of schoolchildren to reason and solve problems by using verbal, quantitative, and spatial (nonverbal) symbols. CogAT is a multilevel test, with Levels 1 and 2 for grades K–3 and Levels A–H for grades 3–12; it takes approximately 90 minutes to complete. Each level contains a Verbal Battery, a Quantitative Battery, and a Nonverbal Battery consisting of two to three subtests. Separate scores obtained on the three batteries and an overall composite score may be converted to various types of norms (standard age scores, national grade and age percentile ranks, grade and age stanines, and normal curve equivalents) based on a national standardization conducted in 2000.

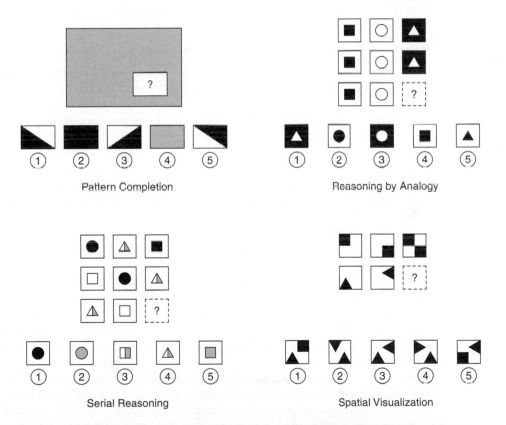

FIGURE 6.2   Sample items from the Naglieri Nonverbal Ability Test-Multilevel Form.

Test of Cognitive Skills.   The Test of Cognitive Skills is a successor to the California Short-Form Test of Mental Maturity and the Short-Form Test of Academic Aptitude. The current edition (TCS/2) of the test consists of four subtests:

> *Sequences:* ability to comprehend a rule or principle implicit in a series of figures, letters, or numbers
>
> *Analogies:* ability to discern various literal and symbolic relationships
>
> *Memory:* ability to recall previously presented picture materials or nonsense words
>
> *Verbal reasoning:* ability to reason deductively, analyze category attributes, and discern relationships and patterns.

Each of the four subtests has different forms at six grade levels: 2–3, 4–5, 6–7, 8–9, 10–11, and 11–12. Administration time is 50 minutes at grades 2–3 and 54 minutes at the other five grade levels. Age or grade percentile, stanine, and standard score norms can be determined for each subtest; the combined scores on all four subtests can be converted to a Cognitive Skills Index (CSI).

Nonverbal and Culture-Fair Group Intelligence Tests

Performance tests designed as individually administered measures of the intellectual abilities of persons with language or cultural handicaps were discussed earlier in the chapter. Complementary instruments that can be administered on a group basis have also been constructed for assessing the intelligence of physically or culturally disadvantaged individuals. The grandfather of these nonverbal tests was the Army Examination Beta, which was developed during World War I to measure the intellectual abilities of illiterate U.S. Army recruits. The Army Beta included tasks such as cube analysis, digit symbols, geometrical constructions, mazes, and picture completions. In addition to its military uses, the test was adapted to the evaluation of unskilled civilian workers. It was updated, restandardized, and republished by The Psychological Corporation in 1974 as the Revised Beta Examination, Second Edition, and again in 1999 as Beta III. Beta III consists of five subtests: Coding, Picture Completion, Clerical Checking, Picture Absurdities, and Matrix Reasoning.

Goodenough–Harris Drawing Test.   Another example of a nonverbal test suitable for group or individual administration is the Goodenough–Harris Drawing Test (by F. L. Goodenough and D. B. Harris). Unlike Beta III, which is a multiple-task test, the Goodenough–Harris requires only that the examinee accomplish the task of drawing pictures of a man, a woman, and the self. Rather than being scored for their artistic merit, the drawings are scored by comparing them with 12 model drawings and for the presence of 73 specific characteristics (e.g., body and clothing details, proportionality of head to trunk). The test is untimed, but it usually takes from 10 to 15 minutes to complete. Norms for children from age 3 to 15 years are reported as standard scores and percentile ranks and separately by sex. Also of interest is a quantitative scoring system, the Draw-A-Person: QSS, developed by J. A. Naglieri to make the scoring of person drawings more objective.

Culture-Fair Tests.   For many years, designers of intelligence tests have been besieged by the criticism that these instruments are loaded with items that are biased toward middle-class Western culture. It was the hope of Goodenough and Harris that their test would measure basic intelligence relatively free of cultural influences, but it became clear that the task of drawing a human figure is significantly affected by specific sociocultural experiences. There have been several other noteworthy attempts to develop a culture-free intelligence test, but these efforts were largely unsuccessful. Consequently, the goal was subsequently modified to that of developing a culture-fair test of intelligence. In designing a *culture-fair test,* efforts are made to use only items related to experiences common to a wide range of cultures. Items involving specific linguistic constructions and other culture-loaded tasks, such as speed of responding, are omitted. In this sense, the Goodenough–Harris test is culturally fair. Two other widely used tests that probably come as close as any others to being culturally fair are Raven's Progressive Matrices and the Culture Fair Intelligence Test.

Raven's Progressive Matrices. This test (by J. C. Raven), which may be administered on either an individual or a group basis, requires the examinee to indicate which of several figures or designs belongs in a given matrix. Developed in Great Britain as a measure of Spearman's general intelligence factor, the Raven's is available in three forms: Standard, Coloured, and Advanced Progressive Matrices. The Standard Form, suitable for ages 6 to 80, can be obtained in five black-and-white sets of 12 problems each and completed in 20 to 45 minutes. The Coloured Form, designed for children aged 5 to 11 years, elderly persons, and mentally and physically impaired persons, takes 15 to 30 minutes. The Advanced Form has an age range of 11 years through adulthood and takes 40 to 60 minutes to complete. The most recent norms, based on British and U.S. samples, are available on the Advanced Form, but all three forms need restandardizing.

Matrix Analogies Test. Similar to but more recently developed than Raven's Progressive Matrices is the Matrix Analogies Test—Expanded Form (by J. A. Naglieri). It consists of nonverbal reasoning items in four categories: Pattern Completion, Reasoning by Analogy, Serial Reasoning, and Spatial Visualization. Examinees (ages 5 to 17 years) are tested in 20 to 25 minutes on 64 abstract designs of the standard progressive matrix type, one design per page. The norms are based on a large, representative sample of individuals of ages 5 to 17 years living in the United States. Raw scores are converted to standard scores, percentile ranks, and stanines by half-year intervals and to age equivalents ranging from 5 to 17 years 11 months. A Matrix Analogies Test-Short Form, consisting of 34 items, is also available.

Culture-Fair Intelligence Tests. This series of tests (by R. B. Cattell) is composed of three scales: Scale 1 for children ages 4 to 8 years and adults with intellectual disabilities; Scale 2 for children 8 to 14 years and adults of average intelligence; and Scale 3 for college students, executives, and others of above-average intelligence. Each scale is composed of four subtests (Series, Classifications, Matrices, and Conditions) for measuring the ability to perceive relationships. In addition to these four culture-fair subtests, Scale 1 contains four subtests for assessing cultural information and verbal comprehension. Scale 1 is untimed, but usually takes about 22 minutes to complete; Scales 2 and 3 take 12½ minutes each.

Naglieri Nonverbal Ability Test. Similar to the Raven's in its use of designs in a matrix-type format is the Naglieri Nonverbal Ability Test—Multilevel Form (NNAT) (by J. A.

Naglieri). Sample items from the NNAT are given in Figure 6.2. The aim of this test, like that of other nonverbal tests, is to provide an unbiased measure of the general mental ability of individuals with limited English-language skills or other learning disabilities. The NNAT–Multilevel Form is appropriate for students in kindergarten through grade 12 and takes approximately 30 minutes to administer. Nonverbal Ability Index Scores and other normed scores based on a standardization sample of over 100,000 students are provided.

Summary.   Instruments such as Raven's Progressive Matrices, the Culture Fair Intelligence Tests, the Naglieri Nonverbal Ability Test, and the Universal Nonverbal Intelligence Test represent commendable efforts to develop tests on which different cultural groups score equally well. It is now recognized, however, that construction of a test to measure cognitive abilities independent of experience is probably impossible. In any event, the results of research conducted in developing countries indicate that differences in general literacy and schooling are more important than language, country, race, or ethnicity as determinants of "cultural" differences in scores on intelligence tests (see Frisby, 1999).

As seen in the Universal Nonverbal Intelligence Test, efforts to develop cognitive abilities tests that are fair to people in different cultures continue, but this does not mean that many older intelligence tests are so culturally biased that they should be abandoned. It is noteworthy that the market in other countries for traditional intelligence tests is much greater than that for "culture-fair" tests (Oakland & Hu, 1993). Apparently, people in non-Western countries are less concerned than middle-class Americans with the culture fairness of traditional Binet-type intelligence tests.

Academic Ability and Admissions Tests

Many group intelligence tests have been designed specifically to measure aptitude for scholastic work and are referred to as *academic ability tests.* Some group intelligence tests have a broader focus than this, but they are still similar in content to academic ability measures: they are heavily loaded with verbal, numerical, and other school-type items.

A number of different tests have been used over the years for college admissions purposes, including the American Council on Education Psychological Examination (ACE), the School and College Ability Tests (SCAT), the College Entrance Examination Board's Scholastic Aptitude Test (subsequently called the Scholastic Assessment Test) (SAT), and the American College Testing Program Assessment (ACT). Because of their widespread use, the last two of these test batteries will be described in some detail.

Scholastic Assessment Test (SAT).   The predecessor of the Scholastic Assessment Test, the Scholastic Aptitude Test (SAT), was originally adapted in 1926 from the Army Examination Alpha. Prior to 1994, the SAT consisted of two sections yielding two scores: Verbal (SAT-V) and Mathematical (SAT-M). Verbal analogies, antonyms, information, reading, comprehension, and sentence completion items made up the Verbal section; arithmetic, algebra, geometry, charts and graphs, and logical reasoning items made up the Mathematical section. Both sections were scored on a standard score scale having a mean of 500 and a standard deviation of 100; scores range from 200 to 800. Although new forms of the SAT were developed every year, scores on each new form were scaled back to the 1941 standardization group. This group consisted of 10,000 mostly White male students from upper-income groups in the northeastern United States who were applying for admission to Ivy League schools. Understandably, high school students in the early 1990s scored somewhat lower than the mean of 500 achieved by that group.

A revision of the SAT, which was first administered on a nationwide basis in March 1994, had two parts: SAT I: Reasoning, and SAT II: Subject Tests. SAT I consisted of Verbal Reasoning and Mathematical Reasoning sections, lasting 75 minutes each. The Verbal Reasoning section consisted of 78 multiple-choice items on Analogies, Sentence Completions, and Critical Reading. The Mathematical Reasoning section consisted of 60 items on Regular Mathematics, Quantitative Comparisons, and Student-Produced Responses. As on previous versions of the SAT, raw scores on the Verbal and Mathematical Reasoning Tests were converted to a standard-score scale having a mean of 500 and a standard deviation of 100. These scores were based on the performance of more than 1 million students who took the test in 1994. The scores were recentered to reflect the larger and more diverse contemporary student population, resulting in an increase in the average Verbal Reasoning score of approximately 80 points and the average Mathematical Reasoning score of around 20 points. In addition to standard scores on the Verbal and Mathematical Reasoning Tests, an SAT score report gave raw scores and percentile ranks for each subtest, score ranges based on the standard error of measurement of the tests, and national and state percentile equivalents for college-bound seniors.

The validity of the SAT is reflected in that the correlation with the first-year-college grade-point average is around .50 (Burton & Ramist, 2001). This is about the same as the correlation between high school grades and first-year-college grade-point average. On the positive side, this means that the SAT alone accounts for 25% of the variance in a college student's performance. When high school grades and SAT are combined, the correlation increases to .60. Critics are quick to point out that the SAT only increases the prediction from using high school grades by themselves by .10. In addition, if the SAT alone accounts for 25% of the variance, then 75% of the variance will be accounted for by other factors.

A more recent version of the SAT, the New SAT 2005, which was first given in 2005, was developed in response to criticisms of previous version of the test. The New SAT consists of a 50-minute Writing Section, a 70-minute Critical Reading Section, and a 70-minute Mathematics Section. The Writing Section, which deals with grammar, usage, and word choice, consists of a series of multiple-choice questions and a required student-written essay. The Critical Reading Section, which deals with critical reading and sentence-level reading, consists of items on reading comprehension, sentence completions, and paragraph-length critical reading. The Mathematics Section consists of two 25-minute and one 20-minute section on number and operations, algebra and functions, geometry, statistics, probability, and data analysis. All three sections are scored on a standard score scale ranging from 200 to 800.

The ACT Assessment.   The second most widely administered college admission examination is the ACT (American College Tests). The 215 multiple-choice questions on the ACT are grouped into four subtests: English, Mathematics, Reading, and Science. Actual testing time for these four subtests is 2 hours and 55 minutes (3½ hours with breaks). In addition to scores on the four subtests, a composite score (average of the four subtest scores rounded to the nearest integer) and seven subscores are reported. The subtest and composite scores range from 1 to 36, with a mean of 18; the seven subscores range from 1 to 18, with a mean of 9. Correlation with first-year-college grade-point average is about the same as for the SAT (.50).

Graduate Record Examinations.   The most popular test for admission to graduate school is the Graduate Record Examinations (GRE). It consists of a General Test to measure aptitude for graduate work and a series of Subject Tests to measure achievement in a particular subject-matter area. The GRE General Test consists of a verbal, a quantitative, and an analytic writing section. The latest version of the GRE General Test emphasizes the assessment of higher-level critical thinking with verbal and quantitative materials and analytic writing skills. The GRE Subject Tests are 3-hour examinations in particular subject-matter areas.

SUMMARY

1. Most theories of intelligence include the following: judgment, understanding, reasoning; abstract thinking; ability to learn; ability to adapt to one's environment; speed of learning; amount of learning; and focusing and sustaining one's ability to achieve a desired goal.

2. Among the most prominent theories of intelligence are those associated with the psychometric approach (Spearman, Thurstone, Guilford, Vernon, and Cattell), the developmental approach (Piaget), and the information-processing approach (Luria, Sternberg, and Gardner). The psychometric approach is derived from an understanding of test responses to tasks considered to measure intelligence. In contrast, the developmental approach emphasizes the types and extent to which a person achieves various sequences in cognitive development. Finally, information-processing approaches focus on the types of processes people go through, such as simultaneous versus sequential.

3. Intelligence tests can be for diagnosis (mentally retarded, gifted), selection, level of disability, interventions for vocational rehabilitation, evaluation of treatment effectiveness, and research on cognitive abilities.

4. The first practical test of intelligence was constructed by Alfred Binet and Théodore Simon during the first decade of the 20th century. The Binet–Simon scales (1905, 1908, 1911), a series of school-related tasks arranged in order of ascending difficulty, yielded a mental age score for each examinee. The Stanford–Binet, authored by Lewis Terman, was first published in 1916 and revised in 1937 and 1960. The test yielded a ratio IQ, defined as IQ = 100(MA/CA), although a deviation IQ could also be computed on the 1960 revision. The fourth edition of the Stanford–Binet involved more sophisticated theory and psychometric methodology, provided for separate scores on 15 tests and four areas, as well as a composite score. The emphasis in designing the fourth edition was not only on identification of mental retardation, but also on providing information for diagnosing specific causes of learning disabilities. Like the SB-IV, the fifth edition of the Stanford–Binet (SB-V) has a hierarchical design. SB-V consists of ten subtests at the lowest level, combined into five composite

factors (Fluid Reasoning, Knowledge, Quantitative Reasoning, Visual–Spatial Processing, Working Memory) at the next level and a general intelligence factor (*g*) at the highest level.

5. Unlike subtests on the Stanford–Binet, which were grouped according to age levels, subtests on the Wechsler scales were grouped into 10 or so categories according to content. Also, scores on the Wechsler scales yielded three kinds of deviation IQs: Verbal, Performance, and Full Scale. In addition to three IQs, the pattern of subtest scaled scores on the Wechsler tests was analyzed with the hope of yielding clinical information that might be useful in the diagnosis of certain personality characteristics and disorders. The three most recently published Wechsler intelligence tests are the WAIS-III for adults, the WISC-IV for school-aged children, and the WPPSI-III for preschool and primary school children.

6. Among other wide-range individual intelligence tests are the Differential Ability Scales (DAS), the Detroit Tests of Learning Aptitude (DTLA), the Kaufman Assessment Battery for Children (K-ABC), the Woodcock–Johnson III Tests of Cognitive Abilities (WJ III), and the Das–Naglieri Cognitive Assessment System (CAS). The last three are especially noteworthy for their grounding in psychometric and neuropsychological theory.

7. Representative of the many special-purpose, individually administered intelligence tests are pictorial tests such as the Columbia Test of Mental Maturity and other single-task tests such as the Porteus Mazes and the Kohs Block Designs. Nonverbal individual intelligence tests designed for individuals with language or physical handicaps include performance test batteries such as the Hiskey–Nebraska Test of Learning Aptitude, the Leiter International Performance Scale, the Comprehensive Test of Nonverbal Intelligence, and the Universal Nonverbal Intelligence Test.

8. Group-administered tests of intelligence are most likely to be used in organizational and school settings. These tests stem from the Army Examinations Alpha and Beta, which were based on the pioneering work of Arthur Otis and other psychologists during World War I. Examples of current group intelligence tests are the Otis–Lennon School Ability Test, the Wonderlic Personnel Test, the Cognitive Abilities Test, and the Test of Cognitive Skills. Nonverbal and presumably culture fair group tests such as the Goodenough–Harris Drawing Test, Raven's Progressive Matrices, the Culture Fair Intelligence Tests, and the Naglieri Nonverbal Ability Test are also available.

9. Certain group tests of academic ability, including the Scholastic Assessment Test (SAT), the American College Tests (ACT), and the Graduate Record Examinations, are used extensively for college, university, and professional school admissions.

MASTERING THE CHAPTER OBJECTIVES

1. *Defining intelligence*
   a. Define intelligence and state why the components of the definition are, in and of themselves, not sufficient.
   b. Ask three people to provide what they think is meant by the term *intelligence.*

2. *Theories of intelligence*
   a. Define the psychometric, developmental, and information-processing approaches to intelligence.
   b. Why is developing a theory of intelligence important for intelligence assessment?
   c. Write a short essay on one of the theories of intelligence.

3. *Applications of intelligence testing*
   a. Name four uses of intelligence testing.
   b. Find three people who have had their intelligence tested and ask them what the results were used for.

4. *Stanford–Binet*
   a. What was the original purpose of the Stanford–Binet and how has this changed with newest revisions?
   b. What is the ratio IQ of a child who is 8 years, 9 months old if his or her score on the Stanford–Binet Intelligence Scale is equal to a mental age of 6 years, 5 months? (See Answers to Quantitative Questions, p. 487.)
   c. Why are deviation IQ scores considered psychometrically superior to ratio IQ scores?
   d. What theory of intelligence is "embedded" in the most recent versions of the Stanford–Binet?

5. *Wechsler intelligence scales*
   a. List and describe current editions of the Wechsler series of intelligence tests, including the age range for which each is appropriate and the subtests on each test.
   b. Compare the Wechsler tests with the older and newer editions of the Stanford–Binet in terms of age range, types of abilities measured, fairness of the tests to physically or culturally disadvantaged people, and other relevant features.

6. *Additional individual wide-range intelligence tests*
   a. Provide a description of the major features of the following: Differential Ability Scales, Detroit Test of Learning Aptitude, Kaufman Assessment Battery for Children, Woodcock–Johnson-III, and the Das–Naglieri Cognitive Assessment System.
   b. Why do you think the CHC and the PASS models of intelligence have been so influential in test development?

7. *Special-purpose individually administered intelligence tests*
   a. Describe three special-purpose tests and explain when they would be most appropriate to use.
   b. What is the difference between a culture-free and a culture-fair test? Is it possible to develop a test of either kind, and, if so, what would it be used for?
   c. What intelligence test(s) would you recommend for administration to each of the following individuals: a 5-year-old child suspected of being mentally retarded; a group of South Sea island aborigines; a 10-year-old child with cerebral palsy; a normal, English-speaking adult; a 7-year-old totally blind child; an adult schizophrenic; a group of culturally disadvantaged elementary school children.

8. *Group intelligence tests*
   a. What are the advantages and disadvantages of group intelligence tests?
   a. Describe the Otis–Lennon, Cognitive Abilites Test, and the Wonderlic.

9. *Academic ability–admissions tests*
   a. Describe the Scholastic Assessment Test, American College Tests, and the Graduate Record Examinations.

    b. How effectively can tests such as the SAT and GRE predict college achievement? Explain why this level of prediction is useful and why it is limited.

EXPERIENCING PSYCHOLOGICAL ASSESSMENT

1. Search the Internet for a popular online test of intelligence. Look through the items and infer what aspects of intelligence seem to be assessed (e.g., abstract thinking). Which aspects of "intelligence" seem to be omitted (e.g., adaptation to environment)?

2. Find three people who have been given a (preferably) individually administered intelligence test. Interview them on what the experience was like and what they understand the results to mean.

......

CHAPTER SEVEN

INDIVIDUAL AND GROUP DIFFERENCES IN COGNITIVE ABILITIES

CHAPTER OBJECTIVES

1. Provide information on the diagnosis, classification, incidence, causes, and treatment of intellectual disabilities (mental retardation).
2. Define learning disabilities, including its subtypes and how they are assessed.
3. Define mental giftedness, describe educational policies for them, and describe research on their development and personalities.
4. Describe the characteristics of creative people and various tests of creativity.
5. Summarize research on the relationship between age and intelligence.
6. Summarize research on the following demographic research related to intelligence: family size, birth order, socioeconomic status, urban–rural region, education, teacher expectation, and ethnicity–race.
7. Summarize research on sex differences in cognitive abilities.
8. Summarize research on heritability and intelligence.

The previous chapter discussed theories and methods of assessing intelligence. This is important information, but it is also essential to know something about the types of areas that are being assessed. Such knowledge allows psychologists and educators understand and elaborate on the meaning of test scores. This chapter is an introductory overview of research concerned with individual and group differences in cognitive abilities. The discussion is limited to descriptions and interpretations of empirical findings from scientific investigations of differences in intelligence and related cognitive variables. In a wider sense, this field is referred to as *differential psychology* (see Aiken's, 1999, *Human Differ-*

ences for a comprehensive coverage of the field). The main focus for this chapter will be on intellectual disabilities, giftedness, creativity, learning disabilities, age, generational differences, and additional correlates of mental abilities, such as sex, nationality, and heredity.

VARIATIONS IN COGNITIVE ABILITIES: INTELLECTUAL DISABILITIES, LEARNING DISABILITIES, GIFTEDNESS, AND CREATIVITY

Of particular interest to psychologists and educators concerned with identifying individuals at all levels of ability and designing programs to treat, train, and educate them are children and adults who have very high or very low mental abilities. The variation among different mental abilities within individuals may, of course, be as great as the differences between individuals. For example, children who make high or low overall scores on intelligence tests do not necessarily score high or low on all cognitive abilities. A person may be good at one cognitive skill, poor at another, and average in still others. In any event, a great deal of professional and popular attention has been given to individuals who make very low or very high scores on tests of overall mental ability or general intelligence. These are the "intellectually disabled" (also "mentally retarded") and "mentally gifted," who, depending on particular circumstances and one's point of view, may be a bane or blessing to society.

Intellectual Disabilities (Mental Retardation)

Binet and Simon's principal reason for constructing the first practical test of intelligence was to identify children who they and other observers felt had little chance of making reasonable progress in regular school classes. Therefore, it is not surprising that one of the most common uses of general intelligence tests has been in diagnosing mental retardation.

Diagnosis and Classification.   A diagnosis of intellectually disabled affects decisions regarding not only educational and employment selection and classification, but also social security benefits, eligibility for the death penalty, and other matters of public policy regarding the intellectually disabled (Kanaya, Scullin, & Ceci, 2003) (see overview in www.nichcy.org/pubs/factshe/fs8txt.htm). Administration of an intelligence test is not mandatory in the diagnosis of intellectually disabled, but intelligence test scores, along with measures of academic and vocational achievement, psychomotor skills, and *adaptive behaviors,* are usually taken into account in making the diagnosis. Adaptive behaviors include communication skills (understanding what is said and being able to answer in a meaningful way), daily living skills (dressing and feeding oneself, going to the bathroom), and social skills. These behaviors may be assessed by an informal analysis of a person's history and present behavior or by administering a standardized instrument, such as the Vineland Adaptive Behavior Scales, the AAMR Adaptive Behavior Scales, or the Scales of Independent Behavior. The examiner fills out the scales from information supplied by a parent, teacher, or other person who is well acquainted with the child's behavior.

Socially derogatory labels such as *moron, imbecile,* and *idiot,* which were used in the early years of the 20th century to designate high, middle, and low grades of "feeble-mindedness," are no longer used by professional psychologists and educators in the United

States. Since the latter part of the 20th century, efforts have been made to replace the term *mental retardation* with a perhaps less stigmatizing term, such as *mental impairment* or, more commonly, *intellectual disabilities*. However *mental retardation* is still commonly used and can be defined as

> significantly subaverage general intellectual functioning existing concurrently with deficits in adaptive behavior and manifested during the developmental period that adversely affects a child's educational performance. [34 *Code of Federal Regulations* 300.7 © (6)]

In general, the *cut score* for mental retardation on an IQ test has been 70 or 75, or two standard deviations below the mean. Below this overall cut score, various systems for classifying different levels of mental retardation that make use of IQ scores have been advocated. Among these are the classification systems of the American Psychiatric Association (APA) and the American Association of Mental Retardation (AAMR).

The American Psychiatric Association (1994) lists three requirements for a diagnosis of mental retardation:

1. Significantly subaverage intellectual functioning: an IQ of approximately 70 or below on an individually administered IQ test (for infants, a clinical judgment of significantly subaverage intellectual functioning).
2. Concurrent deficits or impairments in present adaptive functioning (i.e., the person's effectiveness in meeting the standards expected for his or her age by his or her cultural group) in at least two of the following areas: communication, self-care, home living, social–interpersonal skills, use of community resources, self-direction, functional academic skills, work, leisure, health, and safety.
3. The onset is before age 18. (p. 50)

The four levels of severity in the APA system of classifying mental retardation are *mild mental retardation* (IQ level 50 or 55 to approximately 70); *moderate mental retardation* (IQ level 35 or 40 to 50 or 55); *severe mental retardation* (IQ level 20 or 25 to 35 or 40); *profound mental retardation* (IQ level below 20 or 25). Descriptions of the characteristic behaviors of children in these four categories at three periods of development are given in Table 7.1. As described in this table, the expected behaviors vary with both the degree of retardation and the chronological age of the individual. These behaviors are, of course, norms or averages, and the extent to which the behavior of a particular individual corresponds to the norms varies with his or her sociocultural background, other skills or characteristics, and additional circumstances.

Another four-level classification system, which is parallel to the APA system and sometimes used in schools to emphasize adaptive behavior rather than mental deficiency, is educable *mentally impaired* for children who are mildly retarded, *trainable mentally impaired* for those who are moderately retarded, *trainable (dependent)* for children who are severely retarded, and *custodial (life support)* for those who are profoundly retarded.

Relying less on the concept of IQ than other classification systems is the definition of mental retardation proposed by the American Association of Mental Retardation (AAMR) (2002). This definition describes mental retardation in terms of substantial limitations in present functioning, characterized by significantly subaverage intellectual functioning, manifested before age 18, and existing concurrently with related limitations in two or more of the

TABLE 7.1   Age-Related Behavioral Changes in the Mentally Retarded

---

MILD MENTAL RETARDATION (IQ = 50–70)

Preschool Age (0–5): Slower than average to walk, feed self, and talk, but casual observer may not notice retardation.

School Age (6–21): Learns perceptual–motor and cognitive skills (reading and arithmetic) on third- to sixth-grade level by late teens; can learn to conform socially.

Adult (21 and Over): Usually achieves social and vocational skills needed for maintaining self; requires guidance and help when under unusual economic or social stress.

MODERATE MENTAL RETARDATION (IQ = 35–49)

Preschool Age (0–5): Most development noticeably delayed, particularly in speech; can be trained in a variety of self-help activities.

School Age (6–21): Learns to communicate and take care of elementary health and safety needs; learns simple manual skills, but makes little or no progress in reading and arithmetic.

Adult (21 and Over): Performs simple unskilled or semiskilled tasks under supervised conditions; participates in simple games and travels alone in familiar places; incapable of self-maintenance.

SEVERE MENTAL RETARDATION (IQ = 20–34)

Preschool Age (0–5): Pronounced delay in motor development; little or no speech; benefits from self-help (e.g., self-feeding) training.

School Age (6–21): Usually walks unless locomotor disability present; can understand and respond to speech; can profit from training in health and other acceptable habits.

Adult (21 and Over): Follows daily routines and contributes to self-maintenance; needs direction and close supervision in controlled environment.

PROFOUND MENTAL RETARDATION (IQ BELOW 20)

Preschool Age (0–5): Extreme retardation in all areas; minimal sensorimotor abilities; requires nursing care.

School Age (6–21): Obviously delayed in all areas of development; responds with basic emotions and may benefit from training in use of limbs and mouth; must be closely supervised.

Adult (21 and Over): May be able to walk and talk in a primitive way; benefits from regular physical activity; cannot take care of self, but requires nursing care.

---

following 10 adaptive skill areas: communication, self-care, home living, social skills, community use, self-direction, health and safety, functional academics, leisure, and work.

Rather than listing various levels of retardation and the debilities characterizing each, the AAMR manual focuses on a hierarchy of need supports (intermittent, limited, extensive, pervasive) required for rehabilitating mentally retarded persons. With respect to APA terminology, mildly retarded individuals require intermittent support, moderately retarded individuals require limited support, severely retarded individuals require extensive support, and profoundly retarded individuals require pervasive support in their constructive activities and social functioning.

Incidence and Causes of Intellectual Disabilities.   An estimated 2.5% to 3% of the U.S. population is intellectually disabled, the percentage being lower for females than for males (Twenty-third Annual Report to Congress, U.S. Department of Education, 2001).[1] The number of intellectually disabled European Americans is greater than that in all other ethnic groups, but the percentage of African American schoolchildren who are identified as intellectually disabled is higher than for any other ethnic group, followed by Native Americans, Hispanics, and Asian–Pacific Islanders, in that order (U.S. Department of Education, 1997).

Although both genetic and environmental factors play a role in its etiology, in three-fourths of the cases, the exact cause of intellectual disabilities is unknown. Genetic conditions, such as Down syndrome, fragile X syndrome, and phenylketonuria (PKU), account for a sizable percentage of cases, but problems during pregnancy (fetal alcohol syndrome, rubella, etc.), problems during labor or birth (e.g., oxygen deficiency), and health problems (whooping cough, measles, meningitis) can also cause intellectual disability.

In the United States, mild mental retardation is associated with a number of demographic variables related to low socioeconomic status: low educational level, minority group membership, unemployment or low employment levels, poor nutrition, poor health, and generally substandard living conditions. Neglect, low levels of intellectual stimulation, a paucity of formal learning experiences, inadequate language models, and the unstructured and unpredictable environments in which many children live also contribute to the degree of intellectual disability.

The IQs of intellectually disabled children who are apparently free of organic pathology are generally much closer to the mean IQ of the general population than those with demonstrable organic disorders. The extreme disability of persons falling in the severe and profound categories, and in some cases the moderate category, is due to a variety of disorders leading to central nervous system damage: major gene problems such as galactosemia, gargoylism, phenylketonuria, and Tay–Sachs disease; genetic-dependent conditions such as cretinism, hydrocephaly, and microcephaly; chromosomal abnormalities such as Down syndrome and Klinefelter's syndrome; intrauterine infections; birth trauma (head injury, oxygen deprivation or oversupply); and diseases contracted during infancy (meningitis, encephalitis, lead poisoning, etc.). The most common genetic cause of mental retardation is Down syndrome, and the second most common is fragile-X syndrome. In many cases, intellectually disabled children with no known organic basis for their condition turn out to have fragile-X syndrome (Dykens, Hosdapp, & Leckman, 1994). It is likely that future research will reveal other genetic causes of mental retardation.

Biological factors may also play a role in cultural differences in intellectual disabilities. For example, the conditions listed in the last paragraph account for a relatively small

---

[1]The exact percentage varies, however, with the IQ cut score and the specific test and norms from which it is determined. Flynn (2000) asserts that, because the IQ criterion of 70 for a diagnosis of mental retardation has been changed from norms based on European Americans only to norms based on all Americans, the proportion of individuals who are classifiable as mentally retarded has ranged from a high of 1 in 23 to a low of 1 in 213 during the past 50 years (also see Kanaya, Scullin, & Ceci, 2003).

percentage of the total number of intellectually disabled children in more developed countries, where good maternal and infant health care are the rule. In less developed countries, where malnutrition is more common and health care less adequate, disorders of malnutrition account for a high proportion of cases of retardation.

Prevention and Treatment. Many disorders with which mental retardation is associated may be prevented by screening at birth (e.g., PKU, congenital hypothyroidism, Rh disease, jaundice, Hib diseases, measles, encephalitis, maternal rubella). Mental retardation can sometimes be treated medically (by diet, hormone replacement, vaccines, etc.) when the cause is identified early enough. In most cases, however, the condition is incurable, and training and education rather than physical or chemical treatments are prescribed.

Intellectually disabled persons who receive appropriate educational and social supports over a sustained period of time usually improve. Such care is given mainly at home, though private and state-operated residential facilities are also available. Special education for intellectually disabled and other handicapped children is mandated by law—the Education for All Handicapped Children Act and the Individuals with Disabilities Education Act (IDEA) (P.L. 94-142, 99-457, and 101-476)—and consequently available throughout the United States. Approximately half of all intellectually disabled individuals between the ages of 6 and 21 are taught in separate public or private facilities and the remainder in regular classrooms, resource rooms, public or private residential facilities, or other facilities.[2]

Nationwide projects such as the Abecedarian Project (Campbell & Ramey, 1994; Ramey et al., 2000), the Ypsilanti Project (Schweinhart & Weikart, 1997), and Head Start were based on the idea of modifying and improving intellectual and social development. Such intervention programs produced somewhat greater learning efficiency and social adaptation, but long-term gains in cognitive abilities were minimal (Robinson, Zigler, & Gallagher, 2000). A more likely outcome from these projects was improvements in motivation and specific skills, rather than permanent changes in IQs (Lazar & Darlington, 1982).

The Individualized Family Services Plan (IFSP), an intervention system for children up to age 3 who are suspected of being intellectually disabled, is now available in most localities. IFSP addresses the unique needs of the family so that they can provide the best help for the child. A program for school-aged children, the Individualized Education Program (IEP), which describes the child's unique needs and the services designed to meet these needs, may be worked out cooperatively by the local school staff and the parents.

Learning Disabilities

Difficulties in learning to read, write, spell, or perform arithmetic or other academic skills have traditionally been attributed to intellectual disabilities, physical handicaps, severe emotional problems, or lack of motivation. But even when these factors have been eliminated as possible explanations, there remains a large group of children who experience problems in scholastic achievement. These children are described as having a specific learning disability, or simply a *learning disability (LD)*. Learning disabilities may occur in individuals at any

[2]See statistics at Web site nces.ed.gov/pubs2003/digest02/tables/dt053.asp.

level of intelligence and at any age, but, in contrast to mental retardation, the achievements of LD individuals are significantly below what their general cognitive ability would suggest.

Demographics and Definitions.   Learning disabilities (LDs) constitute the largest hand-icapping condition among children throughout the world (Stanford & Oakland, 2000). An estimated 5 million or more U.S. schoolchildren and youth have one or more disabilities, over half of whom have learning disabilities. Among the learning disabled, males outnum-ber females 2 to 1. Within racial–ethnic groups, the percentage of children with learning disabilities is highest for Native Americans and lowest for Asian–Pacific Islanders (U.S. Department of Education, 1997).

Public Law 101-476, the Individuals with Disabilities Education Act of 1990 (IDEA), defines learning disabilities as follows:

> The term "children with specific learning disabilities" means those children who have a dis-order in one or more of the basic psychological processes involved in understanding or in using language, spoken or written, which disorder may manifest itself in imperfect ability to listen, think, speak, read, write, spell, or to do mathematical calculations. Such disorders in-clude such conditions as perceptual handicaps, brain injury, minimal brain dysfunction, dyslexia, and developmental aphasia. Such terms do not include children who have learning problems which are primarily the result of visual, hearing, or motor handicaps, of mental re-tardation, of emotional disturbance, or of environmental, cultural, or economic disadvantage.

The most frequent signs of learning disabilities in children are these:

Difficulty in understanding and following instructions

Trouble remembering what someone just told them

Failure to master reading, spelling, writing, and/or math skills, and thus failure in schoolwork

Difficulty distinguishing right from left

Difficulty identifying words or a tendency to reverse letters, words, or numbers

Lack of coordination in walking, sports, or small activities, such as holding a pencil or tying a shoelace

Easily loses or misplaces homework, schoolbooks, or other items

Cannot understand the concept of time; confused by "yesterday," "today," "tomorrow"

The most common type of learning disability is *dyslexia,* in which the person has difficulty reading silently or aloud (for a description of learning disabilities types, read www.nlm.nih.gov/medlineplus/learningdisorders.html). When asked to read out loud, a dyslexic child reads slowly, hesitantly, and laboriously. Dyslexic children experience diffi-culties in reading because of problems with phonological coding (i.e., decoding printed let-ters into blended sounds). Dyslexia, which is three to four times as common among males as among females, may be due to an inability to process sounds (*auditory dyslexia*), to dif-ficulty in processing information that has been seen (*visual dyslexia*), or to comprehension disorders or written production problems. Instruments such as the Dyslexia Screening Test and the Dyslexia Early Screen Tests (by R. Nicholson & A. Fawcett; The Psychological Corporation) are useful in identifying dyslexia in schoolchildren and preschoolers.

Nonverbal learning problems in mathematics (*dyscalculia*), handwriting (*dysgraphia*), and spatial cognition are less common than verbal learning problems (Rourke, 1989). Difficulties in learning arithmetic may be related to problems of attention or remembering language or reading, visualizing or writing numbers, and organization and ordering. Up to 10% of learning disabled persons have such problems, as compared with less than 1% percent for the general population.

Children with verbal LDs usually do better on performance tests, which require visuospatial and visuomotor skills, than on verbal tests, which measure language skills. The opposite is true of children with nonverbal LDs: they do better on verbal than on the performance tests.

Causes of Learning Disabilities.   There is considerable debate as to whether LDs are caused by neurological, developmental, or experiential factors, or a combination of these. Neurological conditions associated with LDs may be attributable to prenatal influences, such as viruses, alcohol, or cigarette smoking, or to drugs, such as cocaine, radiation, and other teratogens that can cross the placental barrier and harm the embryo or fetus. Premature birth, low birth weight, and the use of forceps may also play a role in learning disabilities (Bender, 1995). Among postnatal factors that have been investigated as possible causes of LDs are convulsions induced by high fevers or inhaling leaded contaminants (Feldman & White, 1992), diabetes, meningitis, head injury, and malnutrition have also been implicated in certain cases (Hallahan, Kauffman, & Lloyd, 1996). The learning disabilities associated with most of these conditions are typically fine, subtle, or minor rather than gross deviations in visuomotor, language, or quantitative skills.

There is evidence of a genetic basis for certain LDs (e.g., Oliver, Cole, & Hollingsworth, 1991). A related line of research has centered on deficits in the left temporal lobes of the brains of people with verbal learning disabilities. One cerebral structure of interest is the planum temporale, an area on both sides of the brain that is known to play a role in language development. In nondyslexics, the planum temporale on the left side on the brain is noticeably larger than that on the right, but in dyslexics there is no difference in the size of the planum temporale on the two sides of the brain (Leonard et al., 1996).

Diagnosis, Treatment, and Education.   In many large hospitals, comprehensive assessments of children suspected of having learning disabilities are carried out by a team of professionals consisting of a pediatrician, a learning specialist, a psychologist, and a social worker (for guidelines on assessing learning disabilities, see endoflifecare.tripod.com/huntdiseasefaqs/id120.html). These teams perform comprehensive assessments on children suspected of having learning disabilities. The assessment team studies the child's problem, provides a diagnosis, and makes suggestions for educational planning or treatment.

Learning assessments are also provided through the public schools. Teachers may be able to identify learning disabilities by careful observation of children. They may also administer group intelligence tests and/or more specialized instruments, such as the Learning Disability Rating Procedure and the Learning Disabilities Evaluation Scale: Renormed, the McCarthy Screening Test, and the Slingerland Screening Tests for Identifying Children with Specific Language Disability. Administration of a battery of psychological tests, however, requires the services of a school psychologist or clinical psychologist.

In the schools, effective diagnosis and remedial planning for learning disabilities are also a multidisciplinary enterprise involving the child's regular teacher, specialists who are knowledgeable regarding the suspected handicap, and persons experienced in using psychometric instruments to make diagnostic evaluations. The interdisciplinary team's overall evaluation is made on the basis of test scores combined with life history obtained from records and interviews and the results of medical examinations of the child.

In keeping with the guidelines provided by the Education for All Handicapped Children Act of 1975, a diagnosis of specific learning disability is made only when a significant difference is found between a person's ability and achievement in one or more of the following areas: oral expression, listening comprehension, written expression, basic reading skill, reading comprehension, mathematics calculation, or mathematics reasoning. A diagnosis of learning disability should also identify the areas of strength and weakness in the child so that appropriate educational experiences can be designed to assist the child in reaching his or her learning potential.

In light of a diagnosis of a learning disability, an *individual education plan* (*IEP*) consisting of short- and long-term objectives and procedures for obtaining them should be prepared. In addition to a plan for remedying school-related deficits, an effective IEP includes provisions for treating accompanying behavioral problems.

The eligibility criteria for providing services to learning disabled children vary from state to state, but, in general, a diagnosis of learning disability follows the *IQ-achievement discrepancy model*. According to this model, a child is considered to have a learning disability when his or her overall score on a standardized achievement test is at least one standard deviation below his or her score on a co-normed intelligence test. Individual intelligence tests, such as the SB-V, WPPSI-R, WISC-IV, and K-ABC-II, and standardized achievement tests, such as the Peabody Individual Achievement Test—Revised, the Kaufman Test of Educational Achievement, and the Wechsler Individual Achievement Test-II, are appropriate (see Groth-Marnat, 2001; Kaufman & Kaufman, 2001). Perhaps even more widely administered for this purpose is the Woodcock–Johnson III, which includes both an intelligence test battery (WJ-III Tests of Cognitive Ability) and a co-normed achievement test battery (WJ-III Tests of Achievement). Descriptions of these tests are given in Chapters 6 and 9. In addition to intelligence and achievement test batteries, more specialized neuropsychological, developmental, and even personality tests are appropriate in certain cases.

The use of intelligence tests in diagnosing learning disabilities is, however, not acceptable to all educators. For example, the President's Commission on Excellence in Special Education (PCESE) has recommended that the use of intelligence tests for this purpose be discontinued. Members of the commission, along with a number of other observers, maintain that how a child behaves in the classroom and at home is often more indicative of the child's actual ability than his or her scores on an intelligence test (Benson, 2003).

A variety of instructional procedures has been used with LD children, including behavioral analysis and intervention, cooperative learning, peer and aggressive tutoring, and coaching in reasoning skills (Bender, 1995; Kirk, Gallagher, & Anastasiow, 1997; Sullivan, Mastropieri, & Scruggs, 1995). The results of these and other intervention strategies (e.g., biofeedback, relaxation training, multisensory instruction, special diets) have been mixed.

Mental Giftedness

At the other end of the intelligence continuum from mental retardation is mental giftedness (for a scale on giftedness, see www.gifteddevelopment.com/Articles/Characteristics_Scale.htm). The most comprehensive longitudinal study of persons with high IQs was conducted by Lewis Terman and his associates (Terman & Oden, 1959). Several hundred children who had scored in the top 1% of the distribution of IQs on the Stanford–Binet Intelligence Scale were followed up throughout their lives at 5-year intervals from 1921 onward. After Terman's death in 1956, the study was continued by Oden (1968) and Sears (1977). The purpose of the study was to obtain information on occupational success, physical and mental health, social adjustment, and other variables associated with high intelligence. Details on the childhood, education, personality, career(s), family, physical and mental health, and life stresses of the participants, as well as their adjustment to old age, were obtained from questionnaires.

Characteristics of Terman's Kids. The results of the Terman study seemed to contradict a number of popular myths pertaining to the gifted; that bright children are sickly, that they burn out early (early ripe, early rot), and that genius is akin to insanity. These mentally gifted children, or "termites," were physically superior to other children: they were heavier at birth and remained heavier than average, they walked and talked earlier and matured at an earlier age than average, and their general health was better. They also maintained their mental and physical superiority as adults. Compared with average adults, follow-up data revealed that the mentally gifted earned more degrees, attained higher occupational success and salaries, had equivalent or better personal and social adjustment, achieved greater marital success, and were physically healthier. The greater occupational success of the "termites" appears, however, to have been due to their higher educational attainments, rather than their higher IQs per se. When educational level was statistically controlled, IQ scores obtained in childhood had no relationship to occupational achievement. Many of the "termites" failed to live up to their potential, and as adults they expressed regret at not having done so (Gardner, 1997).

Terman's findings of better adjustment and a lower rate of mental disorders among the mentally gifted did not go unchallenged. Hughes and Converse (1962) suggested that the fact that the children were selected initially on the basis of teachers' ratings as well as IQ may have biased the sample in favor of well-behaved children. Terman's gifted children also tended to be above average in socioeconomic status, which is associated with better personal adjustment.

Personalities of the Gifted. Subsequent research also posed questions concerning personality adjustment in the gifted. Webb and Meckstroth (1982) characterized gifted children as more inquisitive, active, and energetic, but also as being perceived by others as obnoxious, unruly, strong willed, mischievous, unmanageable, and rebellious. These researchers noted that intellectually gifted children are often troublesome to their parents and feel troubled themselves. This appears to be particularly true of profoundly gifted children with IQs above 150 than of moderately gifted children with IQs between 130 and 150. Profoundly gifted children can usually read before kindergarten age and are superior in problem solving and other types of abstract thinking. Many are fascinated with numerical and musical patterns and with creating new approaches and solutions (Jackson, 1992). They may accomplish such feats as memorizing an entire musical score, figuring out how to identify all prime numbers, or discovering algebraic rules on their own (Feldman & Goldsmith, 1991; Winner, 1996).

Like other children and adults, mentally gifted individuals are susceptible to psychological disorders (Silverman, 1995). Realizing that they are different from other children, profoundly gifted children may become nonconforming, introverted, and egocentric about their abilities. Presumably aware of the envy of their playmates and burdened by high expectations, they tend to have a higher rate of socioemotional problems. Those who are particularly sensitive and under great stress to perform publicly may become depressed, use drugs, fail to perform up to their capacity, and occasionally drop out of society altogether (Janos & Robinson, 1985; Ochse, 1991).

Mathematically Gifted Children.   Many investigations of children with highly developed abilities in art, mathematics, music, and other special fields have been conducted. For example, Julian Stanley and his coresearchers (Keating, 1976; Stanley, Keating, & Fox, 1974) conducted a series of studies of preadolescents who made standard scores of 700 or above on the Scholastic Aptitude Test-Mathematical (SAT-M). The children were given various psychological tests and monitored while they participated in college mathematics courses. As is true of other mentally gifted children, mathematically talented children often learn complex material without being explicitly taught. The researchers found that not only did such children benefit from college-level instruction in mathematics, but, despite initial concerns that they would be unable to adjust to a college environment, most of them actually adjusted quite well. Unlike some other findings concerning mentally gifted and creative persons, the mathematically talented adolescents in Stanley's study tended to be personally well adjusted and highly motivated (especially in mathematics). Subsequent studies found evidence for enhanced activity in the right cerebral hemispheres of mathematically precocious youth (O'Boyle, Alexander, & Benbow, 1991).

Educating Mentally Gifted and Talented Children.   School administrators and teachers use the terms *gifted* and *talented* to designate children with high intellectual or other cognitive abilities.[3] Children in this category have IQs of 130 or 135 or above (two or more standard deviations above the mean), but teachers' ratings and recommendations and other criteria may also contribute to the designation of a child as gifted or talented (for a scale measuring giftedness, see www.gifteddevelopment.com/Articles/Characteristics_Scale.htm). According to Public Law 95-561,

> Gifted and talented children means children, and whenever applicable, youth, who are identified at the preschool, elementary, or secondary level as possessing demonstrated or potential abilities that give evidence of high performance capability in areas such as intellectual, creative, specific academic, or leadership ability, or in the performing and visual arts and who by reason thereof require services or activities not ordinarily provided by the school.[4]

[3]Other terms (e.g., "individuals with high intelligence, highly capable") have been proposed but have not replaced "mentally gifted" or "mentally talented."

[4]*Congressional Record,* October 10, 1978. Educational Amendments of 1978, 20 USC 2701 (1978); 92 STAT.2143.

According to data published by Office for Civil Rights the U.S. Department of Education (1997), approximately 6% of U.S. schoolchildren are gifted or talented. Slightly larger percentages of females than males and larger percentages of Asian–Pacific Islanders and European Americans than Native Americans, Hispanics, and African Americans are classified as mentally gifted or talented. Some gifted or talented children are exceptional in mathematics, others in verbal reasoning, others in music or art, and others in social leadership.

Strategies for educating gifted and talented children include early school admission, acceleration and grade skipping, honors classes, advanced placement classes, college-level courses, independent study, mentoring, special resource rooms, and special schools (see Benbow & Lubinski, 1997, and read print.ditd.org/floater=108.html). Almost all school systems in the United States now have some sort of special instructional program for gifted children. Students in these programs spend most of their school time in regular classrooms, but they are taken out of class for several hours each week to participate in activities designed specially for the gifted. Regional centers for gifted and talented children and other institutions devoted to students with superior abilities have also been established throughout the United States. In general, gifted students fare well—intellectually, socially, and emotionally—in these programs. However, critics often characterize special programs for the gifted as elitist or undemocratic.

Creativity

Tests of intelligence or scholastic aptitude administered to school-aged children usually do a fair job of predicting short-term school achievement and related criteria. These tests, however, were not designed to measure situational variables, lifelong determination, motivation, or nonscholastic talent of the sort that influences creative performance. It is noteworthy that few, if any, of the intellectually gifted individuals studied by Terman (Terman & Oden, 1959) attained the eminence of a Winston Churchill, an Albert Einstein, or an Ernest Hemingway. Nor did any of them become a famous composer, artist, or poet. In fact, most mentally gifted children do not become highly creative adults (Winner, 2000).

Characteristics of Creative People.　　Thomas Alva Edison held 1,093 patents, Albert Einstein published 248 papers, Pablo Picasso averaged over 200 works of art a year, and Wolfgang Amadeus Mozart had composed more than 609 pieces of music by the time of his death at age 35. These cases illustrate the high inner drive that many creative people possess. Other affective and cognitive traits said to be characteristic of creative people are independence, nonconformity, unconventionalism, greater openness to new experiences, flexibility, and risk-taking boldness (Martindale, 1989). Highly creative individuals tend to be restless and rebellious, desire to alter the status quo, and often experience stress and trauma as children (Goertzel, Goertzel, & Goertzel, 1978).

Based on the results of investigations by MacKinnon (1962) and Wallach and Kogan (1965), it would seem that creativity, especially when accompanied by high intelligence, is not a bad characteristic to possess from a mental health standpoint. In contrast, a study by Jamison (1993) of prominent British artists (novelists, painters, playwrights, poets, and sculptors) found that these individuals were much more likely than less creative people to have been treated for mood disorders (mania and depression). Similar results were found by Andreasen (1987) in a study of 30 faculty members in a writers' workshop: 80% exhibited depression or some other form of mood disorder, and 43% were diagnosed as manic-depressive. The meaning of these findings is not entirely clear, but at least they suggest that creative adults, like gifted children, are no strangers to unhappiness and poor adjustment (also see Ludwig, 1995).

Creativity Tests.   It is sometimes maintained that above-average intelligence is necessary but not sufficient for creative productivity. Beyond a minimum level of intelligence, creative performance seems to depend more on motivation and special abilities than on general mental ability (MacKinnon, 1962). Therefore, investigations of creativity conducted during the past 40 years have focused on identifying other cognitive and affective characteristics that distinguish highly creative from less creative individuals. For example, efforts have been made to develop measures of divergent, as opposed to convergent, thinking ability (Guilford, 1967). On measures of *convergent thinking,* such as problems of the sort found on intelligence tests, there is only one correct answer. In contrast, on tests of *divergent thinking,* examinees are presented with open-ended problems having a number of possible solutions and are scored on the originality of their responses. Unfortunately, this open-endedness creates difficulties in scoring and determining the reliability and validity of these tests. Among the scoring procedures that have been advocated are evaluating answers for both the number of responses given by the examinee (*fluency*) and their originality or uncommonness (*novelty*).

The following items are the types found on tests of creativity:

Consequences Test. Imagine all the things that might possibly happen if all national and local laws were suddenly abolished. (Guilford, 1954)

Remote Associates Test. Find a fourth word that is associated with each of these three words: (a) rat–blue–cottage; (b) out–dog–cat; (c) wheel–electric–high; (d) surprise–line–birthday. (Mednick, 1962)

Unusual Uses Test. Name as many uses as you can think of for (a) a toothpick (b) a brick (c) a paper clip. (Guilford, 1954)

Word Association Test. Write as many meanings as you can for each of the following words: (a) duck; (b) sack; (c) pitch; (d) fair (Getzels & Jackson, 1962; copyright © 1962 by John Wiley & Sons, Inc. Reprinted by permission of John Wiley & Sons, Inc.)

Creativity test batteries, such as the Torrance Tests of Creative Thinking (TTCT) (by E. P. Torrance; Scholastic Testing Service), represent a combination of creativity measures. The TTCT consists of three picture-based exercises (Figural TTCT: Thinking Creatively with Picture) and six word-based exercises (Verbal TTCT: Thinking Creatively with Words). An example of the kinds of items on the Verbal TTCT is to "Write out all the questions you can think of" about a given picture. On one part of the Figural TTCT, the examinee is asked to make a sketch from a basic line. The Verbal TTCT, which takes 45 minutes to complete, is scored on three variables: fluency, flexibility, and originality. The Figural TTCT, which takes 30 minutes to complete, is scored on five variables: fluency, originality, elaboration, abstractness of titles, and resistance to premature closure. The TTCT was restandardized in 1980, and national percentile ranks and standard scores from grade 1 through college and adult level are given in the manual. Although a number of researchers have concluded that the TTCT is an unbiased indicator of giftedness (e.g., Esquivel & Lopez, 1988; Torrance, 1988), the reliabilities of the tests are variable and the results of validity studies are inconclusive (Hattie, 1980).

Evaluation of Creativity Tests.   Tests of creativity frequently have significant correlations with IQ tests, and the former are apparently no more effective than the latter in predicting "creative performance." All things considered, a reasonable conclusion is that it remains to be demonstrated whether effective measures of creativity can be devised. Until a test is designed that is an accurate predictor of performance on a generally accepted criterion of creativity, it would be well to follow McNemar's (1964) advice not to dispose of our general intelligence tests.

RESEARCH ON CORRELATES OF COGNITIVE ABILITIES

From the time of their initial appearance during the first decade of this century, intelligence tests have been a part of numerous investigations concerned with the characteristics, causes, and effects of individual differences in cognitive abilities. Unfortunately, these investigations, which were initiated by Francis Galton during the latter part of the 19th century, have too often been unsystematic and a reflection of convenient correlational methods, rather than of sound research design. Although the results of such studies may be difficult to interpret, they are provocative and must be taken into account by anyone who decides to theorize about the nature and development of human cognition.

Age Differences in Cognitive Abilities

Because all intelligence tests are less than perfectly reliable, a person's score on a particular test changes somewhat with time and testing conditions. Nevertheless, given a relatively stable life situation and optimal testing conditions, scores on intelligence tests are fairly stable during the school years. Scores tend to be less stable during early and middle childhood, but they are more consistent during adolescence. A child's IQ on an individual intelligence test varies about 5 points on the average, and changes of 20 or more points are rare. Large IQ fluctuations are usually traceable to fairly dramatic variations in health or living conditions or to severe emotional experiences and problems.

The older definition of the intelligence quotient as 100 times the ratio of mental age to chronological age implies that, for the IQ to remain stable from year to year, mental age must increase at the same rate as chronological age. The condition that raw scores and mental ages on intelligence tests should rise with age during childhood also applies to tasks that do not yield ratio IQs. The exact form of the function relating raw test scores or mental ages to chronological age depends on the specific test and the intellectual components measured by it.

Cross-Sectional and Longitudinal Studies.   Conclusions from earlier studies of changes in general intelligence with age were typically based on cross-sectional data (Doppelt & Wallace, 1955; Jones & Conrad, 1933; Yerkes, 1921). In an analysis of scores on the Army Examination Alpha administered to U.S. soldiers during World War I, Yerkes (1921) found that average scores on the test declined steadily from the late teens through the sixth decade of life. In another early study, Jones and Conrad (1933) found that Army Alpha scores rose linearly from 10 to 16 years, but then gradually declined to the 14-year level by age 55. Norms for the Wechsler Adult Intelligence Scale (Wechsler, 1955) also indicate that intelligence peaks in youth, though at a somewhat later age than found in earlier studies. Mean Full Scale scores on the WAIS, the WAIS-R, and the WAIS-III all reach a peak in the early 20s, remain fairly constant from that point until the late 20s or early 30s, and then decline steadily throughout later life (Tulsky, Zhu, & Ledbetter, 1997; Wechsler, 1955, 1981).

In contrast to *longitudinal studies,* which compare the performance of the same group of people at different ages, *cross-sectional studies* compare the performance of groups of people (cohorts) who grew up under different environmental circumstances. Differences among cohorts in educational opportunity, which is closely related to intelligence test scores, make it difficult to match people of different ages. Consequently, it is impossible to compare the intelligence levels of people of different ages without confounding the effects of education with those of other test-related experiences.

The steady rise in the average educational and socioeconomic levels of Americans during the last century must be taken into account when interpreting the apparent age decline in cognitive abilities. Because intelligence test scores are positively related to both educational level and socioeconomic status, older adults, who had less formal education and typically lower socioeconomic status when they were young, tend to make significantly lower test scores than younger adults.

Because longitudinal studies of intelligence have most often been conducted on college graduates or other intellectually favored groups, it can be argued that the findings are not necessarily applicable to the general population (Bayley & Oden, 1955; Campbell, 1965; Nisbet, 1957; Owens, 1953, 1966). However, longitudinal investigations conducted on people of average intelligence (Charles & James, 1964; Eisdorfer, 1963; Tuddenham, Blumenkrantz, & Wilkin, 1968) and noninstitutionalized mentally retarded adults (Baller, Charles & Miller, 1967; Bell & Zubek, 1960) have yielded similar results. Mean intelligence test scores increase by small amounts during early adulthood and reach a plateau between the ages of 25 and 30.

People who are below average or fail to make adequate use of their abilities decline somewhat in intelligence during early adulthood, but those of above-average intelligence may show no decline at all or even continue to improve well into middle age. Although the results of both cross-sectional and longitudinal studies reveal substantial declines in cognitive abilities during the eighth and ninth decades, it has been found that such abilities may increase even after age 70 (Baltes & Schaie, 1974; Busse & Maddox, 1985; Schaie & Hertzog, 1983). These studies have been interpreted as indicating that the magnitude of intellectual decline with aging varies with both the nature of the test task and the individual.

Specific Abilities.   General intelligence tests measure a combination of several cognitive abilities, and the pattern of change in performance with age varies with the specific ability.

As seen in the age-related pattern of subtest scaled scores on the WAIS-R (Wechsler, 1981), scores on vocabulary and information tests typically show no appreciable changes with aging, but perceptual–integrative abilities and comprehension of numerical symbols decline more rapidly.

Both cross-sectional and longitudinal methods have shortcomings, and investigations combining the two approaches are required to reach valid conclusions regarding intellectual growth with age. In the Seattle Longitudinal Studies, Schaie (1990, 1994) and his co-workers conducted a series of cross-sectional and longitudinal investigations to analyze age changes in five abilities measured by the SRA Mental Abilities Tests: Verbal Meaning, Spatial Orientation, Inductive Reasoning, Number, and Word Fluency. The findings revealed that the nature of the relationship between test score and chronological age varied with the specific ability and the research methodology. During middle adulthood, the rate of decline was greatest for Spatial Orientation and Inductive Reasoning and less for Word Fluency, Verbal Meaning, and Number. During old age the greatest drop was in scores on Verbal Meaning, a slightly speeded test. Other investigators have found greater age-related decline in the ability to reason and solve problems involving visual and geometric stimuli (fluid intelligence) than in verbal skills (crystallized intelligence) (Christensen et al., 1994; Horn, 1982; Horn & Hofer, 1992).

Schaie and his co-researchers (Baltes & Willis, 1982; Schaie & Willis, 1986; Willis, 1990) concluded that cognitive abilities decline with aging, but they emphasized that these abilities are plastic and that age-related declines may be arrested and even reversed. They maintain that providing varied opportunities for intellectual stimulation and a flexible lifestyle can contribute to the maintenance of an optimal level of cognitive functioning in older adulthood (the so-called "use it or lose it" theory). To test this hypothesis, they devised a set of procedures for training older adults to improve their scores on intelligence tests. The training involved not only instruction in specific cognitive skills, but also procedures for reducing anxiety and increasing motivation. Participants in the training sessions were also encouraged to compensate for their decrements in certain cognitive skills by concentrating less on those skills and more on activities in which their cognitive deficits were less pronounced.

In summary, whether a decrease, no change, or even an increase in cognitive abilities is observed with age depends not only on the research methodology (longitudinal, cross-sectional, or variations on these methods), but also on the specific ability and the person tested. Variations in cognitive abilities during adulthood also depend to some extent on the person's test-related experiences. People who remain intellectually active typically show less decline in intelligence test scores than those who fail to do so. And even when older adults do poorly on intelligence tests, they often possess highly specialized knowledge and skills in areas not covered by the tests. Such abilities can assist older adults in being even more competent than younger adults in dealing with the problems of everyday living.

Terminal Drop.   An apparent exception to the conclusion that the decline in cognitive abilities in old age is gradual and varies in magnitude with the specific ability is a phenomenon referred to as the *terminal drop*. This is a deterioration in cognitive functioning (IQ, memory, cognitive organization), reaction time and other sensorimotor abilities, and personality characteristics such as assertiveness during the last few months or years of life.

Prompting research on the terminal drop was the claim made by a nurse in a home for the aged that she could predict which patients were going to die soon merely by observing that they "seem to act differently" (Lieberman, 1965, p. 181). Subsequent research findings revealed declines in various areas of cognitive and sensorimotor functioning and in the ability to cope with environmental demands in patients who died within a year after being tested (Granick & Patterson, 1972; Lieberman & Coplan, 1969; Reimanis & Green, 1971; Riegel & Riegel, 1972). Riegel and Riegel (1972) noted that the drop was evident as long as 5 years before death, but subsequent research results indicated that it may not begin until about 2 years before death and occurs only in certain skills. White and Cunningham (1988) reported that a terminal drop is shown by decrements in IQ, memory, cognitive organization, sensorimotor abilities, and even personality characteristics. The causes of the terminal drop are not well understood, but a decrease in the efficiency of the cardiovascular system and other vital systems of the body is thought to play an important role.

Generational Changes: The Flynn Effect

Another phenomenon concerned with age changes in intelligence, but in this case changes over generations, is the *Flynn effect.* From an analysis of IQ scores in developed countries over three generations, political scientist James Flynn (1987) concluded that the mean IQ of an average 20-year-old in the 1980s was 15 points higher than that of a comparable person in 1940 and was continuing to increase by an estimated .33 IQ points per year. Generational differences in mean IQ were greater on tests such as Raven's Progressive Matrices, a measure of visuospatial ability, than on the Wechsler and Stanford–Binet tests, which are measures of vocabulary, general information, arithmetic, and other acquired knowledge, as well as visuospatial ability. Flynn concluded that the observed generational increase in mean intelligence test scores is due to environmental rather than genetic factors, but that it could not be attributed solely to improvements in formal schooling. Other possible contributing factors are the greater educational attainments of parents, greater parental attention to children, improved socioeconomic status, better nutrition, fewer childhood diseases, and an increasingly complex technological society. According to Greenfield (1998), much of the IQ increase reported by Flynn is due to the visual effects provided by television, computers, video games, and other technological devices. It has also been noted that severe malnutrition and deficiencies in iodine, iron, and other nutrients associated with lower IQs, as well as shorter statures, have decreased markedly during this century. Lynn (1998) and Sigman and Whaley (1998) found the evidence linking intelligence to improved nutrition to be compelling, but Martorell (1998) concluded that better nutrition is probably not responsible for the Flynn effect. Finally, it should be noted that, although average raw scores on IQ tests have been rising for decades, the question of whether population intelligence really is increasing remains controversial (see Howard, 2001).

Other Correlates of Mental Abilities

Family Size and Birth Order.   The inverse relationship between family size and intelligence has been documented by many studies (Lancer & Rim, 1984; Steelman & Doby, 1983; Wagner, Schubert, & Schubert, 1985), although the results have varied with the research methodology (Armor, 2001; Michalski & Shackelford, 2001). The tendency for mentally duller persons to have larger families is not due entirely to socioeconomic differences between large and small families, because it remains significant even when these differences are taken into account. The relationship between family size and intelligence is certainly multicausal, but not necessarily bidirectional. Parents with low IQs have a tendency to have an above-average number of children, but large families do not necessarily produce children with low IQs. Although it may be reasonable to assume that less attention is given to the cognitive development of children in larger families, this is not always true in modern American society (Rodgers, Cleveland, van den Oord, & Rowe, 2000).

It has been observed since Francis Galton's time that first-born children are more likely than later-born children to become high achievers. Summarizing the results of studies up through the mid-1960s, Altus (1966) concluded that first-borns had a higher percentage of people who were intellectually superior when compared to the population as a whole. First-borns also talk earlier and more clearly, learn to read earlier, and are better at problem-solving and perceptual tasks than later-borns. One possible explanation for these differences is that parents usually treat first-borns (particularly boys) differently from later-borns. Both parents tend to be more attentive and stimulating to their first-born children, spend more time with them; and provide greater encouragement and assistance in walking, talking, reading at the appropriate age, and other developmental tasks (Altus, 1966; Lewis & Jaskir, 1983; MacPhee, Ramey, & Yeates, 1984). The finding that the relationship among family size, birth order, and intellectual abilities is more apparent on verbal than on nonverbal measures of ability is consistent with the parental emphasis on language development in such children (Lancer & Rim, 1984). Differences in parental treatment of first-born and later-born children are also thought to be responsible for first-borns being more serious, responsible, studious, and competitive, whereas later-borns are more outgoing, relaxed, imaginative, and athletic.

Occupational Status. In an open, competitive society such as ours, it is reasonable to expect more highly intelligent people to enter occupations requiring higher cognitive abilities. Likewise, persons of lower intelligence tend to enter occupations for which less ability is needed (for additional intelligence–occupation research, see www.owlnet.rice.edu/~psyc231/Readings/schmidt.htm). Related to this point is one of the most widely cited findings in mental testing differences in mean Army General Classification Test (AGCT) scores of World War II military inductees who had been employed in various civilian occupations (Harrell & Harrell, 1945). The mean AGCT scores computed on over 70 occupational groups showed accountants, lawyers, and engineers to be at the top. Teamsters, miners, and farmers were at the bottom, and other occupational groups were arranged in between in a hierarchy according to their mean scores on the AGCT. As might be expected, there was a wide range of scores within each occupation. For example, some truck drivers scored higher than some teachers. Nevertheless, the AGCT data and scores on other tests (e.g., Reynolds, Chastain, Kauffman, & McLean, 1987) clearly demonstrate the importance of the intelligence variable in the prediction of occupational membership. In general, an abundance of research supports the ability of intelligence test scores to predict occupational achievement, especially for more complex occupations (Brody, 1992; Schmidt & Hunter, 2004).

The role of education, which is significantly related to both intelligence and occupational status, in determining the relationship between the last two variables is not entirely clear. Cronin, Daniels, Hurley, Kroch, and Webber (1975) (also see Brody, 1985) maintained that the correlation between intelligence and occupational status is due to the fact that both variables are correlated with social-class background. They concluded that middle- or upper-class homes are more likely than lower-class homes to prepare children to do well on both intelligence tests and in schoolwork, thus paving the way for them to enter higher-status occupations. The cause–effect sequence may also be something like this: Scoring high on a test of intelligence or scholastic aptitude is usually a requirement for admission to a good college, and graduation from a good college or university (and/or a professional school in some cases) is a requirement for entering a more prestigious occupation.

Socioeconomic Status.   One of the most consistent findings of research on individual and group differences in psychological characteristics is the positive correlation between IQ and socioeconomic status (SES), where SES is defined in terms of parental income, education, and occupation. Higher-average IQs among children in higher social classes have generally been found in these studies, a distinction that holds on both conventional and culture-fair tests of intelligence (Speath, 1976). Whether social-class differences in ability are primarily the results of heredity or environment is debatable, but it is generally agreed that a supportive home environment can exert a significant effect on cognitive abilities.

Because socioeconomic status and educational level are closely related, it is difficult to conclude whether observed differences in IQs are due to differences in education or to some other variable associated with socioeconomic status. Children who score low on intelligence tests tend not only to have less formal education, but also to come from homes that are alienated from the dominant culture and under greater than average economic stress. A language other than standard English is typically the primary means of communication in these homes, and the parents do not emphasize the importance of academic skills or know how to help their children acquire them.

Despite the significant positive correlation between intelligence test scores and socioeconomic status, the two variables are far from interchangeable. Consider, for example, the results of a study conducted by Thomas, Alexander, and Eckland (1979) of the relationships of these variables to school marks: it was found that the positive correlation between IQ and educational attainment remained significant even when socioeconomic status was statistically controlled. On the other hand, when IQ was statistically controlled, the correlation between socioeconomic status and educational attainment was slightly negative. These findings suggest that the correlation between IQ and school marks is not, as some psychologists have asserted, due primarily to differences in social-class background. Rather, it seems that intellectual ability affects both socioeconomic status and educational level. For this reason, it can be argued that a major reason why students with middle-class backgrounds are more likely than those with lower socioeconomic status to be in the top half of their school classes is because they possess greater intellectual ability (Thomas, Alexander, & Eckland, 1979).

Urban and Rural Residence.   Place of residence (urban versus rural) is related to occupational membership, socioeconomic status, and intelligence test scores. Studies conducted in the United States during the first half of the 20th century (see McNemar, 1942) found that children living in rural areas had significantly lower mean IQs than those living in urban areas. Although the urban–rural difference in intelligence test scores has persisted, it is not as pronounced as it was in previous generations. Because of radio, television, better access to schools, other sources of information and intellectual stimulation (e.g., the Internet), and advances in farming technology, rural children of today are exposed to a wider range of environmental stimuli and have greater opportunities to learn than their parents and grandparents. Increased exposure to the wider culture has improved the vocabularies, level of knowledge, and general intellectual awareness of rural children. It was estimated by Reynolds et al. (1987) that improved transportation and communication facilities resulted in a drop from an average difference between urban and rural children of 6 IQ points a generation ago to around 2 points in the 1980s. Furthermore, studies conducted among the Venda of South Africa, the Malays and Chinese of Malaysia, and Nigerians support the conclusion that group differences in performance on intelligence tests reflect differences in social class and education, rather than urban versus rural environment per se (Cronbach & Drenth, 1972; Scribner & Cole, 1973). The same might also be said of differences in the test scores of children living in different sections of metropolitan areas.

The dynamics of the home environment go beyond such variables as family size, birth order, and socioeconomic status. Even more important predictors of the intelligence test scores of young children are parenting style, the provision of a supportive home environment, and other measures of treatment within the home (Molfese, DiLalla, & Bunce, 1997). Be that as it may, the magnitude of these effects on the intelligence test scores of children are not at all clear. The findings of research by Baumrind (1993), Jackson (1993), and Scarr (1992, 1993), for example, indicate that, although the characteristics of the home and parent are significantly related to intelligence test scores in early childhood, by adolescence these effects have become very small.

Teachers' Expectations. Cognitive abilities certainly influence educational achievement, but education also influences abilities. The effects of education on cognitive abilities are sometimes indirect, as revealed by studies of teachers' expectations. The *looking-glass theory*—that people tend to adapt their behavior and self-perceptions to how they believe they are perceived by others—was first proposed by the sociologist H. H. Cooley (1922). Some years later, investigations stemming from the observation that the findings of researchers are often related to their expectations were extended to the classroom situation. These investigations, which involved both socially advantaged and socially disadvantaged children, were concerned with the influence of teachers' expectations and attitudes on the test scores and behaviors of students. A famous, albeit somewhat controversial, experiment of this kind was conducted by Rosenthal and Jacobson (1968) in the elementary schools of a South San Francisco school district.

The purpose of the experiment was to determine the effects of telling teachers that certain pupils would show a "potential spurt" in intellectual ability during the ensuing school year. In September, verbal, reasoning, and total IQ scores for all children in the school were obtained by having them take a nonverbal intelligence tests, the Tests of General Ability (TOGA). Then 20% of the children were labeled "potential spurters," ostensibly on the basis of their TOGA scores, but actually at random, in a report to their teachers.

TOGA was readministered to all the children one semester, 1 year, and 2 years later. Comparisons were then made between the IQ gains of the experimental groups (potential spurters) and those of control groups of children who had not been labeled potential spurters. The IQ gains of the experimental groups in grades 1 through 3 were significantly greater than those of the controls, but the IQ differences between the experimentals and controls in grades 4 through 6 were not significant. Mexican American children and those in the medium-ability track showed the greatest initial gains in total IQ. Boys showed greater average gains in verbal IQ and girls in reasoning IQ. The experimentals also showed greater gains in reading and were rated by their teachers as happier, more intellectually curious, and less needful of social approval than the controls.

Rosenthal and Jacobson could not identify the specific teacher behaviors that produced the changes in IQs for the experimental groups, but they speculated that teachers' higher expectations for these children were communicated by means of facial expressions, postures, touch, and other nonverbal cues. The findings of this experiment were not completely replicated by other investigators, and it was criticized for a number of methodological flaws. Also, a subsequent meta-analysis of studies of the expectancy effect strongly supported the hypothesis that the more closely acquainted teachers are with their pupils, the smaller is the effect of teachers' expectations on children's IQ scores (Raudenbush, 1984).

Nationality.   According to popular dogma, certain nationalities and ethnic groups possess specific personality and behavioral characteristics that distinguish them from other groups of people. Although these stereotypes may contain an element of truth, they are typically overgeneralizations that may serve as justifications for differential treatment or even mistreatment of particular national and ethnic groups. Nevertheless, social scientists have shown considerable interest in the relationships of cognitive variables to nationality, ethnicity, and culture.

A number of early investigations concerned with group differences in intelligence focused on nationality. An influential study conducted in the 1920s concluded that Jewish, Scandinavian, and German immigrants (along with native-born Americans) had higher average intelligence test scores than other immigrant groups in the United States (Hirsch, 1926). These results, which suggested that immigrants from countries in northern and western Europe were more intelligent than those from other countries, made such an impression on the psychologist H. H. Goddard that he lobbied for immigration laws that would restrict admission of all immigrants to the United States except those from northern and western Europe (Gould, 1981). Hirsch's (1926) findings, combined with those of Yerkes (1921), Brigham (1923), and others, were subsequently interpreted as being due to selective migration; significant nationality differences were not found when people were tested in their native countries and in their native language. Brigham (1930), in particular, repudiated his statements concerning nationality differences on the Army Alpha and concluded that the methods used were wrong and that the tests measured familiarity with U.S. language and culture, rather than innate intelligence. In other studies of immigrants it was found that scores on U.S. intelligence tests varied with the similarity between the examinees' native culture and that of the dominant U.S. culture.

Certain features of intelligence tests may contribute to the lower scores of different nationalities and cultures. Preliterate societies, for example, do not always share with Western societies the emphasis on speed, solving problems in the smaller number of steps, the superiority of mental compared to physical manipulations, or that originality is better than conformity (Gill & Keats, 1980). Unlike the more time- and self-centered orientation of Western cultures, people in more traditional societies are likely to associate intelligence with gradualness and patience and to stress cooperation, sociability, and honor (Wober, 1974).

Among other cultural differences that may have an effect on test scores are the Confucian perspective of traditional Chinese culture, which views intelligence as benevolence and doing what is right, and the Taoist perspective on intelligence as including humility, freedom from conventional standards of judgment, and knowledge of oneself and external conditions (Yang & Sternberg, 1997). Intelligence test materials may also be perceived differently by members of different cultures. Ortar (1963) found, for example, that when shown a picture of a head with no mouth Oriental immigrant children in Israel were more likely than native Israeli children to say that the body was missing. And when people in the New Guinea highlands were asked to use a set of blocks to copy a two-dimensional design, many tried to use both the tops and the sides of the blocks.

Race and Ethnicity. One of the most controversial issues in the measurement of cognitive abilities concerns racial differences in IQ. A general finding of research on this topic is that, although the mean IQ of Asian Americans is usually found to be equal or greater than that of European Americans, the mean IQs of Native Americans, Hispanic Americans, and African Americans are significantly lower. Among the various group comparisons, attention has focused on African American–European American differences.

African American–European American Differences. Many social scientists (Klineberg, 1963; Lee, 1951) attributed the results of research on racial differences in cognitive abilities to differences in the cultural environments of African American and European American children; others maintained that the differences have a genetic basis (Eysenck, 1971; Jensen, 1969). After analyzing the findings of research on African American European American differences in intelligence, Jensen (1969) concluded that the frequency of genes carrying higher intelligence is lower in the African American population as a whole than in the European American. The consequence, he maintained, is that African Americans, though equal to European Americans in rote learning ability, are poorer in abstract reasoning and problem solving.

One set of research findings cited by Jensen (1981) to counter a strictly environmentalist explanation of racial differences in intelligence is that Hispanic American and Native American children living under even worse environmental conditions than African Americans had higher mean scores on nonverbal intelligence tests. Also, despite the fact that their parents and grandparents were subjected to severe discrimination during the 19th and 20th centuries, persons of Chinese and Japanese ancestry in the United States excel Caucasians in mean nonverbal intelligence test scores, as well as in educational and occupational achievement, and equal them in their scores on verbal intelligence tests. Finally, Jews, who themselves are no strangers to social discrimination, have consistently scored higher than other groups on measures of verbal intelligence (Vernon, 1985). In many of these groups, however, cultural traditions and family characteristics encourage high achievement even when native endowment is not necessarily superior.

Despite the arguments of Jensen (1980, 1981), Herrnstein and Murray (1994), and others, the question of racial differences in intelligence is far from settled. Research findings indicate that European Americans outscore African Americans by approximately one standard deviation on both the WAIS-R (Reynolds et al., 1987) and the Stanford–Binet: Fourth Edition (Thorndike, Hagen, & Sattler, 1986). There is, however, a great deal of overlap between the IQ distributions of the two ethnic groups: an estimated 15% of African Americans obtain higher IQs than the average European American, and 15% of European Americans score lower than the average African American person (Vernon, 1985). These racial differences in intelligence test scores are attributable to an interactive combination of factors, including the inadequacies of the tests, differences in environments, and genetic differences, but the relative importance of these three sources of variability has not been determined.

It is noteworthy that the mean difference between the scores of European Americans and African American on tests of intelligence and academic achievement has declined during the past few decades. Possible explanations for the narrowing racial gap are increases in spending on education and increased parental education, particularly among African Americans, during recent years (Williams & Ceci, 1997). The difference is also greatly reduced when the groups of African Americans and European Americans are matched for socioeconomic status (Loehelin, 1989).

Japanese–American Differences.   Also relevant to the question of nationality and ethnic-group differences in intelligence is the finding of significantly higher mean IQs in Japanese than in American children (Lynn, 1982). It had been known for many years that the children of Asian immigrants to the United States tended to score at least as high as Caucasian children in this country. Lynn (1982) reported that the difference in mean IQ between Americans and Japanese reared in their own countries is approximately 11 points in favor of the latter group. In fact, it has been estimated that at least 10% of the Japanese population, compared with only 2% of Americans and Europeans, have IQs of 130 or greater.

Several possible explanations have been offered for the difference in mean IQs of Japanese and American children, a difference that has reportedly increased gradually since World War II. Assuming that the samples of Japanese and American children who were tested were equally representative of the specific populations and that the tests were equally appropriate, the most obvious explanation is that the two cultures have different child-rearing and formal educational practices. One biological explanation for the rise in IQ among the Japanese is that, because of improvements in health and nutrition, Japanese children today are better off physically and mentally than their counterparts were in pre–World War II days. Another suggestion is that the IQ increase has been caused by heterosis (hybrid vigor) resulting from a decline in consanguineous (kinship) marriages as large numbers of Japanese moved from small villages to large cities after World War II. Finally, Lynn (1987) proposed that the disparity in intelligence between Caucasians and people with Asian backgrounds is due to genetic differences in brain functioning. He maintained that in people of Asian backgrounds the left cerebral hemisphere evolved structures capable of processing visuospatial information. The result, according to Lynn, is that in Asians a higher proportion of cortical tissue is devoted to the processing of spatial information, and a smaller proportion of cortical tissue is available for processing verbal information. Consequently, linguistic communication, as in reading and writing Kanji, involves spatial skills that normally depend on the right cerebral hemisphere. As reasonable as this explanation of the higher test scores of Japanese children may sound, Brody (1992) concluded that the evidence for Lynn's theory is not persuasive.

Gender Differences.   Differences between the mean intelligence test scores of males and females are sometimes found, but they are usually inconsequential. Research findings indicate, however, that there are sex differences in specific cognitive and perceptual–motor abilities. It should be stressed however, that even though clear differences have been found there is also considerable overlap between males and females. Halpern (1997, 2003) concluded that women do better than men on tasks requiring rapid access to and use of phonological, semantic, and other information in long-term memory. Women are also superior to men on tasks requiring fine-motor dexterity, perceptual speed, and decoding of nonverbal information. Women also have better speech articulation, and lower perceptual thresholds for touch, taste, and odor than men. Men, on the other hand, perform better than women on tasks involving fluid reasoning, transformations in visual working memory, and motor tasks requiring aiming. With respect to academics, women make higher grades in school, in literature and foreign languages in particular. Men do better than women on tests of knowledge in general and on tests of knowledge of geography, mathematics, and science. These findings are, at least in part, a function of differences in the ways in which boys and girls are treated and taught in our society. For example, girls are usually expected to be more accomplished in linguistic and social skills, whereas boys are supposed to perform better in mathematical, mechanical, and related problem tasks.

Not only sex (gender) but also sex hormones have been found to be related to cognitive abilities. For example, Hier and Crowley (1982) obtained a positive correlation between spatial ability and secretions of male sex hormones during puberty. Research findings also suggest that testosterone slows development of the left hemisphere and enhances development of the right hemisphere of the brain; the right hemisphere is associated with the kinds of reasoning skills needed to solve mathematical problems (Christiansen & Knussman, 1987). An additional finding is that women perform better on tests of motor coordination and verbal facility, but poorer on tests of spatial reasoning during times of the month when blood estrogen levels are at a peak (Hampson, 1990; Kimura & Hampson, 1993). Males' scores on tests of spatial skills also fluctuate with their testosterone levels: they are higher in the morning than later in the day, and higher in the autumn than in the spring (Kimura & Hampson, 1994; Moffat & Hampson, 1996).

Various neuropsychological explanations for sex differences in specific cognitive abilities have been proposed. One set of explanations points to the sexual dimorphism of neural structures in the hypothalamus, amygdala, and cerebral cortex. Females have proportionally larger language areas than males (Harasty, Double, Halliday, Kril, & McRitchie, 1997), and the density of neurons in the language areas of females' brains is reportedly greater than those in males' brains (Witelson, Glezer, & Kigar, 1995). The brains of females are also more bilaterally organized than those of males, in that cognitive functions in females are less specific to a particular cerebral hemisphere. Also, the corpus callosum is thicker in females than in males, permitting better conductivity between the two cerebral hemispheres (Innocenti, 1994; Jancke & Steinmetz, 1994; Johnson, Pinkston, Bigler, & Blatter, 1996). Finally, PET (positron emission tomography) scan data point to sex differences in areas of the brain in which the greatest activity takes place while the individual is performing specific cognitive functions (Shaywitz et al., 1995).

Heredity.   Belief in the hereditary determination of intelligence goes back at least as far as the time of Francis Galton in the late 19th century. Alfred Binet did not reject the idea that intelligence is determined by heredity, but he was more interested in the possibility of modifying intellectual abilities by education, training, and environmental intervention (Eysenck, 1984). One of the most outspoken proponents of the notion that intelligence is determined in large measure by heredity was the psychologist H. H. Goddard, who advocated the reconstruction of society along IQ lines (Goddard, 1920).

Most psychologists, child development specialists, and educational researchers would probably agree that general intelligence, or at least a predisposition to develop intellectually, is to some extent inherited (Snyderman & Rothman, 1987). Some genetics researchers view intelligence as a *polygenic* characteristic, that is, one that is shaped to a large extent by the interaction of many minor genes, rather than a single major gene.

Perhaps the least ambiguous method of obtaining information concerning the effects of environment on cognitive abilities would be to conduct an experiment with pairs of monozygotic (identical) twins, who have identical heredities. Some twin pairs would be separated at birth by assigning them to different environments; other twin pairs would be kept together in the same environment. A finding of greater differences in measured abilities between twin pairs reared in different environments than between those reared in the same environment would constitute support for the hypothesis that environment influences cognitive abilities.

Because society will not permit even well-intentioned scientists to move children around like chess pieces, nonexperimental methods of evaluating the relative effects of heredity and environment have been devised. One approach is to compare, at various chronological ages, the IQs of monozygotic twins who have been reared apart. In this way, heredity is effectively held constant while environment is varied, albeit in an unsystematic, uncontrolled manner. Also, the IQs of individuals who have different heredities but live in similar environments, such as nonidentical siblings or unrelated children reared together, can be compared. Comparisons can also be made between the IQs of persons having different genetic relationships and reared in different environments, such as nonidentical siblings and unrelated individuals reared apart.

Despite the difficulty of locating pairs of monozygotic twins who have been reared apart, evidence has been obtained from a number of investigations of this type (see Bouchard, Lykken, McGue, Segal, & Tellegen, 1990; Bouchard & McGue, 1981; Plomin & Foch, 1980, for summaries). In general, it has been found that the correlations between the IQs of monozygotic twins reared together are almost always higher than those of monozygotic twins reared apart. For example, Bouchard et al. (1990) reported correlations between the Wechsler Adult Intelligence Scale (WAIS) IQs of monozygotic twins reared together as .88 for the Verbal Scale, .79 for the Performance Scale, and .88 for the Full Scale; the corresponding values for monozygotic twins reared apart were of .64, .71, and .69. Also, the closer the genetic relationship between individuals, the higher were the correlations between their scores on intelligence tests. Bouchard and McGue (1981) listed the median correlations between the IQs of persons with different degrees of kinship living together as .86 for monozygotic twins, .60 for dizygotic twins, .47 for siblings, .42 for parent and offspring, .33 for spouses, and .29 for adopted or natural siblings. Presumably reflective of the influence of environment on IQ were the lower correlations for corresponding twin pairs reared apart.

Population geneticists often express the results of studies of hereditary differences in terms of a *heritability index* (h^2), defined as the ratio of test score variance due to heredity to test score variance due to a combination of heredity and environment. Although heritability estimates as high as .72 (Plomin, 1990) have been reported, average estimates of h^2 for intelligence in the general population are around .50. This indicates that an estimated 50% of the variance in IQ scores is attributable to genetic factors. It should be cautioned, however, that these numbers reveal nothing about the relative importance of heredity or environment in determining the intelligence of a specific individual; heritability coefficients apply only to populations.

Even the most avid supporter of a genetic basis of intelligence on the one hand or a staunch environmentalist on the other hand recognizes that *both* heredity and environment are important in the formation of cognitive abilities. *Environment* in this context refers not only to the psychosocial, or experiential, environment of the person, but also to the prenatal and postnatal biological environment (nutrition, accidents, etc.). One interpretation of the research data bearing on this matter is that heredity establishes a kind of upper limit to intelligence, a limit attainable only under optimal environmental conditions (Weinberg, 1989).

Another approach to evaluating the differential effects of heredity and environment on cognitive abilities is represented by adoption research, such as the Minnesota Adoption Studies (Scarr & Weinberg, 1983) and the Texas Adoption Project (Horn, 1983). In these investigations the IQs of large samples of adopted children were compared with those of their nonadopted siblings and those of their adoptive and biological parents. Horn's (1983) findings are typical in that the IQs of the adopted children (3 to 10 years old) whom he studied were much closer to those of their biological mothers, from whom they had been separated almost since birth, than to the IQs of their adoptive parents. The IQs of the adolescents in Scarr and Weinberg's (1983) study were also more highly correlated with the IQs of the biological mothers than with those of their adoptive mothers.

Another interesting finding is that the effects of heredity on intelligence tend to increase with age, while the effects of environment, and shared environment in particular, tend to decrease with age (Bartels, Rietveld, Van Baal, & Boomsma, 2002; McGue, Bouchard, Iacono, & Lykken, 1993). A contributing factor is that as children and adults grow older the part of the environment that was more influential earlier in life is replaced by other, nonshared experiences in school, in social interactions with peers, at work, and in other situations.

The fact that genetic influences become even more significant with age was underscored by the results of the Louisville Twin Study (Wilson, 1983). In this investigation of 500 pairs of twins, the IQs of monozygotic twins became more similar but the IQs of dizygotic twins became less similar from infancy to adolescence. The results of the Minnesota Adoption Studies (Scarr & Weinberg, 1983) are consistent with those of the Louisville

Twin Study in finding that the home environment has some impact on IQ, particularly during early childhood, but that the effects of home environment are substantially less than those of heredity. Another finding is that there is still an estimated heritability coefficient of .80 for intelligence test scores even in a sample of adults with a mean age of 66 years (Pedersen, Plomin, Nesselrade, & McClearn, 1992). This indicates that heredity continues to exert a profound influence on IQ scores in later life.

SUMMARY

1. Both intelligence test scores and adaptive behavior are important in the diagnosis of mental retardation. Mental retardation is classified, according to its severity, into four categories: mild, moderate, severe, and profound. Heredity and environment are both determinative and interactive factors in mental retardation, but in the majority of cases the exact cause of the condition is unclear.

2. Specific learning disorders are disabilities in reading, writing, spelling, arithmetic, or other academic skills that cannot be explained by mental retardation, specific sensory–motor handicaps, emotional disorder, or environmental disadvantage. Federal law mandates that learning disabled children must be professionally diagnosed and that an individual education plan should be prepared for each child. A major psychodiagnostic indicator of a learning disability in most states is when a child's score on a standardized achievement test is significantly below his or her score on a co-normed intelligence test. Tests of intelligence and achievement that are employed in the determination of learning disabilities are the WISC-IV and the Wechsler Individual Achievement Tests, the K-ABC and the Kaufman Test of Educational Achievement, and the tests of cognitive abilities and achievement on the Woodcock–Johnson III.

3. The traditional stereotype of mentally gifted children as being physically weak, unhealthy, likely to burn out early, and emotionally unstable is incorrect for the majority of such children and particularly those who are moderately gifted. However, extremely gifted children are reportedly more likely than average to have social and emotional problems. Acceleration, mentoring, enrichment, special classes, and special schools are among the procedures that have been employed in the education of mentally gifted children.

4. Creative performance is not only a function of relatively high intelligence, but also of high motivation, special training, and perhaps other psychological abilities. A major problem in developing useful measures of creativity is defining the criteria of creative performance. Test batteries such as Guilford's Structure-of-Intellect Tests and the Torrance Tests of Creative Thinking are noteworthy examples of instruments designed to assess creativity. The results of recent research suggest that certain kinds of creative performance are associated with mood disorders such as bipolar disorder.

5. Given a relatively stable home environment, adequate nutrition, and appropriate educational experiences, IQ scores remain fairly stable after early childhood. The results of cross-sectional studies depict intelligence as rising into young adulthood and then declining gradually into old age; longitudinal studies find less decline with age. The

rate of decline, or even rise in some cases, is a function of the kinds of activities in which people engage throughout their lives: those who continue to pursue intellectual activities show less intellectual decline than those who evince less interest in continued learning ("use it or lose it" theory). An abrupt decline in the last weeks or months before death in old age is referred to as *terminal drop.*

6. The following demographic findings have been associated with intelligence:
    a. Larger family size is associated with lower average IQs, and first-born children tend to be intellectually superior to later-borns.
    b. Occupational status and socioeconomic status are positively correlated with each other and with intelligence, but it is not clear whether the advantages of higher social-class membership results in children with higher IQs or whether both higher IQs and higher social position are consequences of genetic factors.
    c. People from urban regions tend to have higher IQs than people living in rural areas.
    d. Higher education is associated with higher intelligence.
    e. Teachers' attitudes or expectations concerning what children are capable of achieving may play a role in whether a child fulfills his or her potential.
    f. African Americans have typically scored one standard deviation (15 IQ points) lower than European Americans on IQ tests. However, when participants were matched for socioeconomic status, this difference was greatly reduced. The difference has also decreased over the past 30 years.
    g. Japanese (and Asians in general) score higher (11 IQ points on average for Japanese) than Caucasians on IQ tests.

7. Studies have revealed no consistent gender differences in general mental ability, though each sex tends to be superior to the other in certain specific abilities. Girls are better at rote memory, language-type tasks, perceptual speed and accuracy, and numerical computations. Boys are better in mathematical reasoning, visuospatial ability, mechanical ability, and speed and coordination of large bodily movements. The physiological bases of these differences are most likely related to differences in the development and functioning of the left and right hemispheres of the brain. Differences in other cerebral structures and in the level of testosterone are also associated with gender differences in cognitive abilities.

8. The relative contribution of heredity has been hotly debated. Numerous investigations have led to the conclusion that the heritability coefficient (proportion of variance in the intelligence test scores of the general population accounted for by heredity) is as high as .70; it is also clear that the environment plays an important role in shaping a person's cognitive abilities.

MASTERING THE CHAPTER OBJECTIVES

1. *Intellectual disabilities*
    a. Describe the classification system for mental retardation advocated by the American Association of Mental Retardation and the American Psychiatric Association.

b. Because the method of diagnosing mental retardation, including the cutoff IQ, varies from state to state, it is possible for a child to be mentally retarded in one state and "borderline" or "low average" in another state. What educational, medical, and political consequences might this have?

2. *Learning disabilities*
   a. List four types of learning disabilities.
   b. Describe several causes of learning disabilities.
   c. Pretend you are a psychologist evaluating a person suspected of having learning disabilities. Identify four important things you would consider and name three tests you might use. Why would these tests be appropriate?

3. *Giftedness*
   a. List four findings of Terman's gifted participants.
   b. List five findings of the characteristics derived from other studies of people who are gifted.

4. *Creativity*
   a. List six characteristics of highly creative people.
   b. Test your creative ability by writing down all the possible things you might do with a paper clip, wire clothes hanger, and foot ruler. Have three class mates do the same thing and compare your answers.

5. *Age and intelligence*
   a. Summarize the research on aging and intelligence by describing the abilities that are most likely to decline with age and those that are more stable.
   b. What is the Flynn effect?
   c. What is meant by terminal drop?

6. *Intelligence and demographics*
   a. List seven major findings related to intelligence and demographics (e.g., birth order, occupational status).
   b. What do you think are the major causes of IQ score differences among various ethnic groups (especially African American–European American)?
   c. Design a study to test the hypothesis that the difference between the mean IQs of African Americans and European Americans is *not* significant. Don't be overly concerned with whether your study could actually be conducted, but make certain that extraneous (confounded) variables are controlled.

7. *Sex differences*
   a. List the abilities that females have been found to be superior in compared to males. Then list all those that males have been found to be superior in.
   b. List the physiological reasons that help to explain sex differences in mental abilities.

8. *Heritability of intelligence*
   a. Summarize the sources of evidence for a hereditary component to intelligence.
   b. In a summary of the average correlations between the IQs of persons having different degrees of kinship, Bouchard and McGue (1981) listed the median correlation between the IQs of same-sex fraternal twins reared together as .60 and the median correlation between the IQs of identical twins reared together as .86. A suggested formula for computing the heritability coefficient is

$$h^2 = r_i - r_f / 1 - r_f,$$

where r_i is the correlation between the IQs of identical (monozygotic) twins, and r_f is the correlation between the IQs of same-sex fraternal (dizygotic) twins reared together. Use this formula to compute h^2 and interpret the result. (See Answers to Quantitative Questions, p. 487.)

EXPERIENCING PSYCHOLOGICAL ASSESSMENT

1. List all the demographics related to intelligence. Put a plus by all those that would be correlated with you having higher intelligence (e.g., first-born), a zero if they would not be likely to have any relationship for you (e.g., middle-born), and a minus if they would be correlated with you having a lower intelligence (e.g., rural upbringing or residence). How well do you think these factors predict your intelligence?

2. Once you have listed the sex differences in specific abilities (see question 7a above), identify specific behaviors in everyday life that do or don't seem to support these differences (e.g., observe to see if most females decode nonverbal information more quickly).

CHAPTER EIGHT

NEUROPSYCHOLOGICAL ASSESSMENT

CHAPTER OBJECTIVES

1. Define neuropsychological assessment and describe the types of questions neuropsychological assessment might answer.

2. Discuss the problems in evaluating infants and young children.

3. Describe the following developmental assessment instruments: Gesell Development Schedules, Brazelton Neonatal Behavioral Assessment Scale, Bayley Scales of Infant Development, McCarthy scales, FirstSTEP, and AGA Early Screening Profiles.

4. Describe Luria's PASS model of brain functioning.

5. Overview of frequent neuropsychological symptoms.

6. Describe the following disorders: head injury, tumors, cerebrovascular disease, dementia, and exposure to toxic substances.

7. Describe the fixed battery versus the flexible hypotheses testing approaches in neuropsychology.

8. Describe the Halstead Reitan and Luria–Nebraska batteries.

9. Describe domains of neuropsychological functioning and how these are assessed.

It is often important to understand changes in mental abilities as a person progresses through her or his life-span. Different risks occur at different stages. During infancy and early childhood, there may be developmental delays related to birth complications or genetic disorders. Early and middle childhood may have the first expressions of intellectual disabilities or learning disabilities. Young adults are more likely to have problems related to head injuries or exposure to neurotoxic substances, such as organic solvents or recreational drugs. Finally, people in late adulthood may have cognitive decline due to strokes or the onset of Alzheimer's disease. It is often crucial to identify these changes to provide optimal treatment and help the person make the most of existing abilities.

The field of psychology that evaluates the above areas is referred to as *neuropsychological assessment* (see comprehensive coverage in Groth–Marnat, 2000b, and Lezak, Howieson, & Loring, 2004). The knowledge base of neuropsychological assessment depends on an understanding of the relationship between normal or abnormal brain function and behavior. One way of describing this is that a medical doctor (especially a neurologist) tells you what the *brain* is doing, whereas a neuropsychologist tells you what the *person* is doing as a result of the brain (see descriptions in neuropsychologycentral.com). The core strategy in accomplishing this goal is to evaluate specific components or functions of mental abilities, such as attention, language, memory, and spatial abilities. This information can then be used to answer the following types of questions:

1. Diagnosis (Is the cause of a patient's seizures psychological or is it the result of abnormal brain activity?)
2. Treatment and educational planning (What would be the best educational program given the nature of a child's learning disability?)
3. Legal decision making (Is this older person who is experiencing cognitive decline still able to make legal decisions in a knowing and intelligent manner?)

Many of the tests and knowledge discussed in Chapters 6 and 7 are relevant for neuropsychological assessment. For example, the Wechsler intelligence scales are sensitive to the impact of brain dysfunction. The index scores are particularly helpful in understanding decline in specific aspects of cognitive abilities (see, for example, Psychological Report 6.1 on learning disabilities). However, it is often necessary to include specialized tests or test batteries that have been found to be especially sensitive to brain dysfunction. This chapter will discuss and give examples of these tests and explain the types of procedures that may occur during neuropsychological assessment.

DEVELOPMENTAL ASSESSMENT

Often the first signs of brain dysfunction occur during infancy or early childhood. These might include delays in learning that may be due to low mental ability, sensory and motor handicaps, or neurological disorders of various kinds. As a result, psychologists need to be familiar with the range of instruments needed to detect these early signs of difficulties.

The first studies of human development, which began during the late 19th century, were prompted by the concern expressed by writers and social reformers with the welfare of children and particularly with their health, education, and exploitation in the workplace and elsewhere. This concern led to the child welfare movement and to legislation and public programs directed toward more humane treatment of children. Associated with the child welfare movement was the new science of developmental psychology and research on the physical, cognitive, emotional, and social characteristics of children. Contributing to this research were instruments and procedures designed to measure cognitive, motor, perceptual, emotional, and social development.

Contrary to William James's assertion that, to the newborn baby, the world is only a "booming, buzzing confusion," newborns are able to structure their environment to some extent and make some sense of it. During the first year of life, motor, perceptual, and cognitive abilities develop rapidly, and, combined with ever-growing experience, the world becomes a more meaningful place.

Problems in Testing Infants and Young Children

Testing infants (0 to 1½ years) and preschoolers (1½ to 5 years) can be difficult because of their short attention span and greater susceptibility to fatigue. Young children may also lack motivation to pursue the test tasks. Finally, the characteristics assessed by these infant and early childhood tests are rather unstable. For these reasons, the reliabilities and validities of tests administered to infants and preschoolers tend to be lower than tests designed for school-aged children. Intelligence tests designed for infants and young preschoolers also tend to have low correlations with scores on intelligence tests administered to the same children in later years and are not very accurate predictors of later intellectual development.

One reason why correlations between scores on infant intelligence tests and scores on tests such as the Stanford–Binet Intelligence Scale administered at a later age are low is because of differences in the types of tasks on the two kinds of tests. Infant intelligence tests are primarily measures of sensorimotor development, such as the ability to lift and turn the head, follow a moving object with the eyes, and reach for or grasp an object. In contrast, the items on Binet-type intelligence tests are more linguistic or verbal in nature. After infancy, children have a greater behavioral repertoire and can walk and sit at a table while manipulating the test materials and communicate better with the examiner.

Infant intelligence tests not only have relatively low predictive validities, but their reliabilities are also lower than those of tests administered later during the preschool period. Although the greater distractibility of infants in the testing situation contributes to the lower reliabilities of tests administered to them, bona fide changes in cognitive abilities also occur in younger children.

Not only are preschool-aged children more attentive and motivated than infants in testing situations, but their cognitive abilities appear to be of a different quality. For example, preschoolers are much more interested in words and social interactions than they were during infancy.

Despite their low correlations with later test results, tests administered during infancy are useful in diagnosing mental retardation and organic brain disorders and in screening for developmental disabilities. Research findings have revealed that test scores obtained during infancy are significant predictors of the later intellectual status of mentally retarded and neurologically impaired children (Ames, 1967; McCall, 1979). Although the results of such studies indicate that performance on infant tests can contribute to an understanding of child development and making practical decisions about this age group, test data must be combined with and interpreted in the light of other information about the examinee and an awareness of the limitations of the tests.

Gesell Developmental Schedules

Research begun by Arnold Gesell at the Yale Clinic of Child Development in the 1920s led to an extensive series of investigations of infancy and early childhood that continued for 40 years (see Ames, 1989). A guiding assumption of these studies was that the gross-motor, fine-motor, language, personal–social, and adaptive behavior functions of children follow an orderly maturational sequence. Normative data were collected on the development of motor, linguistic, and personal–social skills, as well as adaptive behavior from birth to age 6. Detailed information on each child was obtained by various methods: home record, medical history, daily record, anthropometric measurements, material observations, reports of the child's behavior at the clinic, normative examination, and developmental ratings. The following excerpt is characteristic of the normative behavioral descriptions provided by Gesell and his co-workers (Gesell & Amatruda, 1941, p. 41):

> The baby can reach with his eyes before he can reach with his hand; at 28 weeks a baby sees a cube; he grasps it, senses surface and edge as he clutches it, brings it to his mouth, where he feels its qualities anew, withdraws it, looks at it on withdrawal, rotates it while he looks, looks while he rotates it, restores it to his mouth, withdraws it again for inspection, restores it again for mouthing, transfers it to the other hand, bangs it, contacts it with the free hand, transfers, mouths it again, drops it, resecures it, mouths it yet again, repeating the cycle with variations—all in the time it takes to read this sentence.

Scores on the Gesell Developmental Schedules, determined from the presence or absence of specific behaviors characteristic of children at certain ages, were summarized in terms of a *developmental age (DA)*. The DA could then be converted to a *developmental quotient (DQ)* by the formula DQ = 100 (DA/CA). However, Gesell did not consider the DQ as equivalent to an IQ.

The Gesel Developmental Schedules were probably used more by pediatricians than by psychologists from the 1920s through the 1940s. Psychologists, particularly those with a strong psychometric orientation, criticized the Gesell Schedules as being too subjective and as poorly standardized. However, a later version of the scales included more objective observational procedures. Knobloch (Knobloch & Pasamanick, 1974; Knobloch, Stevens, & Malone, 1987) provided detailed instructions for making observations on the revised Gesell Developmental Schedules and interpreting them. Norms for preschoolers (2½–6 years) by half-year intervals, but not for infants, were also published (Ames, Gillespie, Haines, & Ilg, 1979).

The Gesell Developmental Schedules were very popular, especially with pediatricians, and revisions of the original schedules were still in use in the 1990s (Ireton, 1992, 1998). However, developmental psychologists went on to construct instruments with better psychometric characteristics than those of the Gesell Schedules. Examples are the California First Year Mental Scale, the Northwestern Intelligence Test, the Griffiths Mental Development Scale, the Merrill–Palmer Scale, and the Cattell Infant Intelligence. Only the last two of these are still in print, and for the most part even they have been superseded.

A more recent derivative of the Gesell Developmental Schedules is Denver-II, a revision of the Denver Developmental Screening Test. Denver-II was designed to assess the personal, social, fine- and gross-motor, language, and adaptive abilities of children from birth to age 6 and to serve as a screening instrument for developmental delays. The 125 items on Denver-II are administered individually in 20 to 25 minutes or in 10 to 15 minutes for the abbreviated version of the test. Results are scored on four areas: Personal–Social, Fine Motor–Adaptive, Language, and Gross Motor. Ratings on five behaviors are also obtained: Typical, Compliance, Interest in Surroundings, Fearfulness, and Attention Span. Denver-II is easy to administer and score, but it has been criticized for the unrepresentativeness of its standardization sample (Hughes, 1995).

Brazelton Neonatal Behavioral Assessment Scale

People are evaluated in many ways, both formal and informal, throughout their lifetime, and sometimes even before they are born. For example, The Rochester Obstetrical Scale consists of a prenatal scale, a delivery scale, and an infant scale. Another measure, the Apgar score, is derived from measurements of heart rate, respiration, muscle tone, reflexes, and color obtained at 1 minute and 5 minutes after birth (Chinn, Drew, & Logan, 1975). Perhaps the most popular neonatal test is the Brazelton Neonatal Behavioral Assessment Scale (NBAS) (Brazelton, 1973, 1984).

The NBAS, which has an age range of 3 days to 4 weeks, is scored on 26 behavioral items and 20 elicited responses, including measures of neurological, behavioral, and social functioning. The items measure hand–mouth coordination, habituation to sensory stimuli, startle responses, reflexes, stress responses, motor maturity, and cuddliness. Despite certain shortcomings (e.g., few normative or validity data and fairly low reliability coefficients), the NBAS continues to be used by pediatricians and child psychologists in both practice and research.

Bayley Scales of Infant Development

The Bayley Scales of Infant Development-Second Edition (BSID-II) (Bayley, 1993) are based on the results of an extensive research program (the Berkeley Growth Study) directed by Nancy Bayley. BSID-II, which was designed for children between 1 and 42 months who are suspected of being at risk for cognitive disabilities, consists of three parts: a Mental Scale yielding a Mental Development Index, a Motor Scale yielding a Psychomotor Development Index, and a Behavior Rating Scale to supplement information from the Mental and Motor Scales. The Mental Scale measures sensory–perceptual abilities, discriminations, and the ability to respond to them; acquisition of object constancy; memory, learning, and problem solving; vocalization; beginning verbal communication; early evidence of the basis of abstract thinking; habituation; mental mapping; complex language; and mathematical concept formation. The Motor Scale measures degree of body control, coordination of large muscles, finer manipulative skills of hands and fingers, dynamic movement, dynamic praxis, postural imitation, and stereognosis. The Behavior Rating Scale measures attention–arousal, orientation–engagement, emotional regulation, and motor quality. The entire test can be administered in 25 to 35 minutes to children under 15 months and in a maximum of 60 minutes to children over 15 months of age.

The BSID-II standardized in the early 1990s on a sample of 850 boys and 850 girls aged 1 to 42 months. The sample was selected in stratified random fashion from four geographical regions and by age, gender, ethnicity, and parental education. The BSID-II manual also provides data on children who were born prematurely, tested positively for HIV, were exposed to drugs during the prenatal period, were asphyxiated at birth, are developmentally delayed or have frequent middle-ear infection, are autistic, or have Down syndrome. An accompanying instrument, the Bayley Infant Neurodevelopmental Screen (BINS), was designed to assess basic neurological functions, auditory and visual receptive functions, and social and cognitive processes in children aged 3 to 24 months. Like other infant intelligence tests, scores on the BSIS-II are not a very good predictor of performance on IQ tests administered later in childhood.

The McCarthy Scales of Children's Abilities and the McCarthy Screening Test

Taking up where the Bayley scales leave off, the McCarthy Scales of Children's Abilities (MSCA) (McCarthy, 1972) were designed for children aged 2½ to 8½ years. These scales yield six measures of intellectual and motor development: Verbal, Perceptual–Performance, Quantitative, General Cognitive, Memory, and Motor. The MSCA was standardized on samples of approximately 100 children in each of 10 age groups, stratified by race, region, socioeconomic status, and urban–rural residence. Unfortunately, data on the validity of the MSCA, published after the author's death, are rather meager.

The McCarthy Screening Test (MST), which was published some years after the MSCA, provides a means of identifying children (ages 4 to 8½ years) who may be at risk for learning problems. The six component scales on the MST are drawn from those on the MSCA.

FirstSTEp and the ESP

Psychological tests used in screening large numbers of children for developmental delays and subsequent in-depth diagnostic testing should comply with the criteria listed in the federal Individuals with Disabilities Education Act (IDEA). Although the MSCA meets the IDEA criteria, two instruments designed specifically with those criteria in mind are the FirstSTEp Screening Test for Evaluating Preschoolers (Miller, 1993) and the American Guidance Service (AGS) Early Screening Profiles (ESP). The psychometric characteristics of both FirstSTEp and the ESP are acceptable for developmental screening instruments, but neither instrument has been used extensively in research.

FirstSTEp is a rapid (15 minutes) test for screening children aged 2.9 through 6.2 years for developmental delays. The 12 subtests, which were designed to create a "game" atmosphere in testing, are classified into three of the five IDEA domains: Cognition, Communication, and Motor. The child's performance on the 12 FirstSTEp subtests is expressed as a composite score interpreted in terms of three classification categories: "within acceptable limits," "caution" (mild to moderate developmental delays), or "at risk" (for developmental delays). Optional Social–Emotional and Parent–Teacher Rating Scales are used to assess the fourth IDEA domain (Attention–Activity Levels, Social Interactions, Personal Traits, and Serious Behavior Problems). An optional Adaptive Behavior Checklist assesses the fifth IDEA domain (Activities of Daily Living, Self-Control, Relationships and Interactions, and Functioning in the Community).

The AGS Earl Screening Profiles (ESP) (by P. Harrison et al., 1990; American Guidance Service) is a brief inventory for determining developmental delays in preschoolers (2 to 6 years, 7 months). It consists of three basic components (profiles) and four supplemental surveys. The profiles take less than 30 minutes to administer, and the surveys take 15 to 20 minutes. The Cognitive–Language Profile consists of tasks for assessing reasoning skills, visual organization and discrimination, receptive and expressive vocabulary, and basic school skills. The Motor Profile assesses gross- and fine-motor skills (e.g, walking a straight line, imitating arm and leg movements, tracing mazes, drawing shapes). The Self-help–Social Profile, a questionnaire completed by a parent or other caretaker of the child, is concerned with the child's typical performance in communication, daily living skills, socialization, and motor skills. The four surveys on the ESP are the Articulation Survey (child pronounces 20 words), Home Survey (parent answers questions about the child's home environment), Health History (parent checks any health problems the child has had), and Behavior Survey (examiner rates attention span, frustration tolerance, response style, and other behaviors of the child during administration of Cognitive–Language and Motor profiles). Scores on the ESP are converted to screening indexes at Level I or to standard scores, percentile ranks, and age equivalents at Level II, indicating whether the child requires further assessment.

Other Developmental Tests

A number of other test batteries and specific tests are available to assess motor, perceptual, cognitive, emotional, and social development during infancy and early childhood. Some of these instruments are merely forms on which a parent, guardian, or other person who is familiar with the child records observations of the child's everyday behavior and characteristics. Other instruments involve the presentation of materials to the child, who is usually told to do something with the materials; the child's responses are then noted and evaluated. Certain psychometric instruments, such as the Peabody Developmental Motor Scales, the Test of Language Development-Primary: Third Edition, and the Developmental Test of Visual Perception-Second Edition were designed to assess development in specific domains. Other instruments, such as those described next, are batteries of tests for evaluating a child's development in several domains.

Developmental Assessment of Young Children (DAYC).   This measure (Voress & Maddox, 1998) is used to identify possible delays in cognition, communication, social–emotional development, physical development, and adaptive behavior development during the first 6 years of life. These five domains reflect areas mandated for assessment and intervention in the Individuals with Disabilities Education Act. Corresponding to each of the five domains is a subtest that, depending on the child's age, can be administered in 10 to 20 minutes. The five domain scores provide information on specific strengths and weaknesses and differentiate between children who are developing normally and those who are significantly below normal in development. The scores may also be used to document progress in developmental abilities as a result of specific intervention programs. Reliability and validity data for the five DAYC domain and composite scores given in the manual (Voress & Maddox, 1998) are very encouraging with respect to DAYC as a measure of development.

Infant–Toddler Developmental Assessment. Another noteworthy domain-centered approach to identifying children from birth to 36 months who are developmentally at risk is represented by the Infant–Toddler Developmental Assessment (IDA) (Provence, Erikson, Vater, & Palmeri, 1995). Rather than being a test battery per se, IDA is a comprehensive, multidisciplinary, family-centered procedure involving a team of professionals who obtain, review, and integrate data from multiple sources. There are six phases in the evaluation process, each of which develops from the preceding one and is completed after team discussion and review. Phase four of the IDA procedures, the Developmental Observation and Assessment Phase, makes use of the Provence Birth-to-Three Developmental Profile. The standardized developmental assessment provided by the Provence Profile employs naturalistic observation and incorporates parent reports of the child's development on eight domains: Gross Motor, Fine Motor, Relationship to Inanimate Objects (Cognitive), Language–Communication, Self-help, Relationship to Persons, Emotions and Feeling States (affects), and Coping. Reliability coefficients for scores on these domains range from the high .70s to the mid-.90s, depending on the child's age. Several types of evidence for the validity of the IDA have also been reported (see Erikson, 1995; Meisels & Fenichel, 1996).

NEUROPSYCHOLOGICAL THEORIES, DISORDERS, AND ASSESSMENT

During ancient times, the Oracle at Delphi advised those seeking his advice to begin by knowing themselves. Despite continuous search and research for nearly two centuries, this has proved to be no simple task. The functioning of the 3 pounds of grayish-pinkish tissue comprising the human brain sometimes appears to defy self-understanding. Still, we now know a substantial amount about the functioning of the four lobes of the cerebral cortex (frontal, parietal, occipital, and temporal) and the subcortical structures of the brain.

Although thought and action typically involve many different areas of the brain, there is a certain degree of specificity or localization of the functioning of the brain. We know, for example, that for most people an area in the left frontal lobe of the cerebral cortex (*Broca's area*) plays an important role in the production of grammatical language and that an area in the left temporal lobe (*Wernicke's area*) imparts meaning to language. We also know that the left parietal lobe is important in visuo-spatial orientation, that the frontal lobes play an important role in abstract thinking and problem solving, and that the hippocampus has a role in the storage of memories. By assessing different neuropsychological functions, it is possible to infer which areas of the brain might be compromised. For example, verbal difficulties are more likely to be associated with difficulties in the left hemisphere, whereas nonverbal (visuospatial) problems can be more clearly linked to the right hemisphere.

Usually, medical procedures such as CT or MRI scans are fairly accurate at identifying locations of the brain that are being compromised. Given this, the greatest value of neuropsychological assessment often is describing how these difficulties are being expressed in behavior or thought. This can then be used to design treatments, decide if a person can function independently, assist with legal decision making, or monitor changes over time.

Various conceptions have been developed to help understand brain–behavior relationships. Figure 8.1 is a diagram of the conceptual framework of neuropsychological functioning similar to that developed by Reitan and Wolfson (1993). This process begins when sensory input is first received by the brain. In order to process this information the brain must focus on and screen the information accurately. This involves comparing the new information with past experience. Depending on the type of information that is received, it may be processed primarily by the left hemisphere for verbal information or primarily by the right hemisphere for nonverbal information. This information may then be stored in long term memory. The highest level of processing involves developing concepts and deciding on how best to proceed with the information. Impairment to any one of these areas of functioning can result in problems that need to be compensated for by the remaining intact functions.

Another general neuropsychological theory, the PASS (planning–attention–simultaneous processing–successive processing) model of cognitive abilities, is based on Aleksandr Luria's conceptualization (Luria, 1973). According to Luria's theory, the cognitive activity of the human brain can be divided into three functional units (Das, Naglieri, & Kirby, 1994). The *first functional unit,* which is considered to be associated with the upper brain stem and the limbic system, is concerned with vigilance or attention and discrimination among stimuli. Although not responsible for receiving and analyzing information, this unit is critical to cognitive processing because it provides a general state of readiness and a

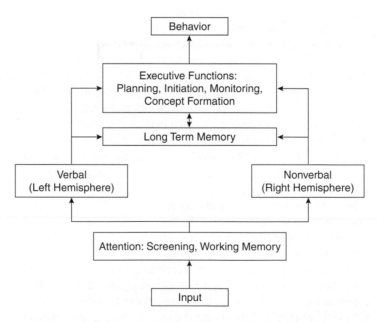

FIGURE 8.1   Model of neuropsychological functioning.

(Adapted from Reitan [1993].)

focus of attention. The *second functional unit,* thought to be associated with the posterior regions of the cerebral hemispheres, including the visual (occipital), auditory (temporal), and general sensory (parietal) areas, is concerned with the reception, elaboration, and storage of information by means of simultaneous and successive processing. The *third functional unit,* which is associated with anterior parts of the cerebral hemispheres, particularly the prefrontal region, is responsible for the programming, regulation, and verification of cognitive activity. This unit regulates the activities of the first functional unit so that behavior will be consistent with the individual's conscious goals and motives. In summary, the first functional unit is said to be responsible for arousal and attention, the second functional unit for reception, analysis, and storage using simultaneous and successive reasoning processes, and the third functional unit for planning, regulating, and verifying mental activity.

A diagram of the PASS cognitive processing model is given in Figure 8.2. The model conceptualizes the three functional units of Luria's theory as operating on the individual's knowledge base. The knowledge base consists of all the information, in both long- and short-term memory, that is available to the individual at processing time. For processing to be effective, this knowledge base must be integrated with the *planning* (third functional unit), *attention* (first functional unit), and *simultaneous and successive* processes (second functional unit) as they are demanded by the particular task. The result of processing, or *output,* involves speaking, writing, or other motoric activities.

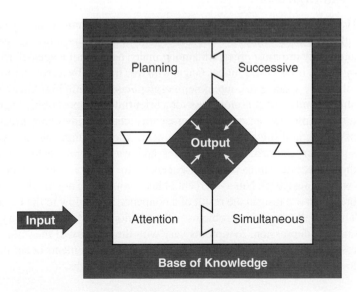

FIGURE 8.2   PASS Cognitive Processing Model.

(From Naglieri, J. *Essentials of CAS assessment.* Copyright © 1999, John Wiley & Sons. This material is used by permission of John Wiley & Sons Inc.)

NEUROPSYCHOLOGICAL DISORDERS

Central to evaluating a person's neuropsychological status is an understanding of the most frequent types of disorders that are likely to be encountered. Neuropsychological symptoms can be expressed in a wide number of ways. This might include problems with attention, motor skills, visuospatial skills, short- and long-term memory, language, and abstract thinking. They can also cause the individual to become hyperactive, impulsive, distractible, and emotionally unstable. An overall decrease in a wide range of abilities caused by organic factors is referred to as *dementia*. Visual problems might include difficulty constructing objects (*visuoconstructive disorders*), neglecting one half of a person's vision (*visual neglect*), or inability to recognize objects (*agnosia*). *Apraxia* is an inability to perform purposeful movements and may include problems with coordination. Paralysis can occur when the motor areas are damaged.

When the language areas of the brain are affected, difficulties in understanding spoken or written language (*aphasia*), as well as impairment in reading ability (*alexia–dyslexia*) and writing (*agraphia–dysgraphia*), may occur. These are often associated with damage to the left hemisphere of the brain and are frequently the result of a stroke or tumor.

Neuropsychological disorders may be caused by aberrations in genetics, development, and aging or by trauma, tumors, chronic alcohol abuse, diet, drugs, microorganisms, or other physical or chemical conditions that affect the functioning of the brain. The most frequently encountered types of neuropsychological disorders are head injuries, cerebrovascular disease, tumors, dementia, and exposure to toxic substances.

Head Injuries

Head injuries are the most common cause of brain damage among adults. They typically result from a fall or motor vehicle accident. Although head injuries can occur to people of all ages, they are most prevalent among males between the ages of 15 and 24. One early case of a head injury was Phineas Gage, who was injured by a crowbar that penetrated his frontal lobes (see video clip content.nejm.org/cgi/content/full/351/23/e21?query=TOC). Remarkably, he only lost consciousness for a brief time and most of his cognitive abilities remained intact. However, he did have personality changes involving greater impulsiveness, poor planning, and impaired social judgment. These changes were severe enough that he had significant interpersonal difficulties and was never able to work again. Unfortunately, there are often long-term consequences to moderate and severe forms of head injury (www.biausa.org). Ninety percent of head injuries do not involve actual penetration into the brain, but are instead the result of a nonpenetrating blow to the head (a *closed head injury*). This usually results in problems with attention, short-term memory, fatigue, headache, and anxiety–depression. Symptoms vary with the severity of the injury, but in some cases can result in permanent difficulties. The greatest improvements occur in the first few weeks following the injury and usually level off after 18 months.

Cerebrovascular Disease

Cerebrovascular disease (stroke) can be caused by either a blockage of blood to a region of the brain (*ischemia*) or bleeding into the brain itself (*hemorrhaging*). Both conditions cause damage to the brain, which mostly occurs in the area in which the bleeding (with hemorrhaging) or oxygen deprivation (with ischemia) occurs. The area of damage largely determines the type of symptoms experienced. For example, aphasia along with sensory and/or motor changes to the right side of the body are most likely to occur for strokes in the left hemisphere. Cerebrovascular disease can potentially occur at any time in the life cycle, but the risk is much higher for persons over 55.

Tumors

A tumor is an abnormal growth of cells that occurs independent of the surrounding tissues. Tumors in the brain typically cause alterations in cognitive and sensory–motor function. These changes often occur for very specific functions. For example, tumors in the right posterior portion of the brain are likely to cause problems with naming or constructing objects. More general changes, such as poor attention and confusion, are likely to be caused by the general swelling of the brain that often accompanies the growth of a tumor. A number of interesting and unfortunate personality changes have occurred in cases with tumors to areas of the brain that regulate emotions. In many cases, individuals have begun to experience emotional instability, including violence. Charles Whitman was a famous case who shot people from a University of Texas building. Upon his death, an autopsy of his brain found a large tumor in his *amygdala.*

Dementia

Dementia is a cluster of symptoms caused by organic factors that includes memory difficulties, language impairment, constructional difficulties, poor executive functioning, mental confusion, poor orientation to the environment, and a decline in social–occupational functioning. There are over 50 causes of dementia, many of which are reversible. For example, dementias caused by drug interactions or thyroid conditions can usually be treated, with the result being a significant improvement in cognitive functioning. The two best-known and most common causes are Alzheimer's disease (www.alzfdn.org/) and vascular dementia (www.strokeassociation.org). Vascular dementia results from damage in the brain due to multiple strokes. Dementia can also be caused by Parkinson's disease, AIDS, toxic conditions, vitamin B12 deficiency, thyroid disorders, or drug interactions. Neuropsychological assessment plays an important role in accurate diagnosis, especially in distinguishing normal from abnormal aging. It may also be useful in distinguishing organically based dementia from *pseudodementia due to depression.*

Exposure to Toxic Substances

Over 50,000 chemicals are currently in use. Many of these, such as lead, mercury, and organic solvents, have been known to cause impairment of brain functioning. In addition, many recreational substances, such as alcohol, ecstasy, and methamphetamine, result in known or suspected neuropsychological symptoms. Identification of these symptoms can be used to help maintain safe work sites, identify the need for treatment, or monitor change over time. In cases where unsafe work safety standards have not been implemented, the quantification of neuropsychological deficits might become part of litigation proceedings.

NEUROPSYCHOLOGICAL TESTING

The basic strategy of neuropsychological assessment is to evaluate each domain of functioning listed in Table 8.1. Tests are typically selected in an effort to provide a complete description of each of these functions (see a brief description of many of these tests on endoflifecare.tripod.com/huntdiseasefaqs/id120.html). The result will be scores on how good the client's abilities are in attention, learning–memory, language, spatial abilities, motor performance, and executive functioning. Different disorders will typically have different patterns of test performance. Thus, a patient with a left hemisphere stroke will be likely to have language difficulties, whereas a patient with early Alzheimer's disease will be expected to have mainly problems with their memory. The data from neuropsychological testing can then be used to answer the sorts of referral questions detailed at the beginning of the chapter.

Formal neuropsychological testing provides crucial information in the form of test scores. However, it is also important to place the scores within the context of information derived from an interview with the client. An important part of the interview is that it provides observations of the person's behavior, including how they describe themselves. For example, a client might state they do not have any problems with their cognitive functioning. In contrast, they may have done poorly on formal testing. This pattern suggests poor awareness of their deficits. The interview also provides essential details of the person's history, which can make test scores more meaningful. Such a history would include information related to their early development, academic performance, interpersonal relations, occupational performance, and details surrounding the onset and course of their illness. Client records, particularly medical reports, also help to make the test scores more meaningful.

To assess the effects of trauma or other causes of injury to the brain, it is important to obtain an estimate of the individual's premorbid cognitive functioning. This may be accomplished in various ways, perhaps most precisely from scores on standardized tests of intelligence or achievement that were administered before the injury occurred. Other indexes of premorbid functioning, though less precise, are educational level and socioeconomic status. In addition, it must be borne in mind that the functions of different areas of the brain vary not only with their location, but also with chronological age, gender, and other demographic factors.

Neuropsychological Screening

Because a complete neuropsychological examination is a time-consuming process, a number of brief screening procedures are available. The results of screening can be used to decide whether to refer for medical examination or if an extensive neuropsychological battery is warranted. Sometimes these screening tests are selected from tests used for assessing neuropsychological functions. Typical examples are the Bender Visual Motor Gestalt Test, Benton Visual Retention Test, and Trail Making. Other tests have been designed specifically for screening purposes. Examples are the Quick Neurological Screening Test, Screening Test for the Luria–Nebraska Neuropsychological Battery, Cognistat, and the Repeatable Battery for the Assessment of Neuropsychological Status.

TABLE 8.1   Frequent Neuropsychological Tests and Functions

Comprehensive Neuropsychological Assessment Batteries
Wechsler Adult Intelligence Scale-III (WAIS-R NI)
Wechsler Intelligence Scale for Children-IV (WISC-IV Integrated)
Halstead–Reitan Neuropsychological Test Battery
Luria–Nebraska Neuropsychological Test Battery

Screening Instruments
Quick Neurological Screening Test-II
Screening Test for the Luria–Nebraska Neuropsychological Battery
Repeatable Battery for the Assessment of Neuropsychological Status

Attention
WAIS-III/WISC-IV Digit Span and Arithmetic subtests
Trail Making

Learning and Memory
Wechsler Memory Scale-III
Test of Memory and Learning
Wide Range Assessment of Memory and Learning
Memory Assessment Scales
Benton Visual Retention Test

Language
WAIS-III/WISC-IV Vocabulary and Information subtests
Boston Diagnostic Aphasia Exam
Dyslexia Screening Test
Western Aphasia Battery

Spatial Abilities
WAIS-III/WISC-IV Block Design subtest
Bender Visual Motor Gestalt Test

Motor Performance
Finger tapping
Grip strength

Executive Functions, Abstraction Ability
WAIS-III Similarities subtest
Category Test
Wisconsin Card Sorting Test

Emotional and Behavioral Functions
Beck Depression Inventory
Child Behavior Checklist
Minnesota Multiphasic Personality Inventory-2
Personality Inventory for Children

Neuropsychological Test Batteries

One strategy of neuropsychological assessment is to use a standard or "fixed" battery that evaluates all or most relevant functions. One advantage of using such a battery is that every client is given the same tests such that comparisons can be readily made between one client and the next. A fixed battery also allows a pattern to emerge in which the client's high and low performances will stand out against a background of average performance.

Wechsler Intelligence Scales.   Most neuropsychologists use all or portions of the Wechsler intelligence scales (WAIS-III/WISC-IV) as a core feature for their evaluations (see Chapter 6). This is because considerable information can usually be obtained by looking at the pattern of Wechsler intelligence scale scores. On a global level, the neuropsychologist can note whether the person's Full Scale IQ is lower than expected. For example, it would be unusual to find an attorney or other professional who had an IQ in the average to low average range. If they had sustained a head injury or a stroke, it would suggest that these events are the cause for this lower than expected performance.

It is also possible to look at more specific scores on the Wechsler intelligence scales. As noted in Chapter 6, the index scores are ideally suited to understanding a person's relative strengths and weaknesses. The Processing Speed Index (speed by which a person solves problems) and Working Memory Index (attention) are generally sensitive to any compromise in cognitive functioning. It would be expected, for example, to see these as the lowest scores following a closed head injury (or many other types of neuropsychological complaints). However, other patterns might emerge as well, depending on the type of injury or illness and the part of the brain that is affected. For example, low scores on the Perceptual Organization Index combined with a much higher score on the Verbal Comprehension Index might indicate damage to the right hemisphere. This is logical given that nonverbal (or visuospatial) abilities are mediated by the right hemisphere, and these nonverbal abilities are measured by the Perceptual Organization Index.

The necessity of obtaining a clearer definition of the effects of organic brain damage on cognitive and behavioral functioning led to the development of a modification of the WAIS-R known as the WAIS-R as a Neuropsychological Instrument (WAIS-R NI) (see Groth–Marnat, Gallagher, Hale, & Kaplan, 2000). Except for some modifications, as in the Object Assembly puzzles, the WAIS-R subtests were retained on the WAIS-R NI. In addition, a number of alternative administrations to the existing subtests were developed. A set of similar procedures has been developed for the WISC-IV and is sold as the WISC-IV Integrated. The central strategy of these alternative administration procedures is to provide a set of procedures that help to partial out the processes a person uses to solve various problems. For example, if a person does poorly on a test requesting that they recall factual information about everyday life, we really don't know if they did poorly because they never knew the correct answers or because, during the testing, they had difficulty retrieving the information. Thus, the WAIS-R NI and WISC-IV integrated provide a series of multiple-choice questions in addition to the standard WAIS-R/WISC-IV verbal questions. If, indeed, information retrieval was the problem (but they knew the answers), then they would be able to recognize the correct answers when they were presented in a multiple-choice format. In addition, an analysis of the types of errors a client makes also yields useful information for diagnosis and rehabilitation.

Halstead–Reitan Neuropsychological Test Battery. Subtests comprising the Halstead–Reitan Neuropsychological Test Battery (Reitan & Wolfson, 1993) are described in Table 8.2. Each of these was selected because it was found to be uniquely suited to detecting brain impairment (so-called *brain-sensitive* tests). Different forms of these tests are included on the Adult Battery (ages 15 years and over), the Older Children's Battery (ages 9 to 14 years), and the Young Children's Battery (ages 5 to 8 years). The tests and procedures tap a number of sensory abilities, perceptual–motor speed and dexterity, expressive and receptive language functions, memory, concept formation, and abstract reasoning. Any of these abilities may be affected by damage to or dysfunction of the central nervous system or to the sense receptors and muscles. Among the more complex tests on the Halstead–Reitan are the Category Test and the Trail Making Test. On the Category Test the examinee deduces general principles from information presented on slides. On the Trail Making Test, he or she draws lines to connect numbered and lettered circles (from 1 to A, from 2 to B, and so on, alternating numbers and letters).

In addition to these "brain-sensitive" tests, the Halstead–Reitan battery also includes the WAIS III/WISC IV and the Minnesota Multiphasic Personality Inventory-2. As a result, it includes a comprehensive assessment of brain and personality function. In addition to its comprehensiveness, it has ample research support. However, it has been criticized for being too long (6 to 8 hours when the WAIS-III/WISC-IV and MMPI-2 are included) and not assessing memory in sufficient depth.

Luria–Nebraska Neuropsychological Battery. This test battery (Golden, Purisch, & Hammeke, 1985) was designed to assess the following functions: cerebral dominance; tactile, visual, and motor functions; perception and reproduction of pitch and rhythm; receptive and expressive speech; reading, writing, and arithmetic; memory; concept formation; and other intellectual processes. Both forms (I and II) of the battery can be scored by computer, but Form I can also be scored by hand. Like the Halstead–Reitan, the Luria–Nebraska provides a comprehensive assessment of neuropsychological functioning. The Luria–Nebraska takes only about one-third as much time to administer as the Halstead–Reitan, but it has been criticized for relying too heavily on language skills and for failing to detect aphasia and certain other neuropsychological disorders adequately.

Tests Organized around Specific Functions. An alternative to the use of a comprehensive fixed battery is to select various tests based on a combination of the referral question, client's presenting symptoms, and how the person performed on tests given earlier in the assessment process. Often the selection of tests is based on testing out various hypotheses related to a client's functioning. This hypotheses-testing approach is flexible and potentially time efficient. Sometimes the tests given to assess the various functions are single, narrow tests. Often, however, the tests are drawn from portions of the test batteries described previously. For example, the Digit Span subtest (repeating sets of numbers forward and backward) from the WAIS-III/WISC-IV is used as one of several tests to evaluate attention. The hypotheses-testing approach has been criticized for focusing too extensively on client weaknesses and does not have as much of a research base as the fixed-battery approach. A major reason for the lack of research is that the test is more difficult to investigate since each case is unique, thereby making it difficult to make generalizations about validity. It should be noted, however, that the contrast between a fixed-battery versus a more flexible hypotheses-testing approach is overly polarized. In actual practice, most neuropsychologists use a core set of procedures (usually the WAIS-III/WISC-IV), but then add to them based on what additional information they would like to obtain.

Typically, a hypotheses-testing approach will investigate each one of a series of client functions. The following listing provides a brief description of the function being assessed, followed by a sample of some of the tests that might be used to assess it.

Attention.   To function effectively, a person must be able to focus on a task. This requires filtering out irrelevant, distracting information. The person must also have the flexibility to shift her or his attention when necessary. A person who becomes overly focused on a task might express this symptomatically by repeating the task again and again (*perseverating*). In contrast, a person who shifts her or his focus too easily might have a high level of distractibility. Optimal attention requires a balance between these two extremes. Since attention is a complex function and easily interacts with other abilities, it is easily disrupted by central nervous system dysfunction.

Both the Digit Span and Arithmetic subtests from the WAIS-III/WISC-IV are good measures of attention. Another frequently used test is Trail Making from the Halstead–Reitan battery (see description in Table 8.2). Trails B is a particularly good measure since it requires the person to shift attention back and forth between ascending numbers and then letters in alphabetical order.

Learning and Memory Functions.   Problems with short- and long-term memory are indicators not only of mental retardation, but of specific learning disabilities, cerebral trauma, neurological disorders, attention-deficit hyperactivity disorder (ADHD), aging, and even emotional disorders. Deficits in recall memory, and free recall in particular, are more pronounced than declines in recognition memory in brain-injured persons. Patients typically show less deficit on tests of recognition or identification memory than on tests of recall memory. They also show less deficit on implicit than explicit memory and less deficit on skill memory than event memory.

Because memory and learning are not unitary capacities, a battery of tests is often needed to identify which aspects of memory and learning have been affected. Such batteries cannot take the place of intelligence tests, which assess a wider range of cognitive functions, but they provide supplementary data and diagnostic clues. The Wechsler Memory Scale-III is the most frequently used memory test and can be administered to clients between the ages of 16 and 89. It measures both auditory–verbal and visual–nonverbal memory in both immediate and delayed (by 20 minutes) recall modes. It has the important advantage of using the same standardization population as the WAIS-III. This means that comparisons of a client who has taken both tests can be readily made.

Three additional popular memory assessment batteries are the Test of Memory and Learning (TOMAL), the Wide Range Assessment of Memory and Learning (WRAML), and the Memory Assessment Scales (MAS). The TOMAL, WRAML, and MAS measure verbal and nonverbal (visual) memory functions. The first two tests are designed for children and adolescents, and the last one for adults. All three batteries are highly reliable mea-

TABLE 8.2   Tests and Procedures for the Halstead–Reitan Neuropsychological Test Battery

Category Test. Measures abstract reasoning and concept formation; requires examinee to find a rule for categorizing pictures of geometric shapes.

Tactual Performance Test. Measures kinesthetic and sensorimotor ability; requires blindfolded examinee to place blocks in appropriate cutout on an upright board with dominant hand, then nondominant hand, then both hands; also tests for incidental memory of blocks.

Speech Sounds Perception Test. Measures attention and auditory-visual synthesis; requires examinee to pick from four choices the written version of taped nonsense words.

Seashore Rhythm Test. Measures attention and auditory perception; requires examinee to indicate whether paired musical rhythms are the same or different.

Finger-Tapping Test. Measures motor speed; requires examinee to tap a telegraph key-like lever as quickly as possible for 10 seconds.

Grip Strength. Measures grip strength with dynamometer; requires examinee to squeeze as hard as possible; separate trials with each hand.

Trail Making, Parts A, B. Measures scanning ability, mental flexibility, and speed; requires examinee to connect numbers (Part A) or numbers and letters in alternating order (Part B) with a pencil line under pressure of time.

Tactile Form Recognition. Measures sensory–perceptual ability; requires examinee to recognize simple shapes (e.g., triangle) placed in the palm of the hand.

Sensory–Perceptual Exam. Measures sensory–perceptual ability; requires examinee to respond to simple bilateral sensory tasks (e.g., detecting which finger has been touched, which ear has received a brief sound); assesses the visual fields.

Aphasia Screening Test. Measures expressive and receptive language abilities; tasks include naming a pictured item (e.g., fork); repeating short phrases; copying task (not a measure of aphasia), included here for historical reasons.

Supplementary. WAIS III, WRAT 3, MMPI 2, memory tests such as Wechsler Memory Scale III, or Rey Auditory Verbal Learning Test.

(Adapted from Robert J. Gregory, *Psychological testing: History, principles, and applications* [4th ed.]. Boston, MA: Allyn and Bacon.Copyright © 2004 by Pearson Education. Reprinted by permission of the publisher.)

sures of memory and learning functions. The MAS manual provides profiles of scores for patients with neurological disorders such as dementia, closed head injury, left-hemisphere lesions, and right-hemisphere lesions.

A shorter (10 minutes), less comprehensive memory test that is useful for screening is the Benton Visual Retention Test. It consists of 10 designs presented individually to the examinee. The examinee is shown each design briefly and then tries to copy it from memory. The small shapes included at the periphery of most of the drawings are considered important in determining the examinee's ability to maintain integrity of the visual field. The Benton is scored based on the number and types of errors. Research with the Benton has provided support for its sensitivity to traumatic brain injury, attention-deficit disorder, and various types of dementia.

Language.   Language difficulties frequently occur with clients having acquired brain injury, especially when the injury is to the left hemisphere. The most common difficulties are the aphasias. Such disorders can involve an extremely diverse set of symptoms including difficulty finding the correct word, poor auditory comprehension, poor articulation, impaired writing, loss of verbal fluency, misspoken words, reading difficulty, and poor repetition of words and sentences.

Extremely valuable information regarding a client's language functions can often be obtained by carefully observing a client's behavior or using informal procedures, such as "repeat these words after me" or "write this sentence." The WAIS-III/WISC-IV Vocabulary, Information, and Similarities subtests (see description in Chapter 6) also provide useful information regarding language functions. A more detailed, comprehensive assessment of language functions may be obtained from specialized batteries such as the Boston Diagnostic Aphasia Exam, Dyslexia Screening Test, and the Western Aphasia Battery.

Spatial Abilities.   In contrast to the mainly language difficulties associated with dysfunction to the left hemisphere, spatial difficulties are more likely to be associated with problems in the right hemisphere. One way of assessing for this is to see how easily a client can reproduce an object. To do this accurately, the client must first perceive it accurately (intact visuoperceptual abilities), then organize where it should be arranged (intact visuospatial abilities), and finally draw it correctly (intact visuomotor abilities).

Useful information regarding spatial abilities can often be determined by noting performance on the WAIS-III/WISC-IV Block Design, Matrix Reasoning, and Picture Completion subtests. A number of scoring procedures have also been developed to evaluate simple drawings, such as a clock, bicycle, or person. A brief and time-honored procedure is the Bender Visual Motor Gestalt Test (Bender, 1938; Canter, 1983), which consists of nine geometric designs on 4- by 6-inch white cards; these are shown one at a time to the examinee, who is told to copy each card. Significant distortions in copying the designs are interpreted as indicating poor spatial (mainly visuoconstructional) abilities. Children aged 8 years and older of average or above-average intelligence usually make no more than two errors on the Bender. Errors considered indicative of organic brain damage include shape distortions; design rotations; problems integrating the design; disproportionate, overlapping, or fragmented drawings; and perseverations (Lacks, 1999).

Motor Performance.   Tests of motor function can be used to detect the subtle difficulties with strength and coordination that are often the result of brain dysfunction. These tests can also be used to identify differences between the left and right side of the body, which may reflect dysfunction in the motor regions of either the left or right hemisphere. In such cases, the difference must usually exceed 20% or more. For example, the Halstead–Reitan Finger Tapping Test (see Table 8.2) requests clients to tap their index finger as rapidly as they can for 10 seconds. If, for example, a client has an average of 50 taps for the right hand (averaged over five different trials), but only 30 taps with the left hand, this represents 40% less taps with the left hand compared to the right hand. This lowered left-hand tapping speed suggests some brain dysfunction to the right hemisphere (since the right hemisphere controls the left side). Grip Strength (see Table 8.2) similarly looks at the difference between the strength of the right hand compared to the left.

Executive Functions, Abstraction Ability. Executive functions refer to a client's ability to regulate and direct his or her behavior. This includes the ability to initiate behavior, plan, monitor, and move toward a goal. If a person has impaired executive abilities, then he or she will exist in a semivegetative state unless someone or something stimulates and organizes his or her actions. This is true even if other cognitive abilities are intact. Another component of executive abilities involves insight. In some cases clients might be completely or partially unaware that they have any cognitive difficulties. This is crucial in treatment planning, since a prerequisite of treatment is that persons must acknowledge they indeed have problems that they need to work on. Often, abstract thinking is also included as part of a person's executive functioning.

An important means of evaluating a client's executive function is through careful observations. Often a parent or spouse can provide useful information. Poor awareness of difficulties would be indicated by family members who describe considerable difficulties versus clients who think they are functioning normally. Additional informal procedures might be to ask clients to plan a birthday party or to describe their perception of the presence and extent of their cognitive difficulties.

Abstract reasoning is often associated with executive functioning. As a result, it is often useful to look at something like the Similarities subtest of the WAIS-III or the Category Test of the Halstead–Reitan (see Table 8.2). Whereas Similarities assesses verbal abstract reasoning, the Category Test is more a measure of nonverbal abstract reasoning. Another measure of nonverbal abstract reasoning is the Wisconsin Card-Sorting Test (WCST) (Heaton, Chelune, Talley, et al., 1993). It is untimed (20 to 30 minutes) and appropriate for a wide age range (6.5 to 80 years). The WCST consists of four stimulus cards and a pack of 64 response cards. Each response card contains one to four symbols (triangle, star, cross, or circle) in one of four colors (red, green, yellow, or blue). The examinee is directed to sort the response cards beneath the four stimulus cards according to a certain principle (color, shape, or number). The examinee is not informed of the sorting principle, but merely whether his or her responses are right or wrong. After 10 consecutive correct responses have been made, the examiner shifts the sorting principle without warning (say from "color" to "form"). Scoring is typically in terms of the number of trials needed to make a certain number of consecutive correct responses using each sorting principle. The revised manual provides normative, reliability, and validity information on the test based on child and adolescent samples.

Emotional Status. In addition to assessing the various cognitive functions, it is also important to understand a client's emotional status. Sometimes emotional difficulties can be the direct result of physical changes in the brain. In other cases, clients have emotional reactions to their perceived loss of functioning. Their level of emotional functioning often needs to be treated to optimize improvement. For example, a depressed client will have a difficult time being motivated to become involved in rehabilitation. Emotional functioning is also useful for predicting outcome. In general, optimistic, extroverted clients have better outcomes than those who are more pessimistic and introverted.

A brief, narrow assessment of a client's level of depression can be obtained using the 21-item Beck Depression Inventory-II or the Geriatric Depression Scale. In contrast, a much more comprehensive evaluation can be obtained with the 567-item Minnesota Personality

Inventory-2. Chapters 17 and 18 describes these and other similar instruments in much greater depth.

Computer-Based Neuropsychological Assessment

Advances in neurophysiology and cognitive psychology, together with improvements in computer technology and psychometric methodology during the past three decades, have led to the increased use of computers for administering, scoring, and interpreting neuropsychological tests. As a result, neuropsychological testing has become faster, more flexible, and more focused; not only the accuracy of responses, but also their speed and even their intensity can be determined by means of computer-based assessment.

Among the many neuropsychological tests with computer-based versions are the Category Test and the Wisconsin Card Sorting Test. Computer software for components of the Halstead–Reitan Neuropsychological Battery and the Luria–Nebraska Neuropsychological Battery is also available. In addition to single tests and test batteries that can be administered either by a human examiner or a computer are instruments administered exclusively by computer. An example is MicroCog: Assessment of Cognitive Functioning, Version 2.4. Designed to assess cognitive functioning in adults aged 18 to 80 years, MicroCog comes in a Standard form requiring 50 to 60 minutes testing time and a Short form requiring 30 minutes. The 18 tests on the Standard form were standardized on 810 adults reportedly representative of the U.S. national population, with separate norms for nine age groups, as well as norms adjusted for educational level. Summary scores are provided for nine areas of functioning: Attention–Mental Control, Memory, Reasoning–Calculation, Spatial Processing, Reaction Time, Information-Processing Accuracy, Information-Processing Speed, Cognitive Functioning, and Cognitive Proficiency. Validity data for various clinical groups (major depression, dementia, schizophrenia, alcoholism, epilepsy, mixed psychiatric, lupus, etc.) and correlations with other neuropsychological tests are given in the MicroCog manual.

SUMMARY

1. Neuropsychological assessment is based on an understanding of how tests of mental abilities can be used to evaluate the relationship between brain functioning and behavior. Behavioral observations, interviews of the patient and other people, neurological tests, brain-imaging procedures, and psychological tests may all contribute to this process. The results of neuropsychological assessment can be used to assist with diagnosis, design treatment, and assist with legal decision making.

2. Testing infants and preschoolers is difficult because they often lack motivation and fatigue easily. One limitation is that the reliabilities between such tests and measurements taken in older childhood and adolescence are generally low since infant and early childhood abilities are more changeable. In addition, the primarily sensorimotor tasks given to infants and preschoolers are very different from the more mental types of tasks given to older children. Despite this, infant intelligence tests are useful in screening for mental retardation, developmental delay, and organic brain disorders.

3. Arnold Gesell and his colleagues at Yale University during the 1920s and 1930s provided developmental norms and tests that served as guidelines and methods for practice and research with children. The Gesell Developmental Schedules, the Bayley Scales of Infant Development (BSID-II), the Denver Developmental Screening Test (Denver-II), and other measures of abilities in infants and young children have contributed to scientific knowledge of child development and disorders. Most tests designed to assess and track delays in the development of young children now follow the criteria specified in the Individuals with Disabilities Education Act (IDEA). Two examples of tests designed specifically according to the five IDEA domains are the First-STEP Screening Test for Evaluating Preschoolers and the American Guidance Service (AGS) Early Screening Profiles. An older but still widely used test that adheres fairly closely to the IDEA criteria is the McCarthy Scales of Children's Abilities.

4. Luria's Planning–Attention–Simultaneous–Successive has been influential in understanding neuropsychological dysfunction and designing cognitive tests. It is based on the three functional units of (1) attention (attention and discrimination of stimuli; located in the brain stem and limbic system), (2) reception, elaboration, storage of information (can be either simultaneous or sequential processing; located in the posterior portion of brain), and (3) planning (programming, regulation, verification; located in the anterior portion of the cortex).

5. Frequent neuropsychological symptoms include dementia (general loss in abilities due to organic factors), visuoconstructive disorders (difficulty constructing objects), visual neglect (neglecting one half of one's visual field), agnosia (inability to recognize objects), apraxia (inability to perform purposeful movements), aphasia (difficulty understanding written or spoken language), alexia and dyslexia (impairment in reading), and agraphia and dysgraphia (impairment in writing).

6. Neuropsychologists typically work with the following types of disorders: head injury, tumors, cerebrovascular disease, dementia, exposure to toxic substances (industrial toxins, alcohol, recreational drugs), and learning disabilities (see Chapter 7)

7. The fixed-battery approach uses a set battery of tests, with every client thereby providing a pattern for strengths and weaknesses and a standard procedure for every patient. A flexible-hypotheses testing approach is highly responsive to the referral question, can be altered depending on incoming information about the client, and is time efficient. However, it tends to be overly focused on deficits and is difficult to research.

8. The Halstead–Reitan Neuropsychological Test Battery is comprised of a series of brain-sensitive tests in combination with the Wechsler intelligence scales and the MMPI-2 (6 to 8 hours). The Luria–Nebraska assesses cerebral dominance; tactile, visual, and motor functions; perception and reproduction of pitch and rhythm; receptive and expressive speech; reading, writing, and arithmetic; memory; concept formation; and other intellectual processes (2 to 3 hours).

9. Neuropsychological tests are typically organized around the following functions: attention, learning and memory, language, spatial abilities, motor performance, executive functions and abstraction, and emotional and behavioral functions. A complete picture of the client's functioning can be determined by his or her performance in each of these areas.

MASTERING THE CHAPTER OBJECTIVES

1. *Neuropsychological assessment*
   a. Define neuropsychological assessment.
   b. What are three typical questions that neuropsychological assessment might be used to answer?

2. *Problems with infant and preschool assessment*
   a. What are three major difficulties with assessing infants and preschoolers?
   b. Why do infant and preschool tests have a difficult time predicting later child abilities?

3. *Common developmental assessment instruments*
   a. Briefly describe the Brazelton Neonatal Behavioral Assessment Scale, the Bayley Scales of Infant Development, and the McCarthy scales.
   b. Compare FirstSTEp with the AGS Early Screening Profiles, and compare DAYC with the Infant–Toddler Developmental Assessment in terms of their purposes, composition, and scoring.

4. *Luria's PASS model*
   a. Describe Luria's PASS model.
   b. How could the symptoms of learning disabilities and ADHD be conceptualized based on the PASS model?

5. *Neuropsychological symptoms*
   a. Define the following: dementia, visuoconstructive disorders, visual neglect, agnosia, apraxia, aphasia, alexia/dyslexia, and agraphia/dysgraphia.
   b. List the types of symptoms you would expect to see with damage to the right hemisphere and to the left hemisphere.

6. *Neuropsychological disorders*
   a. Describe two features of the following disorders: head injuries, cerebrovascular disease, tumors, dementia, exposure to toxic substances.
   b. Describe the symptoms of someone you are familiar with who has one of the disorders you described in question 6a.

7. *Fixed versus flexible battery approaches*
   a. Describe the advantages and disadvantages of the fixed-battery approach.
   b. Describe the advantages and disadvantages of the flexible hypotheses-testing approach.

8. *Halstead–Reitan and Luria–Nebraska batteries*
   a. What are the strengths and weaknesses of the Halstead–Reitan battery?
   b. Describe the Luria–Nebraska battery.

9. *Neuropsychological functions*
   a. Define four neuropsychological functions and state how you would evaluate them.
   b. Why do you think it's more difficult to describe executive functions than the other types of functions?

EXPERIENCING PSYCHOLOGICAL ASSESSMENT

1. Attention is often measured by having a person repeat a series of numbers that have been spoken out loud to them. Develop a string of progressively longer numbers (start with 2, then

3, and so on, all the way to 10 numbers). Now that you have developed this "test," evaluate four people by seeing how many numbers they can repeat without making any mistakes. The numbers might be standardized by developing a list of progressively longer numbers, administered by students in the class, and discussed.

2. Verbal memory is often assessed by reading a short story (paragraph length) to a person and then having them recall as many details as possible. Select (or develop) such a story, read it to four people, and note the differences between how well they did. The story might be standardized by selecting and administering the paragraph, and the results might be discussed in class.

3. Collect as much information as you can on the provisions of various laws concerning the identification, diagnosis, and intervention programs with children who are medically and/or environmentally at risk. Focus on Public Laws 94-142, 99-457, 101-476 (IDEA), 101-336 (ADA), and 102-119.

CHAPTER NINE

STANDARDIZED ACHIEVEMENT TESTS

CHAPTER OBJECTIVES

1. Describe the purpose, standardization, and accountability of achievement tests.
2. Describe what is meant by summative versus formative evaluation and norm-referenced versus criterion-referenced measurement.
3. Define the following four types of standardized achievement tests: survey test batteries, single-subject survey tests, diagnostic tests, prognostic tests.
4. List major considerations in selecting a standardized achievement test.
5. Describe the purpose of and some examples of common achievement test batteries.
6. Describe the purpose of and some examples of common achievement tests in specific areas.

Tests of achievement, defined as the level of knowledge, skill, or accomplishment in an area of endeavor, are the most popular of all psychometric instruments. Counting all classroom tests constructed by teachers and standardized tests sold to schools and other organizations, the number of achievement tests administered easily exceeds other types of psychological and educational tests. A large majority of the 50 states have mandated that students take achievement tests in some grades. Most standardized achievement tests administered in North American schools are in the areas of reading and language arts. Millions of dollars are spent each year on tests in mathematics, science, social studies, and other subject-matter areas as well.

FOUNDATIONS OF ACHIEVEMENT TESTING

Any test of ability (general intelligence, special abilities, achievement) actually measures what people have achieved. The items on tests of intelligence and special abilities, like those on achievement tests, require examinees to demonstrate some accomplishment. Scores on achievement tests are used for many of the same purposes as scores on other tests of general or specific abilities. These purposes include global and diagnostic assessment of individual abilities and evaluation of the effectiveness of educational and social programs.

Educational achievement tests are often better predictors of school marks than tests of intelligence and special abilities, but they cannot completely replace them. The accomplishments or attainments measured by general intelligence tests are broader and are the products of less formal and usually less recent learning experiences than those measured by standardized tests of achievement. Most achievement tests assess knowledge of something that has been explicitly taught, so scores on these tests tend to be influenced more by coaching than scores on tests of intelligence and special abilities.

A distinction between achievement tests and other measures of cognitive abilities can also be made in terms of their different emphases. Achievement tests focus more on the present, that is, on what a person knows or can do right now. On the other hand, tests of intelligence and special abilities focus on the future: they measure aptitude for learning, that is, what a person should be able to do with further education and training.

A number of popular achievement tests are linked to aptitude tests published by the same company and standardized on the same population of students. The combined use of these measures of achievement and aptitude can facilitate the interpretation of achievement test results beyond the information provided by the norms on the test alone. Conclusions can be drawn as to whether students are achieving up to their potential and in what content areas they are most likely to benefit from further instruction and study.

Historical Overview

The introduction of both oral and written tests of achievement in personnel and educational assessment is attributable in some measure to the Chinese experience. The selection of government employees by means of oral examinations began in China around 150 B.C. (Bowman, 1989). Written tests in composition and poetry, recopied and judged by two graders, were first used in China around A.D. 1370. Following the introduction of paper making into Europe, a skill that Europeans learned from the Arabs in the 12th century and that the latter had learned from the Chinese in the 8th century, written examinations began to replace oral examinations in some European universities. The first educational use of written tests in a European university reportedly occurred at Cambridge, England, in 1702, and the University of London was chartered as an examining center for written tests in 1836 (Green, 1991). Not until 1845, however, were written examinations administered on a large scale in the United States (Greene, Jorgensen, & Gerberich, 1954).

By the early 1800s the number of students in urban schools of the United States had grown too large for frequent administration of oral examinations. Nevertheless, oral testing continued to be the principal method for evaluating pupil achievement in this country until the latter half of the 19th century. In 1845, the Boston educator Horace Mann argued persuasively that written examinations, administered and scored under uniform conditions, were better measures of achievement than oral examinations. Mann's influence led the Boston schools to begin administering written examinations to pupils every year. It was hoped that this practice would help determine "the condition, improvement or deterioration of our schools" (Fish, 1941, p. 23). Despite the efforts of Mann and other educators, oral examinations continued to be the principal method of assessing school achievement for many years and were only gradually replaced by written tests. Meanwhile, the scoring of both oral and written tests remained fairly subjective.

The first objective test of achievement, one that could be reliably scored, was a handwriting scale constructed by the Englishman George Fisher in 1864. One year later, in an effort to raise educational standards, New York State initiated the Regents Examinations. In 1897 another important step in educational measurement was taken in J. M. Rice's classic study of the spelling abilities of schoolchildren. The results obtained from administering a 50-word spelling test to 33,000 children led Rice to conclude that as much was learned in 15 minutes as in 40 minutes of daily instruction in spelling. In later studies, Rice devised objective tests to assess the language skills and arithmetic achievements of children. These tests are generally viewed as the forerunner of standardized achievement testing, a foundation subsequently built on by other pioneers in educational measurement.

Several standardized achievement tests were published during the early years of the 20th century under the direction of E. L. Thorndike, whom Ross and Stanley (1954) viewed as the father of the educational testing movement. These tests included C. L. Stone's Arithmetic Test for the Fundamental Operations and the Arithmetic Reasoning Test (1908), S. A. Courtis's Arithmetic Tests Series (1909), and Thorndike's Scale of Handwriting for Children (1909). Demonstrations of the unreliability of grades assigned by teachers, even in more exact subjects such as mathematics (Starch & Elliot, 1913), led to an increased interest in objective, standardized testing. By the end of the 1920s, numerous standardized achievement tests were available, including batteries of measures such as the Stanford Achievement Test (1923) for elementary school pupils and the Iowa High School Content Examination (1924). In 1926, the multiple-choice Scholastic Aptitude Test replaced the essay tests that had previously been administered by the College Entrance Examination Board since the beginning of the century (Donlon, 1984). The new multiple-choice format, together with the invention of automated scoring machines, led to a rapid increase in the use of standardized tests for evaluating pupil achievement.

Rather than being motivated solely by educational and scientific concerns, the growth of achievement testing in the United States has been attributed in part to the fact that both sides in a public debate over public schools found the advocacy and results of testing politically useful (Levine, 1976). Even today standardized testing in the schools continues to have significant political ramifications. The continuing debate concerning nationally administered tests in basic educational subjects (reading, mathematics, etc.) for purposes of accountability in teachers and schools is illustrative of the contemporary politics of testing.

Essay and Objective Tests

Despite hundreds of research studies, the argument over the relative merits of essay and objective tests has never been completely resolved. In fact, it has often been alleged that today's teachers have gone overboard in their use of objective tests to the detriment of students' composition skills. Nevertheless, it is clear that carefully designed objective tests can measure not only memory for facts, but also many of the more complex objectives of instruction that formerly were evaluated only by essay examinations. A noteworthy trend in the past several decades has been toward tests that assess the attainment of higher-order instructional objectives, such as application, analysis, and evaluation. Another trend has been away from standardized achievement tests that attempt to gauge individual attainment of broad educational objectives and toward tests designed specifically for particular textbooks and teaching programs. Finally, in response to the criticism that objective tests foster poor writing and inadequate self-expression, greater emphasis is now placed on standardized essay tests of written expression. Constructed response tests in mathematics and science, protocols from laboratory experiments, and portfolios of work are also being used in an attempt to expand the assessment of student achievement (Aiken, 1998; Linn, 1992, Ch. 5).

Purposes and Functions of Achievement Tests

The basic function of achievement testing is to determine how much people know about certain topics or how well they can perform certain skills. The results of achievement testing inform students, as well as teachers and parents, about the students' scholastic accomplishments and deficiencies. Other functions of achievement testing include advanced placement, course credit, certification, and accountability for the quality of teaching. Such tests can also act as a stimulus for student learning, provide teachers and school administrators with information for planning or modifying the curriculum for a student or group of students, and serve as a means of evaluating the instructional program and staff. The tests measure only a sample of educational achievements, but presumably a representative sample, in a particular subject or grade.

Achievement tests are obviously not the only method of determining the effectiveness of instruction, but they provide measures of the quality of education and can thereby contribute to its improvement. At the very least, scores on achievement tests serve as flags that can alert teachers, school administrators, and parents to the instructional needs of individual students and groups.

Achievement tests cannot assess all objectives or goals espoused by educational philosophers. These tests do not directly measure such affective variables as delight and confidence in thinking, interest in educational subject matter, pleasure in using skills, enjoyment of reading, learning to learn and to cope with change, or the development of interpersonal and social skills. What they can measure, and more accurately than teachers' judgments or other subjective evaluations, is the extent to which students have attained certain cognitive objectives of instruction (Levine, 1976).

High-Stakes and Low-Stakes Testing

The results of testing may be used for multiple purposes concerning individuals and groups. For example, in educational contexts, tests can monitor student achievement and evaluate the effectiveness of educational programs. The extent to which the decisions contributed to test results have a significant impact or consequences for individual students and groups are referred to as the "stakes" of testing. Such decisions may involve the diagnosis of a student as having a learning disability, the appropriate educational program for a student with such a disability, placement of a student in a program for the gifted and talented, and promotion or graduation of a high school student. Other high-stakes decisions to which tests contribute are admission to a certain institution, placement in a desired program, awarded a scholarship, and professional certification or licensing (Heubert & Hauser, 1999).

In contrast to *high-stakes testing, low-stakes testing,* consists of administering a test for informational purposes alone or for highly tentative judgments. For example, test results may be used only to monitor academic progress and provide feedback on that progress to students, teachers, and parents, with no implication of a specific decision to be made (American Educational Research Association et al., 1999).

For whatever purposes they may be used, and whether high- or low-stakes decisions are involved, it is important for all psychometric instruments to measure what they were designed to measure and to do so reliably. When test results are used for high-stakes decisions that have important effects on students' lives, it is particularly important for the quality (validity, reliability, standardization, etc.) of the test to be as high as possible. Extreme care should be employed in administering and scoring the test, the results should be interpreted correctly, and the context in which decisions are made from the scores should be taken into account.

Teacher-Made and Standardized Tests

Standardized achievement tests represent only a fraction of the number of tests administered in the schools; students spend much more time taking teacher-made than standardized tests (Dorr-Bremme & Herman, 1986). Be that as it may, the purposes or functions of achievement testing described in the preceding paragraphs apply to both classroom tests prepared by teachers and standardized tests constructed by professionals in educational measurement. Teacher-made tests differ from standardized tests in certain important respects. A teacher-made test is more specific to a particular teacher, classroom, and unit of instruction and is easier to keep up to date than a standardized test. Consequently, a teacher-made test is more likely to reflect the current educational objectives of a particular school or teacher. Standardized tests, on the other hand, are built around a core of educational objectives common to many different schools. These objectives represent the combined judgments of subject-matter experts, who cooperate with test-construction specialists in developing tests. Standardized achievement tests are also concerned as much or more with understanding and thinking processes as with factual knowledge. Thus, teacher-made tests and standardized tests are complementary rather than opposing methods of evaluating achievement. They measure somewhat different but equally important things, and, depending on the objectives of the particular classroom or school, both kinds of tests should be employed. When a particular standardized test does not assess the educational goals of a certain school system, other standardized tests or even a teacher-made test should be considered.

In addition to being more carefully constructed and having broader content coverage than teacher-made tests, standardized achievement tests have norms and are usually more reliable. For these reasons, standardized achievement tests are particularly useful in comparing individual pupils for the purpose of class placement and in evaluating different curricula by assessing the relative achievements of different schools and districts. The diagnostic function of a test, whereby a person's abilities and disabilities in a certain subject or area are determined, may be served by both teacher-made and standardized tests. However, standardized tests are somewhat more effective for this purpose. Decisions pertaining to the individualization of instruction, the placement of students at particular levels of instruction, and remedial education are also generally made on the basis of scores on standardized rather than teacher-made tests.

Accountability

Test scores have been used not only to assess student performance, but also to evaluate teachers and schools. Holding teachers accountable for the extent of their success in instructing students, or *accountability,* has been a controversial topic in education for many years. Should teachers, who typically are not permitted to select their students but must try to teach everyone assigned to them, be rewarded only when students attain the instructional objectives and not rewarded or even penalized when they fail to do so? As a result of increasing public concern over the failure of schools to do an adequate job of educating students, particular attention has been given to responsibility for teaching effectiveness. Attempts have been made in both the public and private sectors to hold teachers accountable for student learning. In keeping with these efforts, the competencies that students must attain to complete a given grade or course of study or to graduate from high school are specified. Then evaluation of the effectiveness of instruction is based on the attainment of these competencies, as indicated largely by scores on achievement tests.

Unfortunately, many students and parents view formal education from a rather narrow vendor–consumer perspective, in which schools are seen as markets that "sell" educational products to student customers. Such a perspective places the responsibility for student learning almost completely on the teachers, educational materials, and structure and dynamics of the organizations in which learning takes place. Teachers realize, however, that it is difficult if not impossible to teach students who are not interested in learning the subject matter and/or who fail to accept some of the responsibility for their own education. Thus, in addition to "teacher accountability," the importance of "student responsibility" and "parent responsibility" for the learning process needs to be emphasized. The following letter from an eighth-grade teacher is informative:

> I asked eighth-grade students in three math classes to raise their hands if they planned to attend a college or university upon high school graduation. With the exception of two or three students in each class, all hands went up. Yet, approximately half of those who said they planned to pursue a tertiary education had not bothered to complete the math assignment. Many had been too busy watching television, playing video games, talking on the telephone, visiting friends, shopping, or just stalking the streets looking for something to do. Instead of blaming teachers, administrators, and college entrance exams for personal failings, it's time for students and their parents to accept the responsibility for their educational successes or failures. Parents who place a high value on learning and teach self-discipline, respect for others, personal integrity, and plain old hard work have children who are more likely to have the self-confidence and skills to achieve their future goals. (*US News,* April 30, 2001)

Performance Contracting

Accountability is associated with *performance contracting,* that is, making teachers' salaries commensurate with their teaching effectiveness. An important criterion of teaching effectiveness consists of pretest to posttest changes in student knowledge or competency. In using tests to determine the extent to which teachers have fulfilled a contract to teach the educational material to students, the same or equivalent tests are administered at both the beginning and end of an instructional unit or course. Consequently, the greater the gains in student achievement from pretest to posttest are, the higher the teacher's pay. A frequent result of such before-and-after testing is, unfortunately, overattention to the content of the tests at the expense of other important instructional objectives.

When combined with other measures of performance, achievement test scores can and should contribute to decisions regarding accountability and performance contracting. However, they have definite limitations when used for this purpose. It might seem as if determining the significance of differences or changes in test scores would pose no problem. Presumably, all one needs to do is subtract pretest scores from posttest scores and analyze the differences in whatever way is considered appropriate. One drawback of this approach, however, is that raw difference scores can be very unreliable. This is particularly true when the reliability coefficients of the pretest and posttest scores, which, although higher than the reliability of the difference scores, are still fairly low. Another statistical problem encountered in analyzing difference scores is *regression toward the mean*. This is the tendency for examinees whose pretest scores are very low or very high to obtain posttest scores that are closer to the mean. The use of regressed difference scores is often recommended as a way of dealing with regression toward the mean, but such a procedure is not always advisable. More complex statistical procedures for analyzing changes in test scores have been proposed, though all have limitations of one kind or another.

Summative and Formative Evaluation

Traditional educational practice calls for administering an achievement test at the end of an instructional unit or course to determine whether students have attained specified objectives. In this procedure, referred to as *summative evaluation,* a test score is viewed as an end product, or summing up, of large units of educational experience. In contrast to summative evaluation, the need for *formative evaluation* is a consequence of the belief that instruction and evaluation should be integrated. The purpose of formative evaluation is to help both students and teachers focus on the learning experiences needed to move toward mastery of the subject. When evaluation is formative, testing and other methods of assessing educational progress take place continuously during the instructional process. Instructional units are developed that include testing as an ongoing, integral part of instruction, rather than simply a culmination of the process. In this way, the learner's performance is monitored throughout the instructional sequence and can serve to direct review and further learning.

Norm-Referenced and Criterion-Referenced Measurement

Not only has educational measurement traditionally been summative rather than formative; it has also been norm-referenced rather than criterion-referenced. A person's score on a *norm-referenced test* is interpreted by comparing it with the distribution of scores of a particular norm (standardization) group. In contrast, a person's score on a *criterion-referenced test* is interpreted by comparing it with an established standard or criterion of effective performance.[1] This standard may be formulated from a consensus of a group of people in all walks of life who are concerned with education-school teachers and school administrators, parents, measurement experts, and politicians. In terms of content, norm-referenced tests are typically broader and contain more complex tasks than criterion-referenced tests. Consequently, individual differences in scores on a norm-referenced test tend to be greater than those on a criterion-referenced test.

Despite differences in the purpose and design of norm-referenced and criterion-referenced tests, a particular achievement test can function in both ways. How much material a student has learned (criterion-referenced function) and how his or her performance compares with that of other students (norm-referenced function) can frequently be determined by the same instrument.

Criterion-referenced tests designed to measure achievement in single subjects, such as reading or mathematics, as well as batteries of criterion-referenced tests, are available. Another product offered by certain testing companies is single-subject tests combined with matching instructional strategies in these subjects. Customized criterion-referenced tests or banks of criterion-referenced items in a number of subjects are available from certain companies. These custom-built tests have the advantage of being tailored to the objectives of a particular school system, but they also have disadvantages. In addition to the problem of deciding on an acceptable passing score or mastery level on each test, the need for a large number of subtests to measure many different educational objectives requires each subtest to be relatively short; hence its reliability is fairly low. Also, the problem of how the reliabilities and validities of the various subtests and the test as a whole should be determined has not been completely resolved.

National Assessment of Educational Progress

Certain achievement tests are administered on a school-, district-, or state-wide basis to evaluate the educational progress of students and monitor the long-term effectiveness of particular educational programs. The results of such system-wide testing are reported in the media and are often used to support legislative action and expenditures concerned with public education. Although a number of achievement tests are administered on a nationwide basis, no national achievement test is given periodically to evaluate the educational status of representative samples of students from every state. The tests administered by the National Assessment of Educational Progress come closest to meriting this distinction.

A criterion-referenced approach has guided the National Assessment of Educational Progress (NAEP), also known as "The Nation's Report Card." The NAEP is a continuing nationwide survey of the knowledge, skills, understandings, and attitudes of young Americans. Its stated purpose is "to improve the effectiveness of our Nation's schools by making objective information about student performance in selected learning areas available to policy makers at the national, state, and local levels" (Public Law 100-297, sec. 3401). Since 1969, NAEP has periodically assessed the abilities of large samples of Americans in four

---

[1]Some writers (e.g., Anastasi & Urbina, 1997) prefer the term *domain-referenced test* to criterion-referenced test. Both terms indicate that the frame of reference employed in interpreting scores on a test is the content of the test, rather than the sample of examinees on whom the test was standardized.

age groups (9, 13, 17, and 25–35 years) in arts, civics, geography, mathematics, reading, science, U.S. history, and writing. A stratified random sampling procedure has been used in the National NAEP to select a certain number of persons of each gender, socioeducational status, and race from four geographical regions and four types of communities. Although many questions are asked concerning each topic, the fact that both examinees and items are sampled necessitates only one relatively short testing period (50 minutes) for each person. Adults are assessed individually, and younger persons are assessed on both an individual and a group basis. Because the results are expressed in terms of the percentages of people in each age group who possess certain skills and knowledge, examinees' names do not appear on the test papers. Results are reported for the nation as a whole and for specific geographical regions. Long-term results in mathematics, science, and reading are obtained at ages 9, 13, and 17 and in writing for grades 4, 8, and 11.

Since 1990, NAEP assessments have also been conducted on a voluntary basis at the state level. Separate representative samples of students are selected for each participating jurisdiction or state, but results are not representative of the state as a whole.

The NAEP was planned as a continuing program to provide the U.S. public, and especially legislators and educators, with information on the status and growth of educational accomplishments in the United States and the extent to which the nation's educational goals are being met. It was not designed, as some have feared, to evaluate the achievements of specific schools or school districts or as a means of federal control over public school curricula. However, the findings have been analyzed by geographical area, size and type of community, gender, parental education, and ethnic group. Of particular interest are analyses of the effects of federal support and specific types of programs on educational attainment.[2]

TYPES AND SELECTION OF STANDARDIZED ACHIEVEMENT TESTS

There are four types of standardized achievement tests: survey test batteries, survey-tests in special subjects, diagnostic tests, and prognostic tests. Some of these are individual tests designed for administration to one person at a time, but a great majority are group tests that can be given to any number of people simultaneously. The market for highly specialized tests in a particular subject area is rather limited, so standardized achievement tests typically cover broad content areas and deal with matters of general knowledge. Because the curriculum becomes more specialized in the upper grade levels, administration of standardized achievement tests is less common after junior high school.

Survey-Test Batteries

The most comprehensive way of assessing achievement is to administer a survey-test battery, a set of subject-matter tests designed for particular grade levels. The major purpose of administering a battery of tests is to determine an individual's general standing in various

---

[2]NAEP reports and related publications can be obtained from ED Pubs, P.O. Box 1398, Jessup, MD 20794–1398. Telephone: 877-4ED-PUBS. FAX: 301-470-1244. Web URLs: www.ed.gov/pubs/edpubs.html and nces.ed.gov/nationsreportcard.

subjects, rather than his or her specific strengths and weaknesses. Consequently, each test in a survey battery contains a fairly limited sample of the content and skills in a particular subject. Because all tests in a battery are standardized on the same group of people and the scores are expressed on the same numerical scale, a person's performance in different subjects can be compared directly.

Although test batteries provide a more comprehensive assessment of pupil achievement than single tests, they have a number of drawbacks. Despite the longer total administration time for a battery, the tests are shorter than single-survey tests and consequently tend to have lower reliabilities. Of course, not all the tests in a battery need to be administered to a given group of students; the examiner may choose to administer only tests that yield relevant information pertaining to the specific assessment goals.

Single-Subject Survey Tests

Single-subject tests are usually longer and more detailed than comparable tests in a battery and thereby permit a more thorough evaluation of achievement in a specific area. Single-subject tests are not designed to identify specific, detailed causes of high or low performance in a subject; they typically yield an overall score and perhaps a couple of subscores. Because of greater uniformity among different schools in reading and mathematics instruction than in other subjects, standardized tests in these two areas tend to be more valid than, for example, science and social studies tests.

Diagnostic Tests

Diagnostic tests have the function of identifying specific difficulties in learning a subject. To construct a diagnostic test in a basic skill such as reading, arithmetic, or spelling, performance in the subject as a whole is analyzed into subskills, and then groups of items are constructed to measure performance in these subskills. Unlike survey tests, which focus on total scores, diagnostic tests yield scores on each of several subskills. Because differences among scores on the various parts of the tests are interpreted in making diagnoses, the number of items for measuring a particular subskill must be sufficient to ensure that the differences between part scores are reliable. Unfortunately, the number of items comprising part scores are often small and scores on the parts are correlated, resulting in difference scores having low reliability.

Most diagnostic tests are in reading, but diagnostic tests in mathematics, spelling, and foreign languages are also available. A diagnostic test contains a greater variety of items and usually takes longer to administer than a survey test in the same subject. Diagnostic tests may also involve special apparatus, such as a tachistoscope to present reading material for only a brief period of time and an eye-movement camera to track the direction in which the eyes move in reading.

Certain individually administered survey, or global, tests are also used for purposes of educational diagnosis. Examples are the Kaufman Test of Educational Achievement and the Peabody Individual Achievement Test-Revised. Even more global in its diagnostic aims is the Woodcock–Johnson III Tests of Achievement, an individually administered multiple-skills test battery designed to measure general intellectual ability, specific cognitive abilities, oral language, and academic achievement of individuals between 2 and 90 years of age.

Administration of a survey-test battery is a reasonable first step in a testing program, because it provides an overall picture of a person's standing in various subjects. If a second assessment of a person's achievement in a particular area is needed, a single test in the specific subject can be administered. Finally, if it is desirable to make a detailed analysis of a person's disability in reading or mathematics and to determine the causes of the disability, a diagnostic test should be given.

Prognostic Tests

Prognostic tests, which contain a wider variety of items than survey achievement tests in the same subject, are designed to predict achievement in specific school subjects. For example, the purpose of a reading-readiness test administered to a kindergartner or first grader is to predict whether the child is prepared to benefit sufficiently from instruction in reading. At a higher grade level, prognostic tests in mathematics (algebra, geometry) and foreign languages are available for predicting ease of learning these subjects.

Selecting a Standardized Test

Selecting a standardized achievement test is basically a matter of finding an instrument with a content that matches the instructional objectives of the particular class, school, school system, or other organizational unit. This means that the level of knowledge or ability of the examinees and the content and objectives of the curriculum must be determined before deciding which test(s) to administer. Also, the reasons for testing and the way in which the scores are to be used should be considered. There is little purpose in administering a test merely because it looks good and then letting the unused results gather dust in a file drawer or storage cabinet.

Purposes and Practical Considerations.   The manual accompanying a test typically provides details on its potential uses (evaluation, placement, diagnosis of learning disabilities, readiness to learn, curriculum evaluation) and cites supporting evidence. Consequently, before a test is selected, the specific ways in which the scores are to be used should be clarified and test manuals consulted to determine which tests are appropriate for these purposes. In addition to reading the manual, prospective users should examine a copy of the test and even take it themselves to determine whether it is suitable for its intended purposes. Some testing companies also publish specimen sets of tests, consisting of a test booklet, answer sheet, manual, scoring key, and other associated materials. Test catalogs, which are helpful in deciding which tests to administer, are also available by mail and online. Most testing companies have Web sites that describe their purposes, products, and services (see Appendix C).

Another consideration in selecting a test is the degree of cooperation that can be expected from the school or other organization in administering it and interpreting the findings. Also of importance are practical matters, such as cost and time for administration, scoring, and analyzing the results. The machine-scoring services provided by commercial testing firms greatly facilitate the scoring and analysis processes and are usually fairly reasonable in cost.

Reliability, Validity, and Norms.   Frequently overlooked, but often crucial in selecting an achievement test, are its statistical characteristics. The reliabilities of most achievement tests, are in the .80s and .90s, but the meaning of these high coefficients depends on the procedures by which they were obtained. A parallel-forms coefficient is preferable to a test–retest coefficient or an internal-consistency coefficient because the last two are more likely to be inflated by measurement error. To decide whether an achievement test is valid, evidence of its content validity must be obtained by comparing the content of the test with the objectives of the instructional program of interest. An adequately prepared test manual describes the system for classifying the content and behavioral objectives used in constructing the test, and prospective users must decide whether these objectives correspond to their own. When a test is administered for the purpose of predicting later achievement, as in the case of a reading-readiness or other prognostic test, it is also important to obtain evidence of its predictive validity.

In addition to reliability and validity, the adequacy and appropriateness of the norms should be examined before selecting a test. Most well-constructed achievement tests are standardized on representative, national samples, sometimes stratified according to age, sex, geographical region, socioeconomic status, and other relevant variables. Test purchasers who plan to report scores in terms of these norms should make certain that the characteristics of the norm group are similar to those of the students to be examined. For purposes of placement and other comparisons within a given school or school system, local norms may be even more meaningful than national norms.

Users of standardized achievement tests also need to be aware of the fact that, in plotting a student's academic growth by means of normed scores on a standardized achievement test administered at successive grade levels, it is assumed that the different grade-level groups on which the test was standardized are equivalent. For example, demographic changes in the communities from which students in certain schools are drawn may result in significant differences in the composition of student groups at different grade levels. This may happen because of recent migratory influx of people of different socioeconomic, nationality, or ethnic groups. If there is any reason to believe that differences among the norm groups on variables other than those that are growth related are significant, then a student's grade-norm scores, percentile-rank scores, or standard scores on a test cannot be compared accurately across grade levels.

In purchasing a test it is important not to be misled by its name. Experienced test users are well aware of the *jingle fallacy* of assuming that instruments having the same name measure the same thing and the *jangle fallacy* of assuming that instruments having different names measure different things. Before deciding what achievement tests to purchase, novices and experienced testers alike can profit from consulting reviews of tests in *The Mental Measurements Yearbook, Test Critiques,* professional journals, or other sources.

ACHIEVEMENT TEST BATTERIES

Achievement test batteries represent efforts to measure broad cognitive abilities and skills produced by basic educational experiences in core areas. These multilevel batteries of tests assess basic skills in reading, mathematics, language arts, and, at the appropriate grade levels, study skills, social studies, and science.

A representative list of achievement test batteries is given in Table 9.1. Descriptions of these and other commercially available test batteries can be found in the various editions

TABLE 9.1   Representative Achievement Test Batteries

California Achievement Test, Fifth Edition (CAT5) (CTB/McGraw-Hill; grades K–12)

Comprehensive Test of Basic Skills, Fourth Edition (CTBS/4) (CTB/McGraw-Hill; grades K–12)

Iowa Tests of Basic Skills (ITBS), Form M (by H. D. Hoover, A. N. Hieronymus, D. A. Frisbie, & S. B. Dunbar; Riverside Publishing Co.; grades K–12)

Iowa Tests of Educational Development (ITED), Form M (by L. S. Feldt, R. A. Forsyth, T. N. Ansley, & S. D. Alnot; Riverside Publishing Co., grades 9–12)

Kaufman Test of Educational Achievement (KTEA/NU) (by A. S. Kaufman & N. L. Kaufman; American Guidance Services; grades 1–12)

Metropolitan Achievement Tests, Eighth Edition (Metropolitan8) (Harcourt Brace; grades K–12)

Peabody Individual Achievement Test-Revised (PIAT-R/NU) (by F. C. Markwardt, Jr.; American Guidance Service; ages 5–18)

Stanford Achievement Test Series, Ninth Edition (Stanford 9) (Harcourt Brace; grades K–13)

TerraNova Assessment Series (CTB/McGraw-Hill; ages K–12)

Wechsler Individual Achievement Test II (WIAT-II) (The Psychological Corporation, ages 5–19 years)

Wide Range Achievement Test Expanded (*WRAT-Expanded*) (by G. J. Robertson; Wide Range; grades 2–12)

Woodcock–Johnson III Tests of Achievement (WJ-III) (by R. W. Woodcock, K. S. McGrew, & N. Mather; Riverside Publishing; 2–90+ years)

---

of the *Mental Measurements Yearbook, Tests in Print, Tests,* and *Test Critiques* and in the catalogs available from test publishers. These batteries were designed to assess the formal educational achievements of students in kindergarten through senior high school, with an emphasis on the elementary and junior high years.

The testing programs in many grade schools are based on achievement test batteries administered during the fall and spring for the purpose of measuring the general educational attainment and development of students. Test results are of interest to teachers, parents, school administrators, members of school boards, political leaders, and, of course, to the students themselves. A limitation of the battery approach is that some of the tests may not correspond to the particular objectives of a school or school system. Also, not all tests in a given battery have equal reliabilities or validities.

Battery Norms

Since the various subtests at a particular grade level of an achievement test battery were standardized on the same group of people, the resulting unified set of norms permits direct evaluation of a person's relative achievement in several subject areas. If it can be assumed that different grade levels of a test battery were standardized on comparable groups of students, then the cognitive growth of students may also be charted by comparing their scores on the tests comprising the battery over a period of several years. However, this should not be done if there is any doubt about the equivalence or comparability of the different grade-level samples of students on whom the battery was standardized. In addition, the norms with which students' scores are compared should have been obtained by administering the test(s) to the standardization group during the same time of year (fall or spring) as the students whose scores are being evaluated.

Content of Achievement Test Batteries

Because of the greater uniformity of instructional content in elementary school, achievement test batteries are administered most often for the purpose of assessing educational development in the elementary grades. A typical achievement test battery at this level consists of subtests on reading vocabulary, reading comprehension, language usage, spelling, arithmetic fundamentals, and arithmetic comprehension. Subtests to measure study skills, social studies, and science may also be included, but the emphasis is on achievement in basic verbal and quantitative skills. Among popular achievement test batteries at the elementary school level are the Stanford Achievement Test Series, the California Achievement Tests, the Comprehensive Tests of Basic Skills, and the Metropolitan Achievement Tests. These batteries contain tests designed for kindergarten and secondary school, as well as the primary and intermediate grades.

Variability in the academic programs of different high school students makes achievement test batteries less useful in secondary than in the elementary school. Test batteries at the secondary school level also emphasize basic skills in reading, language, and arithmetic, but tests of social studies, science, and study skills are also included. At both the elementary and secondary levels, achievement tests stress general educational development and are not tied to particular courses or schools. Also of interest at the high school level are batteries such as the American College Tests (ACT), which are administered annually for college admissions purposes. The ACT is actually an achievement test battery, but it is somewhat like an aptitude test in that its broad range of content is less related to specific in-school experiences than is that of most achievement tests.

Basic Education Tests

Several achievement test batteries have been designed specifically to measure proficiency in the basic skills of adults with less than a high school education. An example is the Tests of Adult Basic Education (TABE), a multilevel test standardized on adults that measures skills in reading, mathematics, and language. Another test for determining level of development in reading and arithmetic of employees or applicants in a wide variety of occupations and rehabilitation environments is the Reading–Arithmetic Index (RAI). This is an untimed test that takes about 25 minutes to complete the two parts.

Despite the availability of adult basic skills tests, in relatively few businesses and industries are applicants or employees actually tested for literacy. Consequently, many workers are functionally illiterate and must bluff it out in performing a job requiring reading skills. Executives in such companies presumably realize that some of their employees cannot read, write, perform computations, or comprehend English well, but they seem to be limited in what they can do about the problem. This is unfortunate, because illiterate employees are more likely to have accidents and are handicapped in their ability to advance in an organization.

GED Tests

Also appropriate for adults with limited formal education are the Tests of General Educational Development (GED), which is taken by nearly 900,000 adults annually. The GED tests were designed to measure the educational achievements of people with a high school education or equivalent. The full battery, which takes about 7½ hours, consists primarily of multiple-choice items in five areas: writing skills, social studies, science, literature and arts, and mathematics. The writing skills test also includes an essay that documents the test taker's ability to write and communicate effectively. Rather than stressing specific facts and details, items on the GED deal with broad concepts and generalizations based on competencies and knowledge taught in secondary school curricula. Many academic and most business organizations, as well as the U.S. armed forces, accept passing scores on the GED tests as equivalent to a high school diploma (see Web site www.gedtest.org).

ACHIEVEMENT TESTS IN SPECIFIC AREAS

Administration of an achievement test battery has priority in a typical school testing program. When more information on student performance in a particular subject is needed, the usual procedure is to follow the battery with a specific test in the subject. These specific achievement tests have certain advantages over comparable tests in a battery. For example, the fact that a specific subject-matter test contains more items and has a broader subject content than a single test on an achievement battery makes it likely that the former represents the instructional objectives of a wide range of classrooms and schools more adequately. Also, because of its length it is likely to be more reliable than a comparable test on an achievement battery.

A line from an old song, "Reading and writing and 'rithmetic, taught to the tune of a hickory stick," is a testimonial to the time-honored prominence of these subjects in the elementary school curriculum. Hundreds of specific subject-matter tests in reading, mathematics, language, science, social studies, the professions, business, and the skilled trades are available. Other areas in which standardized achievement tests have been published are health, home economics, industrial arts, library usage, literature, the Bible, music, speech, spelling, and driver education. In addition to traditional norm-referenced tests of the survey, diagnostic, and prognostic type, there are many criterion-referenced tests in specific subjects. Also, the emphasis during the past few decades on basic skills competency testing in high schools has led to publication of a number of proficiency tests for assessing the knowledge and skills of junior and senior high students in reading, writing, and mathematics. These survival skills are considered essential for coping with the demands of everyday living.

Reading Tests

Many problems experienced by children in learning school subjects are associated with reading, a common reason for referring a child for psychoeducational evaluation. Difficulties in reading are cumulative and affect performance in almost all schoolwork, so it is important to assess reading level and diagnose deficiencies in this subject early and regularly. Because of their many uses, more reading tests are administered than any other kind of standardized achievement test. Various types of reading tests are available, three major categories are survey tests, diagnostic tests, and reading-readiness tests. Other ways of classifying reading tests are norm-referenced versus criterion-referenced (or both) and silent versus oral reading.

Survey Reading Tests. The main reason for administering a survey reading test is to determine a person's overall reading ability. Tests of this type contain sections of vocabulary items and other sections consisting of paragraphs or passages about which questions are asked. A measure of word knowledge is obtained from the vocabulary items, whereas speed and level of reading comprehension are measured from the paragraphs. Illustrative of the best tests of this type are the Gates–MacGinitie Reading Tests, Fourth Edition. Designed for grades K–12 and Adult Reading, the two forms of this test contain five levels: Pre-Reading (PR), Beginning Reading (BR), 1 and 3, 3–12, and Adult Reading (AR). Beginning reading skills and primary-level developmental reading skills are assessed in the lower levels, and continuing growth in reading competence is measured at the higher levels.

Most survey reading tests employ a multiple-choice format, but an open-ended or constructed-response format is used on the Stanford 9 Open-Ended Reading test. Two other examples of survey reading tests are the Gray Oral Reading Tests-4 and the Test of Reading Comprehension-3. Some survey reading tests, such as the Nelson–Denny Reading Test CD-ROM, can be administered by computer.

Diagnostic Reading Tests. Diagnostic reading tests, which are by far the most common type of diagnostic test, attempt to assess many different factors that affect reading and thereby determine the source of students' difficulties in the subject. Included among these factors are eye–hand coordination, visual and auditory perception, understanding of concepts, and even motivation. A diagnostic reading test may contain subtests on visual and auditory discrimination, sight vocabulary and vocabulary in context, phoneme–grapheme, vowels and consonants, silent and oral reading, spelling, reading comprehension, and rate of comprehension. Because correlations among these subtests are often substantial, the various skills measured by diagnostic reading tests are not necessarily independent. In addition, the reliabilities of the subtests and the test as a whole are frequently not as high as might be desired. Representative of tests in this category are the California Diagnostic Reading Tests, the Stanford Diagnostic Reading Tests-Fourth Edition, and the Woodcock Diagnostic Reading Battery.

Reading-Readiness Tests. As a measure of the extent to which children possess the skills and knowledge necessary for learning to read, a reading-readiness test often predicts achievement in first grade better and requires less administration time than a general intelligence test. Reading-readiness tests contain many of the same types of items as diagnostic reading tests, and certain reading tests contain both diagnostic and prognostic components.

Mathematics Tests

In a manner similar to achievement tests in reading, mathematics achievement tests may be classified as survey, diagnostic, and prognostic.

Survey Mathematics Tests.   Various approaches to instruction are represented by standardized mathematics tests, including a more traditional emphasis in mathematics curricula as well as a more modern emphasis on problem solving, concept development, and reasoning. Certain tests are designed to encompass both modern and traditional emphases in the mathematics curriculum, and instruments reflecting more specialized instructional approaches from primary school through college are available. In general, norm-referenced mathematics tests of the survey type require students to demonstrate an understanding of quantitative concepts and operations and the ability to apply this understanding in solving problems. Tests of proficiency in both general and specific mathematics (algebra, calculus, trigonometry) courses at the high school level are also available through the College-Level Examination Program (CLEP).

Diagnostic Tests in Mathematics.   Although less widely administered than diagnostic reading tests, diagnostic tests in mathematics also represent attempts to break down a complex subject involving a variety of skills into its constituent elements. The items on diagnostic tests of arithmetic and mathematics are based on an analysis of skills and errors in the subject. Knowledge and skills required for applications involving numeration, fractions, algebra, and geometry are tapped by these tests. Two examples of diagnostic mathematics tests are the Stanford Diagnostic Mathematics Test-Fourth Edition and KeyMath-Revised/NU: A Diagnostic Inventory of Essential Mathematics. The former instrument is a group test designed to diagnose the specific strengths and weaknesses in basic mathematical concepts and operations of children in grades 1 through 12. KeyMath is an individually administered test designed to measure the understanding and application of basic mathematics concepts and skills in kindergarten through grade 9.

Prognostic Tests in Mathematics.   A number of tests have been designed to forecast performance in specific mathematics courses, but, compared with prognostic tests in reading (reading-readiness tests), they are not widely used. Two examples are the Orleans–Hanna Algebra Prognosis Test-Third Edition and the Iowa Algebra Aptitude Test, Fourth Edition. Designed to identify which students will be successful and which will encounter difficulties in learning algebra, the Orleans–Hanna assesses aptitude and achievement as well as the interest and motivation in algebra of junior and senior high school students. The questionnaire and work sample items on the test take 40 minutes to complete. The percentile rank and stanine score norms are based on three groups of students: those completing grade 7 mathematics, those completing grade 8 mathematics, and those from the first two groups who completed a 1-year course in algebra during the following year. The Algebra Aptitude Test was designed to assess the readiness of seventh- and eighth-grade students for Algebra I. Its four subtests, which require a total of 50 minutes to complete, measure prealgebra skills in interpreting graphs and written mathematical information, translating word problems into algebraic or equation format, identifying functions, and using symbols.

Language Tests

Language, as generally construed, refers to any means of communication. Although language tests consist primarily of verbal-type items, measures of nonverbal communication for use with hearing-impaired and even normal-hearing people have been developed. Both oral and written language is taught at all levels, and tests appropriate for the entire range of grades are available. Failure to understand certain concepts can act as a communication barrier between teachers and preschool or primary school pupils and consequently have serious effects on children's learning. In recognition of this fact, the Boehm Test of Basic Concepts-Third Edition (for grades K–2) and the Boehm-3 (for ages 3 to 5 years) were designed to measure a young child's mastery of basic concepts of space, quantity, and time (see Figure 9.1).

Despite the availability of tests such as the Boehm, most achievement tests in the language category were designed for secondary school and college students. These instruments,

FIGURE 9.1 Sample items from the Boehm Test of Basic Concepts-Third Edition.
The examinee marks an × on the selected option.

including both English and foreign language tests, are frequently administered in high schools and colleges for the purpose of placing students in English or foreign language courses appropriate to their level of competence.

English Language Tests.   Some of the most severe criticisms of objective tests have come from teachers of English. Still, it is generally recognized that such tests do a fairly respectable job of measuring knowledge of grammar and vocabulary and, to some extent, skill in oral and written expression. The assessment of English language skills constitutes a part of achievement test batteries, but there are also many separate tests of proficiency in English.

Listening, speaking, and writing are obviously part of English usage, and a number of tests have been designed to measure these skills. An example of a test of this type is the OWLS series: Listening Comprehension Scale, Oral Expression Scale, and Written Expression Scale. Each of these tests, which are appropriate for children and young adults, takes less than 25 minutes to complete. The Listening Comprehension Scale measures receptive language, the Oral Expression Scale measures expressive language, and the Written Expression Scale provides an authentic assessment of written language skills. Speaking and listening skills, in either English or Spanish, can also be measured by the Language Assessment Scales-Oral (LAS-O) and the Pre-LAS 2000. The LAS-O is administered to grades 1–12 and the Pre-LAS to preschool children.

Two examples of writing tests are the Test of Written Language-3 (TOWL-3) and the Stanford Writing Assessment Program, Third Edition. Designed for students in grades 2–12, TOWL-3 is a free-response, work-sample measure on which the examinee writes stories about a set of pictures (see Figure 9.2). The stories may be scored on several variables, including theme, vocabulary, syntax, spelling, and style. The Stanford Writing Assessment involves presentation of a series of prompts designed to elicit a writing sample in each of four modes: descriptive, narrative, expository, and persuasive. A Writer's Checklist provides reminders for prewriting, composing, and editing. Writing is scored on ideas and development; organization, unity, and coherence; word choice; sentence and paragraphs; grammar and usage; and mechanics.

Many other achievement tests, such as the CEEB Advanced Placement Tests and the Graduate Record Examinations, also contain a writing (essay) component. Undergraduate and graduate students whose native language is not English may take the Test of Written English (TWE) and the Test of Spoken English (TSE). The TWE, which is administered by Educational Testing Service along with the TOEFL (discussed next), requires examinees to write a 30-minute essay in standard written English in response to a brief essay question or topic. The TSE, which was designed to measure the ability of nonnative speakers of English to communicate orally in English, requires examinees to respond orally under timed conditions to a variety of printed and aural stimuli.

Nonnative English speakers who apply for admission to North American colleges and universities typically take the Test of English as a Foreign Language (TOEFL). TOEFL, a 3-hour multiple-choice examination administered by Educational Testing Service, consists of three parts: Listening Comprehension, which measures the ability to understand spoken English; Structure and Written Expression, which measures the ability to recognize language inappropriate for standard written English; and Vocabulary and Reading Comprehension, which measures the ability to understand technical reading material. Secondary

FIGURE 9.2   Sample pictures from the Test of Written Language-3.
The examinee makes up a story about each of a series of pictures like these two.

(D. Hammill & S. Larson © 1996 by pro.ed, Inc. Used with permission.)

school students who are not native speakers of English and who wish to enroll in full-time educational programs conducted in English may also take the Secondary-Level English Proficiency Test (SLEP). Another English language proficiency test for people whose native language is not English is the Test of English for International Communication (TOEIC). TOEIC, which like TOEFL and SLEP is designed and administered by Educational Testing Service, is the world standard for the assessment of English as used in the global workplace.

Foreign Language Tests.   Survey tests of proficiency in a foreign language typically consist of different forms for students who have completed different amounts and kinds of study of the language. Certain tests reflect the more traditional grammar approach to language instruction, whereas others emphasize comprehension of spoken and written communication. The most popular survey tests of proficiency in foreign languages are Educational Testing Service's Advanced Placement examinations, the CLEP Subject Examinations, and the College Board SAT II tests. Tests in French, German, and Spanish are available in all three of these programs; also available in the Advanced Placement program are tests in Italian and Mandarin Chinese. Separate tests in several foreign languages are also available in the Praxis II: Subject Assessments for beginning teachers. Although most foreign language tests are limited to reading and listening, the Center for Applied Linguistics administers tests of the ability to speak Chinese, Hausa, Hebrew, Indonesian, Portuguese, and other languages.

Social Studies Tests

Topics in social studies, history, economics, and political science are generally thought of in connection with secondary school and college curricula. Social studies, in a less restrictive sense, is also taught in the elementary grades. Among the many tests of achievement in social studies at the secondary school level are the College Board's Advanced Placement Examinations in Economics, Government and Politics, History, Human Geography, and World History; and the CLEP Subject Examinations in American Government, History of the United States I & II, Principles of Macroeconomics, Principles of Microeconomics, Introductory Psychology, Introductory Sociology, and Western Civilization I & II.

Science Tests

Instruction in science, like instruction in mathematics, has changed markedly during the past few decades, making many older tests obsolete or inappropriate for today's science curricula. The Biological Sciences Curriculum Study (BSCS) and the Physical Sciences Study Committee (PSSC) led to the design of specific tests in biology and physics. Comprehensive testing programs in other sciences, such as the American Chemical Society's Cooperative Chemistry Tests, also reflect contemporary approaches to science education. These approaches emphasize the teaching of science content so that it will be usable and important for decision making in everyday life. With this goal in mind, more recently developed science tests require students to discover patterns in sets of data and interpret the meanings of these patterns, rather than merely recalling them. Many older tests have also been revised in an attempt to assess performance in either a modern or traditional science program.

As students progress through junior and senior high school, instruction in general science, biology, chemistry, and physics becomes more concentrated. Useful in evaluating senior high students' knowledge and skills in specific fields of science are the College Board's Advanced Placement examinations in biology, chemistry, environment science, and physics; the CLEP Subject Examinations in general biology, general chemistry, and human growth and development; and the SAT II: Subject Tests. Other science tests for high school and college students include the ACS Examinations and the ACT Proficiency Examinations.

Tests in Higher Education and the Professions

Many institutions of higher learning permit students to earn credit for college courses by obtaining acceptable scores on standardized achievement tests such as those administered by the College Board's Advanced Placement Program (APP), the College-level Examination Program (CLEP), and the ACT Proficiency Examination Program. In addition, colleges, universities, and professional schools use scores on standardized achievement tests as criteria for selecting students. These tests are usually restricted or secure in the sense that they are sold or rented only to certain organizations for administration in connection with specific educational programs.

A set of standardized achievement tests used in selecting students for graduate programs are the Subject Tests of the Graduate Record Examinations (GRE). These tests, which are available in eight subject areas (Biochemistry, Cell and Molecular Biology; Biology; Chemistry; Computer Science; Literature in English; Mathematics; Physics; Psychology) may be taken, along with the GRE General Test, by college students in their senior year who intend to apply for admission to graduate school.

Other examples of standardized tests used for purposes of admission to graduate or professional schools are the Graduate Management Admission Test (GMAT), the Law School Admission Test (LSAT), the Medical College Admission Test (MCAT), and the NLN Achievement Tests in Nursing. Certification or licensing as a lawyer, physician, public accountant, registered nurse, teacher, or professional in certain other fields is also contingent on passing a series of achievement tests (board examinations, bar examinations) in the particular field.

The Praxis Series. Professional Assessments for Beginning Teachers is relied on by 44 states as part of their certification process for beginning teachers. It consists of three parts: Praxis I: Academic Skills Assessment, for measuring reading, writing, and mathematics skills vital to all teacher candidates; Praxis II: Subject Assessment, for measuring teacher candidates' knowledge of the subjects they will teach; and Praxis III: Classroom Performance Assessments, for evaluating the beginning teacher's classroom performance. Praxis I is taken on entering a teacher training program, Praxis II on graduating from college and entering the profession, and Praxis III during the first year of teaching.

Tests for Business and Skilled Trades

Business is a school subject in itself, and business education tests are designed to assess a person's knowledge of the subject. In addition to evaluating the degree of accomplishment in a school subject, achievement tests are used in business and industry for purposes of selection, placement, and promotion. Tests of proficiency in typing, filing, word processing, computing, and other office skills are perhaps the most popular of these measures.

Tests of knowledge and skill in a particular trade (*trade tests*) are widely used for purposes of employee selection, placement, and certification or licensing. A trade test may consist of a series of questions to be answered orally or in writing, or it may be a work-sample task requiring demonstration of a particular skill. Examples of trade, or occupational competency, tests are those available from Educational Testing Service's Chauncey Group. The Chauncey Group, together with its subsidiary Exterior Assessments, has been responsible for the development and administration of dozens of licensure and professional certification examinations. These examinations have been prepared for many major industries and professions (construction, insurance, barbering, cosmetology, real estate, food safety, architecture, securities, nursing, etc.). They may be administered not only in traditional paper-and-pencil format, but also by computer and/or over the Internet. Tests in certain areas include objective or essay questions of the type found on academic achievement tests and situation assessments, such as those designed to determine a person's ability to take appropriate action on each of a set of memos and other communications of the sort usually found in an executive's in-basket, as well as the ability to handle a leaderless group negotiation interview. These kinds of tasks obviously extend beyond the domain of cognitive ability testing and into the realm of personality and social skills assessment.

SUMMARY

1. Achievement tests measure knowledge, are influenced largely by experience, and focus on the present. In contrast, ability tests are more focused on a person's potential and assess what a person will do in the future. Achievements tests can measure not only knowledge of facts, but also comprehension and higher-order thinking. They have been criticized, however, for fostering poor skills in written composition. They can also be used to evaluate students for purposes of grade assignment, promotion, placement, diagnosis of learning difficulties, determination of readiness to learn, and evaluation of curricula and teaching effectiveness (accountability).

2. Educational testing has traditionally been summative (focused on the end product of education), but is also used to help evaluate the process of education (formative). It is usually norm referenced in that a student's scores are compared with a standardization group ("How well did John do compared with other fourth graders?"). It can also be criterion referenced in that comparisons can be made with a standard level of performance ("How well does John know his multiplication tables?"). Also of significance is the use of tests in large-scale educational assessment and planning, as in the National Assessment of Educational Progress.

3. Four types of achievement tests are single-subject survey tests, survey-test batteries, diagnostic tests, and prognostic tests. Survey tests provide an overall appraisal of achievement in a subject, whereas diagnostic tests analyze a person's specific strengths and weaknesses in a subject. Readiness, aptitude, and other prognostic tests attempt to forecast achievement by determining a person's ability to learn certain types of material.

4. Selecting a standardized achievement test can be based on the right type of content, level of cooperation from the school, cost, time for administration, scoring procedures, reliability, and validity. The reliabilities of most achievement tests, determined by test–retest and parallel-forms procedures, are typically in the .80s or .90s. Evidence for content validity is usually of greater concern than other types of validity in evaluating educational achievement tests. Much of this information can be found in the test manual. Additional sources of information concerning achievement tests include publishers' catalogs, test reviews in professional journals, *Tests in Print, The Mental Measurements Yearbooks, Tests, Test Critiques,* specimen sets of tests, and various Web sites (see Appendix C).

5. Various multilevel achievement test batteries are commercially available. They are typically used to monitor how well the student is doing, as well as how effectively the school is teaching. These batteries are commonly administered in elementary and ju-

nior high school. Common examples are the Stanford Achievement Test Series, California Achievement Tests, American College Tests, Tests of Adult Basic Education, and the Tests of General Educational Development.

6. Single-subject tests in reading, mathematics, science, social studies, English, foreign languages, and other areas are also widely administered. Survey reading tests typically measure knowledge of vocabulary and speed and level of comprehension. Diagnostic tests, which are designed to assess specific strengths and weaknesses in a particular subject, are available in reading, arithmetic, and spelling. Various prognostic tests in reading (reading-readiness tests), mathematics, and languages (language aptitude tests) are also available. Achievement tests in social studies (history, economics, political science) and in the natural sciences (general science, biology, chemistry, physics) are available for a wide range of grades and different types of curricula. Tests for admission to schools of nursing (NTE), medicine (MCAT), law (LSAT), management (GMAT), teaching (Praxis), and other professional programs and for determining proficiency in various business occupations and the skilled trades are also used extensively.

MASTERING THE CHAPTER OBJECTIVES

1. *Achievement tests: purpose, standardization, accountability*
   a. List the purpose of standardized achievement tests.
   b. Compare standardized achievement tests with teacher-made tests, listing the merits and shortcomings of each.
   c. What is accountability in education? How is accountability related to performance contracting? List arguments supporting and opposing performance contracting in the schools.

2. *Summative and formative evaluations norm-referenced and criterion-referenced measurement*
   a. How does formative evaluation differ from summative evaluation? How do the two approaches to evaluation conflict with or complement each other? In what way is formative evaluation related to criterion-referenced measurement?
   b. Distinguish between norm-referenced and criterion-referenced measurement. What are the advantages and disadvantages of each?

3. *Four types of achievement tests*
   a. Compare the purposes and design of survey tests, single-subject tests, diagnostic tests, and prognostic tests.
   b. Contrast high-stakes testing with low-stakes testing, including the types of tests and the decisions used with each.

4. *Selecting standardized achievement tests*
   a. What considerations would you make in selecting a standardized achievement test?
   b. Where would you obtain information regarding achievement tests?

5. *Achievement test batteries*
   a. At what grade levels and for what purposes are standardized achievement tests most valid and useful?
   b. What are the advantages and disadvantages in administering an achievement test battery rather than a series of single-subject-matter tests?

6. *Achievement tests in specific areas*
  a. Describe three reasons for administering tests of reading achievement.
  b. What are some of the criticisms that have been directed toward standardized tests of language ability?

EXPERIENCING PSYCHOLOGICAL ASSESSMENT

1. Most departments of psychology and education keep on file specimen sets of standardized achievement tests, including test booklets, answer sheets, scoring keys, manuals, and perhaps other interpretive materials. Prepare a critical review of one of these tests, using the outline in Box 9.1. Whenever possible, you should fill in this outline from information obtained by reading the test manual and examining the test itself. Wait until you have completed your review before consulting published reviews of the test in the *Mental Measurements Yearbooks, Test Critiques,* or other sources.

BOX 9.1
OUTLINE OF A TEST REVIEW

Content. List the title, author(s), publisher, date and place of publication, forms available, type of test, and cost. Give a brief description of the sections of the test, the kinds of items of which the test is composed, and the mental operations or characteristics the test is supposed to measure. Indicate how the test items were selected and whether the construction procedure and/or theory on which the test is based are clearly described in the manual.

Administration and Scoring. Describe any special instructions, whether the test is timed and, if so, the time limits. Give details concerning scoring: as a whole, by sections or parts, and so on. Indicate whether the directions for administration and scoring are clear.

Norms. Describe the group(s) (demographic characteristics, size, etc.) on which the test was standardized and how the samples were selected (systematic, stratified random, cluster, etc.). What kinds of norms are reported in the test manual or technical supplements? Does the standardization appear to be adequate for the recommended uses of the test?

Reliability. Describe the kinds of reliability information reported in the manual (internal consistency, parallel forms, test–retest, etc.). Are the nature and sizes of the samples on which reliability information is reported adequate with respect to the stated uses of the test?

Validity. Summarize available information on the validity (content, predictive, concurrent, construct) of the test included in the manual. Is the validity information satisfactory in terms of the stated purposes of the test?

Summary Comments. Prepare a summary statement of the design and content of the test, and comment briefly on the adequacy of the test as a measure of what it was designed to measure. Does the manual provide satisfactory descriptions of the design, content, norms, reliability, and validity of the test? What further information and/or data are needed to improve the test and its uses?

CHAPTER TEN

APPLICATIONS AND ISSUES IN ABILITY TESTING

CHAPTER OBJECTIVES

1. Introduce the importance of and issues surrounding student academic competence.
2. Describe the criticisms and rebuttals surrounding college entrance examinations and multiple-choice tests in general.
3. Discuss issues on coaching for the college entrance exams.
4. Describe cheating and other reasons why a majority of students might score above average on student competency tests.
5. Describe the issues surrounding the admissibility of intelligence testing in the schools.
6. Discuss fairness in testing and how court rulings have interpreted this in employment settings.

The main reason why tests of abilities are administered in schools, colleges, and other educational institutions is to determine the extent to which students have accumulated specific knowledge and skills, either in or out of formal academic settings. The knowledge should involve not only the simple recall of memorized facts, but also some degree of comprehension and the ability to apply what has been learned to various situations and circumstances. Likewise, the learned skills—cognitive, psychomotor, and social—should be generalizable or transferable to other areas of life. Measurement of these abilities involves not only individuals (students, teachers, administrators, and the like), but also groups of people (classes, schools, school districts, representative samples of residents of states and countries) and the programs or intervention procedures by which changes in knowledge and ability are brought about.

This chapter begins by considering three areas on which educational assessment has concentrated in recent years: student competency, teacher competency, and intervention programs. An analysis of efforts in these three areas should provide a useful overview of the manner in which psychological assessment instruments have been applied for evaluative and selection purposes in schools, colleges, and other organizational programs.

Obviously, applications of ability testing in educational and other organizational settings have not been without controversy and criticism. Rather than sticking their heads in the sand and pretending that critics of psychological and educational testing are merely attempting to feather their own nests, it is scientifically, humanistically, and politically wise for test designers and users to attend to, evaluate, and heed these criticisms. Only in this way can they hope to improve their products and services so that they will be of greater value to society as a whole.

ASSESSMENT IN EDUCATIONAL CONTEXTS

Evaluating Student Competency

It is hardly surprising to hear critics of U.S. public schools proclaim that our schools and students are in trouble. Although over three-fourths of adult Americans are high school graduates, the results of evaluations by the National Assessment of Educational Progress (NAEP) of the knowledge and skills of young Americans reveal persisting deficiencies in reading, writing, science, mathematics, history, civics, and other subject areas. As discussed in Chapter 9, the periodic measurement of students' levels of competency in reading, math, science, writing, history, geography, and other academic areas has been designated as "The Nation's Report Card." The 20 years of results summarized in Table 10.1 indicate that scholastic achievement is low among European American, African American, and Hispanic

TABLE 10.1   Highlights of Findings from 20 Years of NAEP

- Students can read at a surface level, getting the gist of material, but do not read analytically or perform well on challenging reading assignments.

- Small proportions of students write well enough to accomplish the purposes of different writing tasks; most do not communicate effectively.

- Only small proportions of students develop specialized knowledge needed to address science-based problems, and the pattern of falling behind begins in elementary school.

- Students' grasp of the four arithmetic operations and beginning problem solving is far from universal in elementary school; by the time students near high school graduation, half cannot handle moderately challenging mathematics material, including computation with decimals, fractions, and percents.

- Students have a basic understanding of events that have shaped U.S. history, but they do not appear to understand the significance and connections of these events.

- Similarly, students demonstrate an uneven understanding of the Constitution and U.S. government and politics; their knowledge of the Bill of Rights is limited.

(Reprinted with permission of the National Assessment of Educational Progress.)

students alike, and particularly in the last two groups.[1] African American and Hispanic students in the United States have, since the 1970s, improved in reading, mathematics, and science, but their performance remains significantly below that of European American students.

National concern with the low test scores of U.S. high school graduates led to the requirement in a majority of states that students pass a *functional literacy,* or minimum competency, test before receiving a high school diploma. Despite compromises and efforts to make it more acceptable, minimum competency or functional literacy testing has been the subject of continuing debate. Because substantially larger percentages of African American than European American students have failed statewide examinations for high school students, a number of such tests have often been alleged to be discriminatory against minorities (e.g., *Debra P.* v. *Turlington,* 1984). There are also critics who feel that passing an eighth-grade-level test is an inadequate standard for high school graduation and that there is a danger that minimum competency will become the norm. Two other dangers of minimum competency testing are that teachers may end up teaching to the test and that enforcers of the requirement will continue to be besieged by outraged parents whose children have failed the tests.

Regardless of these problems, using tests to assess competency in basic skills and requiring specified minimum scores for high school graduation appear to be here to stay. In many states, accountability through evaluation of student performance is an annual event resulting in the listing in local newspapers of test score averages by school and grade level. Efforts to make such evaluations more useful in educational decision making and resource allocation are indicated by calls for reporting scores on the NAEP tests by state and locality, rather than simply averages for the nation as a whole.

Value-Added Testing

Related to accountability and competency testing is the concept of value-added education and the associated process of value-added testing. In *value-added testing,* student achievements in academic subjects and life skills such as analyzing a newspaper column, a mathematical table, or a television advertisement are assessed before and after a certain period of formal education and study. The difference between pre- and postcourse test scores is a measure of the value added by the educational experience. For example, entering college students may be required to analyze newspaper advertisements, articles, and speeches to demonstrate their mastery of life skills. Retesting at the end of the sophomore year, when they still have sufficient time to make up deficiencies, reveals how much the students have learned in the general education curriculum. Value-added testing is mandated by law and controlled by coordinating boards in certain states, and individual institutions in several other states have incorporated value-added testing into their academic procedures.

---

[1]A history of the world extracted from college students' term papers and exams, ranging from the "Stoned Age" to the "Berlin Mall," describes "Judyism" as a monolithic religion with the god "Yahoo," Gothic cathedrals as supported by "flying buttocks," Hitler as terrorizing his enemies with the "Gespacho," and Caesar as assassinated on the "Yikes of March" while declaring "Me too, Brutus!" (Henriksson, 2001).

Teachers and Testing

Testing in the schools is conducted by school psychologists, guidance counselors, and directors of special education, but most often by the classroom teachers themselves. From their very first day in the classroom, teachers are involved with formal and informal evaluations of students. Such evaluations entail not only observations, classwork, homework, and teacher-made tests, but also standardized tests. The extensive use of standardized tests in schools frequently leads, however, to errors of administration, scoring, and interpretation. Many of these errors are attributable to a lack of training, a lack of concern, or both on the part of test users. Consequently, it is a matter of some importance for teachers, guidance counselors, and others who have testing responsibilities in the schools to be properly trained and informed.

Teacher Training in Testing.   The majority of prospective teachers have some exposure to psychological and educational testing in college courses, but in most cases it is fairly superficial. Many teachers do not understand what is being measured by the tests they administer, nor do they know the meanings of the standard scores entered into a student's permanent record. They often draw sweeping conclusions on the basis of a single test score, failing to take into account the child's developmental history, social competency, or home environment. Therefore, it is essential that more attention be given to this aspect of teacher training. For example, teachers need to realize that scores on tests of intelligence and special abilities should be interpreted in terms of the probabilities that the examinee will succeed in a particular vocation or program of studies. Far too often test scores are viewed as fixed measures of mental status on the one hand or completely as meaningless on the other.

Testing the Teachers.   Increased public concern over the quality of education in the United States has led to another form of involvement of teachers with testing. Nearly all 50 states have implemented some form of teacher-evaluation system. The most widely used test for screening teacher college candidates and beginning teachers and for certifying graduates for general knowledge, professional skills, and subject knowledge is the Praxis Series described in Chapter 9. Of particular interest in the present context is a candidate's performance on Praxis III: Classroom Performance Assessments, which consists of a training and evaluation framework for classroom testing.

Most states require a passing score on a specified test, such as Praxis I, for students to enter teacher-training programs, and almost all states use tests for teacher certification. Tests are also administered for purposes of recertification and allocation of merit pay. In addition to the Praxis series and other tests, several states have implemented formal observation systems for beginning teachers. In these states, fledgling teachers are given assistance in teaching for a trial period, after which a recommendation made to state officials determines whether the candidate will receive regular certification.

Unfortunately, a large percentage of would-be teachers do not perform well on these tests. In many states, for example, one-third or more of the individuals who take Praxis I do not reach the state-established cutoff score for beginning teachers. Also, as a group, students who say they will pursue degrees in education score lower than average on college admissions tests. The lower test scores of preservice and in-service teachers is attributable, at least in part, to the fact that teaching has become less attractive to capable women and minorities in comparison with other more lucrative and prestigious vocations.

Although having to pass licensing exams may make many teachers "testy,"[2] both of the nation's two largest organizations of teachers, the National Education Association and the American Federation of Teachers, support the testing of beginning teachers to ensure that they meet a reasonable standard of competency. Supporters of a national test for prospective teachers argue that it is an indicator of teacher quality and will professionalize the teaching force. By improving the quality of teachers, such a test will also lead to increases in teachers' salaries and overall improvements in the quality of schools.

Teacher competency tests have not gone unchallenged, and legal battles regarding such tests have been fought in several states (e.g., *G. I. Forum et al.* v. *Texas Education Agency et al.,* 2000). A continuing problem concerns the passing standard on the tests: if it is set reasonably high, then large numbers of minority candidates are likely to fail; if it is set too low, individuals of low ability will enter the teaching profession. In addition, certain professional educators have expressed dissatisfaction with the nature of the examinations. Some authorities believe that a blend of tests using computer technology, direct observations of classroom performance, portfolios with documentation of teaching performance and other items, as well as the standardized paper-and-pencil tests, should be employed to evaluate both prospective teachers for hiring and experienced teachers for recertification, promotion, tenure, and merit pay.

CRITICISMS AND ISSUES IN ABILITY TESTING

As witnessed by the number and variety of instruments described in the preceding chapters, the assessment of cognitive, perceptual, and psychomotor abilities has expanded rapidly during this century. The widespread administration of group tests of achievement, intelligence, and special abilities in education, business, and government has contributed to the growth of psychological testing of employees. However, organized labor, maintaining that occupational selection and promotion should be based on experience and seniority rather than test scores, has typically been unsupportive of psychological assessment. Opponents of standardized testing in educational contexts, in particular the use of college entrance examinations and intelligence testing in the schools, have also been outspoken.

Nature and Consequences of Criticisms

The bulk of criticism of psychological and educational testing during the past several decades has been concerned with either the content and applications of tests or the social consequences of relying on test scores to make decisions about people. Testing in general has been attacked on the one hand for invasion of the individual's right to privacy and, on the other hand, for its secretiveness or confidentiality. Ability tests in particular have been faulted for limitations and bias in what they purport to measure.

With respect to their applications, it has been argued that, rather than fostering equality of opportunity, tests have led to maintenance of the status quo and a legitimizing of undemocratic practices by educational institutions, business organizations, and government. More specifically, it has been claimed that tests are often useless as predictors of

[2]See Web site www.education-world.com/a_issues/issues/128.shtml.

behavior, that they are unfair to minority groups, that the results are frequently misinterpreted and misused, and that they promote a narrow and rigid classification of people according to supposedly static characteristics.

Criticisms of psychological and educational testing have frequently created more heat than light, but some of the concerns have stimulated a reevaluation of testing practices. Certain criticisms have led to changes of a technical nature, whereas others have prompted a reexamination of the ethics of testing and the drafting of proposals for an ethical code that would apply to the publishers, distributors, and users of tests.

Legal and ethical issues concerned with the administration of psychological tests and the use of test results were discussed briefly in Chapter 1. As noted there, according to the Family Educational Rights and Privacy Act (1974) test scores and their interpretations kept by educational institutions may be made available to other people only with the *informed consent* of the student or an adult who is legally responsible for the former.

The concept of privileged communication also applies to both test and nontest information. Privileged communication is, however, an all or none affair: a psychologist who is authorized by a client to reveal specific information pertaining to a case must reveal *all* available information that is relevant to the case when ordered to do so by a court of law. Also, whenever a psychologist feels that a client represents a clear and present danger to himself or herself or others, relevant portions of this information must be released to responsible persons without the client's consent. In fact, because the good of society as a whole supersedes a particular individual's right to privacy and privileged communication, a psychologist may be legally obligated to reveal the information (*Tarasoff* v. *Regents of University of California,* 1983).

Whether the administration of psychological tests represents a serious invasion of privacy has been debated at length. It can be argued that if the responses to test questions are of sufficient social value, then people may have to endure some invasion of their privacy. As important as respect for individual rights concerning confidentially of test scores and invasion of privacy may be, these rights must be balanced against society's need for evaluative information of high quality.

Ideally, the results of psychological assessments are treated conscientiously and with an awareness of the limitations of the instruments and the needs and rights of examinees. Unfortunately, the ethical standards of examiners are not always as high as they should be. An awareness of this problem led the American Psychological Association and other professional organizations to adopt codes of ethics pertaining to testing and to impose sanctions against the violation of these codes (American Educational Research Association et al., 1999; American Psychological Association, 1992, 2002, see code 9 on assessment, www.apa.org/ethics/code2002). This represented a step forward in psychological assessment and the practice of psychology in general.

College Entrance Examinations

Large-scale testing programs, in which tests are administered to thousands of students each year, have been special targets of criticism during the past several decades. It has been maintained, for example, that too much school time is spent in administering tests that measure only a few of the variables pertinent to academic achievement and other accomplishments. Of all large-scale testing programs, the most influential and most often attacked are those involving college and university entrance examinations. The Scholastic Assessment Test (SAT), the American College Tests (ACT), and various other instruments fall in this category, but the SAT that has been the target of the most unrelenting criticism.

Most college admissions officers probably assign more weight to high school grades and SAT scores than to performance indicators such as oral interviews, letters of recommendation, extracurricular activities, and portfolio reviews. This is understandable when one considers the low objectivity and poor reliability of many of these measures of personal qualities and performance. For example, due to lack of confidentiality or a concern about it and a strong interest on the part of the letter writer in having the applicant accepted, letters of recommendation are almost always laudatory. For this reason, it has sometimes been said that "One telephone call is worth a dozen letters of recommendation." The same leniency error, in addition to variability in grading standards from school to school, affects the accuracy of high school grades as predictors of performance in college. Personal interviews continue to be of some value in admissions, but they are also limited by the prejudices of the interviewer and the ability of applicants to present themselves in a favorable light.

Despite the fact that few colleges require the submission of SAT scores with an application, the great majority of undergraduate institutions have retained either the SAT or the ACT for admissions and placement purposes. Scores on these tests can also serve as an early warning system and as diagnostic guides for remedial work. The SAT is one of the most carefully designed of all available tests, having high reliability and substantial validity for predicting college grades. These features, however, have not protected it from the rash of criticism to which it has been subjected since the 1950s. The SAT and other psychometric measures of academic promise and progress have often served as whipping boys for shortcomings in the educational system as a whole, an example of blaming the messenger for bringing bad news.

Multiple-Choice Tests

During the 1960s, critics of college entrance examinations and other nationally administered educational tests were particularly outspoken (e.g., Black, 1962; Hoffman, 1962). Of these critics, the most vocal and influential was Banesh Hoffman, who argued that multiple-choice tests (1) favor shrewd, nimblewitted, rapid readers; (2) penalize subtle, creative, more profound persons; (3) are concerned only with the answer and not the quality of thought behind it or the skill with which it is expressed; and (4) have a generally bad effect on education and the recognition of merit. These allegations, however, relied mainly on hypothetical examples and emotionally loaded arguments rather than solid evidence.

Hoffman's criticisms and those of other writers did not go unchallenged. After examining the basic assumptions of various critics of educational testing, Dunnette (1963) concluded that most of the assumptions were erroneous and fallacious and due either to a lack of information or a refusal to recognize that tests are the most accurate means available for identifying merit. Other authorities (e.g., Chauncey & Dobbin, 1963) admitted that tests have limitations but that, when properly used, they can help improve instruction.

Attacks on standardized tests did not disappear with the 1960s, nor were they limited to nonpsychologists. For example, McClelland (1973) argued that, rather than continuing to use measures of what a person already knows as a way of demonstrating his or her capabilities, other measures, such as those that assess the capacity to learn quickly, should be developed.

A criticism that has wide educational and social implications is that not only are multiple-choice tests poor measures of ability and achievement, but that they also encourage inferior teaching and improper study habits. Whether this criticism is justified, teachers are cautioned to be wary of excessive reliance on objective tests and not to neglect traditional essay examinations that require students to explain and support their answers (see Courts & McInerney, 1993; Gifford & O'Connor, 1992). Effective use of essay items requires that scorers evaluate both the content of the answers and the style or skill with which they are expressed. Writing out an answer to a question does not improve the ability to express oneself in writing unless constructive feedback on both the form and content of the answer is provided.

The criticism that multiple-choice tests provide only a glimpse of a student's knowledge at a superficial level and fail to reveal what the student can do with that knowledge has prompted a movement toward *performance-based testing,* or *authentic assessment,* in the public schools. Consisting of open-ended questions and hands-on problem solving in mathematics, science, and certain other subject-matter areas, performance-based tests stress reasoning, analysis, and writing. On such tests, students earn credit not only by giving the right answer but also by demonstrating how they arrived at it. Students may also be required to work in small groups, conducting experiments and sharing interpretations of results or producing something through collective efforts. A collection of student performances or products over a period of time may also be evaluated, a process referred to as *portfolio assessment.* Despite enthusiasm for the new tests, the issues of validity, fairness, cost–benefit ratio, and scoring reliability with respect to performance-based testing remain to be resolved (Baker, O'Neil, & Linn, 1993; Educational Testing Service, 1992).

LEGAL MATTERS AND EDUCATIONAL SELECTION TESTS

Students and their parents have a legal right in most states to information regarding the student's performance on psychological or educational tests, but this does not necessarily mean that actual scores should be reported. Rather, test results should be communicated in such a way that they are not misunderstood or misused and to assist rather than hinder examinees. This caution applies primarily to tests administered to children for diagnostic purposes in clinical or educational contexts. On the other hand, scores on college entrance examinations are routinely reported to test takers and to institutions to which students indicate their scores should be sent. In addition, New York State's truth-in-testing law, enacted in 1979, requires that students who take the SAT or other college admissions tests be given copies of the actual questions and correct answers, as well as copies of their own answer sheets, within a reasonable period of time after taking the test. Two other provisions of the New York State law are that (1) test takers must be told at the time of application how their scores will be computed, what the tester's contractual obligation to them is, and how scores on the test are affected by coaching and various demographic factors, and (2) the test contractor must file information on the test's validity and studies pertaining thereto with the state commission on education. The law also requires that complete editions of the tests be published so that students can practice taking them.

Certain critics of educational testing wish to expand the full-disclosure provisions of the New York law to other states and other examinations, to encourage the use of novel tests to lessen cultural bias, and to make the testing industry more accountable to consumers. Although over two dozen state legislatures, as well as the federal government, have considered laws similar to the one in New York State, the only other state that has enacted a special statute regulating college entrance examinations is California. This law, referred to as the Dunlop Act, requires only that representative samples of tests be provided to the California State Department of Education.

The New York State statute and other pending *truth-in-testing* legislation affect not only the SAT, the ACT, and other undergraduate admissions tests, but also tests for admission to graduate and professional schools. Although the Law School Admission Council and the Graduate Management Admission Council approved disclosure of the results of their tests (LSAT and GMAT), the American Association of Medical Colleges and the American Dental Association voiced strong opposition to truth-in-testing legislation. The former organization, arguing that the New York law violates the copyright on the MCAT, obtained an injunction in 1979 against implementation of the law. In 1990, a federal court found that the New York State statute, which requires publication of materials from the Medical College Admission Test, violates federal copyright law. Despite this ruling, disclosure of test materials continues to be standard practice by testing organizations. Current procedures designed to ensure fair and open testing are an accepted part of test construction, administration, and scoring at Educational Testing Service, the American College Testing Program, and other organizations that design and market tests.

Concern over truth-in-testing legislation has led to improvements in monitoring test questions for cultural or socioeconomic bias. Careful internal review by the ETS professional staff has eliminated bias (ethnic group, gender, etc.) from almost all the thousands of items included on ETS tests each year. The College Entrance Examination Board has also adopted a policy of letting students verify their SAT scores and of public disclosure of SAT items 1 year after the tests have been administered. Test takers can also challenge items on the SAT and other ETS tests and how these examinations are administered.

Effects of Coaching on Test Scores

Prospective applicants to undergraduate or graduate colleges and professional schools are, understandably, interested in improving their scores on qualifying examinations. A consequence of the increasing importance of large-scale nationwide testing has been the publication of test-coaching booklets and the establishment of schools that purport to increase a person's score on a particular test or standardized tests in general. The four most prominent test-coaching organizations are College PowerPrep, Kaplan Inc., The Princeton Review, and test.com inc (see Appendix D for Web sites).

Whether coaching has a significant effect on scores on the SAT and other entrance examinations has been a topic of contention for many years. It is an important issue, for if it can be demonstrated that coaching can improve test scores, then young people who cannot afford it will be deprived of the same opportunity as their more affluent peers.

The results of earlier studies on coaching indicated that its effects are variable, depending on the similarity of the coached material to the test material, the examinee's level of motivation and education, and other factors. Evidence concerning the effects of coaching on the SAT was reported some years ago by the College Entrance Examination Board (1971). The findings indicated that short-term, intensive drill on items similar to those on the SAT did not lead to significant gains in scores, especially on the verbal section of the test. However, this conclusion was questioned by a number of people, in particular Stanley H. Kaplan, director of the largest test-coaching organization in the world. In 1979, the Federal Trade Commission (FTC) released a report of a study of the effects of a 10-week coaching program in three of the Kaplan Educational Centers. Admitting that the study had certain methodological flaws, the FTC nevertheless concluded that performance on both the verbal and mathematical portions of the SAT was improved by coaching courses.

The FTC study and a review of findings by Slack and Porter (1980) were subsequently evaluated by Educational Testing Service. Reanalyzing the data from the FTC investigation, ETS obtained similar findings: inconsistent and negligible effects of coaching for students at two of the Kaplan schools and increases of 20 to 35 points for both verbal and mathematical scores at a third school. Acknowledging that significant increases in test scores may occur when coaching programs involve many hours of course work and assignments, ETS nevertheless maintained that at least part of the gains found at the third school could be attributed to differences in motivation and other personal characteristics.

Summaries of studies conducted during the past two decades on the effects of coaching on SAT scores reveal that intensive drill on items similar to those on the SAT may yield gains of 25 to 32 points on both the verbal and mathematical sections (see review at siop.org/tip/backissues/TipJuly99/4Camara.htm). However, students who merely retake the SAT have gains that are nearly as high (Donlon, 1984). Improvements occur mainly on items with complex or confusing formats and with individuals of poor educational backgrounds (Powers, 1986). The 25 to 32-point gains work out to getting two to four more items correct on the math section and one to two more items correct on the verbal section. In general, however, claims by The Princeton Review (Biemiller, 1986) and other organizations that SAT scores can be increased by 100 points or more are unwarranted (Powers, 1993).

Because most college applicants have more anxiety concerning mathematics than other subjects, brushing up on algebra, geometry, and word meanings just before taking an admissions test may enhance scores. With respect to test-taking procedures, skipping difficult items and coming back to them after completing the rest of the items in that section, looking for reasonable answers on items containing long reading passages, making informed guesses, and the like, will not work wonders but may improve scores somewhat (see the recommendations for test taking on pages 50–52). In any case, in addition to screening new test items for bias, ETS examines new items for their susceptibility to coaching and discards or revises those on which performance can be improved by short-term drill or instruction (Swinton & Powers, 1985).

OTHER ISSUES IN EDUCATIONAL TESTING

Although matters pertaining to the SAT and other national testing programs have received more attention in the media, a number of other matters concerning testing in and for the schools are of concern.

Cheating on Tests

Cheating on tests is a matter of concern at all levels of the educational system (see Cizak, 1999). As test scores have become more important in determining the future educational and professional careers of individuals and in the political arena for assessing schools and other institutions, the temptation to cheat appears to have increased.

Administration of *secure* tests involves standard procedures, such as verifying personal identification, seating examinees in a certain way, careful proctoring, and counting tests and answer sheets to minimize cheating, but none of these procedures entirely eliminates cheating. Pressures from parents, teachers, peers, and students themselves to do well may lead to the theft of tests, copying answers from other students, and cheating in other ways.

In addition to direct observations of cheating on tests or reports by other people that specific students cheated, circumstantial evidence of cheating may be obtained from (1) similar patterns of identical wrong answers by students who sat close to each other during the test (Belleza & Belleza, 1989, 1995) and (2) very large numbers of erasures on answer sheets, primarily from changing wrong answers to right ones. The last technique was used in California during the mid-1980s to confirm suspicions that dramatic increases in test scores in some schools were caused by teachers themselves altering students' answers to items on the California Assessment Program (CAP) tests. The answer sheets from the CAP tests, which measured basic skills in reading, writing, and mathematics and were administered annually in the third, sixth, eighth, and twelfth grades of California public schools, were scored by electronic data scanners. The scanners both scored the answer sheets and counted erasures. Using this procedure in combination with confirmatory clerical work, it was found that in several dozen Los Angeles schools the percentage of erasures on the answer sheets was significantly higher than the expected 3%. Although the resulting furor and associated media coverage precipitated strong protests by the teachers' union and refusals by some teachers to handle the CAP tests, these events led to an investigation of both direct and indirect cheating and tampering with the CAP and CTBS tests (Banks, 1990).

Tampering by teachers with students' answer sheets could not be convincingly denied, but why did they do it? The general answer to this question seems to be that test scores have come to be used so extensively in U.S. society to evaluate individuals, schools, school districts, stages, and even neighborhoods that the pressure on teachers and schools for their students to do well is enormous. Not only have the social pressures on everyone connected with schools resulted in cheating by students and test tampering by teachers, but the latter also frequently "teach to the test." Teaching to and tampering with tests is understandable when one considers the extensive publicity given to test scores by schools, the need to justify increased public expenditures on education, and incentives in which additional funds are allocated to schools when their students score higher on standardized tests.

The time-worn circle in which the state superintendent is badgered by politicians, district superintendents by the state superintendent, school principals by the district superintendent, teachers by principals, students by teachers and parents, and politicians, principals, and teachers by parents leads to a situation in which someone is "always on your back." Principals and other school administrators, who do not have tenure and may be demoted or transferred if students score too low on standardized tests, are particularly susceptible to pressure. Being only human, they may direct this pressure toward teachers to have their schools show up well in the annual roster of test score averages of schools published in local newspapers.

Students, teachers, and school administrators all require some source of motivation to improve the low level to which public education has sunk in many sections of the United States and some means of evaluating the effectiveness of their efforts. However, the atmosphere of paranoia that reportedly permeated the ranks of teachers and administrators in the Los Angeles School District during the test-tampering scandal of 1986–1988 was not beneficial to education in general or to educational testing in particular.

Lake Wobegon Effect

In 1988 it was reported that 70% of the students, 90% of the 15,000 school districts in the United States, and all 50 states were scoring above the national norms on norm-referenced achievement tests administered in elementary schools (Cannell, 1988). This report led to the term *Lake Wobegon effect,* after Garrison Keillor's fictional Minnesota community "where all children are above average." Cannell's findings were supported by the results of a study conducted by the U.S. Department of Education: 57% of elementary school students scored above the national median in reading and 62% above the national median in mathematics. In another survey, conducted by the Friends of Education, it was found that 83% of 5,143 elementary school districts, 73% of 4,501 secondary school districts, and all but two states (Louisiana and Arizona) were "above average" in achievement test scores (Cannell, 1989).

One explanation for the Lake Wobegon effect is that it is a consequence of the tests not being renormed often enough. Another explanation is that it is caused by teachers' coaching students on test questions, allowing them more than the allotted time to take the test, and even altering the completed answer sheets.

Publishers of the standardized achievement tests cited in these studies (CTB/McGraw-Hill, Riverside Publishing Company, and Harcourt Brace) responded that it is expensive to renorm tests as frequently as might be desirable and that improved tests scores may actually indicate that the schools are getting better. Nevertheless, test publishers could undoubtedly do more to emphasize to users of their tests when (the date) and on what samples of students their tests were normed. In particular, it should be made clear whether any groups (e.g., special education students or those with limited English proficiency) were excluded from the norming samples.

While most school officials did not respond in writing or print to Cannell's findings and criticisms, one school assessment expert asserted that it is unethical and unwarranted to assume that cheating has occurred when test scores increase. This official defended the right of teachers to examine the content of a test to determine in which skill areas students need to improve, but not to teach to the test (Landers, 1989).

It is widely recognized that scores tend to creep upward when a particular test battery is administered repeatedly in a school over a period of years. One reason for the increase may be that teachers are teaching to the test, but a likelier explanation is that they are teaching *from* the test (Lenke, 1988). Teachers take note of the areas of the test in which scores are low and attempt to improve students' knowledge and skills in these areas. This is, of course, an appropriate instructional strategy and should not be labeled as cheating. One could also argue that the problem is with norm-referenced tests and that the results of criterion-referenced testing would yield more meaningful information concerning academic strengths and weaknesses and be less subject to misinterpretation. Be that as it may, politicians, parents, and others will undoubtedly continue to demand year-to-year and school-to-school comparative test data to assist in educational decision making.

National Educational Standards and Tests

The nationwide concern that U.S. children are not as well educated in science and mathematics as children in many other countries goes back at least as far as the launching of the first Soviet *Sputnik* in 1957. The results of internationally administered achievement tests subsequently reawakened this concern by revealing that U.S. schoolchildren are behind their counterparts when compared with most other industrialized nations, particularly in mathematics and science (National Center for Education Statistics, November 1996, June 1997, February 1998, 2001).

The National Skills Standards Act, which was incorporated in the Goals 2000: Educate America Act of 1994, established a national skills standards board to develop a voluntary national system of skill standards, assessments, and certifications. It was required under this law that a variety of nondiscriminatory assessment systems—oral and written evaluations, portfolio assessments, performance tests, and others—be devised and applied to monitor the attainment of these standards.

A set of educational standards and the accompanying tests would presumably provide a source of motivation and a guide for improving learning in the public schools and a way of determining the extent of progress in reaching the standards. As seen in the heated debate during the late 1990s concerning the proposed nationwide testing of fourth-graders in reading and eighth-graders in mathematics), bipartisan support for such testing has been difficult to obtain. Conservatives may fear that national tests will be a first step in federal involvement in neighborhood schools and that local schools will be under pressure to adapt their teaching plans to ensure that pupils perform well on the tests. Many liberal representatives are opposed to national testing because they fear that the tests will discriminate against minority children (Shogren, 1997).

In connection with the National Skills Standards Act, there has also been a great deal of discussion among governmental leaders and professionals regarding the development of national tests in English, mathematics, science, history, and geography to be administered on a national level in the fourth, eighth, and twelfth grades. Under the "No Child Left Behind" legislation of President George W. Bush's first administration, federal funding for schools is made contingent on student achievement in mathematics, reading or language arts, and science. Starting in 2005–2006, the mathematics and reading tests are administered at least once during grades 3 to 5, 6 to 9, and 10 to 12; the science tests will not be ushered in until 2007–2008. Different states may give different tests, but all students in a given state are required to take a statewide test to permit comparisons by grade, school, and district. Also, the tests, which cannot be changed from year to year, contain both multiple-choice items and open-ended questions that require students to construct answers and demonstrate critical thinking.[3]

In addition to competency testing in the school grades, efforts have been made to gain support for the development of a national test to determine the extent to which college students have acquired the skills in critical thinking, problem solving, and communication needed to compete in a global economy and exercise the rights and responsibilities of citizenship (Zook, 1993, p. A3). Proposals for such a National Postsecondary Student Assessment, which have been spurred by the demand for accountability in higher education, are also controversial. However, some sort of evaluative procedure to determine whether the large sums of money being spent on higher education are effective in equipping young adults with the analytic skills needed in the workplace is probably forthcoming. The development of such a test or tests would be expensive, but not as costly as having a nation full of poorly educated college graduates.

Intelligence Testing in the Schools

The relationships of educational experience, socioeconomic status, ethnicity, nationality, gender, nutrition, and numerous other psychosocial and biological variables to scores on tests of cognitive abilities have been considered in hundreds of research investigations over the past several decades (see Chapter 7). A continuing question is concerned with the nature of the interaction between heredity and environment in determining scores on intelligence tests. The significance of this question and the social and educational implications of the answers have resulted in legal action in certain states. At issue are questions concerning the utility and bias of intelligence tests: Are these tests useful and fair to all groups of children, or are they biased against certain ethnic groups?

Among the legal cases that have dealt with the administration of intelligence tests in schools are *Stell* v. *Savannah–Chatham County* (1963), *Hobson* v. *Hansen* (1967), *Diana* v. *State Board of Education* (1970), *Guadalupe* v. *Tempe Elementary School District* (1972), *Larry P.* v. *Riles* (1979), *PASE* v. *Hannon* (1980), and *Georgia NAACP* v. *State of Georgia* (1985). A decision that was later reversed by the U.S. Circuit Court of Appeals was handed down in the case of *Stell* v. *Savannah–Chatham County.* The court concluded in this case that, because the IQs of African American children were lower than those of European American children, requiring both groups to integrate in the same schools would be mutually disadvantageous. In *Hobson* v. *Hansen* the court ruled that group tests of ability discriminate against minority children and therefore cannot be used to assign students to different ability tracks. In *Diana* v. *State Board of Education,* the court ruled that traditional testing procedures cannot be used for the placement of Mexican American children in EMR classes in California and that special provisions (e.g., bilingual assessment) must be used to test minority children. The court's decision in *Guadalupe* was to have students tested in

---

[3]See Web site www.ed.gov/policy/elsec/leg/esea02/pg2.

their primary language and to eliminate unfair portions of the test. It was also decreed that IQ scores must be at least two standard deviations below the mean and that other determiners, such as measures of adaptive behavior, must be included in making decisions on whether children should be classified as mentally retarded.

In his book *Bias in Mental Testing,* Jensen (1980) asserted that neither verbal nor nonverbal tests of intelligence are biased in any meaningful way against native-born minorities in the United States. Jensen maintained that tests of intelligence and other cognitive abilities have predictive validity for all ethnic groups and that the tests are not responsible for differences among these groups. As expressed in the decision in *Larry P.* v. *Riles* (1979), Judge Robert Peckham of the Federal District Court of San Francisco disagreed with Jensen. After concluding that IQ tests denied the five African American plaintiffs in a class action suit equal protection under the law, Judge Peckham ordered a continuation of his earlier ban on IQ testing for the placement of African Americans in California public school classes for educable mentally retarded children. Thus, it was ruled that individually administered tests of intelligence are biased against African Americans and that the California State Department of Education could not use these tests for educational diagnosis or placement of African American children. Contributing to this decision was the fact that a disproportionate number of African American children had been assigned to EMR classes, which Judge Peckham labeled "dead-end education." Consequently, it was stipulated that the proportion of African American children in EMR classes should match their proportion in the general population of schoolchildren. In 1986, Judge Peckham reissued his ruling prohibiting the use of IQ tests in the public schools of California, even when parental consent had been obtained. The court's decision in *Larry P.,* however, did not ban the use of all intelligence testing in California public schools, and such tests continued to be administered for certain purposes.

Less than a year after the judicial decision in *Larry P.* v. *Riles,* another federal judge, John F. Grady, rendered a very different decision in a similar case in Illinois. In this case, *PASE* (Parents in Action on Special Education) v. *Hannon* (1980), it was decreed that the WISC, WISC-R, and Stanford–Binet tests, when used in conjunction with the statutorily mandated ["other criteria"] for determining an appropriate educational program for a child (under Public Law 94–142) . . . do not discriminate against African American children (p. 883). As a result, intelligence tests continued to be administered for special class placement in Illinois public schools and in the schools of many other states. Similar to the decision in *PASE* v. *Hannon,* the court ruled in *Georgia NAACP* v. *State of Georgia* (1985) that intelligence tests do not discriminate against African American children. Also contrary to the ruling in the *Larry P.* case, it was concluded in the *Georgia* decision that the presence of disproportionate numbers of African American children in EMR classes does not constitute proof of discrimination. Finally, in September of 1992 Judge Peckham lifted the ban on intelligence testing in California public schools on the grounds that it was unfair to African American parents who wanted the tests to be used in the class placement of their learning disabled children (Bredemeier, 1991). This ruling effectively nullified his earlier (1986) prohibition against the use of intelligence tests in the public schools of California. A review of these and other court cases concerned with intelligence testing in the schools reveals that the judicial decisions have varied not only from state to state, but also with the political climate of the times.

Although the use of intelligence tests may sometimes encourage discrimination and even contribute to a self-fulfilling prophecy, a number of psychologists and educators maintain that there are advantages to using intelligence tests for placement purposes. Many children who are referred by teachers as in need of special education are found not to be so when they are retested. In fact, if the tests were not used, more minority children would probably be assigned to special education classes. And even those who are placed in such classes on the basis of low test scores often profit from special education to such an extent that their IQs are raised and they become ineligible for these services. Finally, it might be asked what happens to children who need special education but are not identified because intelligence tests are not used. How many schoolchildren fall further behind each year because they are deprived of an education appropriate to their abilities by being placed in regular classes?

EMPLOYMENT TESTING AND BIAS

Equal in importance to issues surrounding the use of tests in schools and colleges is the question of the fairness of these instruments for purposes of job selection, placement, and promotion. As a result of the growing concern over civil rights, the matter became increasingly important during the 1960s and 1970s. Because employment tests had, at the time, been validated principally on members of the dominant European American culture, it was reasonable to ask whether they had any validity for African Americans and other minorities. Such was the situation in the *Myart* v. *Motorola* (1964) case, in which the issue was whether a test that was being used for selection purposes was racially discriminatory.

Equal Employment Opportunity Legislation

The Civil Rights Act of 1964 came in the wake of the Motorola case and other criticisms of psychological testing. Title VII of this act specifically prohibited discrimination on the basis of race, color, national origin, sex, or religion.[4] A Supreme Court ruling on Title VII occurred in the case of *Griggs et al.* v. *Duke Power Company* (1971), which dealt with a suit brought against the Duke Power Company by African American employees. The suit challenged Duke Power's earlier requirement of a high school diploma and new hiring and promotion policies requiring designated minimum scores on the Wonderlic Personnel Test and the Bennett Test of Mechanical Comprehension. Chief Justice Warren Burger, who wrote the majority opinion in this case, concluded that "If an employment practice which operates to exclude Negroes cannot be shown to be [significantly] related to job performance, the practice is prohibited" (*Griggs et al.* v. *Duke Power Company,* 1971, p. 60). But Justice Burger also stated that

> nothing in the [Civil Rights] Act precludes the use of testing or measuring procedures; obviously they are useful. What Congress has forbidden is giving these devices and mecha-

---

[4]Also concerned with fair employment practices are the Age Discrimination in Employment Act of 1967 (ADEA) and the Americans with Disabilities Act of 1990 (ADA). The ADEA prohibits discrimination against employees or applicants age 40 or older in all aspects of the employment process. Under the ADA, qualified individuals with disabilities must be given equal opportunity in all aspects of employment.

nisms controlling force unless they are demonstrably a reasonable measure of job performance. Congress has not commanded that the less qualified be preferred over the better qualified simply because of minority origins. Far from disparaging job qualifications as such, Congress has made such qualifications the controlling factor, so that race, religion, nationality, and sex become irrelevant. (*Griggs* v. *Duke Power Company,* 1971, p. 11)

The intent of the Supreme Court decision in *Griggs et al.* v. *Duke Power* was to require employers to demonstrate that the skills measured by their selection tests and other hiring procedures are job related. The immediate effect of the decision was a reexamination and in some situations a discontinuance of certain job-selection tests by business and industrial organizations. Congress subsequently concluded that Title VII of the Civil Rights Act of 1964 had not been adequately enforced and that discrimination against minorities and women was continuing. This conclusion led to a revision of the Civil Rights Act—the Equal Employment Opportunity Act of 1972. The Equal Employment Opportunity Coordinating Council (EEOCC), which was established by the Equal Employment Opportunity Act, then prepared a set of guidelines, *The Uniform Guidelines on Employee Selection Procedures.* These guidelines described procedures for employers, labor organizations, and employment agencies to follow in showing

that any selection procedure which operates to disqualify or otherwise adversely affect members of any racial, ethnic, or sex group at a higher rate than another group, has been validated in accord with these guidelines, and that alternative employment procedures of equal validity which have less of an adverse effect are unavailable. (U.S. Equal Employment Opportunity Commission, 1973, p. 20)

The guidelines further state that to be adjudged a valid predictor of performance the test or combination of tests should normally account for at least half the reliably measurable skills and knowledge pertaining to the job.

The law concerning the disparate impact of employment practices with respect to certain groups was extended in three subsequent cases—*United States* v. *Georgia Power Company* (1973), *Albemarle Paper Co.* v. *Moody* (1975), and *Washington* v. *Davis* (1976). In the case of *Albemarle Paper Co.* v. *Moody,* after finding the company's testing program inadequate, the court maintained that, even if a test is valid but adversely impacts the employment of certain groups, the organization should make every effort to find a less biased selection device. The legal definition of *adverse impact* follows the four-fifths rule, according to which a condition of adverse impact is viewed as being present if one group has a selection rate that is less than four-fifths (80%) of that of the group with the highest selection rate. For example, if 100 European Americans and 100 African Americans apply for a job and 60 European Americans (the highest group) are hired, then a condition of adverse impact may be said to exist if fewer than (4/5)60 = 48 African Americans are also hired. Under the EEOC guidelines, employers are required to adopt selection techniques having the least adverse impact. In *Washington* v. *Davis,* the court expanded the criterion to which selection tests should be related to include performance in job-training programs.

A 1978 revision of the EEOC Guidelines on Employee Selection (U.S. Equal Employment Opportunity Commission, 1978) was not as strict as the original version of the guidelines in requiring employees to conduct differential validity studies. Like its predecessor, the revised guidelines were designed to require employers to justify the use of tests and other selection procedures that exclude disproportionate numbers of minority group members and women. The guidelines describe three validation methods on which employers may rely: criterion-related validity, content validity, and construct validity. But they are not clear on how large the validity coefficients should be. In addition, although the revised guidelines state that using tests is legitimate when the scores are related to job performance, they do not specify what is meant by "job-related criteria."

Job relatedness is an important concept in this context, because the use of tests that have an adverse impact is often justified on the basis of the claim that they are job related. The failure of the EEOC guidelines to make clear what is meant by job-related criteria and other problems of clarity in the guidelines prompted many business and service organizations to suspend the use of job-selection tests altogether.

Clearly, the implication of the EEOC guidelines was that employment managers need to conduct validation studies of all their selection procedures, not just psychological tests, to determine if they are significantly related to job success. In *Watson* v. *Fort Worth Bank and Trust* (1988), the Court ruled that subjective employment devices such as interviews can be validated and that employees may claim adverse impact resulting from promotion practices based on interviews. Costly though it may be, interviews and other methods that are less objective than tests must be subjected to scrutiny by means of appropriate validity studies.

Another interesting court case concerned with fair employment practices was *Wards Cove Packing Company* v. *Antonio* (1989). The plaintiffs in this case were Filipino and Eskimo workers in salmon canneries in Alaska, who claimed that the company was keeping them out of better paying jobs such as machinery repair. The judicial decision in this case is important because it shifted the burden of proof to the employee to show that the psychological test being used for promotion purposes was not valid and reliable. Concern over this decision, which reversed a central theme of the *Griggs* v. *Duke Power* case, led to the Civil Rights Act of 1991. This act reaffirmed the principles under Title VII of the Civil Rights Act of 1964, but clarified the condition that the burden of proof lies with the employer. Another important provision of the act effectively outlawed the use of differential cutoff scores by race, gender, or ethnic background, the impact of which was a shift away from the quota system that had been in effect for over two decades. In short, it was stipulated that

> It shall be an unlawful employment practice for a respondent in connection with the selection or referral of applicants or candidates for employment or promotion to adjust the scores of, use different cutoff scores, or otherwise alter the results of employment related tests on the basis of race, color, religion, sex, or national origin.

Other lawsuits related to educational and employment selection have been concerned with the effects of affirmative action or quotas in denying university admission to Asian and European Americans who possess the requisite qualification. Although the court has upheld selection or admissions procedures that favor underrepresented groups (e.g., *United States* v. *City of Buffalo,* 1985), proposals to do away with legislatively mandated affirmative action requirements in schools and in the workplace became very significant during the 1990s.

Test Fairness

As the EEOC guidelines imply, psychological and educational tests standardized on European American samples are unacceptable for use in selecting African Americans and other minority group applicants. The use of such tests with groups other than those on which they were standardized raises the issue of test fairness. The concept of fairness in psychological and educational assessment has a more statistical meaning than that implied by the EEOC guidelines. The traditional point of view in psychological measurement is that the *fairness* of a test for different groups depends on whether applicants with the same probability of doing well on a performance criterion have the same likelihood of being selected. According to this definition, even if the mean test score of one group is lower than that of another, the test is not necessarily unfair. African Americans or other minorities in the United States may attain lower average scores than European Americans on employment tests, but it reveals nothing about the fairness of the tests in the technical sense. Regardless of any difference in mean test scores for two different groups, it has traditionally been maintained that a job-selection test is fair if it predicts job success equally well for all applicant groups.

After calling attention to a statistical flaw in the traditional (equal regression) definition of test fairness, Thorndike (1971) proposed an alternative definition. Thorndike's *constant ratio* definition specifies that qualifying scores on a test should be established in such a way that different groups of applicants are selected in proportion to the number of each group capable of attaining an acceptable level on the performance criterion. For example, if 30% of all European American applicants and 20% of all African American applicants are judged capable of performing a given job, then qualifying scores on a selection test should be set in such a way that 30% of European American applicants and 20% of African American applicants are hired.

Another definition of test fairness was suggested by Cole (1973). She proposed that separate cutoff scores for the two or more different groups of applicants be established in such a way that the probability of selection is the same for potentially successful applicants in each group. Assume, for example, that two different groups are composed of 50 and 100 applicants each. If it has been previously determined that 50% of all applicants can perform the job satisfactorily, then $50\% \times 50 = 25$ applicants in the first group and $50\% \times 100 = 50$ applicants in the second group should be selected. A similar quota selection procedure was suggested by Dunnette and Borman (1979). In their proposal, however, the percentage of applicants to be selected is determined beforehand; then separate regression equations are applied to each group.

The revised EEOC guidelines admit that test fairness is not a fixed concept and that experts may disagree on its meaning. Whatever definition of fairness may be preferred, the relative seriousness of errors of incorrectly rejecting and incorrectly accepting applicants must be taken into account. This implies that the fairness of a test is a relative matter, depending on whether it is considered more serious to reject an applicant who would have succeeded (*false negative*) or to accept an applicant who will fail (*false positive*). Social conscience may dictate that the former error is more serious, whereas considerations of safety and profit point to the latter error as being of greater concern. Viewed from this perspective, the meaning of fairness is a matter of social policy rather than psychometrics alone.

Even when the test as a whole is considered fair, it is possible for individual items to be unfair or biased toward a particular group. For example, certain items may present a stereotyped view of minorities and women according to occupation, education, family, and recreation or in other ways (Tittle, 1984). To identify and guard against item bias, test publishers typically conduct judgmental reviews to detect stereotyping and familiarity of test content to particular groups. Various statistical procedures have also been devised to determine the presence of item bias or differential item functioning (DIF). Among these procedures are transformed item-difficulty indexes, biserial correlations to determine item discriminations, item characteristic curves, and variants of chi square, such as the Mantel–Haenszel statistic (Cole & Moss, 1989; Scheuneman & Bleistein, 1989).

Construction of item characteristic curves is one of the most descriptive ways of detecting item bias. According to this approach, a test item is unbiased if its characteristic curve is the same for the groups being compared. In other words, examinees of equal ability, regardless of the group to which they belong, have equal probabilities of getting the item right. Experimental studies in which the content of a test is varied to determine if different groups respond differently and factor-analytic studies to determine whether the responses of different groups yield the same factors have also been conducted to investigate test and item bias (Cole & Moss, 1989; Tittle, 1984).

A kind of compromise solution to the problem of item bias was worked out in 1984, when the Educational Testing Service agreed to an out-of-court settlement of a suit charging social bias on insurance licensing examinations in Illinois. According to the terms of the settlement, it was agreed that in constructing the insurance examinations ETS would first use items on which African Americans and European Americans scored most alike. This approach, referred to as the *Golden Rule settlement* after the insurance company involved in the suit, was subsequently used in a number of other states. Be that as it may, the Golden Rule settlement was subsequently the subject of considerable debate and opposition (*Educational Measurement,* 1987, *6*(2); Anrig, 1987; Denton, 1988).

SUMMARY

1. Requiring students to pass a minimum competency test before being awarded a high school diploma and requiring teachers to pass a professional competency test before being hired or retained are common practices in the United States. Some colleges and universities have also implemented a value-added approach to the assessment of changes in knowledge and skills during the undergraduate years. Competency testing of both high school students and teachers has gained momentum in recent years. In addition to evaluating both students and teachers, tests and related instruments are used to evaluate educational programs or curricula and to determine the effectiveness of other intervention procedures and programs.

2. The content and applications of standardized tests of cognitive abilities have been under attack for many decades. Multiple-choice tests have been accused of penalizing creative thinkers, focusing on a specific answer rather than the quality of responses, and encouraging teachers to teach to the test. High-stakes entrance examinations such

as the SAT have been criticized as being invalid indicators of what they purport to measure, as invading the individual's right to privacy, as unfair to both favored and disadvantaged students, and as fostering poor study habits and unethical social and economic practices. This has resulted in a review of test procedures, rebuttals to many of these accusations, guidelines on not giving too much reliance on them, and the use of performance-based and portfolio assessment. In addition, truth-in-testing legislation was prompted by the demand for the testing industry to become more open and responsible to the public. Although only New York and California have passed such legislation, Educational Testing Service and other large-scale testing organizations have become more open with their tests and procedures and more socially sensitive to the design and uses of their products.

3. The extent to which coaching for the SAT and other similar tests can actually increase scores has been both controversial and the results have been equivocal. Reviews of research indicate that increases in SAT scores due to coaching are typically 25–32 points which are equivalent to getting an additional two to four items correct on the math section and one to two more items correct on the verbal sections. However, for some individuals, gains can be 100 points or more.

4. It has been noted that a majority of students score above the mean in achievement tests. This may be due to actual improvement in education but may also be the result of teachers who teach to the test, tampering by teachers, repeated use of the tests, and student cheating.

5. Legislation and litigation regarding civil rights and equal employment opportunity have led to the regulation of test usage in business and industry. Federal guidelines for employee selection procedures describe the characteristics that test and nontest measures should possess to be acceptable and valid techniques for employee selection and placement.

6. The question of the fairness of tests for minority and disadvantaged groups led to new definitions of *fairness*. Legal and technical issues stemming from consideration of the concepts of fairness and differential prediction have alerted professional psychologists, employment managers, and the general public to the need for more responsible use of tests and other assessment procedures.

MASTERING THE CHAPTER OBJECTIVES

1. *Issues surrounding student academic competence*
   a. List arguments for and against competency testing of (1) high school students, (2) prospective school teachers, and (3) experienced teachers.
   b. What would you imagine would be the impact of eliminating all competency testing?

2. *College entrance and multiple-choice exams*
   a. Discuss specific objections to standardized tests in general and multiple-choice tests in particular.
   b. Describe criticisms of the SAT and the responses of the College Entrance Examination Board and Educational Testing Service to these criticisms.

3. *Coaching for college entrance exams*
   a. How effective is preparation for taking the SAT?
   b. Name three issues that make it difficult to determine the effectiveness of SAT coaching.

4. *Cheating and above-average performance*
   a. What is the impact of the extensive pressure to do well on the SAT and other national tests?
   b. List three reasons why a large majority of students might perform above average on academic competency testing (the Lake Wobegon effect).

5. *Admissibility of intelligence testing in schools*
   a. Review judicial decisions regarding the use of intelligence tests for special class placement in the schools.
   b. If you were the parent of a minority student who was performing poorly in school, what are reasons why you would or would not want to have your child evaluated using an intelligence test?

6. *Fairness in intelligence testing and related court rulings*
   a. Review legislation enacted by the U.S. Congress and judicial decisions pertaining to employment testing, beginning with Title VII of the Civil Rights Act of 1964.
   b. What are the EEOC, Thorndike's, and Cole's (1973) definitions of fairness in tests? Why do different definitions of test fairness exist?
   c. Refer to the 30 paired scores in Table A.2 of Appendix A (p. 449). Assume that X is a score on a job-selection test and Y is a job performance rating. Also assume that the 30 paired scores were obtained from a majority group of applicants for the job, whereas the following 30 paired scores were obtained from a minority group of applicants.

X	Y	X	Y	X	Y	X	Y
40	64	34	41	52	46	50	39
62	48	48	44	42	38	32	30
40	32	56	64	18	26	68	42
52	40	48	36	46	34	60	60
36	31	24	54	64	65	44	48

Now assume that 50% of the majority group applicants, 25% of the minority group applicants, and 40% of all applicants perform the job satisfactorily ($Y = 50$ or higher). Is the test fair according to the traditional definition of fairness? According to Thorndike's definition? According to Cole's definition? What are the percentages of false positives and false negatives in each group, and how do they affect the fairness of the test? (See Answers to Quantitative Questions, pp. 487–488.)

EXPERIENCING PSYCHOLOGICAL ASSESSMENT

1. Investigate the test-coaching schools, test-coaching courses, and published materials on test coaching available in your geographical area. Try to locate six or so students who have been coached or prepared for the SAT, the GRE, or some other nationally administered test for a fee. Did these students feel the coaching worthwhile? What evidence, if any, was cited by the providers of the courses for the beneficial effects of coaching?

■ ■ ■ ■ ■

CHAPTER ELEVEN

TESTING SPECIAL ABILITIES

CHAPTER OBJECTIVES

1. Discuss conceptual issues (including validity) related to achievement tests, aptitude tests, and tests of specific abilities.
2. Discuss concepts (including validity) of psychomotor tests along with relevant examples.
3. Discuss concepts and provide examples of tests of mechanical and clerical abilities.
4. Describe tests of artistic and musical abilities.
5. Describe multiple-aptitude test batteries, including strategies of profile interpretation.
6. Describe the Differential Aptitude Tests, Multidimensional Aptitude Battery-II, General Aptitude Battery, and the Armed Services Vocational Aptitude Battery.

Vocational assessment focuses on understanding the optimal fit between various vocations and a person's abilities, interests, and personality. Accordingly, the next three chapters will elaborate on each of these areas. One of the best predictors of whether a person will do well is if they have a high aptitude for a certain type of activity. Some people have high mechanical abilities and thus excel in such jobs as engineering or automotive repair. Another person might have poor mechanical abilities, but instead have excellent artistic abilities and might be best suited for work as an interior designer or fine artist. Thus, a vocational counselor needs to fully understand a person's pattern of strengths and weaknesses in order to advise a client regarding appropriate training programs so that they can then enter suitable occupations.

CONCEPTS AND CHARACTERISTICS

There is often confusion regarding the differences among aptitudes, achievement, and abilities. In a sense, the term *aptitude* is a misnomer if it is meant to imply that what is being measured is an inborn, unchangeable characteristic. Early mental testers aspired to measure hereditary characteristics, for they assumed that all people whom they examined had equal opportunities to profit from the experiences on which the test materials were based. This assumption, however, was incorrect: experiences, and hence opportunities to learn, are never exactly the same for different people, particularly people of different social classes or cultures.

It is now generally recognized that aptitude tests are, to a large extent, measures of achievement. Such achievement is a complex product of the interaction between hereditary and environmental influences. The difference between *aptitude tests* and *achievement tests* is further blurred in that both types of tests can predict future accomplishment. Thus, achievement tests can also be considered tests of aptitude.

Because of confusion over the difference between aptitude and achievement, it has been recommended that the two terms be replaced with the single term *ability*. Then, depending on the purpose for which it is used—to assess current knowledge and understanding or to predict future performance—a test of ability could be either a measure of achievement or aptitude. But it is a mistake to assume that the distinction between aptitude and achievement is inconsequential. As an illustration of the functional difference between measures of these two variables, consider the results of a study by Carroll (1973). Prior to a foreign language course, students were given a foreign language aptitude test and a foreign language achievement test. At the end of the course, the achievement test was re-administered and it was found that scores increased. This reflected the benefit they received from the training. In contrast, aptitude test scores remained essentially unchanged. This supports the concept that, at least under some circumstances, performance on aptitude tests is not affected by achievement.

General and Specific Abilities

The intelligence tests discussed in Chapters 6 through 9 are measures of *general* aptitude, in that scores on these tests represent a composite of cognitive abilities and can be used to forecast achievement and other behaviors in a wide range of situations. In fact, scores on general intelligence tests are often better predictors of success in educational and employment situations than are combined scores on measures of special abilities (Schmidt & Hunter, 2004). But the fact that general intelligence tests measure a hodgepodge of specific aptitudes or abilities is a two-edged sword. In this fact lie both the strength and weakness of these kinds of tests.

Because intelligence tests measure an assortment of abilities, they have what Cronbach (1970) referred to as *broad bandwidth*. An advantage of their broad content is that intelligence tests are moderately effective in predicting a wide range of performance criteria. A longer test of one of the special abilities measured by an intelligence test, that is, an instrument with a narrower bandwidth, presumably has greater *fidelity*. In other words, it would be expected to measure a specified variable more precisely and do a better job of predicting a narrower range of criteria.

Noting the significant positive correlations among measures of special abilities, Vernon (1979) concluded that general intelligence is more important than special abilities in determining occupational success (Neisser et al., 1996; Schmidt & Hunter, 2004). To the extent that this is true, it is probably due to the fact that criteria of occupational success, like scores on intelligence tests, are the complex products of many variables. In other words, occupational criteria have broad bandwidth and hence are likely to be predicted more accurately from a combination of measures, rather than by scores on a single test of special ability.

Origins of Vocational Testing

One event that stimulated the development of tests of special abilities during the first half of the 1920s and the 1930s was the growth of *scientific management.* Proponents of scientific management in business and industry felt that both employees and employers would benefit if psychological tests could be devised to help match people with jobs. They maintained that the use of tests would result in employees being selected for and placed on jobs they could perform most effectively. Selecting more competent employees and assigning them to jobs for which they were best suited would, by increasing productivity, benefit both employees, employers, and the organization as a whole.

During the Great Depression years of the 1930s, when matters related to employment were of particular concern to government, research and development programs at the University of Minnesota and elsewhere resulted in the construction of a series of special abilities tests for use in vocational counseling and employee selection and placement. From these programs and subsequent efforts came not only numerous single-ability measures, but also several batteries of tests.

Validity of Special Abilities Tests

Because tests of aptitudes or special abilities are designed with differential prediction in mind, it is reasonable to ask how successful they are in predicting who will succeed and who will fail in particular occupations or training programs. That is, just how valid are vocational aptitude tests? The answer is that, in general, the validities of these tests are not very high. The average validity coefficients of different kinds of aptitude tests for predicting performance in various job categories are typically in the .20s and almost never above the .30s (Ghiselli, 1973). These very modest coefficients underscore the limitations of these kinds of tests for predicting performance on the job.

One issue is that job success depends on many more factors than just ability. These might include interpersonal relationships, motivation, personality, or the extent to which the person can adapt to the managerial style or organizational climate. Some factors that predict success are often extremely difficult to predict. For example, incidental or fortuitous events, such as economic and social changes, might influence the employment situation. These unforeseen events can affect the predictive validity of tests in organizational and industrial contexts. Within this multifaceted aspect of job success, it is understandable that the correlation between ability measures and job success is rarely above .30.

Validity is also affected by problems in specifying and measuring criteria of job success. Possible criteria might include peer ratings, employer ratings, economic output, or level of satisfaction. Despite their limitations, tests of special abilities can still assist in determining what occupation or training program is most suitable for a given person. The tests are certainly limited when used alone, but their value increases when the scores are combined with other types of information (interests, motivation, attitudes, etc.).

Even the relatively modest validity coefficients of most special abilities tests are not fixed: they vary with the nature of the criterion, the situation, and the people being examined. For example, a validity coefficient is likely to be higher when a test is validated against grades in a training program than when it is validated against ratings of actual on-the-job performance. A validity coefficient also tends to be higher when the test is administered and the criterion data collected fairly close together in time than when there is a long delay between administration of the test and collection of the criterion data.

Situational variability in a validity coefficient is seen when the correlation between scores on an ability test and ratings of job performance are lower in one organization than another. Research has demonstrated, however, that many job-selection tests have a great deal of *validity generalization;* that is, they are valid across a wide range of situations (e.g., Schmidt & Hunter, 2004; Schmidt et al., 1993). Nevertheless, the validity of a test varies to some extent with both the situation and the characteristics of the people who are tested. It may vary with the sex, ethnicity, and socioeconomic status of the examinees, as well as their vocational interests, motivation, and personality characteristics. Such individual and group differences, which influence, or moderate, the correlation between a test and a criterion measure, are referred to as *moderator variables.*

Organizations are like people in that they are motivated not only to survive, but also to grow; in fact, in our dynamic society organizations must expand or, in the long run, they will fail. Consequently, from the perspective of the organization, an important factor in deciding whether to use a specific test in selecting, placing, or promoting personnel is whether the test contributes to the economic well-being of the organization. The cost of administering the test must be weighed against the benefits to the organization from using it, and studies of the validity of the test can contribute to measuring these benefits. A test should not only be a valid and efficient predictor of job performance; it should also be an independently valid predictor. Why use the test if other, cheaper methods are available for identifying good workers and predicting how they will perform?

Economic benefit to an organization is, of course, not the only reason for determining the validity of a test for a specific purpose in a specific situation. An important legal reason for conducting validity studies in business and industry centers on the question of bias or fairness. For example, it may be that the test–criterion correlation is significantly higher with one ethnic or gender group than another. If so, it is unfair to use the same prediction equation with both groups. The *fairness,* or relative freedom from bias, of the test must be demonstrated if it is to be used for selection or classification purpose.

Performance and Paper-and-Pencil Tests

The first tests of special abilities were performance tests that required examinees to construct something or manipulate physical objects in certain ways. Such *apparatus* tests are frequently more interesting than paper-and-pencil tests, especially to examinees who have reading problems. But the reliabilities of speeded performance tests are typically lower than those of comparable paper-and-pencil tests. These tests are also time consuming and expensive to administer. Furthermore, correlations between scores on performance tests and paper-and-pencil measures of the same ability are far from perfect. Despite the shortcomings of performance tests, *work-sample tests* (or *job-replica tests*) that require examinees to complete a sample of tasks similar to those comprising a certain job are among the most useful measures of ability in specific occupational contexts.

In-Basket Technique and Assessment Center

An interesting example of a work-sample test is the *in-basket technique.* This procedure was devised originally for evaluating school administrators, but it has been used subsequently with other kinds of administrators or executives. On an in-basket test, candidates for an administrative position are presented with samples of items of the sort typically found in an administrator's in-basket (letters, memos, notes, directives, reports, telephone messages, e-mail, faxes) requiring some kind of action. They are asked to indicate what action should be taken on each item, and their responses are evaluated according to experts' judgments of the appropriateness of their responses.

The *assessment center* approach, which was introduced by the American Telephone and Telegraph Company in the 1950s, combines the in-basket technique with other simulation tasks, such as management games and group problem-solving exercises (as in the Leaderless Group Discussion Test). Interviews, psychological tests, and other methods of appraisal are also used in this approach. The assessment center has been employed less as a selection technique than as a means of evaluating managerial-level personnel for promotion and classification. Six to twelve candidates are brought to a specific location, where they are observed and assessed by other executives and by each other for several days. The principal criteria on which the candidates are evaluated are degree of active participation, organizational skills, and decision-making ability.

Because the in-basket technique and other simulation tasks are realistic, it might seem that they would be highly valid. The candidates, however, are aware of being "on stage" as it were, and they may role play or in other ways behave differently than they would in an actual administrative situation. Expense and time constraints also prohibit using such simulation techniques for anything other than the assessment of fairly high level management personnel.

SENSORY–PERCEPTUAL AND PSYCHOMOTOR SKILLS

It is important, and in many cases mandated by government and other organizations, for the sensory–perceptual and psychomotor abilities of both children and adults to be evaluated periodically. It should be noted, however, that it is illegal to reject a job applicant whose physical limitations do not interfere with his or her job performance. At the same time, employees may sue a company if they experience injury on a job for which they lack the physical skills to perform effectively. For these reasons, employers must make certain that the sensory–perceptual and psychomotor skills requirements of employees are job relevant. Except in cases of gross deficiency, however, it is not always apparent when a defect in physical functioning is present. Depending on whether the handicap can be corrected or compensated for and the degree to which it affects job performance, the applicant may or may not be admitted or hired. Current practice, bolstered by the Americans with Disabilities Act (ADA), favors hiring or admitting handicapped persons and taking steps to minimize the debilitating effects of the handicaps.

Tests of Vision and Hearing[1]

Both visual and auditory acuity may be checked by various kinds of tests, some of which (Snellen chart, watch test, etc.) are very simple and others (ophthalmoscope, audiometer, etc.) much more complex. Simple tests of vision and hearing can usually be administered by a teacher or personnel assistant, but a more in-depth examination of vision and hearing requires the services of a professional optometrist, ophthalmologist, or audiologist.

A complete vision examination involves tests of near and far acuity in each eye and both eyes together, muscular balance of the eyes at near and far distances, depth perception, and color vision. Instruments such as the B & L Vision Tester (from Bausch & Lomb) have been used for visual screening in industrial contexts. The results of testing with this instrument are evaluated in terms of a number of *visual job families,* depending on what visual abilities are essential for particular occupations. Color vision tests can contribute to selection on jobs such as air traffic controller, designer, electrician, lab technician, mechanic, and press operator. A typical color vision test consists of a series of *pseudoisochromatic cards* containing a numeral or design made up of colored dots against a background of contrasting dots. The Dvorine Color Vision Test (by I. Dvorine) is a widely used test of this type.

Good hearing, as well as good vision, is important in many occupations, particularly on jobs such as sonar operator. Auditory acuity can be determined roughly by a *watch test,*[2] but a professional hearing test involves the use of an *audiometer.* The results of an audiometric test are plotted as a graph (*audiogram*) showing the sensitivity of each ear to pure tones spanning the frequency range of human hearing. A person's ability to locate the direction from which sounds are coming may also be determined. Another important characteristic of hearing is the ability to discriminate between stimuli of different pitch or loudness.

Tests of Psychomotor Abilities[3]

Tests of psychomotor skills were among the first measures of special abilities to be constructed. Many of the available tests of this type were introduced during the 1920s and

---

[1]Detailed examples of 12 tests of sensory–perceptual abilities (near vision, far vision, visual color discrimination, night vision, peripheral vision, depth perception, glare sensitivity, hearing sensitivity, auditory attention, sound localization, speech recognition, and speech clarity) are given on pages 61–75 of Fleishman and Reilly (1995).

[2]On this test, depending on how quiet the examination room is, a person with normal hearing should be able to hear a "dollar watch" ticking from a distance of 30 to 40 inches from his or her ear.

[3]Detailed examples of tests of 10 psychomotor abilities (control precision, multilimb coordination, response orientation, rate control, reaction time, arm–hand steadiness, manual dexterity, finger dexterity, wrist–finger speed, speed-of-limb movement) are given on pages 38–50 of Fleishman and Reilly (1995). Examples of tests of 9 physical abilities (static strength, explosive strength, dynamic strength, trunk strength, extent flexibility, dynamic flexibility, gross body coordination, gross body equilibrium, stamina) are given on pages 51–60 of the same source.

1930s to predict performance in certain skilled jobs or trades. Subsequently, the Air Force Personnel and Training Research Center made a comprehensive analysis of psychomotor abilities involved in performance as a pilot. Particularly important in these analyses were tests for performance on flight simulators, such as the Link Trainer and the Complex Coordination Test. On the latter, the examinee uses three controls similar to a stick and rudder to match a pattern of stimulus lights on a vertical panel simulating the movements of an airplane in flight.

Speed, strength, and agility all contribute to effective psychomotor performance. Measures of these characteristics are widely used in selecting workers for various kinds of jobs and are valid predictors of performance in physically demanding work (see Blakley, Quinones, Crawford, & Jago, 1994; Hogan & Quigley, 1994). In addition to measures of isometric strength, tests of precision and steadiness of various manipulations with fingers, hands, arms, and legs are available. Some of these tests require small muscular movements, some large, and others both small and large movements.

To illustrate the available psychomotor skills tests, selected measures of gross movements, fine movements, or a combination of gross and fine movements will be described. The majority of these instruments are appropriate for both adolescents and adults and are scored in terms of the number of task units completed in a specified time or the time required to complete the entire task.

Gross Manual Movements. An example of an older test that was designed to measure speed and accuracy of gross finger, hand, and arm movements is the Stromberg Dexterity Test (by E. L. Stromberg). On this test the examinee is required to place 54 biscuit-sized, colored discs (red, yellow, blue) in a prescribed sequence as rapidly as possible (Figure 11.1). This test has been used as a measure of manual dexterity in laundry workers, punch press operators, machine molders, assemblers, and welders. The Minnesota Rate of Manipulation

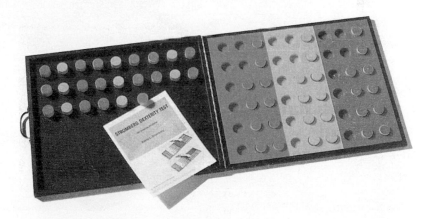

FIGURE 11.1   Stromberg Dexterity Test.

Test consists of a 60-hole board with blocks that are red on one side and yellow on the other. The test is divided into five subtests, on which the blocks are turned, moved, and placed in certain ways. On the Placing Test portion, for example, the blocks are placed into the holes on the board; on the Turning Test portion, the blocks are turned over and replaced in the board.

Fine Manual Movements.   Representative of tests requiring manipulation of small parts are the Purdue Pegboard and the Crawford Small Parts Dexterity Test. Scores on these tests have been found to have significant correlations with performance in occupations such as instrument mechanic, engraver, etcher, precision electronics assembler, and watch repairperson.

The Purdue Pegboard consists of five tasks (right hand, left hand, both hands, right plus left plus both, assembly) for measuring the hand–finger–arm dexterity required for certain kinds of manual work. On the first part of the test, the examinee puts pins into holes, first with the right hand, then with the left, and finally with both hands. On the second part of the test, the examinee puts a pin into a hole, places a washer and collar over the pin, puts another pin into a hole, and so on (Figure 11.2).

The Crawford Small Parts Dexterity Test, a measure of eye–hand coordination and fine-motor dexterity, consists of two parts. On the first part, examinees use tweezers to insert pins into holes and place collars over them. On the second part, the examinee places screws into threaded holes and screws them down with a screwdriver (Figure 11.3).

Gross and Fine Manual Movements.   A psychomotor skills test that combines finger dexterity with gross movements of the arms and hands is the Bennett Hand–Tool Dexterity Test (by G. K. Bennett). On this test the examinee is required first to unfasten 12 nuts from

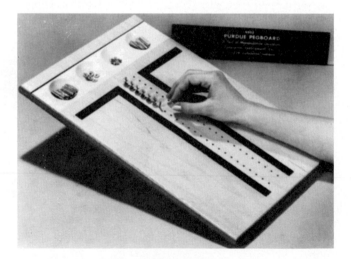

FIGURE 11.2   Purdue Pegboard.

(Courtesy of Lafayette Instrument Company.)

FIGURE 11.3   Crawford Small Parts Dexterity Test, Part II.

(From the *Crawford Small Parts Dexterity Test.* Copyright © 1946, 1956, 1981 by Harcourt Assessment, Inc. Reproduced with permission. All rights reserved.)

FIGURE 11.4   Bennett Hand–Tool Dexterity Test.

(From the *Bennett Hand-Tool Dexterity Test.* Copyright © 1969 by Harcourt Assessment, Inc. Reproduced with permission. All rights reserved.)

12 bolts of three different sizes mounted on the left side of a frame and then to reassemble the nuts and bolts on the right side of the frame (Figure 11.4). Scores consist of the time needed to complete the task. Norms are given in the manual for various groups of industrial applicants.

Reliability and Validity of Psychomotor Tests

The reliabilities of psychomotor abilities tests are lower on the average (.70s and .80s) than the reliabilities of other tests of special abilities. One reason for the relatively low reliability coefficients of psychomotor abilities tests is that the scores are highly susceptible to practice (Fleishman, 1972).

Generally, tests of psychomotor abilities have not proved very useful in vocational counseling. Their validities are usually lower than those of tests of mechanical and clerical ability. Measures of psychomotor skills have been more useful in predicting performance in training programs than in forecasting job proficiency. They also have higher validities for predicting performance on repetitive jobs, such as routine assembly and machine operation, than on complex jobs involving higher-order cognitive and perceptual abilities (Ghiselli, 1973).

MECHANICAL ABILITY

A certain minimum level of psychomotor skill is needed for almost any occupation involving the operation of machinery. Above this minimum level, spatial perception, mechanical knowledge, and other cognitive abilities are more important determiners of performance. One of the first and most frequent kinds of special ability to be measured is mechanical ability. There is some evidence for a weak general factor of mechanical ability, but the tests that have been devised to measure it involve a variety of perceptual–motor and cognitive abilities. These are tests of psychomotor skills such as speed and muscular coordination, perception of spatial relations, and comprehension of mechanical relations. The psychomotor components of various mechanical ability tests, like psychomotor tests in general, have low correlations with each other. Nevertheless, the correlations among total scores on different mechanical ability tests are often fairly substantial.

One interesting, if not surprising, finding is the presence of gender differences in scores on tests of mechanical ability. Males typically score higher on measures of spatial and mechanical comprehension, whereas females score higher on measures of fine manual dexterity and certain aspects of perceptual discrimination. These differences become more pronounced in junior and senior high school, and social factors undoubtedly play a role in determining them.

Spatial Relations Tests

An intensive analysis of mechanical ability conducted by D. G. Paterson and his co-workers at the University of Minnesota during the late 1920s led to the construction of three tests: the Minnesota Mechanical Assembly Test, the Minnesota Spatial Relations Test, and the Minnesota Paper Formboard (Paterson, Elliott, Anderson, Tooks, & Heidbreder, 1930). The first of these, a work-sample test, required examinees to reassemble a set of disassembled mechanical objects. The task demanded manual dexterity and space perception, in addition to mechanical comprehension. The second and third instruments in the series were tests of space perception, which was known to be an important factor in occupations involving mechanical tasks. As the name implies, space perception is the ability to visualize objects in three dimensions and manipulate them to produce a particular configuration.

One descendant of the above tests was the Minnesota Spatial Relations Test, Revised Edition. This test, designed for ages 16 and over, assesses spatial visualization and three-dimensional object manipulation. It consists of four formboards (A, B, C, D) and two sets of geometrically shaped blocks. One set of blocks fits into the recesses of boards A and B, and the second set fits into the recesses of boards C and D. The test begins with the blocks scattered outside the recesses, and the examinee is told to pick up the blocks and place them in their proper recesses on the board as quickly as possible.

Another descendant of the Minnesota Mechanical Ability Test is the Revised Minnesota Paper Formboard Test (Likert & Quasha, 1995). This paper-and-pencil adaptation of the Minnesota Spatial Relations Test was designed for grades 9–16 and adults. It consists of 64 multiple-choice items, each containing a frame showing a geometric figure divided into several parts and five answer frames containing an assembled form (Figure 11.5). The examinee's task is to select the one answer frame out of five showing how the disassembled geometric figure will look if the parts are joined together. The Minnesota Paper Formboard has proved useful in predicting grades in shop and engineering courses, as well as supervisors' ratings and production records in inspection, packing, machine operation, and other industrial occupations. Scores on the test are also related to achievement in dentistry and art. Although the Minnesota Paper Formboard Test was intended to be a more efficiently administered version of the Minnesota Spatial Relations Test, the correlation between scores on the two tests is substantially lower than the parallel-forms reliability coefficient of the former.

Other Paper-and-Pencil Measures of Mechanical Ability

Neither spatial nor mechanical ability consists of a single factor. For example, Carroll (1993) identified five factors in tests of spatial ability: visualization, speeded rotation, closure speed, closure flexibility, and perceptual speed. The results of factor analysis also indicate that performance on tests of mechanical ability is a function of spatial ability, general reasoning ability, and mechanical knowledge and experience (Alderton, 1994). All these factors contribute to scores on tests of mechanical comprehension, which are designed to evaluate an understanding of mechanical principles involved in a range of practical situations. Two examples of tests of this kind are the Test of Mechanical Concepts (from Pearson Reid London House) and the Bennett Mechanical Comprehension Test (BMCT; Bennett, 1994). The two forms (S and T) of the BMCT consist of drawings and questions concerning the operation of mechanical relationships and physical laws in practical situations (Figure 11.6). The average score and reliability of the BMCT are lower for women than for men, and separate norms are provided for each sex. Evidence for the validity of the test is found in its modest correlations with performance in a variety of mechanical, technical, and manufacturing jobs.

There are two or more parts in the upper left-hand corner for each of the problems shown below. Choose from among the five figures labeled A, B, C, D, E, the one that shows how the parts in the upper left-hand corner would look if fitted together. The correct answer is shown for Problem 1.

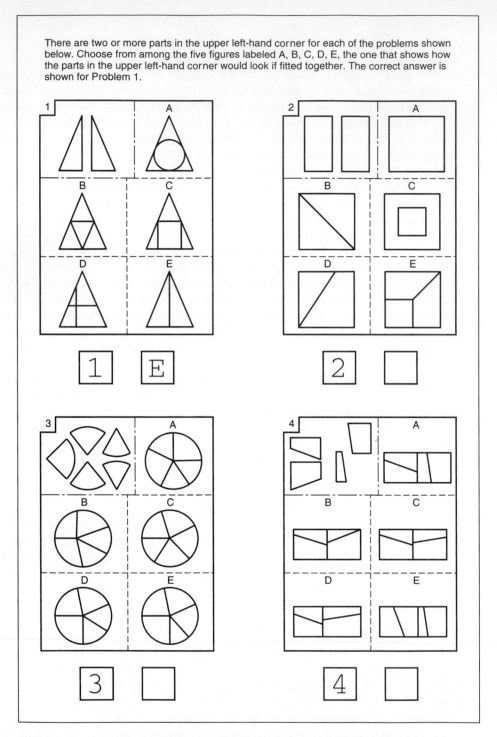

FIGURE 11.5 Sample items from the Minnesota Paper FormBoard-Revised.

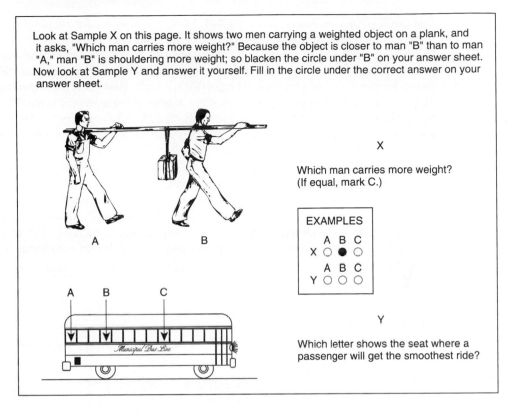

FIGURE 11.6   Sample items from the Bennett Mechanical Comprehension Test.

(From the Bennett Handtool Dexterity Test. Copyright © 1969 by Harcourt Assessment, Inc. Reproduced with permission. All rights reserved.)

CLERICAL AND COMPUTER-RELATED ABILITIES

Like many other categories of ability, clerical ability is not a unitary factor distinct from general intelligence. Manual dexterity and speed of perceiving similarities and differences are necessary in clerical work, but verbal and quantitative abilities are also important. Consequently, many tests of clerical ability contain items similar to those found on general intelligence tests, as well as items to measure perceptual speed and accuracy.

In addition to the more general tests of clerical ability, several tests have been designed to measure stenographic aptitude. Also available are tests of the ability to learn the complex clerical and problem-solving tasks of computer programming and computer operation.

Representative Tests of General Clerical Ability

Commercially distributed tests of clerical ability vary in content from the simple number and name checking tasks of the Minnesota Clerical Test to the combined general intelligence and perceptual–motor tasks of the newer Clerical Abilities Measures. The Minnesota Clerical

Test (MCT) (Andrew, Paterson, & Longstaff, 1979) was designed for use in selecting clerks, inspectors, and other specialists in occupations involving speed of perceiving and manipulating symbols. It consists of two parts, Number Comparison (8 minutes) and Name Comparison (7 minutes), on which the examinee inspects 200 pairs of numbers and 200 pairs of names for errors and checks identical pairs (Figure 11.7). Both parts are scored by the formula "rights minus wrongs." The test–retest reliabilities of the scores are in the .70s and .80s. Percentile norms for students, by sex and grade (7–12), and for groups of clerical workers and applicants are given in the manual. The scores are moderately correlated with teachers' and supervisors' ratings on clerical work.

In contrast to the Minnesota Clerical Test, which measures only perceptual speed and accuracy, the Clerical Abilities Battery is composed of seven tests designed to measure a variety of clerical skills: Filing (5 minutes), Copying Information (5 minutes), Information Comparison (5 minutes), Using Tables (5 minutes), Proofreading (5 minutes), Basic Math Skills (15 minutes), and Numerical Reasoning (20 minutes). Percentile norms based on several well-defined clerical populations are available on both forms A and B of the test.

If the two names or the two numbers of a pair are exactly the same, make a check mark (✓) on the line between them; if they are different, make no mark on that line.

Samples done correctly
of pairs of *Numbers*

79542 _____ 79524
5794367 __✓__ 5794367

Samples done correctly
of pairs of Names

John C. Linder _____ John C. Lender
Investors Syndicate __✓__ Investors Syndicate

Now try the samples below.

(1) New York World _____ New York World
(2) Cargill Grain Co. _____ Cargil Grain Co.

(3) 66273894 _____ 66273984
(4) 527384578 _____ 527384578

FIGURE 11.7 Sample items from the Minnesota Clerical Test.

ARTISTIC AND MUSICAL ABILITIES

The abilities measured by spatial, mechanical, and clerical aptitude tests are important in engineering, mechanics, office work, dentistry, and to some extent in the production of art and music. Tests of artistic and musical abilities have been the objects of decades of research, and some of them possess at least modest validity. However, research concerned with the assessment of these abilities is no longer pursued as energetically as it once was (Carson, 1998).

Tests of Artistic Ability

As the phrase "beauty is in the eye of the beholder" implies, the ultimate judge of artistic merit is the observer. Because taste in art varies greatly with the person, from culture to culture, and from one generation to the next, it is not surprising that criteria of artistic ability are difficult to specify. Notwithstanding the many problems of defining reliable criteria and constructing tests to predict them, a number of tests of visual art ability and musical ability have been published. However, many of these tests are old and are no longer commercially available.

Some years ago researchers at the University of Minnesota found a positive correlation between scores on spatial perception tests, such as the Minnesota Paper Formboard, and artistic ability (Paterson et al., 1930). Spatial ability, of course, is not the only factor in artistic ability; judgment, manual dexterity, creative imagination, and other factors also play a role. Furthermore, a person who can recognize good art is not necessarily able to produce it. For this reason, it is important to distinguish between measures of esthetic appreciation (judgment and perception) and work-sample measures of productive skill in art. Illustrative of tests of art judgment and perception are the Meier Art Judgment Test, the Meier Aesthetic Perception Test (Meier, 1942), and the Graves Design Judgment Test (Graves, 1948). Unlike the Meier Art Judgment Test, which uses famous works of art as test materials, the Graves employs two- and three-dimensional abstract designs to elicit artistic judgments. An example of a performance test in art is the Horn Art Aptitude Inventory (Horn & Smith, 1945), which requires the examinee to sketch common objects and geometric figures and to make sketches from sets of basic lines in rectangular frames.

Musical Ability Tests

The relative importance of innate ability, motivation, instruction, and practice in determining musical talent is not clear. There is some evidence of a weak general factor of musical ability, but most investigations have found that several abilities contribute to musical accomplishment. One such factor is the ability to discriminate among different pitches—the perfect pitch that presumably has characterized many famous musicians. As revealed by research employing brain-scanning techniques, neuropsychological factors are important in determining perfect pitch (e.g., Schlaug, Jaencke, Huang, & Steinmetz, 1995).

The oldest musical ability test, the Seashore Measures of Musical Talents, was a product of the pioneering research of Carl Seashore and his colleagues at the University of

Iowa during the 1920s and 1930s (Seashore, 1939). In contrast to the musical ability tests developed later, the stimulus materials on the Seashore tests consisted of a series of musical tones or notes, rather than meaningful musical selections. This analytic, atomistic approach to measuring musical ability was severely criticized, and, as a result, several tests with more complex musical content were developed. Among these tests are omnibus measures, such as the Drake Musical Aptitude Test (Drake, 1954) and the Musical Aptitude Profile (by E. E. Gordon; from GIA Publications).

The Musical Aptitude Profile (MAP) is a tape-recorded test consisting of 250 original short selections for violin and cello played by professional musicians. No previous knowledge of musical or historical facts is required. The MAP consists of three tests measuring seven components: Tonal Imagery (Melody and Harmony), Rhythm Imagery (Tempo and Meter), and Musical Sensitivity (Phrasing, Balance, and Style). The latest revision of the MAP takes approximately 3½ hours to administer and can be scored manually.

Other music tests designed by E. E. Gordon and published by GIA Publications include the following:

Advanced Measures of Music Audiation. A 20-minute test of music aptitude for college students that yields tonal, rhythm, and composite scores.

Instrument Timbre Preference Test. Assists students 9 years and older to select an appropriate brass or woodwind instrument to learn to play.

Harmonic Improvisation Readiness Record and Improvisation Readiness Record. Designed to serve as objective aids to teachers (grade 3 through music graduate school) to help students improvise music.

Iowa Tests of Music Literacy. A nationally standardized music achievement test for grades 4–12; designed to evaluate growth, diagnose strengths and weaknesses, and compare relative standing of students in music achievement.

MULTIPLE-APTITUDE TEST BATTERIES

It is often useful in vocational counseling, as well as in job classification and placement, to assess skills and knowledge in several different areas. A counselor may decide to administer a set of separate, single tests of abilities, but this may not be the most efficient procedure. Furthermore, it is likely that the single tests will have been standardized on as many different groups of people as there are tests. Because the norm groups can vary in significant ways, it is difficult to make a meaningful comparison between a person's score on one test and his or her scores on other tests.

Separate tests of special abilities certainly have a place, particularly in personnel selection and screening, but such tests are less useful in vocational counseling and classification. The emphasis in the employment scene has shifted somewhat during the past few decades from selecting only the "cream of the crop" to classifying and placing workers on jobs most suited to their abilities and needs. Consequently, the administration of tests comprising a multiple-aptitude battery, which are designed to match people having particular ability patterns to specific jobs, is considered more effective than administering a series of unrelated tests designed to select only the best and screen out all others. Unlike single tests of special abilities, which may be of either the paper-and-pencil or performance type, a typical multiple-aptitude battery involves no apparatus other than paper and pencil and can be administered simultaneously to a large group of students, job applicants, military inductees, or other groups.

Because cognitive abilities are less specific during the elementary school years, administration of an expensive, time-consuming, multiple-aptitude battery is usually not recommended prior to junior high school. During the junior high years, as their cognitive abilities are becoming differentiated with maturity and experience, students are beginning to make career explorations and plans, as well as deciding what academic courses to take. To assist them in these efforts, many school systems administer a multiple-aptitude test battery in the eighth or ninth grade. The information provided by the battery of tests can increase students' awareness of their strengths and weaknesses and thereby provide guidance in making occupational and educational decisions.

Rather than administering a long series of special abilities tests or a multiple-aptitude battery, a vocational counselor may decide to use a general intelligence test plus one or more tests of special abilities. There is certainly nothing wrong with this strategy, because the verbal and quantitative abilities measured by intelligence tests are important in a wide range of academic and vocational pursuits. In addition to evaluating several special abilities, many aptitude batteries contain a general intelligence test. This provides the combined advantages of more efficient administration and comparable norms on all tests.

Score Differences and Profile Interpretation

The statistical procedures of factor analysis (see Appendix A) have been used in the construction of a number of aptitude test batteries. Even on batteries not constructed by factor-analytic methods, the results of studies employing these methods have usually been considered in constructing the items and defining the variables to be measured.

Items on the Differential Aptitude Tests, one of the most popular test batteries used in academic counseling at the high school level, were selected to have high correlations with other items on the same subtest, but low correlations with items on other subtests. The final result was a set of internally consistent subtests having low correlations with each other. It was important for the correlations among subtests to be low; otherwise, the overlap among the abilities measured by different subtests would be too great for differential interpretation of subtest scores.

Reliability and Standard Error of Score Differences.   The magnitudes of correlations among different subtests in the same battery are often appreciable, and the fact that the subtests are fairly short causes their reliabilities to be fairly low. Not only does the reliability of the differences between scores on two tests vary directly with the reliabilities of the tests, but it also varies inversely with the correlation between the tests. The sizable correlation between two given subtests, combined with their low reliabilities, causes the reliabilities of the differences between scores on the subtests also to be low.

A formula for the reliability of the differences (r_{dd}) between the scores of the same people on two tests or subtests having equal variances is

$$r_{dd} = \frac{r_{11} + r_{22} - 2r_{12}}{2(1 - r_{12})},$$
(11.1)

where r_{11} is the reliability of the first set of scores, r_{22} is the reliability of the second set of scores, and r_{12} is the correlation between the two sets of scores. For example, assume that the reliability of pretest scores is $r_{11} = .90$, the reliability of posttest scores is $r_{22} = .80$, and the correlation between pretest and posttest scores is $r_{12} = .70$. Then the reliability of the difference between pretest and posttest scores is

$$\frac{.90 + .80 - 2(.70)}{2(1 - .70)} = .50.$$

When the reliability of the differences between scores on two subtests is low, the difference between a person's scores on the subtests must be fairly large to be significant. To illustrate this principle, suppose that the reliability of T scores on the spatial relations test of an aptitude battery is .85, and the reliability of T scores on the mechanical ability test of the same battery is .90. An approximate value of the standard error of the differences (s_{ed}) between scores on two tests having equal standard deviations may be computed from

$$s_{ed} = s\sqrt{2 - r_{11} - r_{22}},$$
(11.2)

where r_{11} and r_{22} are the test–retest reliabilities of the two tests, and s is the standard deviation of the scores on each test. Recalling that the standard deviation of T scores equals 10, when scores on both tests are expressed as T scores, formula 11.2 becomes

$$s_{ed} = 10\sqrt{2 - .85 - .90} = 5.$$

Consequently, to be fairly certain (say, with probability .95) that the difference between a person's scores on these two tests is not due to chance, the difference should be at least $1.96 \times 5 = 9.8$ T-score units.

Score Profile.   The process of interpreting a person's score on a multiple-aptitude battery consisting of several tests standardized on the same or equivalent norm groups begins with the construction of a score profile. A *score profile,* which is a line graph or bar graph of scores on different tests, provides a picture of the person's strengths and weaknesses in various aptitude areas. From the norms, it is possible to construct a profile of a person's scores on the various tests for use in academic or vocational counseling. Rather than plotting a person's scores as specific points on a graph, the scores may be represented as a series of horizontal or vertical bars spanning one or two standard errors of measurement on either side of the score (see Figure 5.2 on p. 95). Then, if the vertical bars for two tests do not overlap, the difference between the person's scores on those two tests may be interpreted as significant.

Comparing the profile of a person's scores on a multiple-aptitude battery with the average score profile of people in selected occupations can be of help in vocational counseling and occupational selection and placement. Although workers within the same occupation differ to some extent in their ability patterns, certain job families seem to require a particular set of abilities. Similar profiles on a multiple-aptitude battery indicate similar patterns of abilities.

Differential Aptitude Tests. A number of aptitude test batteries have been designed for and standardized mainly in school situations and used as predictors of scholastic achievement. One prominent test battery of this sort is the Differential Aptitude Tests (DAT) (Bennett, Seashore, & Wesman, 1984). The DAT has been used primarily for educational and vocational counseling of junior- and senior-high students, but it has also been used in basic adult education, community college, vocational–technical, and correctional programs.

There are three versions of the DAT: the DAT for Selection, the DAT for Schools, and the DAT for Guidance. The DAT for Selection consists of two components, a General Abilities Battery and a Technical Abilities Battery, depending on the different aptitudes required for different areas of employment. The General Abilities Battery consists of three tests: Verbal Reasoning, Numerical Reasoning, and Abstract Reasoning. The Technical Abilities Battery is comprised of tests of Numerical Reasoning, Abstract Reasoning, Mechanical Reasoning, and Space Relations.

The DAT for Schools and the DAT for Guidance consist of all eight tests listed above. The goal of both the DAT for Selection and the DAT for Schools is to measure a person's capacity to succeed in a variety of careers. The DAT for Guidance aims to assess aptitudes relating to job suitability and performance for school leavers and adults. Each test comprising these three batteries has paper-and-pencil administration and takes 10 to 30 minutes to complete.

In addition to the traditional paper-and-pencil versions, computerized adaptive forms of all eight DAT tests are available. Using item-response theory, the adaptive versions present a subset of test items that are most appropriate for the person being tested.

The internal consistency reliability coefficients of the eight tests range from .82 to .95, and the parallel forms coefficients range from .73 to .90. The correlations among the tests range from nearly zero between Perceptual Speed and Accuracy and other tests in the battery to as high as .70 between the Reasoning and Language Usage tests. Extensive data presented in the manual indicate that the tests on the DAT, and especially the Verbal Reasoning + Numerical Reasoning composite, are valid predictors of high school and college grades. The DAT is also useful in predicting job level within occupations, but the norms for various occupations are limited. Consequently, the DAT should be used cautiously as a differential predictor of vocational success.

Multidimensional Aptitude Battery-II

The Multidimensional Aptitude Battery-II (MAB-II; Jackson, 1998) is a group-administered adaptation of the Wechsler Adult Intelligence Scale-Revised. Like the WAIS-R, the MAB-II consists of two scales (Verbal and Performance) with five subtests each. The five

Verbal subtests are Information, Comprehension, Arithmetic, Similarities, and Vocabulary. The five Performance subtests are Digit Symbol, Picture Completion, Spatial, Picture Arrangement, and Object Assembly. The time limit for each subtest is 7 minutes, so the entire battery can be completed in less than 1½ hours. IQs and standard scores on the Verbal, Performance, and Full Scale Batteries, as well as subtest scale scores, age-corrected scale scores, and a narrative report of the scores and their interpretation, may be obtained from the computer-scoring service of Sigma Assessment Systems. A sample profile of scores on the MAB-II is given in Figure 11.8.

The MAB-II manual (Jackson, 1998) reports test–retest reliabilities over a period of 45 days as .95 for Verbal, .96 for Performance, and .97 for Full Scale scores. In a study of 500 individuals aged 16 to 20, internal consistency coefficients for Verbal, Performance, and Full Scale IQs were in the high .90s. Correlations between MAB scores and WAIS-R IQs in a sample of 145 adults were .94 for Verbal, .79 for Performance, and .91 for Full Scale WAIS-R scores. The results of factor analyses of scores on the subtests indicate that, like the WAIS-R, the MAB-II measures a general intelligence factor, as well as separate verbal and performance factors.

Scales	Scores Raw	SS	Age Corrected Scaled Scores SS
Information	40	83	80
Comprehension	24	62	59
Arithmetic	17	67	64
Similarities	24	56	53
Vocabulary	25	54	53
Digit Symbol	24	56	52
Picture Completion	24	58	54
Spatial	35	62	59
Picture Arrangement	7	42	37
Object Assembly	8	47	44

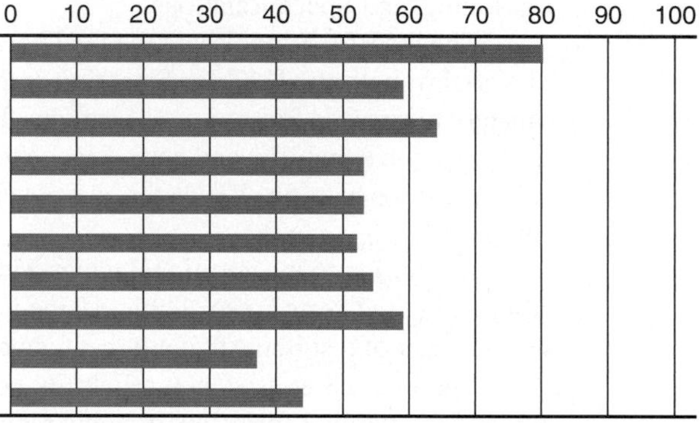

The Raw Score for each test indicates the number of questions that the respondent answered correctly. The first set of Scaled Scores (SS) are not age-based and are used to calculate Verbal, Performance and Full Scale IQ scores. The Age-Corrected Scaled Scores (SS) and the associated bar graph compare the respondent's results with those of people in the same age group.

Scales	Scores Sum	IQ	Intelligence Quotient (IQ)
Verbal	322	120	
Performance	265	100	
Full Scale	587	112	

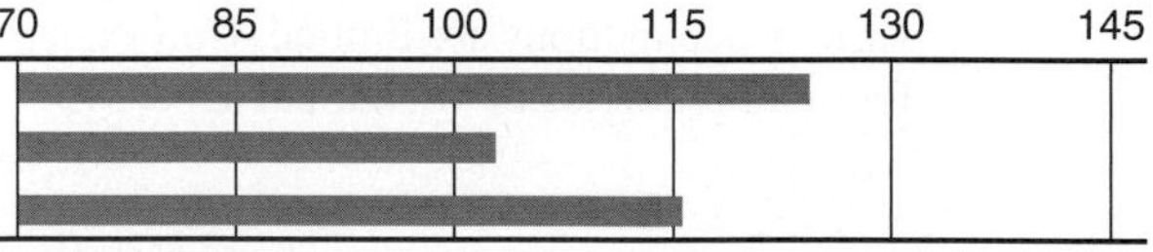

FIGURE 11.8   Profile of scores on the Multidimensional Aptitude Battery-II.

(Reproduced by permission of Sigma Assessment Systems, Inc., P.O. Box 610984, Port Huron, MI 48061-0984. Tel. 800-265-1285. www.sigmaassessmentsystems.com.)

General Aptitude Test Battery

Several multiple-aptitude test batteries have been designed specifically for personnel selection and placement in business and industry. Among these are the General Aptitude Test Battery, the Flanagan Aptitude Classification Tests, the Flanagan Industrial Tests, and the Employee Aptitude Survey. One of the oldest of the industrially oriented test batteries was constructed in the 1930s by the staff of the Minnesota Employment Stabilization Research Institute (MESRI). The MESRI battery contained tests of general intelligence, as well as numerical ability, perceptual ability, mechanical ability, and psychomotor ability. Profiles of the average scores on the tests obtained by clerks, mechanical workers, salespersons, and many other occupational groups were established as a set of *occupational ability patterns* (*OAPs*) with which individual performance could be compared.

The OAP approach of the MESRI battery was retained in the development of the General Aptitude Test Battery (GATB) of the U.S. Employment Service. The GATB, designed on the basis of job analyses and a factor analysis of 59 tests, is composed of 8 short paper-and-pencil and four apparatus tests. These 12 tests in combination yield scores on nine major aptitudes and skills required for occupational success: General Learning Ability (G), Verbal (V), Numerical (N), Spatial(S), Form Perception (P), Clerical Perception (Q), Motor Coordination (K), Finger Dexterity (F), and Manual Dexterity (M). Raw scores on these nine variables are converted to percentile ranks or standard scores having a mean of 100 and a standard deviation of 20. Th composite scores are obtained from appropriate combinations of scores on the nine factors: Cognitive = G + V + N, Perceptual = S + P + Q, and Psychomotor = K + F + M.

A person's standard scores on the GATB variables can be compared with those of the 36 or so occupational ability patterns (OAPs) determined from an analysis of the GATB scores of people in over 800 jobs. An OAP consists of the set of minimum GATB scores considered essential for effective performance in an occupation.

The entire GATB takes 2½ hours to administer and is appropriate for senior-high students (usually twelfth-graders) and adults. Test–retest and parallel-forms reliability coefficients for the separate tests range from .80 to .90, with a standard error of measurement of approximately 7 points for the standard scores. The validities of the nine aptitude scores and the 36 OAPs for predicting occupational and academic criteria of success range from .00 to the .90s.

The GATB has been one of the most widely used vocational counseling and job-placement tools for students in grades 9–12 and adults and is probably the most appropriate test battery for that purpose. Because of the alleged unfairness of the GATB to minority groups, in 1981 a system of *race norming* of the scores was put in place as part of the affirmative action program of the U.S. Department of Labor. This policy consisted of using separate percentile norms for European Americans, African Americans, and Hispanics and reporting only the in-group percentile ranks of applicants. Critics viewed this practice, however, as *reverse discrimination,* and in 1990 use of the GATB was suspended by the Department of Justice until such time as issues regarding fairness and reverse discrimination could be settled. The U.S. Congress also inserted language in the Civil Rights Act of 1991 to the effect that separate norms and score adjustments can no longer be applied to differentiate among groups. The U.S. Employment Service subsequently resumed use of the GATB, but score reports to employers are no longer race normed. Rather, raw scores on the various tests constituting the battery are converted to standard scores based on combined norms for all racial groups.

Armed Services Vocational Aptitude Battery

Beginning with the Army Examinations Alpha and Beta in World War I, over the years various tests have been used to select and classify personnel in the U.S. Armed Services. The Army General Classification Test (AGCT) and the Navy General Classification Test (NGCT) were administered to millions of military recruits during and after World War II to classify them for skilled and unskilled jobs, to select those who could profit from further training, and to reject those who, because of low mental ability, were considered unfit for military service (see Harrell, 1992). Some years after World War II, the Armed Forces Qualification Test (AFQT) replaced the AGCT and NGCT.

During the 1970s, the Armed Services Vocational Aptitude Battery (ASVAB) became the uniform selection and classification test for the joint armed services (for general information, see www.afsc.org/youthmil/tests.htm). The current form of this battery (ASVAB, 18/19), which is the most widely administered multiple-aptitude test in the United States, consists of 10 tests:

General Science (GS): 25 items measuring knowledge of the physical and biological sciences

Arithmetic Reasoning (AR): 30 items measuring ability to solve arithmetic word problems

Word Knowledge (WK): 35 items measuring ability to select the correct meaning of words presented in context and to identify the best synonym for a given word

Paragraph Comprehension (PC): 15 items measuring ability to obtain information from written passages

Numerical Operations (NO): 50 items measuring ability to perform arithmetic computations

Coding Speed (CS): 84 items measuring ability to use a key to assign code numbers to words

Auto & Shop Information (AS): 25 items measuring knowledge of automobiles, tools, and shop terminology and practices

Mathematics Knowledge (MK): 25 items measuring knowledge of high school mathematical principles

Mechanical Comprehension (MC): 25 items measuring knowledge of mechanical and physical principles and the ability to visualize how illustrated objects work

Electronics Information (EI): 20 items for measuring knowledge of electricity and electronics

Working time per ASVAB test ranges from 3 minutes for Numerical Operations to 36 minutes for Arithmetic Reasoning, a total of 144 minutes for all 10 tests. Standard *T* scores and percentile score bands are reported for each test and three composites: Verbal Ability (VA) = WK + PC, Math Ability (MA) = AR + MK, and Academic Ability (AA) = VA + MA. Scores on four occupational composites may also be computed as appropriate combinations of scores on the 10 basic tests: Mechanical & Crafts (MC); Business & Clerical (BC); Electronics & Electrical (EE); Health, Social & Technology (HST).

A person's performance on the ASVAB can be depicted as a series of percentile score bands indicating the ranges within which the person's true scores on the tests probably fall. In addition to the plot of same grade–same sex percentile score bands, both same grade–same sex and same grade–opposite sex *T* scores can be plotted. Two other pieces of information included on the profile sheet are the person's primary and secondary ASVAB codes and Military Careers Score. The codes are interpreted by a special OCCU-FIND in a workbook designed to help examinees identify military occupations with which their scores have the best match. The Military Careers Score, which is used in conjunction with graphs in a *Military Careers* booklet shared with the examinee, assist in the process of estimating his or her chances of qualifying for enlisted occupations in the military (see U.S. Department of Defense, September 1995).

Internal consistency reliability coefficients range from the low .70s to the low .90s for the 10 ASVAB tests and from the low to mid-.90s for the three composite scores. The alternate forms reliability coefficients are mostly in the .70s and .80s for the 10 tests and in the .90s for the composites. Extensive data on the validity of the ASVAB for both military and civilian occupations are given in the *Technical Manual for the ASVAB 18/19* (U.S. Department of Defense, December 1999). As with the DAT, because the same tests may appear in different ASVAB composites, the composites are positively correlated. Consequently, the information provided by various tests is often redundant and reflective more of general cognitive ability than of specific differential aptitudes.

In addition to a standard paper-and-pencil version, a computer-administered version of the ASVAB (the CAT-ASVAB) that employs adaptive testing methodology is available. The CAT-ASVAB has the advantages of less administration time, increased test security, greater precision of measurement at the extremes of ability, immediate performance feedback to examinees, and flexible starting times (see Segall & Moreno, 1999).

Diagnostic Assessment and Work Keys

Since their inception in the 1920s, the construction and use of multiple-aptitude tests has been based on the reasonable assumption that different educational programs and occupations require different human abilities. Ideally, when used for either counseling or placement purposes, such multiscore instruments serve the diagnostic function of determining the sorts of programs or jobs for which people are most suited. In the future, these diagnostic assessments will undoubtedly be more individualized and adaptive and administered either in a face-to-face situation or by computer. One scenario views the diagnostic testing process as beginning with a brief challenge test, followed by probes to identify the component skills in an area in which the examinee has problems, construction of a profile of the examinee's strengths and weaknesses, and the presentation of remedial instruction or training. The diagnostic tests will be aimed primarily at helping students and job applicants learn and succeed, rather than simply providing scores for institutional or organizational decision making, and will guide instruction and training on a continuing basis, rather than merely comparing performances among test takers.

For many years aptitude test batteries such as the DAT, the GATB, and the ASVAB have been administered in school and employment contexts to provide individuals with assistance in making educational and vocational decisions. A related, but more sophisticated and closely coordinated procedure developed by the American College Testing Program appears to have even greater utility. This procedure, known as the Work Keys System, consists of three components or stages: (1) a job analysis or *profiling* process to determine the levels of skills required for competent performance in specific jobs; (2) assessment of people's workplace skills, and (3) instructional support to help educators teach the required skills. During stage 1, intensive focus groups composed of workers who actually perform a certain job are conducted by *job profilers* to identify the skills and skill levels required for a particular job. The result is a job profile that gives employers, students, applicants, and schools a single frame of reference for understanding the skills that are needed to qualify for the job. At stage 2, students or applicants desiring employment in the particular job are administered proficiency tests in each of the following areas that are relevant to the position: applied math, applied technology, listening, locating information, observation, reading, teamwork, and writing. Individuals' scores on these assessments are then compared with the particular job profile to reveal any *skill gaps*. At stage 3, the resulting information obtained in stage 2 is used not only to provide feedback to those who have taken the tests, but also to train them in the skills needed for the particular job. The required training to reduce the diagnosed skill gaps consists of computer-based and classroom instruction calibrated to specified Work Keys targets.

In addition to serving as a basis for remedial instruction, matching students' scores against job profiles can also help educators target school curricula that need improving. Furthermore, corporation executives and work-force development agency administrators can use the information on discrepancies between employee assessment scores and job profiles to modify their training and recruiting programs and allocate the needed funds for the required modifications (Doebele, 1999).

SUMMARY

1. Tests of aptitudes or special abilities focus on the future, that is, on measuring the potential to profit from further training or experience in a certain area. Tests of special abilities have narrower bandwidths than conventional intelligence tests and, as a result, are better predictors of more specific accomplishments, but poorer predictors of complex criteria such as academic achievement. Though certain tests of special abilities are of the work-sample or performance type, paper-and-pencil tests are more widely administered. Predictive validities of aptitude tests are typically fairly low, but scores on such tests can contribute to the prediction of various performance criteria when used in combination with other measures of ability, as well as with scores on measures of interests, personality, motivation, and past performance.

2. Psychomotor abilities appear to be highly specific, and scores on tests of these abilities frequently have lower reliabilities than other ability tests, partially because scores are very susceptible to practice effects. Examples of psychomotor tests are the Minnesota Rate of Manipulation Test for measuring gross manual movements, the Crawford Small Parts Dexterity Test for measuring fine manual movements, and the Bennett Hand-Tool Dexterity Test for measuring both gross and fine manual movements. Reliabilities of these tests are somewhat low and, although they can predict performance on repetitive, routine jobs (e.g., assembly lines), they are not good at predicting more complex aspects of jobs.

3. Tests of mechanical ability and clerical ability were among the first standardized measures of special abilities to be constructed. However, neither mechanical ability nor clerical ability is a unitary psychological dimension. Tests of mechanical ability may involve psychomotor skills, in addition to perception and mechanical comprehension. Examples of tests of mechanical ability are the Bennett Mechanical Comprehension Test and the Test of Mechanical Concepts. Tests of clerical ability may measure perceptual speed and accuracy, as well as verbal and numerical ability. Representative tests of clerical ability include the Minnesota Clerical Test and the Clerical Abilities Battery.

4. Among other special abilities for which tests have been devised are artistic and musical ability. Most of the older tests of artistic and musical ability are, however, no longer commercially available. Some tests of artistic ability measure art appreciation (judgment and perception), while others assess artistic performance or knowledge of art. Two of the most popular tests of art appreciation have been the Meier Art Judgment and Aesthetic Appreciation Tests and the Graves Design Judgment Test. The Seashore Measures of Musical Talents, the oldest published test of musical ability, emphasizes discrimination, judgment, and memory for tones or tonal combinations. Several other musical ability tests, for example, the Musical Aptitude Profile, involve judgment and discrimination of meaningful music. Success in either music or art also depends on other factors than talent.

5. Multiple-aptitude batteries are designed to measure individual strengths and weaknesses in a variety of ability areas. Differences among a person's scores on an aptitude battery should be interpreted cautiously and viewed as significant only if they are greater than one or two times the standard error of measurement of the score differences. In addition, scores on an aptitude battery alone are inadequate for effective academic or vocational counseling. Past performance, interests and motivation, personality characteristics, and situational factors must also be taken into account. Because the tests on a multiple-aptitude battery are generally shorter than tests of single aptitudes, the former usually have lower reliabilities and hence greater standard errors of measurement than the latter. Certain multiple-aptitude batteries, for example, the General Aptitude Test Battery, are based on the results of factor analysis; other aptitude batteries, for example, the Differential Aptitude Tests, are not.

6. The Differential Aptitude Tests has been one of the most useful batteries for academic counseling, whereas the General Aptitude Test Battery has been used more extensively in vocational counseling. The Armed Services Vocational Aptitude Battery

(ASVAB), the most widely administered of all multiple-aptitude batteries, is used for selection and occupational placement purposes in the U.S. military and for counseling high school students who are interested in military careers.

MASTERING THE CHAPTER OBJECTIVES

1. *Achievement, aptitude, and special abilities*
   a. Empirical support for a distinction between aptitude and achievement was obtained some years ago in a cross-sectional investigation by Burket (1973). It was found that achievement scores *increased* with increasing grade level when aptitude scores were held constant, but aptitude scores *decreased* with increasing grade level when achievement scores were held constant. These findings, combined with those of other investigators (e.g., Carroll, 1973), may be interpreted in terms of the following descriptive equation: achievement = aptitude × experience. Explain.
   b. Give two reasons for using tests of specific abilities. Give two reasons not to use them.
   c. What is meant by work-sample tests, the in-basket technique, and assessment centers?

2. *Psychomotor tests*
   a. Identify at least two tests in each of the following categories: psychomotor abilities, spatial ability, mechanical ability, clerical ability, artistic ability, and musical ability.
   b. Describe two reasons why tests of psychomotor abilities have not proved to be useful in vocational selection.

3. *Mechanical and clerical abilities*
   a. Summarize the gender differences that have been found on tests of mechanical abilities. What do you think are the reasons for these differences?
   b. Describe the Minnesota Clerical Test and the Clerical Abilities Test.

4. *Artistic and musical abilities*
   a. Describe three strategies tests used for measuring artistic ability and three used for measuring musical ability.
   b. Describe three reasons why nearly all tests of artistic and musical abilities are no longer published or used.

5. *Multiple aptitude batteries*
   a. What are the advantages and disadvantages of administering an aptitude test battery rather than several single tests of special abilities?
   b. Why is it important to use statistical procedures in profile analysis?
   c. John makes a T score of 65 on the verbal comprehension test and a T score of 75 on the numerical reasoning test of a multiple-aptitude test battery. If the reliabilities of the two tests are .90 and .85, respectively, can the examiner be 95% sure that John is poorer in verbal comprehension than in numerical ability? Support your answer with appropriate computations (see Answers to Quantitative Questions, p. 488).

6. *Examples of multiple aptitude batteries*
   a. Write a critical review of any of the separate tests of special abilities described in this chapter; follow the outline given in Exercise 1 of the Experiencing Psychological Assessment section in Chapter 9.
   b. List the four main features of the Differential Aptitude Tests, Multidimensional Aptitude Battery-II, General Aptitude Battery, and the Armed Services Vocational Aptitude Battery.

EXPERIENCING PSYCHOLOGICAL ASSESSMENT

1. Arrange to visit the administrative offices of your local school district and interview the school psychologist or director of special education about the psychological tests administered by these professionals. For example, what tests are used in assessing the special abilities or disabilities of students? How often are students tested or screened for visual problems? Prepare a report of your findings.

2. Arrange to visit a local optometrist or ophthalmologist and ask him or her to describe the procedures and instruments used in testing a person's vision. What aspects of vision are measured routinely, and which are measured only under special circumstances? Prepare a report of your findings.

CHAPTER TWELVE

VOCATIONAL INTERESTS

CHAPTER OBJECTIVES

1. Introduce the measurement of vocational interests including history, how interests develop, heredity, and stability.
2. Discuss the validity of interest inventories.
3. Describe the Strong Interest Inventory and the Kuder Interest Inventory.
4. Discuss interests and personality with a focus on Holland's theory and the Self-Directed Search.
5. Describe general- and special-purpose inventories, including the Jackson Vocational Interest Survey.
6. Discuss how to help people using vocational counseling.

Scores on tests of intelligence and special abilities are among the best predictors of educational and occupational success. Such tests are measures of *maximum performance,* in that they indicate what a person is capable of achieving under optimum conditions. Questionnaires and inventories of preferences and other affective variables generally contribute less than cognitive measures to the prediction of success in school and on the job, but they are very useful in educational and vocational counseling. These measures of *typical performance* often add significantly to information obtained from measures of ability and past performance.

One shortcoming of affective assessment instruments is that most of them are not as objective and therefore not as reliable as cognitive tests. It is even debatable whether questionnaires, self-report inventories, and other affective measuring instruments deserve the title of *tests.* Nevertheless, many affective instruments have very respectable reliabilities, appreciable validities for certain purposes, and other characteristics of good tests.

Three affective variables that have received a great deal of research attention are *interests, attitudes,* and *values.* Measures of interests are the topic of the present chapter, and measures of attitudes and values are considered in Chapter 13. Chapters 14 through 18 complete our survey of affective measures with an examination of various types of personality assessment procedures and instruments.

FOUNDATIONS OF INTEREST MEASUREMENT

People with similar interests, personalities, and values will be likely to seek out similar jobs. An underlying premise, then, is that we can help people select possible vocations by understanding these variables. Information on a person's *interests,* or preferences for certain kinds of activities and objects, can be obtained in various ways. The most direct method, simply asking a person what he or she is interested in, has its pitfalls. For example, people often have little insight into what their vocational interests are or what particular occupations entail. Nevertheless, these *expressed interests* are sometimes better predictors than less directly obtained information and should not be overlooked in vocational counseling situations. The results of an extensive investigation by Flanagan, Tiedeman, and Willis (1973) showed, for example, that various occupational groups were more disparate in their expressed interests, rather than in their cognitive abilities. For example, engineering students scored much higher than average on mechanical–technical and physical science interests, whereas law students scored higher on public service (politics), literary–linguistic activity, business, and sales interests.

Other methods of determining interests include observations of behavior, such as participation in various activities, inferring a person's interests from his or her knowledge of special terminology or other information about specific occupations, and administering one of the dozens of available interest inventories.[1] These four approaches to interest measurement (asking for expressions of interests, deducing interests from observed behavior, inferring interests from performance on tests of abilities, and determining interests from paper-and-pencil inventories) are applicable to the assessment of the basic interest groups originally described by Super and Crites (1962). These eight interest groups are scientific, social welfare, literary, material, systematic, contact, esthetic expression, and esthetic interpretation.

History and Current Scene

Beginning with the work of E. L. Thorndike (1912) and others, research on interests has not been limited to applied contexts; many studies of the origins and dynamics of interests have been conducted. However, standardized methods of measuring interests were developed initially for purposes of vocational counseling and selection. James Miner is credited with making the first systematic attempt to design criterion-related and content-validated measures of vocational interests. An interest questionnaire constructed by Miner in 1915 was the stimulus for a historic seminar on interest measurement at Carnegie Institute of Technology in

---

[1]A rough indicator of interest in a particular object, person, or situation may also be obtained by physiological procedures such as pupillometric (Hess, 1965) or phallometric (Harris & Rice, 1996; Pithers & Laws, 1995) measurement.

1919 and led to the construction of standardized vocational interest inventories. A participant in the seminar was E. K. Strong, Jr., who, encouraged by the success of one of his doctoral students (K. Cowdery) in differentiating between engineers, lawyers, and physicians on the basis of their interests, expanded these efforts by launching a research program to differentiate among persons in many different vocations on the basis of their interests (see Donnay, 1997). The research of Strong and his students led to the development of the Strong Vocational Interest Blank for Men and a companion instrument for women in the late 1920s and 1930s. Other noteworthy events in the history of interest measurement were the publication in 1939 of the Kuder Preference Record and the research on objective measures of interests conducted by U.S. Army Air Corps psychologists during World War II. Many interest inventories were published after the war, but modifications of Strong's and Kuder's original instruments continued to be the most popular.

Today, interest inventories are administered for a number of reasons in a variety of settings. Traditionally, these instruments have been used principally in occupational and educational counseling in high schools, colleges, and vocational rehabilitation contexts. They have also been used extensively in research on individual and group differences, both in basic research to determine the nature, origins, and effects of interests and in applied research for vocational counseling, selection, and placement. Other applications of interest inventories include assisting individual's questioning their initial vocational decisions or seeking more challenging positions and those who are confronted with plateaus in their careers, facing layoffs, or making preretirement decisions (Hansen & Dik, 2004). Academic and vocational counselors and psychological researchers are undoubtedly the largest groups of users of vocational interest inventories, but industrial consultants, career-development managers, and human resources practitioners also find them helpful.

Development of Interests

Where do interests come from? How do they develop and change over time? The vocational interests of young children typically have an element of fantasy. Children fantasize about being glamorous, talented, heroic, or adventurous, but such fantasies may have little to do with their abilities or knowledge of what particular occupations entail. Children normally progress from a fantasy stage to a transition stage in late childhood and early adolescence and finally to a more realistic stage in the development of vocational interests during late adolescence and early adulthood.

Although vocational interests do not become very specific, realistic, or stable until high school and beyond, the general direction of a person's interests may be apparent fairly early in life. Young children tend to engage in activities that they view as appropriate and avoid activities that they consider inappropriate for themselves. They also make distinctions between people roles and life roles. According to Anne Roe and her coauthors (Roe & Klos, 1969; Roe & Siegelman, 1964), vocational interests, and hence career choices, result from the kinds of relationships that children have with their families. A warm, accepting family atmosphere tends to create a "people" orientation, whereas a cold, aloof family atmosphere is more likely to result in an "object" or "thing" orientation. From a social learning perspective, interests are viewed as the results of differential reinforcement for engaging in certain activities, coupled with imitation and modeling of people who are important to the individual.

The Role of Heredity

Environment certainly affects interests to a substantial degree, but the findings of a study by Grotevant, Scarr, and Weinberg (1977) suggest that a child is born with a hereditary predisposition to be interested in certain things. In this study of 114 biologically related families, many significant correlations between children's and parents' scores on an interest inventory were found. In contrast, few significant correlations were found between the interests of parents and children in 109 adoptive families. Biologically related children were more similar in their interest patterns than nonbiologically related children, and the interests of same-sex pairs of children were more similar than those of opposite-sex pairs. The results of a widely cited Minnesota study of identical twins reared apart also indicated that the correlations between the interests of identical twins are greater than those between the interests of other family pairs (Bouchard et al., 1983; also see Betsworth et al., 1994; Maloney, Bouchard, & Segal, 1991; Waller, Lykken, & Tellegen, 1995). Because identical twins have identical heredities, these findings have been interpreted as demonstrating the influence of heredity on interests. In general, evidence from behavior genetics studies demonstrates that 40% to 50% of the variance in vocational interests is attributable to genetics. According to Lykken, Bouchard, McGue, and Tellegen (1993), the genetic influence operates through gene environment interaction, in that people with a particular genetic makeup are exposed to particular experiences and activities. Furthermore, vocational interests are more likely to be the consequences of nonshared environmental influences that are unique to the individual, rather than environmental influences that are shared with other people (Betsworth et al., 1994; Maloney et al., 1991).

A common belief is that parental behavior is more influential than heredity in shaping children's interests. In contrast, Sandra Scarr and her colleagues concluded that what parents do apparently has little effect on children's interests (Grotevant, Scarr, & Weinberg, 1977). Rather than trying to force or lead children into certain interest areas, these researchers recommended that parents provide their children with a variety of experiences and models. The children will then have a better opportunity to develop whatever interest predispositions or inclinations toward specific activities they naturally possess.

Granting that people tend to be interested in things that they do well and that heredity plays a significant role in determining both abilities and temperament, it is plausible that heredity affects interests indirectly by way of abilities, temperament, and physical structure. For example, a person with a genetically based high level of activity, but a modest level of intelligence, will probably have little interest in becoming a theoretical physicist who spends most of the time thinking about scientific problems. On the other hand, a temperamentally energetic and physically able person may show greater interest in becoming a professional athlete.

Stability of Interests

Individual patterns of likes and dislikes begin developing long before the individual has had experiences with specific occupations. These early interests are relatively unstable, but by the time a child has reached the ninth grade, and almost certainly by the eleventh grade, his or her preferences for specific types of activities have become fairly well established.

Longitudinal studies spanning two decades or more have demonstrated that interests are fairly stable after the late teens (Hansen, 1988; Strong, 1955). Using archival data from the Strong Interest Inventory, Hansen (1988) found that the interests of both women and men were very stable over extended periods of time, as long as 50 years. On the other hand, a person's interests can change even in adulthood, and particular caution should be exercised in interpreting the results of interest inventories administered before the ninth grade (Crites, 1969).

VALIDITY OF INTEREST INVENTORIES

Because of the importance of academic and vocational guidance, commercially available interest inventories have been almost as popular as tests of general intelligence and special abilities. Compared with cognitive measures, however, interest inventories do not predict school grades or occupational performance as accurately (Campbell & Hansen, 1981; Schmidt & Hunter, 2004). Despite this, interest inventories are able to make predictions above and beyond merely using ability measures. On the average, scores on interest inventories correlate around .20 to .30 with school marks, whereas scores on general intelligence tests correlate around .50 with the same criterion. Even though interest inventories are not as good a predictor of job performance, they are good at predicting person–environment fit as it relates to occupational selection, persistence, and satisfaction (Tinsley, 2000). Because people are more likely to avoid occupations that they dislike than they are to enter occupations that they like, low scores on interest inventories tend to be more predictive of what a person avoids doing than high scores are of what he or she is inclined to do (Dolliver, Irvin, & Bigley, 1972; Zytowski, 1976).

Faking

As is also true of ability tests, the validity of interest inventories in predicting occupational choice is affected by test-taking factors and personal characteristics. Whether or not they are intentionally faked, responses to interest inventories may not indicate the true interests of people. Interest inventories can certainly be faked. Bridgman and Hollenbeck (1961) found, for example, that when directed to do so, college students filled out an interest inventory (Kuder Form D) in such a way that their responses were very similar to those of people who were employed in the specified occupations.

Simply because interest inventories can be faked does not necessarily mean that they will be. Interest inventories are less useful when it is advantageous to give false reports, which is more likely when the scores are used for educational or employment selection purposes. Responding falsely to an interest inventory is, however, much less likely when it is administered for purposes of academic and vocational counseling. Even when people might seem to benefit from giving untruthful answers to an interest inventory, they usually do not seem to do so. For example, the Strong Vocational Interest Inventory (SVIB) was used for many years to select individuals for advanced training in the U.S. Navy. Under such circumstances, it might be supposed that faking would be a problem. However, this was not found to be the case (Abrahams, Neumann, & Gilthens, 1971). The mean scores of a group of young men who took the SVIB as part of a Navy scholarship application were very similar to the scores that they made in high school a year before or in college a year after applying for the scholarship. In addition, correlations between the interest score profiles obtained under the scholarship application condition and those obtained under routine testing conditions were in the .90s. It might have been advantageous for the applicants to produce a more favorable outcome by faking, but they did not appear to do so to any appreciable degree.

Response Sets

Although not the same as intentional faking, the tendency to respond to the structure rather than the content of test items (*response sets*) can also result in inaccurate scores on interest inventories. Of particular concern are the response sets of *acquiescence,* or agreeing rather than disagreeing when uncertain, and *social desirability,* or giving a more socially desirable response. One technique designed to minimize these response sets is the *forced-choice* format. Items having this format consist of two or more descriptive statements that are equal in social desirability, but different in content and validity. On a forced-choice interest item, examinees are instructed to indicate which of the activities described in the three or four choices they would most like to do and which they would least like to do. Unfortunately, people sometimes find the forced-choice format awkward and frustrating.

Socioeconomic Status

One demographic factor that is significantly related to responses to vocational interest inventories, and consequently to their validity, is the socioeconomic status of the respondent. Working-class people do not always have an opportunity to cultivate their interests or to train for and enter occupations that are appealing to them. To these individuals, monetary security is a more important factor in employment decisions than satisfying one's interests. This is one reason why, for many years, psychologists showed little inclination to construct inventories to measure the vocational interests of people who were planning to enter unskilled, semiskilled, or even skilled occupations. Because money seemed to be a more important occupational determinant than satisfying vocational interests, the development of interest inventories for nonprofessional occupations was viewed as unproductive. Consequently, early interest inventories were designed almost entirely for use in counseling young people who were planning to enter a profession. The situation changed somewhat after World War II, but the principal focus of interest inventories remained on the professions.

At the high end of the socioeconomic scale are children of wealthy families; such children may have strong vocational interests, but familial and societal expectations and traditions are often more important than individual interests in determining their career choices. Children in wealthy families may not be permitted to do what they like, either because the status or monetary rewards of occupations in which they are interested are not high enough or because parents expect their children to follow in their footsteps or even surpass the parents' own accomplishments. On the other hand, young people in the upwardly mobile middle class are more likely to try to improve their chances of success by entering occupations in which they have strong interests, perhaps even if they do not possess the requisite abilities. For this reason, scores on interest inventories have traditionally been more predictive of occupational choice for middle-class than for upper- and working-class people (McArthur & Stevens, 1955; Miller, 1999). In any event, many of the occupations in the modern workplace do not provide satisfaction for the interests of persons employed in them (Warnath, 1975). So what do people do when they discover that there are large discrepancies between what they would like to do and what they must do to survive? In most cases, rather than jeopardizing their security in a relentless pursuit of their vocational interests and ambitions, they are much more likely to adjust their aspirations so that they are closer to what is actually possible for them to attain (Gottfredson & Becker, 1981).

STRONG INTEREST INVENTORIES

Two of the first and most prominent inventories for measuring vocational interests were designed by E. K. Strong, Jr., and G. F. Kuder. As a result of research conducted during the 1920s, Strong discovered consistent, significant differences in self-reports of what people liked and disliked. He decided to devise an inventory to assess individual differences in interests, beginning with the construction of a variety of items concerning preferences for specific occupations, school subjects, amusements, activities, and types of people. These items, in addition to a scale for rating individual abilities and characteristics, were then administered to groups of men employed in specific occupations. By comparing the responses of men in these occupational groups to those of men in general, Strong was able to develop several dozen occupational scales consisting of items that significant numbers of men with specific occupations answered differently from men in general. This Strong Vocational Interest Blank for Men was the first standardized and commercially distributed measure of interests. Several years later, when it became clear that the interests of women were not limited to clerical work, school teaching, nursing, and housewifery, a companion instrument, the Strong Vocational Interest Blank for Women, was devised.

For various reasons, including the desire to comply with Title IX of the Civil Rights Act of 1964 and to counter allegations of sexism, the men's and women's forms of the Strong Vocational Interest Blank®[2] were combined in 1974 into a single instrument, the Strong–Campbell Interest Inventory (SCII). An effort was made to remove sex bias in the content of the items and the occupational labels and to create a more gender-free inventory. It was recognized, however, that gender bias had been reduced but not entirely eliminated on the SCII. The SCII was further revised in 1985 and 1995 and renamed simply the Strong Interest Inventory (SCI).

Format of the Strong Interest Inventory

The Strong Interest Inventory™ (SII from CPP; see www.cpp-db.com/products/strong/index.asp)[3] consists of 317 items grouped into the following eight parts:

   I. *Occupations.* Each of 135 occupational titles is responded to with like (L), indifferent (I), or dislike (D).
  II. *School Subjects.* Each of 39 school subjects is responded to with like (L), indifferent (I), or dislike (D).
 III. *Activities.* Each of 46 general occupational activities is responded to with like (L), indifferent (I), or dislike (D).

---

[2]*Strong Vocational Interest Blank* and *SVIB* are registered trademarks of Stanford University Press.

[3]*Strong Interest Inventory* and *SII* are trademarks of Stanford University Press.

IV. *Leisure Activities.* Each of 29 amusements or hobbies is responded to with like (L), indifferent (I), or dislike (D).

V. *Types of People.* Each of 20 types of people is responded to with like (L), indifferent (I), or dislike (D).

VI. *Preference between Two Activities.* For each of 30 pairs of activities, preference between the activity on the left (L) and the activity on the right (R), or no preference ( ), is indicated.

VII. *Your Characteristics.* Each of 12 personal characteristics is responded to with Yes, ?, or No, depending on whether they are self-descriptive.

VIII. *Preference in the World of Work.* For each of six pairs of ideas, data, and things, preference between the item on the left (L) and the item on the right (R), or no preference ( ), is indicated.

Although the items, format, and administration procedure of the Strong Interest Inventory were essentially unchanged from the previous edition, the profile was expanded to include 211 occupational scales (102 pairs with separate scales for men and women and 7 scales for occupations represented by a single gender).

Scoring

The SII is scored only by computer, and the item weights and scoring procedures are a trade secret. Completed inventories are sent to CPP, Inc. for scoring, profiling, and interpretation (www.skillsone.com/index.asp), or they can be scored and interpreted by software sold to users.[4] The Strong Profile report displays the examinee's scores on hundreds of scales; other types of reports, such as the Strong Interpretive Report, which provides detailed graphic information on the examinee's occupational interests and tailored descriptions of the best occupations for him or her, are also available.

The SII is scored on five groups of measures: Administrative Indexes, General Occupational Themes, Basic Interest Scales, Occupational Scales, and Personal Style Scales. Before attempting to interpret a person's scores on the last four categories, scores on three Administrative Indexes should be checked: the Total Responses Index; the "Like," "Indifferent," and "Dislike" Percent Indexes; and the Infrequent Responses Index. The Total Responses Index should not fall below 300 (out of 317); the "Like," "Indifferent," and "Dislike" Percent Indexes should not fall outside the range of 14 to 60; and the Infrequent Responses Index should not be less than zero (Harmon, Hansen, Borgen, & Hammer, 1994). The Administrative Indexes are listed at the bottom of page 6 of the six-page "Snapshot: A Summary of Results."

As shown in Figure 12.1 (p. 282), the SII is scored on six General Occupational Themes. These six themes, which are described in Table 12.1 (p. 290), are based on the six categories of Holland's (1985) *vocational personalities:* Realistic (R), Investigative (I), Artistic (A), Social (S), Enterprising (E), and Conventional (C). The examinee's standard *T*

---

[4]The SII is also available through the Internet to qualified individuals who already have an account set up with Consulting Psychologists Press.

STRONG INTEREST INVENTORY

GENERAL OCCUPATIONAL THEMES

BASIC INTEREST SCALES

KEY (Sample Scores)

The phrase printed below the scale name compares your interests to those of people of your own gender. The upper bar shows the range of scores for a group of women from many occupations; the lower bar, the range of scores for a group of men. The number in the right-hand column, represented by the dot, is your score compared to both men and women.

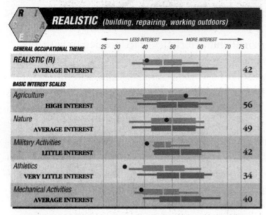

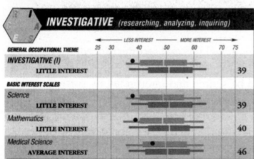

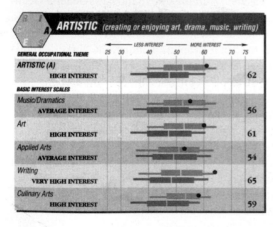

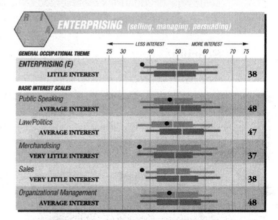

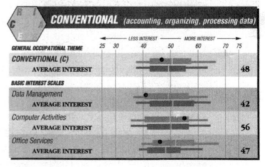

CONSULTING PSYCHOLOGISTS PRESS, INC. • 3803 E. Bayshore Road, Palo Alto, CA 94303

FIGURE 12.1   Sample profile of scores on the Strong Interest Inventory.

(Modified and reproduced by special permission of the Publisher, CPP, Inc., Mountain View, CA 94043 from the Strong Interest Inventory® Instrument.© 1933, 1938, 1945, 1946, 1966, 1968, 1974, 1981, 1985, 1994 by CPP, Inc. Further reproduction is prohibited without the Publisher's written consent. Strong Interest Inventory is a registered trademark of CPP, Inc.)

score and his or her score position in the range of the middle 50% of the norm groups of men and women, on each RIASEC theme and the three to five Basic Interest Scales falling under it. As can be easily noted, the client's main interests are in the Conventional area (note scores related to Office Management, etc.). The 25 Basic Interest Scales were constructed by grouping items having high intercorrelations. Scores on these scales represent the strength and consistency of special areas of interest (Agriculture, Science, Music–Dramatics, Teaching, Public Speaking, Data Management, etc.). T scores on the scales are designated as Very Little Interest, Little Interest, Average Interest, High Interest, or Very High Interest.

Each of the Occupational Scales was constructed by comparing the responses of men or women employed in a particular occupation with the responses of a reference group of men or women in general. All but seven of the Occupational Scales were matched with opposite-gender scales and standardized separately by gender. A person's raw score on a given occupational scale is determined by adding the numerical weights assigned to his or her responses on the scale. The assigned weight depends on the direction in which the item discriminates between men or women employed in that occupation and men or women in general. After all weights corresponding to a person's responses to the items on a particular scale have been added, the obtained raw score is converted to a standard T score that varies directly with the degree of similarity between the examinee's responses and those of the specific occupational group.

Profiles of T scores and ranges of the middle 50% of scores in the norm groups of men and women on the four Personal Style Scales are given. These are bipolar scales with the following definitions:

Work Style: "Works with ideas/data/things" versus "Works with people"
Learning Environment: "Practical" versus "Academic"
Leadership Style: "Leads by example" versus "Directs others"
Risk Taking/Adventure: "Plays it safe" versus "Takes chances"

Scores on the Personal Style Scales are also helpful in vocational counseling and career exploration.

Psychometric Characteristics

The developmental sample for the Strong Interest Inventory consisted of over 55,000 people in 50 occupations who took the inventory in 1992–1993. However, only 9,467 women and 9,484 men from this group were used as general reference samples. This was sufficient to permit accurate validation of old occupational scales and the development of new ones. With respect to the reliability of the SII, high internal consistency and test–retest coefficients of scores on the General Occupational Themes, Basic Interest Scales, Occupational Scales, and Personal Style Scales have been obtained in groups of college students and employed adults. Cronbach alpha coefficients for the General Occupational Themes range from .90 to .94 in the reference sample of men and women, and test–retest coefficients over a 3- to 6-month i terval in a sample of 65 employed women and 75 employed men range from .84 to .92. Coefficient alpha for the Basic Interest Scales ranges from .74 to .94 in the reference sample, and the test–retest coefficient in a sample of approximately 200 men and women ranges from .82 to .94. For the Personal Style Scales, alpha ranges from .78 to .91 in the reference sample; the test–retest coefficient (1- to 4-month interval) in a sample of

128 women and 103 men ranges from .81 to .92. The great majority of the test–retest coefficients in samples of college students and employed adults for the Occupational Scales were also in the .80s and .90s.

Various kinds of evidence pertaining to the content, concurrent, predictive, and construct validity of the SII are reported in the manual (Harmon et al., 1994). Content validity is perhaps the easiest type to establish: an analysis of the composition of the 1994 SII supports the claim of content validity for this instrument. Ranking mean scores on the General Occupational Themes, Basic Interest Scales, Personal Style Scales, and Occupational Scales on the 109 occupational groups provides evidence for concurrent and construct validity, as do correlations between similar measures on other interest inventories, such as the ability to predict college major (Ralston, Borgen, Rottinghaus, & Donnay, 2004) and matching interests with occupations (Dik & Hansen, 2004). In addition, the results of predictive validity studies conducted with previous editions of the Strong (Campbell, 1971; Hansen & Campbell, 1985) have been extrapolated to the 1994 edition.

KUDER INTEREST INVENTORIES

In contrast to the varied item format of the Strong Interest Inventory, G. F. Kuder employed a forced-choice item format in designing his interest inventories. To construct his first inventory, the Kuder Vocational Preference Record, Kuder administered a list of statements concerning activities to college students and determined from their responses which items clustered together. The results led to the construction of 10 groups of items having low correlations across item groups, but high correlations within groups. The 10 item groups were Outdoor, Mechanical, Computational, Scientific, Persuasive, Artistic, Literary, Musical, Social Service, and Clerical. Then triads of items, each member of a triad belonging to a different interest group or area, were formed and administered in forced-choice format. In this way, interests in the 10 different areas were pitted against one another.

Items on the Kuder inventories consist of three statements of activities, and examinees are directed to indicate which activity they *most* prefer and which they *least* prefer. For example, a person might indicate that they would most like to visit a museum and least like to visit an art gallery. Another response to a question might indicate they would most like to collect coins and least like to collect stones.

There are both advantages and disadvantages to the forced-choice item format. Although it tends to minimize certain response sets (acquiescence, social desirability, etc.), people sometimes find the format awkward. Another problem is the ipsative nature of responses to forced-choice items: by accepting or rejecting an activity in one area, the respondent fails to select or reject an activity in another area. For this reason, it is impossible to obtain uniformly high or uniformly low scores across all interest areas. A typical score pattern consists of high scores on one or more areas, low scores on one or more areas, and average scores on the remaining areas.

Three different Kuder inventories are currently commercially available (from National Career Assessment Services): the Kuder™ General Interest Survey, the Kuder™ Occupational Interest Survey, and the Kuder Career Search™ (www.kuder.com/custom/user_manual/).

Kuder™ General Interest Survey

This inventory, which was designed for grades 6–12 and takes 45 to 60 minutes to complete, consists of 168 triads of statements describing various activities; one activity in each triad is to be marked "Most Preferred" and one "Least Preferred." Responses are scored on 10 general-interest areas: Outdoor, Mechanical, Computational, Scientific, Persuasive, Artistic, Literary, Musical, Social Service, and Clerical, plus a Verification (V) scale indicating whether the responses were marked conscientiously. Separate percentile norms for four groups (males and females in grades 6–8 and males and females in grades 9–12) were obtained in 1987. The availability of separate gender norms permits examinees to compare their scores with those of both boys and girls. The narrative report format provides a rank-order listing of percentiles in the 10 interest areas, as well as the three themes in Holland's RIASEC system on which the examinee ranks highest with respect to other males and with respect to other females. Although the provision of separate gender norms helps to control for gender bias resulting from combined norms, differences in the interests of males and females can be seen in the fact that, on average, boys score higher on the Mechanical, Computational, Scientific, and Persuasive scales, while girls score higher on the Artistic, Literary, Musical, Social Service, and Clerical scales.

Kuder™ Occupational Interest Survey

This inventory, which was designed for students in grades 11 and 12, college students, and adults, consists of 100 triads of statements describing various activities; one activity in each triad is to be marked "Most Preferred" and one "Least Preferred." In addition to the traditional paper-and-pencil form, which takes 30 to 40 minutes to complete, a personal computer version of the inventory is available. Scoring consists of comparing the examinee's responses with those of people who were reportedly satisfied with their occupational choices; responses are also compared with those of college students majoring in particular fields of study. A person's score on any of the occupational or college-major scales is a modified biserial correlation coefficient (*lambda coefficient*) between his or her responses to the items and the proportion of individuals in the specified occupational or college major group who endorsed each item. The higher the lambda coefficient is, the more closely the person's score resembles the interest pattern of the corresponding occupational group or major. A narrative report of scores lists the lambda coefficients for occupational and college-major scales by gender of the norm group. The highest lambda coefficients are emphasized in score interpretation, the associated occupations or majors being those in which the examinee's interests are greatest. However, it is recommended that occupations or majors having lambda coefficients within .06 units of the highest coefficients also be considered.

Reliability and Validity

The short-term test–retest reliability coefficients of the two Kuder inventories described above are in the .80s and .90s, and the scores have been found to be fairly stable over a decade or more (Zytowski, 1976). In general, the evidence indicates that the content validities of both inventories are satisfactory. With respect to the predictive validity of the second inventory, Zytowski (1976) found that over half the individuals who had taken it 12 to 19 years earlier had entered occupations on which they had scored within .07 to .12 points of their highest lambda coefficients.

Kuder Career Search™

This latest member of the Kuder family of interest inventories consists of 60 forced-choice item triads written at a sixth-grade reading level (www.kuder.com/custom/user_manual/). It was designed for grade 7 through adulthood and is available in English or Spanish and in Internet-based, mail-back, and self-scored formats. The scores are based on Kuder's 10 scales and six Career Clusters.

The Kuder Career Search with Person Match™ includes all the features of the Kuder Career Search™ plus data based on a Person Match™ procedure. This procedure consists of matching the examinee's responses to the 60 item triads to those of "a criterion pool of real people with unique interests and ways of doing their jobs." The score report lists the closest 25 Person Matches™ to the examinee's responses. The individuals constituting the 25 top matches represent a variety of careers, but have in common the fact that their interest patterns closely resemble those of the examinee.

INTERESTS AND PERSONALITY

According to a holistic conception of personality, interests and abilities are characteristics of personality. Consequently, interest inventories are also personality inventories, and personality inventories also reflect interests (Holland, 1999). Rather than developing by chance, interests are, according to Darley and Hagenah (1955), reflections or expressions of deep-seated individual needs and personality traits. Consistent with this viewpoint is the observation that, as psychoanalysts have maintained since Freud's time, vocational selection is influenced by personality traits.

Psychoanalytic Theory of Interests

Freud and other psychoanalysts emphasized the roles of *sublimation* (the channeling of frustrated sexual or aggressive drives into substitute activities) and *identification* (patterning one's behavior after another person) in the formation of vocational interests. With respect to sublimation, a person with strong sadistic impulses might become interested in being either a butcher or a surgeon, a person with strong exhibitionistic needs might become an actor or other performer, and a person whose sexual impulses are frustrated might write romantic poetry or select a career concerned with decoration, display, and other emphases on the body (modeling, acting, sports, etc.). Although evidence for the operation of sublimation in determining vocational interests and choices is far from clear-cut, data pertaining to the role of identification with parents and significant other people in a person's life are more impressive (Crites, 1969; Heilbrun, 1969; Nachmann, 1960; Steimel & Suziedelis, 1963).

Related, but not restricted to a psychoanalytic perspective on interests, is research linking vocational and educational interests to specific needs and scores on other personality characteristics (e.g., Utz & Korben, 1976). For example, it has been reported that people with scientific interests tend to be more introversive, that interest in selling is associated with aggressiveness, and that people with strong literary and esthetic interests are more likely to possess psychoneurotic characteristics (Osipow, 1983; Super & Bohn, 1970). Other researchers (e.g., Siegelman & Peck, 1960; Sternberg, 1955) have described specific patterns of personality characteristics that are associated with the choice of college major or career.

Roe's Theory and Related Inventories

Based to some extent on psychoanalytic theory and Maslow's (1954) hierarchy of needs, as well as her own research, Anne Roe (1956; Roe & Klos, 1969; Roe & Siegelman, 1964) concluded that the primary factor in career choice is whether the individual is person oriented or nonperson oriented. Roe's revised theory contains two independent dimensions or continua. On the first (*orientation*) dimension, occupational roles are classified as ranging from orientation toward purposeful communication at one end through orientation toward resource utilization at the other end. On the second (*people versus things*) dimension, occupational roles range from interpersonal relations at one extreme to orientation toward natural phenomenon at the other end. A third (*level*) dimension, low versus high, consists of the skill level required by an occupation (unskilled, skilled, professional). Although these three basic dimensions are a central feature of Roe's theory, the theory is actually much more elaborate and has influenced the development of several interest inventories. Three of these instruments are the COPS Interest Inventory, the Hall Occupational Orientation Inventory, and the Vocational Interest Inventory.

COPS Interest Inventory (COPS).   The eight major interest clusters measured by this inventory are represented around the circle in Figure 12.2. The horizontal axis of the figure corresponds to the people versus things dimension, the vertical axis corresponds to the orientation dimension, and the distance from the center of the circle corresponds to the level dimension in Roe's person–environment model. The COPS, which takes 20 to 30 minutes working time and another 15 to 20 minutes for self-scoring, can be administered to junior high students and beyond.

Hall Occupational Orientation Inventory (HOOI).   This inventory, which focuses on 22 job and personality characteristics, is appropriate for individuals from grade 3 through adulthood. It consists of 112 forced-choice items focusing on eight occupational areas: Service, Business Contact, Organization, Technical, Outdoor, Science, General Culture, and Arts and Entertainment.

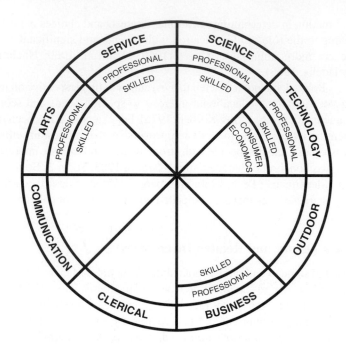

FIGURE 12.2   Eight occupational interest clusters assessed by the COPS Interest Inventory.

(COPSystem Examiner's Manual copyright © 1995 EdiTS Publishers.)

Holland's Instruments and Theory

As depicted in Figure 12.3 and described in Table 12.1, Holland's (1985) RIASEC model conceptualizes the relationships between personality and interests in terms of six types of vocational personalities. Corresponding to these six personality types are six model environments. Each environment is sought by persons with corresponding skills, abilities, attitudes, values, and personality traits.

According to Holland, the behavior of a person in a particular environment is determined by the interaction between personality and the type of environment. People tend to seek environments that are congruent with their personalities, and they are generally happier, more satisfied, and more productive in these environments than in environments that are incongruent with their personalities (Tinsley, 2000). Both the personality types and the environmental types are, however, idealizations, and a given individual or environment is typically a composite of more than one ideal type.

Some of the 15 pairs of personality types in Holland's model are more closely related to each other and hence more consistent. The *consistency* of a person's interest pattern is indicated by the extent to which he or she scores high on types of interests that are close to each other on the hexagonal model. Because the investigative (I) and conventional (C) types are closer to the realistic (R) type on the model, they are more consistent with it. On the

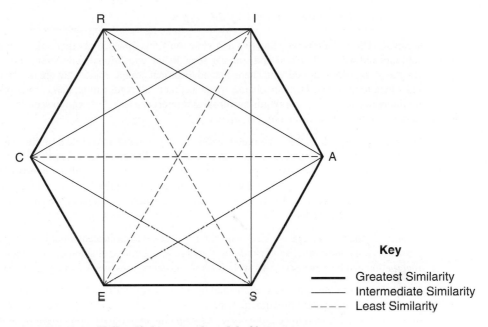

FIGURE 12.3 Holland's hexagonal model of interests.

other hand, the artistic (A) and enterprising (E) types are closer to and hence more consistent with the social (S) type.

Other important concepts in Holland's theory are differentiation, identity, congruence, and calculus. A person who has only one or two high scores has a greater degree of *differentiation* than a person with several high scores. High consistency and differentiation of personality types are characteristic of people who cope effectively with their vocational problems. A second concept, *identity,* may be either personal or environmental. An individual with a sense of *personal identity* has a clear and stable picture of his or her goals, interests, and talents; this condition is associated with having a small number of vocational goals in a few major categories. *Environmental identity* is concerned with whether the goals, tasks, and rewards of the environment are stable over time. A third concept, *congruence,* refers to the fact that different personality types function best in different environments: Does the environment provide opportunities and rewards that are congruent with the person's abilities and preferences? Finally, the concept of *calculus* refers to the fact that personality types or environments can be ordered according to a hexagonal model in which the distances between personality types or environments are consistent with the theoretical relationships between them.

For many years Holland's model of vocational personalities has served as a stimulus and guide for research on career interests and choices, and, when complemented by measures of vocational aspiration, it has achieved notable successes. In addition, the variables in the RIASEC model have been shown to be closely related to several of the Big Five personality variables (Tokar & Fischer, 1998; Tokar & Swanson, 1995) (see Chapter 17).

TABLE 12.1 Descriptions of the RIASEC Types

Realistic. People of this type like to manipulate tools, machines, and other objects and to be outdoors and work with plants and animals; they dislike educational and therapeutic activities. They tend to possess athletic, mechanical, and technical competencies, but are deficient in social and educational skills. They are characterized as practical, conforming, and natural people who are likely to avoid situations requiring verbal and interpersonal skills and to seek jobs such as automobile mechanic, farmer, or electrician.

Investigative. People of this type prefer activities that demand a great deal of thinking and understanding, for example, scientific enterprises. They like to observe, learn, investigate, analyze, evaluate, and solve problems, but tend to avoid situations requiring interpersonal and persuasive skills. Such people are characterized as rational, cautious, curious, independent, introversive. They are more likely to be found in fields such as chemistry, physics, biology, geology, and other sciences.

Artistic. People of this type are imaginative, introspective, complicated, emotional, expressive, impulsive, nonconforming, and disorderly. They prefer unstructured situations in which creativity or imagination can be expressed. Jobs such as actor, musician, or writer are likely to appeal to them.

Social. People of this type are verbally and interpersonally skilled. They like to work with people—developing, enlightening, informing, training, curing, and helping or supporting them in various ways. They tend to be humanistic and empathic and to have good teaching abilities, but minimal mechanical and scientific abilities. They are viewed by others as cooperative, friendly, helpful, persuasive, tactful, and understanding and are likely to be found in clinical or counseling psychology, speech therapy, teaching, and related fields.

Enterprising. People of this type are described as aggressive, ambitious, energetic, domineering, pleasure seeking, self-confident, and sociable. They tend to have high verbal and leadership abilities; they like to influence and persuade others and to lead or manage organizations for economic gain. They prefer jobs such as manager, business executive, or salesperson.

Conventional. People of this type are described as conscientious, efficient, inflexible, obedient, orderly, persistent, and self-controlled. They tend to have good arithmetic and clerical skills and to be adept at filing, record keeping, and data processing. These skills are congruent with an emphasis on business and economic achievement, leading to jobs such as banker, bookkeeper, and tax expert.

Despite this, Tinsley (2000) concluded that Holland's model did not predict work satisfaction and other predictors of occupational outcome. Holland (1996) has maintained, however, that the model should be revised to include the idea that different belief systems are characteristic of different personality types and are promoted by different environments. He proposed to increase the explanatory power of the model by selectively incorporating into it the concepts of career beliefs and strategies.

Self-Directed Search. Two vocational interest inventories constructed on the basis of Holland's theory are the Self-Directed Search and the Vocational Preference Inventory (from PAR). The Self-Directed Search (SDS)-Form R, which is one of the most widely used career interest inventories, consists of an assessment booklet designed to help the user to make a thoughtful evaluation of his or her own interests and abilities and an Occupations Finder for actively exploring the entire range of possible occupations. The SDS yields scores on the six RIASEC variables listed in Table 12.1. The norms are incorporated in a three-letter occupational code, and the Occupations Finder contains over 1,100 occupational titles keyed to the code. The SDS and the Occupations Finder have been used extensively in many contexts, including the ASVAB Career Exploration Program of the U.S. Department of Defense (1999).

Vocational Preference Inventory. Also based on Holland's theory that occupations are describable in terms of personality characteristics is the Vocational Preference Inventory (VPI), a supplement to the Self-Directed Search and other interest inventories. Respondents indicate whether they like or dislike each of more than 160 different occupations on the VPI, and their responses are scored on the six RIASEC variables and five additional scales: Self-Control, Status, Masculinity–Femininity, Infrequency, and Acquiescence. The first six (RIASEC) scores can be used with the SDS Occupations Finder for purposes of career exploration and vocational guidance. Different patterns of high scores on these six types result in assignment of the examinee to different vocational categories. For example, a person who scores high on the Conventional, Enterprising, and Social scales falls in the same category as advertising agents and sales representatives.

World-of-Work Map

Also based on Holland's RIASEC model, in combination with Dale Prediger's work-task dimensions, is the World-of-Work Map illustrated in Figure 12.4. The pattern of responses on the American College Testing Program's UNIACT Interest Inventory can be plotted on this map and can serve as a basis for visiting and exploring regions in the world of work. Groups of similar jobs (job families) covering nearly all jobs in the United States are plotted in the 12 regions of the map. The location of a job family on the map is based on four primary work tasks:

> *Data:* Facts, numbers, files, accounts, business procedures
> *Ideas:* Knowledge, insights, theories, new ways of saying or doing something
> *People:* Care services, leadership, sales
> *Things:* Machines, tools, living things, and materials such as food, wood, or metal

At the edge of the map are six general areas of the world of work and the related RIASEC types.

Gender Differences

Also reflective of personality differences are the sex-stereotyped patterns of scores obtained on the Strong Interest Inventory, the Vocational Preference Inventory, the Vocational Interest Inventory, and other measures of interests. For example, females tend to score higher than males on the Social, Artistic, and Conventional themes, whereas males score

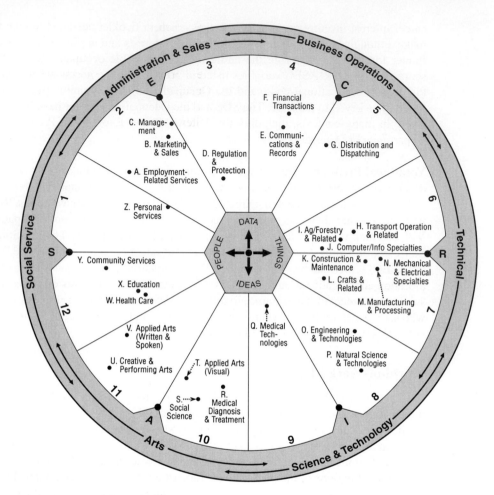

FIGURE 12.4 ACT's World-of-Work Map. See text for explanation.

higher than females on the Realistic, Investigative, and Enterprising themes of the Vocational Preference Inventory (Gottfredson, Holland, & Gottfredson, 1975; Prediger & Hanson, 1976). Similar gender differences have been found in scores on the Vocational Interest Inventory and the Strong Interest Inventory. It has been argued that such differences are due to items that focus on specific activities or materials with which one sex has more experience than the other. Examples are carpentry and automobile-repairing items on Holland's Realistic scale, which are more familiar to males; redesigning the items to include a sewing machine or a blender might make them more familiar to females.

It has been alleged, with some justification, that earlier editions of the Strong and other early interest inventories contributed to gender discrimination by directing young women into traditional women's occupations such as teaching, nursing, and clerical work (Diamond, 1979). Responding to the allegation of gender bias, developers of the Strong Interest Inventory and certain other psychometric instruments constructed unisex forms of the instruments. Furthermore, combined gender norms, as well as the traditional separate-sex norms, were provided. To eliminate gender differences in responses, certain instruments, such as the revised version of the Vocational Interest Inventory and the UNIACT Interest Inventory, utilize sex-balanced items. These items are those that were endorsed by approximately equal percentages of men and women. Perhaps an even more effective way of reducing or eliminating gender differences in scores on interest inventories is to provide equal opportunities, encouragement, and experiences for both sexes in a variety of activities, both traditionally male and traditionally female.[5]

Personality Inventories and Interests

Personality inventories such as those described in Chapter 17 usually contain a number of items concerning interests, attitudes, and values. For this reason, scores on many of these inventories provide information that is useful in academic and vocational counseling. One such inventory is the 16 Personality Factor Questionnaire (16 PF, see detailed description in Chapter 17). The 16 PF can be scored and interpreted by computer on occupational variables corresponding to Holland's RIASEC themes. The resulting profile of scores on these variables can be compared with the profiles of dozens of occupations to determine the similarity between the respondent's interests and those of each occupational group.

OTHER GENERAL- AND SPECIAL-PURPOSE INTEREST INVENTORIES

Although the inventories designed by Strong, Kuder, and Holland have been the most pop ular of all standardized psychometric instruments for assessing interests, many other general- and special-purpose measures of interests have been constructed. The majority of these instruments focus on vocational interests, but several have also been designed primarily to measure interests in school-related activities and various kinds of leisure activities. An illustration is the Leisure Search Inventory (by J. J. Liptak; JIST Works), which is designed to measure the leisure interests of students in junior high school or above. The results may be used in career guidance or employment counseling and to help the person to turn his or her leisure interests into career or employment opportunities.

In addition to surveying interests, the Campbell Interest and Skill Survey (CISS) (from NCS Pearson) provides for self-reports of the respondent's confidence in his or her ability to perform various skills. Many special-purpose inventories for assessing the interests of children, the disadvantaged, and people who plan to enter nonprofessional occupations have also been published.

---

[5]Concern over sex discrimination, as well as the nature and origin of sex differences in psychological characteristics, also stimulated the development of a number of measures of gender role, prominent among which are the Bem Sex-Role Inventory and the Personal Attributes Questionnaire.

Jackson Vocational Interest Survey

One of the most carefully designed and validated of all general interest inventories is the Jackson Vocational Interest Survey (JVIS) (from Sigma). Based on the results of an extensive research program directed by D. N. Jackson, the JVIS consists of 289 forced-choice pairs of statements describing job-related activities. The statements comprising an item pair refer to two equally popular interests, and examinees are told to indicate a preference between them. Designed for high school age and beyond, the JVIS takes 45 to 60 minutes to complete. Initial scoring is on 34 basic interest scales representing 26 work-role and eight work-style dimensions. Definitions of these dimensions were refined by referring to job descriptions in the *Dictionary of Occupational Titles*. Another approach to scoring the JVIS is in terms of 10 occupational themes (Expressive, Logical, Inquiring, Practical, Assertive, Socialized, Helping, Conventional, Enterprising, and Communication). These themes are based on Holland's six *vocational personalities* themes and a factor analysis of responses to the JVIS. Scores on the 10 themes are fairly reliable: internal consistency coefficients range from .70 to .92, and test–retest coefficients over a period of 4 to 6 weeks range from .69 to .92 for the 34 Basic Interest Scales. With respect to the validity of the JVIS, a large study conducted at Pennsylvania State University found that JVIS profiles did a better job of predicting choice of academic major than any previously reported combination of interest and aptitude measures. JVIS profiles for various job groups are included in the revised manual.

Reviewers of the JVIS have praised its careful construction and factorially pure scales, but it has been noted that more evidence for its validity is needed (Davidshofer, 1985; Thomas, 1985). However, the revised manual (Jackson, 2000) provides a substantial amount of new documentation concerning the psychometric characteristics of the JVIS.

Inventories for Children and the Disadvantaged

Because the vocational interests of children are often neither highly developed nor realistic, interest inventories have been designed mainly for individuals in junior high school and beyond. However, several interest inventories can be administered to elementary school children (grades 3–7). Examples are the HALL Occupational Orientation Inventory-Intermediate and the Wide Range Interest-Opinion Test (WRIOT). These inventories serve to introduce and familiarize children with a wide range of activities and occupations in relation to their current interests, experiences, abilities, and ambitions. The Intermediate HALL contains 110 school-related items designed to complement awareness-development programs and focuses on 22 work and personality characteristics.

The WRIOT and various other instruments (e.g., the Geist Picture Interest Inventory and the Reading-Free Vocational Interest Inventory) were developed primarily for culturally and educationally disadvantaged young people. Rather than words, phrases, or statements, these instruments employ as test materials pictures of people engaged in certain activities. The WRIOT consists of 150 sets of three drawings, presented in booklet or filmstrip form, of people engaged in various activities with which physically or mentally handicapped individuals can identify. The WRIOT can be completed in 40 to 60 minutes by individuals ranging in age from 5 years to adulthood. Likes and dislikes are selected in a forced-choice format, and responses are scored on 18 interest clusters (art, sales, management, office work, mechanisms, machine operation, athletics, etc.) and eight attitude clusters (sedentariness, risk, ambition, sex stereotype, etc.). Job title lists are available for each of the 18 interest clusters.

On the Geist Picture Inventory (from WPS), respondents circle the one of three pictures that they prefer. The inventory takes about 25 minutes to complete and is scored on 12 areas. On the Reading-Free Vocational Interest Inventory, examinees mark preferences for each of 55 sets of three drawings depicting job tasks. The drawings represent the kinds of tasks or occupations in which mentally retarded individuals can be productive and proficient (automotive, building trades, clerical, animal care, food service, patient care, horticulture, housekeeping, personal service, laundry, or materials handling).

The Ashland Interest Assessment was designed for adolescents and adults with learning disabilities, developmental handicaps or delays, limited familiarity with English, limited access to education, chronic unemployment, brain injury, or chronic emotional or psychiatric conditions. The 144 pairs of activities associated with the particular occupations that make up this inventory are printed in large type and at a grade 3 reading level. The respondent selects the activity from each item pair that he or she would most like to engage in. An illustrative item is

> Clean carpets   A
> Deliver furniture   B

The inventory is scored on 12 scales: Arts and Crafts, Food Service, Sales, Protective Service, Mechanical, Plant or Animal Care, Personal Service, Clerical, General Service, Health Care, Construction, and Transportation.

Interests in Nonprofessional Occupations

Certain scales on the Strong Interest Inventory, the Kuder Occupational Interest Survey, and other general-interest inventories pertain to interests in nonprofessional occupations, but none of these inventories was designed expressly for this purpose. Since the 1950s, a number of inventories focusing on the skilled trades have been constructed that use somewhat simpler content and vocabulary than the Strong and Kuder. One such instrument is the Career Assessment Inventory.

The Vocational Version of the Career Assessment Inventory (CAI) was modeled after the Strong inventories and has sometimes been referred to as "the working man's Strong Interest Inventory." Responses to the 305 items on the CAI are made on a 5-point scale (L = like very much, l = like somewhat, I = indifferent, d = dislike somewhat, and D = dislike very much). The items, written at a sixth-grade level and covering activities, school subjects, and occupational titles, can be answered in 30 to 45 minutes.

The computer-based report of T scores on the CAI consists of four sections: I. Administrative Indices (Total Responses, Response Consistency, Response Percentages on Activities, School Subjects, Occupations); II. General Themes (Realistic, Investigative, Artistic, Social, Enterprising, Conventional); III. Basic Interest Area Scales; and IV. Occupational Scales. The 25 Basic Interest Area Scales and the 111 Occupational Scales are grouped under Holland's six themes. Scores on four special Scales (Fine Arts–Mechanical, Occupational Extroversion–Introversion, Educational Orientation, and Variability of Interests), a computer-generated narrative report, and a counselor's summary are provided. From a psychometric viewpoint, the CAI is well designed and has good reliability. A 370-item Enhanced Version of the CAI, which can be scored on more professional occupations than the Vocational Version, is also available. Both the Vocational and Enhanced Versions can also be scored on General Occupational Themes based on Holland's RIASEC model.

USING INTEREST INVENTORIES IN COUNSELING

People often choose to enter an occupation for which there is a poor person–vocation fit. For example, a woman might want to be an attorney due to its perceived status and high income. After placing many years into training, she may only discover that her personality is not congruent with the sorts of demands required of this profession. In addition, people are often unrealistic in making career plans. Many more high school students expect to graduate from college than actually do, and the career aspirations of college graduates are often incompatible with the opportunities available in many careers. Career aims and decisions are affected not only by environmental factors such as the economic situation and the kinds of jobs available, but also by gender, socioeconomic status, physical and mental abilities, interests, and knowledge of particular occupations. Consequently, counselors have the crucial task of evaluating a person's abilities, interests, personality, resources, and opportunities to assist him or her to make optimal decisions. Vocational counselors must be ready to listen, inform, and advise; they should be prepared to obtain personal data from students and other counselees and supply them with information on training programs and occupations.

Vocational counseling must be conducted with caution. Both jobs and students are multifaceted and dynamic: they possess many different features, and these features change with time. The job of a psychologist, for example, may involve different activities in different situations, and the nature of the job has changed over the years. Even in the same situational context and time period, there is usually enough diversity in most jobs for people with different abilities, interests, and personality to adapt and perform satisfactorily.

Interests Are Not Abilities

Despite the need for a flexible, probabilistic approach to vocational counseling, counselors must make some interpretation of scores on psychological tests and inventories. One obvious distinction is between aspirations on the one hand and interests and abilities on the other. Although scores on vocational interest inventories may have significant correlations with measures of cognitive abilities, the correlations are typically fairly low (Hansen, 1984; Randahl, 1991; Swanson, 1993).

Individual aspirations are often colored by false perceptions of what a particular activity or occupation entails. For example, a person who aspires to become a nurse may picture herself or himself as a Florence Nightingale, helping suffering humanity and basking in the praises and love of other people. He or she may be unaware of the fact that nursing involves a great deal of standing and walking, emptying bed pans, adjusting to diverse sleeping patterns, and listening to endless complaints. Consequently, effectiveness in nursing may depend more on having a good pair of feet, tolerance for strong odors, ability to adjust to various work hours, and unlimited patience than on a love of humanity.

In interpreting the results of an interest inventory, counselors should be aware of and attempt to clarify the difference between interests and abilities. It is not uncommon for a person to conclude from the results of an interest inventory that he or she has the abilities required for success in a certain occupation, when actually all that has been shown is that his or her interests are similar to those of persons in that occupation. Because people often fail to distinguish between interests and abilities, it is unwise to leave the task of interpreting a self-administered inventory to the counselee.

The fact that correlations between measures of interests and abilities tend to be rather low indicates that many people do not possess the abilities needed to succeed on jobs in which they are interested or that they may not be interested in jobs for which they have the required abilities. For this reason, scores on interest inventories should be employed in vocational counseling in the light of other information about the counselee. Additional information that may facilitate vocational decision making can be obtained from the individual's accomplishments (grades, awards, extracurricular activities, community service, etc.), experiences, and level of motivation.

A motivational variable to which abilities, interests, and performance are moderately related is *self-efficacy*. Associated with the notion of self-concept, self-efficacy is defined as the individual's judgment concerning his or her ability to accomplish a particular task in a certain situation. Betz (1992, 1994) recommended that vocational counselors attempt to enhance counselees' self-efficacy with respect to particular coursework or occupations by encouraging and arranging for success experiences in specific areas of endeavor. Clarifying the circular relationships among self-efficacy, success, and interest, Lent, Lopez, and Bieschke (1991) maintain that "past success experiences in a particular performance domain may promote self-efficacy; viewing oneself as efficacious likely enhances interest in that domain; and such interest then motivates further expposure to, and choice of, correspondent educational and vocational activities" (p. 429).

Realizing the difficulties of explaining to students, parents, and others the relationships of interests, abilities, motivation, past achievement, and financial status to academic and vocational success, experienced vocational counselors should have available many sources of information and explanation pertaining to the world of work. In addition to such source books as the *Dictionary of Occupational Titles (DOT)* (U.S. Department of Labor, 1991, 1993),[6] the *Occupational Outlook Handbook, 2000–2001* (Bureau of Labor Statistics, 2000), and the *Occupational Outlook for College Graduates* (Bureau of Labor Statistics, 1996), vocational counselors should have a supply of various career exploration and development materials published by commercial testing companies and by the U.S. Department of Labor. Much of the career information that was formerly available only in book form can now be obtained online from the Bureau of Labor Statistics and other public and private organizations. Examples of such resources are the *Occupational Outlook Handbook* (stats.bls.gov/ocohome), the

---

[6]O*NET, the Occupational Information Network, a database that includes information on the knowledge, skills, abilities, interests, preparation, contexts, and tasks associated with 1,122 occupations, has recently replaced the *Dictionary of Occupational Titles* (see Web site www.doleta.gov/programs/onet/).

Career Guide to Industries, 2000–01 Edition (stats.bls.gov/cghome.htm), and the *Occupational Outlook Quarterly* (stats.bls.gov/opub/ooq/ooqhome.htm). Two useful Web sites for grade school students are the BLS Career Information (www.bls.gov/K12/html/edu_over.htm), which provides elementary school pupils with an introduction to career guidance information, and ACT's Career Planning Survey (www.act.org/cps/index.html), a comprehensive career guidance program for preparing students in grades 8–10 to make informed educational and career decisions early in high school.

Computer-Based Career Counseling

A number of computer-assistance guidance systems designed to help students to explore their interests, values, attitudes, abilities, and personalities and make realistic career decisions are available. Examples of career guidance programs and their Web sites are ETS's SIGI PLUS (www.ets.org/sigi/index.html), ACT's DISCOVER (www.act.org/discover), ACT's Career Planning Survey (www.act.org/cps/indes.html), National Career Assessment Services' Career Planning System (www.kuder.com/kcps.asp), and the University of Oregon's Career Information System (oregoncis.uoregon.edu).

The System of Interactive Guidance and Information (SIGI PLUS) is an interactive computer program developed by Educational Testing Service to help users to make informed and rational career decisions. According to ETS, SIGI PLUS "helps users evaluate their values, interests, skills and resources and relate these characteristics to the rewards, satisfactions, activities and requirements they seek in a career." However, because ETS believes that expressed interests are at least as accurate as inventoried interests, SIGI PLUS does not include an interest inventory. Similar to SIGI PLUS are DISCOVER Career Guidance and Information Software System (for high school, colleges, and agencies serving adults) and DISCOVER Intermediate School Version. Users reportedly find these computer programs enjoyable and profitable, and several sessions with them can be followed by discussions with an experienced career counselor. College students and counselors in training have assigned high ratings to SIGI PLUS and DISCOVER (Kapes, Borman, & Frazier, 1989; Peterson, Ryan-Jones, Sampson, Readon, et al., 1994).

SUMMARY

1. The serious use of interest inventories in vocational and academic counseling and placement began with the construction of the Strong Vocational Interest Blanks and the Kuder Vocational Preference Record. The results of longitudinal studies have shown that interests are mainly learned (family interaction patterns, childhood fantasies), but can also be influenced by genetics and temperament. After middle adolescence, interests are very stable.

2. Interest inventories have low correlations with school grades (.20 to .30 compared with ability measures of .50). They are better predictors of vocational choice and satisfaction and are especially good predictors of which vocations a person will avoid. Since interest inventories are used almost exclusively for personal growth and awareness, rather than decisions related to hiring and promotion, there is little motivation

to fake the results. However, it is possible to fake interest inventories, and they are susceptible to response sets.

3. The most recent version of the Strong Interest Inventory consists of 317 items grouped into eight categories. It is scored on 6 general occupational themes, 25 basic interest scales, 211 occupational scales, 4 personal style scales, and 3 administrative indexes. Scoring keys for the occupational scales were developed empirically by comparing the responses of people in general with those of people employed in particular occupations. Scores on the Strong Interest Inventory are fairly reliable and valid predictors of occupational persistence and satisfaction, but not necessarily occupational success. G. F. Kuder constructed several interest inventories consisting of a series of forced-choice item triads. The Kuder Vocational Preference Record, the Kuder General Interest Survey, and the Kuder Occupational Interest Survey are three instruments of this sort. The last of these instruments, like the Strong Interest Inventory, can be scored on a number of empirically derived occupational scales, but the first two are scored only on general-interest scales. All these inventories are appropriate for high school students and adults. A recent addition to the Kuder family of instruments is the Kuder Career Search.

4. The relationships of interests to personality are emphasized in the research of Anne Roe and John Holland and instruments stemming from their research. Holland's Self-Directed Search and Vocational Preference Inventory are two of the most popular of all interest inventories. Holland's RIASEC (Realistic, Investigative, Artistic, Social, Enterprising, and Conventional) model of interests has also influenced the development and scoring of several other interest inventories.

5. In addition to inventories scored according to broad interest areas and adult occupations, a number of instruments are available for assessing the interests of children, the disadvantaged, and those planning to enter nonprofessional occupations. The Jackson Vocational Interest Survey is a 289-item, forced-choice instrument that evaluates 10 occupational themes (Expressive, Logical, etc.).

6. Vocational counseling requires a broad knowledge of the world of work and skilled integration of ability test scores, measures of interest, biographical data, and behavioral observations. Computer-based assessment can greatly help this process.

MASTERING THE CHAPTER OBJECTIVES

1. *Introduction to vocational interest measurement*
   a. Describe the factors that influence the development of interests.
   b. Develop a life history outline of how your interests and career aspirations have changed over time. Why do you believe these changes occurred?

2. *Validity of interest inventories*
   a. What validity support is there for interest inventories? How do they compare with ability measures?
   b. What are response sets? Why are they of particular concern in designing inventories to measure interests and personality characteristics? What can be done to counter the effects of response sets on scores on these inventories?

3. *Strong and Kuder interest inventories*
   a. Compare the Strong Interest Inventory (SII) with the Kuder Occupational Interest Survey (KOIS) in terms of design, scoring, and interpretation.
   b. On the SII and the KOIS, why are the correlations between occupational scales having the same or very similar names often not very high? What theoretical and practical significance might this have?

4. *Interests, Personality, and the Self-Directed Search*
   a. Defend the thesis that interests are personality characteristics and therefore that interest inventories are measures of personality. Cite specific theories, research findings, and instruments to support your position.
   b. In J. L. Holland's theory of interests and personality, certain interest clusters are characteristic of people with certain personality traits and point to certain vocations or careers. Without looking at the personality–job description list below, rate yourself on a scale of 1 to 10 on whether you feel you are Realistic, Investigative, Artistic, Social, Enterprising, and Conventional (or take one of the instruments in Question 2 of Experiencing Psychological Assessment). Theoretically, the following job listings should correspond to your interest or personality type:

   Realistic: Jobs such as automobile mechanic, farmer, or electrician.

   Investigative: Jobs in fields such as chemistry, physics, biology, geology, and other sciences.

   Artistic: Jobs such as actor, musician, or writer.

   Social: Jobs in clinical or counseling psychology, speech therapy, teaching, and related fields.

   Enterprising: Jobs such as manager, business executive, or salesperson.

   Conventional: Jobs such as banker, bookkeeper, and tax expert.

   To what extent did your interest type match up with the above list of vocations? Are these suggested vocations consistent with the ones that you feel that you are truly interested in and have the abilities and personality to be successful in?
   c. Write the letter of the interest area in the right column that corresponds to the personality characteristic in the left column. You may put more than one letter from the right column opposite the adjective in the left column.

1. active	a. artistic
2. aggressive	b. clerical
3. attractive	c. computational
4. charming	d. literary
5. conscientious	e. mechanical
6. conservative	f. musical
7. conventional	g. outdoor
8. cooperative	h. persuasive
9. courageous	i. scientific
10. dependable	j. social service
11. friendly	
12. intelligent	
13. inventive	
14. logical	
15. methodical	
16. organized	
17. original	

18. pleasant
19. practical
20. precise
21. serious
22. sociable
23. strong
24. sympathetic
25. thoughtful

Compare your responses with those of your classmates and friends. Was there any consistency in the way that different people matched the items in the left column with those in the right column? What do the results tell you about the relationships of personality to vocational interests? Are some personality characteristics associated with interests in a wide variety of occupations, whereas others are associated with a more narrow range of occupations?

5. *General- and special-purpose inventories*
   a. List three reasons why inventories designed for nonprofessional occupations developed so much later than those for professional groups.
   b. Consider the following five interest inventories:
   a. Career Assessment Inventory
   b. Kuder Occupational Interest Survey
   c. Self-Directed Search
   d. Strong Interest Inventory
   e. Wide Range Interest–Opinion Test

Which of these inventories would you recommend for the following situations?
1. Counseling a college freshman or sophomore on choice of major and vocation
2. Setting up a counseling program for students admitted to a vocational high school with a variety of different trade programs
3. Helping tenth-graders to explore careers and consider various occupational choices
4. Helping a group of physically and mentally handicapped individuals to consider a variety of activities with which they can identify
5. Helping a counseling service work with college graduates who are uncertain about their future careers
6. Introducing and familiarizing a group of elementary school children with a wide range of career activities and occupations

6. *Vocational counseling*
   a. Give three reasons why it would be important to consult with a vocational counselor regarding scores on interest inventories.
   b. What effects do you believe computer or online administration and scoring of vocational interest inventories have or will have on the process of career familiarization, search, counseling, and decision making?

EXPERIENCING PSYCHOLOGICAL ASSESSMENT

1. Many Web sites enable you to take an interest inventory online. For example, you might log on to CPP, Inc. to take the Strong Interest Inventory (www.skillsone.com/index.asp). However, this needs to be done under the direction of a qualified person and a fee is involved.

2. Take the Self-Directed Search online (www.self-directed-search.com/index.html, fee of $9.95). For a rough approximation of Holland's types, you might try a free but unvalidated service such as www.careerkey.org/english/index.html. How accurate do you feel the above measures are (including the Strong Interest Inventory if you took it)? How close do the findings align with your career aspirations? Are there any careers you have considered that are not congruent with your personality? If so, why do you think this occurred?

3. Log on to the following three Web sites, and explore the career-related information provided:

   www.bls.gov/k12/htm/edu_over.htm
   www.act.org/cps/index.html
   www.kuder.com/kcps.asp

....

CHAPTER THIRTEEN

ATTITUDES AND RELATED PSYCHOSOCIAL CONSTRUCTS

CHAPTER OBJECTIVES

1. Describe Thurstone, Likert, and Guttman scales.
2. Describe sources for finding attitude scales.
3. Describe issues related to the reliability and validity of attitude scales.
4. Describe what a value scale is, including as examples the Rokeach Value Survey and the Values Scale.
5. Describe what is meant by personal orientation and give examples of how it is measured (Bem Sex-Role Inventory, Sex-Role Egalatarianism Scale, Personal Orientation Inventory, and the Life-Orientation Inventory).

An *attitude* is a learned predisposition to respond positively or negatively to a specific object, situation, institution, or person. As such, it consists of cognitive (knowledge or intellective), affective (emotional and motivational), and performance (behavioral or action) components. Though the concept of attitude is similar in some respects to interest, opinion, belief, or value, there are differences in the manner in which these terms are used. An *interest* is a feeling or preference concerning one's own activities. Unlike *attitude*, which implies approval or disapproval (a moral judgment), being interested in something simply means that a person spends time thinking about it or reacting to it, regardless of whether these thoughts and behaviors are positive or negative. An *opinion* is a specific reaction to certain occurrences or situations, whereas an *attitude* is more general in its effects on responses to a broad range of people or events. Furthermore, people are aware of their opinions, but they may not be fully conscious of their attitudes. Opinions are similar to *beliefs,* in that both are judgments or acceptances of certain propositions as facts, but the factual supports for opinions are usually weaker than those for beliefs. Finally, the term *value* refers to the importance, utility, or worth attached to particular activities and objects, usually as ends, but potentially as means as well.

ATTITUDE MEASUREMENT

Different methods can be used to obtain information concerning a person's attitude, values, and orientation. This includes attitude scales, surveys, and inventories. These rely to a large extent on an examinee's ability to provide a self-report of these variables. In contrast, projective techniques, physiological indicators, and measures of implicit associations are more indirect means of assessing attitudes and values. Perhaps the most straightforward procedure is direct observation, that is, observing how the person behaves in relation to certain things. What does the person actually do or say in situations in which the attitude, object, or event is present? Willingness to do a favor, sign a petition, or make a donation to some cause is an example of behavioral measures of attitudes. Despite this diversity of approaches, the most frequent means of assessing attitudes is through traditional attitude scales.

Traditional Attitude Scales

The most popular method of measuring attitudes is to administer an *attitude scale* consisting of a set of positive and negative statements concerning a specific concept (e.g., a group of people or an institution). Total score on an attitude scale is determined from the aggregated responses of the examinee to the statements, the specific scoring method depending on the type of scale (see an example of teacher attitudes toward mainstreaming at www .ericdigests.org/pre-927/teacher.htm).

One of the first attitude scales was the Bogardus Social Distance Scale (Bogardus, 1925), on which respondents ranked various racial and religious groups in order of acceptance. In administering this *cumulative scale,* respondents were instructed to indicate the degree to which they accepted various social or religious groups in various capacities. Items were arranged in a hierarchy such that a positive response to a given item implied a positive response to all preceding items in the hierarchy. The Bogardus scale proved useful in research on regional differences and other variables associated with racial prejudice, but it permitted attitude measurement on only an ordinal scale and was somewhat crude by present-day standards. Better measures of attitudes resulted from the research of Louis Thurstone, Rensis Likert, Louis Guttman, and other psychometricians.

Thurstone Scales.   During the late 1920s, Louis Thurstone and his co-workers attempted to measure attitudes on an interval measurement scale, on which equal differences in scale values correspond to equal differences in attitude strength, by using the methods of *pair comparisons* and *equal-appearing intervals.* Construction of an attitude scale by either of these methods begins by collecting a large number of statements expressing a wide range of positive and negative feelings toward a given topic. The next step in the method of pair comparisons is for a large number of experts to compare the statements with each other and indicate which statement in each pair expresses a more positive attitude toward the topic.

Because making the numerous comparisons required by this procedure is rather cumbersome and time consuming, the method of equal-appearing intervals proved more popular.

In the method of equal-appearing intervals, the 200 or so statements expressing attitudes toward something (person, object, event, situation, or abstraction) are sorted into 11 categories by a large sample of judges. These categories range from least favorable (category 1) to most favorable (category 11) toward the thing in question. The judges are instructed to think of the 11 categories as lying at equal intervals along a continuum. After all judges have completed the sorting process for all statements, a frequency distribution is constructed for each statement by counting the number of judges who placed the statement in each category. Next, the median (*scale value*) and semi-interquartile range (*ambiguity index*) for each statement are computed from the corresponding frequency distribution. Then the statements are rank ordered according to their scale values, and 20 or so statements are selected for the finished scale. In a true interval scale, the difference between the scale values of any two adjacent statements will be equal to the difference between the scale values of any other pair of adjacent statements. Furthermore, the ambiguity indexes of all statements should be low.

A portion of one of the many attitude scales constructed by this method is shown in Form 13.1. Note that the scale values of the statements, which are concerned with attitudes toward capital punishment, range from 0.1 (highly negative toward) to 11.0 (highly positive toward). A person's score on such a scale is the median of the scale values of the statements she or he checks.

Thurstone and his co-workers constructed some 30 attitude inventories by the method of equal-appearing intervals, most of which had reliabilities in the .80s. Remmers (1960) generalized the equal-appearing intervals procedure in his nine Master Attitude Scales, which measure attitudes toward any school subject, vocation, institution, defined group, proposed social action, practice, homemaking activity, as well as individual and group morale and the high school.

Despite the fairly high reliabilities of instruments constructed by the method of equal-appearing intervals, the procedure has been criticized for the great amount of work involved in scale construction, the lack of uniqueness of a respondent's score, and the effects of the judges' own attitudes on the scale values of statements (Selltiz, Wrightsman, & Cook, 1976). Considering the ready availability of computers and other time-saving devices, the first criticism is not so serious. The second criticism refers to the fact that the same score, which is simply the median scale value of the statements checked, may be obtained by checking a different combination of statements and therefore is not unique. The third criticism refers to the fact that not everyone is capable of playing the role of neutral judge. It was found in one study (Goodstadt & Magid, 1977), for example, that nearly 50% of the college students who served as judges responded to a pool of attitude statements in terms of their own personal agreement or disagreement with the items. Bruvold (1975) concluded, however, that careful instruction of the individuals who are doing the judging reduces the judgmental bias to a level that does not seriously distort the equal-interval properties of these scales. A final criticism, which is not limited to Thurstone-type attitude scales, is that scores on these scales represent measurement at only an ordinal rather than an interval level. Actually, the level of measurement of attitudes scales constructed by the

FORM 13.1   Twelve of the Twenty-Four items on a Scale of Attitudes toward Capital Punishment

Directions: This is a study of attitude toward capital punishment. Below you will find a number of statements expressing different attitudes toward capital punishment.

✓ Put a check mark if you agree with the statement.
✗ Put a cross if you disagree with the statement.

Try to indicate either agreement or disagreement for each statement. If you simply cannot decide about a statement, you may mark it with a question mark. This is not an examination. There are no right or wrong answers to these statements. This is simply a study of people's attitudes toward capital punishment. Please indicate your own convictions by a check mark when you agree and by a cross when you disagree.

Scale Value	Item Number	
(0.1)	12	I do not believe in capital punishment under any circumstances.
(0.9)	16	Execution of criminals is a disgrace to civilized society.
(2.0)	21	The state cannot teach the sacredness of human life by destroying it.
(2.7)	8	Capital punishment has never been effective in preventing crime.
(3.4)	9	I don't believe in capital punishment, but I'm not sure it isn't necessary.
(3.9)	11	I think the return of the whipping post would be more effective than capital punishment.
(5.8)	18	I do not believe in capital punishment, but it is not practically advisable to abolish it.
(6.2)	6	Capital punishment is wrong but is necessary in our imperfect civilization.
(7.9)	23	Capital punishment is justified only for premeditated murder.
(9.4)	20	Capital punishment gives the criminal what he deserves.
(9.6)	17	Capital punishment is just and necessary.
(11.0)	7	Every criminal should be executed.

(Reprinted from Peterson & Thurstone, 1933.)

method of equal-appearing interval scales probably lies somewhere between the ordinal and interval levels of measurement.

Likert Scales.   The procedure devised by Rensis Likert has become the most popular of all attitude-scaling procedures. This is because it is both simple and versatile. As with Thurstone's method of equal-appearing intervals, Likert's *method of summated ratings* begins with the collection or construction of a large number of item statements expressing a variety of positive and negative attitudes toward a specific object or event. Suggestions for constructing these attitude statements are given in Table 13.1.

After a preliminary set of statements has been devised, 100 to 200 selected people—not necessarily expert judges—are told to indicate on a 4- to 7-point scale the extent to which they agree or disagree with each statement. In the typical case of a 5-point scale, positively worded items are scored 0 for strongly disagree, 1 for disagree, 2 for undecided, 3 for agree, and 4 for strongly agree; negatively worded items are scored 4 for strongly dis-

TABLE 13.1 Suggestions for Constructing Statements for a Likert-Type Attitude Scale

1. The statements should refer to the present, rather than the past.

2. The statements should not be factual or interpretable as factual.

3. The statements should not be interpretable in more than one way.

4. The statements should be relevant to the psychological concept under consideration.

5. The statements should be simple sentences containing only one thought, rather than compound or complex sentences.

6. Statements containing double negatives, words not likely to be understood by the respondents, words having more than one meaning, nonspecific adjectives or adverts (for example, many, sometimes), or universals such as all, always, none, or never should be avoided.

7. Slang and colloquialisms, which tend to make statements ambiguous and unclear, should be avoided.

agree, 3 for disagree, 2 for undecided, 1 for agree, and 0 for strongly agree. The respondent's total score on the initial set of attitude items is computed as the sum of his or her scores on the individual items. After obtaining the total scores for all respondents on the initial item set, a statistical procedure (*t*-test or item-discrimination index) is applied to each item. Then equal numbers of positively and negatively worded items (typically 10 of each) that significantly differentiate respondents whose total scores fall in the upper 27% from those whose fall in the lower 27% are selected. A person's score on the scale is the sum of the numerical weights (0, 1, 2, 3, or 4) of the responses he or she checks.

Not all published attitude scales designated as Likert scales were actually constructed by item-analysis procedures. In many cases, a set of declarative statements, each with five agree–disagree response categories, is simply put together as an instrument without any specific theoretical construct in mind or without following Likert's procedure. Consequently, one cannot be certain that a questionnaire that looks like a Likert scale was actually constructed by the Likert scaling procedure.

Despite misuses of the method of summated ratings, it has several advantages over the method of equal-appearing intervals (Selltiz et al., 1976). Because it does not require expert, unbiased judges, constructing a Likert scale is easier than constructing a Thurstone scale. Also, unlike Thurstone scales, Likert scales permit the use of items that are clearly related to the attitude being assessed as long as they are significantly correlated with total scores. Finally, a Likert scale is likely to have a higher reliability coefficient than a Thurstone scale consisting of the same number of items. Like Thurstone scales, however, Likert scales have been criticized for the fact that different patterns of responses can yield the same score and that at best the scores represent ordinal measurement.

Guttman Scales. Less popular than the Thurstone and Likert procedures is a third attitude-scaling procedure, the Louis Guttman's *scalogram analysis*. The purpose of scalogram analysis (Guttman, 1944) is to determine whether responses to items selected to measure a given attitude fall on a single dimension. When the items constitute a true, unidimensional Guttman scale, the respondent who endorses a particular item also endorses every item having a lower scale value. This condition is more likely to be met with cognitive test items than with attitude statements or other affective items.

As with Bogardus's (1925) approach to attitude scale construction, the goal of scalogram analysis is to produce a cumulative, ordinal scale. Guttman realized the difficulty of constructing a true interval scale with attitude items, but he felt that it could be approximated. The extent to which a true scale is obtained is indicated by the *reproducibility coefficient,* computed as the proportion of actual responses that fall into the perfect pattern of a true Guttman scale. That is, what proportion of the respondents who endorse a particular item endorse all items below it on the scale? An acceptable value of the reproducibility coefficient is around .90.

An illustrative response matrix for computing the reproducibility coefficient for a seven-statement Guttman scale administered to 10 people is given in Box 13.1. Observe that the respondents (rows) are arranged in order according to the total number of + responses, where + indicates agreement and − indicates disagreement with the attitude expressed in the particular statement. The number of + responses (p) for each statement is then counted, and a dividing line is drawn under the row corresponding to the pth response. For example, there are nine + responses in the column for statement 5, so a horizontal line is drawn under the ninth entry in that column. In a cumulative Guttman scale, all responses above this line should be + and all responses below it should be −. Because the − response in the ninth row and the + response in the tenth row of column 5 are deviations from this ideal pattern, they are counted as errors. Consequently, there are two errors for statement 5. The number of errors for the remaining statements are determined similarly, yielding a total of $E = 8$ errors for all seven statements combined. Next we compute the total number of responses as the number of statements times the number of responses as $N =$ rows $\times$ columns $= 10 \times 7 = 70$. The reproducibility coefficient (R) is then computed from the formula

$$R = 1 - \frac{E}{N} = 1 - \frac{8}{70} = .886. \tag{13.1}$$

Since the lowest acceptable value of R for a true Guttman scale is .90, the reproducibility coefficient for this seven-item scale is unacceptable evidence for these statements forming a Guttman scale.

Other Attitude-Scaling Procedures

A number of other procedures have been applied to the process of attitude scale construction, including the semantic differential technique, Q-technique, magnitude estimation, expectancy-value scaling, and facet analysis. The first two of these are discussed in Chapter 16.

Magnitude Estimation.   In this method, which is based on a psychophysical procedure for scaling stimulus intensities, the respondent assigns a numerical value to each of a series of stimuli varying across a range of intensities. The responses of a representative sample of people are then averaged and plotted against the actual stimulus intensities. A similar procedure has been used to scale perceptions of social or political events, such as the serious-

BOX 13.1

RESPONSE MATRIX FOR COMPUTING THE REPRODUCIBILITY COEFFICIENT OF AN ILLUSTRATIVE SEVEN-ITEM GUTTMAN SCALE

| Respondent | STATEMENT | | | | | | | Total |
	3	1	7	6	5	4	2	(+)
I	+	+	+	+	+	+	+	7
B	+	+	+	+	+	−	+	6
A	−	+	+	−	+	−	+	4
E	−	+	+	−	+	−	+	4
H	−	+	+	−	+	+	−	4
J	−	+	+	−	+	−	+	4
D	−	+	+	−	+	−	−	3
C			∣		∣			2
F	+	−	−	−	−	−	−	1
G	−	−	−	−	+	−	−	1
Total (+)	3	7	8	2	9	2	5	
Errors	2	0	0	0	2	2	2	

ness of various criminal offenses (Sellin & Wolfgang, 1964). The averaged ratings given to each of the events are plotted against a measure of actual values, such as the monetary cost of an offense. This technique has also been used to scale other social perceptions or attitudes, such as the popularity of political candidates, by having respondents draw a line whose length reflects the strength of their feelings or attitudes toward the person, object, or event.

Expectancy–Value Scaling.   This approach to attitude scaling was proposed by Fishbein and Ajzen (1975). The respondent begins by indicating the extent to which he or she approves of a set of affective or value dimensions (the affective or value component). The respondent is then asked to indicate the extent to which he or she believes that each dimension applies to the issue under consideration (the cognitive or expectancy component). Combining each expectancy with its corresponding value yields an E–V score. For example, one investigation described by Fishbein and Ajzen (1975) evaluated preferences between various energy technologies (nuclear, fossil fuel, tidal power, etc.). Respondents began by indicating their degree of liking or disliking for each of the following relevant dimensions as a feature of each technology: low cost, risk of catastrophe, long- and short-term pollution, and favorable technological spin-off. Next the respondents indicated, in terms of a probability figure, the extent to which each dimension characterized each technology. High probabilities were associated with liked dimensions and low probabilities with disliked dimensions. Thus, a favored technology was identified by high probabilities and a disfavored technology by low probabilities being assigned on most or all of the dimensions.

Facet Analysis.   One criticism of scalogram analysis, which applies to the methods of equal-appearing intervals and summated ratings as well, is that attitudes are complex, multidimensional states that can rarely be represented by a single score. Another criticism is that the dimensionality of an attitude scale may vary with the sample of respondents. In any event, Guttman's subsequent research on attitude measurement, which he labeled "smallest space analysis," or *facet analysis,* bears little resemblance to his earlier interest in *scalogram analysis. Facet analysis* is a complex, a priori, multidimensional paradigm for item construction and analysis that can be applied to any attitude object or situation (Castro & Jordan, 1977). The procedure has been used to construct cross-cultural attitude–behavior scales regarding a number of psychosocial conditions and situations, including mental retardation and racial–ethnic interaction (Hamersma, Paige, & Jordan, 1973).

Multidimensional Procedures.   It has become increasingly evident during the past two or three decades that attitude measurement is, in the strict sense of the term, multidimensional and that more complex assessment procedures are necessary. The use of factor analysis with attitude instruments is now fairly common. A trend away from unidimensional scales is evident in the increasing use of such methods as multidimensional scaling, latent structure analysis, latent partition analysis, and the repertory grid technique in the scaling of attitudes (see Ostrom, Bond, Krosnick, & Sedikides, 1994; Procter, 1993).

Sources of Attitude Scales

Many different inventories and scales for assessing social attitudes, political attitudes, and occupational attitudes are described in a series of books published by the Institute for Social Research at the University of Michigan (e.g., Robinson, Shaver, & Wrightsman, 1991; Robinson, Shaver, & Wrightsman, 1999). Other sources include the *American Social Attitudes Data Sourcebook, 1947–78* (Converse, Dotson, Hoag, & McGee, 1980) and *A Sourcebook of Harris National Surveys: Repeated Questions, 1963–76* (Martin & McDuffee, 1981). Dozens of attitude measures in a wide range of areas are also listed in *Tests in Microfiche* (Educational Testing Service) and in Volume 5 of the *ETS Test Collection Catalog* (1991) (Web sites www.ets.org and ericae.net/testcol.htm). Another source of information on published inventories, questionnaires, and scales of attitudes and values are the Web sites of the publishers and distributors of psychological assessment instruments (see Appendix C).

   Among the attitudes that have been assessed and studied extensively are, in alphabetical order, attitudes toward aged (old) people, AIDS, computers, Congress, day care, disabled persons, drinking, the environment, gays and Lesbians, gender role, gifted children, mainstreaming, mathematics, politicians, premarital sex, the president, race (ethnic group), school, science, sex, smoking, teachers, testing, women, and work. Several publishers and distributors of psychological assessment instruments market attitude questionnaires and scales. In addition to ready-made attitude instruments, computer software for generating one's own instruments is available from certain business organizations. An example is Easy.Gen Employee Attitude Survey Generator (from Wonderlic Personnel Test, Inc.). This computer software package designs attitude questions and select questions from a database of 515 questions covering 41 topics. It also administers attitude questionnaires and produces graphs and reports of results.

Reliability and Validity of Attitude Measures

Because of their homogeneity of content, the internal consistency reliability coefficients of scores on both published and unpublished attitude scales are usually in the .80s or even .90s. Test–retest reliabilities tend to run a bit lower, but are still fairly high for Thurstone- and Likert-type scales.

In addition to actual changes in attitudes produced by some manipulated condition, a number of situational and procedural variables can affect the reliability of an attitude instrument. Among these are conditions of administration, number of response categories, and method of scoring. Standardization of a psychometric instrument implies standard, uniform conditions of administration. Nevertheless, it is frequently impossible to keep the conditions of administration constant when attitude data are collected in different kinds of situations. Because reliability implies consistency of differentiation among persons, the reliability of a psychometric instrument tends to be lower when the conditions under which the instrument is administered have different effects on the scores of different people. For example, the scores of younger children are affected more than those of older children by variations in conditions of administering attitude scales. Consequently, it is not surprising that the obtained reliability coefficients of attitude scale scores increase with the chronological age of the respondents.

Another factor that can influence the reliability of an attitude scale is the number of response categories. Scores on instruments with a larger number of item-response categories tend to have larger variances, and hence higher reliabilities, than scores on instruments with smaller numbers of response categories. This is one possible reason why scores on Likert-type scales tend to be more reliable than those on Thurstone-type scales. There is, however, a limit to how much reliability can be raised by increasing the number of response categories. Although it may seem reasonable that increasing the number of response categories beyond five would have a significant effect on reliability, this is not generally true. Likert-type scales with six, nine, or even more response categories do not have appreciably greater reliability coefficients than those with the traditional five categories. When a rating scale has a large number of categories, it appears that raters are unable to make the finer discriminations required and therefore use only some of the categories. A possible exception to this rule occurs when the range of attitudes toward a specified concept is small, in which case increasing the number of response categories to six or seven can have a small enhancing effect on reliability (Masters, 1974).

It has also been suggested that increasing the number of response categories can improve the overall reliability if responses are transformed to normal deviate (z) scores

(Wolins & Dickinson, 1973). This technique is one of the many efforts to raise the reliability and validity of attitude measures by some kind of item-weighting or component-weighting procedure. Unfortunately, with respect to their reliability, none of the various differential weighting schemes has been found superior to more traditional scoring procedures. This is particularly true when the number of items on a single-score instrument is large.

On certain kinds of attitude items, including some Thurstone-type scales, there is a middle or neutral response category (?, Don't know, Uncertain, etc.) in addition to the bipolar Yes–No categories. Use of this neutral category by respondents varies with the instructions, context, and type of attitude object. Alwin and Krosnick (1991) found, however, that the reliability of multicategory measures of sociopolitical attitudes was not enhanced by explicitly providing a "don't know" option. On the other hand, on two- and three-category formats, inclusion of a neutral response category may improve reliability somewhat (Aiken, 1983b). For this reason, inclusion of a neutral response category is generally recommended on scales consisting of items that would be scored dichotomously.

With respect to their validity, scores on attitude scales tend to make small but significant contributions to the prediction of performance in organizational and other settings. Attitude measures have not generally correlated very highly with actual behavior, and research reviews have concluded that they are not very accurate predictors of specific behaviors. Ajzen and Fishbein (1977) maintained, however, that specific behavior can be predicted from measures of attitude toward the specific behavior, especially when attitude statements are expressed in behavioral terms.

MEASUREMENT OF VALUES

The *values* held by a person—the usefulness, importance, or worth attached to particular activities or objects—are related to, but not identical to, interests and attitudes. Compared with attitudes, values are viewed as more central to personality and more basic to the expression of individual needs and desires. The concept of *value* is, of course, not restricted to psychology and sociology, but is used in philosophy, religion, economics, and other fields as well.

Psychometric instruments measuring values have been used in a wide variety of research studies throughout the world to compare the work-related, moral, child-rearing, and other values of different cultures. Many older instruments designed to measure values, such as the popular Study of Values (Allport, Vernon, & Lindzey, 1960), were similar in content to inventories of interests, attitudes, and beliefs. Many of these instruments, which proved to be incompatible with subsequent conceptions of values (Braithwaite & Scott, 1991), are now out of print. An exception is the Rokeach Values Survey.

Rokeach Value Survey

Milton Rokeach, who conducted extensive international and cross-cultural research on the topic, defined a value as "a relatively enduring organization of beliefs around an object or situation predisposing one to respond in some preferential manner" (Rokeach, 1968,

p. 112). He maintained that there are two kinds of values: those concerned with modes of conduct (*instrumental values*) and those concerned with end states (*terminal values*). Although vocational psychologists have in large measure limited their attention to terminal values, Rokeach defined several subcategories of both instrumental and terminal values and designed an instrument to measure them.

Rokeach classified instrumental values as being of two kinds: *moral values* and *competence values.* The former category is concerned with interpersonal modes of conduct, which produce guilt feelings when violated. The latter category, or competence values, has to do with intrapersonal, self-actualizing modes of conduct, violations of which lead to feelings of inadequacy. Terminal values are also subdivided into *personal values* and *social values.*[1] Personal values, which include such end states as peace of mind and salvation, are self-centered. Social values, which include end states such as equality and world peace, are societally centered.

The Rokeach Value Survey consists of a series of 18 instrumental and 18 terminal value terms or phrases for assessing the relative importance of these values to people. The respondent is directed to place the 18 items in each list in rank order according to their importance to him or her. No other instrument attempts to measure as many values, a fact that, coupled with speed of administration and scoring and inexpensiveness, has contributed to its popularity. The Rokeach Value Survey has adequate reliability for differentiating among groups, a purpose for which it has been employed in hundreds of investigations for three decades. People of different nationalities and in different walks of life rank the items on the Rokeach Value Survey differently. For example, Israeli students assigned the highest rankings to "a world at peace" and "national security," whereas U.S. students placed higher value on "a comfortable life" and "being ambitious" (Rokeach, 1973, 1979). In another cross-cultural study of value systems, university students in Australia gave significantly higher ranks than university students in China to the following values of the Rokeach survey: an exciting life, world at peace, family security, happiness, inner harmony, being cheerful, being forgiving, being helpful, being honest, being loving, and being responsible. In contrast, the Chinese students assigned significantly higher ranks than the Australian students to a world of beauty, national security, pleasure, social recognition, wisdom, being ambitious, being capable, being courageous, being imaginative, being intellectual, being logical, and being self-controlled (Feather, 1986).

Vocational Values

One change that has occurred in the measurement of values during recent years is the inclusion of such measures within broad-based inventories oriented toward vocational counseling and attitudes or motivations toward work. However, the titles of a number of published instruments designed specifically to assess occupational choices and satisfactions still contain the term values. Among these are the Work Values Inventory and the Values Scale. The vocational values measured by these instruments vary from person to

---

[1]The distinction between personal and social was also included in a later definition of a value as "an enduring belief that a specific mode of conduct or end-state of existence is personally or socially preferable to an opposite or converse mode of conduct or end-state of existence" (Rokeach, 1973, p. 5).

person, within the same person from time to time, and with the nature of the job. Super (1973) found, for example, that people in upper-level occupations were motivated more by the need for self-actualization, which is an intrinsic goal, while extrinsic values were more likely to be subscribed to by people in lower-level occupations.

The Values Scale.   This instrument was developed by the Work Importance Study, an international consortium of vocational psychologists from North America, Asia, and Europe. It possesses characteristics of both the Work Values Inventory and Rokeach's Value Survey. The purpose of the consortium and The Values Scale was to understand values that individuals seek or hope to find in various life roles and to assess the relative importance of the work role as a means of value realization in the context of other life roles. The Values Scale consists of 106 items, takes 30–45 minutes to complete, and is scored for 21 values (five items per value):

Ability utilization	Creativity	Social interaction
Achievement	Economic rewards	Social relations
Advancement	Life-style	Variety
Esthetics	Personal development	Working conditions
Altruism	Physical activity	Cultural identity
Authority	Prestige	Physical prowess
Autonomy	Risk	Economic security

The reliabilities of all scales are adequate for individual assessment at the adult level; the reliabilities of ten scales are high enough for individual assessment at the college level, and the reliabilities of eight scales are adequate at the high school level. The means and standard deviations for three samples (high school, college, adult), as well as data on the construct validity of the instrument, are given in the manual.

PERSONAL ORIENTATIONS

Similar to inventories of interests and values are measures of *personal orientations*. One example of a personal orientation is the extent to which an individual tries "to be all that he can be"—to fulfill his or her potential or become *self-actualized*. Other concepts concerned with personal orientation on which measures have been designed and research conducted are life orientation (Dudek, & Makowska, 1993; Madhere, 1993), moral orientation (Liddell, Halpin, & Halpin, 1992), interpersonal orientation (Silva, Martinez, Moro, & Ortet, 1996), and sex (gender) role.

Bem Sex-Role Inventory

Development of a number of measures of sex role during the past 30 or so years was prompted in large measure by concern over gender discrimination and an interest in the nature and origin of sex differences in psychological characteristics. One of the most prominent instruments of this type is the Bem Sex-Role Inventory (BSRI) (Bem, 1974; published by Mind Garden). The short form of the inventory (Short BSRI), which was designed to classify individuals according to their sex-role orientation, consists of 60 words or phrases to be rated on a 7-point scale on which 1 means "never or almost never true" and 7 means "always or almost always true." Twenty of the items refer to characteristics considered significantly more desirable in men than in women (e.g., aggressive, ambitious), 20 items refer to characteristics considered significantly more desirable in women than in men (e.g., affectionate, cheerful), and 20 items are presumably sex neutral (e.g., adaptable, conscientious). Scores on three scales—Masculinity (M), Femininity (F), and Androgyny (A)—are determined first. Next, the examinee is placed in one of the following four categories according to his or her scores on the M, F, and A scales. Masculine (above median on M and below median on F), Feminine (above median on F and below median on M), Androgynous (above median on both M and F), or Undifferentiated (below median on both M and F).

The test–retest and internal-consistency reliabilities of the Short BSRI are generally satisfactory, but the validity data are fairly meager. In addition, researchers are cautioned not to rely on the norms reported in the manual: they are based solely on samples of Stanford University undergraduate students.

Sex-Role Egalitarianism Scale (SRES)

Another inventory concerned with psychological and behavioral differences between the sexes is the Sex-Role Egalitarianism Scale (SRES) (by L. A. King & D. W. King; from Sigma Assessment Systems). Designed to measure attitudes toward the equality of men and women, the SRES contains 95 attitudinal statements to be answered on 5-point scales. The items are written at a sixth or seventh-grade level and require approximately 25 minutes to answer. The five 19-item scales on the SRES cover the following domains: Marital Roles, Parental Roles, Employment Roles, Social–Interpersonal–Heterosexual Roles, and Educational Roles.

The internal-consistency, test–retest, and alternate forms reliabilities of the SRES are fairly high. With respect to its validity, relationships between the SRES and other variables, as well as group differences in the scores, support the convergent, discriminant, and construct validity of this instrument (King & King, 1993).

Personal Orientation Inventory (POI)

This widely used inventory (by E. L. Shostrom; from EdITS) was designed to measure values and behaviors that are important in the development of self-actualizing people. Such people develop and use all their potential and are free of the inhibitions and emotional turmoil that characterize less self-actualized people. The POI consists of 150 forced-choice items appropriate for high school and college students and adults. It is scored first on two major orientation ratios: Time Ratio (Time Incompetence–Time Competence) and Support Ratio (Outer Support–Inner Support). The Time Ratio indicates whether the respondent's time orientation is primarily in the present, past, or future. The Support Ratio indicates whether the respondent's reactivity orientation is basically toward other people or toward the self. After these two ratios have been computed, scores on the following 10 scales are determined:

Self-Actualizing Value. Affirmation of primary values of self-actualizing people

Existentiality. Ability to situationally or existentially react

Feeling Reactivity. Sensitivity of responsiveness to one's own needs and feelings

Spontaneity. Freedom to react spontaneously to be oneself

Self-Regard. Affirmation of self because of worth

Self-Acceptance. Affirmation of self or acceptance of self despite weaknesses or deficiencies

Nature of Man. Degree of the constructive view of the nature of man, masculinity, and femininity

Synergy. Ability to be synergistic, to transcend dichotomies

Acceptance of Aggression. Ability to accept one's natural aggressiveness as opposed to defensiveness, denial, and repression of aggression

Capacity for Intimate Contact. Ability to develop contactful, intimate relationships with other human beings, unencumbered by expectations and obligations

Percentile norms based on a sample of 2,607 western and midwestern college freshmen (1,514 males and 1,093 females), in addition to mean scores and profiles based on a smaller sample of adults, are given in the manual. Test–retest reliabilities of the individual scales, computed on a sample of 48 college students, are moderate (mostly in the .60s and .70s). Correlations with other personality scales and other evidence from the validity of the POI are also given in the manual.

Life-Orientation Inventory

This inventory (Udai, 1995) is used in organizational or career contexts for human resource development and research purposes. It permits applicants, employees, or counselees to evaluate their life-style orientations with respect to the concepts of *enlarging* or *enfolding.* An enlarging life-style is oriented toward innovation, change and growth, whereas an enfolding life-style is oriented toward the goals of traditional stability and inner strength. There are two scales, A and B. Scale A consists of 14 item activities pertaining to the enlarging and enfolding orientations. The respondent indicates on a 5-point scale, the amount of time that he or she spends on the activity. On the six pairs of forced-choice items on Scale B, the respondent indicates the importance of each of two activities to him or her.

SUMMARY

1. Attitudes are learned predispositions to respond positively or negatively to some object, person, or situation. As such, they are characteristics of personality, though at a more superficial level than temperaments or traits. Attitudes can be assessed in a number of ways, the most popular being attitude inventories or scales. Procedures for constructing attitude scales were devised by Thurstone (method of equal-appearing intervals), Likert (method of summated ratings), and Guttman (scalogram analysis).

Other attitude-scaling techniques include the semantic differential, Q-sorts, magnitude estimation, expectancy-value scaling, facet analysis, and a number of multivariate statistical procedures.

2. Judging from the variety of available instruments, one can have an attitude toward almost anything (e.g., any school subject, vocation, defined group, institution, proposed social action, or practice). The great majority of the hundreds of attitude scales and questionnaires listed in various reference sources are not standardized since they were designed for particular research investigations or applications. However, many standardized instruments for assessing attitudes toward school and school subjects, work and work supervisors, and other kinds of human activities are available from commercial test publishers.

3. The reliability of attitude scales is highest when administration is standardized, participants are adolescents or adults (rather than children), there are higher numbers of response categories (although five seems to be optimal for Likert scales), there is the inclusion of an "uncertain–don't know" category, and there are a larger number of items. Attitude measures have not been found to predict behavior, although this correspondence has been found to increase when item content is linked to specific behaviors.

4. Value relates to the usefulness, importance, or worth of something or somebody. They are thus more central to personality in that they relate to unique expressions of needs and desires. The Rokeach Value Survey consists of 18 terminal values (relating to personal and social end states) and 18 instrumental values (relating to moral and competent behaviors). It has stimulated a large amount of research on political–ideological values and conceptions of the good life. The Values Scale evaluates the life roles and relative importance of work. It consists of 106 items that measure the relative importance of 21 values, such as achievement, economic rewards, and working conditions.

5. Personal orientations, such as self-actualization and sex-role identification, cut across a wide range of personality variables, such as orientation to life, sex roles, or morals. The Bem Sex-Role Inventory has been used in numerous investigations to differentiate between masculine, feminine, and androgynous roles. Results of research with this inventory and similar instruments indicate that masculinity and femininity are two different psychological constructs and not simply polar opposites on a single dimension. Three additional multiscale measures of personal orientations discussed in this chapter are the Sex-Role Egalitarianism Scale, the Personal Orientation Inventory, and the Life-Orientation Inventory. The first of these instruments measures attitudes toward the equality of men and women, the second measures various aspects of self-actualization, and the third evaluates life-style orientation in terms of enlarging and enfolding processes.

MASTERING THE CHAPTER OBJECTIVES

1. *Thurstone, Likert, and Guttman scales*
   a. Describe and create one item each for a Thurstone, Likert, and Guttman scale.

b. In the process of constructing an attitude scale by Thurstone's method of equal-appearing intervals, each of 50 judges sorts 200 attitude statements into 11 piles. The numbers of judges who place statements X, Y, and Z into each of the 11 categories are given in the three frequency distributions listed below. Compute the scale value (median) and ambiguity index (semi-interquartile range) of each statement by methods described in Appendix A. Use the pile number (1, 2, . . . , 11) plus .5 as the upper exact limit of the interval. (See Answers to Quantitative Questions, p. 488.)

PILE NUMBER	STATEMENT D	STATEMENT N	STATEMENT X
1			8
2			17
3		6	10
4		10	9
5		13	6
6	3	8	
7	7	6	
8	9	4	
9	13	3	
10	10		
11	8		

c. Using the procedure outlined in Box 13.1, compute the reproducibility coefficient for the following data. The rows of the matrix will have to be rearranged in appropriate order before making the computations. (See Answers to Quantitative Questions, p. 488.)

	ATTITUDE STATEMENT					
Respondent	1	2	3	4	5	6
A	+	+	+	+	+	+
B	−	−	+	+	+	−
C	−	−	−	−	+	−
D	+	+	+	+	+	−
E	−	−	+	+	+	+
F	−	−	+	−	+	+
G	−	−	+	+	−	−

2. *Sources for finding attitude scales*
    a. Select a topical area such as AIDS, moral values, abortion, or an aspect of foreign policy. Describe how you would find a previously developed attitude scale to be used for a survey on this topic.
    b. Write five attitude questions for the topical area you selected in part (a).

3. *Issues related to the reliability and validity of attitude scales*
    a. Pretend you have given the attitude scale you developed in 2b, but found the reliability was moderately low. Describe three things you might do to increase its reliability.
    b. Rewrite the questions in 2b so that they will be most likely to predict relevant behaviors.

4. *Values*
   a. Describe the Rokeach Value Survey and The Value Scale.
   b. Describe how The Value Scale might be useful in vocational selection.

5. *Personal orientation*
   a. How is sex-role orientation related to sexual orientation? Would you expect men who score high on the Femininity scale of a personality or interest inventory to be gay and women who score high on a Masculinity scale to be lesbians? Why or why not?
   b. During the past few years, the terms *family values* and *Christian values* have been used extensively by politicians, social reformers, and the media in general. What are family values and how are they similar to and different from Christian values? Construct five items that might be used for a scale measuring family values. What kinds of people would you expect to score high and what kinds of people would you expect to score low on your scale?

EXPERIENCING PSYCHOLOGICAL ASSESSMENT

1. Read an opinion poll such as an ongoing one about crime at www.pollingreport.com/crime.htm. Take two of the questions that have been used and change them to Likert, Guttman, and Thurstone items.

2. Retype the statements in Form 13.1 (p. 306) in order of their item numbers, renumber the statements from 1 to 12, and omit the scale values. Next, make multiple copies of this attitude scale and administer it to several people. Determine each respondent's total score on the scale by adding the scale values of the statements that he or she checked and dividing the sum by the total number of statements (12). Ask the respondents to explain the reasons for their attitudes toward capital punishment and summarize the results. What personality variables do you believe are related to attitudes toward capital punishment?

■ ■ ■ ■ ■

CHAPTER FOURTEEN

PERSONALITY ASSESSMENT: ORIGINS, APPLICATIONS, AND ISSUES

CHAPTER OBJECTIVES

1. Define personality.
2. Describe the precursors to personality theory: phrenology, physiognomy, graphology, and the word-association test.
3. Describe the major theories of personality: type, trait, psychoanalytic, phenomenological, social learning, and empirical.
4. Elaborate on the uses and misuses of personality assessment: ethical problems and interpreting data.
5. Describe the following methods of clinical assessment: mental status exam, case study, psychodiagnosis, and case conference.
6. Introduce the following applications of personality assessment: marital–family, health, and legal.
7. Introduce the following issues and controversies in personality assessment: objections by the public, polygraph–integrity testing, employee selection, validity, ethnic–gender bias, clinical versus statistical prediction, traits versus situations, and idiographic versus nomothetic.

Personality assessment presupposes that there are characteristics that define the difference between various people and that these differences can be accurately measured. These may include an extremely wide number of characteristics, such as values, traits, personal identity, sense of humor, interpersonal warmth, behavioral styles, world view, and acculturation. These characteristics are socially constructed in that they allow us to form socially shared descriptions of persons living within our culture. Thus, when a person is described as dominant, confident, articulate, these words have a shared meaning for other people within our culture. They are also enduring in that they are more likely to be expressed across a wide variety of situations over a period of time. Thus, if a person is dominant and confident, we will expect him or her to act in these ways in many different situations. While it is true to say that everyone has all personality traits within them, a description of their personality should indicate the relative strengths of the various traits. This pattern of strong and weak characteristics forms a profile that enables us to describe how one person is different from another.

Personality also refers to clusters of related dimensions that enable us to describe how a person behaves, feels, and interacts with others. Thus, a dominant person will likely be active in positions of leadership, feel confident, and interact with others by directing their behavior. The fact that a personality characteristic has a cluster of related characteristics is crucial in interpreting personality tests. To merely state that a person is dominant and leave it at that tells us only minimal information about the person. Only when we widen our description does the interpretation become more interesting and relevant. Thus, persons who are dominant are likely to have the following qualities: they need to be in control, have a history of being successful, believe they can act in ways that are more effective than others, are persuasive, and under stress are more likely to act on their environment to create change. This knowledge about various personality characteristics allows us to make a full, useful, and rich description of the person who is being assessed. A final feature of personality is that it motivates the person to act and feel in certain ways. Thus the above description emphasizes that personality:

1. Is comprised of socially constructed descriptions
2. Is enduring
3. Is expressed in a wide number of situations
4. Allows prediction of behaviors, feelings, and interactions
5. Has related characteristics
6. Is motivational

Given the above definition, it follows that methods of assessing personality should include a broad range of cognitive, affective, and interpersonal variables. In Chapters 6 and 11 we studied cognitive abilities and achievement. While these variables are not the same as personality, they do interact with and are influenced by personality. In contrast, interests, attitudes, and values (see Chapters 12 and 13) are more closely aligned with what we think of as personality. Other emotional, temperamental, and stylistic characteristics, which have traditionally been labeled *personality variables,* are also important in understanding and predicting human behavior. This chapter provides general background material and applications concerning personality assessment. The following four chapters deal with more specific methods for assessing personality: observations, interviews, ratings, personality inventories, and projective techniques.

PSEUDOSCIENCES AND OTHER HISTORICAL ANTECEDENTS

As with intelligence testing, personality assessment developed partly from research on individual and group differences. Many antecedents of contemporary personality assessment can be found in the history of abnormal psychology and psychiatry. The history of science is replete with examples of beliefs or doctrines that had many adherents at one time, but subsequently were proved to be partially or totally incorrect. Among these pseudoscientific doctrines are phrenology, physiognomy, and graphology.

Phrenology, which relatively few people believe in today, was viewed seriously by many famous men and scholars during the late 18th and early 19th centuries. According to proponents of phrenology, the development of specific areas in the human brain is associated with certain personality characteristics and mental disorders. Among the personality traits supposedly related to protuberances in certain regions of the brain are agreeableness, combativeness, and acquisitiveness (Figure 14.1). A natural consequence of this belief is that personality can be analyzed by fingering a person's head for "bumps" over specific brain areas that are presumably associated with certain characteristics. Phrenology had a great deal of influence on 19th-century psychiatry and on *faculty psychology,* a notion that affected the school curriculum of the time. According to faculty psychology, the mind consists of a number of faculties that can be developed by mental exercise (e.g., by studying Latin, Greek, geometry, and other difficult subjects), just as the body can be developed by physical exercise.

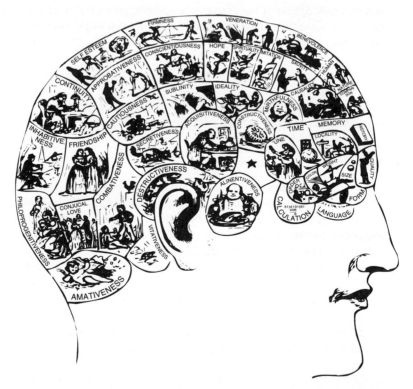

FIGURE 14.1   Phrenologist's Chart of Brain Functions. Localization of Various Affective and Cognitive Faculties as Depicted by a 19th-Century Phrenologist. Phrenology was a pseudoscience, and no one places much credence in it today.

(Corbis.)

Physiognomy, another pseudoscience, is concerned with determining temperament and character from external features of the body and especially the face. Remnants of physiognomy can be seen in contemporary personnel evaluation and assessment procedures, for example, in the requirement that a photograph of the applicant must accompany an application for employment. Another personality assessment device associated with physiognomy is the Szondi Test, which consists of six sets of photographs, eight pictures per set, of mental patients with different diagnoses (e.g., hysteria, catatonia, paranoia, depression, or mania). Examinees select the two pictures that they like most and the two that they dislike most in each set. The basic assumption underlying the Szondi Test is that the facial features of the mental patients depicted in the 12 selected and 12 rejected photographs have a personal meaning for the respondent. The latter's needs and personality are presumably similar to those of the patients depicted in the photographs. Because no consistent evidence for the validity of the Szondi Test in personality analysis or psychiatric diagnosis has been found, the test has been largely discredited.

Belief in *graphology,* which is concerned with analyzing personality by studying handwriting samples, is perhaps even more widespread than belief in physiognomy. Although it makes sense that handwriting, which is a type of stylistic behavior, can reflect personality characteristics, even experienced handwriting analysts are not known for the accuracy of their interpretations. Physiognomy and graphology are somewhat more reputable than phrenology, but many of the claims of their proponents are just as wrong.

Not all pre-20th-century attempts to develop a science of personality assessment should be labeled pseudosciences. Very reputable, although not always successful, were the efforts of Francis Galton, Emil Kraepelin, and Alfred Binet. In 1884, Galton proposed to measure emotions by recording changes in heartbeat and pulse rate and to assess good temper, optimism, and other personality traits by observing people in contrived social situations. Kraepelin, who is best known for his system of classifying mental disorders, developed the *word-association technique* in 1892. Also during the 1890s, Alfred Binet devised methods for studying the personality characteristics of eminent persons.

Despite a few promising beginnings in the 19th century, genuine progress in personality assessment was not made until the 20th century. Particularly noteworthy in this regard are Carl Jung's word-association tests for detecting and analyzing mental complexes (1905), Robert Woodworth's Personal Data Sheet, the first standardized personality inventory to be administered on a mass basis (1919), and Hermann Rorschach's Inkblot Test (1920).

THEORIES OF PERSONALITY

Almost everyone has some theory as to why people behave as they do. These theories of human nature and behavior typically consist of overgeneralizations or stereotypes, but they serve as rough guides to expectations and action. Sometimes a person's very survival depends on the ability to understand and predict the behavior of other people.

Realizing that everyone is different from everyone else and that human behavior can be very complex, personality theorists have learned to be suspicious of commonsense explanations. Certain psychologists, impressed by the individuality and intricacy of human actions, have despaired of finding general principles or laws to explain personality. They reject the *nomothetic approach,* the search for general laws of behavior and personality, as unrealistic and inadequate to the task of understanding the individual. Instead, they advocate an *idiographic approach* that advocates the study of the unique individual as a lawful, integrated system worthy of study in its own right (Allport, 1937).

There are many other differences among personality theories, one being the relative emphasis placed on heredity and environment as molders of behavior. Theorists also differ in the extent to which they emphasize internal, individual characteristics or traits, rather than situational variables, as determiners of behavior. As these and other points of debate among psychologists suggest, there is no generally accepted theory of personality. On the contrary, theories and research findings pertaining to the origins, structure, and dynamics of personality are continually emerging and changing. Still, it is important for anyone who is interested in psychological assessment to be aware of the various theories of personality and to be skeptical of untested theories. Despite their shortcomings, theories can serve as motivators and guides in the measurement and understanding of personality. Theories provide frames of reference—ideas concerning the dynamics and development of personality and behavior—for interpreting assessment findings. In this respect, the theories proposed and tested by professional psychologists are presumably more useful than commonsense theories.

Type Theories

One of the oldest approaches to understanding personality is the notion of fixed categories or types of people. Galen, a physician in ancient Rome who subscribed to Hippocrates' doctrine of four body humors (blood, yellow bile, black bile, and phlegm), maintained that there are four corresponding temperament types. The *sanguine type,* with an excess of blood, was said to be vigorous and athletic; the *choleric type,* with an excess of yellow bile, was easily angered. The *melancholic type,* with an excess of black bile, was generally depressed or sad, and the *phlegmatic type,* with an excess of phlegm, was chronically tired or lazy. Like phrenology and other pseudoscientific notions, the humoral theory is now only of historical interest (but see Figure 14.2). Based somewhat more securely on observational data, but still highly tentative and overgeneralized, are the body-type theories of Ernest Kretschmer, Cesare Lombroso, and William Sheldon.

The idea that personality is associated with physique has intrigued many philosophers and poets. Shakespeare declared as much in several of his plays. For example, in Act I, Scene II of *Julius Caesar,* Caesar says:

> Let me have men about me that are fat.
> Sleek-headed men, and such as sleep a-nights.
> Yond Cassius has a lean and hungry look;
> He thinks too much; such men are dangerous.

Less poetic but perhaps more systematic than the writings of famous authors were the descriptions of the scientist Ernst Kretschmer (1925). Kretschmer concluded that both a tall, thin body build (*asthenic*) and a muscular body build (*athletic*) are associated with withdrawing tendencies (schizoid personality). A short, stout body build (*pyknic*), on the other hand, was said to be associated with emotional instability (cycloid personality). A related typology was proposed by Sheldon, Stevens, and Tucker (1940). Their three-component *somatotype* system classified human physiques according to the degree of fatness (*endomorphy*), muscularity (*mesomorphy*), and thinness (*ectomorphy*). Body builds representing extremes of these three components are presumably related to the following respective temperament types: endomorphy to viscerotonia (sociable, jolly, loves food), mesomorphy to somatotonia (athletic, aggressive), and ectomorphy to cerebrotonia (introversive, studious).

Body-type theories are intriguing, but the scientific validity is mixed. There are many exceptions to the hypothesized relationships between physique and temperament, and different interpretations have been given to these relationships. Furthermore, contemporary psychologists object to typologies because they place people in categories and assign labels to them. Not only does labeling overemphasize the internal causation of behavior, but it may also act as a self-fulfilling prophecy in which people become what they are labeled as being. Thus, a person who is labeled an *introvert* may be left alone by would-be friends, causing him or her to become even more socially isolated. Similarly, an *extrovert* may become more outgoing or sociable because other people expect him or her to behave in that way.

Trait Theories

Less general than personality types are personality traits. Gordon Allport, an early personality theorist, began his research on traits by listing 17,953 words in the English language that refer to characteristics of personality and then reducing them to a smaller list of trait names (Allport & Odbert, 1936). He defined a *trait* as a "neuropsychic structure having the capacity to render many stimuli functionally equivalent, and to initiate and guide equivalent (meaningfully consistent) forms of adaptive and expressive behavior" (Allport, 1961, p. 347). To Allport, *personality* consisted of the dynamic organization of the traits that determine a person's unique adjustment to the environment.

Another trait theorist, R. B. Cattell, classified traits in four ways: common versus unique, surface versus source, constitutional versus environmental mold, and dynamic versus ability versus temperament. Common traits are characteristics of all people, whereas unique traits are peculiar to the individual. A person's surface traits are easily observed in behavior, but his or her source traits can be discovered only by the statistical procedures of factor analysis (see Appendix A). Constitutional traits depend on heredity, and environmental-mold traits depend on environment. Finally, dynamic traits motivate the person toward a goal, ability traits determine the ability to achieve the goal, and temperament traits are concerned with the emotional aspects of goal-directed activity. Cattell's trait theory, which is much more elaborate than this brief description indicates, has served as a framework for several personality inventories, one being the 16 Personality Factor Questionnaire.

Many other psychologists, including Henry Murray, J. P. Guilford, and Hans Eysenck, constructed theories and conducted research on personality traits. The methods of factor analysis have been applied to much of this research, yielding a variety of personality dimensions. The two basic dimensions of Eysenck's system, introversion–extroversion and stability–instability, are depicted in Figure 14.2. The positions of the 32 personality variables on the vertical and horizontal axes of this figure indicate the direction and magnitudes of these characteristics on the two dimensions.

Psychoanalytic Theory

Sigmund Freud is considered to be the father of psychoanalysis. In the first two decades of the 20th century he organized a set of beliefs based primarily on careful clinical observation and his own extensive self-analysis. The view of personality he developed was based on struggles between that part of ourselves that demands immediate gratification (the *id*), a second component that tells us ideally what we should do (our conscience or the *superego*), and the reality part that must deal with the conflict between these two opposing forces (the

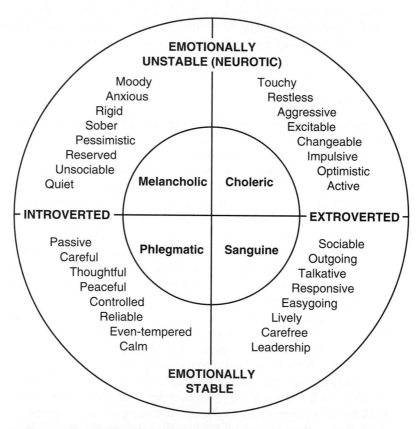

FIGURE 14.2　Eysenck's Dimensions of Personality.

(From Kluwer Academic Publishers/Plenum, *Publishing Personality and Individual Differences*, 1958, by H. J. Eysenck and M. W. Eysenck. Copyright © Springer Science and Business Media. Reprinted with kind permission.)

ego). Much of the struggles, conflict and compromise among these three components occurs beyond our awareness. A second major component of his theory was that we go through stages of psychosexual development (*psychosexual stages*). How we resolve these stages forms the template for how we will deal with challenges as an adult. These are the much popularized *oral* (birth to 1½), *anal* (1½ to 3), *phallic* (3 to 6), *latency* (6 to early adolescence), and *genital* (adolescence–adulthood) stages. A third major component is that we develop defense mechanisms to deal with internal conflicts. Thus we might use *projection* by denying our internal unacceptable feelings and attributing them to others. Such a process is both a denial of the feelings ("not me, its him") as well as an expression ("now I am justified in feeling anger since that *other* person is hostile").

In the nearly 100 years since Freud first developed his principles, they have gone through considerable development, elaboration, and empirical testing. Weston (1998) summarized empirical support for five essential propositions of psychoanalysis (see www.psychsystems.net/lab/SciLeg.pdf). The first is that there is an unconscious. This unconscious mediates both thoughts and emotional processes. For example, many people enhance their self esteem (and thus reduce anxiety) by automatically constructing thoughts that present themselves in a highly favorable manner (the so-called "self serving bias"). As a general rule, people view themselves in a more favorable manner than more objective observers. A second proposition is that we struggle with conflicting feelings. The process of dealing with these feelings occurs on both a conscious and unconscious level (*parallel processes*). However, much of our conflict occurs below the threshold of consciousness. The unconscious works to develop compromises between the multiple and often conflicting feelings.

A third central proposition of psychoanalysis is that many stable personality traits, interpersonal patterns, and styles of attaching to others are strongly molded in childhood. For example, a child who learns that showing affection or touching in childhood is a source of anxiety is likely to transfer these feelings into adulthood. Certainly, part of the stability of traits is due to genetics. However, early childhood patterns help to modify and differentiate the expression of more general, genetically based characteristics. A fourth proposition is that, as we develop, we form mental representations of self, others, and relationships. These relate to how we attach ourselves to others, level of self-esteem, feelings toward intimacy, style of responding to threatening events, and capacity to invest emotionally. Most current psychoanalytically oriented therapists give a primary emphasis to understanding these mental representations. Not only do they work with clients to understand these representations, but they also work with them to develop strategies of optimizing the quality of their current life. This is very different from the classical Freudian approach that had the client passively lie on a couch, free associate, and try to recover and gain insights into deeply repressed childhood memories (sort of like an archaeological expedition).

A fifth proposition is understanding how children deal with their early psychosexual feelings as they move through their development. A particularly crucial focus is how they later form and maintain intimate relationships as adolescents and adults. Freud proposed the development of the *oral* or *anal* personality style. He also stressed the importance of resolving conflictual feelings toward parents (mainly the *Oedipus complex*). Many of Freud's descriptions have been found to be either too general, culturally and historically specific, or just plain wrong. However, research has found support for later psychoanalytically inspired constructs of identity, intimacy, and how we initiate and generate useful behaviors. This

involves a stagelike process in which people perceive others in progressively more complex, less self-centered ways, learn to invest emotionally in others, and behave in a manner
that is based on principles of morality, rather than egocentricity.

Freud's theories have been hotly debated since their inception. Criticisms have centered around too much reliance on uncontrolled clinical observation, statements that are un-
verifiable, overly focused on sexuality, lack of support for many of Freud's classical stages,
placing too much emphasis on early childhood, being overly male oriented, and being too
specific to Freud's historical, cultural, and personal context. By expanding basic psychoanalytic principles into the five more general propositions outlined above, they can more easily overlap with and be informed by more current thinking and trends in research. It also
helps to highlight areas that can be more readily and usefully assessed. Instead of trying to
assess a person's "Oedipus complex," it is more useful to ask how they can assess patterns
of attachment, mental representations of the self, or the most frequently used strategies for
reducing anxiety.

Considerable effort has been placed into assessing psychoanalytically based or psychoanalytically inspired constructs. For example, the *hystrionic personality* is attention
seeking and dramatic and quickly becomes involved with others. Their interpersonal relationships are often problematic since they are superficial and dependent, repress negative
feelings, and express these unacceptable feelings through physical symptoms. The assessment of this style is part of standard objective tests such as the Minnesota Multiphasic Personality Inventory-2 and the Millon Clinical Multiaxial Inventory (see Chapter 17). Since
many psychoanalytic constructs involve unconscious processes that are not directly accessible to the individual, many self-report techniques have been considered inappropriate. As
a result, methods to access these more implicit processes have been developed. The most
frequently used are projective techniques that involve having the client respond to an ambiguous stimulus such as an inkblot or picture of people doing something or having them
complete a fragment of a sentence (see Chapter 18). When the client fills in the ambiguous
information, it is believed that they express the structure or content of their unconscious
processes.

Phenomenological Theories

Stemming from a philosophical tradition that emphasized the analysis of immediate, personal, subjective experience, phenomenological (humanistic or "self") theorists maintain
that trait theorists and others who attempt to divide personality into a set of components do
an injustice to its integrated, dynamic organization. Consequently, phenomenological theorists have been critical of psychoanalytic, trait-factor, and behavioral approaches to understanding personality. In contrast to traditional psychoanalysis, which emphasizes the
fundamental importance of sexual and aggressive impulses, the unconscious, and psychosexual stages of development, phenomenologists stress perceptions, meanings, feelings,
and the self. Phenomenologists view people as responding to the world in terms of their
unique, private perceptions of it. These perceptions are determined by experiences and the
meanings attached to these experiences in an effort to fully realize one's potential. The part
of the environment that is perceived and has meaning for the individual is known as the *phe-*

nomenal field, a portion of which (the *self*) is related to the individual in a personal way. Finally, the totality of the good and bad evaluations given by a person to the self are referred to as the *self-concept.*

According to Abraham Maslow, Carl Rogers, and other phenomenological theorists, everyone goes through a process of striving to attain a congruence or harmony between the real and ideal selves, or *self-actualization.* The basic direction of existence is toward self-actualization and positive relations with others, but this effort can be inhibited in various ways. Carl Rogers pointed out that most people are not open or willing to accept the full range of their experiences. In the process of growing up, they learn that they are objects of *conditional positive regard,* in which their behavior is deemed acceptable by parents and other significant persons only if it conforms to expected standards (*conditions of worth*). Consequently, the child, who eventually becomes an adult, learns to recognize and accept only a part of his or her experiences. The result is an incompletely functioning individual who cannot become fully functioning until other people treat him or her with *unconditional positive regard.* This is when the individual is accepted regardless of what he or she is or does.

Clinical practitioners who espouse phenomenological theory tend to prefer case studies and open or unstructured interviews, rather than objective psychological tests and procedures. Carl Rogers was not a great believer in the value of personality assessment instruments, and phenomenological, or self, theory has not been as influential as trait-factor and psychoanalytic theories in the development of such devices. Still, many instruments and procedures for assessing feelings and attitudes toward the self have been based on a phenomenological conception of personality. Examples are sorting lists of adjectives that describe the self (Q-sorts; see Chapter 16) and inventories such as the Tennessee Self-Concept Scale, Coopersmith Self-Esteem Inventories, and the Personal Orientation Inventory (see Chapter 13).

Social Learning Theory

Many other theoretical concepts have influenced the development of personality assessment instruments. Among these are George Kelly's (1955) theory of personal constructs and the cognitive-behavioral approach of social learning theorists such as Julian Rotter, Albert Bandura, and Walter Mischel.

Rotter's Theory.   The first *social learning theory* as such was that of Julian Rotter (1954), who attempted to integrate the traditional behavioristic position on the role of reinforcement in learning with the cognitive conceptualizations of Kurt Lewin and other field theorists. Rotter was not the first to note that most human behavior is learned in a social context, but he made a more conscious effort than his predecessors to develop a systematic theory of how this takes place. Rotter distinguished between reinforcements and cognitions: reinforcements result in movement toward or away from a goal, whereas cognitions are internal states such as expectancy and reinforcement value. The term *expectancy* refers to a person's estimate of the subjective probability that a specific behavior performed in a certain situation will lead to reinforcement. Two *generalized expectancies* measured and investigated by Rotter and others are locus of control and interpersonal trust. *Locus of* *control* refers to the typical direction from which people perceive themselves as being controlled (internal, or from within oneself, versus external, or by other people). *Interpersonal trust* is concerned with the extent to which a person believes that other people tell the truth.

According to Rotter, reinforcement is important for performance, but not all reinforcements are equally valued by the individual. Even when the probabilities of occurrence of different reinforcements are equal, certain objects or actions will have greater *reinforcement value* than others. Both reinforcement value and expectancies are affected by the psychological relevance or meaning of the situation to the individual, and they must be understood in order to predict how the person will behave in this situation.

Bandura's Observational Learning Theory.   More important for the development of techniques for modifying maladaptive behavior than for influencing the design of personality assessment instruments is Bandura's (1977) social learning theory. Conceptualizing psychological functioning as the reciprocal interactions of behavioral variables, person variables (cognitions and other internal states), and environmental variables, Bandura emphasized that a human being is not a passive, push-button automaton that acts only when acted on. People both influence and are influenced by the social environment, in which learning takes place by observation, imitation, and modeling. Unlike more traditional behaviorists, such as Clark Hull and B. F. Skinner, Bandura maintained that much learning takes place without reinforcement, in the absence of rewards and punishments, but that reinforcement is important in determining when learned behavior occurs. Particularly significant in the learning process is modeling the behavior of others. The effectiveness of modeling depends on the personal characteristics of the model and the learner's motivational level. Aggression, fears, sex-typed behaviors, and many other emotional and stylistic reactions are, according to Bandura, learned by observation and modeling.

Bandura also emphasized the fact that learning and behavior are mediated by perceptions and cognitions: people use internal, symbolic representations of their environments, and it is these representations that mediate changes in behavior. By visualizing the consequences of their actions, people learn to regulate their behavior.

Empirical Approaches to Personality Assessment

Rather than being designed according to a formal theory of personality, many personality assessment instruments have been constructed on a purely empirical basis. For example, items on the various scales of the Minnesota Multiphasic Personality Inventory (MMPI) were selected on the basis of their ability to distinguish between two contrasting groups of people (normals and selected psychiatric patient groups). No specific theory of personality was implied or involved in this empirical procedure; MMPI items were simply validated against the specific criteria of psychiatric diagnoses in various samples of mental patients.

A number of assessment instruments have been developed in the context of investigations of personality and behavior disorders. These efforts, though not completely devoid of theoretical foundations, have not been restricted to a single theoretical position. Examples of tests derived from this perspective are the Millon Clinical Multiaxial Inventory, California Psychological Inventory, Personality Assessment Inventory, and the NEO-PIR.

USES AND MISUSES OF PERSONALITY ASSESSMENT

Personality assessment procedures and instruments are used in schools, clinics, hospitals, prisons, and other settings where the results contribute to the process of making decisions about people. Ideally, the results are treated conscientiously and with an awareness of the limitations of the assessments and the needs and rights of examinees. To practice competently, a number of guidelines need to be followed.

Ethical Problems

Among the methods used in personality assessment are observations, interviews, rating scales, checklists, self-report inventories, and projective techniques. Sometimes these methods have been misapplied by untrained or unethical persons, resulting in a black mark for psychological testing as a whole. It is not difficult for a person who has read a bit of psychology to obtain a few paper-and-pencil instruments and pretend to be a personality analyst. Like fortune tellers and other charlatans, these would-be psychodiagnosticians deal in generalities, truisms, and other statements that seem specific to a given individual, but actually apply to most people. To demonstrate this "*Barnum effect* (there is a fool born every minute)," consider the following "personality profile":

> You have a great need for other people to like and admire you. You have a tendency to be critical of yourself. You have a great deal of unused capacity you have not turned to your advantage. While you have some personality weaknesses, you are generally able to compensate for them. At times you have serious doubts as to whether you have made the right decision or done the right thing. (Sundberg, 1955)

These are statements that can make palm readers, astrologers, and other fortune tellers rich. Virtually everyone given these "interpretations" feels they are remarkably accurate (Glick, Gottesman, & Joltan, 1989). However, this is because they are so general and universal that they can apply to anyone. Unfortunately, they are not really informative since they don't consider a person's uniqueness.

A great deal of training and experience is needed to become a skilled observer and interpreter of human personality. Teachers, personnel managers, and other nonpsychologists can often apply rating scales and checklists in a sensitive, sensible manner, but the administration and interpretation of personality inventories and projective techniques are restricted to psychologists and other professionals with sufficient training. Because these topics are very personal and should be handled with care, we need to be cautious in administering and interpreting the results of any personality assessment device. Both the examinee's right to privacy and natural concern over his or her own emotional stability and mental health should be respected.

In addition to ensuring privacy and other ethical issues, it is also essential to ensure the validity of assessment. This can be compromised if an examiner either exaggerates the problems ("fakes bad") or minimizes the problems by only describing positive features ("fakes good"). Using more unobtrusive measures, which are often considered less susceptible to faking, may reduce faking, but at the same time introduce problems of quantification and interpretation (see Chapter 18).

Interpreting Assessment Data

Even when carefully constructed and validated measures of personality are used, it is a cardinal rule that the resulting interpretations should be viewed as hypotheses to be confirmed or disconfirmed by subsequent information. The results of personality assessment are neither exact nor final, and they can be viewed in different ways by different examiners. This becomes embarrassingly obvious when different psychologists or psychiatrists, acting as expert witnesses in a court case, differ radically in their interpretations of the same assessment findings. Given the subjective nature of some psychological assessments, such embarrassments may be unavoidable when the two parties in a legal dispute have different objectives.

Several additional recommendations concerning the collection and interpretation of personality assessment data can be made (adapted from Sundberg, 1977):

1. Survey the examinee's overall life situation and problems and then obtain more details in areas of particular relevance to the assessment.
2. Be sensitive to the sociocultural and ethnic background of the examinee, as well as his or her age and sex, if relevant.
3. Use more objective, as opposed to subjective, techniques and data whenever possible.
4. Obtain the *right kind* of information, not just *more* information, about the specific situation and purposes of the assessment.
5. Avoid too much speculation in interpreting results and predicting behavior; be especially careful in making predictions concerning behavior having a low probability of occurrence.
6. If possible, check your findings and interpretations with those of other psychological assessors, and keep a record of your agreements and disagreements, successes and failures.
7. Communicate your findings in writing in a style that can be understood by the people for whom the report is intended.

CLINICAL ASSESSMENT

Although clinical psychologists usually spend more time on treatment, consultation, research, teaching, and other activities than on psychological assessment, many clinicians find objective tests such as the MMPI and projective tests such as the Rorschach useful in psychodiagnosis and treatment planning (Beutler & Groth-Marnat, 2003). Clinical assessment for diagnosis and treatment planning takes place in a variety of settings. These include mental health settings for purposes of diagnosis, treatment, and residential placement; medical settings as an aid in evaluating the psychological aspects of illness and planning for rehabilitation; educational settings as an aid in formulating proper remediation measures; and legal settings to assist courts in sanity hearings, custodial decisions, and determining personal injury.

Once the need for clinical assessment has been recognized, goals can be set and decisions made regarding the kinds of data needed to attain the goals. The general goals of clinical assessment are to provide an accurate description of the patient's (client's) problem(s), to determine what interpersonal and environmental factors precipitated and are sustaining the problem(s), and to make predictions concerning outcomes with and without intervention (Beutler, Groth-Marnat, & Rosner, 2003). Obtaining the kind of information required in clinical settings often necessitates a thorough case study.

Mental Status Examination and Clinical Case Study

Clinical psychologists are frequently asked to conduct a *mental status examination* to obtain information about a person's emotional state (affect and mood), intellectual and perceptual functioning (attention, concentration, memory, intelligence, and judgment), and style and content of thought processes. Such an evaluation also includes information on the client's speech, psychomotor activity, general appearance, and attitude and insight into his or her condition. This information is obtained from a combination of formal testing, along with behavioral observations and detailed interviews of the person and those who know him or her well. In conducting a thorough case study, information on the client's background and character is provided by the client and significant other people, and follow-up data are collected over a period of time. Information on the family, the culture, health history, developmental history, educational history, economic history, legal history, and the person's activities and thoughts may all be elicited (Kazdin, 2003). After the assessment data have been obtained and integrated, a report summarizing the findings and describing the person's strengths and weaknesses is prepared. Recommendations for clinical, educational, or vocational interventions may be made in the report.

When a case study is conducted to determine the cause(s) of a specific psychological problem, hypotheses or conclusions pertaining to causation may be formulated and specific recommendations made concerning treatment (psychotherapy, drugs or other medical treatment, special education, etc.). A follow-up assessment to evaluate the effectiveness of the prescribed treatment program should also be conducted after an appropriate time interval.

Despite its yield of potentially useful information for constructing an overall picture, as well as providing an in-depth understanding of the individual, a clinical case study has some notable weaknesses. These include the introspective nature of the data (memory is rarely completely accurate), the fact that the person conducting the study is frequently biased in selecting and evaluating certain kinds of data or measurements, and the limited generalizability of the findings across situations or circumstances encountered by the person. Employing a variety of assessments in a systematic sample of situations can help reduce, if not eliminate, misinterpretations and overgeneralizations. It also helps for clinicians to be aware of and work to counter various types of biases they might have in making their conclusions (Garb, 2005).

Psychodiagnosis

Psychodiagnosis is the process of examining a person from a psychological viewpoint to determine the nature and extent of a mental or behavioral disorder. In the traditional *medical model* of mental disorders, the psychodiagnostician observes, interviews, and tests the patient to determine the presence or absence of certain psychological (and physical) symptoms. The diagnostician then compares the patient's symptoms with standard descriptions of abnormal behavior to determine in which category of disorders the patient best fits. The end result of this process is the assignment of a psychiatric classification to the patient, as specified in the *Diagnostic and Statistical Manual of Mental Disorders-IV* (DSM-IV-TR) (American Psychiatric Association, 2000) or the *International Classification of Diseases* (*ICD-10*) (World Health Organization, 1992). In addition to diagnosing the disorder, a *prognosis,* or prediction of probable outcome, is sometimes made.

Case Conference

A written report is only one way in which the results of a psychometric evaluation are communicated to those who have a legitimate right to know. Clinical-case conferences or consultations in mental health contexts and parent–teacher or parent–counselor conferences in school settings may occur both before and after a psychological evaluation. When conducting a posttest conference with a person who is unsophisticated in psychological terminology, such as a typical parent, the examiner should describe, in language appropriate to the listener, the test results and whatever conclusions can reasonably be drawn from them. In general, qualitative rather than quantitative descriptions and interpretations should be employed. The purpose and nature of the tests, why these particular tests were selected, and the limitations of the tests and results should also be discussed. Descriptive statements, rather than labels, and score ranges that take into account the standard error of measurement, rather than specific scores, should be used. Consultation also involves a discussion of options and decisions for treatment, remediation, rehabilitation, or other intervention and the provision of information on referral sources. Following the consultation, the examiner should send a copy of the examination report to the referral source and other responsible parties who have a need and a right to know.

OTHER AREAS OF APPLICATION OF PERSONALITY ASSESSMENT

Three other areas in which there has been an increased demand for psychological services during the past decade are marriage and family, health, and legal (forensic) matters. These areas have attracted the attention of research psychologists and other professionals who are interested in developing psychometric instruments for research and applications in these areas. Many colleges and universities have established graduate programs in these areas, and measurement and research pertaining to them are extensive.

Marital and Family Assessment

A number of psychometric instruments have proved useful in identifying, diagnosing, and making prognoses concerning marital and family problems. Checklists, rating scales, inventories, and other devices are available for premarital advising, identifying sources and possible solutions for family disagreements and problems, and helping victims of divorce to adjust to their lives. Traditional inventories and projectives, such as the MMPI-2, Millon Clinical Multiaxial Inventory, the 16 Personality Factor Questionnaire (16 PF), and the

Rorschach Inkblot Test, are frequently administered to analyze marital and family problems. Also available are checklists (e.g., the Marital Evaluation Checklist), inventories (e.g., the Marital Attitude Evaluation, Marital Satisfaction Inventory, and Family Assessment Measure), and special projective techniques (e.g., the Family Relations Test: Children's Version and Family Apperception Test). Another useful psychometric instrument, the Family Environment Scale (from Consulting Psychologists Press), was designed to assess the social climate of family systems and determine how the characteristics of the family interact. This questionnaire can be used to identify family strengths and problems and important issues for family treatment. Information provided by all these instruments should be supplemented by sensitive interviewing and observations of couples and family members in face-to-face social interactions.

Health Psychology

Health psychology has been defined as the "educational, scientific, and professional contributions of the discipline of psychology to the promotion and maintenance of health, the prevention and treatment of illness, and the identification of etiological and diagnostic correlates of health, illness, and related dysfunction" (Matarazzo, 1980, p. 815). Interest in the role of attitudes, self-efficacy, and other psychological factors or personality variables in health is not limited to psychosomatic disorders, such as duodenal ulcers and migraine headaches, but includes cardiovascular disorders, cancer, and other life-threatening illnesses. Psychologists are called on not only to identify psychological factors that are related to various medical conditions and to help diagnose specific disorders, but also to assist in planning treatments or other intervention procedures. The field of *behavioral medicine,* a subspecialty of health psychology, has made significant contributions to the treatment and management of patients by behavior-modification techniques and other procedures. The concept of health has also come to have a broader connotation than just the absence of disease. As used by social and behavioral scientists, in particular, health now refers to *positive wellness* and the attainment of a good *quality of life.*

Several health-related personality inventories are available for assisting in the formulation of comprehensive treatment plans for adult medical patients. Among these are the Alcohol Use Inventory (from NCS Assessments) for assessing the nature of an individual's pattern of alcohol usage, the Eating Disorders Inventory-2 (from Psychological Assessment Resources) for assessing symptoms and thought patterns associated with anorexia and bulimia, and the Millon Behavioral Health Inventory (from NCS Assessments) for assisting in the formulation of comprehensive treatment plans for adult medical patients. The number of commercially available checklists, rating scales, and other questionnaires concerned with health-related matters has increased markedly in recent years. Included among these are instruments designed to identify health problems in general and specific health areas, questionnaires of opinions and beliefs pertaining to health, measures of stress and ways of coping with it, measures of pain perception and control, and measures of anxiety, depression, substance abuse, violence, and suicide potential.

Related to personal efficacy and control are *attributions,* or explanations that people provide for the causes (internal or external) of their behavior. Two instruments designed to study the role of attributions, and the related concept of *locus of control,* in determining behavior are the Health Attribution Test (from IPAT) and the Health Locus of Control Scale (Wallston & Wallston, 1981).

Another variable that has played a central role in the field of health psychology is *stress*. Among the commercially available instruments with the word *stress* in the title are the Daily Stress Inventory and the Parenting Stress Index (both from Psychological Assessment Resources). Other stress-related instruments are the Coping Resources Inventory (from Consulting Psychologists Press) and the Hassles and Uplifts Scale (from Mind Garden). Related to the measurement of stress or stress reactions is the field of *behavioral toxicology,* which is concerned with the assessment of performance under adverse environmental circumstances.

Legal Psychology

Legal psychology is concerned with psychological aspects of law and law enforcement (see Goldstein, 2003). Psychologists who are employed in law-enforcement contexts are typically clinicians who possess a wide range of skills and perform a variety of tasks. They may use tests, questionnaires, and interviewing procedures to help to select law-enforcement personnel. They may serve as human relations experts and staff developers who conduct workshops and in other ways train police officers in techniques of intervening in crises such as domestic arguments and hostage taking. They may counsel or conduct group and individual psychotherapy with officers and their families. They may also contribute to the evaluation of staff development programs in law-enforcement contexts and conduct research on the training and treatment of law-enforcement personnel.

A branch of legal psychology known as *forensic psychology* is concerned primarily with evaluating defendants in court cases to determine whether a client has sustained a personal injury, is competent to stand trial, or would make a good parent (in child-custody decisions) and whether they are dangerous and/or likely to be recidivists. In court cases, psychologists may be asked by either the prosecution or the defense to examine a plaintiff for signs of mental disorder, dangerous or violent behavior, competency to stand trial, capacity to handle his or her own affairs, inability to serve as a suitable parent in a child-custody hearing, and for many other purposes.

Not only the defendant but also other persons (witnesses and others) associated with a legal dispute may require a psychological examination. Psychologists may be asked for an opinion regarding an unknown or apprehended criminal, whether a child will be better off if placed with one of the parents or with another person, and even how potential jurors are likely to vote in a specific trial. For example, an expert in personality analysis may be called on to assist in the process of jury selection in criminal or civil trials.

Competency and Insanity.   The opinions and recommendations of psychologists in matters dealing with the issue of competency (competency to stand trial, civil commitment, understanding of Miranda rights, capacity to sign a will) have been increasingly sought in recent years. Competency to stand trial has to do with whether a defendant understands the charges against him or her and can assist in his or her own defense. As stated by the U.S. Supreme Court in *Dusky* v. *United States* (1960), the defendant must possess "sufficient present ability to consult with his lawyers with a reasonable degree of rational [and] factual understanding of the proceedings against him." This means that usually, but not always, persons who are mentally retarded, acutely psychotic, or suffering from debilitating neurological disorders are considered incompetent to stand trial. Incompetency is, however, not synonymous with *insanity.* Whereas legal insanity pertains to the mental state of the defendant at the time that the crime was committed, the condition of incompetency is a continuing one. A person may be found "competent to stand trial" and yet adjudged "not responsible by reason of insanity."

The McNaughten Rule, the Durham decision, and the Model Penal Code have all influenced legal tests for insanity in the United states. Although insanity pleas are permissible in the great majority of states, several states have completely abolished such pleas. The standard of legal insanity applied most frequently by the judicial system in the United States is the Model Penal Code proposed by the American Law Institute (ALI) and adopted in 1972. The ALI definition states:

> A person is not responsible for criminal conduct, i.e., insane if, at the time of such conduct, as a result of mental disease or defect, he lacks substantial capacity either to appreciate the criminality (wrongfulness) of his conduct, or to conform his conduct to the requirement of the law. (American Law Institute, 1956)

Among the procedures and tools employed by psychologists in assessing competency are interviewing guides and competency screening instruments such as the Georgetown Screening Interview for Competency to Stand Trial (Bukatman, Foy, & De Grazia, 1971), the Competency Screening Test (Lipsitt, Lelos, & McGarry, 1971), the Competency Assessment Instrument (McGarry et al., 1973), and the Georgia Court Competency Test (Wildman et al., 1980). The Rogers Criminal Responsibility Assessment Scales (from Psychological Assessment Resources) may be administered to determine criminal responsibility according to the degree of psychological impairment that is significant in determining insanity under the ALI standard. The five scales on this instrument assess Patient Reliability, Organicity, Psychopathology, Cognitive Control, and Behavioral Control at the time of the crime that the patient is alleged to have committed. Neuropsychological tests may also be administered to defendants in insanity pleas.

Two of the most commonly administered tests in forensic contexts are the MMPI-2 and Rorschach (see Chapters 17 and 18). In addition to its many other applications in jurisprudence, the MMPI-2 can contribute to the identification of defensiveness (unwillingness to tell the truth) and provide information pertaining to additional matters of personal behavior that are of concern in court trials. The Rorschach is another workhorse in legal settings, but neither the MMPI-2 nor the Rorschach in and of themselves will provide clear answers to legal questions.

Sex and Violence.   With respect to sexual offenses, the Clarke Sex History Questionnaire for Males (Langevin, 1983), which was designed to assess types and strength of sexually anomalous behavior, may be of help to forensic psychologists.

Although no test has been developed that, by itself, can predict violent behavior, the MMPI can contribute to forecasting dangerous or violent behavior. The widely administered Hare Psychopathy Checklist-Revised (R. D. Hare; Psychological Assessment Resources) is also useful. A number of behavioral indicators, such as a recent history of violence, substance abuse, breakup of a marriage or love relationship, discipline or termination at work, and access to weapons such as guns, can also contribute to the prediction of violent behavior (Monahan & Steadman, 2001). A combination of personal history and test data may be used to derive an estimate of the probability of violent behavior. Determining the potential for violent behavior is important, not only in parole hearings and other matters concerning convicted criminals, but also in the selection and promotion of police officers and other peace-keepers.

Violence may be expressed toward adults or children, but in recent years the legal system and society as a whole have become sensitized to allegations of physical abuse of children. In cases of alleged mistreatment of children, observations, interviews, figure drawing tests, and doll play can contribute to the determination or prediction of physical or sexual abuse of children.

Child Custody. Child-custody evaluations may entail parent interviews focusing on child-rearing practices, in addition to the administration of tests of intelligence and personality. Measures of parents' knowledge and attitudes concerning child-rearing practices may also contribute to decisions in child-custody cases. Gordon and Peck's (1989) Custody Quotient, which yields ratings on 10 parenting factors, can be helpful in this regard.

A comprehensive system for evaluating parents and children in cases of child abuse or mistreatment is the Uniform Child Custody Evaluation System (from Psychological Assessment Resources). A complete evaluation with this system entails completing 10 general data and administrative forms, 9 parent forms, and 6 child forms. Included in the parent forms are a complete family–personal history, two interviews, a parent abilities checklist, observations of parent–child interactions, a home visit observation, and several other forms.

Evaluation of children in custody cases may involve administration of standardized psychometric instruments such as the Comprehension subtest of the WPPSI-R or WISC-IV, storytelling tests, and the Bricklin Perceptual Scales (Bricklin, 1984). The latter instrument focuses on understanding the child's perceptions of his or her parents in four areas: competence, supportiveness, follow-up consistency, and possession of admirable personality traits. It is customary to talk with the child and perhaps employ other techniques (doll play and figure drawings concerning family living situations, sentence-completion tests, etc.) to determine whether the child has a preference regarding his or her future living and visitation arrangements. It must be acknowledged, however, that the stated preferences and reports of preschoolers with average or below-average intelligence are frequently not very reliable and are influenced too much by recent events to be taken at face value.

ISSUES AND CONTROVERSIES IN PERSONALITY ASSESSMENT

Like measures of cognitive abilities, measures of personality have been criticized by psychologists and nonpsychologists alike. Perhaps because their applications are less extensive and less crucial, personality assessment instruments have not been criticized by the general public as much as ability tests. The relatively poor measurement characteristics of many personality tests, however, have not escaped professional and public notice.

Objections by the Public: Texas Test Burning and Project CAMELOT

Some of the most extreme negative comments concerning these instruments are found in books by Whyte (1956) and Gross (1962, 1965) on the applications of personality tests in business and industry. Objections made by Whyte (1956), along with objectionable content of items, even led to a public burning of certain attitude scales and other questionnaires and tests by order of the Houston School Board in 1959. Parents objected to their children being required to respond true or false to items such as these:

> I enjoy soaking in the bathtub.
> A girl who gets into trouble on a date has no one to blame but herself.
> If you don't drink in our gang, they make you feel like a sissy.
> Dad always seems too busy to pal around with me. (Nettler, 1959, p. 682)

Another event concerning psychological testing and social science research in general that led to strong emotional reactions in the mid-1960s was Project CAMELOT. Financed by the U.S. government, this project was designed to study the psychological causes of counterrevolution and counterinsurgency in Latin American. Both the Latin American public and certain U.S. congresspersons reacted rather heatedly when they became aware of the project, precipitating a congressional investigation of psychological testing in government, industry, and education. One issue aired at length during the inquiry was the administration of personality test items concerning sex and religion to job applicants, such as these: (1) My sex life is satisfactory, (2) I believe in God, (3) I don't get along very well with my parents. The congressional hearings did not result in a discontinuance of such tests, but the political concern associated with the hearings prompted psychologists and other assessment specialists to pay more attention to the ethics of psychological assessment.

More recently, Paul (2004) has pointed out her belief that personality tests reduce our sense of humanness by assigning limiting labels; "tests substitute a tidy abstraction for a real, rumpled human being, a sterile idea for a flesh-and-blood individual." She also states that tests often ask intrusive questions and have limited accuracy, and the interpretation of scores are subject to biases on the part of persons making the interpretations. She agrees with most professional psychologists that tests need to be selected that have good psychometric qualities, and interpretations need to be based not just on scores, but on understanding the overall context of the person.

The Polygraph and Integrity Testing

Theft is a big problem in U.S. business and industry, with perhaps billions of dollars in materials and products being stolen each year. Consequently, corporation executives are alert to any legal means for detecting dishonesty among employees or applicants. For years, polygraph (lie-detector) tests, which typically measure heart rate, respiration rate, blood pressure, and changes in skin resistance, were used by business and industrial organizations to identify thieves and deceivers among their employees. However, most research has not supported the accuracy of polygraph testing (www.psychologymatters.org/polygraphs .html). In 1988, the U.S. Congress passed the Employee Polygraph Protection Act, which banned most uses of polygraphs in preemployment interviews in government and the private sector. Despite this, heated debates related to its accuracy and appropriateness continue (www.apa.org/monitor/jun98/lie.html). Subsequently, a number of paper-and-pencil tests of honesty or integrity were introduced. Some states have also contemplated banning these tests, though a task force of the American Psychological Association concluded that "honesty tests, when used appropriately and in conjunction with additional selection procedures, have demonstrated useful levels of validity as selection procedures" (APA task force, 1991, p. 6).

The practice of integrity testing in business and industry remains controversial, and there are many unresolved issues and unanswered questions regarding the construct of honesty and the testing of integrity. The matter continues to be discussed at length in the professional literature, which should help to clarify the issues and improve the psychometric qualities of the instruments and the social sensitivity with which they are used (Camara & Schneider, 1994; Lillienfeld, Alliger, & Mitchell, 1995; Ones, Viswesvaran, & Schmidt, 1995).

Personality Testing for Employee Selection

Related to the debate over integrity testing is a situation regarding the administration of a true–false personality test that occurred in the case of *Soroka* v. *Dayton–Hudson Corporation* (1991). The dispute was concerned with PsychScreen, a personality inventory developed from the MMPI and the CPI that the Target Stores' management had administered to applicants for the position of security guard. This inventory had been used previously for screening applications for positions in law enforcement, air-traffic control, and nuclear power plants, in which security was of the utmost importance. Legal council for the plaintiff argued that the following kinds of items on Psychscreen were discriminatory with regard to religious and sexual preferences:

> I believe in the second coming of Christ.
> I believe there is a devil and a hell in afterlife.
> I am very strongly attracted to members of my own sex.
> I have never indulged in any unusual sex practices. (Hager, 1991, p. A-20)

Attorneys for Dayton–Hudson Corporation argued that such questions were effective in identifying emotionally unstable persons, who could not be expected to perform effectively in the position of security guard. The appellate court concluded, however, that questions on religion and sex violate a job seeker's right to privacy and consequently ruled in favor of the plaintiff.

Appealing this ruling to the California Supreme Court, the American Psychological Association pointed out that items such as those on PsychScreen should not be considered singly, but rather collectively, in evaluating their effectiveness in detecting emotional instability. Still, it can be argued that questions concerning sexual and religious preferences, which may contribute slightly to the prediction of job performance, but almost certainly are not directly job relevant, have no place on employment screening tests.

Personality assessment is also cited in federal legislation dealing with fair employment practices. For example, the roles of personality inventories and projective techniques in the employee selection process are brought into question in the Americans with Disabilities Act of 1990 (ADA). According to the provisions of this act, when employment test results are reported in terms of diagnostic labels such as "depression" or "anxiety," the tests are considered to be medical procedures. Consequently, according to the ADA, the tests cannot be administered until a conditional offer of employment has been made (U.S. Equal Employment Opportunity Commission, 1994). Tests of cognitive abilities and physiological states may also be considered parts of a medical examination and therefore subject to the same restrictions. However, there are few general rules in this process, and decisions are made on a case by case basis.

Validity of Personality Tests

Questions of what is measured by personality tests, whether these variables are worth measuring, and how best to interpret and apply the results have received extensive scrutiny during the past few decades. This has resulted in the psychometric qualities of many personality assessment instruments being carefully evaluated and debated. The greatest concerns have been directed toward projective instruments. In contrast, objective instruments are generally considered to have better psychometric properties. However, their reliabilities and validities are not as good as most ability measures. In addition, the validity coefficients of personality tests generally decline markedly over time and situations.

In certain areas, the theoretical underpinnings and the criteria against which personality tests are validated need to be improved. The disease model of mental disorders and the associated diagnostic classification system (DSM-TR) (American Psychiatric Association) are in many respects unreliable and have limited validity (Beutler & Malik, 2002). In many cases, clinicians do not agree on which diagnosis a person has. Even when a correct diagnosis is given, it does not lead to a clear plan on what the best treatment might be. Despite this, many personality inventories try to lead the clinician as closely as possible to a psychiatric diagnosis. Another matter of concern is the misinterpretation of the results of personality assessments. Errors of interpretation can occur through failure to consider the base rate, or the frequency of the event (criterion) to be predicted. Misinterpretations can also occur when clinicians do not consider test scores within the context of the person. In addition, "clinical insight" or "intuition" is often little better than a collection of superficial stereotypes, truisms, and overgeneralizations (Garb, 1998, 2005).

There are certainly an impressive array of techniques that have been employed in personality assessment. However, these have often resulted in considerable variability in how successful they are in achieving their goals. For example, the vast majority of interpretations based on human figures have not been supported (Groth-Marnat, 1999a; Groth-Marnat & Roberts, 1998). Despite this, projective techniques such as human figure drawings have sometimes contributed to clinical or selection decisions. In contrast, other research has been more supportive. For example, scales on the MMPI have generally been able to detect 80% of those who were faking good or faking bad (see Groth-Marnat, 2003, pp. 240–247). In legal cases where people might be inappropriately using the legal system for personal gain, this is potentially very important information. In addition, the use of the MMPI along with medical information has been found to increase the accuracy of physicians' diagnosis (Schwartz & Wiedel, 1981). Combining measures of cognitive abilities with measures of temperament and motivation may also increase the predictability of job-performance criteria. For example, Gottfredson (1994) suggested that employment selection may be improved by identifying the less cognitive elements of job performance and administering measures of these elements (e.g., certain personality traits) along with aptitude tests. She maintained that such noncognitive predictors may reduce possible adverse impacts from using cognitive predictors alone and at the same time enhance the validity of these predictors. Gottfredson admitted, however, that the contribution made by affective variables, over and above that made by a cognitive test battery alone, in forecasting occupational performance is probably fairly small in most instances. Finally, personality measures have been successful in predicting what type of psychological treatment will be most likely to help people with certain personality patterns (Beutler, Clarkin, & Bongar, 2000).

The validity of personality tests cannot be resolved without better research and development, but such efforts should be undertaken with a socially responsible attitude and a respect for the rights of individuals (see Messick, 1995). The variable validity of personality tests also means that test users should possess and apply a solid understanding of technical matters pertaining to test norms, design, reliability, and validity. There should also be a *science of practice* in which professional psychologists should keep records of and learn from their "hits" and "misses." In the long run, this kind of information serves as a check on the validity of tests achieving their stated purposes.

Ethnic and Gender Bias

Related to both ethical issues and the question of test validity is the matter of whether personality tests are biased against a particular race, gender, or other demographic group. For example, Gynther (1981) found that the MMPI profiles of blacks showed a greater degree of psychopathy than those of whites. Some years later, Dahlstrom and Gynther (1986) concluded that these differences were valid and not the consequence of ethnic group bias in the MMPI. Nevertheless, in revising the MMPI an effort was made to eliminate both ethnic-group and gender bias. Subsequent comparisons of the MMPI-2 scores of African American and Anglo-American men found a number of significant differences between the two groups (Ben-Porath, Shondrick, & Stafford, 1995; Frueh, Smith, & Libet, 1996). However, it is still unclear whether these differences represent "true" differences between the groups or are the result of error and therefore represent bias. For example, African Americans may have higher scores on suspiciousness due to the impact of being subjected to discrimination. On the other hand, this may be merely due to test error.

Although there has been relatively little systematic research on the personality test scores of different ethnic, social-class, or nationality groups in recent years, research on gender bias has flourished. A traditional response to gender differences in test scores has been to provide separate norms for males and females, but efforts have also been made to construct test items that are not biased toward either sex. Such efforts are routine in constructing periodically revised ability tests, such as the SAT and GRE. With regard to affective instruments, the development of MMPI-2 and the 1994 edition of the Strong Interest Inventory, in particular, involved painstaking efforts to eliminate gender bias.

Clinical and Statistical Prediction

The statistical (or actuarial) approach to data collection and behavior prediction consists of applying a statistical formula, a set of rules, or an actuarial table to assessment data. This can be done by a human being or, what has become common practice in recent years, by a computer following an interpretive program. In contrast, the clinical, or impressionistic, approach involves making intuitive judgments or drawing conclusions on the basis of subjective impressions combined with a theory of personality. Impressionistic interpretations are made not only on the basis of interviews, biographical data, and other clinical information, but also more "objective" information, such as personality ratings and test scores.

An early review of research comparing clinical and statistical approaches to prediction concluded that in 19 out of the 20 studies examined the statistical approach was either superior or equal in effectiveness to the clinical approach (Meehl, 1954). This set off 50 years of fiery debate ("seer versus sign"), with Meehl's conclusions generally being supported (Grove, Zald, Lebow, Snitz, & Nelson, 2000).

Although the studies summarized by Meehl (1954) and later by Groves et al. (2000) provided impressive support for the conclusion that personality diagnoses and behavior predictions are more accurate when a statistical rather than a clinical approach is employed, Lindzey (1965) demonstrated that an expert clinician can sometimes make highly accurate diagnoses. For example, by using only the information obtained from administering the Thematic Apperception Test, a clinical psychologist proved to be 95% accurate in detecting homosexuality. The statistical approach of employing only certain objective scores obtained from the TAT protocols was significantly less accurate.

Other studies have also found that, under certain circumstances, trained practitioners employing data from a variety of sources (case history, interview, test battery, etc.) are better predictors than actuarial (statistical) formulas (e.g., Goldberg, 1970; Holt, 1970; Wiggins & Kohen, 1971). Debate over the relative effectiveness of the clinical and statistical approaches to personality assessment has subsided, but research on this issue continues. For example, Gardner, Lidz, Mulvey, and Shaw (1996) compared the accuracy of an actuarial with a clinical procedure in predicting violent behavior by mentally ill persons. The patients were followed for 6 months from their release into the community after having been seen in a psychiatric emergency room. As in the great majority of earlier comparisons of clinical and actuarial approaches to prediction, the latter proved superior to the former on a number of criteria. In other words, the rates of false-positive and false-negative errors were lower with the actuarial approach. Actuarial predictions based only on patients' histories of violence were more accurate than clinical predictions, and actuarial predictions that did not use information on patients' histories were also more accurate than clinical predictions. This indicates optimal clinical practice should use acturial rather than clinical methods when predicting violence (Monahan & Steadman, 2001).

Validity of Clinical Judgment

Given the general finding that acturial formulas are more accurate than clinical impressions, it then becomes important to understand possible sources of clinician error. We also need to determine how it might be improved (see Weston & Weinberger, 2004). It is also important to gain better strategies on how computers using acturial formulas and clinicians can interact to maximize the advantages of each approach (Lichtenberger, in press). Even though psychodiagnosis requires extensive training and experience, the probability of making a mistake can be appreciable. Because of selective perception, selective remembering, insufficient experience, inadequate follow-up, and faulty logic, clinicians make errors in diagnosis and other types of judgments. Some of the most common types of errors are illusory correlation, not taking into account base rate (frequency) data, hindsight bias, and overconfidence (see Garb, 1998, 2005).

Illusory correlation involves judgments that are based on the number of times (correlates) a certain sign or indicator and a specific disorder seem to have occurred together. The reason why this can be illusory, or incorrect, is that the clinician overlooks the fact that they have failed to occur together even more often. Psychodiagnosticians commit this error when they notice or recall whatever fits their expectations and ignore or forget whatever is contrary to these expectations. For example, large eyes drawn on human figure drawings is often considered to be a sign of paranoia despite the fact that there is no empirical support for this conclusion.

A second source of error in clinical judgments may occur when clinicians do not take into account *base rate,* which is the proportion of people in a particular population who possess a specific characteristic or condition. For example, 80% of patients in a psychiatric hospital might be schizophrenic (a very high base rate). Thus it will be very easy to diagnose schizophrenia in a psychiatric hospital since, if you diagnose everyone there as schizophrenic, chance means you will be correct 80% of the time. Even if clinicians are correct 90% of the time, they will only be performing 10% above chance level. In contrast, suicide has a very low frequency of occurrence (low base rate). Thus it will be much more difficult to accurately predict its occurrence such that the error rate will be much higher. However, the consequences for misdiagnosis may be considerable. Thus clinicians need to balance their error rates with the possible consequences to the client.

A third source of error that detracts from clinical judgments is the *hindsight bias* or believing that, after an event has already occurred, one could have predicted it if he or she had been asked to do so. An illustration of this error is concluding that an acquaintance who has committed a violent act was always overly aggressive and disturbed.

A fourth source of error in clinical judgments is *overconfidence* in one's judgments, despite evidence to the contrary. For example, simply formulating a rule such as "psychotics are pale" may be sufficient to convince the clinician that it is a valid symptom. Interestingly, confidence tends to be fairly high for clinicians with minimal knowledge regarding a phenomenon. As their knowledge increases, their confidence goes down until they become very knowledgeable, at which time it becomes only moderate (Garb, 1998, 2005).

Traits and Situations

The emphasis on situations, as opposed to traits, as determiners of behavior goes back to the Hartshorne and May (1928). They found that lying and cheating among children was not due so much to character traits as to the external situation. Four decades later, Mischel (1968) summarized evidence for the conclusion that, although behavioral correlates of cognitive abilities are fairly consistent across different situations, personal–social behavior is highly dependent on the specific situation. Mischel concluded that inferences regarding personality dynamics or traits are less useful than knowledge of the situation itself in predicting behavior. He argued that assessments of generalized traits of personality are not particularly helpful, because such traits are frequently not generalizable across situations. Rather than analyzing personality into a complex of traits or factors, Mischel (1986) proposed a social-learning approach. This approach emphasizes that people learn to make different responses in different situations, and the accuracy with which a person's behavior in a specific situational context can be predicted must take into account the learning history of that person in similar situations.

It is certainly true that social norms, roles, and other group-related conditions exert powerful effects on people and may override temperament or personal style as determiners of individual thoughts and actions. When a social situation remains fairly constant, people tend to suppress their idiosyncrasies and adjust their behavior and thinking to the social expectations, rewards, and punishments provided in this situation. It has been amply demonstrated by research in social psychology and by candid television programs that when in Rome all kinds of people "do as the Romans do." Acceptance of this truism does not mean, however, that individual personality plays no role whatsoever in determining behavior.

Evidence pertaining to the trait–situation controversy is not all in favor of situationism. A number of investigators (e.g., Bem & Allen, 1974; Chaplin & Goldberg, 1984; Underwood & Moore, 1981) have found that the consistency of traits across situations is itself an individual difference variable. Regardless of the external circumstances, some people are more consistent than others in their behavior, and they are generally aware of how consistently they behave. In the investigation by Bem and Allen, people who believed themselves to be fairly consistent in friendliness and conscientiousness tended to be so; those who identified themselves as less consistent tended to be that way.

Research has also demonstrated that some behaviors are more consistent than others. Certain behaviors are narrowly situation specific, whereas other behaviors that do not require specific eliciting stimuli occur in a wide range of situations and hence are more reflective of broad personality variables (Funder & Colvin, 1991). Additional support for trait consistency comes from the field of behavioral genetics (Benjamin, Ebstein, & Belmaker, 2002).

Reviewing Mischel's position and subsequent evidence, a reasonable conclusion is that there is little support for a strict situationist viewpoint regarding personality. Rather, it is best to emphasize that behavior is a joint product of personality characteristics and the particular situation in which the behavior occurs. In certain (strong) situations, the features of the situations themselves are more important in determining how people behave; in other (weak) situations, personality characteristics are more influential. People with certain personality traits also tend to seek out situations having certain characteristics. Not only are people affected by specific situations, but to some extent they also choose the situations that will affect them.

Idiographic and Nomothetic Approaches

Allport (1937) stated that the *idiographic approach* holds that every person is a lawful, integrated system that must be studied as an individual, in his or her own right. Rather than attempting to interpret test scores, inventories, rating scales, and similar standardized instruments with respect to norms, psychologists of an idiographic persuasion study the unique consistencies and variations in the person, as noted in observations, interviews, and personal records (diaries, biographies, etc.). In contrast, the *nomothetic approach* relies heavily on group norms or averages; general laws of personality and behavior that are applicable to all people are sought and applied. Originally, these two positions were posed as polar opposites, with proponents heatedly arguing for one approach or the other. Like many great debates in the field, the controversy has become muted with the passage of time. Instead of an either–or position, it is now acknowledged that both positions have benefits and limitations.

SUMMARY

1. Personality is comprised of socially constructed descriptions, is enduring, is expressed in a wide number of situations, and is motivational. It allows prediction of behaviors, feelings, and interactions, and each description has related characteristics.

2. Early precursors of personality assessment include phrenology (based on the size of specific bumps on the scalp as reflecting personality characteristics), physiognomy (external features can indicate personality characteristics), graphology (handwriting analysis), and word-association tests (associations to words reflect different aspects of personality).

3. Although certain instruments are designed on a purely empirical basis, many assessment devices are constructed in the context of a theory of personality. Psychoanalytic theory considers unconscious processes, the resolution of conflicted feelings that are simultaneously mediated by conscious and unconscious processes, the impact of early childhood experiences on personality, the understanding of mental representations of the self and others, and the development of identity as a result of working through a progression of psychosexual feelings. Type theory studies fixed categories or types of people, such as Sheldon's observations that certain personality types seemed to be associated with body types (somatotypes). Trait theory is similar, but emphasizes traits as adaptive, dynamically organized, based on motivation, and organized according to various dimensions. For example, Eysenck described unstable (neurotic)–stable and introverted–extroverted dimensions. Phenomenological theories focus on a person's experience and sense of self, especially as they relate to self-

actualization and developing a positive sense of self-regard. Social-learning theory is based on how our interactions with others develops our beliefs about the self (expectations, interpersonal trust, self-efficacy) through imitation, modeling, and vicarious trial and error learning. Empirical strategies are based on measuring the relation between answers to sets of questions and personality as measured through behavior, symptom patterns, ratings by others, or other personality tests.

4. Ethical issues relate to the use of truisms (the Barnum effect), overpathologizing, confidentiality, ensuring accuracy of interpretations, and faking. Guidelines have been developed on how to optimally work with these issues.

5. Clinical psychologists administer tests and other psychometric instruments for screening, psychodiagnosis, treatment planning, and research in mental health clinics and other settings. Of particular importance are mental status examinations, which assess the intellectual, perceptual–motor, and emotional status of patients by means of in-depth interviews, questionnaires, rating scales, and related psychometric procedures. After completing a psychodiagnostic examination of a person, a clinical case conference is held to explain the results to family members and others who have a right to know.

6. Marital and family assessment evaluates family interaction, marital satisfaction, and parenting styles. Health psychologists analyze the role of psychological factors in physical illness and assist in planning and implementing prescribed treatments for such conditions. Among the many activities of legal or forensic psychologists are the psychological evaluation of offenders and other parties in judicial cases concerned with questions of competency to stand trial, responsibility for criminal acts, and the custody of minors.

7. Negative reactions from the public relate to intrusive questions, the use of test questions for assessment, possible bias (gender, ethnic), labeling, and the use of unvalidated procedures such as polygraph (lie) detectors. Research and practice guidelines have been established to work with how culture, ethnicity, and gender affect personality assessment. Efforts have been made to eliminate or at least to control for gender bias in interest inventories and other affective measures by rewriting items to make them relevant and fair to both males and females and by providing both separate and combined sex norms. Even though efforts have been made to construct gender- and race-free assessment instruments, clinicians still need to carefully study these factors in each case and modify their interpretations accordingly. Other issues regarding personality assessment include the relative validity of such procedures, the relative effectiveness of clinical and statistical prediction, the relative importance of traits and situations as determiners of behavior, and the relative value of examining the uniqueness of the individual (idiographic approach), as opposed to searching for general laws of behavior that are applicable to all people (nomothetic approach).

MASTERING THE CHAPTER OBJECTIVES

1. *Define personality*
   a. Define what is meant by personality.

    b. Consider a person who you feel has a strong personality trait (e.g., warm, shy, assertive). Consider how this characteristic involves each of the six components described at the beginning of the chapter (p. 321).

  2. *Precursors of personality assessment*
    a. Define what is meant by phrenology, physiognomy, graphology, and word-association tests.
    b. Click on to quackwatch.com and read what they say about graphology and phrenology. Why do you feel graphology might lay a greater claim to being a valid method than phrenology?

  3. *Major theories of personality*
    a. Describe the major concepts of trait theory, psychoanalytic theory, phenomenological (self) theory, and social-learning theory. Which theory is most appealing to you in terms of its explanatory power and congruence with your own personal theory of human personality?
    b. What is meant by an empirical approach to personality assessment? What are possible advantages over theoretical approaches?

  4. *Uses and misuses of personality assessment*
    a. List and briefly define four possible ethical issues related to personality assessment.
    b. Describe five guidelines that can help increase the accuracy of interpreting assessment data.

  5. *Clinical assessment*
    a. What is involved in a mental status exam?
    b. List four sources of error when doing psychodiagnosis. What do you think can be done to minimize these sources of error?

  6. *Applications of personality assessment*
    a. What is involved in health psychology assessment?
    b. Differentiate between the legal concepts of competency and insanity. What psychological assessment instruments or techniques can contribute to decisions concerning competency and insanity?

  7. *Issues and controversies in personality assessment*
    a. List and briefly describe four issues in personality assessment that the public has objected to.
    b. What is *clinical prediction,* and how does it differ from *statistical prediction*? Which is more effective and why?

EXPERIENCING PSYCHOLOGICAL ASSESSMENT

  1. Read an example of a legal report of a client with a question as to whether or not he could comprehend the Miranda rights (www.psychologyandlaw.com/tomjones.htm).

  2. Obtain a sample of three people's handwriting and explain that you will give them a handwriting analysis. Then give them the Barnum statements on p. 331, followed by a series of questions asking them to rate how accurate they feel the handwriting analysis is. To what do you attribute the responses?

■ ■ ■ ■ ■

CHAPTER FIFTEEN

OBSERVATIONS AND INTERVIEWS

CHAPTER OBJECTIVES

1. Describe principles of observation, including critical incidents, incident sampling, time sampling, participant observation, situational testing, training observers, nonverbal behaviors, self-observation, and content analysis.

2. Describe biographical data as used in psychobiography and employment selection.

3. Describe interviewing and interviewing techniques.

4. Define the methode clinique, stress interviewing, and cognitive interviewing.

5. Discuss the reliability and validity of interviews.

6. Describe behavioral assessment, including behavior analysis, observational methods, self-monitoring, and behavioral interviewing.

There are many ways of obtaining information about personality, the most popular of which are considered in the next four chapters. Some of these approaches to personality assessment are based on theory; others are more empirical or fact oriented. Some are more direct; others are indirect or even convoluted. Some are elaborate and expensive; others are simple and economical. This chapter deals with what may be considered the most empirical and direct, but not necessarily the least expensive, of all personality assessment procedures: observing and interviewing. These procedures, which may be used as primary or secondary sources of information about people and for other purposes than personality assessment, involve the seemingly superficial but often intricate acts of looking and listening. When employed by astute but considerate individuals, they can supply a wealth of information on a person's typical ways of acting and thinking. On the other hand, when the observer or interviewer is unskilled, insensitive, or biased, the results can be useless and even misleading.

OBSERVATIONS

The most widely employed and probably the most generally understood and acceptable method of personality assessment is some form of observation. Observation, which is basic to all science, consists of the observer simply taking note of certain events, such as particular behavior, and usually making a record of what is observed. The most common procedure is the *uncontrolled observation* of behavior "on the wing," with no attempt to restrict it to a particular situation or set of circumstances. Observing the activities of children on a playground and the behavior of people in a waiting line are examples of such uncontrolled, or *naturalistic,* observation. An illustration of uncontrolled observation in the world of work is the *critical incidents technique* (Flanagan, 1954). Supervisors and others who are familiar with a certain job are asked to identify specific behaviors that are critical to performance or that distinguish between good and poor workers on the job. These behaviors, or *incidents,* are critical, because they have either highly positive or highly negative consequences. Examples are "secures machinery and tidies up place of work when finished" and "follows up customers' requests promptly." Identification of a large number of such incidents provides valuable information on the nature of the job and the requirements for performing it effectively.

Observations may be uncontrolled and yet systematic and objective. For example, teachers can be trained to make objective observations of the behavior of schoolchildren and accurate *anecdotal records* of whatever behavior seems significant. A well-trained teacher–observer indicates in the anecdotal record precisely what was observed and distinguishes it from the interpretation placed on it. The observer realizes that when Johnny pinches Mary it is not always an act of aggression.

Improving the Accuracy of Observations

Training observers to be as objective as possible, by not letting their own personal biases and needs affect what they observe and separating observation from interpretation, is one of several recommended guidelines for improving the validity of observational data. Another guideline is to observe a limited number of specific behaviors, which are defined beforehand. Employing several observers and collecting a large, representative sample of observations can also improve the accuracy of observations. Obtaining a representative sample of behavior is, however, time consuming and expensive. To reduce the volume of data collected in continuous observation, the *incident sampling* technique of noting and recording only specific events or incidents, say of aggressive behavior, is appropriate. Further improvements in the efficiency of observation may be obtained by *time sampling,* that is, making a series of observations lasting only a few minutes each over a period of a day or so (see Haynes & Heiby, 2004).

Participant Observation

Also relatively uncontrolled is *participant observation,* in which the observer is part of the observational situation. Participant observation has been used extensively by cultural anthropologists, so much so that at one time it was remarked that a typical aborigine family consisted of a mother, a father, two children, and a cultural anthropologist! Realizing that they must take into account the likelihood that the observer's own behavior will affect the reactions of other people in the situation, proponents of this research method argue that active involvement in a situation can provide insights that are unobtainable by other means.

Situational Testing

In addition to relatively uncontrolled observations, prearranged, contrived, or controlled observations are made with the purpose of determining how people (and animals) behave in various situations. For example, a developmental psychologist may set up an observational situation beforehand to determine if children will cheat or behave honestly under a prearranged set of conditions. Or by watching the behavior of children in a gamelike situation involving dolls or other toys, an observer may obtain confirming or disconfirming evidence of whether they are victims of abuse. For example, the "What If" Situations Test was designed to assess the abilities of preschoolers to recognize, resist, and report inappropriate touching.

A classic series of studies that used a controlled observational procedure known as *situational testing* was the Character Education Inquiry (Hartshorne & May, 1928). In these investigations, children were surreptitiously provided with an opportunity to demonstrate their honesty, altruism, and other character traits. For example, to test for honesty, the investigators placed the children in a situation where some coins could be stolen and in another situation where test answers could be copied, presumably without being detected. Among the findings of the studies were that older children, less intelligent children, children of lower socioeconomic status, and more emotionally unstable children tended to be less honest in all the situations. Perhaps the most important outcome of the Hartshorne and May studies was that honesty and other character traits varied as much with the specific situation as with the individual. In other words, the degree of honesty, altruism, or other ethical behavior manifested by children depended greatly on the situations in which they were observed.

Situational testing of military personnel was introduced by the Germans and subsequently adapted by the British and U.S. armed forces during World War II. A series of simulated situational tests for selecting espionage agents was designed by the U.S. Office of Strategic Services (OSS), the forerunner of the CIA. As in the Hartshorne and May (1928) studies, deception of the candidates was involved. For example, in the "wall problem" a group of men was assigned the task of crossing a canyon. Unknown to the real candidate, the men designated to assist him were *plants,* rather than actual candidates. One plant acted as an obstructor by making unrealistic suggestions and insulting or worrisome remarks; another plant pretended not to understand the task and passively resisted directions from the candidate. Not realizing that the other candidates were cooperating with the examiners, the real candidate was observed during his efforts to complete the task in the face of these frustrating circumstances. It was difficult to determine the effectiveness of these procedures as selection methods, however, and they were never adequately validated.

Situational testing has been used in other assessment programs, for example, observing how applicants to a clinical psychology program would respond when shown a videotape of a client. One interesting variation is the Leaderless Group Discussion (LGD) test, in which several executive candidates discuss an assigned topic for 30 to 50 minutes while their individual performances are observed and rated. The ratings made by the observers, as well as those of other candidates, may be in terms of the degree of ascendance, task facilitation, and sociability shown by each candidate. In spite of the real-life quality of situational testing, it is never possible to duplicate the actual situations that the examinees may face. Furthermore, the candidates frequently catch on to the deception. Even in the OSS assessment program, some candidates realized that the tests were rigged. Due in large measure to the "fakability" of situational tests and problems in arranging the situations and evaluating the results objectively and consistently, the reliabilities and predictive validities of these tests are frequently too low to justify the cost.

One strategy for reducing the intrusiveness of the observer is to observe the participants through a television monitor. By remaining unseen, the observer minimizes the effect of the behavior of the people who are being observed. Whenever people realize that they are being observed, they may behave unnaturally or act as if they were on stage (role playing). For this reason, observations for the purposes of personality assessment are usually made as unobtrusively as possible. In *unobtrusive observation,* the performer is unaware of the observer's presence, and therefore the behavior of the former is not influenced by the knowledge of being watched. Either controlled or uncontrolled observation may be unobtrusive, and even participant observation can be relatively unobtrusive when the observer takes steps to be accepted by the people who are being observed.

Clinical Observations

A clinical or school psychologist who is examining a child interacts with the child as a special kind of participant observer. Consequently, psychological examiners must be careful not to let their own presence and actions provoke atypical behavior in the child. The examiner's observations, which must be as unobtrusive as possible, are an important part of the psychological report. Observations should be communicated as objective, verifiable behaviors, rather than in psychological terminology that may mean different things to different readers.

Much of what is known about personality dynamics and mental disorders has been obtained from observations of people in clinical settings. Clinical observations are obviously not completely objective: both parties in a clinical situation affect each other's behavior. Consequently, the accuracy of clinical observations and the interpretations given to them should be verified by other people and procedures.

An alert clinical observer notes a variety of details: what the examinee is wearing and whether he or she is well groomed; if and how the examinee shakes hands and looks at the examiner; how the examinee sits, stands, and walks; what facial expressions, body movements, and voice tones are characteristic. These are nonverbal behaviors and, when interpreted properly, can provide better insight into personality than a record limited to what the examinee actually says.

Training Observers

More important than special procedures and devices in ensuring the accuracy of observations is training observers to be as perceptive and objective as possible. Because they filter their observations through their own personal biases and desires, observers who are not sensitive to this fact often have a great deal of difficulty making accurate observations and separating observation from interpretation or fact from opinion.

The training of observers begins by describing the form or schedule on which the observations are to be made and going over the objective definition of each target behavior and how its occurrence and duration are to be recorded. Observers should be told what to look for and how to record their observations clearly, objectively, and unobtrusively; how to distinguish between what is observed and how it is interpreted; and how to become more aware of the effects of their personal biases and other factors on which they observe and report. The trainer points out common errors made in recording behaviors and the importance of not letting one's own biases, expectancies, personality, attitudes, or desires interfere with what is being observed.

Since prior knowledge about certain people may lead to assumptions or expectations that they should behave in a certain way, observers should be supplied only with information that is absolutely essential for them to have concerning the persons who are to be observed. To minimize the bias in observations created by a desire to provide the researcher or supervisor with supporting data, observers should be given minimal information concerning the purposes of the research project and no details on the specific hypotheses or expected outcomes. Whenever they are visible to the persons who are being observed, observers should be cautioned to remain as inconspicuous and unobtrusive as possible, remaining in the background and recording what is seen and heard without any display of emotion, approval, or disapproval. Observer trainees should also be provided with an opportunity to practice or role play their observational activities and to have their performance evaluated before making genuine observations. To ensure higher reliability of observations, two or more observers are preferable to one. It is also preferable to define the behaviors to be observed as specifically as possible, rather than designating them with overly general descriptive categories.

Nonverbal Behavior

Most people realize that interpersonal communication is not entirely verbal, but they are usually unaware of the extent to which movements of their hands, eyes, and mouth, as well as body postures and voice tones, are interpreted as messages. As suggested by the following quotation, Sigmund Freud was well aware of these nonverbal cues: "He that has eyes to see and ears to hear may convince himself that no mortal can keep a secret. If his lips are silent, he chatters with his fingertips; betrayal oozes out of him at every pore" (Freud, 1905, p. 94).

A great deal of research has been conducted on nonverbal behavior, including *kinesics* (movements of body parts), *proximics* (distance between communicants), and *paralinguistics* (tone of voice, rate of speaking, and other nonverbal aspects of speech). According to the findings of one investigation, 65% to 90% of the meaning in interpersonal communications comes from nonverbal cues (Mehrabian & Weiner, 1967).

It has been found that certain types of nonverbal cues are more important than others in message transmission. Kinesics are particularly important, followed by proximics, paralinguistics, and even *culturics* (style of dress, culturally based habits or customs, etc.). Most people are probably right more often than wrong in interpreting nonverbal messages, but mistakes do occur. The poker-faced gambler and the glad-handed salesman or politician are renowned for their ability to deceive and manipulate other people by means of nonverbal behavior. Nonverbal behaviors and characteristics are interpreted more accurately when the observer has some knowledge of the specific situation or context in which the behavior occurs. In addition, some people are better than others at interpreting nonverbal behavior, an ability that appears to be related to personality, but not to intelligence.

The PONS.   Rosenthal, Hall, DiMatteo, Rogers, and Archer (1979) devised the Profile of Nonverbal Sensitivity (PONS) to assess individual differences in the ability to interpret nonverbal communications. The PONS consists of a 45-minute film in which viewers are presented with a series of stimuli such as facial expressions or spoken phrases heard as tones or sounds, but not as words. After each stimulus is presented, the viewer selects the most appropriate of two descriptive labels. The authors of the PONS report that men and women who make high scores on the test tend to have fewer friends, but warmer, more honest, and more satisfying sexual relationships, than those who make low scores.

Reasoning that sensitivity to nonverbal messages is an important ability for diplomats, David McClelland used the PONS in an applicant screening program for the U.S. Information Agency. Short, taped segments from the test were played to USIA job applicants, who were then asked to indicate what emotion was being expressed. It was found that applicants who scored high on the PONS were viewed by their colleagues as significantly more competent than those who scored low (Rosenthal et al., 1979, pp. 304–306).

Unmasking the Face.   Another contribution to the assessment of nonverbal behavior is the Facial Action Coding System (FACS). Designed by Ekman and Friesen (1978, 1984), the FACS material consists of 135 photographs of various facial expressions for training observers in scoring dozens of facial action units. Kaiser and Wehrle (1992) subsequently developed a method, based on the FACS, for automated coding of facial behavior in computer-aided test or game situations. Also useful in training observers to judge emotion from facial expressions is Friesen and Ekman's Pictures of Facial Affect. This is 110 black and white pictures expressing fear, anger, happiness, sadness, surprise, or danger (plus a neutral expression).

Self-Observation and Content Analysis

Many people typically spend considerable time observing themselves, and it is a useful method of collecting observational data for both research and clinical purposes. Self-observation is not only an economical research procedure, but it is one of very few ways to get at private thoughts and feelings. Other techniques are hypnosis, narcoanalysis (interviews assisted with a sedative), free association, and projective techniques (see Chapter 18). A problem with self-observations is that they are likely to be even more biased than observations made by others. People are seldom entirely objective in describing their own thoughts and behavior (Wolff & Merrens, 1974). As with observations made by others, however, people can be trained to make more objective, systematic self-observations (Thoreson & Mahoney, 1974). They can learn to distinguish between what they actually feel, think, or do and what they should or would like to feel, think, or do. Research findings show, for example, that having an opportunity to "see ourselves as others see us" can make our self-perceptions and self-evaluations more like those of other people. For example, Albright and Malloy (1999) confirmed the hypothesis that observing a videotape of oneself in social interaction increases the accuracy of predicting others' judgments of oneself.

A wealth of self-observation data can be accumulated by keeping a continuous written record of our thoughts, feelings, and actions. Unfortunately, it is not always clear what to do with such an abundance of data, that is, how to analyze or interpret it. As seen in the *content analysis* of diaries, autobiographies, letters, drawings, and other personal documents, important insights into personality and behavior can be obtained by interpreting self-observational data (Allport, 1965). But the complexity and laboriousness of content analysis have kept this interpretive approach from being applied routinely in clinical and other applied contexts (see review by Wrightsman, 1994).

BIOGRAPHICAL DATA

Psychobiography

In addition to their potential uses in clinical diagnosis, personal documents such as diaries, letters, and autobiographies provide a rich source of information for psychobiographers (psychobiography.com/faq). *Psychobiography* is actually a subcategory of psychohistory: both employ psychological concepts and theories to reconstruct and interpret happenings that occurred in the past. More specifically, *psychohistory* is concerned with the analysis, by means of history and psychology, of events such as the Salem witchcraft trials or the rise of Nazi Germany. The term *psychobiography,* on the other hand, refers to the psychological exploration of a person's life (Wrightsman, 1994).

Psychobiographical studies of many famous people, including political leaders such as Adolf Hitler (Binion, 1976; Langer, 1972), Mohandas Gandhi (Erikson, 1969), and a number of U.S. presidents (Brodie, 1983; Freud & Bullitt, 1967; Glad, 1980; Kearns, 1976; Mazlish, 1973), have been conducted for both theoretical and practical purposes (see Nixon, www.ralphmag.org/nixon.html). Among the practical reasons are to provide opposition leaders or others who must deal with certain political figures with insights into the personalities and behaviors of those leaders and predictions as to what they might do under certain circumstances. These were the motives behind Freud and Bullitt's (1967) psychobiography of Woodrow Wilson and Langer's (1972) psychobiography of Adolf Hitler.

Psychobiography has been criticized for a number of factual, theoretical, cultural, and logical errors. Wrightsman's (1994) review is very critical of the approach, but critics such as Elms (1976) and Cocks and Crosby (1987) have made suggestions for improving psychobiographical procedures. They argue that a psychobiographical analysis should not be made unless sufficient information is available on the person's life or at least on those areas or periods that are being analyzed. Furthermore, other psychological theories other than classical psychoanalysis should be applied to the analysis. Finally, the preconceptions and biases of psychobiographers should be acknowledged and controlled.

In addition to autobiographies and other personal documents, the biographical information recorded on application blanks, in letters of recommendation, and in the answers given to biographical (biodata) inventories may provide insights into personality characteristics. These sources are used extensively in employment and admissions decisions, but they may also prove valuable in personality assessment and in the diagnosis of behavioral disorders and their causes (see Stokes, Mumford, & Owens, 1994).

Biographical Data in Employment Contexts

Biographical data concerning a person's characteristics, experiences, and accomplishments are based on observations by the person himself or herself, as well as on those of other people (see Stokes & Cooper, 2004). Usually obtained from applications blanks and other self-report forms, biographical information is useful for decision-making purposes in educational, medical, recreational, employment, and other contexts. The most systematic research and applications with biographical data have, however, occurred in employment situations. Although much of this information is highly factual and objective (applicant's name, birth date, marital status, etc.), a substantial amount is obtained from self-observations and the respondent's impressions of the interpersonal environment.

Applications and Recommendations.   Among the first things required of a job applicant are a letter of application and/or a completed application blank. A completed application blank is both a formal request for employment and a brief description of the applicant's fitness for the job. Following a series of identifying questions (name, address, employment desired, etc.), detailed background information (education, physical handicaps, military record, previous employment and experience) is requested. In most cases, a section of the blank is also provided for references.

Whether elicited by letter, telephone, interview, or questionnaire, information from an applicant's listed references can be useful despite some obvious limitations. Letters of recommendation probably have the most serious limitations in that they often provide a biased description of the applicant. In fact, praise is so common in letters of recommendation that personnel administrators and other selection officials often become overly sensitized to anything less than very positive statements concerning the applicant. There is also a tendency to interpret short letters as indicative of disapproval and longer letters as more complimentary. Because former employers or other reference sources are reluctant to reveal negative information about a person in writing, one telephone call is sometimes worth a dozen letters of recommendation.

Biographical Inventories.   Formal biographical inventories, or biodata forms, consist of a variety of items pertaining to the life history of an applicant (family relationships, friendships, extracurricular activities, interests, etc.). A great deal of research on longer forms of the weighted application blank has been conducted with employees at all levels of an organization (Schoenfeldt & Mendoza, 1994; Stokes et al., 1994).

Not only do biographical inventories have a great deal of content validity, but they are also effective predictors of performance in a variety of job contexts, ranging from unskilled work to high-level executive responsibilities (Childs & Klimoski, 1986; Drakeley, Herriot, & Jones, 1988). Ability to predict job performance ranges between .28 to .48 (Stokes & Cooper, 2004). In many instances the validity of these inventories is also generalizable from one context to another (Rothstein, Schmidt, Erwin, Owens, & Sparks, 1990). Despite these advantages, biographical inventories are not widely used for personnel selection purposes (Hammer & Kleiman, 1988). One explanation is that legal problems are associated with requests for certain kinds of information (e.g., age, sex, ethnicity, religion, marital status, number of children) on application blanks and biographical inventories. Furthermore, applicants may object to certain items (personal finances, family background, and other intimate details) as being too personal or otherwise offensive (Rosenbaum, 1973). This is unfortunate, because responses to these items are frequently good predictors of employee performance.

INTERVIEWS

Interviewing is one of the oldest and most widely used methods of personality assessment. An interview not only yields much of the same kind of data as observations, but it also provides information on what a person says and how he or she says it. The interviewee's nonverbal behavior, including body postures and poise, gestures, eye movements, and the quality and pattern of speech, is important and should be noted. The major emphasis in interviewing, however, is on the content of the verbal statements made by the interviewee. Sommers-Flanagan and Sommers-Flanagan (2003) summarize that interviewing involves a professional relationship in which the client and interviewer are motivated to accomplish a mutually agreed on goal. The interaction is based on both client and interviewer working to accomplish this goal. The resulting information consists of details of the interviewee's background or life history, in addition to data concerning feelings, attitudes, perceptions, and expectations.

Interviews are used in many different contexts and for a variety of purposes. In research contexts, they are used for polling and surveys and for obtaining in-depth information on personality and behavior to test some hypothesis or theoretical proposition. In employment situations, interviews are used for employee selection and screening, evaluation or appraisal, troubleshooting, and termination. In clinical contexts, *intake interviews* of patients and their relatives are essential in collecting case history information for making medical and/or psychological diagnoses (*diagnostic interviews*). In addition, *therapeutic interviews* are part of the psychological treatment process, and *exit interviews* are designed to determine whether an institutionalized individual is ready to be released.

Whatever the context and purposes of interviewing, it requires skill and sensitivity and may be very time consuming and laborious. Interviewing is as much an art as a science, and some interviewers are more effective than others in establishing rapport and getting interviewees to open up. The procedure varies with the purposes of the interview, but, as in any interpersonal situation, the outcomes depend on the personality and actions of both the interviewer and interviewee. Thus, an interview is not a one-way, question and answer situation in which the interviewer remains unaffected. In almost every case it is a dynamic, two-way interchange in which the participants mutually influence each other.

Interviewing can be an end in itself, but it may also function as a get-acquainted or warming-up process designed as a lead-in to other assessment procedures. Most clinical and counseling psychologists like the face-to-face closeness of an interview because it enables them to get a feel for the patient (client) and his or her problems and characteristics. Clinical psychologists, personnel psychologists, employment counselors, and other human service professionals usually believe that the time and expense of an interview are justified, because personal information obtained in this way is not available by any other means. Applicants, counselees, and patients usually express feelings of being more involved when interviewed than when they are merely asked to fill out paper-and-pencil questionnaires or application blanks and are not given an opportunity to communicate their problems, needs, opinions, and circumstances in a face-to-face manner.

Interviewing Techniques

A personal interview can take place anywhere, but it is usually better to conduct it in a quiet room free from distractions. Both the interviewer and the interviewee should be comfortably seated and facing each other. Because interviewing is a complex interpersonal skill and to some extent a function of the interviewer's interpersonal style, effective interviewing is not easily taught. Attention to the following recommendations, however, can improve your interviewing skills.

Professional interviewers are usually friendly but neutral, interested but not prying or overly demonstrative in reacting to interviewees. They are warm and open, accepting interviewees for what they are without showing approval or disapproval. They do not begin with leading questions of the "How often do you beat your wife?" type and do not ask questions that imply a certain answer (e.g., "You still do that, don't you?"). By timing the questions properly and varying their content according to the situation, good interviewers are able to develop a conversation that flows from topic to topic. Pauses or silences cause them no discomfort: they allow the interviewee sufficient time to answer a question completely and listen to the answer without interrupting. In addition, they pay attention not only to what the interviewee says, but also to how it is said. Realizing that the interviewer's behavior (activity level, amount and speed of talking, etc.) tends to be imitated by the interviewee, interviewers are patient and comfortable and do not hurry the interviewee. Skilled interviewers also check their understandings, impressions, and perceptions of interviewees' answers to clarify them and make certain that they do not misunderstand. Interviewers may ask direct questions to fill in gaps in their understanding of interviewees. However, they are not voyeurs who relentlessly probe and keep the interview focused on highly personal and emotional material.

Although the characteristics of good interviewers described here are generally applicable, the specific techniques vary with the theoretical orientation (behavioral, client centered, psychoanalytic, etc.) of the interviewer, as well as the goals and stage of the interview. The age, sex, ethnicity, attractiveness, health, intelligence, personality, and other characteristics of the interviewee and interviewer may also affect the process and progress of an interview. Most interviewers outside clinical contexts, as well as many clinicians, are fairly eclectic in their orientation, following no particular theory of personality, but applying relevant concepts from a variety of theories.

Structured Versus Unstructured Interviews.   The degree to which an interview is *structured* depends primarily on the goals of the interview, but it is also important to consider the characteristics of the participants (e.g., see cpmcnet.columbia.edu/dept/scid/). Some interviewees respond more readily to a relatively unstructured, open-ended approach; others communicate more relevant information when the interviewer follows an interviewing guide and asks very structured questions. Interviewers may also feel more comfortable and obtain a greater amount of personal information by asking a series of questions similar to those found on an application blank or personal history form. Less experienced interviewers typically find it easier to handle a structured interview, the results of which can be readily quantified for purposes of analysis. Experienced interviewers may prefer greater flexibility in the content and timing of interview questions, in other words, less structure.

More skill and time are required to conduct an interview in an unstructured or open-ended manner in which the interviewer can follow up interesting leads or concentrate on details of greater significance. To accomplish this, the interviewer encourages the interviewee to feel free to talk about his or her problems, interests, behaviors, or whatever else seems relevant to the goals of the interview. These goals also affect the amount of structure in an interview. When answers to a large number of specific questions are required, as in an employment selection situation, a fairly structured approach is appropriate. When the goal is to obtain an in-depth picture of personality or to define the nature of certain problems and their causes, less structure is called for. Whether highly structured or relatively open ended, the sequence of questions usually proceeds from general to specific and from less personal to more personal topics. Most professional interviewers are able to vary their approach with the personality of the person being interviewed and the objectives of the interview. They begin by asking a series of nonthreatening, open-ended questions to establish rapport and get the conversation going and then become more specific in questioning as the interview proceeds.

Interview Topics and Questions.   The specific questions asked depend on the purposes of the interview, but it is helpful to plan an interview by outlining the topics to be covered, if not the specific questions to be asked. A topical outline for a life history interview is given in Table 15.1. A complete life history interview, whether conducted in a clinical, social service, employment, or research context, requires obtaining the kinds of information listed in this table. Not all these topics need to be covered in a specific situation: the interviewer can concentrate on the areas considered most important. In any event, the specific interview questions, framed in language with which the interviewee is familiar and comfortable, can be developed from the outline in Table 15.1.

Clinical Interviews

Clinical interviews are conducted for intake purposes at a social agency or mental hospital; diagnostic interviews are used to determine the causes and correlates of an individual's problems, and therapeutic interviews (counseling, psychotherapy) are directed toward helping. Table 15.2 is a list of recommendations to be followed in conducting a clinical interview. Many of these recommendations are not restricted to clinical interviews, but apply to other types of verbal interchanges as well.

When conducted properly, a diagnostic or therapeutic interview can provide a great deal of information about a person: the nature, duration, and severity of his or her problems; how

TABLE 15.1 Information to Record in an Interview

Identifying data: Name, age, sex, education, ethnic group, nationality, address, date of birth, marital status, date of interview, and so forth.

Purpose(s) of interview: Employment, psychiatric intake, psychodiagnostic, problem solving or troubleshooting, performance evaluation, termination or exit.

Physical appearance: Clothing, grooming, physical description (attractiveness, unusual features, etc.), obvious or apparent physical disorders or disabilities.

Behavior: Attitudes and emotions (cooperative, outgoing or reserved, friendly or hostile, defensive, etc.); motoric behavior (active versus passive, posture, gait, carriage); level of intellectual functioning (bright, average, retarded as estimated from vocabulary, immediate and long-term memory, judgment, abstract thinking); signs of mental disorder (distorted thought processes: bizarre constructions, thought blocking, etc; distorted perceptions: delusions, hallucinations, disorientation in time or space, etc.; inappropriate or extreme emotional reactions: depression, mania; unusual mannerisms, postures, or facial expressions).

Family: Parents, siblings, other family members; sociocultural group; attitude(s) toward family members.

Medical history: Present health, health history, physical problems.

Developmental history: Physical, intellectual, language, emotional, and social development; irregularities or problem of development.

Education and training: Schools attended, performance level, adjustment to school, plans for further education and training.

Employment: Nature and number of jobs or positions held, military service (rank and duties), job performance level(s), job problems.

Legal problems: Arrests and convictions, nature of misdemeanors or felonies.

Sexual and marital history: Sexual activities and problems, marriages, martial problems, separations and divorce(s), children.

Interests and attitudes: Hobbies, recreational activities, social activities and attitude(s) toward others, level of self-acceptance and satisfaction, aspirations or goals.

Current problems: Description of problem(s), including onset, duration, frequency, and severity; plans for solving it (them).

the problems are manifested (inwardly or outwardly); what past influences are related to present difficulties; the interviewee's resources and limitations for coping with the problems; the kinds of psychological assistance that the interviewee has had in the past; and the kinds of assistance that are expected and might be of help now (www.mentalhealth.com/bookah/p44-dq.html#Head4).

Methode Clinique and Morality Research

The clinical method of interviewing, in which the interviewer asks probing questions to test the limits or obtain in-depth information about a person, was employed extensively by Sig-

TABLE 15.2   Recommendations for Conducting a Clinical Interview

Assure confidentiality.
Convey a feeling of interest and warmth (rapport).
Try to put the interviewee at ease.
Try to get in touch with how the interviewee feels (empathy).
Be courteous, patient, and accepting.
Encourage the interviewee to express his or her thoughts and feelings freely.
Adjust the questions to the cultural and educational background of the interviewee.
Avoid psychiatric or psychological jargon.
Avoid leading questions.
Start with open-ended questions and proceed to more direct ones.
Use humor sparingly, and only if appropriate and not insulting.
Listen without overreacting emotionally.
Attend not only to what is said, but also to how it is said.
Take notes or make a recording as inconspicuously as possible.

mund Freud, Carl Jung, Jean Piaget, and many other famous psychologists. The use of clinical interviewing in research, referred to as the *methode clinique,* requires considerable skill.

An example of a research instrument involving the use of the methode clinique is Lawrence Kohlberg's Moral Judgment Scale. Kohlberg (1969, 1974) maintained that the development of personal morality progresses through three ascending levels, consisting of two stages each. At the lowest level (*premoral level*), moral judgments are guided either by punishment and obedience or by a kind of naive pleasure–pain philosophy. At an intermediate level (*morality of conventional rule conformity*), morality depends either on the approval of other people ("good boy–good girl" morality) or on adherence to the precepts of authority. In the first stage of the last level (*morality of self-accepted moral principles*), morality is viewed in terms of acceptance of a contract or democratically determined agreement. In the second stage of the last level, the individual has developed an internal set of principles and a conscience that direct his or her judgment and behavior.

The Moral Judgment Scale is administered by presenting nine hypothetical moral dilemmas and obtaining the examinee's judgments and reasons for the judgments pertaining to each dilemma. One such dilemma, the case of Heinz and the druggist, is as follows:

> In Europe, a woman was near death from a special kind of cancer. There was one drug that the doctors thought might save her. It was a form of radium that a druggist in the same town had recently discovered. The drug was expensive to make, but the druggist was charging ten times what the drug cost him to make. He paid $200 for the radium and charged $2000 for a small dose of the drug. The sick woman's husband, Heinz, went to everyone he knew to borrow the money, but he could only get together about $1000 which is half of what it cost. He told the druggist that his wife was dying, and asked him to sell it cheaper or let him pay later. But the druggist said, "No, I discovered the drug and I'm going to make money from it." So Heinz got desperate and broke into the man's store to steal the drug for his wife. (Kohlberg & Elfenbeim, 1975)

Scoring the examinee's moral judgments and reasons for the judgments concerning stories such as this consists of clinical interviewing combined with rather subjective evaluations of the participant's responses in terms of Kohlberg's stages. In addition to the subjectivity of scoring, several other criticisms have been made of Kohlberg's approach to moral development. A review of evidence concerning the approach pointed out several conceptual and methodological problems, including problems in the derivation, administration, and scoring of the Moral Judgment Scale (Kurtines & Greif, 1994).

Stress Interviewing

The usual rule of cordiality toward the interviewee is suspended in a *stress interview*. The goal of stress interviewing, which is used in clinical, selection, and criminal interrogation contexts, is to determine the ability of the person to cope with or solve a specific problem under emotionally stressful conditions. Stress interviewing may also be appropriate when time is short or when the interviewee is very repetitive, emotionally unresponsive, or very defensive. An attempt is made to produce a valid emotional response—to get beneath the superficial social mask (*persona*) of the interviewee—by asking probing, challenging questions in a kind of police interrogation atmosphere. A great deal of professional expertise is obviously required to make a stress interview appear realistic and to keep reactions from getting out of hand.

Cognitive Interviewing

Eyewitness information is clearly important in criminal investigation, but police typically receive inadequate training in interviewing cooperative witnesses. An interviewing procedure that has been taught to many police interviewers who conduct criminal interrogations is *cognitive interviewing*. This procedure was developed by Geiselman, Fisher, MacKinnon, and Holland (1985) to obtain more detailed, accurate information from eyewitnesses to criminal acts. The original version of the cognitive interviewing procedure consists of (1) inducing the eyewitness to mentally re-create the original context of the crime, (2) instructing the eyewitness to report everything that he or she observed, (3) having the eyewitness recall the features and events of the crime scene in a variety of orders, and (4) having the eyewitness describe the event from a variety of perspectives. This basic procedure has been enhanced to address the social dynamics and communication between the interviewer and the eyewitness (Fisher, McCauley, & Geiselman, 1994). Research findings indicate that more correct details are produced by cognitive than by structured interviews (Mantwill, Koehnken, & Aschermann, 1995; .org/640/00memon.ci_review.html).

Personnel Interviewing

Almost all production and service organizations use interviews, not only for selecting, classifying, and placing employees, but also for counseling, troubleshooting, termination (exit interview), and research (see Dipboye, Wooten, & Halverson, 2004; Sommers-Flanagan & Sommers-Flanagan, 2003). Because the interviewing process is expensive and time consuming, it is reasonable to wonder if it is the most efficient procedure for obtaining data on job applicants. Much of the information from a structured interview, which is the preferred approach in most employment settings, can be obtained from an application blank or questionnaire. However, job applicants are often more willing to reveal matters of significance in the personal atmosphere of an interview than in writing. In most organizational settings, for all but the lowest-level jobs, a personnel interview is the final step in the employee selection process.

A variety of information about an applicant is usually available to employment interviewers, including that supplied by the completed application form, letters of recommendation, test scores, and the like. The interviewer's task is to integrate the information obtained from all these sources and the personal interview to make a recommendation or job decision.

An employment interviewer must be cautious in asking questions regarding sensitive private matters, not only because they may place the interviewee under an emotional strain, but also because it may be illegal to ask them. Examples of questions that are and are not legally permissible are given in Box 15.1.

Reliability and Validity of Interviews

Interviewing is an important psychological tool, but it shares with observational methods the problems of reliability and validity. Reliability demands consistency, but interviewers vary in their appearance, approach, and style and, consequently, the impression that they make on interviewees. Differing impressions result in differences in behavior: a person may be friendly and outgoing with one interviewer, whereas with another he or she becomes hostile and remote. In addition, the interviewer's perceptions of the interviewee can be distorted by his or her own experiences and personality.

The reliability of an interview is usually determined by comparing the ratings given to the interviewee's responses by two or more judges. These reliabilities have large variability ranging from .23 to .97 (Mdn =.57) for ratings of personality characteristics to −.20 to .85 (Mdn = .53) for ability ratings (Arvey & Campion, 1982). Reliabilities are usually higher when the questions are specific and relate directly to the rated behaviors and are also higher when the interview is structured or at least semistructured (Campion, Pursell, & Brown, 1988; Dipboye et al., 2004). Even when the questions are fairly objective and specific and asked in a structured format, however, the interrater reliabilities of interview data are usually no higher than .80.

When conducting an interview, the interviewer is the assessment instrument. Consequently, many of the reliability problems of interviews are related to the characteristics and behavior of the interviewer. Because the interviewer is almost always in charge in an interviewing situation, his or her personality and biases are usually more important than those of the interviewee in determining the kind of information elicited. The socioemotional tone of an interview is determined more by the interviewer's actions than by those of the interviewee: the interviewer determines what will be focused on, and the length of the interviewee's answers is directly related to the length of the questions asked by the interviewer. In addition to being overly dominant, the interviewer may fail to obtain complete, accurate information by asking the wrong questions, by not encouraging complete answers or not allowing enough time for them, and by recording the responses incorrectly.

■ ■ ■ ■ ■

BOX 15.1

PERMITTED AND NONPERMITTED EMPLOYMENT QUESTIONS

Interpretive guidelines issued by the Equal Employment Opportunity Commission indicate that it is permissible to ask the following questions in an employment interview:

How many years experience do you have?
(To a housekeeper) Why do you want to return to work?
What are your career goals?
Who have been your prior employers?
Why did you leave your last job?
Are you a veteran? Did the military provide you with job-related experience?
If you have no phone, where can we reach you?
What languages do you speak fluently?
Can you do extensive traveling?
Who recommended you to us?
What did you like or dislike about your previous jobs?
What is your educational background? What schools did you attend?
What are your strong points? Weaknesses?
Do you have any objection if we check with your former employer for references?

On the other hand, it is considered legally unacceptable to ask the following questions in an employment interview:

What is your age?
What is your date of birth?
Do you have children? If so, how old are they?
What is your race?
What church do you attend?
Are you married, divorced, separated, widowed, or single?
Have you ever been arrested?
What kind of military discharge do you have?
What clubs or organizations do you belong to?
Do you rent or own your own home?
What does your wife (husband) do?
Who lives in your household?
Have your wages ever been attached or garnished?
What was your maiden name (female applicants)?

Other shortcomings of interviewers are the tendency to give more weight to first impressions and to be affected more by unfavorable than by favorable information concerning an interviewee. Errors that affect ratings also occur in interviewers' judgments. An example is the *halo effect* of making consistently favorable or unfavorable judgments on the basis of a "general impression" or a single prominent characteristic of the interviewee. This occurs when a person who is actually superior (or inferior) on only one or two characteristics is given an overall superior (or inferior) evaluation. In addition, a *contrast error* of judging an average interviewee as inferior if the preceding interviewee was clearly superior, or as superior if the preceding interviewee was clearly inferior, can occur.

Because an interviewer's impressions are influenced by the neatness, posture, and other nonverbal behaviors of the interviewee, as well as by the latter's verbal responses, prospective interviewees would do well to prepare themselves mentally and physically for an interview. In the case of an employment interview, the interviewee should have some knowledge of the organization and its philosophy. The interviewee should be prepared to give a synopsis of his or her background and aspirations, but refrain from making controversial comments or engaging in bad habits such as smoking or nail-biting during the interview (see Box 15.2).

The validity of interviews, like their reliability, is extremely variable, ranging from −.05 to +.75 (Arvey & Campion, 1982). Validity increases as the structure increases. For example, Wiesner and Cronshaw (1988) found that the overall validity of unstructured employment interviews was .20, whereas structured interviews had validity coefficients of .63. Unfortunately, most people overrate the accuracy of conclusions reached through interviews for both employee selection and clinical diagnosis (Arvey, 1979; Reilly & Chao, 1982). Interviews can be made more valid by carefully planning and structuring them and

---

■ ■ ■ ■ ■ ▬▬▬

BOX 15.2
DON'TS FOR EMPLOYMENT INTERVIEWS AND RÉSUMÉ BLOOPERS*

MAJOR "DON'TS" FOR INTERVIEWS
Don't ask "How long is this going to take?"
Don't say "I'm a people person."
Don't say "I left my last three positions because my boss picked on me."
Don't ask "How much vacation am I going to get?"
Don't say "I'm not sure what I want to do."
Don't ask "Can you sign my unemployment card?"
Don't wear a blue metallic cocktail dress.
Don't wear short shorts.
Don't leave your tattoo exposed.
Don't bring your cell phone.

SOME FAVORITE RÉSUMÉ BLOOPERS
"My career objection is . . ."
"Experienced in private relations"
"Skilled in proolreading"
"I want to work for a company where I can be depreciated."
"I have WordPurpose and Locust skills."
"I want a position to pay my bills."

*Compiled by Snelling Personnel Services.

by thoroughly training interviewers (Maurer & Fay, 1988). The results of an interview have higher validity when the interviewer (preferably more than one) focuses on specific information and responses are evaluated question by question (preferably by two or more evaluators), rather than as a whole. To facilitate this process, the entire interview should be electronically recorded for later playback and evaluation. In this way, the task of interpreting an interviewee's responses can be separated more effectively from the actual interviewing process. But even a videotape recording, and especially an audiotape recording, of an interview are not sufficient. Spoken words and pictures are not always clear, and the emotional tone and contextual variables are frequently missed in an electronic recording. For this reason, an alert human observer who takes good notes is needed to supplement an electronic recording of an interview.

Interviewing by Computer

Psychodiagnostic interviewing can often be automated by storing a set of questions and instructions in a computer. The computer asks a question, receives an answer, and decides (*conditionally branches*) what question to ask next. The branching strategy has been applied effectively in patient data systems in many psychiatric hospitals.

Computer interviewing for purposes of obtaining case histories, conducting behavior assessments, focusing on specific problems, identifying target symptoms, and assisting in psychiatric diagnosis has been growing in recent years. An example of computer software packages for psychodiagnostic interviewing and report preparation is the Diagnostic Interview for Children and Adolescents-IV (DICA-IV) Computer Program for Windows (by W. Reich, Z. Weiner, & B. Herjanic; Multi-Health Systems). Computer-assisted telephone interviewing (CATI) may be conducted with instruments such as the Primary Care Evaluation of Mental Disorders (Kobak et al., 1997), the Present State Examinations (Dignon, 1996), and the Diagnostic Interview Schedule (Alhberg, Tuck, & Allgulander, 1996; Bucholz, Marion, Shayka, Marcus, & Robins, 1996). "Talking computers" that conduct interviews on sensitive topics, particularly in cases of child abuse, are also available (e.g., Romer et al., 1997).

As with other psychometric applications of computers, the advantages of interviewing by computer are efficiency, flexibility, and reliability. Computer-based interviewing saves professional time, permits a broader coverage of topics, and is more flexible than a series of questions asked by a human interviewer. In general, there is a high degree of agreement between information obtained by computer interviewing and information elicited by standard psychiatric interviews and questionnaires. Most people do not object to being interviewed by a computer and, in fact, may be more willing to divulge personal information, particularly of a sensitive nature, to an impersonal, nonjudgmental computer than to a human interviewer (Farrell, 1993; Feigelson & Dwight, 2000; Supple, Aquilino, & Wright, 1999).

Among the disadvantages of computer-based interviewing are that it may be necessary to abbreviate or bypass the system in crisis cases, it has limited utility with children and adults of low mentality, and it may not be flexible enough to use with the wide range of problems and symptoms found in psychiatric patients. Other potential disadvantages of computer-based interviewing include difficulties in handling anything other than structured, verbal information and an inability to tailor the wording of questions to the person and the context. A sequential, unstructured interview in which successive questions are determined by the interviewee's responses to previous questions is more difficult to program than a structured interviewing procedure in which the same questions are asked of every interviewee.

Behavior Analysis and Assessment

The term *behavior modification* refers to a set of psychotherapeutic procedures based on learning theory and research and designed to change inappropriate behavior to more personally and/or socially appropriate behavior. The inappropriate behaviors may be excesses, deficits, or other inadequacies of action that are correctable through behavioral techniques such as systematic desensitization, counterconditioning, and extinction. Among maladaptive behaviors that have received special attention from behavior therapy are specific fears (or phobias), smoking, overeating, alcoholism, drug addiction, underassertiveness, bedwetting, chronic tension and pain, and sexual inadequacies. Although these target behaviors have typically been rather narrowly defined, more cognitively inclined behavior therapists have also tackled more general problems, such as negative self-concept and identity crisis. Furthermore, the target behaviors consist not only of nonverbal movements, but also of verbal reports of thoughts and feelings.

Behavior Analysis

Behavior therapists attempt to understand behavior by identifying its antecedents, including both the social learning history and current environment, and the results or consequences of this behavior. A fundamental principle of behavior modification, based on laboratory studies of operant learning, is that behavior is controlled by its consequences. In designing a program to correct problem behavior, we must identify not only the conditions that precede and trigger the behavior, but also the reinforcing consequences that sustain it. Using this approach, the process of behavior modification is preceded by a *functional analysis* of the problem behavior(s). The analysis consists of an A–B–C sequence in which A stands for the antecedent conditions, B the problem behavior, and C the consequences of this behavior. B is modified by controlling for A and altering C. The antecedents and consequences of the target behavior may be overt, objectively observable conditions or covert mental events reported by the person whose behavior is to be modified.

Behavior Assessment

Behavior assessment has multiple functions, including identifying target behaviors, alternative behaviors, and causal variables; designing intervention strategies; and reevaluating target and causal behaviors (Haynes & Heiby, 2004). Various procedures are employed, including observations and interviews, in addition to checklists, rating scales, and questionnaires completed by the patient or by a person acquainted with the patient.

Observational Methods.   The observational procedures employed in a behavior analysis involve taking note of the frequency and duration of the target behaviors and the particular contingencies (antecedents and consequences) of their occurrence. Depending on the context and the age of the patient, behavior observations can be made and recorded by teachers, parents, nurses, nursing assistants, or any other person who is acquainted with the patient.

Self-Monitoring.   Perhaps the easiest and most economical way to determine how frequently and under what conditions a particular target behavior occurs is self-observation. Although self-observation is not always reliable, people can be trained to make accurate and valid observations of their own behavior (Kendall & Norton-Ford, 1982). In self-observation for purposes of behavior analysis and modification, the person is instructed to carry at all times materials such as a note pad, a wrist counter, and a timer to keep a record of occurrences of the target behavior and the time, place, and circumstances under which it occurs. Self-observation, or *self-monitoring,* can be fairly reliable when the patient is carefully trained. Sometimes the very process of self-monitoring—observing and tabulating occurrences of specific behaviors an individual would like to change—results in a decrease of the problematic behavior. For example, heavy smokers tend to smoke less when they keep a record of how often, how long, and in what circumstances they smoke. By making themselves more aware of smoking, it becomes less automatic and more under conscious control.

Behavioral Interviewing.   Behavioral interviewing is a type of clinical interviewing in which the focus is on obtaining information to plan a program of behavior modification. This entails objectively describing the problem behaviors, as well as the antecedent conditions and the reinforcing consequences, to the interviewee. Successfully conducting such an interview requires encouraging and teaching the interviewee to respond in terms of specific behaviors, rather than in the more customary language of motives and traits. After obtaining the necessary information to develop a program of behavior modification, it is explained to the person and he or she must be motivated to stick with the program.

SUMMARY

1. Observations and interviews are the most widely used, but not necessarily the most valid, methods for assessing personality. Observations may be controlled or uncontrolled and formal or informal. Other types of observations are naturalistic, participant, and self-observations. Naturalistic observations occur in naturally occurring rather than prearranged situations. Critical incidents are important behavioral events that highlight some crucial aspect of behavior. Incident sampling is the recording of only specific types of behavior when they occur, whereas time sampling is making a series of behavioral observations for a set period of time. Participant observations are made when the observer becomes a participant in the group that is being observed. Situational testing occurs when a simulation is set up and behaviors are observed based on the simulation. The personal documents resulting from self-observations are assessed by means of content analysis. The reliability and validity of objective observations may be improved by time and incident sampling, careful training of ob-

servers, conducting the interview as unobtrusively as possible, and electronic recording. Observers should be trained to attend to both verbal and nonverbal behaviors.

2. Information on a person's life history can be obtained efficiently from an application blank or biographical inventory, in addition to conversing with people who know the person. Letters of recommendation are also used extensively, but they are often of questionable value. This is particularly true when the recommender knows that the letter may be read by the person about whom it is written. Sometimes a psychobiography is developed based on records of a person's life. These can be used to help predict how a person might respond to future types of situations.

3. Depending on their purposes and the skills of the interviewers, interviews may be structured, semistructured, or unstructured. Structured interviews have the advantage of being easier to follow, covering all necessary areas, and having fairly good reliability and validity. However, due to their lack of flexibility, they may not explore crucial but unexpected areas and may have minimal rapport. Flexible interviews can explore novel aspects of the person and may have better levels of rapport, but their reliability and validity are generally lower than for more structured interviews. Interviews may be conducted for clinical, educational, employment, and other purposes. Good interviewing skills involve being warm, open, and accepting; taking careful behavioral observations; checking for understanding; understanding the context of the person's life; and being sensitive to cultural and gender issues. Often interviewers begin with open-ended questions and then become more closed-ended to clarify specific areas of information that were not clear.

4. The methode clinique requires considerable skill since it requires interviewers to explore and test the limits of of an interviewee's experience. Stress interviews involve the use of a confrontational approach designed to break down resistance and defenses. Cognitive interviewing is designed to optimize the accuracy of eyewitness reports during police interrogation. It covers an interviewee's experience and memory of a situation in a systematic manner.

5. The reliability and validity of interviews is extremely variable since they can be reduced by variations in selecting what information to pursue, halo effects, contrast error, incorrect recording of answers, and failure to obtain complete information. Despite these sources of error, people overrate their accuracy. Interview reliability and validity can be improved by increasing the structure of the interview, thorough training of interviewers, multiple ratings of the same area, rating specific questions, and making an objective recording of the results of the interview. A number of standard interview schedules, primarily for use in clinical situations, have been published. In addition to traditional face-to-face interviewing, some interviews are conducted by computer and/or over the telephone.

6. Both observation and interviewing are used in behavior analysis and in designing behavior-modification programs. Behavior analysis consists of the application of various techniques to obtain information about a patient whose behavior is maladaptive in some way. A behavior analysis results in the specification of antecedent conditions (A), maladaptive target behaviors (B), and the consequences of these behaviors (C). Behavioral assessment is done through observational methods, self-monitoring, and behavioral interviewing.

MASTERING THE CHAPTER OBJECTIVES

1. *Principles of observation*
   a. Provide brief definitions of critical incidents, incident sampling, time sampling, participant observation, situational testing, nonverbal behaviors, self-observation, and content analysis.
   b. What are the assets and limitations of observation (think of their relative simplicity, objectivity, reliability, and validity)?
   c. In what kinds of situations or circumstances would it be appropriate to use participant observation? What kinds of information can participant observation be expected to provide, and what are its shortcomings?

2. *Biographical data*
   a. Describe how a psychobiography is different from a regular biography.
   b. How would you design a selection procedure using biographical data? What are the assets and limitations of such a procedure?

3. *Interviewing*
   a. How is an interview different from an ordinary conversation?
   b. What are the characteristics that make a good interview?
   c. What are the advantages and disadvantages of structured versus unstructured interviews?

4. *Specialized interviews*
   a. Define what is meant by the methode clinique, stress interviewing, and cognitive interviewing.
   b. What are some guidelines in conducting a personnel interview?

5. *Reliability and validity of interviews*
   a. Summarize the reliability and validity of interviews.
   b. What can be done to improve their reliability and validity?

6. *Behavior assessment*
   a. Describe what is meant by behavior analysis, observational methods, self-monitoring, and behavioral interviewing
   b. What kinds of problems do you feel are most appropriate for behavioral assessment? Why?

EXPERIENCING PSYCHOLOGICAL ASSESSMENT

1. Select a person in one of your classes as a subject for observation, preferably someone whom you do not know and toward whom you have neutral feelings. Observe the person over a period of three or four class meetings and inconspicuously record what he or she does and says. Try to be as objective as possible, looking for consistent, typical behaviors, as well as noting responses that occur infrequently. At the end of the observation period, write a two- to three-page characterization of the person. Without having access to any other information about the person (what other students say about the person, how well he or she does in college, etc.), how would you describe his or her personality and characteristic behavior? Finally, check your observations against those of other people who know or have observed this person. After this experience of close observation using a time sampling technique, how do

you feel about objective observation as a method of assessing personality? Is it reliable, valid, and useful?

2. Review the discussion of interviewing procedures in this chapter and other interviewing guidelines available to you. Then conduct a structured personal interview of someone you do not know well. Write up the results as a formal report, giving identifying information, a summary of the interview findings, and recommendations pertaining to the interviewee.

3. Prepare a list of questions to be asked during an employment interview, and conduct the interview with an acquaintance of yours. Feel free to deviate from the interview schedule if you think of questions that are more pertinent to the person's (applicant's) performance on the job(s) for which he or she is applying. Make certain that all questions are both relevant and legally permissible.

CHAPTER SIXTEEN

CHECKLISTS AND RATING SCALES

1. Define checklists and describe how to select and score them.

2. Describe the different types of checklists, including the following examples: Adjective Checklist, Multiple Affect Adjective Checklist-Revised, State–Trait Anxiety Inventory, Child Behavior Checklist, Teacher's Report Form, Revised Behavior Problem Checklist, and the Symptom Checklist-90-R.

3. Describe different formats for rating scales, including numerical scales, unipolar and bipolar scales, semantic differential, graphic rating scale, visual analogue scale, standard rating scale, behaviorally anchored scales, forced-choice scales, and Q-sorts.

4. Describe types of rating scales.

5. Discuss the problems with rating scales.

Information obtained from observations and interviews, whether formally or informally, can be recorded in a variety of ways. Because of the large mass of data produced in lengthy observational and interviewing sessions, the findings are almost always summarized in some form. Together with a condensed written description, checklists and rating scales are useful devices for summarizing data obtained from observations and interviews. Whereas checklist items usually require only dichotomous (check–not check, yes–no, etc.) responses, three choices (check yes, check no, or do not check) are provided on some checklists. On rating scales, respondents are required to make evaluative judgments on an ordered series of three or more categories.

Exceeded in popularity only by achievement tests, checklists and rating scales are convenient, economical, and versatile psychometric instruments. They can be easily constructed, conveniently administered with only paper and pencil, used to describe oneself or someone or something else, and adapted to the measurement of a wide range of behaviors, personal characteristics, and other objects, events, or conditions. Hundreds of checklists and rating scales are commercially available. These instruments may be administered alone or in combination with other methods for evaluating people and other things.

CHARACTERISTICS OF CHECKLISTS

A *checklist* is a relatively simple, highly cost effective, and fairly reliable method of describing or evaluating a person. It consists of a list of words, phrases, or statements descriptive of a person or some other object or event. They are more easily constructed than rating scales or personality inventories and often just as valid and can be administered as self-report or observer-report instruments. Respondents are instructed to check, underline, or otherwise indicate which word(s) or phrase(s) is descriptive of themselves (self-checking) or of someone or something else. Because, unlike rating scales, checklists do not require respondents to make explicit decisions about the quality, frequency, or intensity of behaviors and characteristics, they are more efficient. Rating scales can provide more detailed information than checklists, but it takes longer to complete them. Consequently, there is perhaps a kind of speed–accuracy trade-off between the two kinds of instruments.

Checklists are used extensively in clinical, educational, and industrial–organizational contexts. Although some checklists are standardized, commercially available instruments, many checklists have been prepared for special purposes or for use in specific contexts. For example, the checklist in Form 16.1 is a nonstandardized instrument designed to measure Type A behavior. Two other examples of nonstandardized checklists are the Social Readjustment Rating Scale (Holmes & Rahe, 1967) and the Behavioral Checklist for Performance Anxiety (Paul, 1966).

Social Readjustment Scale

The Social Readjustment Scale (SRS) was designed to study the effects of life changes, both negative and positive, on behavior and physiological reactions to the stress produced by such changes (Holmes & Rahe, 1967). The theory on which the 43-item SRS is based assumes that the greater the degree of readjustment in a given year, the higher is the probability that the respondent will develop a stress-related illness. Each item on the SRS has a scoring weight of 0 to 100, depending on the degree of readjustment required by the event described in the item. After evaluating criticisms concerning the SRS, Scully, Tosi, and Banning (2000) concluded that it is a useful tool for stress researchers and practitioners.

Behavioral Checklist of Performance Anxiety

A second checklist that is not commercially available, the Behavioral Checklist for Performance Anxiety, is shown in Form 16.2. This instrument is used to assess the effects on anxiety of a type of behavior therapy known as *systematic desensitization*. An advantage of this and similar checklists is that they can be completed repeatedly or periodically to determine whether changes in behavior have occurred as a result of treatment. A check is made in each

FORM 16.1   Descriptive Checklist

Directions: Make a check mark on the line for every item that is descriptive of you.

___ 1. achievement oriented	___ 11. emotionally explosive
___ 2. aggressive	___ 12. fast worker
___ 3. ambitious	___ 13. hard worker
___ 4. competitive	___ 14. highly motivated
___ 5. constant worker	___ 15. impatient
___ 6. dislikes wasting time	___ 16. likes challenges
___ 7. easily angered	___ 17. likes to lead
___ 8. easily aroused to action	___ 18. likes responsibility
___ 9. easily frustrated	___ 19. restless
___ 10. efficient	___ 20. tries hard to succeed

---

box in Form 16.2 to indicate the occurrence of the corresponding behavior during the designated time period (1 through 8).

Selecting a Checklist

Although nonstandardized checklists such as the above are not necessarily makeshift or shoddy, rarely are they adequately validated. Consequently, it is uncertain whether the checklist is serving its intended purposes. For this reason, it is wise to consider one of the many commercially available checklists before constructing a new one. Checklists of adaptive behavior, developmental progress, health problems, personal characteristics, personal history, personal problems, and psychopathological symptoms are all commercially available. There are checklists for anxiety, depression, hostility, psychopathy, and mental status, as well as checklists for marital, sexual, and interpersonal relations in adults (see Aiken, 1996). Whether standardized or not, or commercially available or not, the following questions should be considered in selecting any checklist or rating scale:

1. What variables (constructs) are measured by the instrument, and how are they defined?
2. What is the rationale on which the instrument is based (a specific theory of personality or behavior, previous research findings, etc.)?
3. What special training or specific conditions are required for using the instrument? By whom and under what conditions (environmental context, materials, etc.) can it be used?
4. How is the instrument scored, and what materials are needed to score it? Can it be scored quickly and accurately by hand, or is a computer or other scoring machine needed?
5. Has the instrument been standardized? If so, was the standardization group representative of the people who will be evaluated with the instrument?
6. What kinds of evidence are presented for the reliability of the instrument (test–retest, parallel forms, internal consistency, or other)?
7. What kinds of evidence for the validity (content, criterion related, construct) of the instrument are presented or available from other sources?

FORM 16.2   Behavioral Checklist for Performance Anxiety

BEHAVIOR OBSERVED	TIME PERIOD							
	1	2	3	4	5	6	7	8
1 Paces								
2 Sways								
3 Shuffles feet								
4 Knees tremble								
5 Extraneous arm and hand movement (swings, scratches, toys, etc.)								
6 Arms rigid								
7 Hands restrained (in pockets, behind back, clasped)								
8 Hand tremors								
9 No eye contact								
10 Face muscles tense (drawn, tics, grimaces)								
11 Face deadpan								
12 Face pale								
13 Face flushed (blushes)								
14 Moistens lips								
15 Swallows								
16 Clears throat								
17 Breathes heavily								
18 Perspires (face, hands, armpits)								
19 Voice quivers								
20 Speech blocks or stammers								

Scoring Checklists

A checklist consisting of a set of discrete, unrelated items is usually not scored as an aggregate, but rather responses to individual items are examined, both within and across respondents. The number of respondents who answer a given item can, of course, be determined and compared with the number who answer each of the other items.

Conventional scoring of responses to interrelated sets of checklist items designed to measure the same variable typically begins by giving 1 point to each checked item and 0 points to each unchecked item; a score of 1 is given if checking the item indicates a favorable response, and a score 0 if checking it indicates an unfavorable response toward whatever the variable expressed in the item may be. Scoring weights other than 0 and 1 are assigned in certain cases, as when the items are scaled according to their importance. When the number of items is large, however, giving different weights to different items generally has little effect on the reliability or validity of the instrument. When a number of respondents evaluate the same person on a checklist, a group score on each item may be determined by counting the number of respondents who checked the item.

When respondents are not instructed to check a certain number of items, different respondents may check different numbers of items. Because this *frequency–response set,* as it is sometimes called, can have a pronounced effect on overall scores, some method of compensating for it is needed. For example, separate norms on the various scales of the Adjective Check List (ACL) are provided for each of five "Number Checked" interval groups. To convert a person's raw score on the ACL scales to standard scores, the scorer uses the raw score-to-standard score conversion tables listed for the group, in which the "Number Checked" interval contains the number of adjectives checked by the person. Other methods of statistically controlling for the frequency response set are described by Aiken (1996).

Reliability and Validity

Scores (0's and 1's) on the individual items on a checklist have lower reliabilities than sums of scores on several items. Reliability coefficients for summed scores across items may be determined by means of the test–retest, internal consistency, and parallel forms methods described in Chapter 5. The reliabilities of checklists determined by these procedures are typically lower than those for cognitive tests. An alternative approach to determining the reliability of sets of checklist items is the method of interchecker agreement or concordance. This method consists of computing a single agreement score (phi) from the concordance of the check-mark configurations of two or more checkers (Sinacore, Connell, Olthoff, Friedman, & Gecht, 1999).

With respect to the validity of checklists, research findings indicate that checklist scores have significant correlations with a wide range of performance criteria. Scores on checklists of employee performance, treatment effectiveness, and other criteria are also significantly related to scores on various predictor variables. For example, Boyle and his associates (Boyle et al., 1996, 1997) found that both the reliability and validity coefficients of checklists of psychiatric disorders were similar to if not higher than those of interviews. And MacRae et al. (1995) found that checklist scores tended to correlate higher with physicians' ratings than scores on databases completed by students. In a study of the psychometric properties of a standardized-patient checklist and rating-scale form for assessing interpersonal and communication skills, Cohen et al. (1996) found that the reliability of the rating form was slightly higher than that of the checklist. However, self-ratings have been found to have only low to moderate correlations (.30 to .68) with ratings by informants who are familiar with the person doing the self-rating (Achenbach, Krukowski, Dumenci, & Ivanova, 2005).

TYPES AND EXAMPLES OF CHECKLISTS

Adjective Checklists

Very popular and easy to construct is a checklist consisting of a series of adjectives, such as aggressive, ambitious, competitive, efficient, explosive, impatient, irritable, restless, and tense. People of whom these nine adjectives are descriptive are sometimes designated as Type A personality (see Form 16.1 and *Experiencing Psychological Assessment*, Exercise 3). Two of the most popular standardized adjective checklists are the Adjective Check List (ACL) (from CPP) and the Multiple Affect Adjective Checklist (from EdITS).

Adjective Check List (ACL).   The Adjective Check List (ACL) consists of 300 adjectives arranged alphabetically from *absentminded* to *zany*. Examinees take 15 to 20 minutes to mark the adjectives that they consider to be self-descriptive. These responses may then be scored on the 37 scales described in the ACL manual: 4 modus operandi scales, 15 need scales, 9 topical scales, 5 transactional analysis scales, and 4 origence–intellectence (creativity and intelligence) scales. Scores on the modus operandi scales (total number of adjectives checked, number of favorable adjectives checked, number of unfavorable adjectives checked, communality) pertain to the manner in which the respondent has dealt with the checklist. The need scales (scales 5 to 19) are based on Edwards's (1954) descriptions of 15 needs in Murray's (1938) need-press theory of personality. Each topical scale (scales 20 to 28) assesses a different topic or component of interpersonal behavior (e.g., counseling readiness, personal adjustment, creative personality, masculine attributes). The transactional analysis scales (scales 29 to 33) are described as measures of the five ego functions in Berne's (1966) transactional analysis. The origence–intellectence scales (scales 34 to 37) are described as measures of Welsh's origence–intellectence (creativity and intelligence) dimensions of personality.

For purposes of interpretation and counseling, raw scores on the ACL are converted to standard T scores. As an illustration, the 37 T scores and the associated profile of the cases described in Psychological Report 16.1 are given in Table 16.1. The T scores are interpreted with reference to norms based on samples of 5,236 males and 4,144 females in 37 states. Profiles and associated interpretations for six sample cases, one of which is summarized in Report 16.1, are also provided. The internal consistency reliabilities of most of the 37 scales are reasonably high, but test–retest reliability data are limited. The manual reports test–retest reliability coefficients for the separate scales ranging from .34 for the high-origence, low-intellectence scale to .77 for the aggression scale (median of .65) and also describes many uses of the ACL and research investigations in which it has been used.

Reviews of the ACL have been fairly positive, concluding that the instrument is well developed (Teeter, 1985; Zarske, 1985). The scales are significantly intercorrelated and therefore should not be interpreted as independent factors. A factor analysis that one of the authors (L. A.) of this book conducted on the 15 need scales (scales 5 to 19) yielded three factors: Self-confidence or Ego Strength, Goal Orientation, and Social Interactiveness or Friendliness. The ACL has been used primarily with normal adolescents and adults, and its validity in psychodiagnosis and treatment planning has not been determined. It has been found most useful in research on the self-concept.

PSYCHOLOGICAL REPORT 16.1   Case Description
Accompanying Adjective Check List Scores in Table 16.1

This 19-year-old undergraduate student majoring in biology maintained an A grade average and planned to go to graduate school. She was brought up in a close-knit, large family and had warm feelings about her parents and her childhood. Before college, she had always lived in small towns or semirural areas. Coming to an urban college required quite an adjustment, but she liked the excitement and stimulation of city life. She retained her religious beliefs and regularly attended church. She viewed herself as a political and economic conservative. Her life history interviewer described her in the following way:

> She is an intelligent, vivacious, attractive young woman, enthusiastic about her life at the university. Although she views herself as introverted, her behavior is more extroverted; she was talkative, outgoing, candid, and not hesitant to assume a leadership role. Her parents were strict, expected the children to assume responsibilities, and placed a high value on academic achievement. She described her mother as a demanding, extremely shy woman who participated in social activities from a sense of duty. She said her father was somewhat intimidating, but affectionate; she feels closer to him now than she did when she was growing up. Being at school—away from home and the relative isolation of that environment—is very exciting.

Scores on her ACL profile are in agreement with the case history data and staff evaluations. Moderate elevations occur on the scales for Achievement, Self-confidence, and Personal Adjustment and scores of 60 or greater on the scales for Ideal Self, Creative Personality, and A-2 (high origence, high intellectence). The ACL profile also revealed scores of 60 or greater on the scales for Favorable, Communality, Femininity, Critical Parent, and A-4 (low origence, high intellectence). Although the staff rating of 54 on Femininity was above average for the sample of 80 students included in this project, it is not as high as the score of 69 on her self-descriptive ACL. Because she had scores greater than 50 on both Masculinity and Femininity, she is in the androgynous cell in the interaction diagram between the two scales. The profile also reveals elevated scores on *both* Favorable and Unfavorable, which suggests she is more complex, internally differentiated, and less repressive than her peers.

Multiple Affect Adjective Checklist-Revised.   The Multiple Affect Adjective Checklist-Revised (MAACL-R) (Zuckerman & Lubin, 1985) consists of 132 adjectives and is available for administration in two forms: trait ("In General") and state ("Today"). Depending on the form, examinees check the adjectives that indicate how they generally feel (on the trait form) or how they feel today or at present (on the state form). Both forms have been shown to discriminate between patients with affective disorders and patients with other disorders or from nonpatients. Standard T scores on both the trait and state forms are obtained on five basic scales: Anxiety (A), Depression (D), Hostility (H), Positive Affect (PA), and Sensation Seeking (SS). Two summary standard scores, Dysphoria (Dys = A + D + H) and Positive Affect and Sensation Seeking (PASS = PA + SS), may also be computed. Norms for the trait form of the MAACL-R are based on a representative nationwide sample of 1,491 individuals aged 18 years and over; norms for the state form are based on a (nonrepresentative) sample of 538 students at a midwestern college. With the exception of the Sensation Seeking scale, the internal-consistency reliability coefficients for both the trait and

TABLE 16.1 Scales and Sample *T* Scores on the Adjective Check List

SCALE NAME AND DESIGNATION	*T* SCORES FOR THE CASE IN REPORT 16.1	SCALE NAME AND DESIGNATION	*T* SCORES FOR THE CASE IN REPORT 16.1
Modus Operandi		*Topical Scales*	
1. Total number of adjectives checked (No Ckd)	37	20. Counseling readiness (Crs)	55
		21. Self-control (S-Cn)	48
2. Number of favorable adjectives checked (Fav)	62	22. Self-confidence (S-Cfd)	59
		23. Personal adjustment (P-Adj)	53
3. Number of unfavorable adjectives checked (Unfav)	59	24. Ideal self (Iss)	64
		25. Creative personality (Cps)	63
4. Communality (Com)	68	26. Military leadership (Mls)	52
		27. Masculine attributes (Mas)	54
Need Scales		28. Feminine attributes (Fem)	69
5. Achievement (Ach)	57		
6. Dominance (Dom)	50	*Transactional Analysis*	
7. Endurance (End)	53	29. Critical parent (CP)	62
8. Order (Ord)	57	30. Nurturing parent (NP)	48
9. Intraception (Int)	57	31. Adult (A)	56
10. Nurturance (Nur)	44	32. Free child (FC)	46
11. Affiliation (Aff)	53	33. Adapted child (AC)	41
12. Heterosexuality (Het)	46		
13. Exhibition (Exh)	44	*Origence–Intellectence*	
14. Autonomy (Aut)	49	34. High origence, low intellectence (A-1)	47
15. Aggression (Agg)	58		
16. Change (Cha)	58	35. High origence, high intellectence (A-2)	64
17. Succorance (Suc)	41		
18. Abasement (Aba)	56	36. Low origence, low intellectence (A-3)	44
19. Deference (Def)	49	37. Low origence, high intellectence (A-4)	63

(Modified and reproduced by special permission of the Publisher, CPP, Inc., Mountain View, CA 94043 from *The Adjective Check List Manual* by Harrison G. Gough, Ph.D., and Alfred B. Heilbrun, Jr., Ph.D. All rights reserved. Further reproduction is prohibited without the publisher's written consent.)

state scales are adequate. The test–retest reliabilities are satisfactory for the trait scales, but low for the state scales, as might be expected from momentary fluctuations in attitudes and behavior. The results of validity studies on various populations, including normal adolescents and adults, counseling clients, and patients from clinics and state hospitals, are reported in the MAACL-R manual (Zuckerman & Lubin, 1985). Scores on the MAACL-R correlate in the expected direction with other measures of personality (e.g., the Minnesota Multiphasic Personality Inventory, the Profile of Mood States, peer ratings, self-ratings, and psychiatric diagnoses).

State–Trait Anxiety Inventory (STAI). The State–Trait Anxiety Inventory (Psychological Assessment Resources) is a 20-item, self-report inventory that readily allows examiners to determine the extent and nature of a person's anxiety. This makes it very useful for planning, monitoring, and evaluating psychological treatment. As the title suggests, effort was placed into distinguishing between the more transitory (state) from the more enduring (trait) aspects of anxiety. Test–retest reliability over a 30- to 60-day interval was good for trait anxiety ($r = .73–.86$) and, as expected, low for state anxiety ($r = .36$ for females and .51 for males). Much higher internal consistency reliabilities were found for both state ($r = .88–.93$) and trait ($r = .92–.94$) anxiety (see Groth-Marnat, 2003). The validity of the STAI is supported (Groth-Marnat, 2003; Spielberger & Reheiser, 2004) in that high scores were associated with diagnoses of anxiety disorders. The STAI has also been found to correlate with other measures of anxiety and is sensitive to the impact of a wide number of interventions. However, it has been difficult to determine optimal cutoff scores for the presence of an anxiety disorder. In addition, factor analysis has found that it is not a pure measure of anxiety, but seems to be associated with the more general characteristic of negative affect, as well as depression. Despite these limitations, it is an ideal instrument for treatment planning, which is reflected in its widespread use in clinical and research settings.

Problem Checklists

A number of checklists have been designed to identify behavioral problems in children, one of the oldest being the Mooney Problem Checklists. One of the most frequently cited instruments of this type is the Child Behavior Checklist (CBCL). Like the Mooney Problem Checklists, the CBLC is a *broadband instrument* that provides a fairly comprehensive overview of social, behavioral, and emotional functioning. Another example of a broadband problem checklist is the Revised Behavior Problem Checklist (RBPC). Unlike the Mooney, which is a *self-report instrument,* the last two checklists are *informant instruments* that are completed by a parent or teacher. Strictly speaking, they are rating scales rather than checklists, in that responses are made on multiple categories.

Child Behavior Checklist.   This instrument was designed to assess the behavioral problems and competencies of children as reported by their parents or others who know the child well. The parent version of the CBCL consists of 118 behavior problem items to be rated on a scale of 0 (behavior "not true" of child), 1 (behavior "sometimes or somewhat true" of child), and 2 (behavior "very true or often true" of child). Scores on the social competency items are summed as Activities, Social, and School subscores.

The CBCL was standardized in 1981 on 1,300 students in the Washington, D.C., area, and separate norms by gender and three age levels (4 to 5, 6 to 11, 12 to 16 years) on eight to nine factors are provided in the manual (Achenbach & Edelbrock, 1983). The norms yield six different Child Behavior Profiles on eight to nine factors; they are grouped into Externalizing, Internalizing, and Mixed Syndromes. Test–retest reliability coefficients on the behavior problems and social competence variables are moderate to high, while those of the indexes of parental agreement are mixed. A substantial amount of validity data has been collected on the CBCL (Greenbaum, Dedrick, & Lipien, 2004). For example, CBCL scores are significantly correlated with scores on similar instruments, such as the Conners Parent Rating Scale (Conners, 1973; Conners & Barkley, 1985) and the Revised Behavior Problem Checklist (Quay & Peterson, 1983).

Teacher's Report Form.[1] A parallel version of the Child Behavior Checklist, the Teacher's Report Form (TRF) (Achenbach & Edelbrock, 1986), is completed by teachers or teacher aides. The TRF provides a picture of the problem and adaptive behaviors of children in school settings. Respondents indicate on a 3-point scale ("not true," "somewhat or sometimes true," "very often true") how frequently specific behaviors occurred during the past 2 months. The child's academic performance is rated on a 5-point scale ("far below grade" through "far above grade"), and four items concerned with adaptive behavioral functioning are rated on a 7-point scale ("much less" through "much more"). The TRF was initially standardized on a sample of 6- to 11-year-old boys, but norms on other groups of children have also been determined. Reported reliability and validity data for the TRF appear to be satisfactory (Edelbrock & Achenbach, 1984). For example, comparisons between the TRF scores of clinical and nonclinical groups of children, in addition to a comparison of children in regular classes with those in special education, have yielded significant results. Correlations of children's TRF scores with their observed behaviors have also been found to be significant (Edelbrock, 1988). A Youth Self-Report Form (YSR) of the CBCL, designed for 11- to 18-year-old boys and girls, is also available (Achenbach & Edelbrock, 1987). Both the TRF and the YSR have received high marks from reviewers as instruments for documenting the problem behaviors of children and adolescents (Christenson, 1992). Users of these instruments should note, however, that they can contribute to the processes of clinical interviewing and clinical decision making, but they are not adequate, stand-alone instruments for diagnostic or classification purposes.

Revised Behavior Problem Checklist (RBPC). Similar to the Mooney checklists, this 89-item instrument (from PAR) was designed to identify problem behaviors in individuals aged 5 to 18 years (Quay & Peterson, 1983). It has been used to screen for behavior disorders in schools, as an aid in clinical diagnosis, to measure behavior change associated with psychological or pharmacological interventions, as part of a battery to classify juvenile offenders, and to select samples for research on behavior disorders in children and adolescents. It can be completed by a teacher, parent, or other observer in approximately 20 minutes and scored on six subscales: conduct disorder, socialized aggression, attention problems–immaturity, anxiety–withdrawal, psychotic behavior, and motor tension–excess. *T* score norms based on teachers' ratings are available for grades K–12. The interrater reliability coefficients for the six subscales are moderate to high, but the test–retest reliabilities are somewhat lower. Analysis of the construct validity of the RBPC indicates that it represents a consensus of what is known about maladaptive child behavior.

Symptom Checklists

More clinically oriented than adjective checklists or checklists of problem behaviors are symptom checklists such as the Mental Status Checklist Series and the Derogatis Symptom Checklist Series. Each of the two Mental Status Checklists consists of 120 items of the sort

---

[1]The Child Behavior Checklist, the Teacher's Report Form, and the Youth Self-Report Form are available from T. M. Achenbach & C. Edelbrock, Department of Psychiatry, University of Vermont.

included in a comprehensive mental status examination of an adult: presenting problem, referral data, demographics, mental status, personality function and symptoms, diagnosis, and disposition.

The most popular clinical instrument in the Derogatis Symptom Checklist Series is the Symptom Checklist-90-Revised (SCL-90-R) (Derogatis, 1994; from NCS Assessments). Mental health professionals can administer the SCL-90-R in 12 to 15 minutes to evaluate adolescent or adult psychiatric patients at intake, to screen for psychological problems, to monitor patient progress or changes during treatment, and to assess posttreatment outcomes (www.pearsonassessments.com/tests/scl90r.htm). The SCL-90-R is scored on nine primary symptom dimensions: Somatization, Obsessive Compulsive, Interpersonal Sensitivity, Depression, Anxiety, Hostility, Phobic Anxiety, Paranoid Ideation, and Psychoticism. The level or depth of a disorder, the intensity of the symptoms, and the number of patient-reported symptoms are indicated by three different scales. Norms for nonpatient adults, nonpatient adolescents, psychiatric outpatients, and psychiatric inpatients are available (Groth-Marnat, 2003). Reliability (internal consistency) for the nine primary symptom dimensions ranged from a low of .79 for Paranoid Ideation to a high of .90 for Depression. Test–retest reliability over a 1-week duration ranged from a low of .78 for Hostility to a high of .90 for Phobic Anxiety. Validity is supported in that scores on the SCL-90-R have been found to correlate with similar scales and relate to expected diagnostic groups (i.e., scores on the Paranoid Ideation dimension were associated with persons diagnosed with paranoid conditions). The SCL-90-R was also correlated with the general level of distress a person was experiencing (see Groth-Marnat, 2003).

STRATEGIES FOR CONSTRUCTING RATING SCALES

Rating scales, which were introduced as psychological research instruments by Francis Galton during the latter part of the 19th century, are popular assessment devices in clinical, school, employment, sports, and entertainment contexts. Ratings may be made either by the ratee (the person being rated) or another rater. Rating scales are generally viewed as less precise than personality inventories and more superficial than projective techniques. Whether this perception is correct, rating scales have the dual advantages of economy and versatility of construction and scoring.

An alternative to a rating scale is a ranking scale, on which respondents assign ranks of 1 to *n* to *n* people, objects, or events (see Experiencing Psychological Assessment, Exercise 4). Although ranking instruments are fairly simple to construct, they are often cumbersome to use: the rankers may have difficulty making the large number of comparisons required by the ranking procedure. Scoring the responses to a ranking instrument is not particularly difficult (see Chapter 3), but statistical analysis of the results poses some problems.

It is not particularly difficult to construct a rating scale. All we need do is designate or define the objects to be evaluated, the attributes or characteristics of the objects to be rated, and the categories (anchors) or continuum on which the ratings will be made. Sometimes this can be based on an underlying theory or deductive basis. For example, ratings of the use of defense mechanisms may be based on existing lists derived from psychoanalytic theory. It is also possible to form items based on a factor analysis of the variable in question. For example, ratings of various abilities can be based on factor analytic studies of intelligence. Finally, items might be determined based on how well they correlate with external measures of interest. Any items that do not have good correlations with these external measures can be deleted from the scale.

These three strategies for constructing rating scales are, of course, not mutually exclusive: two or all three may be employed at some juncture in the process of constructing a particular rating scale. Furthermore, the strategies are not limited to rating scales. The construction of checklists, personality inventories, projective techniques, and other personality assessment devices may all rely on one or more of these strategies (see also Chapter 17 for strategies of scale construction).

FORMATS FOR RATING SCALES

Just as there are various strategies for constructing rating scales, there are different formats for presenting and responding to items on these instruments. Among the formats are numerical scales, visual analogue scales, semantic differential scales, graphic rating scales, standard rating scales, behaviorally anchored scales, and forced-choice scales.

Numerical Scale

On this type of rating scale, a person, object, or event is assigned one of several numbers corresponding to particular descriptions of the characteristics being rated. All that is required is for the ratings to be made on an ordered scale on which different numerical values are assigned to different locations. Form 16.3 is an illustrative instrument containing 15 numerical rating scales that can be used to rate oneself or someone else. Responses are scored on five personality variables: agreeableness, conscientiousness, extroversion, neuroticism, and openness. Scores on each variable range from 0 to 18.

Unipolar and Bipolar Scales

Numerical rating scales, and many other types of scales as well, may be either unipolar or bipolar. On a *unipolar scale,* the attribute being rated (e.g., aggressiveness) is seen as one-dimensional and thereby as increasing from a minimum to some maximum amount; the scale values (anchors) are a series of increasing integers. The anchors on a 5-point scale, for example, may be 0, 1, 2, 3, 4 or 1, 2, 3, 4, 5. On a *bipolar scale,* the rated attribute is viewed as varying in two directions (e.g., submissive–aggressive); consequently, the middle of the scale is represented as 0, and the two ends (poles) are the maximum negative and positive integers. For example, the numerical categories on a 5-point bipolar scale are –2, –1, 0, 1, 2.

A unipolar scale is typically scored by giving 0 points to ratings in the category corresponding to the lowest amount of the rated attribute. In contrast, higher scores are given to higher scoring attributes. These are calculated by using using the formula $c - 1$, where c

FORM 16.3   Five-Variable Personality Rating Scale

Directions: For each item, check the number between the pair of adjectives corresponding to your description of yourself.

1. affectionate	1 2 3 4 5 6 7	reserved
2. calm	1 2 3 4 5 6 7	worrying
3. careful	1 2 3 4 5 6 7	careless
4. conforming	1 2 3 4 5 6 7	independent
5. disorganized	1 2 3 4 5 6 7	well organized
6. down to earth	1 2 3 4 5 6 7	imaginative
7. fun loving	1 2 3 4 5 6 7	sober
8. helpful	1 2 3 4 5 6 7	uncooperative
9. insecure	1 2 3 4 5 6 7	secure
10. prefer routine	1 2 3 4 5 6 7	prefer variety
11. retiring	1 2 3 4 5 6 7	sociable
12. ruthless	1 2 3 4 5 6 7	soft-hearted
13. self-disciplined	1 2 3 4 5 6 7	weak-willed
14. self-pitying	1 2 3 4 5 6 7	self-satisfied
15. suspicious	1 2 3 4 5 6 7	trusting

Scoring formulas for the five variables are as follows:

Agreeableness = 5 + item 12 + item 15 – item 8

Conscientiousness = 13 – item 3 + item 5 – item 13

Extroversion = 13 – item 1 – item 7 + item 11

Neuroticism = 13 + item 2 – item 9 – item 14

Openness = item 4 + item 6 + item 10 – 3

is the number of rating categories. Item scores may then be summed to yield a partial score on a particular group of items or a total score on the entire instrument.

The scoring of ratings on bipolar scales involves two steps. First, the same number of points (0 to $c – 1$) as on a unipolar scale is assigned to the successive ratings, from the lowest to the highest category. Second, points are subtracted from each of the category points in step 1. For example, when there are five bipolar categories, 0, 1, 2, 3, and 4 points are first assigned to the successive rating categories. Subtracting $(5 - 1)/2 = 2$ from each of these values yields $-2, -1, 0, 1$, and 2, which are the item scores for ratings in the five successive categories of the bipolar scale. As with ratings on a unipolar scale, the resulting item scores may then be added to provide either a part or total score.

Semantic Differential

A type of numerical rating scale that has frequently been used in research on personality and social psychology is the *semantic differential.* Osgood, Suci, and Tannenbaum (1957) devised this method for their studies of the connotative (personal) meanings that concepts such as *father, mother, sickness, sin, hatred,* and *love* have for different people. When taking a semantic differential instrument, the person rates a series of concepts on several 7-point, bipolar adjectival scales. For example, the concept *mother* might be rated by making a check mark on the appropriate line segment on each of the following three scales:

$$\text{BAD} \ \_\_\_:\_\_\_:\_\_\_:\_\_\_:\_\_\_:\_\_\_:\_\_\_ \ \text{GOOD}$$
$$\text{WEAK} \ \_\_\_:\_\_\_:\_\_\_:\_\_\_:\_\_\_:\_\_\_:\_\_\_ \ \text{STRONG}$$
$$\text{SLOW} \ \_\_\_:\_\_\_:\_\_\_:\_\_\_:\_\_\_:\_\_\_:\_\_\_ \ \text{FAST}$$

After all concepts of interest have been rated on the various scales, responses to each concept are scored on several *semantic dimensions* and compared with responses to the remaining concepts. The main connotative meaning (semantic) dimensions that have been determined by factor analysis of ratings of a series of concepts on a large number of these adjectival scales are *evaluation, potency,* and *activity.* A *semantic space* may then be constructed by plotting a person's scores on the rated concepts on each of these three dimensions. Concepts falling close to each other in the semantic space presumably have similar connotative meanings for the rater.

Graphic Rating Scale

Another popular type of rating scale is a *graphic rating scale,* an example of which is

How well does this person cooperate in a group?

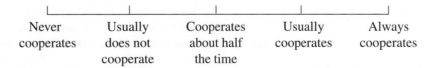

Never	Usually	Cooperates	Usually	Always
cooperates	does not	about half	cooperates	cooperates
	cooperate	the time		

The rater marks an × or check mark on each of a series of lines such as this containing descriptive words or phrases pertaining to a certain characteristic or trait. Typically, a verbal description of the lowest degree of the characteristic is given at the extreme left end of the line, a verbal description of the highest degree of the characteristic at the extreme right end of the line, and descriptions referring to intermediate degrees of the characteristic at intermediate points on the line.

Visual Analogue Scale

In clinical contexts it is often difficult to determine the intensity of a patient's subjective experience (of pain, anxiety, substance craving, etc.). One technique that has been used to estimate the intensity of such experiences is a *visual analogue scale* (Wewers & Low, 1990). The patient may be instructed, for example, to point to or mark the place on the line corresponding to the intensity of the anxiety or pain that he or she is currently experiencing. A young child may be asked to point to the picture of a face in a graded series of smiling and frowning faces that best indicates how he or she feels. The following scales are examples of visual analogue scales with numerical anchors.

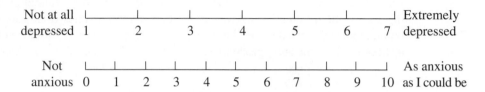

An example of a visual analogue scale with verbal anchors is

Not   MILD   MODERATE   SEVERE   As anxious
anxious   as I can be

Visual analogue scales like these can be administered periodically to measure changes in feelings or moods (e.g., Stern's Visual Analog Mood Scales) over time, but they have limitations.

This technique is perhaps more accurate than simply asking patients to tell how they feel in their own words, but some patients have difficulty understanding the procedure and representing subjective experiences such as pain, anxiety, and depression on visual analogue scales.

Standard Rating Scale

On a *standard rating scale,* the rater supplies or is supplied with a set of standards for evaluating the persons to be rated (the *ratees*). An example of a standard rating scale is the *person-to-person scale,* which is constructed for rating individuals on a specified trait such as leadership ability. The rater is asked to think of five people falling at different points along a hypothetical continuum of leadership ability. Then the rater compares each ratee with these five individuals and indicates which of them is most like the ratee in leadership ability.

Behaviorally Anchored Scales

Developed by Smith and Kendall (1963) and based on Flanagan's (1954) *critical incidents technique,* behaviorally anchored scales represent attempts to make the terminology of rating scales more descriptive of actual behavior and hence more objective. Understandably, terms such as *anxiety, self-confidence,* and *aggressiveness* and other nouns or adjectives used in traditional trait-oriented rating scales may be interpreted differently by different raters. This is particularly true when raters receive little or no training in how to interpret the terms.

Construction of a behaviorally anchored rating scale begins by convening a group of individuals who possess expert knowledge of a particular job or situation. Then, by means of discussion and deliberation, these individuals attempt to reach a consensus on a series of behaviorally descriptive critical incidents from which an objective, highly reliable rating scale can be constructed. Behavioral descriptions that survive repeated reevaluation by the group, or by other groups, may then be prepared as a series of items to be rated. We might expect that the emphasis on observable behavior and the concentrated group effort in devising behaviorally anchored scales would make them psychometrically superior to other types of rating scales. Furthermore, the fact that the scale-construction process requires group involvement and consensus, and hence a greater likelihood of group acceptance, would seem to be an advantage. Research findings indicate, however, that behaviorally anchored rating scales are not necessarily superior to graphic rating scales (Kinicki & Bannister, 1988).

Two variations of behaviorally anchored scales are *behavioral expectation scales* (*BES*) and *behavioral observation scales* (*BOS*). On BES scales, critical behaviors are rated in terms of expectations rather than actual behaviors. Ratings on BOS scales are made in terms of the frequency (never, seldom, sometimes, generally, always) with which each of a set of critical behaviors is observed during a specified time period. Some researchers have concluded that in employment contexts the BOS method is preferable to the BARS method (Wiersma & Latham, 1986).

Forced-Choice Scale

On a *forced-choice rating scale*, the rater is presented with two or more descriptions and told to indicate which best characterizes the person to be rated. If there are three or more descriptions, raters may also be asked to indicate which is least descriptive of the ratee. On an item containing four descriptions, for example, two of the descriptions are equally desirable and two are equally undesirable. The rater is told to select the statement that is most descriptive and the one that is least descriptive of the ratee. Only one desirable statement and one undesirable statement actually discriminate between high and low ratees on the criterion, but the raters presumably do not know which statements these are. A hypothetical example of a four-statement, forced-choice item for rating leadership is

_____ Assumes responsibility easily.
_____ Doesn't know how or when to delegate.
_____ Has many constructive suggestions to offer.
_____ Doesn't listen to others' suggestions.

(Reader: Can you tell which statement is keyed as "desirable" and which one is keyed as "undesirable"?)

Raters sometimes find the forced-choice format cumbersome, but it is considered fairer than the person-to-person rating technique. The forced-choice technique also has the advantage of controlling for certain errors in rating, such as constant errors, the halo effect, contrast error, and proximity error.

Q-Sorts

Q-sorts are similar to rating scales, but they also possess certain features of checklists. The *Q-sort technique,* pioneered by Stephenson (1953), requires the respondent to sort a set of descriptive statements into a series of piles ranging from "most characteristic" to "least characteristic" of himself or herself or an acquaintance. The respondent is asked to arrange the statements so that a specified number fall in each pile and produce a normal distribution of statements across piles.

Q-sort statements may be prepared specifically for a certain investigation, but standard decks of statements are available. One commercially distributed set, the California Q-Sort Revised (Adult Set), consists of 100 cards containing statements descriptive of personality; also available from Consulting Psychologists Press is a Child Set.

Certain investigations of changes in self-concept resulting from psychotherapy or other interventions have required the research subjects to make before and after Q-sorts of a series of statements to describe their feelings and attitudes (e.g., Rogers & Dymond, 1954). When the real- and ideal-self sorts are more alike after intervention than they were before, it may be concluded that the intervention experience was effective.

PROBLEMS WITH RATINGS

A variety of errors may be made when making ratings, among which are constant errors, the halo effect, contrast errors, and the proximity error. As with most other assessment methods, raters are not equally prone to these errors. The amount of error depends on a large number of factors, including observational ability, amount of experience, rater personality, interpersonal skills, perceptiveness, and freedom from judgmental bias.

Errors in Rating

Constant errors occur when the assigned ratings are higher (*leniency* or *generosity error*), lower (*severity error*), or more often in the average category (*central tendency error*) than they should be. All raters are susceptible to the *ambiguity error* of failing to interpret items correctly because they are worded poorly, insufficient information is provided, or the scale anchors are not described or placed properly.

Another type of rating error, the *halo effect,* occurs when raters have a tendency to respond on the basis of a general impression of the ratee or to overgeneralize by giving favorable ratings to all traits merely because the ratee is outstanding on one or two. A halo effect may also be negative, in which case one bad characteristic spoils the ratings on all other characteristics. Related to the halo effect is the *logical error* of assigning similar ratings on characteristics that are perceived by the rater as logically related.

The term *contrast error* has been employed in at least two senses. In one sense it refers to the tendency to assign a higher rating than justified if the immediately preceding ratee received a very low rating or to assign a lower rating than justified if the preceding ratee received a very high rating. In a second sense, contrast error refers to the tendency of a rater to compare or contrast the ratee with the rater himself or herself in assigning ratings on certain behaviors or traits.

A *proximity error* occurs when the rater tends to assign similar ratings to a person on items that are placed close together on the printed page. Likewise, if a person is consistently rated high, low, or average on the majority of a set of items that are close together on the printed page, he or she may receive similar ratings on other items located near these items. Another proximity factor, the *most recent performance error,* occurs when a ratee is judged on the basis of his or her most recent behavior, rather than on a more representative sample of the behavior.

Errors in rating can also occur when raters possess inadequate information about the persons being rated. Consequently, the raters may be overly influenced by irrelevant or incorrect communications regarding the ratee and attach too much importance to insignificant details concerning him or her. Faced with insufficient knowledge about the ratee, raters may fall back on stereotypes concerning human nature, remember only information that confirms their beliefs about the ratee and people in general, and be swayed more by their feelings than by correct information. Raters may also commit the *fundamental attribution error* of interpreting the ratee's behavior in the rating situation as being due to internal or dispositional factors, rather than to the nature of the rating situation itself.

Improving Ratings

It is not easy to make reliable and valid judgments of people under the best of circumstances and particularly so when the behaviors or characteristics are poorly defined or highly subjective. Not only are personal biases likely to affect ratings, but raters are often not sufficiently acquainted with ratees to make accurate judgments. Training in how to make ratings more objective—by being aware of the various kinds of errors that can occur in rating, becoming more familiar with the persons and traits being rated, and omitting items that the rater feels unqualified to judge—can improve the accuracy of ratings (Stamoulis & Hauenstein, 1993; Sulsky & Day, 1994). Combining the responses of several raters can also balance out the response biases of individual raters (Achenbach et al., 2005). Greater reliability and validity of ratings may be attained by designing items more carefully, stating them in precise behavioral terminology, arranging the items on the rating sheets so that they can be read and scored more easily and accurately, and making certain that the individual items and the rating form as a whole are not excessively long.

Research on job ratings has shown that the most reliable ratings are those given by the ratee's peers (Imada, 1982; Wexley & Klimoski, 1984). Ratings by subordinates, superiors, peers, and self do not always agree, but combining ratings from these four sources may result in greater reliability and validity than from any of the sources by themselves (Harris & Schaubroeck, 1988). Finally, careful attention to the design of rating scales, by defining the points (*anchors*) clearly with precise behavioral descriptions of the characteristics to be rated, contributes to the validity of ratings.

STANDARDIZED RATING SCALES

The great majority of rating scales are nonstandardized, special-purpose instruments designed for particular research investigations. Nevertheless, many standardized scales for rating the behavior and personality traits of children and adults are commercially available. Scales for rating the developmental status and behaviors of mentally retarded, learning disabled, emotionally disturbed, and physically handicapped children are especially popular. Scales for rating anxiety, depression, hostility, and other clinical symptoms are also widely used.

Researchers in the fields of child development, special education (e.g., autism, ADHD, speech and language impairments, mental retardation), and school psychology, in particular, have constructed dozens of rating instruments for assessing behavioral changes resulting from specific educational, therapeutic, and other intervention programs. Many of these instruments are oriented toward behavior assessments, whereas others have a trait–factor orientation and still others were developed in a psychodynamic, psychiatric context and thereby contain associated terminology. Furthermore, many standardized interview and observation instruments involve ratings of behavior and personality and hence consist in part of rating scales.

Computer-based reports are available for many commercially distributed rating scales and checklists. In addition, a number of rating scales and checklists can be administered by computer. For example, computer-administered versions of clinician-administered rating scales, some employing *interactive voice responding* (*IVR*), are available for the assessment of anxiety, depression, obsessive–compulsive disorder, and social phobia. In their review of computer-administered clinical rating scales, Kobak, Greist, Jefferson, and Katzelnick (1996) concluded that patients were generally more honest with the computer than with other presentation methods and often preferred it when revealing sensitive information pertaining to suicide, alcohol or drug abuse, sexual behavior, and HIV-related symptoms. The reviewers concluded that, when used with established ethical guidelines, computers are reliable, inexpensive, accessible, and time efficient in the assessment of psychiatric symptoms.

SUMMARY

1. Checklists are listings of characteristics or behaviors in which the examinee makes a series of dichotomous decisions (yes–no, true–false, etc.). These provide an objective record of the results of observations and interviews and can also be used to determine whether changes have occurred as a result of a particular treatment, educational program, or other intervention procedure. They can be selected based on the following considerations: type of variable, rationale or theory, training required to administer it, ease of scoring, type of standardization, reliability, and validity. Scoring is usually comprised of simply adding up the number of items that have been endorsed, although sometimes different weightings can be given to the different items.
2. Checklists can be used to evaluate traits, behavioral problems, and symptoms. Examples of commercially developed checklists include the Adjective Check List, Multiple Affect Adjective Checklist-Revised, State–Trait Anxiety Inventory, Child Behavior Checklist, Teacher's Report Form, Revised Behavior Problem Checklist, and the Symptom Checklist-90-R.

3. Rating scales are somewhat more complicated to construct in that they require multi-category evaluative decisions. A similar procedure is a ranking scale in which examinees are requested to assign ranks to a person, situation, or trait. Rating scales can be constructed by defining the attribute to be rated and assigning some form of rating category (anchor). The design can be based on an underlying theory, factor analysis, and selecting or deleting items based on how effectively they correlate with the variable of interest.

4. Valid rating scales require judgments (ratings) concerning behaviors, personality traits, and other characteristics of individuals (ratees) to be made by objective, unbiased raters. A variety of formats has been used in constructing rating scales, including numerical scales, unipolar or bipolar scales, semantic differential, graphic rating scale, visual analogue scale, standard rating scale, behaviorally anchored scales, forced-choice scales, and Q-sorts. There are advantages and disadvantages to each type of scale, and each is more useful for some purposes than for others.

5. Among the many different types of errors that can occur in making ratings are leniency–generosity, severity, central tendency, ambiguity, halo effect, logical error, contrast error, proximity error, most recent performance error, and the fundamental attribution error. The forced-choice rating procedure, on which the rater is required to choose between two equally desirable descriptions and perhaps between two equally undesirable descriptions as well, controls for some of these errors, but it is cumbersome to use and disliked by many raters. Ratings may be transformed to standard scores as a statistical control for constant errors. Perhaps the most effective procedure for reducing the effects of all types of errors in rating is to train raters carefully and familiarize them with the various kinds of errors that can be made. When rating scales are constructed carefully and made as objective as possible and the raters are thoroughly trained, reliability coefficients in the .80s or even the .90s may be attained. Averaging the ratings of several raters also improves the reliability coefficient of a rating scale.

MASTERING THE CHAPTER OBJECTIVES

1. *Checklists: definitions, selection, scoring*
   a. Define what is meant by a checklist.
   b. What considerations would you have in selecting a checklist and how are they scored?

2. *Types of checklists*
   a. Briefly describe the following commercially available checklists: Adjective Checklist, Multiple Affect Adjective Checklist-Revised, State–Trait Anxiety Inventory, Child Behavior Checklist, Teacher's Report Form, Revised Behavior Problem Checklist, and the Symptom Checklist-90-R.
   b. What is meant by a broadband, self-report, and informant instrument?

3. *Constructing rating scales*
   a. Describe how you would construct a rating scale.
   b. Study the examples of rating scales given in the chapter (Form 16.3 and Experiencing Psychological Assessment, Exercises 3 and 4), and identify whether they were based on theory, factor analysis, or external correlations. Explain why you think this is the case.

4. *Formats for rating scales*

   a. Define the following formats of rating scales: numerical scales, unipolar or bipolar scales, semantic differential, graphic rating scale, visual analogue scale, standard rating scale, behaviorally anchored scales, forced-choice scales, and Q-sorts.

   b. Study the examples of rating scales given in Experiencing Psychological Assessment, Exercises 3 and 4, and identify the type of format that was used.

5. *Problems with rating scales*

   a. Define the following problems with rating scales: leniency–generosity, severity, central tendency, ambiguity, halo effect, logical error, contrast error, proximity error, most recent performance error, and the fundamental attribution error.

   b. Describe what can be done to reduce these errors.

EXPERIENCING PSYCHOLOGICAL ASSESSMENT

1. Construct a 10-item checklist of behaviors that are symptomatic of depression and a second 10-item checklist of behaviors that are symptomatic of anxiety. Make copies of your two checklists and administer them to 12 people. Score the checklists by counting the number of items checked by the respondent. Compute and interpret the correlation between the respondents' scores on the two checklists.

2. One problem with the research literature on Type A behavior is that different assessment methods (e.g., interview and questionnaire) do not yield the same results. Although questionnaires such as the Jenkins Activity Survey are more efficient than interviews, Rosenman (1986) and others have rejected such self-report measures because Type A personalities presumably have little insight into their own behavior. One way of testing this hypothesis is to compare self-ratings of behavior with ratings of behavior made by unbiased observers. With this in mind, select a few individuals who seem to fit the following description of the Type A personality:

   > A personality pattern characterized by a combination of behaviors, including aggressiveness, competitiveness, hostility, quick actions, and constant striving.

   Administer the checklist in Form 16.1 (p. 374) to each person, and then have someone who knows the person well fill out the same checklist to describe this person. Use an appropriate statistical procedure to compare the self-ratings and the ratings by others.

3. On a scale of 1 to 10, where 1 is the lowest rating and 10 is the highest rating, rate each of the following adjectives according to how descriptive it is of (a) your *real self* (the way you actually are), (b) your *ideal self* (the way you would like to be), and (c) other *people in general*.

	YOUR REAL SELF	YOUR IDEAL SELF	OTHER PEOPLE IN GENERAL
brave	_____	_____	_____
careful	_____	_____	_____
cheerful	_____	_____	_____
conscientious	_____	_____	_____
considerate	_____	_____	_____
courteous	_____	_____	_____
creative	_____	_____	_____

dependable	____	____	____
energetic	____	____	____
friendly	____	____	____
good looking	____	____	____
helpful	____	____	____
honest	____	____	____
humorous	____	____	____
intelligent	____	____	____
organized	____	____	____
patient	____	____	____
strong	____	____	____
studious	____	____	____
trusting	____	____	____

Evaluate your responses by the following procedure: Compute the sum of the absolute values of the differences between the ratings assigned to (a) your real self and your ideal self, (b) your real self and the selves of other people in general, and (c) your ideal self and the selves of other people in general. Compute the percent congruency coefficient for each of the three comparisons by dividing the sum by 180 and subtracting the resulting quotient from 1. The closer the congruency coefficient is to 1.00, the more similar the two selves are. Interpret your results in terms of Rogers's self-theory or social-learning theory.

4. Rank, from 1 to 12, each of the following sets of three adjectives in terms of how descriptive each set is of you personally. A rank of 1 means that the three adjectives are completely descriptive of you, and a rank of 12 means that the three adjectives are not at all descriptive of you.

____ **1.** pioneering, enthusiastic, and courageous
____ **2.** stable, stubborn, and well-organized
____ **3.** intellectual, adaptable, and clever
____ **4.** sensitive, nurturing, and sympathetic
____ **5.** extroverted, generous, and authoritative
____ **6.** critical, exacting, and intelligent
____ **7.** harmonizing, just, and sociable
____ **8.** secretive, strong, and passionate
____ **9.** honest, impulsive, and optimistic
____ **10.** ambitious, hard working, and cautious
____ **11.** original, open-minded, and independent
____ **12.** kind, sensitive, and creative

According to astrology, the personality characteristics of an individual are determined by the zodiacal sign of his or her birthdate. The 12 zodiacal signs and the corresponding dates are as follows:

1. Aries: March 21–April 19
2. Taurus: April 20–May 20
3. Gemini: May 21–June 21
4. Cancer: June 22–July 22
5. Leo: July 23–August 22
6. Virgo: August 23–September 22

7. Libra: September 23–October 22
8. Scorpio: October 23–November 21
9. Sagittarius: November 22–December 21
10. Capricorn: December 22–January 19
11. Aquarius: January 20–February 18
12. Pisces: February 19–March 20

Does the number of your zodiacal sign correspond to the number of the item triad that you gave a rank of 1? Compare your results with those of your classmates, friends, and relatives. Is this a fair test of the validity of the process of analyzing personality in terms of zodiacal signs? Why or why not? Do you believe in astrology? Defend your answer. (Adapted from Balch, W. R. [1980]. Testing the validity of astrology in class. *Teaching of Psychology, 7*[4], 247–250.)

CHAPTER SEVENTEEN

OBJECTIVE PERSONALITY INVENTORIES

CHAPTER OBJECTIVES

1. Discuss issues related to truthfulness, reliability, and validity.
2. Describe the four Beck inventories, as well as other examples of single-construct inventories.
3. Describe the content-based strategy, as well as the examples of the Myers–Briggs Type Indicator and the Personality Research Form.
4. Describe the factor-analytic approach to test development.
5. Describe the 16PF, Adult Personality Inventory, Eysenck Personality Questionnaire, and the NEO-PIR.
6. Discuss criterion keying.
7. Describe the MMPI/MMPI-2.
8. Describe the California Psychological Inventory, Personality Inventory for Children, Millon Clinical Multiaxial Inventory, the Basic Personality Inventory, and the Personality Assessment Inventory.

There are literally hundreds of objective personality inventories. They all have in common the fact that they ask clients to give answers to fixed-response formats. These vary in length from a single word (the client might circle that they feel they are "trustworthy" or "shy") to a full sentence (the client answers "True" to "I like parties where there's lots of exciting people"). Thus the information is usually based on self-report by the client. Objective personality inventories also have very specific rules for administration and scoring so that an untrained person or even a computer can perform these clerical functions. In some instances a client can respond to questions on a computer and, when finished, the scores and interpretation appear on a screen seconds later. These tests are called *objective* both because the format is structured and because the scoring and interpretation are based on statistical comparisons with a normative group. Thus there is little room for more subjective scoring by the psychologist doing the testing.

This chapter provides an overview of single-construct personality tests, as well as multiconstruct inventories. The multiconstruct inventories are organized around their having been designed based primarily on content–theoretical, factor-analytic, or criterion-keyed strategies. However, this distinction is sometimes less than clear, since many tests have used a combination of these strategies. The tests described are representative and have been selected for inclusion based on their being frequently used, well designed, and extensively researched.

TRUTHFULNESS, RELIABILITY, AND VALIDITY

Personality inventories consist of items concerning personal characteristics, thoughts, feelings, and behavior. As on an interest inventory, a rating scale, or a checklist, respondents mark items on a personality inventory that they judge to be descriptive of themselves or, in certain cases, of someone whom they know well. The validity of any of these tests rests on the assumptions that examinees are telling the truth, that they are valid judges of themselves, and that the questions are clear. If any of these assumptions is incorrect, then the validity of personality assessment is compomised.

False (Untruthful) Responses

As emphasized throughout this textbook, a psychometric instrument cannot provide valid results unless it is responded to consistently and honestly. Because many of the items on personality inventories require respondents to admit to things that they might not wish to, but would rather present themselves in the most favorable light, the question of truthfulness of the responses is a serious one.

Truthfulness in responding can be a serious problem on personality inventories. Respondents may be unwilling to tell the truth, or they may not even know the truth about themselves and consequently provide incorrect information. Hardly surprising is the research finding that people can respond to personality inventories in a distorted fashion when instructed to do so. But for fear of being detected or for whatever reason, lying or faking on psychological inventories is not as common in counseling or job-placement situations as we might suspect (Schwab & Packard, 1973). In many cases, special validation scoring keys have been designed to detect dissimulation or faking on some inventories. Scores obtained from applying these keys do not always reveal if the respondent has been careless or untruthful, but they provide one check on the validity of the findings.

Intentional deception, either to make oneself appear worse (*fake bad*) or better (*fake good*) than one is, is not the only factor affecting the accuracy of responses to a personality inventory. Response tendencies or sets, such as acquiescence, social desirability, overcautiousness, and extremeness, also influence score validity. Of particular concern are the response sets of *acquiescence* (the tendency to agree rather than disagree when in doubt) and *social desirability* (the tendency to respond in a more socially acceptable manner). As with faking good and faking bad, special scoring keys have been devised on certain inventories to detect or compensate for these response sets. Typically, a person's scores on such *validity scales* are inspected before evaluating scores on other (content or diagnostic) scales. Because scores on validity scales do not necessarily reveal faking and response sets, it is best to use personality inventories as aids in decision making only when respondents have nothing to lose by answering thoughtfully and truthfully, and nothing to gain by failing to do so.

Norms, Reliability, and Validity

Scores on personality inventories are usually interpreted with reference to a set of norms based on the responses of selected groups of people. Since the standardization samples are often fairly small and perhaps unrepresentative of the intended (target) population, the norms must be interpreted cautiously. Furthermore, the scores and norms obtained on some personality inventories, particularly those consisting of items having a forced-choice format, are *ipsative*. This means that a person's score on one scale is affected by his or her scores on the remaining scales. Ipsative scores compensate for each other, so a person's scores on all scales cannot be in the same direction (high or low). This makes it difficult to compare the scores of different people on a particular scale or variable.

Situational factors usually have more influence on personality than they do on a person's ability. For example, a person's level of dominance will vary according to the situation he or she is in. In contrast, their ability remains relatively constant. Thus personality is less stable than ability. The result of this is that personality tests have lower reliabilities than tests of ability or achievement.

In addition to modest reliabilities, personality inventories have lower validities than ability or achievement tests. Faking and response sets partially account for these lower validities. Another factor affecting the validity of personality inventories is the susceptibility of users to the *jingle fallacy* of believing that groups of items (scales) with similar names measure the same variable. This can occur, for example, when scores on the anxiety or depression scale of one inventory have only modest correlations with similarly labeled scales on another inventory. On the other hand, a high correlation between scores on the scales of two different inventories may be illusory, because the method of responding to the two scales is similar, regardless of their content.

SINGLE-CONSTRUCT AND SYMPTOM INVENTORIES

Although people have undoubtedly been evaluating the personalities of others since the dawn of human history, the formal beginnings of personality assessment go back only to the early 20th century. The first personality inventory of any importance, the Personal Data Sheet, was constructed during World War I by R. S. Woodworth to screen U.S. Army recruits for emotional disorders. This single-score instrument consisted of 116 yes–no questions concerning abnormal fears, obsessions, compulsions, tics, nightmares, and other feelings and behaviors. Here are four illustrative items from the Personal Data Sheet are:

Do you feel sad and low-spirited most of the time?
Are you often frightened in the middle of the night?
Do you think you have hurt yourself by going too much with women?
Have you ever lost your memory for a time? (DuBois, 1970, pp. 160–163)

Another early personality inventory scored on a single variable was the A-S Reaction Study, a multiple-choice instrument designed by G. W. Allport and F. H. Allport in 1928 to measure the disposition to be ascendant or submissive in everyday social relationships.

Today, many single-score or single-construct inventories are available. Examples of the psychological constructs that inventories have been designed to measure are altruism, anger, anxiety, depression, hopelessness, hostility, risk taking, self-concept, self-esteem, sensation seeking, and stress. Among the most popular of the single-construct measures are the Beck inventories and various measures of self-concept and self-esteem.

Beck Inventories

The four instruments in this group are the Beck Depression Inventory, Beck Anxiety Inventory, Beck Hopelessness Scale, and Beck Scale for Suicide Ideation (by A. T. Beck; Psychological Corporation). All four inventories have been favorably reviewed with respect to their content, administration, and scoring (Carlson, 1998; Dowd, 1998; Fernandez, 1998; Groth-Marnat, 2003; Hanes, 1998; Stewart, 1998; Waller, 1998a, 1998b). The inventories consist of 20 to 21 items each and can be completed in 5 to 10 minutes. The Beck Depression Inventory (BDI) and its revision, the BDI-II (Beck & Steer, 1993), are the most popular and, in fact, among the most widely researched of all personality inventories (home.san.rr.com/edwardpierce/Beck.htm). The 21 sets of items on the BDI-II, which were written in compliance with the DSM-IV guidelines for the diagnosis of depression, were designed to assess the nature and intensity of depression in normal and psychiatric patients (www.cps.nova.edu/~cpphelp/BDI2.html). The items are comprised of four statements arranged in order of increasing severity with respect to a particular symptom of depression and focus on symptoms present during the preceding 2 weeks. Separate scores may be determined on the two subscales (cognitive–affective and somatic–performance), as well as a total score. A total score of 0 to 9 is classified as normal, a total score of 10 to 18 as mild–moderate depression, a total score of 19 to 29 as moderate–severe depression, and a total score of 30 and above as extremely severe depression.

Internal consistency (coefficient alpha) reliabilities of total scores are as high as .92. The validity of the BDI and BDI-II is supported in that scores on the BDI/BDI-II have moderate to high correlations with external ratings of depression, can distinguish the level of adjustment within groups of psychiatric patients, and are adequate at differentiating symptoms of anxiety from those of depression (see Groth-Marnat, 2003). Factor analyses have found that the items comprised physiological symptoms (e.g., loss of energy, changes in sleep patterns) and thoughts or feeling related to depression (e.g., dislike of self, suicidal thoughts).

Similar in format to the Beck Depression Inventory is the 20-item Beck Hopelessness Scale (BHS). It was designed to measure three major aspects of hopelessness: feelings about the future, loss of motivation, and expectations. BHS scores are moderately correlated with those on the BDI, but the former instrument is considered to be a better predictor of suicide intention and behavior than the latter. The internal consistency reliabilities reported in the 1988 BHS manual are reasonably high (.82 to .93 in seven norm groups). The test–retest reliability coefficients are, however, very modest (.69 after 1 week and .66 after 6 weeks). This suggests that hopelessness may be fairly changeable. Reviews of the BHS have concluded that it has adequate reliability and is well constructed and well validated (Dowd, 1992; Owen, 1992).

Two other Beck scales similar in format to the BDI and BHS are the Beck Anxiety Inventory (BAI) and the Beck Scale for Suicide Ideation (BSSI). Like the other Beck scales, these newer instruments were designed for adults from 17 to 80 years and are available in both English and Spanish. The BAI was designed to measure the severity of anxiety in adolescents and adults and has been found to discriminate between anxious and nonanxious diagnostic groups. The anxious groups included patients with agoraphobia, panic disorder, social phobia, obsessive–compulsive disorder, and generalized anxiety. The BSSI was designed to evaluate suicidal thinking and attitudes and thereby to identify individuals at risk for suicide. The internal-consistency reliabilities of the BAI and the BSSI are high, but the test–retest reliabilities are more modest. Studies of the clinical validity of the two instruments are generally very supportive (BAI: Beck, 1990; and BSSI: Beck, 1991).

Self-Concept and Self-Esteem

The *self-concept,* which consists of how a person views himself or herself, depends on the person's comparisons of his or her physical characteristics, abilities, and temperament with those of other people. The self-concept also includes the attitudes, aspirations, and social roles of the person. Whereas self-concept refers to the ideas or beliefs that an individual has about himself or herself, *self-esteem* consists of how the self is evaluated by the person. People may come to evaluate themselves highly (high self-esteem) or lowly (low self-esteem).

Q-Sorts, which were discussed in Chapter 16, are measures of self-concept based on a rating or sorting technique. Among the older measures of self-concept and self-esteem that are still commercially available are the Coopersmith Self-Esteem Inventories (from Consulting Psychologists Press), the Piers–Harris Children's Self-Concept Scale (from Western Psychological Services), and the Tennessee Self-Concept Scale (from Western Psychological Services). Other popular inventories of self-concept and self-esteem are the Behavioral Academic Self-Esteem (from Consulting Psychologists Press), the Dimensions of Self-Concept (from EdITS), the Student Self-Concept Scale (from American Guidance Service), and the Self-Esteem Index (from pro.ed).

Inventories for Diagnosing a Specific Disorder

Anxiety, depression, hostility, and many other conditions are symptomatic of various psychological disorders, and inventories for assessing these symptoms may be administered for diagnostic purposes. In addition, inventories designed to identify or diagnose a specific disorder are available. There are inventories for alcoholism, antisocial personality, borderline personality, burnout, eating disorders, neuroticism, panic, agoraphobia, psychopathic personality, social phobia, substance abuse, trauma, and other psychopathological conditions.

Many of these inventories yield multiple scores, but the emphasis remains on a single disorder or syndrome.

Particularly noteworthy among inventories that focus on a specific disorder are those concerned with anorexia, bulimia, and other eating disorders. The most popular and widely researched of these instruments are the Eating Inventory (from Psychological Corporation) and the Eating Disorder Inventory (from Psychological Assessment Resources). The second edition of the latter instrument, the Eating Disorder Inventory-2 (EDI-2; www.cps.nova.edu/~cpphelp/EDI2.html), was designed to assess a broad range of psychological features of eating disorders, such as anorexia nervosa and bulimia nervosa, in patients as young as 11 years. It consists of 91 forced-choice items (64 original items plus 27 additional items), each of which is rated by the respondent (age 12 and over) on a 6-point scale ranging from "always" to "never." Responses are scored on eight original subscales (Drive for Thinness, Ineffectiveness, Body Dissatisfaction, Interpersonal Distrust, Bulimia, Perfectionism, Maturity, Fear, and Interoceptive Awareness) and three provisional subscales (Impulse Regulation, Social Insecurity, and Asceticism www.parinc.com/samprpts/EDI_2.htm). The significant positive correlations among the majority of the scales show, however, that they do not represent independent dimensions. The majority of the correlations of the EDI-2 scales with scores on several personality inventories and clinicians' ratings are modest but significant. Sample cases and a few research studies are also described in the manual. From these data, it can be tentatively concluded that the EDI-2 is a useful clinical screening tool and outcome measure and a valuable adjunct to clinical judgments concerning patients with eating disorders. It has received favorable reviews as a clinical tool in dealing with anorexia nervosa, bulimia, and other eating disorders (e.g., Ash, 1995; Schinke, 1995).

INVENTORIES BASED ON CONTENT VALIDATION

It would seem logical that if you want to find something out about something, you ask. The questions asked should be based on the sorts of things you would like to know. If you want to know if a person is introverted, you would develop a series of questions asking such things as how much time they like to spend alone, whether they tend to do most of the talking versus most of the listening, and the extent they feel comfortable in groups. The development of such questions is essentially based on developing items that correspond to the content of what you are trying to measure. This content is typically derived from an understanding of the construct based on theory, clinical experience, or research. For example, depression is often conceptualized as being comprised of affective ("I feel sad much of the time"), cognitive ("I don't think I'm a worthy person"), and physiological ("I'm lacking in energy") components. A content-based questionnaire would thus want to have an even balance of items reflecting these three components of depression.

The first multiscore, or multiphasic, adjustment inventory was the Bernreuter Personality Inventory (1931). It consisted of 125 items to be answered yes, no, or ? by high school students, college students, or adults. By assigning different numerical weights to different items, the Bernreuter was scored on six variables: Neurotic Tendency, Self-sufficiency, Introversion–Extroversion, Dominance–Submission, Sociability, and Confidence. Many other multiscore personality inventories have been published since 1930. Another example of an older inventory of this type is the Edwards Personal Preference Schedule (by A. L. Edwards; Psychological Corporation), which was based on Henry Murray's need–press theory of personality. Because it is concerned with reasoning and often guided by a theory of personality, rather than empirical tryouts and statistics, the content-validated approach has sometimes been referred to as the rational or a priori method of instrument construction. Two examples of content-validated inventories that are based, at least to some extent, on a theory of personality are the Myers–Briggs Type Indicator and the Personality Research Form.

Myers–Briggs Type Indicator

The Myers–Briggs Type Indicator (MBTI) (by K. C. Briggs and I. B. Myers; Consulting Psychologists Press; www.cpp.com/products/mbti/index.asp) is composed of a series of two-choice items concerning preferences or inclinations in feelings and behavior. There are four forms (G, F, K, and J), containing 126 to 290 items per form. Based on Carl Jung's theory of personality types, the MBTI is scored on four bipolar scales: Introversion–Extroversion (I–E), Sensing–Intuition (S–N), Thinking–Feeling (T–F), and Judging–Perceptive (J–P). Combinations of scores on these four two-part categories yield 16 possible personality types. Thus, an ENFP type is a person whose predominant modes are Extrovert, Intuition, Feeling, and Perceptive, whereas an ISTJ type is a person whose predominant modes are Introvert, Sensing, Thinking, and Judging. Unfortunately, the fact that no measures of test-taking attitude are provided can lead to errors in diagnosis and screening with the MBTI.

Percentile norms for the four indicator scores, based on small samples of high school and college students, are given in the MBTI manual (Myers & McCaulley, 1985). Split-half reliabilities of the four indicators are reported as being in the .70s and .80s, and a number of small-scale validity studies are also described. Although the conceptualization of personality in terms of types is not viewed favorably by many psychologists, an impressive array of materials on the Myers–Briggs Type Indicator is available from Consulting Psychologists Press. These include various interpretive guides, books, and workshop materials. Profiles of scores and several types of reports can be prepared by a computer, and other resources and services for users are also available.

Personality Research Form

Based to a large extent on Henry Murray's trait theory of personality and focusing on areas of normal functioning rather than psychopathology, the Personality Research Form (PRF) (by D. N. Jackson, Sigma Assessment Systems) is a set of five true–false inventories designed for grade 6 through adulthood. Each of the 15 scales on Forms A and B and the 22 scales on Forms AA, BB, and E consists of 20 true–false items. In addition to the content scales, there are two scales to detect an invalid profile. One scale identifies those who are faking bad (Infrequency Scale consisting of rarely marked items), and Forms AA, BB, and E have a scale to detect faking good (the Social Desirability Scale).

The PRF was standardized on 1,000 male and 1,000 female college students. Internal consistency and test–retest reliability coefficients for scores on the 14 content scales common to all five forms cluster around .80, but the reliabilities of the six additional content scales on Forms AA, BB, and E are in the .50s. Validity coefficients obtained by correlating the content scales with behavior ratings and a specially devised trait-rating form are in the .50s. Evidence for the convergent and discriminant validity of the PRF, using peer ratings and data from hundreds of studies, is reported in the manual.

INVENTORIES BASED ON FACTOR ANALYSIS

If we were to ask people to describe individuals they are familiar with, we would eventually come up with hundreds if not thousands of descriptions. They might include things such as kind, generous, shy, introverted, thrifty, reflective, wise, confident, and outgoing. A rational analysis of these descriptions indicates that some seem to be similar, whereas others are very different. For example, descriptions such as introverted and reflective seem to share some similarities. In contrast, descriptions such as shy and emotionally open would seem to be very dissimilar. An important aspect of theory and research in personality is, of course, to see how these clusters of descriptions are organized. This extends to personality assessment in that we are similarly concerned with how tests can be designed to assess these core aspects of personality. In the above listing of personality descriptions, we have rationally considered the pattterns these descriptions have to each other. *Factor analysis* does this in a far more precise, empirical, and detailed manner by calculating all the possible intercorrelations between various descriptions (see Appendix A, pp. 453–456). These descriptions are in the form of test items. The result is a series of items that are highly correlated and form clusters or *factors*. The higher the correlations among the various items, the stronger they relate to the factor. The factors are then named according to what the content of the correlated items appears to represent. The meaning of the factors can be refined by studying the various nuances and subcomponents in the content of the items.

The exact number and names of the core aspects of personality have been hotly contested in the field. Early work by Guilford and his co-workers calculated the intercorrelations among items from a wide number of personality inventories. They came up with 10 traits, including such descriptors as Friendliness, Emotional Stability, and Ascendance (dominance). An outgrowth of this research was the Guilford–Zimmerman Temperament Survey (Guilford & Zimmerman, 1956), which included 30 items to measure each of the 10 traits. R. B. Cattell later identified 16 Personality Factors, which could be further reduced to five Global Factors (the "Big Five"; see Wiggins & Trapnell, 1997). A frequent list labels these as **O**penness, **C**onscientiousness, **E**xtroversion, **A**greeableness, and **N**euroticism. Note that these can be easily remembered by using the acronym **OCEAN.**

What is not quite as clear is the exact names that should be given to these factors. For example, there is consensus on the name of the Extroversion (versus Introversion) factor but the Openness to Experience factor is sometimes referred to as Receptivity (versus Toughmindedness). This highlights the fact that, although the process of factor analysis is statistical and objective, naming the factors that emerge is far more subjective. It is largely based on a rational consideration of content of the adjectives–items that emerge following factor analysis. Another controversial area is that, although there is agreement on the number of factors, there is far less agreement on the number and subcomponents of these factors. The next section will describe both the 16 PF and the NEO-PI-R. Both of these conceptualize variations on the Big Five components, but have different descriptions of how these five factors can and should be broken down and measured.

16 Personality Factor Questionnaire

The most comprehensive series of factor-based inventories for assessing personality in both children and adults was designed by R. B. Cattell and published by the Institute for Personality and Ability Testing (www.16pfworld.com/questionnaire.html). Cattell began his personality research with a list of approximately 18,000 personality-descriptive adjectives that had been gleaned by Allport and Odbert (1936) from dictionaries. By combining terms having similar meanings, the list was first reduced to 4,500 "real" traits and then to 171 trait names; subsequent factor analyses of scores on these trait dimensions produced 31 surface traits and 12 source traits of personality. Cattell devised a number of measures of these traits and four others isolated in his later work, but his major product was the 16 Personality Factor Questionnaire (16 PF).

The fifth edition of the 16 PF consists of 185 three choice items, including 10 to 15 items for each of the 16 primary factor scales (Russell & Karol, 1994). The items on the fifth edition of the 16 PF reflect modern language usage and were screened for ambiguity, as well as gender, race, and cultural bias. The overall readability of the inventory is at the fifth-grade level, and total testing time is 35 to 50 minutes. In addition to the 16 primary factors, the 16 PF can be scored, by hand or computer, on three Validity Indexes and five Global Scores (second-order factors). These indexes (Impression Management, Infrequency, and Acquiescence) provide a preliminary check on the validity of the responses.

The computer-generated 16 PF Score Summary contains narrative interpretations of the Validity Indexes, the Global Scores, cognitive and perceptual functioning, interpersonal style, intimate relationships, occupational considerations, personality dynamics, and therapeutic and counseling issues. The normative data for the 16 PF are based on the 1990 U.S. Census, and combined gender norms are available. In addition to improved construction and norms, the scales on the 16 PF Fifth Edition have higher reliabilities than those of previous editions. Internal consistency reliabilities range from .64 to .85, with an average of .74; test–retest reliabilities average around .80 over a 2-week interval and .70 over a 2-month interval.

Updated norms for the 16 PF Fifth Edition Questionnaire became available in early 2002. These norms are based on the responses of adults in a sample stratified to match the 2000 Census figures from the general U.S. population.

Adult Personality Inventory

The Adult Personality Inventory (API) (by S. F. Krug; MetriTech) is a 324-item self-report inventory for assessing personality in normal adults and can be scored on 21 content scales and 4 validity scales. The content scales consist of seven personality characteristics (Extroverted, Adjusted, Tough-minded, Independent, Disciplined, Creative, and Enterprising), eight interpersonal styles (Caring, Adapting, Withdrawn, Submissive, Uncaring, Non-Conforming, Sociable, and Assertive), and six career or life-style factors (Practical, Scientific, Aesthetic, Social, Competitive, and Structured).

The API was standardized on 1,000 adults, and separate norms for men and women are available. The norms, however, have been criticized as unrepresentative (D'Amato, 1995). The reliability and construct validity information reported in the manual is very limited. The internal consistency and test–retest reliability coefficients average around .75. Despite these shortcomings, the API has been used in various counseling and personnel contexts. The availability of accompanying Career Profile computer software has contributed to the popularity of this inventory with practitioners and researchers.

Eysenck Personality Questionnaire

The Eysenck Personality Questionnaire (EPQ) (by H. Eysenck; EdITS), a revision of the Eysenck Personality Inventory and the Junior Eysenck Personality Inventory, represents a more parsimonious conception of personality than that reflected in Cattell's inventories. Two earlier inventories designed by Eysenck, the Maudsley Personality Inventory and the Eysenck Personality Inventory, were scored on the dimensions of Neuroticism (N) and Extroversion (versus Introversion) (E) that emerged from his factor-analytic research. A measure of Psychoticism (P) and a Lie Scale (L) were added in constructing the EPQ.

The EPQ has a wide age range (7 through adulthood) and takes only 10 to 15 minutes to complete. Test–retest reliabilities of the N, E, P, and L scales of the EPQ range from .78 to .80 over a 1-month interval; internal-consistency coefficients are in the .70s and .80s. Norms on the two forms (A and B), based on U.S. college students and adults, are appropriate for individuals aged 16 years and above. Norms on the Junior EPQ were obtained from samples of 7- to 15-year-old children. The EPQ and its predecessors have been used extensively in personality research, though less frequently in clinical and other applied contexts. Eysenck (1965, 1981) used scores on the E and N factors in particular to predict how people react in certain experimental situations. He also related personality patterns to body type.

NEO Personality Inventory

The NEO Personality Inventory-Revised (NEO-PI-R) and an abbreviated version, the NEO Five-Factor Inventory (NEO-FFI) (by P. T. Costa, Jr., & R. R. McCrae; Psychological Assessment Resources), are based on the five-factor model described above. Each of the two forms (R and S) of the NEO-PI-R consists of 240 items to be rated on a 5-point scale and requiring approximately 30 minutes to complete. The NEO-FFI consists of 60 items and takes only 10 to 15 minutes to complete. Both the NEO-PI-R and the NEO-FFI are scored for the three N–E–O *domains* (factors): Neuroticism (N), Extroversion (E), and Openness to Experience (O), plus Agreeableness (A) and Conscientiousness (C). Each of these five domains is further subdivided into six scorable *facets,* as follows:

> *Neuroticism:* Anxiety, Hostility, Depression, Self-consciousness, Impulsiveness, Vulnerability
>
> *Extroversion:* Warmth, Gregariousness, Assertiveness, Activity, Excitement-seeking, Positive Emotions
>
> *Openness to Experience:* Fantasy, Aesthetics, Feeling, Actions, Ideas, Values

Agreeableness: Trust, Modesty, Compliance, Altruism, Straightforwardness, Tender-mindedness

Conscientiousness: Competence, Self-discipline, Achievement Striving, Dutifulness, Order, Deliberation

The internal consistency reliability coefficients of scores on the domain scales range from .86 to .95 for the NEO-PI-R and .68 to .86 for the NEO-FFI. Since the NEO-PI-R facet scales consist of fewer items than the domains, the internal consistency coefficients were generally lower (ranging from .56 to .90). Test–retest reliabilities computed over a 6-month period range from .86 to .91 for the domain scales and from .56 to .90 for the facet scales. Extensive factor analysis has provided strong support for at least three of the five domains (factors). Further support for the validity of the NEO-PI-R has been found in correlations with many related measures (typically ranging in the .80s).

INVENTORIES BASED ON CRITERION KEYING

Criterion keying (also called empirical criterion keying) has guided the development of many modern tests, the most famous of which is the Minnesota Multiphasic Personality Inventory. The name of this strategy can be used to logically understand its approach. The *criterion* portion refers to the use of some outside comparison or contrast group that has some identified characteristic. The contrast (criterion) group may be depressed, extroverted, anxious, or any number of other qualities. Items are then designed based on what seem like reasonable questions to differentiate a group from another comparison group without the characteristic. So far, this sounds like the content approach to scale construction. However, the items are then tested to see how well they differentiate the two (or more) groups. The ultimate selection of these items is based not on the content of the items, but on how effectively they discriminate between the different groups. "Good" items are ones that, based on statistical analysis, are effective at making the discriminations. The selected items are then *keyed* in the direction that indicates they are good discriminators. Thus *criterion keying* means items are "keyed" in the direction that allows them to make the required discrimination between groups with known qualities (or "criterion").

The Minnesota Multiphasic Personality Inventory

The first edition of the MMPI was designed in the early 1940s by S. R. Hathaway and J. C. McKinley to assess personality characteristics that are indicative of psychological abnormality in adults. Although it has to a large extent been replaced by a second edition (MMPI-2), the design, validation, and use of the original MMPI provided a background and guidelines for other personality inventories developed by the empirical approach.

The original 550 statements on the MMPI, which were answered yes, no, or cannot say, were concerned with attitudes, emotions, motor disturbances, psychosomatic symptoms, and other reported feelings and behaviors indicative of psychiatric problems. Each of the nine scales on which the MMPI was scored consisted of items that were answered differently by psychiatric patients in a specified diagnostic group than by a control group of normal people. The nine clinical scales, together with the Si (Social Introversion) scale and the four validity scales (*?, L, F, K*), are described in Table 17.1. Many special scales (e.g., accident proneness, anxiety, ego strength, originality) were developed from the MMPI item pool during the course of thousands of research investigations conducted over a half-century.

TABLE 17.1   Descriptions of Validity and Clinical Scales on the Original MMPI

Validity (Test-taking Attitude) Scales

? (Cannot Say)   Number of items left unanswered.

L (Lie)   Fifteen items of overly good self-report, such as "smile a lot."   (Answered True)

F (Frequency or Infrequency)   Sixty-four items answered in the scored direction by 10% or less of normals, such as "People are plotting against me." (True); high scores indicate a fake bad pattern.

K (Correction)   Thirty items reflecting defensiveness in admitting to problems, such as "Very sensitive to criticism."   (False)

Clinical Scales

1 or Hs (Hypochondriasis)   Thirty-three items derived from patients showing abnormal concern with bodily functions, such as "Chest pains."   (True)

2 or D (Depression)   Sixty items derived from patients showing extreme pessimism, feelings of hopelessness, and slowing of thought and action, such as "Life is worthwhile."   (False)

3 or Hy (Conversion Hysteria)   Sixty items from neurotic patients using physical or mental symptoms as a way of unconsciously avoiding difficult conflicts and responsibilities, such as "Heart pounds a lot."   (True)

4 or Pd (Psychopathic Deviate)   Fifty items from patients who show a repeated and flagrant disregard for social customs, an emotional shallowness, and an inability to learn from punishing experiences, such as "Activities and interests criticized."   (True)

5 or Mf (Masculinity–Femininity)   Sixty items from patients indicating the extent they endorse items more frequently endorsed by members of the opposite sex, such as males answering "Arrange flowers." (True)

6 or Pa (Paranoia)   Forty items from patients showing abnormal suspiciousness and delusions of grandeur or persecution, such as "Evil people trying to influence my mind."   (True)

7 or Pt (Psychasthenia)   Forty-eight items based on neurotic patients showing obsessions, compulsions, abnormal fears, and guilt and indecisiveness, such as "Habitually save things."   (True)

8 or Sc (Schizophrenia)   Seventy-eight items from patients showing bizarre or unusual thoughts or behavior, who are often withdrawn and experiencing delusions and hallucinations, such as "Feel things aren't real." (True); and "Don't like people close to me."   (True)

9 or Ma (Hypomania)   Forty-six items from patients characterized by emotional excitement, overactivity, and flight of ideas, such as "Sometimes happy or sad for no reason."   (True)

0 or Si (Social Introversion)   Seventy items from persons showing shyness, little interest in people, and insecurity, such as "Like parties."   (False)

Before attempting to interpret scores on the clinical or special scales of the MMPI, scores on the four validity scales should be inspected. The first of these, the (*?*) *Cannot Say* score, is the total number of items that the examinee answered "cannot say" or did not answer. A high *Cannot Say* score is interpreted as defensiveness in responding. The raw lie (*L* or fake good) score is the number of items answered in such a way as to place oneself in a more favorable light, while the infrequency (*F* or fake bad) score is the number of items answered so as to place oneself in a less favorable light. People often fake good to obtain something pleasant, whereas they fake bad to avoid something unpleasant, such as going to prison, military service, or other disliked outcomes. The *K* score is a measure of overcriticalness or overgenerosity in evaluating oneself. High scorers on the *K* scale tend to deny personal inadequacies and deficiencies in self-control; low scorers are willing to say socially undesirable things about themselves.

The MMPI-2

A revision of the MMPI was undertaken in the 1980s for the following reasons: to provide new, up-to-date norms; to broaden the item pool with content not represented in the original version; to revise and reword the language of some of the existing items that were dated, awkward, or sexist; and to provide separate forms of the inventory for adults and adolescents (www.pearsonassessments.com/tests/mmpi2htm). All 550 items on the original MMPI were retained in the Adult and Adolescent revised versions, but 14% of them were changed because of dated language or awkward expressions. Words or phrases that were more characteristic of the 1940s (streetcar, sleeping powder, drop the handkerchief, etc.) were omitted, and other modifications were made to update statements (e.g., "I like to take a bath" became "I like to take a bath or shower"). As on the original form, items on the revised MMPI were written at a sixth-grade level. The Adult Version (MMPI-2) contained 154 new experimental items designed to assess certain areas of psychopathology (such as eating disorders, Type A personality, and drug abuse) that were not well represented in the original MMPI. The Adolescent Version (MMPI-A) contained 104 new items concerned specifically with adolescent problems. In addition, the tendency for normal adolescents in a temporary state of turmoil to score like adult psychopaths on the original MMPI was corrected.

Designed to be suitable for nonclinical as well as clinical uses, the MMPI-2 consists of 567 true–false questions written at an eighth-grade level and takes about 90 minutes to complete. The validity scales and the 10 basic clinical scales are scored from the first 370 items, whereas the content scales are scored on items 371 to 567 (see Table 17.2). Numerous additional scales (referred to as either supplementary or research scales) have been developed through researching the meanings of various combinations of items. Indeed, it has been said with some justification that there have been more scales derived from the MMPI than there are items.

As can be noted by comparing Tables 17.1 and 17.2, the MMPI-2 has the same clinical (basic) scales as the MMPI. However, the original range of scores for the MMPI was not uniform around the *T* scores. What this means is that the percentile distributions varied from one scale to another such that a *T* score of 65 on one scale might have had 98th percentile ranking but the same *T* score of 65 on another scale might have had a different percentile

TABLE 17.2   Validity and Basic (Clinical) MMPI-2 Scales

NAME (ABBREVIATION)	INTERPRETATION OF HIGH SCORES
Validity Scales	
Lie (L)	Naive, obvious exaggeration of positive qualities
Infrequency (F)	Exaggeration of negative qualities
Correction (K)	Defensiveness, subtle exaggeration of positive qualities
Variable response inconsistency (VRIN)	Inconsistent (contradictory) responses suggesting random responding based on similar *and* opposite items
True response inconsistency (TRIN)	Inconsistent (contradictory) responses based on opposite contents
Basic (Clinical) Scales	
Hypochnodriasis (Hs)	Extreme concern with physical malfunctioning
Depression (D)	Sadness, pessimism, hopelessness, low self-esteem, unhappiness
Hysteria (Hs)	Immature, attention seeking, low insight, use of denial, unexplained physical symptoms
Psychopathic deviance (Pd)	Antisocial, angry, self-centered, alienated from self and/or society, exploits others for own needs
Masculinity–femininity (Mf)	High number of female interests (for males) or high number of male interests (for females)
Paranoia (Pa)	Hypersensitive to real or imagined criticism, suspiciousness, possible delusions
Schizophrenia (Sc)	Disorganized or unusual thoughts, poor reality contact, perceptual–motor–sensory abnormalities
Hypomania (Ma)	High energy, euphoric, speeded activity, poor impulse control, poor judgment, unable to sleep
Social introversion (Si)	Shy, withdrawn, limited need to be with people, possible social anxiety
Content Scales	
Anxiety (ANX)	Generalized anxiety, worries, insomnia, tension, problems with concentration, ambivalence
Fears (FRS)	Specific and multiple fears (fear of dirt, open spaces, nuisance animals, blood, etc.)
Depression (DEP)	Sadness, feeling empty, guilt, cries easily, sensitive to rejection, feels hopeless and helpless
Health concerns (HEA)	Physical complaints, low energy, worried or nervous regarding physical functioning, maladjusted
Bizarre mentation (BIZ)	Psychotic thoughts (delusions, hallucinations, disorganized thoughts), paranoid beliefs
Anger (ANG)	Poor control of anger, impatient, irritable, loss of control, possible abuse of others

TABLE 17.2   Continued

Cynicism (CYN)	Distrusts others, fears being exploited by others, negativity toward others
Antisocial practices (ASP)	Difficulties with law or school system, lying, stealing, cheating, thinks like a criminal
Type A (TPA)	Hardworking, driven, impatient, annoyed by interruptions, blunt, petty, competitive
Low self-esteem (LSE)	Extremely aware of faults, lack of confidence, feels of little significance, feels disliked by others
Social discomfort (SOD)	Withdrawn, shy, prefers to be alone, introverted, uneasy with people
Family problems (FAM)	Unhappy (possibly abusive) childhood, marital difficulties, family discord
Work interference (WRK)	Personal problems interfere with work, career indecision, dislike of co-workers, worry, tension
Negative treatment indicators (TRT)	Distrust or dislike of helping professionals, low self-disclosure, resistant to change, gives up easily

ranking. This made it difficult to compare various scales. In contrast, the MMPI-2 developed *T* scores so that they were uniform.

To provide a more representative sample of U.S. adults than its predecessor, the MMPI-2 was standardized on 1,138 male and 1,462 female residents (ages 18 to 90) of the United States. The standardization sample was selected, according to 1980 census data, on the basis of geographical distribution, ethnic and racial composition, age and educational levels, and marital status. Reliability data reported in the MMPI-2 manual (Hathaway & McKinley, 1989) are based on relatively small samples (82 men and 111 women); test–retest coefficients for scores on the basic scales range from .58 to .92. Some of the low–reliability coefficients, coupled with the fairly sizable standard errors of measurement, indicate that differences in scores on the various scales should be interpreted cautiously.

Interpretation of MMPI-2 Profiles

Figure 17.1 is a profile of scores on the MMPI-2 obtained by the 60-year-old businessman described in Psychological Report 17.1. Note that scores above a *T* score of 65 are considered interpretable. The higher the score, the stronger the meaning is for the person. Although a generally high profile on the clinical scales suggests serious psychological problems, a high *T* score on a given clinical scale is not necessarily indicative of the disorder with which the scale is labeled. For this and other reasons, the clinical scales are referred to by their numerical designations. Rather than being based on a single score, a personality analysis is made on the basis of the pattern displayed by the entire group of scores. Often these are summarized by 2-point codes such that a person with the highest scores on scales 1 and 3 would be given a 13/31 code. Extensive research has been conducted to understand the meanings of the different code types.

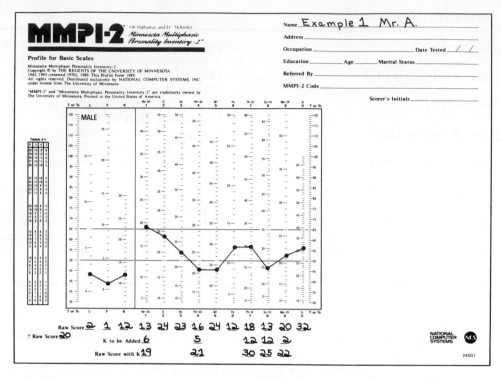

FIGURE 17.1 Sample Profile of Scores on the MMPI-2. See Psychological Report 17.1.

(From *Minnesota Multiphasic Personality Inventory-2 (MMPI-2) Profile for Basic Scales.* Copyright © 1989 by the Regents of the University of Minnesota. Reproduced by permission of the publisher. All rights reserved. MMPI-2 and Minnesota Multiphasic Personality Inventory-2 are trademarks owned by the University of Minnesota.)

There are frequent clusters or classic patterns of scale elevations. Scale 2 is considered to be a measure of depression and scale 7 a measure of anxiety, tension, or alertness to unknown danger. Because depression and anxiety are common symptoms of mental disorder, psychiatric patients typically have high scores on scale 2, scale 7, or both. This 27/72 code type points to a combination of anxiety and depression. Other patterns of high scores indicate other symptoms. For example, high scores on scales 4 and 9 suggest impulsiveness, low frustration tolerance, rebelliousness, and hostile aggression. High scores on scales 6 and 8 point to withdrawal, apathy, and paranoid delusions.

Special terms have become associated with certain patterns of high scores on the MMPI clinical scales. Scales 1, 2, and 3 are referred to as the *neurotic triad,* because persons with high scores on these scales often have psychoneurotic problems. When the *T* scores on all three scales are above 70, but scale 2 is lower than scales 1 and 3, the configuration is referred to as a *conversion V* and is associated with a diagnosis of conversion hysteria. At the other end of the profile, scales 6 through 9 are referred to as the *psychotic tetrad* because of their association with psychotic problems. A configuration in which the *T* scores on scales 6 through 9 are all above 70, but the *T* scores on scales 7 and 9 are lower than those

PSYCHOLOGICAL REPORT 17.1   Interpretative Report of Scores on MMPI-2 Profile in Figure 17.1

Mr. A was seen in a medical outpatient service complaining of a variety of abdominal pains and distress. He is a 60-year-old businessman, white, married, with 2 years of college. Little evidence could be found for an organic basis for his complaints, and he was referred for psychological assessment.

The profile he obtained on the MMPI-2 is shown in Figure 17.1 (12/21 code type) and, even though scale 2 is below a *T* score of 65, it is still interpretable since it is so close to this cutoff. All the traditional validity indicators are below the mean and suggest that he was very cooperative with the test. There is no evidence of defensiveness or of intention to distort his self-presentation on the inventory. His L and K scores fell in the ranges that raise the possibility that he was deliberately faking a poor adjustment, but his score on the F scale does not indicate that this is true. The correlates of these validity indicators suggest that this man is open, conventional, likely to display his problems, but is not in the midst of a serious emotional crisis.

On scale 1, his highest clinical score, he earned a *T* score of 66. A score in the high range on this scale suggests that he is rather self-centered and demanding, pessimistic and defeatist in his view of the future, and is likely to overreact to any real problems. It is likely Mr. A will have numerous physical complaints that will shift to different places on his body.

His second highest score is on scale 2 and it falls in the moderate range. This score also suggests that he is pessimistic and discouraged about the future. He is dissatisfied with himself or the world, is worrying and moody. His temperament is introverted, but he is a responsible and modest individual.

Slight elevations on scales 6, 7, and 0 suggest that Mr. A is responsible, hardworking, and reserved.

Individuals with 12/21 profiles show an exaggerated reaction to physical disorders, are prone to fatigue, and are often shy, irritable, reclusive, and depressed. Visceral pain, overconcern with bodily functions, and lack of insight are prominent features.

The scale by scale analysis of this man's profile highlights some hypochondriacal and depressive trends in an introverted, moody, and hardworking man. The code-type characteristics are present but only to a moderate degree, as would be expected for profile elevations of this magnitude.

These characterizations are clearly borne out in the background information about Mr. A. He was married at the age of 25 to his present wife; there have been no marital difficulties. However, Mrs. A has recently quit her job, which resulted in a loss in the family income. They have one child, a son age 25, who is living away from home.

Mr. A has consulted his family physician very frequently in the last year and has made three visits to a Veterans Administration outpatient clinic in the last few months. In addition to his abdominal symptoms, Mr. A has had problems sleeping, complains of chronic fatigue, a loss of interest in sex, and recurring fears of death. He has also lost considerable weight and has had difficulty concentrating in his work. Sedatives have not been helpful. The present diagnostic impression is that Mr. A is suffering from dysthymia (moderate depression) with hypochondriacal features.

on scales 6 and 8, is referred to as a *paranoid valley* and suggests a diagnosis of paranoid schizophrenia.

Computer-Based Test Interpretation (CBTI)

Hundreds of CBTI programs and services are now commercially available, including programs that score and interpret the results of tests of cognitive abilities, neuropsychological functioning, and personality. Psychological Report 17.1, for example, was generated by a program for interpreting the MMPI-2. Many companies provide computerized test interpretation and reporting services, as well as hardware and software for computer-based testing. Computerized reports are available for such areas as clinical evaluation, forensic applications, vocational decisions, and client feedback.

The programs that generate CBTI reports represent either a distillation of clinical experience or a conglomeration of statistical relationships between what people report on a personality inventory or other psychometric device and how they actually behave. In the clinical approach, the diagnostic program essentially mimics the clinical judgments of experienced psychodiagnosticians. In the statistical, or actuarial, approach, the reported interpretative statements are based on significant differences between the responses of two contrasting groups of people, those independently assigned to one diagnostic group and those assigned to another.

Whether the program follows the more popular clinical approach or the statistical–actuarial approach, the rules or algorithms used in generating CBTI reports range in difficulty from (1) a simple procedure in which a given score or score range is connected to a set of short interpretative paragraphs, all the way through (2) a complex set of if–then decision rules in which a particular pattern of subscores leads to a given interpretive statement. However, even the most complex interpretations are usually not as individualized as those devised by professional psychologists, who use not only test scores, but also additional information (history, behavioral observations, additional test scores). The algorithms and decision trees followed in various CBTI programs result in the same data producing the same set of verbal statements. The reader of such a report may be impressed by its scientific aura, it is also appropriate to be somewhat skeptical (Groth-Marnat & Schumaker, 1989). Murphy and Davidshofer (1994) suggested that the more a CBTI report says about a person, the less likely it is to be true. Butcher, Perry, and Hahn (2004) similarly pointed out that approximately half of all interpretations in a computerized report will be false. This highlights the importance of integrating interpretations with existing information to help counter inaccuracies (Lichetenberger, in press). Clearly, CBTI reports are not an adequate substitute for clinical judgment, and trained clinicians should review and perhaps fine-tune them with information obtained from other sources.

California Psychological Inventory

Of the many empirically validated, MMPI-like inventories for normal individuals, the most popular and extensively researched is the California Psychological Inventory (CPI). Designed by Harrison Gough, half of the 480 true–false statements on the original version of this inventory of adolescent and adult personality characteristics were taken from the MMPI and the remaining half were new. Unlike the MMPI clinical scales, which are concerned primarily with maladjustment and psychiatric disorders, the CPI scales assess more positive, normal, and interpersonal aspects of personality (it is sometimes referred to as the "sane person's MMPI").

CPI Scales.   The original (1957) CPI was scored for the starred (*) scales listed in Table 17.3, three of which, Well-being, Good Impression, and Communality, are validity scales. The first two validity scales were constructed from items that normal people tended to answer in a certain way when asked either to fake bad (Well-being) or to fake Good (Good Impression), whereas the Communality score is simply a count of highly popular responses. Eleven of the 15 remaining scales, like those on the MMPI, were selected using a criterion-keying approach. The other four scales (Social Presence, Self-acceptance, Self-control, and Flexibility) were developed using a content-based approach.

CPI™ Third Edition. The first revision of the CPI (1987) comprised 462 items retained or reworded from the original 480-item CPI. A subsequent third edition (1996) contained 434 of these items (Gough & Bradley, 1996). The revised CPI™, Third Edition, is scored on 20 Folk Scales consisting of the original 18 CPI scales plus Empathy and Independence (see Table 17.3). It is also scored on three Vector (or factor) Scales and 13 Special Purpose Scales, five of which are listed in Table 17.3. The three vector scales represent a theoretical model containing three major themes: role, character, and competence. The theme on the first vector (v.1) measures the extent a person is oriented toward being internal (introverted) versus external (extroverted). It is related to scores on Capacity for Status, Dominance, Self-acceptance, Sociability, and Social Presence. The second vector (v.2) measures norm favoring versus norm questioning, which involves interpersonal values of the sort assessed by the Responsibility, Socialization, and Self-control scales. The third vector (v.3) measures competence or realization, and is a combination of scores on Achievement via Conformance, Achievement via Independence, Intellectual Efficiency, Well-being, and Tolerance scales. The three vector scores are uncorrelated, but they are significantly related to scores on the folk-concept scales.

Scores on v.1 and v.2 were classified separately to yield a fourfold typology: alpha, beta, gamma, and delta. *Alphas* are externally oriented and norm favoring; *betas* are internally oriented and norm favoring; *gammas* are externally oriented and norm doubting; *deltas*

TABLE 17.3   Folk and Special Scales on the California Psychological Inventory, Third Edition

FOLK SCALES		SPECIAL SCALES AND INDEXES
*Dominance	*Communality	Managerial Potential
*Capacity for Status	*Tolerance	Work Orientation
*Sociability	*Well-being	Leadership Potential Index
*Social Presence	*Achievement via	Social Maturity Index
*Self-acceptance	Conformance	Creative Potential Index
Independence	*Achievement via	
Empathy	Independence	
*Responsibility	*Intellectual Efficiency	
*Socialization	*Psychological-Mindedness	
*Self-control	*Flexibility	
*Good Impression	*Femininity–Masculinity	

*Scales on original version of California Psychological Inventory.

are internally oriented and norm doubting. Alphas are described as "ambitious, assertive, enterprising, outgoing, and self-seeking"; betas are "cautious, conservative, conventional, moderate, and unassuming"; gammas are "adventurous, clever, headstrong, progressive, and rebellious"; deltas are "preoccupied, quiet, reserved, sensitive, and worrying."

The third structural scale (v.3) is based on a continuum of levels of competence. The lowest levels are described as poorly integrated, with little or no realization of the positive potential of the type. The middle levels have average ego integration, with moderate realization of the positive potential of the type. Finally, the highest level is described as having "superior ego integration, with good realization of the positive potential of the type (the type being alpha, beta, gamma, or delta).

Test–retest reliabilities over 1 year were variable, with the lowest being .51 for flexibility and a high of .84 for Femininity–Masculinity (median $r = .68$). Internal consistency was also variable with a low of .43 for Femininity–Masculinity and a high of .85 for Well-being (median $r = .76$) (Gough & Bradley, 1996). Predictive validity indicates that scores on the CPI correspond with descriptions made by people who are familiar with them (Gough & Bradley, 1996). It has also been found to predict such things as grade-point average, recidivism among forensic populations, and police performance (see Groth-Marnat, 2003). The CPI has been used to identify and develop successful employees and leaders, create efficient and productive organizations, and promote teamwork. Limitations of the CPI are that little research has been done in clinical settings, there is considerable item overlap between the scales (with resulting high correlations among many of the scales), and little research has been done on the meaning of two-point code types.

Personality Inventory for Children

Because of the low reading comprehension of most children, self-report inventories are less reliable and less valid when used with children. Although there are numerous inventories on which children rate themselves, instruments on which adults rate children are often more valid. An example is the Personality Inventory for Children, Second Edition (PIC-2) (by D. Lachar & C. P. Gruber; Western Psychological Services; see Lachar, 2004). Consisting of 275 true–false items concerning child behavior, the PIC-2 can be completed in 40 minutes by a parent, usually the mother, or another caregiver. Responses are scored on three response validity scales (Inconsistency, Dissimulation, Defensiveness) and nine adjustment scales (Cognitive Impairment, Delinquency, Family Dysfunction, Impulsivity and Distractibility, Psychological Discomfort, Reality Distortion, Social Skill Deficits, Social Withdrawal, Somatic Concern). Each adjustment scale is scored on two or three subscales.

A shorter version of the PIC-2, the Behavioral Summary, may be used for screening, research, or monitoring behavior change. It consists of the first 96 items and is scored on eight adjustment scales. Two other instruments in the PIC-2 family are the Personality Inventory for Youth (PIY), a self-report inventory for children (grades 4–12), and the Student Behavior Survey (SBS), a child-rating scale completed by teachers.

The PIC-2 was standardized on 2,306 parents of children in grades K–12 in 23 urban, rural, and suburban schools in 12 states. Additional data were collected on a sample of 1,551 parents whose children had been referred for educational or clinical intervention.

Millon Clinical Multiaxial Inventory

The Millon Clinical Multiaxial Inventory-III (MCMI-III) was designed using a combination of criterion keying, theory, and internal consistency. It was developed to assess personality disorders and clinical syndromes related to DSM-IV and coordinated with Theodore Millon's theory of personality (Millon, Millon, & Davis, 1997; www.pearsonassessments .com/tests/mcmi_3.htm). In revising the MCMI-II to produce the MCMI-III, 95 of the 175 items were reworded or replaced for closer alignment of the inventory with the DSM-IV. Of the 24 diagnostic scales on the MCMI-III, 14 are personality pattern scales that coordinate with disorders on Axis II (personality disorders) of DSM-IV, and 10 are clinical syndrome scales associated with disorders on Axis I (clinical disorders) of DSM-IV. In addition, there are three modifying indexes and a validity index to detect careless, confused, or random responding (see Table 17.4).

The MCMI-III can be administered to adults (18+ years) in approximately 25 minutes in clinical situations where people are evaluated for emotional, behavioral, or personal difficulties. Raw scores on the various scales are weighted and converted to *base rate scores,* which take into account the incidence of a particular characteristic or disorder in the general population. By determining the occurrence of a particular personality disorder or trait in a specific population, the raw scores can be transformed so as to maximize the ratio of the number of correct classifications (true positives) to the number of incorrect classifications (false positives).

In addition to scores on the MCMI-III, NCS Assessments provides a computerized treatment-oriented narrative report, including statements on the validity of the responses, interpretations for both DSM-IV Axis I and Axis II disorders, comments regarding noteworthy responses made by examinees, parallel DSM-IV multiaxial diagnoses, and therapeutic implications. A capsule summary section of the report reviews the severity of the symptoms and briefly describes indications on Axes I and II of the DSM-IV and related treatment considerations.

The normative sample consisted of 1,000 males and females representing a wide variety of psychiatric diagnoses. Reliability is excellent, given that alpha coefficients range from .66 to .89 for the personality scales and .71 to .90 for the clinical syndrome scales. Test–retest reliabilities range from .84 to .96 for the clinical syndrome scales. Validity is supported in that most of the correlations between the MCMI-III and external measures have been in the expected direction (i.e., MCMI-III Major Depression scale and the Beck Depression Inventory was .74). In addition, the MCMI-III has been able to predict diagnoses at an accuracy rate ranging between .30 and .80 above chance (or base rate) occurrence (see Millon & Meagher, 2004)

Personality Assessment Inventory

The Personality Assessment Inventory (PAI) (by L. C. Morey; Psychological Assessment Resources; see Morey & Boggs, 2004) was developed using a combination of content and criterion-keying strategies. It consists of 344 4-point (F = False, Not At All True; ST = Slightly True; MT = Mainly True; VT = Very True) items written at a fourth-grade level. As a multidimensional alternative to the MMPI, the PAI was designed to provide information

TABLE 17.4 MCMI-III Scales

SCALE NAME	MEANING OF HIGH SCORES
Modifying Indexes	
Disclosure	Faking good (low scores), faking bad (high scores)
Desirability	Faking good
Debasement	Faking bad
Validity	Random responding
Clinical Personality Pattern Scales	
Schizoid	Detached, withdrawn, loner, distant, passive
Avoidant	Socially inept, anxious, self-critical, isolated, rejected
Dependent	Inadequate, agreeable, needs guidance, docile
Histrionic	Dramatic, emotional, active, colorful, attention seeking
Narcissistic	Self-important, immature, confident, pretentious
Antisocial	Competitive, impulsive, provocative, violent, cynical
Aggressive (Sadistic)	Hard-headed, intolerant, aggressive, callous, cruel
Compulsive	Conforming, disciplined, restrained, meticulous
Passive–Aggressive (Negativistic)	Resentful, oppositional, guilty, conflicted, moody
Self-defeating (Masochistic)	Aggrieved, feels victimized, unhappy, self-effacing, servile
Severe Personality Pathology Scales	
Schizotypal	Eccentric, disorganized, isolated, bizarre, apathetic
Borderline	Unstable, moody, unpredictable, self-destructive
Paranoid	Suspicious, defensive, superior, touchy, hostile
Clinical Syndrome Scales	
Anxiety Disorder	Tense, apprehensive, indecisive, hyperalert
Somatoform Disorder	Conflicts expressed through physical complaints
Bipolar: Manic Disorder	Mood swings; elation to depression
Dysthymia	Sad, pessimistic, hopeless, helpless, introverted
Alcohol Dependence	Problem drinking, impulsive, self-indulgent
Drug Dependence	Drug abuse, self-indulgent, narcissistic
Severe Clinical Syndrome Scales	
Thought Disorder	Bizarre, fragmented, disorganized thoughts
Major Depression	Hopeless, fearful, pessimistic, ruminates, sad
Delusional Disorder	Paranoid, persecutory thoughts, suspicious, hostile

relevant to clinical diagnoses, treatment planning, and screening for psychopathology in adults aged 18 and older. It can be scored on four validity scales (Inconsistency, Infrequency, Negative Impression, Positive Impression), 11 clinical scales (Somatic Complaints, Anxiety, Anxiety-Related Disorders, Depression, Mania, Paranoia, Schizophrenia, Borderline Features, Antisocial Features, Alcohol Problems, Drug Problems), five treatment scales (Aggression, Suicidal Ideation, Stress, Nonsupport, Treatment Rejection), and two interpersonal scales (Dominance, Warmth). Ten scales are subdivided into 31 conceptually distinct subscales.

The U.S. norms for the PAI are based on a normative sample of U.S. adults aged 18 years and older, stratified by gender, race, and age according to 1995 U.S. Census projections. Norms are also available on large samples of adult clinical patients and college students and on samples in other countries and cultures.

Reviews of the PAI have been generally positive (Boyle, 1995; Kavan, 1995; White, 1996), and an extensive amount of research has been conducted with it with various groups, particularly in clinical and forensic contexts (e.g., Edens, Hart, Johnson, Johnson, & Olver, 2000; Hays, 1997; Rogers, Ustad, & Salekin, 1998; Wang et al., 1997). The number of research citations of the PAI in PsycINFO since 1995 has been higher than that for any other personality inventory except the MMPI-2. According to Piotrowski's (2000) summary of survey findings, the PAI ranks among the most frequently used objective personality tests in practice and clinical training.

SUMMARY

1. Faking is unusual when people respond to objective personality inventories. Patterns of faking include fake bad, fake good, acquiescence, or responding in a socially desirable fashion. These can occur due to personal gain or poor insight. Since this can seriously compromise test validity, many personality inventories have developed special scales to detect various patterns of faking.

2. The Beck inventories are widely used examples of single-construct inventories. They are comprised of 20 to 21 items and assess the nature and extent of depression (Beck Depression Inventory-II), hopelessness (Beck Hopelessness Scale), anxiety (Beck Anxiety Inventory), and suicidal thoughts (Beck Scale for Suicide Ideation). Since they are brief and have good psychometric qualities, they are ideal for use in planning, monitoring, and evaluating the outcome of treatment. Single-construct inventories are also available for the assessment of self-concept (Coopersmith Self-Esteem Inventories, Tennessee Self-Concept) and diagnosing specific disorders (Eating Disorder Inventory-2).

3. Content strategies of test development use a rational, often theoretically based, understanding of a construct to generate test questions. Examples of inventories based on content (theory) are the Edwards Personal Preference Schedule, the Myers–Briggs Type Indicator, and the Personality Research Form.

4. Factor analysis correlates descriptions of people to determine the items that form clusters (factors).

5. Among the inventories based on the results of factor analysis are the Guilford–Zimmerman Temperament Survey, the 16 Personality Factor Questionnaire, the

Adult Personality Inventory, the Eysenck Personality Questionnaire, the NEO Personality Inventory, and the NEO Five-Factor Inventory.

6. Criterion keying (also called empirical criterion keying) first develops a series of items that, based on their content, seem like they might differentiate among various groups of people with known characteristics. However, the ultimate selection of these items is based on a statistical analysis of how effectively they actually perform this function. In other words, the items are retained and *keyed* in the direction that allows for the identification of the *criterion* (group with the known characteristic).

7. The most famous criterion-keyed personality inventory, and the one on which the greatest amount of research has been conducted, is the Minnesota Multiphasic Personality Inventory (MMPI/MMPI-2). The MMPI/MMPI-2 was designed to differentiate among various diagnostic groups on nine clinical scales by analyzing differences in the responses of normal people and patients having specific psychiatric diagnoses. The MMPI/MMPI-2 may be scored on many other scales as well, including validity scales (*?, L, F, K*). Validity scales on the MMPI and other personality inventories are scored to determine whether the items have been answered properly and to adjust scores on content scores for faking and response sets. Numerous computer-scoring and interpretation programs have been developed for the MMPI/MMPI-2. Computer-based test interpretation, which began with work at the Mayo Clinic in the early 1960s on interpretive scoring of the MMPI, has expanded to include the scoring and interpretation of dozens of cognitive and affective instruments by hundreds of commercial organizations.

8. The criterion-keyed procedure by which the MMPI was constructed was also employed in preparing the California Psychological Inventory, the Personality Inventory for Children, and related instruments. Other noteworthy personality inventories designed on the basis of criterion keying, as well as theory and sophisticated psychometric procedures, include the Millon Clinical Multiaxial Inventory-III, the Basic Personality Inventory, and the Personality Assessment Inventory.

MASTERING THE CHAPTER OBJECTIVES

1. *Truthfulness, reliability, and validity*
   a. List five reasons why someone might fake their responses on a personality inventory.
   b. Write five true–false items pertaining to personality characteristics that you think would be answered true more often by people wanting to fake bad than those answering truthfully. Then write five items that you believe would be answered "true" more often by people wanting to fake good than those answering truthfully.

2. *Beck and other single-construct inventories*
   a. Briefly describe the Beck Depression Inventory, Beck Hopelessness Scale, Beck Anxiety Inventory, and the Beck Scale for Suicide Ideation.
   b. Give three reasons why you believe the Beck scales are optimal for planning, monitoring, and evaluating the outcome of mental health interventions.

3. *Content strategies of test development*
   a. Describe the content (theoretical) strategy of test development.
   b. Briefly describe the Myers–Briggs Type Indicator and the Personality Research Form.

4. *Factor analytic approach to test development*
   a. Describe the factor analytic approach to test development.
   b. List the sequence of steps (at least four) you would go through if you wanted to develop a multiconstruct factor analytically based test of positive aspects of human functioning.

5. *Examples of factor analytically based tests*
   a. Briefly describe the 16PF and Adult Personality Inventory.
   b. Briefly describe the Eysenck Personality Questionnaire and the NEO-PIR.

6. *Criterion-keying strategies of test development*
   a. Describe the sequences involved in criterion keying.
   b. List and describe three personality inventories designed according to each of the following strategies: content validated, factor analyzed, criterion keyed.

7. *MMPI/MMPI-2*
   a. Describe the method and rationale for the development of the MMPI-2.
   b. List five reasons why the MMPI-2 has been so popular.

8. *Examples of criterion-keyed tests*
   a. Briefly describe the California Psychological Inventory, and Personality Inventory for Children.
   b. Briefly describe the Millon Clinical Multiaxial Inventory, Basic Personality Inventory, and Personality Assessment Inventory.

EXPERIENCING PSYCHOLOGICAL ASSESSMENT

1. In recent years, there has been a great deal of discussion in the psychological literature concerning the variable of optimism–pessimism. Using a rational (content-based) understanding of the construct, design an optimism–pessimism inventory consisting of 10 items. Five of the items should be worded in a positive (optimistic) direction and the other five in a negative (pessimistic) direction. Using any response format that you like and appropriate directions, label your inventory an Attitude Questionnaire. Type your inventory on one side of a sheet of paper, make several copies, and administer them to the same number of people. Obtain comments on your inventory from the examinees and others, and make changes in wording or format as needed.

2. Arrange to take the Myers–Briggs Type Indicator, the California Psychological Inventory, or another personality inventory and have your scores interpreted by a qualified person. Are your scores consistent with your own assessment of your personality? What criticisms of the inventory do you have to offer?

3. Take an online Big Five personality test at www.personal.psu.edu/faculty/j/5/j5j/IPIP/. Are your scores consistent with your own assessment of your personality? What criticisms of the inventory do you have to offer?

4. Depression and anxiety are the two most frequently presented clinical symptoms. To familiarize yourself with screening tests for these problems, read through the tests described on www.depression-screening.org/screeningtest/screeningtest.htm and www.med.nyu.edu/psych/screens/anx.html. Be sure to read and follow the guidelines included in the disclaimers.

. . . . .

CHAPTER EIGHTEEN

PROJECTIVE TECHNIQUES

CHAPTER OBJECTIVES

1. Describe what is meant by projective technique.
2. Summarize the criticisms and rebuttals of projective assessment.
3. Describe sentence-completion procedures and projective drawings.
4. Describe Rorschach scoring and interpretation and why it has been so controversial.
5. Describe the Thematic Apperception Test and its variations.

Projective technique is a term coined by Lawrence Frank (1939) for psychological assessment procedures in which respondents *project* their inner needs and feelings onto ambiguous stimuli. The stimuli are relatively unstructured materials and/or tasks that a person is asked to describe, tell a story about, complete, or respond to in some other way. In contrast to more direct personality inventories and rating scales, projective techniques are usually less obvious in intent and therefore presumably less subject to faking and response sets. Because the stimulus materials or tasks are relatively unstructured in content and open-ended in terms of the responses elicited, it is assumed that the structure imposed by the respondent is a reflection, or *projection,* of his or her individual perceptions of things. It is also assumed that less structured materials have a greater likelihood of revealing important facets of personality than more structured ones. This grouping of assumptions is also referred to as the *projective hypothesis.*

Early approaches to projective testing were strongly influenced by psychoanalytic theory. This is reflected in that the greatest development of and reliance on projective tests occurred between 1930 and 1960 when psychoanalysis was the predominant force in psychology and psychiatry. Thus examiners might have looked for information on how a client perceives Oedipal situations or what their predominant defense mechanisms were. This has evolved into a much broader approach that includes not only psychoanalytic formulations, but also a person's perceptual–cognitive style and how people construct a story of their lives, internalized images of other people, and how they experience their world (Hilsenroth, 2004). The result is an understanding of a person's internal world of images and fantasy. This is very different from most other forms of assessment that evaluate more observable dimensions, such as traits, interests, and behaviors.

Controversy over projective testing has been one of the greatest debates in the field of psychology. Advocates state projectives provide knowledge of important dimensions of a person's functioning that cannot be obtained through other means. They have been described as X-rays of the mind or a sort of "open sesame" into the unconscious. Over the past two decades, considerable research has been conducted, organized, and cited in an attempt to support these claims. In contrast, critics have pointed out that norms are flawed, scoring is subjective (and therefore unreliable), client responses can be overly influenced by situational factors, there is overreliance on impressionistic interpretations, clinicians often disagree on interpretations, and much of the research is flawed (www.psychologicalscience.org/newsresearch/publications/journals/sa1_2.pdf). Based on these difficulties, critics have concluded that projectives are pseudoscience and believe that training programs should not "waste time" teaching projectives, that projectives should be "abandoned in clinical practice," and that there should be a moratorium on their use.

Despite the above criticisms, projective testing continues to be popular. Recent surveys of practice indicate that three (Rorschach, Thematic Apperception Test, House–Tree–Person) of the 10 most frequently used tests by clinical psychologists are projectives (see Table 1.3; from Camara et al., 2000). Clearly, many professionals who are working face to face with clients feel that they are valuable tools. It is also clear that many academics (and many practitioners) feel that such faith is misguided and potentially hazardous to clients. Table 18.1 summarizes some of the more important issues in the debate. One important thing to keep in mind is that the degree of support for a particular projective test will vary from test to test. For example, it is easier to score and research responses to a set of inkblots than for a storytelling test. This is because inkblot responses are simpler (i.e., "bat," "moth") than the far more complex data found in a story. A second thing to consider is that the way in which projectives are used varies widely. One practitioner might administer a Rorschach and carefully score it according to a well-standardized system. Interpretations might be conservative and based primarily on categories that have been well validated. In contrast, another clinician might administer a Rorschach and then provide an intuitive, impressionistic interpretation. This diversity means that making generalizations about projectives is difficult. This is very different from objective personality tests that have a standard set of administrative and scoring procedures, as well as more fixed (often computer-based) procedures for interpretation.

To better understand the diversity in interpreting projective drawings, let's consider the following situation. A psychologist has requested a client to draw a picture of a person. The size, erasures, eyes, and degree of distortion are noted. Previous psychologists working with human figure drawings have suggested the following interpretations:

> *Large size of figure:* indicates emotional expansiveness or acting-out behavior.
> *Small size of figure:* emotional constriction, withdrawal, or timidity.
> *Erasures around buttocks or genitals:* indicates anxiety related to sexuality.
> *Large eyes:* hypervigilance, paranoid tendencies.
> *Distorted drawing:* disorganized thought processes, poor awareness of reality.

TABLE 18.1   Criticisms and Rebuttals of Projective Testing

CRITICISM	REBUTTAL
Poor interrater reliability	Good interrater reliability has been demonstrated for well-developed scoring systems when raters are properly trained.
Poor test–retest reliability (low stability)	Good stability has been demonstrated for constructs expected to be stable, but low stability has been found for changeable characteristics.
Flawed or nonexistent norms	Norms have been a problem in the past, but have been updated.
Unsupported research for many interpretations	This varies according to interpretive category, but many interpretations do have good research support.
Interpretations are subjective	This varies according to test, scoring or interpretive system, and how the "test" is used (formally vs. impressionistically).
Contrary to claims, results can be faked	Many research studies indicate faking is difficult.
Poor predictions of external behavior	Projectives are more concerned with internal structure and images that are not expected to necessarily correspond to external behavior.
Generally poor validity	A number of meta-analyses indicate validity is comparable to commonly used objective personality tests.

These interpretations may appear plausible, but they are primarily based on an assumed parallel (or assumed "isomorphy") between features of the drawing and aspects of the person. Thus large drawings would reflect an expansive person who is prone to acting out. They are also based on clinical anecdotes that seem to confirm specific interpretations. Often practitioners can readily give examples in which the large size of a drawing did indeed reflect a person with expansive, acting-out tendencies. This is despite the fact that in most cases this finding did not occur among people with known expansiveness or acting out. The result is an example of illusory correlation. As a result, such interpretations should be viewed only as possibilities or reasonable hypotheses that may or may not be confirmed by other sources of information regarding a person. In contrast to the above approach, there is moderate research support for some interpretations of human figures drawings using formal scoring systems. These include identifying the presence of brain damage, impulsiveness, and level of cognitive development (see Groth-Marnat, 1999a). Using this more structured, empirically based approach is more likely to provide accurate interpretations. Since it is difficult to know whether a more intuitive, impressionistic or a more formal, empirical approach is used, it makes it very difficult to generalize regarding whether the Draw-a-Person "test" as a whole is a valid procedure or not. It depends in part on how it is used.

The option of using projectives either impressionistically or formally presents a dilemma. An impressionistic, qualitative approach opens up the possibility for rich, symbolically meaningful information about the examinee. This can be used to develop numerous hypotheses. For example, the play, *A Streetcar Named Desire,* depicts a traumatized fading Southern belle. She is admitted to a psychiatric hospital where a psychologist gives her a Rorschach. One of her responses is "It's a butterfly, a fragile and exquisite creature who once roamed free, but now, is caught in the net of a naturalist. It will be pinned down and studied with a cold eye by a man who has no sense that it was once a living, breathing, vibrant being." This vividly captures her image and experience of her current world. However, the process of giving this response a formal score where it can be compared to a normative group loses this richness and meaning. This is despite the fact that formal scoring and interpretation are likely to meet psychometric standards for reliability and validity. Thus a formal approach may meet psychometric standards, but is likely to lose depth and richness. In contrast, an impressionistic, symbolical approach has the potential to capture personally meaningful information about the person, but will rarely meet psychometric standards.

In addition to reliability and validity are issues related to the type and cost of information derived from projective assessment. Many psychologists greatly value information regarding a client's internal world of images and fantasies. Accordingly, they attend to these types of client experiences when working with them. Projective techniques for this group of psychologists would be very relevant. In contrast, other psychologists are much more concerned with external behaviors and how the client's thoughts alter these behaviors. As a result, they would not be likely to value information derived from projective assessment. A final factor is that projective testing takes extensive time to learn, administer, score, and interpret. Contrast this with the cost-containment climate of health care, along with high demands on teaching a wide number of skills in graduate training programs. As a result, providers need to carefully weigh the value of the information with the cost of obtaining it (Groth-Marnat, 1999b). Often, projective testing is considered to be neither time nor cost effective.

WORD ASSOCIATIONS AND CONSTRUCTIONS

Various projective techniques have been devised to detect less obvious motives, conflicts, problems, and other covert intrapersonal characteristics. Of these, semistructured techniques such as word associations and sentence completions are perhaps closest to self-report inventories in terms of design, format, and objectivity.

Word Associations

The method of word association was introduced by Francis Galton in 1879 and first applied clinically by Carl Jung (1910) to detect clusters of unconscious images (or "complexes"). A series of words is read aloud to a person who has been instructed to respond to each with the first word that comes to mind. Clinical applications of the technique involve interspersing selected emotionally loaded words or words of special significance to the person within a set of neutral words. In addition to significant verbal associations and delays in responding, the degree to which certain words are emotionally arousing may be determined by measuring skin conductance, muscle tension, respiration rate, blood pressure, pulse rate, voice tremors, or other physiological reactions to the stimulus words. An extension of this is the use of a polygraph to detect lying by noting high-emotional responses to certain events concerning a crime about which the respondent has some knowledge (a so-called "lie detector" test).

As with all projective techniques, responses on a word-association test should be interpreted within a context of other information about the person. A general principle that has guided psychoanalytic interpretations of language is that nouns are more likely than verbs to be disguised expressions of needs and conflicts. This is so because, according to psychoanalytic theory, it is easier to alter the object of a desire (a noun) than its direction (a verb).

Many clinical psychologists prefer to construct their own word lists, but standardized lists are available. An example is the Kent–Rosanoff Free Association Test, a standard list of 100 words and associations to them given by 1,000 adults. The Kent–Rosanoff, which was published originally in 1910, is one of the oldest psychological tests in use (Isaacs & Chen, 1990). Another standard word list was provided by Rapaport, Gill, and Schafer (1968) and used for diagnostic purposes at the Menninger Clinic.

Sentence Completions

Asking a person to complete specially prepared incomplete sentences is a flexible, easily administered projective technique first described by Payne (1928). A variety of sentence fragments or *stems* related to possible areas of emotional arousal and conflict can be constructed. The following are illustrative:

> My greatest worry is _____.
>
> I only wish my mother had _____.
>
> The thing that bothers me most is _____.
>
> I don't like to _____.

It is assumed that the respondent's wishes, desires, fears, and attitudes are reflected in the way he or she completes the sentences.

Despite the fact that they are more obvious than many other projective techniques, sentence completions are considered to be one of the most valid of all projective techniques for diagnostic and research purposes (Haak, 1990; Lah, 1989). The reliability and validity of sentence completions are higher when the responses are scored and interpreted objectively, rather than impressionistically. As with the MMPI and other criterion-keyed instruments, empirical keys have been constructed for both word associations and sentence completions.

Sentence-completion tests may be constructed for a particular clinical case or personality research study, but several instruments of this kind are commercially available. Examples are the Sentence Completion Series and the EPS Sentence Completion Technique (both from Psychological Assessment Resources) and the Rotter Incomplete Sentences Blank, Second Edition (by J. B. Rotter; Psychological Corporation).

Rotter Incomplete Sentences Blank, Second Edition (RISB).   Each of the three forms (high school, college, adult) of the RISB consists of 40 sentence fragments written mostly in the first person and requiring 20 to 40 minutes to complete. Responses are scored for conflict (C) or unhealthy response (e.g., I hate . . . almost everyone.); positive response (P) (e.g., The best . . . is yet to come.); and neutral response (N) (e.g., Most girls . . . are females.). Failing to respond or making a response that is too short to be meaningful is counted as an omission. Scoring weights for C responses are C1 = 4, C2 = 5, and C3 = 6, from lowest to highest degree of conflict expressed. Scoring weights for P responses are P1 = 2, P2 = 1, and P3 = 0, from least to most positive response. N responses receive no numerical weight. After scoring the responses to all sentence fragments, an overall adjustment score is obtained by adding the weighted ratings in the conflict and positive categories. The overall adjustment score ranges from 0 to 240, higher scores being associated with greater maladjustment. The second (1992) edition of the RISB manual contains a number of case examples to demonstrate the scoring of this instrument.

Research has shown that the RISB correctly classifies most respondents into adjusted and maladjusted categories and hence can be used in screening for overall maladjustment. The latest (1992) norms provide cutoff scores based on adjusted and nonadjusted samples. The 1992 manual also contains an updated review of research studies that substantiate the reliability, validity, and clinical utility of the RISB (Rotter, Lah, & Rafferty, 1992).

Rosenzweig Picture-Frustration Study

Another projective device on which examinees construct verbal responses to partially verbal stimuli is the Rosenzweig Picture-Frustration Study (by S. Rosenzweig, Psychological Assessment Resources). Each of the three forms (child, adolescent, adult) of this instrument consists of 24 cartoons depicting individuals in frustrating situations (see Figure 18.1). The

FIGURE 18.1   An Item from the Rosenzweig Picture-Frustration Study.

(Copyright © 1964 by Saul Rosenzweig. Reproduced by permission.)

examinee is asked to indicate, by writing in the blank box over the frustrated person's head, a verbal response that might have been made by this anonymous person (Figure 18.1). Responses are scored according to the direction and the type of aggression expressed. Included under direction of aggression are extraggression (outwardly, toward the environment), intraggression (inwardly, toward oneself), and imaggression (avoidance or nonexpression of aggression). Included under type of aggression are obstacle-dominance or O-D (the frustrating object stands out), etho-defense or E-D (the examinee's ego predominates to defend itself), and need-persistence or N-P (the goal is pursued despite the frustration). Scores are interpreted in terms of frustration theory and available norms on the instrument. The Rosenzweig Picture-Frustration Study has been used in a large number of research investigations throughout the world concerned with the nature of frustration and its relationships to other variables (see Rosenzweig, 1978).

Projective Drawings

Procedures requiring oral or written responses to words and sentences are only one of many construction tasks characterized as projective techniques. Other nonverbal materials that have been employed are clay paints, building materials, and colored chips. Handwriting analysis, although it has not received wide acceptance among psychologists, also has devotees (Holt, 1974). Even more popular have been instruments such as the Draw-a-Person Test (Machover, 1971) and the House–Tree–Person Technique (Buck, 1992) that require respondents to make drawings of people or other objects.

Draw-a-Person Test (DAP).   On this test the respondent makes drawings of people of the same and the opposite sex. The drawings are interpreted in terms of the placement of various features of the drawings (sex, quality, position, clothing, etc.). Particular aspects of the drawings are considered to be indicative of certain personality characteristics or psychopathological conditions. Drawings that are leaning to the side suggest the person is feeling emotionally off balance. Large drawings point to acting out of impulses, and dark, heavy shading suggests strong aggressive impulses. Small drawings, few facial features, or a dejected facial expression point to depression, few body periphery details indicate suicidal tendencies, and few physical features suggest psychosis or organic brain damage (see Groth-Marnat, 1999a). Machover (1971) maintained that a disproportionately large or small head (the center of intellectual power, control of body impulses, and social balance) is indicative of functional difficulties in these areas. Although many of these interpretive signs and generalizations were reportedly based on clinical experience and may make psychoanalytic and even common sense, they have not held up under close scrutiny. Some evidence has been found for a relationship between the judged quality of the drawings and overall psychological adjustment (Lewinsohn, 1965; Roback, 1968), but research has not supported most of the psychodynamic interpretations of Machover and others.

   Naglieri, McNeish, and Bardos (1991) developed Draw-a-Person: Screening Procedure for Emotional Disturbance to be used as a screening test for children suspected of behavior disorder and emotional disturbance. This approach to scoring the DAP has met with some success in the diagnosis of problem children (Naglieri & Pfeiffer, 1992). A number of other variations on the DAP Test, such as having the respondent draw pictures of several objects, a group of people, or a story, have been published. Two of these are the

House–Tree–Person Technique and the Kinetic Drawing System for Family and School. The former instrument (by J. N. Buck & W. L. Warren; Western Psychological Services) requires the respondent to make freehand drawings of a house, a tree, and a person. The drawings may be scored quantitatively on a number of variables, but they are usually interpreted impressionistically and holistically.

Kinetic Drawing System for Family and School.   On this projective technique (by H. M. Knoff & H. T. Prout; Western Psychological Services), the child or adolescent examinee is first asked to draw a picture of his or her family doing something. After the drawing has been completed, the respondent is asked to identify each family member in the drawing, describe what he or she is doing in the picture and why, and to talk about their relationships with each other. A similar procedure is followed in administering the school portion. In interpreting the drawings, the examiner attempts to clarify their meanings and to determine what covert processes may have influenced their construction. Two of the most psychologically important features of the drawings are the types of activities the examinees are engaged with and the extent to which the activities interact.

THE ROSCHACH

The Swiss psychiatrist Hermann Rorschach developed a series of inkblots in 1921. He administered them in a standard manner as a means of studying personality. These inkblots have remained virtually unchanged to the present time and consist of ten 5½- by 9½-inch cards (from Hogrefe & Huber). Each card contains one bilaterally symmetrical, black-and-white (five cards), red-and-gray (two cards), or multicolored (three cards) inkblots against a white background similar to the one in Figure 18.2. The cards are presented individually and

FIGURE 18.2   An Inkblot Similar to Those on the Rorschach Psychodiagnostic Technique.

viewed at no greater than arm's length; turning the cards is permitted. Examinees are told to report what they see in the blot or what it might represent (www.phil.gu.se/fu/ro.html).

After all cards have been presented, the examiner again shows the examinee each card and asks what features (shape, color, shading, etc.) determined his or her responses. Following this *inquiry* phase, there may be a further period of *testing the limits* to discover whether the examinee can see certain things in the cards.

A number of scoring procedures for the Rorschach have been developed. The most extensively used, well researched, and psychometrically sound is Exner's comprehensive system (Exner, 2003). Every response is scored on the following categories:

> *Location:* Sections of the blot that determined the percept: the whole blot (*W*), a common detail (*D*), an uncommon detail (*Dd*), or, if the white space on the card was used, (*S*).
>
> *Determinant:* Features of the percept that determined the response: form (*F*), color (*C*), shading-texture (*T*), shading-dimension (*V*), shading-diffuse (*Y*), chromatic color (*C*), achromatic color (*C'*), movement (*M*), or combinations of these.
>
> *Content:* Anatomy (*An*), blood (*Bl*), clouds (*Cl*), fire (*Fi*), geography (*Ge*), nature (*Na*), and so forth.
>
> *Popularity:* Whether the response is a popular (*P*) or an original (*O*) one.

The number of responses in each category and certain ratios derived from them guide the interpretation of the test protocol as a whole. Since there are a large number of calculations, computer-assisted programs are available to increase clerical efficiency (e.g., Rorschach Interpretive Assistance program by J. E. Exner, Jr., and I. B. Weiner; Psychological Assessment Resources). The scores and related calculations are then used for interpretation. For example, a large number of small, detailed responses is said to indicate compulsivity, and white-space responses presumably point to oppositional tendencies. Responding to the colored areas of the inkblot is thought to reflect how the person responds to emotions. If they have a high number of responses that exclusively respond to color (so-called Pure C responses; e.g., "bright red blood"), it suggests they are easily overwhelmed by emotions. A complete absence of color responses suggests they try to exclude emotions from their experience. A high number of human movement responses (e.g., "two people playing drums") suggests that the examinee's imagination is well developed. The ratio of the number of human movement responses to the number of color responses (*experience balance*) is said to be related to the degree to which a person is thought-minded (internally oriented), rather than acting on their feelings (externally oriented). Also important in evaluating a Rorschach protocol is the accuracy of responses, that is, how well the responses fit the respective parts of the blots (good, poor, and indeterminate). A high number of poor responses indicates they do not see the world the way most people do (see Psychological Report 18.1). This can reflect creativity or, if the responses are distorted and bizarre, schizophrenia. A high number of Popular (frequently perceived responses) also indicates they see the world the way most people do. However, too many Popular responses suggest overly conventional, rigid thinking. Delays in responding may be interpreted as anxiety.

The above approach is based on a reliable scoring system that compares a client's responses to norms. As noted, high or low numbers of responses in various categories are then

PSYCHOLOGICAL REPORT 18.1   Rorschach Evaluation

Name of Examinee: Joe   Sex: Male
Age: 19   Education: 9th grade
Date of testing: 6/19/2005
Test administered: Rorschach

Referral question: Joe is a 19-year-old, single, Hispanic male with 9 years of education who has been living in a semihomeless condition for the past 4 years and using various recreational drugs. He was admitted to a 1-month rehabilitation program with a somewhat flat affect and self-reported symptoms of anxiety, depression, low self-esteem, and difficulty communicating. His psychiatrist was considering the possibility of antipsychotic medication, but wanted additional information regarding the possibility of a subtle, undiagnosed thought disorder (schizophrenia).[a]

Background information: Both parents had been involved with drug abuse, but there was no clear history of family psychiatric difficulties. Joe was diagnosed with learning difficulties at age 6. He always felt as if he was different and recalls having difficulty talking to females and experiencing thoughts of infinity and that God was against him. He began taking Ritalin and later Adderall. At age 12, these began to be used as recreational drugs and at 15 he began using marijuana, L.S.D., and amphetamines. Work history has been minimal, and he has never had a relationship with a female other than an occasional date. He now presents with a combination of substance abuse, depression, and anxiety. Eye contact was good and he was easily able to focus on, understand, and answer questions.

Selected[b] Rorschach results:

Number of responses = 17	Whole: 88%	Detail: 12%	
Pure form responses = 14	M = 1	Form/color = 1	Pure color, color/form = 0
Form minus = 27%	Form unusual = 47%	Form plus = 11%	Popular = 2
Total human content = 18%	Human response = 1	Human fantasy = 2	
Aspiration index: 15:1	Experience balance = 1:0	Stress tolerance = .5 W:M 15:1	

Interpretation and impressions: Joe looks at the overall situation, but neglects to take in many relevant details (88% of responses were Whole). This suggests that he has difficulty organizing many aspects of his life. One important way that he copes is to almost completely neglect his emotional responses (nearly a complete absence of Color responses). A further strategy is to withdraw from human contact (only 3 human responses). When he does perceive people, it is often colored by fantasy images (2 of the 3 human responses were fantasy images). Thus he copes by ignoring complexities, blocking out emotions, and withdrawing from human contact. This seems to be partially effective in that his ability to tolerate stress is fairly effective (Stress tolerance = a low .5). In addition, Joe does not see the world the way most people see it (Form minus = 27%, Form unusual = 47%, Popular = 2). Despite being unusual, his perceptions are neither bizarre, disorganized, overly paranoid, nor seem delusional. Instead they are lacking in complexity and focus on fairly obvious aspects of his world.

   Summary and recommendations: Although Joe's thoughts are somewhat similar to those of a person diagnosed with schizophrenia, they are not sufficiently bizarre or disorganized for him to be given this diagnosis. Instead, they are overgeneralized, pay little attention to detail, are poorly organized, and exclude affect. Given this pattern, he would likely benefit from long-term treatment that focuses on organizing his thoughts and resolving patterns of interpersonal relationships and uses medical interventions targeted toward his depression and anxiety (rather than toward a thought disorder). Any interventions should emphasize extremely clear communication, extensive support, and a collaborative style and have a clear contract regarding roles and commitment toward change.

---

[a]Although many aspects of the Rorschach are controversial, it is generally agreed that it is able to detect subtle thought disorders.
[b]An actual Rorschach protocol will have numerous scores, ratios, and indexes. These few were selected since most were discussed in the text and because they are such clear findings in this particular case.

used to make various interpretations. In contrast, responses may also be interpreted in terms of content. The response given earlier in the chapter by the protaganist of *A Streetcar Named Desire* is an example of a response that lends itself to a content interpretation. Another example is aggressive tendencies noted by a large number of explosions or blood. Unreal characters such as ghosts and clowns may suggest an overinvestment in fantasy life and difficulty identifying with real people. Masks are interpreted as role playing to avoid exposure, food is interpreted as dependency needs or emotional hunger, death as loneliness and depression, and eyes as sensitivity to criticism. This approach has the advantage of developing potentially rich, meaningful descriptions of the client. However, it runs the risk of being subjective and reflecting the interpreter's processes as much (or possibly more) than the client's.

The main debates regarding projective techniques have focused on the Rorschach. Virtually every aspect has been challenged. These challenges have been responded to by Rorschach proponents (refer to Table 18.1; www.psyc.jmu.edu/cipsyd/rorschach/ wheredowego.pdf). For example, Meyer et al. (2002) responded to criticisms of Rorschach reliability by analyzing eight data sets. He concluded that interrater reliability was excellent (range from .82 to .97). One criticism has been that 200 of the 700 protocols used to norm the Comprehensive System were found to be duplicates. This was used to question all previous research using these norms (Garb, 1999). Exner (2004) has responded by both collecting new norms and pointing out that, using only the 500 "true" protocols, one still came up with similar norms as when the 200 duplicates were included. Meta-analyses of the Rorschach have generally supported its validity as being comparable to the MMPI (ranging from .40 to .50; e.g., Meyer, 2004; Parker, Hanson, & Hunsley, 1988). In contrast, Hunsley and Bailey (2001) reanalyzed these data and concluded that the Rorschach had only a low validity of .29 (in contrast to the MMPI's validity of .48). Meyer (2004) has countered with meta-analyses of a wide variety of tests and concluded that not only does the Rorschach have reasonable validity, but this validity is also similar to many tests used in medicine (www.psyc.jmu.edu/cipsyd/rorschach/factfiction.pdf).

As can be seen from the above information, the debate is both extensive and complex. It involves many thousands of studies. Sometimes it seems these studies are like the Rorschach itself in that different people extract very different meanings from them. What has clearly emerged is that there is tremendous variability in the degree of support for various Rorschach categories. Thus we should not try to look at the Rorschach as a whole, but instead consider specific aspects of it. Even the strongest critics agree that some of the categories are valid. But there is also general agreement that many categories have not been adequately researched or, if they have been researched, the findings are equivocal (see Groth-Marnat, 2003). Probably the best way of resolving this controversy is to develop as much consensus as possible on those categories that do have good to adequate validity. These can be maintained in current interpretive systems, whereas questionable categories should be removed. The result would be a "leaner" but better validated, more user friendly, and less controversial instrument.

Holtzman Inkblot Technique

The Holtzman Inkblot Technique (HIT) (by W. H. Holtzman; The Psychological Corporation) represents an attempt to construct a more objective and valid inkblot test than the

Rorschach. The two parallel forms of the HIT (A and B) consist of 45 blots each, and the examinee is limited to one response per blot. Each blot was selected on the basis of high-split-half reliability and an ability to differentiate between normal and pathological responses. The HIT blots are more varied than those on the Rorschach: some are asymmetrical and some have colors and different visual textures. The HIT can be scored on 22 response categories developed by computer analysis of hundreds of test protocols. The percentile norms for these 22 scores are based on eight groups of people, normal and pathological, ranging in age from 5 years to adulthood. A variation of the HIT is the HIT 25 (Holtzman, 1988), which requires two responses to each of 25 cards selected from the HIT Form A.

The procedures by which the HIT was constructed and standardized were more like those of a personality inventory than other projective techniques, so it is not surprising that its reliability is higher than that of the Rorschach. For example, the HIT has demonstrated promise in the diagnosis of schizophrenia, in that it correctly classified 26 of 30 schizophrenics and 28 of 30 normal college students (Holtzman, 1988; also see Swartz, 1992). As with the Rorschach, however, greater clarity regarding its validity needs to be done.

THE THEMATIC APPERCEPTION TEST
AND ITS VARIATIONS

After the Rorschach, the next most popular projective technique is the Thematic Apperception Test (TAT) (by H. A. Murray; Harvard University Press). The TAT consists of 30 black-and-white picture cards (four overlapping sets of 19 cards each for boys, girls, men, and women) depicting people in ambiguous situations, plus one blank card. Administration of the TAT begins by asking the examinee to tell a complete story about each of the 10 or so picture cards selected as appropriate for his or her age and sex. The examinee is told to devote approximately 5 minutes to each story, telling what's going on now, what thoughts and feelings the people in the story have, what events led up to the situation, and how it will turn out. For example, one of the pictures shows a young woman in the foreground and a weird old woman with a shawl over her head grimacing in the background. The following story was told by a young college woman in response to this picture:

> This is a women who has been quite troubled by memories of a mother she was resentful toward. She has feelings of sorrow for the way she treated her mother; her memories of her mother plague her. These feelings seem to be increasing as she grows older and sees her own children treating her the same way as she treated her mother. She tries to convey the feeling to her children, but does not succeed in changing their attitudes. She is living the past in her present, because this feeling of sorrow and guilt is reinforced by the way her children are treating her.

From stories such as this, information concerning the dominant needs, emotions, sentiments, complexes, and conflicts of the storyteller and the pressures to which he or she is subjected are reportedly obtained. As suggested by the above story, responses to TAT pictures may be particularly useful in understanding the relationships and difficulties between the respondent and his or her parents.

When interpreting TAT stories, it is assumed that respondents project their own needs, desires, and conflicts into the stories and characters. The traditional interpretation procedure is a fairly subjective, impressionistic process centering on an analysis of the needs and personality of the main character (the *hero* or *heroine*), who presumably represents the examinee, and the environmental forces (*press*) impinging on the main character. The frequency, intensity, and duration of the story are all taken into account in the interpretation.

The following are illustrative of the TAT responses or signs that certain psychologists consider indicative of mental disorders of various kinds: Slowness or delays in responding suggest depression; stories by men that involve negative comments about women or affection for other men are indicative of relationship difficulties; overcautiousness and preoccupation with details are signs of obsessive–compulsive disorder. In addition to identifying these patterns of pathology, the TAT also provides information on the content of a person's thoughts. This is in contrast to the Rorschach, which clarifies the underlying structure of personality.

TAT stories can be influenced by situational factors such as mood, sleep deprivation, stress, and differences in instruction. This has resulted in relatively low test–retest reliability. Another limitation of the TAT is that normative data are either lacking or inadequate. The result has been that interpretation is typically impressionistic and highly dependent on the skill of the individual clinician. Despite this trend toward impressionistic interpretation, scores determined by one of several systematic procedures for recording and analyzing the stories have been found to be fairly reliable and valid (Bellak & Abrams, 1997; Groth-Marnat, 2003; Meyer, 2004). These systematic procedures have been used to understand such things as the strengths of various needs, ego defense mechanisms, problem-solving style, and internal images of people (Moretti & Rossini, 2004).

Modifications of the TAT

The TAT pictures have been criticized for depicting scenes of limited cultural diversity and for not including children or older populations. As a result, various modifications have been constructed for non-Whites, children, and older adults. On the assumption that Blacks identify more closely with pictures of other Blacks than Whites, 21 of the original TAT pictures were redrawn with Black figures and published as the Thompson Modification of the TAT (Thompson, 1949). Also noteworthy is TEMAS (Tell-Me-a-Story), which was designed specifically for use with urban Hispanic children (Costantino, 1978; Costantino, Malgady, & Rogler, 1988). The 23 chromatic pictures on TEMAS depict Hispanic characters interacting in urban settings involving negative and positive emotions, cognitions, and interpersonal activities. Two other special versions of the TAT are the Senior Apperception Test and the Children's Apperception Test (Bellak & Abrams, 1997).

Children's Apperception Test.   Based on the assumption that young children (3 to 10 years) identify more closely with animals than with humans, the Children's Apperception Test (CAT-A) consists of 10 pictures of animals in various situations. The Children's Apperception Test-Human Figures (CAT-H), an extension of the CAT-A to older children, consists of pictures of humans in situations paralleling those of the CAT-A animal pictures. The stories on both the CAT-A and the CAT-H are interpreted from the viewpoint of psychodynamic theory, specifically in terms of conflicts, anxiety, and guilt. A checklist, the Haworth

Schedule of Adaptive Mechanisms, is available to assist in interpreting CAT-A and CAT-H stories.

Roberts Apperception Test for Children (RATC).   This test (from Western Psychological Services; McArthur & Roberts, 1982) was designed for children aged 6 to 15 years, but is also usable with families. The 27 stimulus cards (line drawings of adults and children in modern clothing) on the test emphasize everyday interpersonal situations, including family confrontation, parental conflict, parental affection, observation of nudity, and school and peer interpersonal events, in addition to situations of the sort found on the TAT and CAT.

The RATC is administered in two overlapping sets of 16 cards each, one set for boys and one for girls. Explicit guidelines are provided for scoring the stories with respect to adaptive and maladaptive functioning on the following scales: Reliance on Others, Support-Other, Problem Identification, Unresolved Problems, Anxiety, Support-Child, Limit Setting, Resolution, Aggression, Depression, and Rejection. Three other dimensions, Atypical Response, Maladaptive Outcome, and Referral, serve as critical indicators. Raw scores on each area are converted to standard scores based on norms, by age and sex, obtained on 200 Caucasian children. A supplementary set of pictures designed specifically for Black children is also available.

Children's Apperceptive Story-Telling Test (CAST).   The Children's Apperceptive Story-Telling Test (from pro.ed; Schneider, 1989) is based on Adlerian theory and designed to evaluate the emotional functioning of children aged 6 through 13. CAST consists of 31 colorful pictures to which children make up stories (Schneider, 1989; Schneider & Perney, 1990). It was constructed to be racially sensitive and was standardized on a sample of 876 U.S. children selected as representative. CAST is scored on four factors: adaptive, non-adaptive, immature, and uninvested. Internal-consistency and test-retest reliability coefficients of the factor scores are in the .80s and .90s. Some evidence for the content, criterion-related, and construct validity, including score profiles for several clinical groups of children (attention deficit, conduct, anxiety, opposition, and depressive disorders) is reported in the manual.

Senior Apperception Technique.   This test, which was designed specifically for older adults, consists of 16 pictures about which examinees are asked to tell stories. The pictures reflect themes of loneliness, uselessness, illness, helplessness, and lowered self-esteem, in addition to positive and happier situations. As in the case of the Gerontological Apperception Test (Wolk & Wolk, 1971), a similar instrument, responses to the pictures on the Senior Apperception Technique reflect serious concerns over health, getting along with other people, and being placed in a nursing or retirement home. Both tests have been criticized for inadequate norms and possible stereotyping of the elderly.

PROSPECTS FOR PERSONALITY ASSESSMENT

Personality assessment is one of the core activities of most professional psychologists. This is particularly true for psychologists working in clinical, forensic, medical, and counseling settings. It has been found to be useful in both describing a client's current functioning and predicting future behavior. Typical referral questions include the following:

Who will benefit from which type of therapy?
Which offenders are likely to reoffend?
Has a client really benefited from intervention?
Are a patient's seemingly medical symptoms actually due to psychological factors?
Does a client have a subtle, underlying psychotic disorder?
Is this person likely to be malingering?
What are this person's personality strengths?

Professional psychologists confront these types of issues on a regular basis. They are challenging questions and providing accurate, useful answers is crucial. One of the best tools to help address these issues has been personality assessment. From this perspective, personality assessment is a robust, extensively used procedure with demonstrated efficacy.

Despite the demonstrated usefulness of personality assessment, it clearly has its limitations. A major one is that personality only accounts for approximately 20% of why people function and act the way they do. Other factors are the situation, how the person interacts with the situation, and miscellaneous factors (e.g., chance events, types of interpersonal relationships). Importantly, error is built into personality assessment. No matter how hard we try, we still can only hope to account for something in the range of 20% for why people behave as they do. While this is certainly important information, it is also somewhat humbling to consider how much we still do not know.

Over the past decade, personality assessment has been criticized from both within and without the field. It should be clear from the previous discussion that the scientific basis and usefulness of projective tests have been strongly challenged. Additional criticisms are that personality assessment focuses too much on what's wrong with people (rather than what they do well), is not sufficiently linked to treatment planning, does not relate sufficiently to a person's everyday behavior, and does not do an adequate job of taking cultural factors into account (Groth-Marnat, 1999b, 1999c). The greatest external criticisms (and threat) have been from managed care that often perceives personality assessment as neither crucial for treatment planning nor cost effective. As a result, reimbursement has been greatly reduced, with a corresponding reduction in the amount of testing psychologists provide. The field has responded to these criticisms by working to more closely link assessment with treatment planning, expanding the assessment of positive functioning, demonstrating the cost effectiveness of assessment, providing evidence for the scientific basis of personality assessment (including projectives), making greater links to a person's everyday functioning, and demonstrating greater sophistication and sensitivity toward cultural variables.

The future is always difficult to predict. Despite this, it is tempting to briefly play Nostradamus (see Groth-Marnat, 2000a). Assessment will certainly continue incorporating the innovations in scale construction that were discussed previously in the book. These include item-response theory, adaptive administration, and more sophisticated methods of making predictions. At the forefront will be developments in computer technology. This might include such things as ready access to formulas for predicting behavior or virtual reality presentations. For example, a person's personality might be assessed by noting their typical reactions to virtual reality interpersonal transactions. The result may be that traditional paper–pencil responses to test items will become used less and less frequently. TAT-type tests might use voice-activated technology to automatically record and content analyze a person's narrative, which could then be rapidly generated into computer-based interpretations. Computers may also combine traditional test responses with physiological monitors such as EEG, heart rate, and skin conductance. Artificial intelligence could be used to continually improve behavioral predictions by integrating client responses with constantly updated databases. A crucial factor then would be how we can optimally interact with computers (Lichtenberger, in press). Finally, genetic analysis might help to evaluate those characteristics (e.g., introversion–extroversion, neuroticism) that have a significant genetic loading. Groth-Marnat has estimated that the following scenario might occur sometime around the year 2050:

> Development of the first fully integrated assessment system using a combination of artificial intelligence, interactive virtual reality/hologram, physiological monitors, massive interlinked norms, valdity/predictions based on new theories of predicting behavior, branching strategies, genetic measures, in session as well as ongoing everyday life measures. (Groth-Marnat, 2000a, p. 361)

Although this might seem part science fiction, nearly all the above technologies are already present. They are not being used primarily due to their high cost. But the history of technology consistently demonstrates that new technologies are initially very costly, but, if they are sufficiently useful, the cost decreases, resulting in widespread use.

The above advances will present new challenges. As with any technologies, they have the potential to improve our lives, enrich how we interact with each other, and optimize what we can do with our lives. They can also be intrusive and confining and can limit who and what we can become. Although we are already confronting each of these issues, advanced technology will certainly intensify their relevance. It will ultimately depend on you, the readers of this book, to provide guidance. After reading the past many pages of material, you will now be the wise consumers who should be well equipped to challenge or confirm stereotypes, better understand test results, vote on relevant legislation, educate colleagues, and perhaps administer, interpret, and develop tests.

SUMMARY

1. Projective techniques request people to respond to an unstructured stimulus (inkblot, picture, blank paper, sentence stem). Interpreting the stimulus allows them to project aspects of themselves into their response. Proponents claim that this accesses deeper aspects of a person's functioning that the person may not be aware of. It is often thought that more ambiguity increases the possibility that more and deeper aspects of the person will be projected.

2. Projective techniques have been criticized as having poor reliability and subjective scoring, being susceptible to faking, and having flawed or nonexistent norms, unsupported validity, and subjective interpretations. Rebuttals have been given for each of

these criticisms. However, it is difficult to generalize to all projectives since there is so much diversity among various projective techniques. There is also diversity in how they are used; some practitioners use formal scoring and give only conservative interpretations, whereas others use a more informal, impressionistic approach. The formal approach has the advantage of having better psychometric properties, but loses out on unique, symbolical meanings that may describe the client's experience. In contrast, an informal impressionistic approach may strive for possibly meaningful interpretations, but will sacrifice psychometric rigor.

3. Word-association tests have examinees say the first thing that comes to mind in response to a list of words. In contrast, sentence-completion procedures (such as the Rotter Incomplete Sentence Blank) give a sentence fragment (or "stem") and have the examinee finish off the sentence. Projective drawings request the examinee to draw a picture of a person (or a house–tree–person or a picture of themselves doing something). Scoring and interpretative approaches show extreme variability in their degree of structure and amount of validity.

4. The Rorschach requests examinees to respond to a set of 10 inkblots. The responses are scored based on such features as whole versus detail, why they saw the image they did (form, color, movement), content (human, animal, anatomy), and number of populars (responses that many people make). The number and proportion of these responses are considered to reveal how examinees organize aspects of their actual lives. Some people describe a high degree of detail (versus global responses), respond with a high number of color responses, and vary in the degree their perceptions are organized and resemble other people's. It thus assesses the structure of personality. The validity of the Rorschach has been one of the greatest debates in psychology.

5. The Thematic Apperception Test consists of pictures that a person is asked to tell stories about. The narrative content is then analyzed to better understand needs, interpersonal relations, motivations, and other aspects of personality. The TAT is considered to assess the content of personality. Numerous variations of the TAT have been developed, including the Senior Apperception Test, Children's Apperception Test, Roberts Apperception Test, and the Children's Apperceptive Story-Telling Test (CAST).

MASTERING THE CHAPTER OBJECTIVES

1. *Projective techniques*
    a. What is the projective hypothesis?
    b. What are the supposed advantages of projective techniques?

2. *Criticisms and rebuttals of projective techniques*
    a. What are the criticisms of projective techniques and what are the rebuttals to these criticisms?
    b. Given your own values regarding internal and external aspects of the person, psychometric rigor, and world view, do you think you would use projective techniques? Why or why not? If yes, where do you stand on the formal–structured versus informal–impressionistic continuum of using them?

3. *Sentence completion and projective drawings*
    a. What are three advantages of sentence-completion procedures?
    b. Describe the support for the validity of projective drawings.
    c. What are some threats to the validity of projective drawings (be sure to include assumed isomorphy and illusory correlation)?

4. *Rorschach scoring, interpretation, and controversy*
    a. Define what is meant by Rorschach scorings for location, determinants, content, and popularity.
    b. Ask someone to give three responses to the inkblot in Figure 18.2 and then, to the best of your ability, score these responses according to location, determinants, content, and popularity (you may need to consult your instructor or refer to a guidebook, such as Groth-Marnat, 2003).
    c. Describe four interpretive signs for the Rorschach (e.g., what does it mean if someone gives no or very few "color" responses?).
    d. Give four reasons why the Rorschach has been so controversial.

5. *The Thematic Apperception Test and its variations*
    a. Describe the features, administration, and scoring of the TAT.
    b. Give three reasons why it is difficult to establish the validity of the TAT.
    c. What are three reasons why it was necessary to develop variations of the TAT? Give three examples of variations.

EXPERIENCING PSYCHOLOGICAL ASSESSMENT

1. Construct 10 incomplete sentences pertaining to matters of concern to college students. Type (double-space) the sentence fragments on a sheet of paper and make several copies. Administer your sentence completion test to a group of college students; tell them to complete every sentence fragment with a word or phrase that has a personal meaning or refers to a matter of concern to them. Study the responses given to the sentence fragments, and try to analyze them in terms of the personalities of the respondents. Write a report summarizing your findings.

2. Test out the validity of four features of the House–Tree–Person using the following procedure:
    a. Ask several people to make the following four ratings on a scale from 1 to 10: (1) how close they feel to their mother, (2) how close they feel to their father, (3) the amount of power their mother had in the family, and (4) the amount of power their father had in the family. You may need to exercise some flexibility or even do some preselection if a prospective participant comes from a more complicated family (e.g., single parent, parents divorced or remarried several times, etc.).
    b. On a single page of unlined paper have them each draw a picture of a house, a tree, and a person. Drawings should be done using a pencil and they should be told to take their time (i.e., make sure it is three dimensional, not a stick figure).
    c. Note that the tree is considered to represent the father, the house the mother, and the drawing of the person represents the person who has done the drawing. The relative proximity and size of the house, tree, and person are said to represent various family relationships. Check to see if this is true by comparing the ratings made by your participants with the size and proximity of the drawings (i.e., if they rated themselves as being much closer

to their father than to their mother, is this also reflected in the drawings? Is this also true of the ratings of relative power in the family?

  d. Was the above exercise a good test of the validity of the House–Tree–Person? Why or why not?

3. Look through several popular magazines and either cut out or photocopy five pictures of people in ambiguous situations. It should not be immediately obvious what the people in the pictures are doing or thinking. Present the pictures, one at a time, to several people, and ask them to tell a story about each picture. Tell them that they should include in their stories what is going on now, what led up to it (what happened before), and how it will turn out. Interpret the stories in terms of common themes, the actions and feelings of the main characters, the pressures and frustrations occurring in the stories, whether the stories are generally pleasant or unpleasant, and whether the endings are upbeat or downbeat (comedic or tragic). Are there common elements in all the stories? Can you tell anything from these stories about the personality, attitudes, and feelings of the storyteller?

DESCRIPTIVE STATISTICS

APPENDIX OBJECTIVES

1. Describe scales of measurement and frequency distribution, including score intervals, histogram, frequency polygon, and normal curve.
2. Describe measures of central tendency, including mode, median, mean, percentile, decile, and quartile.
3. Describe measures of variability, including range and standard deviation.
4. Describe correlation and linear regression.
5. Explain multiple regression and factor analysis.

Any kind of physical measurement (of size, weight, coloration, etc.) made on living things will vary across individual members of a species. Human beings differ physically from each other in many ways, in height, weight, blood pressure, visual acuity, and so on. Individual differences in these physical variables, in addition to cognitive abilities, personality traits, and behaviors, are appreciable. Among other things, people differ in their abilities, interests, attitudes, and temperaments. Some of these individual differences can be measured more precisely than others, as reflected in the type of measurement scale.

SCALES OF MEASUREMENT

The measurement of physical and psychological variables may be characterized by degree of refinement or precision in terms of four levels or scales: nominal, ordinal, interval, and ratio. Measures on a *nominal scale* are used merely to describe or name, rather than to indicate the order or magnitude of something. Examples of nominal measurement are the numbers on athletic uniforms or numerical designations of demographic variables such as sex (e.g., male = 1, female = 2) and ethnicity (White = 0, Black = 1, Hispanic = 3, Asian = 4). Such numbers are a convenient way of describing individuals or groups, but it makes no sense to compare the numbers in terms of direction or magnitude.

Somewhat more refined than nominal measurement is measurement on an *ordinal scale*. Numbers on an ordinal scale refer to the ranks of objects or events on some variable. For example, numbers designating the order of finishing in a race or other contest are on an ordinal scale.

A third level of measurement is an *interval scale,* on which equal numerical differences correspond to equal differences in whatever characteristic is measured. The Celsius scale of temperature is an example of an interval scale. For example, the difference between 40°C and 60°C is equal, both numerically and in terms of temperature (heat), to the difference between 10°C and 30°C. Standard scores on intelligence tests are also considered to be interval-level measurements.

The highest, or most refined, level of measurement is a *ratio scale.* This type of scale has the characteristics of an interval scale as well as a true zero: a value of 0 on a ratio scale signifies a complete absence of whatever is being measured. Measurements made on a ratio scale allow numerical ratios to be interpreted in a meaningful way. Height, for example, is measured on a ratio scale. So if John is 6 feet tall and Paul is 3 feet tall, it is correct to say that John is twice as tall as Paul. Many physical variables are measured on ratio scales, but most psychological characteristics are not. Scores on psychological tests represent measurement on an ordinal or, at most, an interval scale. For this reason, even if Frank's score on an intelligence test is 150 and Jim's score is 50, we cannot conclude that Frank is three times as intelligent as Jim. But if the scores on the test are interval-level measures and Amy makes an IQ score of 100, it can be said that the difference in intelligence between Frank and Amy (150 − 100) is equal to the difference in intelligence between Amy and Jim (100 − 50).

FREQUENCY DISTRIBUTIONS

The range and distribution of individual differences in physical and mental characteristics may be depicted by means of a frequency distribution of scores on a test or some other psychometric instrument. In its simplest form, a *frequency distribution* is a list of possible scores and the number of people who made each score. Assume that, on a five-item test, 1 point is given for each correct answer. Then the possible scores are 0, 1, 2, 3, 4, and 5. If 25 people take the test, the frequency distribution of their scores might look something like this:

SCORE	FREQUENCY
5	1
4	4
3	9
2	6
1	3
0	2

Note that one person answered all five items incorrectly, nine people answered three items correctly, and one person answered all five items correctly.

Score Intervals

When the range of scores on a test is large, say 25 points or more, it may be convenient to group the scores into intervals. To illustrate, intelligence quotient (IQ) scores on the Wechsler Adult Intelligence Scale (WAIS) range from approximately 43 to 152. Computations made on these scores may be simplified by grouping them into intervals of 5 IQ points, starting with the interval 43–47 and counting up through the interval 148–152 (see column 1 of Table A.1). This gives 22 intervals, instead of the 110 intervals (IQs from 43 through 152) that would result if an interval were allotted to every possible score. Using the smaller number of intervals has little effect on the accuracy of the statistics computed from the frequency distribution of WAIS IQ scores, and it is a more efficient way of describing the scores.

Histogram and Frequency Polygon

A frequency distribution of scores can be plotted graphically as a histogram or a frequency polygon. To construct a *histogram,* the exact limits of the score intervals must first be determined. The *exact limits* of an interval are computed by subtracting .5 from the lower limit and adding .5 to the upper limit of the interval. For example, the exact limits of the interval 43–47 in Table A.1 are 42.5 and 47.5, and the exact limits of the interval 148–152 are 147.5 and 152.5. After the exact limits of all intervals have been computed, the frequency corresponding to each interval is plotted as a vertical bar, with a width spanning the exact limits and a height proportional to the number of scores falling on the interval. Figure A.1 is a histogram of the frequency distribution in Table A.1.

TABLE A.1 Frequency Distribution of Full-Scale IQs on WAIS*

IQ INTERVAL	NUMBER OF EXAMINEES (FREQUENCY)	IQ INTERVAL	NUMBER OF EXAMINEES (FREQUENCY)
93–97	255	148–152	1
88–92	220	143–147	0
83–87	135	138–142	3
78–82	107	133–137	12
73–77	55	128–132	26
68–72	49	123–127	64
63–67	18	118–122	145
58–62	11	113–117	165
53–57	6	108–112	224
48–52	3	103–107	274
43–47	1	98–102	278

*Data from D. Wechsler, *The Measurement and Appraisal of Adult Intelligence,* 4th ed. Baltimore: Williams & Wilkins, 1958, p. 253.

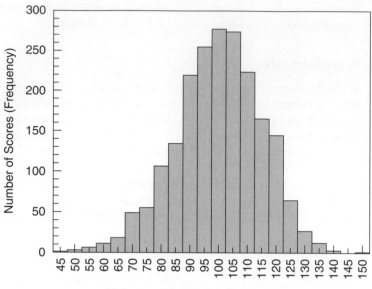

FIGURE A.1   Histogram of Frequency Distribution in Table A.1.

A frequency distribution can also be represented by a series of connected line segments. In Figure A.2, the points corresponding to the frequencies and midpoints of the score intervals in Table A.1 have been joined to form a *frequency polygon*.

Normal Curve

The frequency polygon in Figure A.2 is not a smooth curve, but it is similar in shape to a symmetrical, bell-shaped curve. More people made scores of approximately 100 (actually 98 to 102) than any other score, and successively fewer people made scores lower or higher than 100. If the frequency polygon were perfectly symmetrical, smooth, and bell-shaped, it would look like Figure A.3.

The graph in Figure A.3, which can be described by a mathematical equation, is called a *normal curve*. The scores on the base axis of this curve are *standard scores (z scores)*, the computation of which is described in Chapter 4. These z scores serve as a convenient, standard method of expressing and comparing the scores of the same person on two or more tests or the scores of two or more people on the same test.

A certain percentage of the area under the curve in Figure A.3 lies between any two z scores. This percentage may correspond to the percentage of a group of people whose raw test scores, when converted to z scores, fall within the range of the two z scores. For example, 19.15% of the area under the curve and, consequently, 19.15% of a normal distribution of test scores fall between $z = 0$ and $z = .5$ (or $z = 0$ and $z = -.5$). On the other hand, only 1.66% of the area under a normal curve lies between $z = +2.0$ and $z = +2.5$ (or $z = -2.0$ and $z = -2.5$).

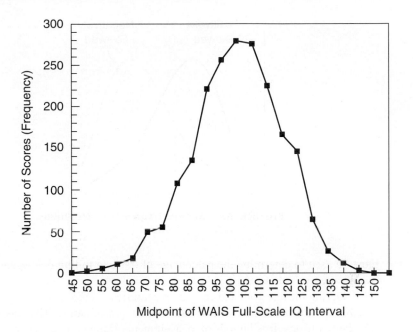

FIGURE A.2   Frequency polygon of frequency distribution in Table A.1.

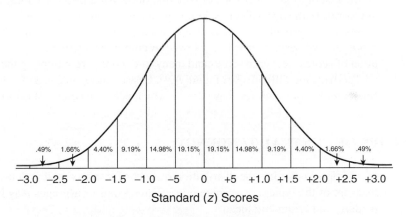

FIGURE A.3   Standard normal distribution.

The theoretical range of z scores in a normal distribution is minus infinity $(-\infty)$ to plus infinity $(+\infty)$, but over 99% of the area under the normal curve (or 99% of a normal distribution of test scores) falls between z scores of -3.00 and $+3.00$. When converting a raw test score to a z score, the result, of course, is not always one of the 13 z scores listed on the horizontal axis of Figure A.3. A special table like that in Appendix B or a computer program

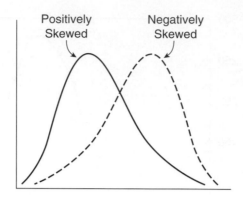

FIGURE A.4   Skewed frequency distributions.

must be used to determine the percentage of the area falling below, and by subtraction between, any two values of *z*.

During the late 19th and early 20th centuries, there was much speculation concerning
whether the normal curve expressed an inherent law of nature. The reason for this belief was
that the frequency distributions of measurements made on many characteristics of living or-
ganisms are approximately normal in shape. In fact, much of the mathematical theory of statistical inference, which is so important in psychological and educational research, is based
on the assumption of a normal distribution of measurements. We must be careful, however,
not to glorify the normal curve. Although many tests are constructed in such a way that their
scores are approximately normally distributed, the frequency distributions of other test
scores are very asymmetrical, or skewed. A common situation is a *positively skewed* distribution of scores (few high scores and many low scores), representing the results of a test that
was perhaps too difficult (see Figure A.4). Less common is a *negatively skewed* distribution
(many high scores and few low scores), which occurs when a test is too easy.

MEASURES OF CENTRAL TENDENCY

In addition to plotting the distribution of a set of test scores, it is convenient to have some
measure of the typical or average score. Three kinds of averages may be computed: mode,
median, and arithmetic mean.

Mode

The *mode* of a set of test scores is the score obtained by the largest number of people. In the
five-item test referred to earlier, more people (9) made a score of 3 than any other score, so
the mode is 3. When test scores are grouped into intervals, the mode is the midpoint of the
interval containing the largest number of scores. The score interval 98–102 in Table A.1 contains the largest number of scores (278); the midpoint of that interval, $(98 + 102)/2 = 100$,
is the mode of that frequency distribution.

As seen in the frequency polygon in Figure A.2, the mode is the score corresponding to the highest point in a frequency distribution. Figure A.2 pictures a *unimodal* distribution having one peak. Sometimes a frequency distribution has more than one peak; it is *bimodal* if it has two peaks and *multimodal* if it has more than two.

Median

The *median* (Mdn) of a set of scores is the middlemost score, that is, the score below which half the scores fall. The median of 7, 6, 9, 5, and 3 is 6, because 6 is in the middle when these five scores are ranked from highest to lowest. When the number of scores is even, the median is defined as the mean of the two middlemost scores.

It takes a few steps to compute the median of a frequency distribution, but it can be found fairly quickly by interpolating within the interval in which it falls. To illustrate the procedure, the median of the frequency distribution in Table A.1 will be computed. The total number of scores is 2,052, so the median is the IQ score below and above which .5(2,052) 1,026 scores fall. By successively adding the frequencies in column 2 of Table A.1, we find that there are 860 scores up through the interval 93–97 and 1,138 scores up through the interval 98–102. Expressed in terms of the exact upper limits of the intervals, we say that 860 scores fall below 97.5 and 1,138 scores fall below 102.5. Because the median is the score below which 1,026 scores fall, it is between 97.5 and 102.5. To find the exact median, we form the ratio $(Mdn - 97.5)/(102.5 - 97.5) = (1026 - 860)(1138 - 860)$. Solving this equation yields a value of 100.49 for the median.

The procedure described above for finding the median of a frequency distribution may be simplified as

$$Mdn = L + \frac{w(.5n_t - n_b)}{n_i} \tag{A.1}$$

In this formula, L is the lower exact limit and w the width of the interval containing the median, n_t is the total number of scores in the distribution, n_b is the number of scores falling below the interval containing the median, and n_i is the number of scores falling on the interval containing the median.

Summation Operator

Before considering the procedure for computing the arithmetic mean, you should become familiar with the special symbol $\sum$. This symbol, the Greek letter capital sigma, is a shorthand way of designating the mathematical operation of summation. Thus,

$$\sum X = X_1 + X_2 + X_3 + \cdots + X_n.$$

To illustrate, consider the three scores $X_1 = 2$, $X_2 = 4$, and $X_3 = 1$. The sum of these scores is $\sum X = 2 + 4 + 1 = 7$. Similarly, the sum of squares of the three scores is

$$\sum X^2 = X_1^2 + X_2^2 + X_3^2 = 2^2 + 4^2 + 1^2 = 4 + 16 + 1 = 21.$$

The sum of the products of two variables X and Y, is expressed as

$$\sum XY = X_1Y_1 + X_2Y_2 + X_3Y_3.$$

If $Y_1 = 3$, $Y_2 = 5$, $Y_3 = 2$ and the X values are the same as those in the preceding problem,

$$\sum XY = 2(3) + 4(5) + 1(2) = 6 + 20 + 2 = 28.$$

Arithmetic Mean

Although the mode is easy to compute, it is greatly affected by the shape of the frequency distribution of scores. The median, which is less affected by the shape of the frequency distribution, is the preferred measure of central tendency when the distribution is highly asymmetrical, or skewed. Because the median is cumbersome to work with in statistical theory, the arithmetic mean is the most popular measure of central tendency (average). The arithmetic mean of a set of scores (X's) is determined by adding the scores and dividing the resulting sum by the number of scores:

$$\overline{X} = \sum X/n. \tag{A.2}$$

The mean of the X scores in the preceding problem is $7/3 = 2.33$.

When scores are grouped in the form of a frequency distribution, the mean can be found more quickly by (1) multiplying the midpoint (X_i') of each interval by the frequency (f_i) on the interval, (2) adding these fX' products, and (3) dividing the resulting sum of products by the total number of scores (n):

$$\overline{X} = \sum X'/n \tag{A.3}$$

For example, the arithmetic mean of the five-item problem described earlier is computed as

$$\frac{2(0) + 3(1) + 6(2) + 9(3) + 4(4) + 1(5)}{25} = \frac{63}{25} = 2.52.$$

As an exercise, you should verify that the arithmetic mean of the frequency distribution in Table A.1 is 99.96.

PERCENTILES, DECILES, AND QUARTILES

The median is sometimes referred to as the 50th percentile, because 50% of the scores fall below the median. A frequency distribution may be divided into 100 percentiles; the *pth percentile* is the value below which *p* percent of the scores fall. For example, the 25th percentile is the value below which 25% of the scores fall, and the 75th percentile is the value below which 75% of the scores fall. Any percentile can be computed by a procedure similar to that described for finding the median.

In addition to percentiles, a frequency distribution may be divided into tenths (*deciles*), fifths (*quintiles*), or fourths (*quartiles*). The fourth decile (or 40th percentile) is the value below which four-tenths of the scores fall, and the third quartile (or 75th percentile) is the value below which three-fourths of the scores fall. Note that the 50th percentile, the fifth decile, and the second quartile are all equal to the same numerical value.

MEASURES OF VARIABILITY

A measure of the average or central tendency does not, by itself, provide an adequate analytic description of a sample of scores. Frequency distributions of scores differ not only in their averages, but also in their degree of variability (spread), symmetry, and peakedness. Three measures of variability will be described: the range, the semi-interquartile range, and the standard deviation.

Range and Semi-Interquartile Range

The simple *range*, defined as the highest score minus the lowest score, is the easiest measure of variability to compute.[1] The range of the scores in the five-item problem described previously is $5 - 0 = 5$, and the range of the IQ scores in Table A.1 is $152 - 43 = 109$. Because it is markedly affected by a single very high or very low score, in most cases the range is a poor measure of variability. A modified type of range known as the *semi-interquartile range* is sometimes used as an index of variability when the distribution of scores is highly skewed. The semi-interquartile range, or *Q*, is computed as one-half the difference between the 75th percentile (third quartile) and the 25th percentile (first quartile).

As an exercise, you should verify that, for the frequency distribution in Table A.1, the first quartile is 90.41, the third quartile is 110.33, and the semi-interquartile range is 9.96. The two quartiles may be found by the same sort of linear interpolation procedure that was used to compute the median. Because the first quartile is the score below which .25(2052) = 513 scores fall, we interpolate within the interval 87.5 to 92.5. Then the first quartile is determined by solving for Q_1 in the expression

$$\frac{Q_1 - 87.5}{92.5 - 87.5} = \frac{513 - 385}{605 - 385}.$$

To find the third quartile, which is the .75(2052) = 1,539th score, we interpolate within the interval 107.5 to 112.5. Then the third quartile is computed by solving for Q_3 in the expression

$$\frac{Q_3 - 107.5}{112.5 - 107.5} = \frac{1539 - 1412}{1636 - 1412}.$$

---

[1]This is the *exclusive range*. The *inclusive range* is equal to the exclusive range plus 1.

Standard Deviation

The most common measure of variability, the *standard deviation,* is appropriate when the arithmetic mean is the reported average. The standard deviation of a sample of scores may be computed from

$$s = \sqrt{\frac{\sum X^2 - (\sum X)^2/n}{n-1}}$$ (A.4)

For example, to find the standard deviation of 7, 6, 9, 5, and 3, we begin by computing $\sum X = 30$ and $\sum X^2 = 200$. Therefore,

$$\frac{\sum X^2 - (\sum X)^2/n}{n-1} = \frac{200 - 30^2/5}{4} = 5.$$

which is the *variance* of our five numbers. Extracting the square root of the variance yields 2.24, the standard deviation.

By setting $\sum X = \sum f(X')$ and $\sum X^2 = \sum f(X'^2)$, where f is the frequency and X' the midpoint on an interval, we can use formula A.4 to compute the standard deviation of a frequency distribution. As an exercise, you should confirm that the standard deviation of the frequency distribution of the five-item problem referred to previously is 1.26, and the standard deviation of the frequency distribution in Table A.1 is 14.85.

CORRELATION AND SIMPLE LINEAR REGRESSION

The method of correlation has been employed extensively in the analysis of test data, and it is also very important in classical test theory. Correlation is concerned with determining the extent to which two sets of measures, such as intelligence test scores and school marks, are related. The magnitude and direction of the relationship between two variables is expressed as a numerical index known as the *correlation coefficient.* Of the many different types of correlation coefficient, the Pearson *product–moment coefficient,* or *r,* is the most popular. It ranges in value from −1.00 (a perfect inverse relationship) to +1.00 (a perfect direct relationship). The Pearson *r* is, however, not the only correlation coefficient that is used in analyzing and applying test scores. For example, the point–biserial coefficient, which is described in Chapter 4, is used extensively in item analysis.

Computing the Product–Moment Coefficient

Table A.2 illustrates the initial computations in determining the correlation coefficient between 30 pairs of *X–Y* scores. Let *X* be an ability test score and *Y* a job performance rating. Thus, person 1 scored 44 on the ability test and 69 on the performance rating, whereas the corresponding scores for person 2 are 38 and 46. The column headings indicate the steps in computing *r:*

1. Compute X^2, Y^2, and XY for each person (columns 4, 5, and 6).
2. Add the *X, Y, X^2, Y^2,* and *XY* columns (columns 2 through 6) and substitute these sums into the following formula:

$$r = \frac{n \sum XY - (\sum X)(\sum Y)}{\sqrt{[n \sum X^2 - (\sum X)^2][n \sum Y^2 - (\sum Y)^2]}}. \quad \text{(A.5)}$$

Since $\sum X = 1,498, \sum Y = 1,511, \sum X^2 = 79,844, \sum Y^2 = 79,641,$ and $\sum XY = 77,664,$

$$r = \frac{30(77,664) - (1498)(1511)}{\sqrt{[30(79,844) - (1498)^2][30(79,641) - (1511)^2]}} = .524.$$

TABLE A.2   Computing Sums for Determining Product–Moment Correlation

(1) PERSON	(2) X	(3) Y	(4) X^2	(5) Y^2	(6) XY
1	44	69	1,936	4,761	3,036
2	38	46	1,444	2,116	1,748
3	56	51	3,136	2,601	2,856
4	54	44	2,916	1,936	2,376
5	66	53	4,356	2,809	3,498
6	52	49	2,704	2,401	2,548
7	46	43	2,116	1,849	1,978
8	36	35	1,296	1,225	1,260
9	44	37	1,936	1,369	1,628
10	60	69	3,600	4,761	4,140
11	22	31	484	961	682
12	72	47	5,184	2,209	3,384
13	56	45	3,136	2,025	2,520
14	52	41	2,704	1,681	2,132
15	50	39	2,500	1,521	1,950
16	64	65	4,096	4,225	4,160
17	40	36	1,600	1,296	1,440
18	28	59	784	3,481	1,652
19	68	70	4,624	4,900	4,760
20	48	53	2,304	2,809	2,544
21	32	51	1,024	2,601	1,632
22	74	63	5,476	3,969	4,662
23	42	54	1,764	2,916	2,268
24	50	52	2,500	2,704	2,600
25	40	49	1,600	2,401	1,960
26	58	48	3,364	2,304	2,784
27	62	60	3,844	3,600	3,720
28	54	64	2,916	4,096	3,456
29	60	55	3,600	3,025	3,300
30	30	33	900	1,089	990
Sums:	1,498	1,511	79,844	79,641	77,664

The Meaning of Correlation

The method of correlation is useful in the field of psychological testing for a number of reasons, among which is the fact that correlation implies predictability. The accuracy with which a person's score on measure Y can be predicted from his or her score on measure X depends on the magnitude of the correlation between scores on the two variables. The closer the correlation coefficient is to an absolute value of 1.00 (either +1.00 or −1.00) the smaller the average error made in predicting Y scores from X scores. For example, if the correlation between tests X and Y is close to +1.00, it can be predicted with confidence that a person who makes a high score on variable X will also make a high score on variable Y, and a person who makes a low score on X will make a low score on Y. On the other hand, if the correlation is close to −1.00, it can be predicted with some confidence that a person who scores high on X will score low on Y, and a person who scores low on X will score high on Y. The closer the value of r is to +1.00 or −1.00, the more accurate the prediction will be; the closer r is to .00, the less accurate the prediction will be. Predicting a person's score on one variable from his or her score on the other variable will be no better than chance.

It is important to remember that correlation implies prediction, but it does not imply causation. The fact that two variables are related does not mean that one variable is necessarily a cause of the other. Both variables may be influenced by a third variable, and the correlation between the first two is a reflection of this common cause. For example, it can be demonstrated that the mental ages of a group of children with a wide range of chronological ages is positively correlated with their shoe sizes. Neither mental age nor shoe size is a cause of the other, but rather the positive correlation between these two variables is due to the influence of a third variable, maturation or physical growth, on both mental age and shoe size. The fact that two variables are significantly correlated facilitates predicting performance on one from performance on the other, but it provides no direct information on whether the two variables are causally connected.

Simple Linear Regression

The product–moment correlation coefficient, which is a measure of the *linear* relationship between two variables, is actually a by-product of the statistical procedure for finding the equation of the straight line that best fits the set of points representing the paired X–Y values. To illustrate the meaning of this statement, the X–Y pairs of values listed in Table A.2 are plotted as a *scattergram* in Figure A.5. Clearly, all 30 points do not fall on the same straight line, but a line can be fitted through the points in such a way that the sum of the squared vertical distances of the points from the line is as small as possible. A formula for finding this *least squares regression line* is

$$Y_{\text{pred}} = r \frac{s_y}{s_x} (X - \overline{X}) + \overline{Y}, \tag{A.6}$$

where $\overline{X}$ and $\overline{Y}$ are the means and s_x and s_y the standard deviations of the X and Y variables. For the data in Table A.2, $\overline{X} = 49.93$, $\overline{Y} = 50.37$, $s_x = 13.19$, $s_y = 11.04$, and $r = .52$. Entering these numbers into formula A.6 and simplifying yields the linear equation

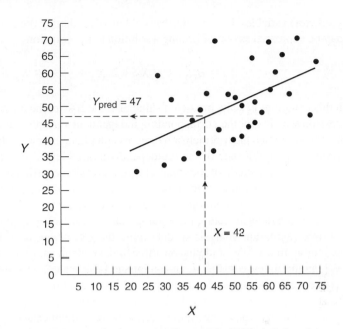

FIGURE A.5 Scattergram of scores in Table A.2 showing regression line and illustrative problem.

$Y_{pred} = .44X + 28.64$. Using this equation, a person's score on variable Y can be predicted with better than chance accuracy from his or her score on variable X. For example, as illustrated by the dashed lines in Figure A.5, if $X = 42$, $Y_{pred} = .44(42) + 28.64 = 47.12$. This means that, if a person makes a score of 42 on the X variable, the best estimate of his or her score on the Y variable is approximately 47.

MULTIPLE REGRESSION AND FACTOR ANALYSIS

Many other statistical procedures are employed in analyzing test scores and using them for evaluative and prediction purposes. Among these procedures are multiple regression analysis, discriminant analysis, profile analysis, multidimensional scaling, and factor analysis. All these topics are considered in detail in books on advanced statistics and psychometrics (e.g., Nunnally & Bernstein, 1994), so in the interest of space only the first and the last will be considered here.

Multiple Regression

Simple linear regression analysis involving one independent (X) variable can be extended to two or more independent variables. Let Y represent a criterion variable such as academic achievement or job performance, and let $X_1, X_2, X_3, \ldots, X_n$ represent a series of n independent (predictor) variables. In symbols, the problem of predicting the criterion from these variables may be expressed as one of finding a solution to the equation

$$Y_p = B_1X_1 + B_2X_2 + B_3X_2 + \cdots + B_nX_n + A.$$

In this equation, Y_p is the predicted value of Y, the B's are the unstandardized (raw score) regression weights for the corresponding independent variables, and A is a constant denoting the point at which the n-dimensional regression plane intersects the Y-axis. The relative importance or significance of the n independent variables in predicting the criterion is indicated by the magnitude of the standardized regression coefficients (β's), which are equal to $\beta_i = (s_i/s_y)B_i$. An index of the combined accuracy of the independent variables in predicting the criterion is R, the multiple correlation coefficient.

As a practical example, assume that a researcher is interested in conducting a multiple regression analysis to determine the effectiveness of the scores of a group of beginning first-grade students on three independent variables (a reading-readiness test $[X_1]$, an intelligence test $[X_2]$, and an integer $[1 = $ male, $2 = $ female] indicating the child's sex [gender] $[X_3]$) in predicting scores (Y_p) on a reading achievement test administered to the students at the end of the first grade. The required computations for this multiple regression analysis can be accomplished easily by computer using a statistical package such as SPSS.

The computer input for the problem may be the students' scores on the three tests and the coded value for sex or, alternatively, the correlations among all four variables. Let us assume that the correlations among the four variables have already been computed. Noting that the subscripts 1, 2, and 3 refer to independent variables 1, 2, and 3 and the subscript y to the dependent variable, these correlations are $r_{12} = .466$, $r_{13} = .055$, $r_{23} = .072$, $r_{y1} = .612$, $r_{y2} = .541$, and $r_{y3} = .197$. In addition to the correlations among the variables, we need to enter their means and standard deviations into the computer. They are $\overline{X}_1 = 49.0$, $\overline{X}_2 = 102.8$, $\overline{X}_3 = 1.48$, $\overline{Y} = 26.0$, $s_1 = 10.3$, $s_2 = 14.7$, $s_3 = .501$, and $s_y = 8.10$.[2]

A typical multiple regression program computes, along with other statistics, the standardized (β) and unstandardized (B) regression weights for the independent variables, the Y intercept, the multiple correlation coefficient (R), the standard errors of the regression weights, and critical ratios for determining the statistical significance of the regression weights. For the above problem, the beta weights (β's) are $\beta_1 = .4556$, $\beta_2 = .3179$, and $\beta_3 = .1490$; the B weights are $B_1 = .3583$, $B_2 = .1752$, and $B_3 = 2.4098$; and the Y-intercept (A) is $= -13.1338$. Therefore, the raw-score (unstandardized) regression equation is

$$Y_p = .3583X_1 + .1752X_2 + 2.4098X_2 - 13.1338$$

Statistical tests performed on the regression weights indicate that they are all significant, with the first independent variable being the strongest predictor and the second inde-

[2]These values were taken from a problem described on pages 137 and 138 of Glass and Hopkins (1996)

pendent variable being the next strongest. The overall effectiveness of the three predictors, in combination, in predicting scores on the criterion variable is indicated by a multiple correlation coefficient of $R = 0.693$, a highly significant value.

There are many other aspects to regression analysis, and entire books have been written on the subject. This very brief treatment, which has barely scratched the surface of an important statistical technique in psychometrics, should serve to whet the reader's appetite for more comprehensive treatments (e.g., Kleinbaum, Kupper, Muller, & Nizam, 1998).

Factor Analysis

The major purpose of *factor analysis* is to reduce the number of variables in a group of measures by taking into account the overlap (correlations) among them. In the field of psychological testing, the problem is to find a few salient factors that account for the major part of the variance of a group of scores on different tests. The many different procedures for extracting these factors from test scores are all based on a fundamental theorem: The observed (total) variance of a test (s_{obs}^2) is equal to the sum of the variance due to factors that the test has in common with other tests (s_{com}^2), the variance specific to the test itself (s_{spe}^2), and the variance produced by errors of measurement (s_{err}^2). Consequently, formula 5.1 in Chapter 5 (page 88) may be rewritten as

$$s_{obs}^2 = s_{com}^2 + s_{spe}^2 + s_{err}^2. \tag{A.7}$$

In formula A.7, what was referred to in Chapter 5 as the true variance of a test (s_{tru}^2) is partitioned into common-factor variance and specific-factor variance. The portion of the observed variance due to common factors is called the test's *communality,* whereas the portion of the observed variance due to specific factors is its *specificity.* From these definitions and formulas 5.2 and A.7, we may write the equation

$$\text{reliability} = \text{communality} + \text{specificity.} \tag{A.8}$$

One component of this equation, the communality of a test, is obtained from the results of a factor analysis involving the test. Then, if the test's reliability is known, its specificity can be found by subtraction. An illustrative factor analysis should clarify these matters.

One way to begin a factor analysis of the scores of n people on a group of tests is to compute the correlations among all the tests and cast them into the form of a matrix. This has been done in Table A.3 with the average correlations among the 13 WISC-III subtests for all ages in the test standardization sample ($n = 1,880$). Notice that the matrix is symmetrical; that is, the correlations in a given row are identical to those in the corresponding column. In addition, there are no entries on the diagonal running from the upper-left corner to the lower-right corner of the matrix.

The decision concerning what values to place on the diagonal of the matrix—the reliabilities of the tests, estimates of their communalities, or all 1.00's—depends on the particular factor-analysis procedure or theory followed by the researcher. In one type of factoring procedure, the *centroid method,* estimates of the communalities of the tests are placed on the diagonal of the correlation matrix. On the other hand, the *principal components method*

TABLE A.3   Matrix of Average Correlations among WISC-III Subtests

SUBTEST	1	2	3	4	5	6	7	8	9	10	11	12	13
1. Information		.66	.57	.70	.56	.34	.47	.21	.40	.48	.41	.35	.18
2. Similarities	.66		.55	.69	.59	.34	.45	.20	.39	.49	.42	.35	.18
3. Arithmetic	.57	.55		.54	.47	.43	.39	.27	.35	.52	.39	.41	.22
4. Vocabulary	.70	.69	.54		.64	.35	.45	.26	.40	.46	.41	.35	.17
5. Comprehension	.56	.59	.47	.64		.29	.38	.25	.35	.40	.34	.34	.17
6. Digit Span	.34	.34	.43	.35	.29		.25	.23	.20	.32	.26	.28	.14
7. Picture Completion	.47	.45	.39	.45	.38	.25		.18	.37	.52	.49	.33	.24
8. Coding	.21	.20	.27	.26	.25	.23	.18		.28	.27	.24	.53	.15
9. Picture Arrangement	.40	.39	.35	.40	.35	.20	.37	.28		.41	.37	.36	.23
10. Block Design	.48	.49	.52	.46	.40	.32	.52	.27	.41		.61	.45	.31
11. Object Assembly	.41	.42	.39	.41	.34	.26	.49	.24	.37	.61		.38	.29
12. Symbol Search	.35	.35	.41	.35	.34	.28	.33	.53	.36	.45	.38		.24
13. Mazes	.18	.18	.22	.17	.17	.14	.24	.15	.23	.31	.29	.24	

requires placing 1.00's on the diagonal. Without belaboring the question of which diagonal entries are best, it should be emphasized that the choice affects both the number of factors extracted and the obtained weights (*factor loadings*) of each test on each factor. The following factor analysis was conducted by the principal components method, using 1.00's on the diagonal of the correlation matrix.

Factoring the Correlation Matrix.   The immediate result of a typical factor analysis is an original (unrotated) factor matrix such as that in columns *A, B,* and *C* of Table A.4. Observe that factor analysis has reduced the number of variables or psychological dimensions from 13, which is the total number of subtests on the WISC-III, to 3, the number of common factors extracted. The decimal numbers in each column of the factor matrix are the loadings of the 13 WISC-III subtests on that factor. For example, the Information subtest has a loading of .78 on factor *A,* but loadings of only −.33 and .03 on factors *B* and *C.* Each factor loading is the correlation between a particular subtest and that factor. The square of the loading of a given subtest on a factor is the proportion of the total variance of the subtest scores that can be accounted for by that factor. Thus, $(78)^2 = 0.61$ means that 61% of the variance of the scores on the Information subtest can be accounted for by factor *A.* Only $(−.33)^2 = .11$, or 11%, of the variance of the Information subtest scores can be accounted for by factor *B,* and $(.03)^2 = .0009$, or .09%, of the variance of the Information subtest scores can be accounted for by factor *C.*

The sum of the cross-products of the corresponding factor loadings of any two subtests in Table A.4 is an estimate of the correlation between those two subtests. For example, the correlation between the Information and Arithmetic subtests is estimated from the loadings in the original factor matrix to be $.78(.74) + (−.33)(−.10) + (.03)(.12) = .61$. This is a fairly close approximation to the actual correlation of .57 (see Table A.3). The accuracy with which the correlation matrix is reproduced by estimates determined from the factor

TABLE A.4 Original and Rotated Factor Matrices

Subtest	ORIGINAL FACTOR MATRIX			ROTATED FACTOR MATRIX			Communality
	A	B	C	A'	B'	C'	
Information	.78	−.33	.03	.80	.25	.09	.71
Similarities	.78	−.34	.02	.81	.25	.08	.72
Arithmetic	.74	−.10	.12	.65	.26	.28	.57
Vocabulary	.79	−.34	.10	.83	.19	.13	.74
Comprehension	.70	−.29	.14	.75	.14	.16	.61
Digit Span	.51	−.02	.28	.45	.06	.36	.34
Picture Completion	.66	.01	−.35	.43	.61	.02	.56
Coding	.44	.55	.54	.10	.09	.88	.79
Picture Arrangement	.60	.16	−.08	.34	.45	.27	.39
Block Design	.75	.18	−.26	.41	.66	.22	.65
Object Assembly	.66	.22	−.36	.31	.71	.14	.62
Symbol Search	.62	.48	.30	.23	.32	.74	.70
Mazes	.37	.42	−.45	−.06	.71	.11	.52

loadings depends on the extent to which the obtained factors account for the total variance among the subtests.

Rotating the Factors. A process known as *factor rotation* may be applied to the original factor matrix to increase the number of high and low positive loadings in the columns of the factor matrix. The result is a simpler configuration of factor loadings, thereby facilitating interpretation of the factors. Depending on the particular rotation method selected, either uncorrelated (*orthogonal*) or correlated (*oblique*) factors may be obtained. Some factor analysts prefer orthogonal rotation, while others like oblique rotation. The rotated factor matrix in Table A.4 (columns A', B', and C') was produced by orthogonal (varimax) rotation of the original factor matrix, so the rotated factors are uncorrelated.

Interpreting the Rotated Factors. Having completed the statistical computations involved in factoring the correlation matrix and rotating the extracted factor matrix, we are now ready to examine the pattern of high and low loadings of each test on every factor. The higher a particular loading is, the more important the factor is on the given test. As shown in Table A.4, the Information, Similarities, Vocabulary, and Comprehension subtests have loadings of over .70 on factor A'. Because these are verbal subtests, factor A' might be labeled a *verbal* factor. Several other subtests also have appreciable loadings on factor A', so this factor actually comes close to what is meant by a *general cognitive factor* (*g*). The Picture Completion, Block Design, and Object Assembly subtests have moderate to high loadings on factor B'. Considering the kinds of tasks comprising these three subtests, factor B' may be labeled a *spatial–perceptual* or *spatial imagery* factor. Finally, the Coding and

Symbol Search subtests, both of which involve transforming one set of abstract symbols to another, have high loadings on factor C'. This appears to be a fairly specific factor consisting of perceptual speed and accuracy and freedom from distractibility.

Communality and Specificity.   The last column in Table A.4 contains the communalities of the 13 WISC-III subtests, computed as the sum of squares of the rotated factor loadings on a given subtest. For example, the communality of the Information subtest is $(.80)^2 + (.25)^2 + (.09)^2 = .71$, so 71% of the variance of the scores on the Information subtest can be accounted for by factors A', B', and C'. If the reliability of the Information subtest is known, formula A.8 can be used to compute the subtest's specificity. Also, subtracting the communality from 1.00 yields the proportion of the total subtest variance that is attributable to a combination of specific factors and error variance. For the Information subtest, this figure is $1.00 - .71 = .29$; that is, 29% of the total variance of the scores on the Information subtest can be explained by specific factors and errors of measurement. Knowing that the estimated reliability of the Information subtest is .84, we can subtract its communality (.71) and find that the specificity of this subtest is .13 (see formula A.8).

SUMMARY

1. The four types of measurement scales are nominal (a simple naming), ordinal (based on a ranking), interval (equal numerical differences), and ratio (interval scale with a true zero). A statistical analysis of test scores begins with the construction of a frequency distribution of the number of people making each score or whose scores fall within a specified interval. Frequency distributions may be represented pictorially as histograms or frequency polygons. The normal curve is a theoretical frequency polygon that is basic to much test theory, and it is used for a variety of purposes. Nonnormal, asymmetrical frequency distributions may be skewed either to the right (positively skewed) or to the left (negatively skewed).

2. Three measures of the central tendency or average of a group of scores, the mode, median, and mean, may be computed from raw scores or from a frequency distribution. The mode is the most frequently occurring score, the median is the value below which 50% of the scores fall, and the arithmetic mean is the sum of the scores divided by the number of scores. Percentiles represent a value that indicates the percent that all other scores fall beneath. Percentiles can be divided into deciles (indicating a grouping of 10% of the values), quintiles (indicating a grouping of a fifth or 20% of the group), or quartiles (indicating a grouping of a quarter or 25% of the group).

3. Three measures of variability or spread of a group of scores are the range, the semi-interquartile range, and the standard deviation. Of these, the standard deviation is the most popular and the most appropriate measure of variability when the arithmetic mean is the reported average. For comparison and interpretive purposes, raw scores may be converted to standard z scores, percentiles, and other transformed scores.

4. The product–moment correlation coefficient, which is a number between −1.00 (perfect negative correlation) and +1.00 (perfect positive correlation), is a measure of the

magnitude and direction of the relationship between two variables. A significant correlation between two variables facilitates the prediction of a person's score on one variable from his or her score on the other variable. A high correlation between two variables should not, however, be construed as implying a causal connection between them. Although causation implies correlation, correlation does not imply causation.

5. Correlations among variables may be used in simple and multiple linear regression analyses to make predictions of scores on a dependent (Y or criterion) variable from scores on one or more independent (X or predictor) variables. Correlational procedures are also used in factor analysis to determine the dimensions or factors that different tests have in common. Factor analysis of the scores obtained by a large sample of people on a group of tests or items consists of extracting the factors, rotating the factor axes, and interpreting the resulting factors. Factors are interpreted by inspecting the loadings of the various tests on the factor. Computation of the communality (common factor variance) and specificity (specific factor variance) can also contribute to the factor interpretation process.

MASTERING THE APPENDIX OBJECTIVES

1. *Scales of measurement and frequency distribution*
   a. Define the following types of scales: nominal, ordinal, interval, and ratio.
   b. Define a frequency distribution, histogram, normal curve, and what is meant by standard scores.
   c. Construct a histogram and a superimposed frequency polygon using the following frequency distribution of scores obtained by a group of 50 students on a test:

TEST SCORE INTERVAL	NUMBER OF STUDENTS
96–100	6
91–95	8
86–90	15
81–85	10
76–80	7
71–75	4

(See Answers to Quantitative Questions, p. 489.)

2. *Measures of central tendency*
   a. Define the mode, median, arithmetic mean, percentile, decile, quintile, and quartile.
   b. Using the table in question 1a, compute the arithmetic mean, median, 25th percentile, 75th percentile, and semi-interquartile range of the scores.
   c. Using the table in Appendix B, find the percentage of the area under the normal curve falling below each of the following z scores: -2.575, -2.33, -1.96, -1.645, $.00$, 1.645, 1.96, 2.33, and 2.575. Next, find the z scores below which 10, 20, 30, 40, 50, 60, 70, 80, and 90 percent of the area under the normal curve falls. (See Answers to Quantitative Questions, p. 489.)

3. *Measures of variability*
   a. Define what is meant by the range and standard deviation.
   b. Calculate the mean and standard deviation for variable *X* using the following table, which depicts pairs of *X* and *Y* scores of 30 people.

X	Y	X	Y	X	Y	X	Y	X	Y
32	46	28	23	37	28	36	21	42	27
35	26	32	20	27	13	31	14	39	46
20	8	45	24	37	22	35	18	34	16
41	42	29	13	23	34	43	47	33	30
25	28	46	40	30	31	34	27	29	26
38	25	40	37	36	39	39	32	24	7

4. *Correlation and linear regression*
   a. Define what is meant by correlation and linear regression.
   b. Using the table in question 3b, compute the following: arithmetic means and standard deviations of *X* and *Y*, product–moment correlation between *X* and *Y*, and regression line for predicting *Y* from *X*. Make a graphical plot (*scattergram*) of the *X*, *Y* points, and draw the regression line of *Y* on *X*. (See Answers to Quantitative Questions, p. 489.)
   c. Whenever the frequency distribution of a group of scores is markedly skewed in either a positive (to the right) or negative (to the left) direction, the median is considered to be a better, less biased measure of central tendency than the arithmetic mean. Why?

5. *Multiple regression and factor analysis*
   a. Describe what is meant by multiple regression and factor analysis.
   b. What is the purpose of conducting a multiple-regression analysis on a set of psychometric data? What is the purpose of conducting a factor analysis?
   c. Consult the PsycLIT or PsycINFO databases for the last several years and find two research studies in which a multiple-regression procedure was used and two other studies in which a factor analysis was used. Summarize the procedure used and the results obtained.

AREAS UNDER
THE NORMAL CURVE

To find the proportion of the area under the normal curve falling below a specific z value, locate the z value in the first column and top row of the table. The decimal number at the intersection of the appropriate row and column is the corresponding proportion of the area under the curve. For example, to find the area below $z = 1.57$, find the intersection of 1.5 in the first column and .07 in the top row. The resulting value is .9418, so 94.18% of the area under the curve falls below $z = 1.57$. Conversely, to locate the value of z below which a specified proportion of the area under the curve falls, begin by finding that proportion in the body of the table. Then find the z value in the corresponding row and column. For example, to find the value of z below which 67% of the area under the curve falls, begin by locating .6700 in the body of the table. It is at the intersection of the row labeled .4 and the column labeled .04, so the corresponding z value is .44.

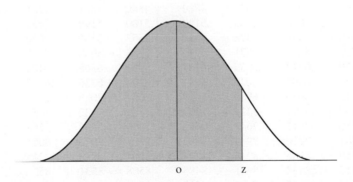

z	.00	.01	.02	.03	.04	.05	.06	.07	.08	.09
−3.0	.00135	.00131	.00126	.00122	.00118	.00114	.00111	.00117	.00104	.00100
−2.9	.0019	.0018	.0018	.0017	.0016	.0016	.0015	.0015	.0014	.0014
−2.8	.0026	.0025	.0024	.0023	.0023	.0022	.0021	.0021	.0020	.0019
−2.7	.0035	.0034	.0033	.0032	.0031	.0030	.0029	.0028	.0027	.0026
−2.6	.0047	.0045	.0044	.0043	.0041	.0040	.0039	.0038	.0037	.0036
−2.5	.0062	.0060	.0059	.0057	.0055	.0054	.0052	.0051	.0049	.0048
−2.4	.0082	.0080	.0078	.0075	.0073	.0071	.0069	.0068	.0066	.0064
−2.3	.0107	.0104	.0102	.0099	.0096	.0094	.0091	.0089	.0087	.0084
−2.2	.0139	.0136	.0132	.0129	.0125	.0122	.0119	.0116	.0113	.0110
−2.1	.0179	.0174	.0170	.0166	.0162	.0158	.0154	.0150	.0146	.0143
−2.0	.0228	.0222	.0217	.0212	.0207	.0202	.0197	.0192	.0188	.0183
−1.9	.0287	.0281	.0274	.0268	.0262	.0256	.0250	.0244	.0239	.0233
−1.8	.0359	.0351	.0344	.0336	.0329	.0322	.0314	.0307	.0301	.0294
−1.7	.0446	.0436	.0427	.0418	.0409	.0401	.0392	.0384	.0375	.0367
−1.6	.0548	.0537	.0526	.0516	.0505	.0495	.0485	.0475	.0465	.0455
−1.5	.0668	.0655	.0643	.0630	.0618	.0606	.0594	.0582	.0571	.0559
−1.4	.0808	.0793	.0778	.0764	.0749	.0735	.0721	.0708	.0694	.0681
−1.3	.0968	.0951	.0934	.0918	.0901	.0885	.0869	.0853	.0838	.0823
−1.2	.1151	.1131	.1112	.1093	.1075	.1056	.1038	.1020	.1003	.0985
−1.1	.1357	.1335	.1314	.1292	.1271	.1251	.1230	.1210	.1190	.1170
−1.0	.1587	.1562	.1539	.1515	.1492	.1469	.1446	.1423	.1401	.1379
−0.9	.1841	.1814	.1788	.1762	.1736	.1711	.1685	.1660	.1635	.1611
−0.8	.2119	.2090	.2061	.2033	.2005	.1977	.1949	.1922	.1894	.1867
−0.7	.2420	.2389	.2358	.2327	.2296	.2266	.2236	.2206	.2177	.2148
−0.6	.2743	.2709	.2676	.2643	.2611	.2578	.2546	.2514	.2483	.2451
−0.5	.3085	.3050	.3015	.2981	.2946	.2912	.2877	.2843	.2810	.2776
−0.4	.3446	.3409	.3372	.3336	.3300	.3264	.3228	.3192	.3156	.3121
−0.3	.3821	.3783	.3745	.3707	.3669	.3632	.3594	.3557	.3520	.3483
−0.2	.4207	.4168	.4129	.4090	.4052	.4013	.3974	.3936	.3897	.3859
−0.1	.4602	.4562	.4522	.4483	.4443	.4404	.4364	.4325	.4286	.4247
−0.0	.5000	.4960	.4920	.4880	.4840	.4801	.4761	.4721	.4681	.4641
0.0	.5000	.5040	.5080	.5120	.5160	.5199	.5239	.5279	.5319	.5359
0.1	.5398	.5438	.5478	.5517	.5557	.5596	.5636	.5675	.5714	.5753
0.2	.5793	.5832	.5871	.5910	.5948	.5987	.6026	.6064	.6103	.6141
0.3	.6179	.6217	.6255	.6293	.6331	.6368	.6406	.6443	.6480	.6517
0.4	.6554	.6591	.6628	.6664	.6700	.6736	.6772	.6808	.6844	.6879
0.5	.6915	.6950	.6985	.7019	.7054	.7088	.7123	.7157	.7190	.7224
0.6	.7257	.7291	.7324	.7357	.7389	.7422	.7454	.7486	.7517	.7549
0.7	.7580	.7611	.7642	.7673	.7704	.7734	.7764	.7794	.7823	.7852
0.8	.7881	.7910	.7939	.7967	.7995	.8023	.8051	.8078	.8106	.8133
0.9	.8159	.8186	.8212	.8238	.8264	.8289	.8315	.8340	.8365	.8389
1.0	.8413	.8438	.8461	.8485	.8508	.8531	.8554	.8577	.8599	.8621
1.1	.8643	.8665	.8686	.8708	.8729	.8749	.8770	.8790	.8810	.8830
1.2	.8849	.8869	.8888	.8907	.8925	.8944	.8962	.8980	.8997	.9015
1.3	.9032	.9049	.9066	.9082	.9099	.9115	.9131	.9147	.9162	.9177
1.4	.9192	.9207	.9222	.9236	.9251	.9265	.9279	.9292	.9306	.9319

z	.00	.01	.02	.03	.04	.05	.06	.07	.08	.09
1.5	.9332	.9345	.9357	.9370	.9382	.9394	.9406	.9418	.9429	.9441
1.6	.9452	.9463	.9474	.9484	.9495	.9505	.9515	.9525	.9535	.9545
1.7	.9554	.9564	.9573	.9582	.9591	.9599	.9608	.9616	.9625	.9633
1.8	.9641	.9649	.9656	.9664	.9671	.9678	.9686	.9693	.9699	.9706
1.9	.9713	.9719	.9726	.9732	.9738	.9744	.9750	.9756	.9761	.9767
2.0	.9772	.9778	.9783	.9788	.9793	.9798	.9803	.9808	.9812	.9817
2.1	.9821	.9826	.9830	.9834	.9838	.9842	.9846	.9850	.9854	.9857
2.2	.9861	.9864	.9868	.9871	.9875	.9878	.9881	.9884	.9887	.9890
2.3	.9893	.9896	.9898	.9901	.9904	.9906	.9909	.9911	.9913	.9916
2.4	.9918	.9920	.9922	.9925	.9927	.9929	.9931	.9932	.9934	.9936
2.5	.9938	.9940	.9941	.9943	.9945	.9946	.9948	.9949	.9951	.9952
2.6	.9953	.9955	.9956	.9957	.9959	.9960	.9961	.9962	.9963	.9964
2.7	.9965	.9966	.9967	.9968	.9969	.9970	.9971	.9972	.9973	.9974
2.8	.9974	.9975	.9976	.9977	.9977	.9978	.9979	.9979	.9980	.9981
2.9	.9981	.9982	.9982	.9983	.9984	.9984	.9985	.9985	.9986	.9986
3.0	.9987	.9987	.9987	.9988	.9988	.9989	.9989	.9989	.9990	.9990

MAJOR SUPPLIERS OF PSYCHOLOGICAL AND EDUCATIONAL ASSESSMENT MATERIALS

Academic Therapy Publications, 20 Commercial Boulevard, Novatao, CA 93939-6191. Telephone: 415-883-3314, 800-422-7249. FAX: 415-883-3720. Web URL: www.atpub.com.

Allyn and Bacon, Department 893, 160 Gould Street, Needham Heights, MA 02194-2310.

The American College Testing Program (ACT), P.O. Box 168, Iowa City, IA 52243-0168. Telephone: 319-337-1000. FAX: 319-337-1551. Web URL: www.act.org.

American Guidance Service, Inc. (AGS), 4201 Woodland Road, Circle Pines, MN 55014-1796. Telephone: 612-786-4343, 800-328-2560. FAX: 612-786-9077. E-mail: agsmail@agsnet. Web URL: www.agsnet.com.

American Psychiatric Press, Inc., 1400 K Street NW, Suite 1101, Washington, DC 20005.

Assessment Systems Corporation, 2233 University Avenue, Suite 200, St. Paul, MN 55114-1629. Telephone: 651-647-9220. FAX: 651-647-0412. E-mail: info@assess.com. Web URL: www.assess.com.

Australian Council for Educational Research Ltd., 347 Camberwell Road (Private Bag 55), Camberwell, Victoria, Australia 3124. Telephone: (03) 9835 7447. FAX: (03) 9835 7499. E-mail:sales@acer.edu.au. Web URL: www.acer.edu.au.

Behavior Science Systems, Inc., P.O. Box 580274, Minneapolis, MN 55458. Telephone: 612-929-6220. FAX: 612-920-4925.

The College Board, 45 Columbus Avenue, New York, NY 10023-6992. Telephone: 212-713-8390. Web URL: www.collegeboard.org.

CCP, Inc. 1855 Joaquin Road, Suite 200, Mountain View, CA 94043. Telephone: 650-969-8901, 800-624-1765. FAX: 650-969-8608. Web URL: www.cpp-db.com.

C.P.S., Inc., P.O. Box 83, Larchmont, NY 10538. Telephone: 914-833-1633. FAX: 914-833-1633.

Denver Developmental Materials, Inc., P.O. Box 6919, Denver, CO 80206-0919. Telephone: 800-419-4729. FAX: 303-355-5622.

Department of Defense, Manpower Data Center, DoD Center Monterey Bay, 400 Gigling Road, Seaside, CA 93955-6771. Telephone: 831-583-2400, Ext. 4284.

DLM Resources, One DLM Park, Allen, TX 75002. Telephone: 800-527-4747.

EdITS/Educational and Industrial Testing Service, P.O. Box 7234, San Diego, CA 92167-0234. Telephone: 619-222-1666, 800-416-1666. FAX: 619-226-1666. E-mail: edits@worldnet.att.net. Web URL: www.edits.net.

Educational Testing Service, Rosedale Road, Princeton, NY 08541-0001. Telephone: 609-921-9000. FAX: 609-734-5410. Web URL: www.ets.org.

Educators Publishing Service, Inc., 31 Smith Place, Cambridge, MA 02138-1089. Telephone: 800-225-5750. FAX: 617-547-0412. E-mail: cps@epsbooks.com. Web URL: www.epsbooks.com.

ETS Test Collection, Educational Testing Service, Princeton, NJ 08541. Telephone: 609-734-5686. Web URL: www.ets.org.

General Educational Development Testing Service of the American Council on Education (GED), One Dupont Circle NW, Suite 250, Washington, DC 20036-1163. Telephone: 202-939-9490. FAX: 202-775-8578. E-mail: ged@ace.nche.edu. Web URL: www.gedtest.org.

Harcourt Brace Educational Measurement, 555 Academic Court, San Antonio, TX 78204-2498. Telephone: 512-299-1061, 800-228-0752. FAX: 800-232-1223. E-mail: customer_service@hbtpc.com. Web URL: www.hbcm.com.

Harvard University Press, 79 Garden Street, Cambridge, MA 02138. Telephone: 800-448-4083. E-mail: hup@harvard.edu. Web URL: www.hup.harvard.edu.

Hawthorne Educational Services, Inc., 800 Gray Oak Drive, Columbia, MO 65201. Telephone: 800-542-1673. FAX: 800-442-9509.

Hilson Research, Inc., P.O. Box 150239, 82-88 Abingdon Road, Kew Gardens, NY 11415-0239. Telephone: 800-926-2258. Fax: 718-849-6238.

Hogan Assessment Systems, Inc., P.O. Box 521176, Tulsa, OK 74152-1176. Telephone: 918-749-0632. FAX: 918-749-0635. E-mail: aferg@webzone.net. Web URL: www.hoganassessments.com.

Hogrefe & Huber Publishers, P.O. Box 2487, Kirkland, WA 98083. Telephone: 800-228-3749. FAX: 424-823-8324. E-mail: hh@hhpub.com. Web URL: www.hhpub.com.

IDS Publishing P.O. Box 389, Worthington, OH 43085.

Industrial Psychology International Ltd., 4106 Firestone Road, Champaign, IL 61821. Telephone: 800-747-1229. FAX: 217-398-5798.

Institute for Personality and Ability Testing (IPAT), P.O. Box 1188, Champaign, IL 61824-1188. Telephone: 800-225-IPAT. E-mail: custserv@ipat.cfom. Web URL: www.ipat.com.

Management Research Institute, Inc., 11304 Spur Wheel Lane, Potomac, MD 20854. Telephone: 301-299-9200. FAX: 301-299-9227. E-mail: mrieaf@aol.com.

Multi-Health Systems, Inc., 908 Niagara Falls Boulevard, North Tonawanda, NY 14120-2060. Telephone: 800-456-3003 or 416-492-2627. FAX: 888-540-4484 or 416-492-3343. E-mail: customerservice@mhs.com. Web URL: www.mhs.com.

National Career Assessment Services, Inc., 601 Visions Parkway, P.O. Box 277, Adel, IA 50003. Telephone: 800-314-8972. FAX: 515-993-5422. E-mail: ncasi@ncasi.com. Web URL: www.kuder.com.

NCS Assessments, P.O. Box 1416, Minneapolis, MN 55440. Telephone: 800-627-7271. FAX: 800-632-99011. Web URL: assessments.ncspearson.com.

NCS London House, 9701 West Higgins Road, Suite 170, Rosemont, IL 60018-4720. Telephone: 800-221-8378. Web URL: londonhouse.ncspearson.com.

NFER-Nelson Publishing Company Ltd., Darville House, 2 Oxford Road East, Windsor-Berkshire, SL4 lDF, England.

Personnel Decisions International, 2000 Plaza VII Tower, 45 South Seventh Street, Minneapolis, MN 55402-1608.

pro.ed, 8700 Shoal Creek Boulevard, Austin, TX 78757-6897. Telephone: 512-451-3246, 800-897-3202. FAX: 800-397-7633. Web URL: www.proedinc.com.

Psychological Assessment Resources, Inc. (PAR), P.O. Box 998, Odessa, FL 33556-0998. Telephone: 813-968-3003, 800-331-8378. FAX: 800-727-9329. Web URL: www.parinc.com.

The Psychological Corporation, 555 Academic Court, San Antonio, TX 78204-2498. Telephone: 800-211-8378. FAX: 800-232-1223. E-mail: customer_service@HBTPC.com. Web URL: www.PsychCorp.com.

Psychological Publications, Inc., P.O. Box 3577, Thousand Oaks, CA 91361-0577. Telephone: 800-345-8378. FAX: 805-373-1753. E-mail: TJTA@aol.com. Web URL: www.TJTA.com.

Publishers Test Service, 2500 Garden Road, Monterey, CA 93940-5379. Telephone: 800-538-9547.

Reitan Neuropsychology Laboratory/Press, P.O. Box 66080, Tucson, AZ 85728-6080. Telephone: 520-577-2970. FAX: 520-577-2940. E-mail: reitanlab@aol.com.

Riverside Publishing, 425 Spring Lake Drive, Itasca, IL 60143-2079. Telephone: 800-323-9540. FAX: 312-693-0325. Web URL: www.riverpub.com.

Scholastic Testing Service, Inc. (STS), 480 Meyer Road, P.O. Box 1056, Bensenville, IL 60106-1617. Telephone: 800-766-7150 or 800-642-6STS. FAX: 630-766-8054. E-mail: ststesting@email.com. Web URL: www.ststeesting.com.

Sigma Assessment Systems, Inc., 511 Fort Street, Suite 435, P.O. Box 610984, Port Huron, MI 48061-0984. Telephone: 800-265-1285. FAX: 800-361-9411. E-mail: SIGMA@sigmaassessmentsystems.com. Web URL: www.sigmaassessmentsystems .com.

Slosson Educational Publications, Inc., P.O. Box 280, East Aurora, NY 14052-0280. Telephone: 716-652-0930, 800-828-4800. FAX: 800-655-3840. Web URL: www.slosson.com.

Swets Test Services, P.O. Box 820, 2160 Sz Lisse, The Netherlands. Telephone: +31 252 435375. FAX: +31 252 435671. E-mail: dvants@swets.nl. Web URL: www .swetstest.nl.

University of Minnesota Press, Test Division, Mill Place, Suite 290, 111 Third Avenue, South, Minneapolis, MN 55401-2520.

U.S. Military Entrance Processing Command Testing Directorate, 2500 Green Bay Road, North Chicago, IL 60064-3094.

Vocational Research Institute (VRI), 1528 Walnut Street, Suite 1502, Philadelphia, PA 19102. Telephone: 800-874-5387. FAX: 215-875-0198. E-Mail: info@vri.org. Web URL: www.vri.org.

Western Psychological Services (WPS), 12031 Wilshire Boulevard, Los Angeles, CA 90025-1251. Telephone: 310-478-2061, 800-648-9957. FAX: 310-478-7838.

Wide Range, Inc., P.O. Box 3410, Wilmington, DE 19804-0250. Telephone: 302-652-4990, 800-221-9728. FAX: 302-652-1644. Web URL: www.widerange.com.

Wonderlic Personnel Test, Inc., 1795 N. Butterfield Road, Libertyville, IL 60048-11238. Telephone: 800-323-3742. FAX: 847-680-9492. Web URL: www.wonderlic .com.

WEB SITES OF ORGANIZATIONS CONCERNED WITH PSYCHOLOGICAL TESTING AND ASSESSMENT

American Counseling Association (ACA): www.counseling.org

American Council on Education (ACE): www.acenet.edu

American Educational Research Association: www.aera.net

American Psychological Association: www.apa.org/science/testing.html

American Speech–Language–Hearing Association (ASHA): www.asha.org

The Association for Assessment in Counseling: aac.ncat.edu

Association of Test Publishers: www.testpublishers.org

Buros Institute of Mental Measurements: www.unl.edu/buros

College PowerPrep: www.powerprep.com

Educational Resources Information Center (ERIC): www.ericae.net\

Educational Testing Service (ETS): www.ets.org

Graduate Record Examinations (GRE): www.gre.org

International Personnel Management Association (IPMAAC): www.ipmaac.org

Kaplan, Inc.: www.kaplan.com

National Academy of Science's Board on Testing and Assessment (BOTA): www4.nationalacademies.org/dbasse/bota.nsf

National Association of School Psychologists (NASP): www.naspweb.org

National Association of Test Directors (NATD): www.naspweb.org

National Center for Research on Evaluation, Standards, and Student Testing (CRESST): www.cse.ucla.edu/

National Council on Measurement in Education (NCME): www.ncme.ed.uiuc.edu

Princeton Review: www.review.com

Society for Industrial and Organizational Psychology (SIOP): www.siop.org

Test.com, Inc.: www.test.com

GLOSSARY

ABC approach. Behavioral assessment approach, involving the identification of the antecedent events (A) and consequences (C) of the behavior (B). The behavior is modified by controlling for A and changing C.

Ability test. A test that measures the extent to which a person is capable of performing a certain task or occupation.

Academic aptitude. The ability to learn school-type tasks; also called scholastic aptitude. Many intelligence tests are basically measures of academic aptitude.

Accommodation. (1) In J. Piaget's theory of cognitive development, the modification of schema as the result of experience. (2) A change in how a test is administered or how the examinee is permitted to respond.

Achievement. The degree of success or accomplishment in a given area or endeavor; a score on an achievement test.

Acquiescence response set (**style**). Tendency of a person to answer affirmatively (yes or true) to personality test items and in other alternative response situations.

Adaptive behavior. The extent to which a person is able to interact *effectively and appropriately with the environment.*

Adaptive testing. Testing procedure, usually computer based, in which the specific items presented vary with the estimated ability or other specified characteristics of the examinee and his or her responses to previous items.

Adjustment. Ability to cope in social situations and achieve satisfaction of one's needs.

Adverse impact. A situation in which the selection rate is substantially lower for members of one race, sex, or ethnic group than for another.

Affective assessment. Measurement of noncognitive (nonintellective) variables or characteristics. Affective variables include temperament, emotions, interests, attitudes, personal style, and other behaviors, traits, or processes typical of an individual. (See *cognitive assessment*)

Age equivalent score. (See **age norm**)

Age norm. Median score on an aptitude or achievement test made by children of a given chronological age.

Age scale. A test on which the items are grouped by age level.

Agnosia. Partial or total inability to recognize sensory stimuli.

Alexia. Impairment of reading ability.

Alternate-forms reliability. An index of reliability (coefficient of equivalence) determined by correlating the scores of individuals on one form of a test with their scores on another form.

Alzheimer's disease. A chronic brain syndrome, usually occurring in older adulthood, characterized by gradual deterioration of memory, disorientation, and other features of dementia.

Amygdala. Portion of the limbic system in the brain that is primarily responsible for regulating emotion.

Analogies test. A test that requires the examinee to determine a relationship, similarity, or difference between two or more things. Example: Roses are to red as violets are to (a) blue, (b) green, (c) orange, (d) yellow.

Analytic scoring. Scoring procedure for essay tests in which different scores are assigned to aspects of content and style of the *examinee's responses.*

Anchor test. A common set of items on each of several forms of a test used to equate scores on the several forms.

Anecdotal record. A written record of behavioral observations of a specified individual. Care must be taken to differentiate between observation and interpretation if the record is to be objective.

Apgar rating. A rating score, determined at 1 minute and at 5 minutes after birth, for evaluating neonates. A rating of 0 to 2 is assigned to measurements of heart rate, respiration, muscle tone, reflexes, and color. A sum of ratings between 7 and 10 is normal for newborns.

Aphasia. Defect in the ability to communicate (speak, write, sign) and/or comprehend spoken or written language caused by disease or injury to the brain.

Apraxia. Inability to make voluntary movements (e.g., inability to use an object properly), although not paralyzed or otherwise impaired in sensory of motor abilities.

Aptitude. Capability of learning to perform a particular task or skill. Traditionally, aptitude was thought to depend more on inborn potential than on experience and practice.

Aptitude test. A measure of the ability to profit from additional training or experience, that is, become proficient in a skill or other ability.

Arithmetic mean. A measure of the average or central tendency of a group of scores. The arithmetic mean is computed by dividing the sum of the scores by the number of scores.

Assessment. Appraising the presence or magnitude of one or more personal characteristics. Assessing human behavior and mental processes includes such procedures as observations, interviews, rating scales, checklists, inventories, projectives techniques, and tests.

Assessment center. Technique, used primarily in the selection of executive personnel, for assessing the personality characteristics and behavior of a small group of individuals by having them perform a variety of tasks during a period of a few days.

Assimilation. In J. Piaget's theory of cognitive development, the process of fitting new experiences into preexisting mental structures.

Assortative mating. Nonrandom mating between individuals possessing similar characteristics.

Ataxia. Loss of muscular coordination, particularly of the extremities.

Attitude. Tendency to react positively or negatively to some object, person, or situation.

Attitude scale. A paper-and-pencil instrument consisting of a series of statements concerning an institution, situation, person, or event. The examinee responds to each statement by endorsing it or indicating his degree of agreement or disagreement with it.

Audiometer. An instrument for measuring auditory acuity that presents pure tones of varying intensities and frequencies in the normal range of hearing. Hearing is tested in each ear. The results are plotted as an audiogram, a graph of the examinee's auditory acuity at each frequency and for each ear.

Aunt Fanny error. Accepting as accurate a trivial, highly generalized personality description that could pertain to almost anyone, even one's Aunt Fanny.

Authentic assessment. Assessment of performance on realistic or real-life tasks or actual situations.

Automated assessment. Use of test-scoring machines, computers, and other electronic or electromechanical devices to administer, score, and interpret psychological assessments.

Average. Measure of central tendency of a group of scores; the most representative score.

Bandwidth. L. J. Cronbach's term for the range of criteria predictable from a test; the greater the number of criteria that a test can predict, the broader its bandwidth. (See *fidelity*)

Barnum effect. Accepting as accurate a personality description phrased in generalities, truisms, and other statements that sound specific to a given person, but are actually applicable to almost anyone. Same as Aunt Fanny error.

Basal age. The highest year level on an intelligence test, as on older editions of the Stanford–Binet, at and below which an examinee passes all subtests.

Base rate. Proportion of individuals in a specified population having a certain characteristic, condition, or behavior.

Basic skills test. Measurement of competence in reading, elementary mathematics, or other skills required in most training and employment settings.

Battery of tests. A group of aptitude or achievement tests measuring different things, but standardized on the same sample, thus permitting comparisons of a person's performance in different areas.

Behavior analysis. Procedures that focus on objectively describing a particular behavior and identifying the antecedents and consequences of the behavior. Behavior analysis may be conducted for research purposes or to obtain information in planning a behavior modification program.

Belief bias. The tendency for preexisting beliefs to distort logical reasoning, making invalid conclusions appear valid or valid conclusions appear invalid.

Bias. Any one of a number of factors that cause scores on psychometric instruments to be consistently higher or lower than they would be if measurement were accurate. Illustrative of factors that result in bias is the leniency error—the tendency to rate a person consistently higher than he or she should be rated.

Bimodal distribution. A frequency distribution having two modes (maximum points). (See *frequency distribution; mode*)

Broca's area. Area in the left frontal portion of the cerebral cortex; concerned with the control of speech. Patients with damage to Broca's area have difficulty enunciating words correctly and speak in a slow, labored manner. (see *Wernicke's area*)

Case study. Detailed study of an individual, designed to provide a comprehensive, in-depth understanding of behavior and personality. Information for a case study is obtained from biographical, interview, observational, and test data.

CATI. Computer assisted telephone interviewing. The items on a questionnaire are read aloud by the interviewer from a computer monitor, and the respondent's answers are recorded and analyzed by the computer. Depending on the respondent's answer, the computer can skip certain items.

Ceiling age. The minimum age or year level on a test, such as the Stanford–Binet, at which an examinee fails all subtests. (See *basal age*)

Central tendency. Average, or central, score in a group of scores; the most representative score (e.g., arithmetic mean, median, mode).

Classification. The use of test scores to assign a person to one category rather than another.

Clinical (impressionistic) approach. Approach to behavioral prediction and diagnosis in which psychologists or psychiatrists assign their own judgmental weights to the predictor variables and then combine them in a subjective manner to make diagnoses and prognoses.

Closed head injury. Brain injury caused by a nonpenetrating blow to the skull.

Cloze technique. Testing procedure in which words are deleted at random from a written text passage and the examinee is directed to replace them. The extent to which the examinee can make sense of the passage

and be successful at filling in the blanks is a measure of his or her reading ability.

Cluster sampling. Sampling procedure in which the target population is divided into sections or clusters. The number of units selected at random from a given cluster is proportional to the total number of units in the cluster.

Coaching. Short-term instruction designed to improve the test scores of prospective test takers. The instructional activities include practice on various types of items and test-taking strategies.

Coefficient alpha. An internal-consistency reliability coefficient, appropriate for tests comprised of dichotomous or multipoint items; the expected correlation of one test with a parallel form containing the same number of items.

Coefficient of equivalence. A reliability coefficient (correlation) obtained by administering two different forms of a test to the same people. (See *alternate-forms reliability*)

Coefficient of internal consistency. Reliability coefficient based on estimates of the internal consistency of a test (e.g., split-half coefficient and alpha coefficient).

Coefficient of stability. A reliability coefficient (correlation) obtained by administering a test to the same group of examinees on two different occasions. (See *test–retest reliability*)

Coefficient of stability and equivalence. A reliability coefficient obtained by administering two forms of a test to a group of examinees on two different occasions.

Cognition. Having to do with the processes of intellect; remembering, thinking, problem solving, and the like.

Cognitive assessment. Measurement of intellective processes, such as perception, memory, thinking, judgment, and reasoning. (See *affective assessment*)

Cognitive style. Strategy or approach to perceiving, remembering, and thinking that a person seems to prefer in attempting to understand and cope with the world (e.g., field independence–dependence, reflectivity–impulsivity, and internal–external locus of control).

Communality. Proportion of variance in a measured variable accounted for by variance that the variable has in common with other variables.

Component processes. According to Sternberg's theory, the cognitive processes or mental components, including metacomponents, performance components, acquisition components, retention components, and transfer components.

Composite score.   The direct or weighted sum of the scores on two or more tests or sections of a test.

Concordance reliability.   Several raters or scorers make numerical judgments of the amount of a characteristic or behavior shown by a large sample of people. Then a coefficient of concordance—an index of agreement among the judgments of the scorers or raters—is computed.

Concrete operations stage.   In J. Piaget's theory of cognitive development, the stage (7 to 11 years of age) during which a child develops organized systems of operations by the process of social interaction, with a corresponding reduction in self-centeredness.

Concurrent validity.   The extent to which scores obtained by a group of people on a particular psychometric instrument are related to their simultaneously determined scores on another measure (criterion) of the same characteristic that the instrument is supposed to measure.

Confidence interval.   A range of values within which one can be fairly certain (usually 95% or 99% confident) that a person's true score (or difference between scores) on a test or a criterion variable falls. (See *standard error of measurement* and *standard error of estimate*)

Confidence weighting.   Objective scoring procedure in which the numerical weights assigned to correct responses to test items depend on the degree of confidence stated by the examinee that his or her responses are correct.

Confirmation bias.   Tendency to seek and remember information that is consistent with one's beliefs or preconceptions.

Construct.   A variable or concept that a test is designed to measure.

Construct validity.   The extent to which scores on a psychometric instrument designed to measure a certain characteristic are related to measures of behavior in situations in which the characteristic is supposed to be an important determinant of behavior.

Constructed response item.   A question or problem that is answered with a written, pictorial, graphical, or other construction. Also known as an open-ended item.

Content analysis.   Method of studying and analyzing written (or oral) communications in a systematic, objective, and quantitative manner to assess certain psychological variables.

Content validity.   The extent to which a group of people who are experts in the material with which a test deals with agrees that the test or other psychometric instrument measures what it was designed to measure.

Contrast error.   In interviewing or rating, the tendency to evaluate a person more positively if an immediately preceding individual was given a highly negative evaluation or to evaluate a person more negatively if an immediately preceding individual was given a highly positive evaluation.

Convergent thinking.   Using facts and reason to produce a single correct answer.

Convergent validity.   Situation in which an assessment instrument has high correlations with other measures (or methods of measuring) the same construct. (See *discriminant validity*)

Correction for attenuation.   Formula used to estimate what the validity coefficient of a test would be if both the test and the criterion were perfectly reliable.

Correction for guessing.   A formula, applied to raw test scores, to correct for the effects of random guessing by examinees. A popular correction-for-guessing formula requires subtracting a portion of the number of items the examinee answers incorrectly from the number he or she answers correctly.

Correlation.   Degree of relationship or association between two variables, such as a test and a criterion measure.

Correlation coefficient.   A numerical index of the degree of relationship between two variables. Correlation coefficients usually range from -1.00 (perfect negative relationship), through .00 (total absence of a relationship), to +1.00 (perfect positive relationship). Two common types of correlation coefficient are the product–moment coefficient and the point–biserial coefficient.

Creativity test.   A test that assesses original, novel, or divergent thinking.

Criterion.   A standard or variable with which scores on a psychometric instrument are compared or against which they are evaluated. The validity of a test or other psychometric procedure used in selecting or classifying people is determined by its ability to predict a specified criterion of behavior in the situation for which people are being selected or classified.

Criterion contamination.   The effect of any factor on a criterion such that the criterion is not a valid measure of an individual's accomplishments. Aptitude test scores may be used to predict grades in school, but when teachers use scores on an aptitude test to decide what grades to assign to students, the grades are not a valid criterion for validating the aptitude test; the criterion has become contaminated.

Criterion-referenced test. A test that has been designed with very restricted content specifications to serve a limited range of highly specific purposes. The aim of the test is to determine where the examinee stands with respect to certain educational objectives. (See *norm-referenced test*)

Criterion-related validity. The extent to which a test or other assessment instrument measures what it was designed to measure, as indicated by the correlation of test scores with some criterion measure of behavior.

Critical incident. A behavior that is considered critical to effective performance on a job (e.g., "cleans up work area before leaving," or "treats customers cordially").

Cross-validation. Readministering an assessment instrument that has been found to be a valid predictor of a criterion for one group of persons to a second group of persons to determine whether the instrument is also valid for that group. There is almost always some shrinkage of the validity coefficient on cross-validation, since chance factors spuriously inflate the validity coefficient obtained with the first group of examinees.

Crystallized intelligence. R. B. Cattell's term for mental ability (knowledge, skills) acquired through experience and education.

CT scan (computerized tomography). X-ray-based diagnostic procedure in which a three-dimensional representation of the brain is generated by computer.

Culture-fair test. A test composed of materials to which all sociocultural groups have presumably been exposed. The test does not penalize any sociocultural group because of lack of relevant experience. Attempts to develop culture-fair tests have not proved very successful.

Cutoff score (cut score). All applicants falling below the cutoff score on a criterion are rejected, and all applicants falling at or above the cutoff score are accepted. The cutoff score depends on the validity of the test, the selection ratio, and other factors.

Decile. One of nine score points that divide a score distribution into 10 equal parts.

Dementia. A general decline in cognitive functioning due to organic factors.

Derived score. A score obtained by performing some mathematical operation on a raw score, such as multiplying the raw score by a constant and/or adding a constant to the score. (See *standard score, T score, z score*)

Developmental age. Score on the Gesell Developmental Schedules.

Developmental quotient (DQ). An index, roughly equivalent to a mental age, for summarizing an infant's behavior as assessed by the Gesell Developmental Schedules.

Deviation IQ. Intelligence quotient (IQ) score obtained by converting raw scores on an intelligence test to a score distribution having a mean of 100 and a fixed standard deviation, such as 16 for the Stanford–Binet or 15 for the Wechsler tests.

Diagnostic interview. An interview designed to obtain information on a person's thoughts, feelings, perceptions, and behavior; used in making a diagnostic decision about the person.

Diagnostic test. An achievement test composed of a number of areas or skills constituting a certain subject, with the purpose of diagnosing an individual's relative strengths and weaknesses in the areas. Diagnostic tests are available in reading, arithmetic, and spelling.

Differential item functioning (DIF). A test item is easier or more discriminating in one group than in another.

Discriminant validity. Situation in which a psychometric instrument has low correlations with other measures of (or methods of measuring) different psychological constructs.

Distracter. Any of the incorrect options on a multiple-choice test item.

Divergent thinking. Creative thinking that involves more than one solution to a problem.

Domain-referenced test. (See *criterion-referenced test*)

Down syndrome (mongolism). A disorder characterized by a flattened skull; thickened skin on eyelids; short, stubby fingers and toes; coarse, silky hair; short stature; and moderately low intelligence. An extra chromosome is found in the twenty-first position in karyotypes of Down syndrome cases.

Dynamic assessment. A test–teach–test approach to assessment in which a person is tested (pretested), then given practice on the test materials, and finally tested again (posttested). The change in performance level from pretest to posttest is a measure of learning potential. (See *zone of potential development*)

Dyscalculia. Inability to perform arithmetical operations.

Dyslexia.   Reading disorder associated with impairment of the ability to interpret spatial relationships or to integrate auditory and visual information.

Ectomorph.   In Sheldon's somatotype system, a person with a tall, thin body build; related to the cerebrotonic (thinking, introversive) temperament type.

Educable mentally retarded (EMR).   Children characterized by a mild degree of mental retardation (IQ = 51 to 69). Such children are capable of obtaining a third- to sixth-grade education and can learn to read, write, and perform elementary arithmetic operations.

Ego.   According to psychoanalytic theory, that part of the personality (the "I" or "me") that obeys the reality principle and attempts to mediate the conflict between the id and superego.

Electroencephalograph (EEG).   Electronic apparatus designed to detect and record brain waves from the intact scalp.

Electromyograph (EMG). Electronic apparatus designed to measure muscular activity or tension.

Elimination scoring.   Scoring procedure in which, rather than marking only the one best answer for an item, the examinee indicates which options are incorrect.

Empirical scoring.   A test development strategy in which an examinee's responses are chosen/not chosen for inclusion on a test based on how well they can detect people in certain criterion groups, such as schizophrenics or physicians. This scoring procedure is employed with various personality and interest inventories.

Endomorph.   In Sheldon's somatotype system, a person having a rotund body shape (fat); related to the viscerotonic (relaxed, sociable) temperament.

Equal-appearing intervals (method of).   Method of attitude scaling devised by L. L. Thurstone, in which a large sample of "judges" sort attitude statements into 11 piles according to the favorableness of the attitude expressed in the statement. The scale value of a statement is computed as the median and the ambiguity index as the semi-interquartile range of the judges' ratings.

Equilibration.   In J. Piaget's theory of cognitive development, the process by which a child comes to know and understand the environment by interacting with it. Equilibration involves the processes of assimilation and accommodation.

Equipercentile method.   Traditional method of converting the score units on one test to the score units on a parallel test. The scores on each test are converted to percentile ranks, and a table of equivalent scores is produced by equating the score at the *p*th percentile on the first test to the score at the *p*th percentile on the second test.

Equivalent forms.   (See *parallel forms*)

Error of measurement.   The difference between an observed score and the corresponding true score on a test.

Essay test.   A test on which examinees are required to compose rather lengthy answers to a series of questions. The answers are evaluated subjectively by the teacher or another evaluator. (See *objective test*)

Estimated learning potential (ELP).   An estimate of a child's ability to learn, derived from measures obtained in the *System of Multicultural Pluralistic Assessment* (*SOMPA*). The ELP takes into account not only the child's IQ on the Wechsler Intelligence Scale for Children-Revised or the Wechsler Preschool and Primary Scale of Intelligence, but also family size, family structure, socioeconomic status, and degree of urban acculturation.

Evaluation.   To judge the merit or value of an examinee's behavior from a composite of test scores, observations, and reports.

Exceptional child.   A child who deviates significantly from the average in mental, physical, or emotional characteristics.

Expectancy effect.   Effect of teacher expectations on the IQ scores of pupils; more generally, the effect of a person's expectations on another person's behavior.

Expectancy table.   A table giving the frequency or percentage of examinees in a certain category (score interval) on a predictor variable (test) who would be expected to fall in a certain category (score interval) on the criterion variable.

Expected growth.   Average change in test scores occurring over a given time period in persons of specified age, grade level, or other characteristics.

Experiential intelligence.   According to Sternberg, the ability to cope effectively with novel tasks.

Explicit memory.   Intentional, conscious memory.

Extrovert.   C. G. Jung's term for people who are oriented, in thought or social orientation, toward the external environment and other people, rather than toward their own thoughts and feelings.

Face validity.   The extent to which the appearance or content of the materials (items and the like) on a test or other psychometric instrument is such that the instrument appears to be a good measure of what it is supposed to measure.

Factor. A dimension, trait, or characteristic of personality revealed by factoring the matrix of correlations computed from the scores of a large number of people in several different tests or items.

Factor analysis. A mathematical procedure for analyzing a matrix of correlations among measurements to determine what factors (constructs) are sufficient to explain the correlations.

Factor loadings. In factor analysis, the resulting correlations (weights) between tests (or other variables) and the extracted factors.

Factor rotation. A mathematical procedure applied to a factor matrix for the purpose of simplifying the matrix for interpretation purposes by increasing the number of high and low factor loadings in the matrix. Factor rotation may be either *orthogonal,* in which case the resulting factors are at right angles to each other, or *oblique,* in which the resulting factor axes form acute or obtuse angles with each other.

Fairness. On an aptitude test, the extent to which scores are unbiased, that is, equally predictive of the criterion performance of different groups.

False negative. Selection error or diagnostic decision error in which an assessment procedure incorrectly predicts a maladaptive outcome (e.g., low achievement, poor performance, or psychopathology).

False positive. Selection error or diagnostic decision error in which an assessment procedure incorrectly predicts an adaptive outcome (e.g., high achievement, good performance, or absence of psychopathology).

Fantasy stage. The earliest stage in the development of interests, in which a child's interest orientations are not based on an accurate perception of reality.

Fidelity. The narrowness of the bandwidth of a test or other measuring instrument. A test with high fidelity is a good predictor of a fairly narrow range of criteria. (See *bandwidth*)

Field dependence. A perceptual style in which the perceiver relies primarily on cues from the surrounding visual environment, rather than kinesthetic (gravitational) cues, to determine the upright position in the rod-and-frame test.

Field independence. A perceptual style in which the perceiver depends primarily on kinesthetic (gravitational) cues, rather than visual cues from the surrounding environment, to determine the upright position in the rod-and-frame test.

Fixed-alternative question. A multiple-choice question consisting of a stem and several possible answers.

Flexilevel test. A test consisting of items arranged in order of difficulty and on which every examinee starts in the middle. When an item is answered correctly, the next more difficult item is present; when an item is answered incorrectly, the next easier item is presented, and so on.

Fluid intelligence. R. B Cattell's term for inherent, genetically determined mental ability, as seen in problem-solving or novel responses.

Forced-choice item. Item on a personality or interest inventory arranged as a dyad (two options), a triad (three options), or a tetrad (four options) of terms or phrases. The respondent is required to select an option viewed as most descriptive of the personality, interests, or behavior of the person being evaluated and perhaps another option perceived to be least descriptive of the personality, interests, or behavior of the person being evaluated. Forced-choice items are found on certain personality inventories, (for example, the Edwards Personal Preference Schedule, interest inventories (Kuder General Interest Survey), and rating forms to control for response sets.

Formal operations. The final stage (11 to 15 years) in J. Piaget's cognitive development sequence, in which the child can now use logic and verbal reasoning and perform higher-level, more abstract mental operations.

Formative evaluation. Evaluation of performance for the purpose of improving instruction or determining areas of strength and weakness for purposes of enrichment or remedial instruction. (See *summative evaluation*)

Four-fifths rule. Selection rule that any procedure resulting in a selection rate for any race, gender, or ethnic group that is less than four-fifths (80%) of that of the group with the highest rate has an adverse impact and is consequently illegal.

Frequency distribution. A table of score intervals and the number of cases (scores) falling within each interval.

Frontal lobe. Portion of the cerebral cortex in the frontal lobes anterior to the central fissure.

Fundamental attribution error. Tendency to attribute one's own behavior to situational influences, but to attribute the behavior of other people to dispositional factors.

G factor. The single general factor of intelligence postulated by Spearman to account for the high correlations among tests of intelligence.

Generalizability coefficient. A numerical coefficient that is an index of the degree of generalizability (i.e., reliability) from sample to population. A generalizability coefficient takes into account one or more sources of error in generalizing from sample to population. It is computed as a ratio of the sum of variances of the test score components under consideration to this sum, plus the weighted sum of the error variances in the situation.

Generalizability theory.   A theory of test scores and the associated statistical formulation that conceptualizes a test score as a sample from a universe of scores. Analysis of variance procedures are used to determine the generalizability from score to universe value, as a function of examinees, test items, and situational contexts. A generalizability coefficient may be computed as a measure of the degree of generalizability from sample to population.

Golden rule.   Compromise worked out between the Golden Rule Insurance Company and Educational Testing Service, in which ETS agreed to construct an examination for insurance salespeople consisting of items that showed the least amount of disparity between white and black applicants.

Grade norm (grade equivalent score).   The average of the scores on a test made by a group of children at a given grade level.

Graduated prompting strategy.   Dynamic assessment procedure in which the examiner presents a series of behavioral hints to teach the rules needed for successful completion of a test task. The hints or prompts, which are generated from a predetermined script, rather than the examinee's responses, are fairly general to begin, but become more specific as needed.

Graphic rating scale.   A rating scale containing a series of items, each consisting of a line on which the rater places a check mark to indicate the degree of a characteristic that the ratee is perceived as possessing. Typically, at the left extremity of the line is a brief verbal description indicating the lowest degree of the characteristic, and at the right end is a description of the highest degree of the characteristic. Brief descriptions of intermediate degrees of the characteristic may also be located at equidistant points along the line.

Graphology.   The analysis of handwriting to determine the character or personality of the writer.

Group test.   A test administered simultaneously to a group of examinees by one examiner. (See *individual test*)

Guess-who technique.   Procedure for analyzing group interaction and the social stimulus value of group members, in which children in a classroom or other group situation are asked to "guess who" possesses certain characteristics or does certain things.

Halo effect.   Rating a person high on one characteristic merely because he or she rates high on other characteristics.

Hemorrhaging.   Bleeding that can, for example, refer to bleeding internal to the brain that can result in brain damage.

Heritability index (h^2).   Ratio of the test score variance attributable to heredity to the variance attributable to both heredity and environment.

Hierarchical model.   P. E. Vernon's tree model of intelligence, consisting of a general factor at the highest level, two major group factors, verbal–educational and practical–mechanical–spatial, at the second level, and a number of minor group factors at a third level.

High-stakes testing.   Testing that contributes to educational, legal, employment, treatment, or other important decisions regarding individuals or groups.

Holistic scoring.   Scoring procedure, as on essay test items, in which a single score is assigned in terms of the examinee's overall performance, rather than by assigning different points to different features of the response. (See *analytic scoring*)

IDEA.   Individuals with Disabilities Act.

Ideal self.   In C. R. Rogers' phenomenological theory, the self a person would like to be, as contrasted with the person's *real self.*

Identification.   Taking on the personal characteristics of another person, as when a developing child identifies with a significant "other" person. Also, in psychoanalytic theory, an ego defense mechanism for coping with anxiety.

Idiographic approach.   Approach to personality assessment and research in which the uniqueness of the individual is emphasized rather than how he or she compares to general (or normative) principles of behavior. (See *nomothetic approach*)

IEP.   Individualized education plan; consists of short- and long-term educational objectives for a particular pupil, typically learning disabled, and procedures for obtaining them.

Implicit memory.   Memory occurring without conscious intent to remember.

In-basket technique.   A procedure for evaluating supervisors or executives in which the candidate is required to indicate what action should be taken on a series of memos and other materials of the kind typically found in a supervisor's or executive's in-basket.

Incident sampling. In contrast to *time sampling,* an observational procedure in which certain types of incidents, such as those indicative of aggressive behavior, are selected for observation and recording.

Incremental validity. An increase in validity produced by a new test over and above that obtained with existing selection procedures.

Individual test. A test administered to one examinee at a time.

Informed consent. A formal agreement made by a person, or the person's guardian or legal representative, with an agency or someone else to permit use of the person's name and/or personal information (test scores and the like) for a specified purpose.

Insanity. A legal term for a disorder of judgment or behavior in which a person cannot distinguish between right and wrong (*McNaghten rule*) or cannot control or manage his or her actions and affairs.

Intelligence. Many definitions of this term have been offered, such as "the ability to judge well, understand well, and reason well" (A. Binet) and "the capacity for abstract thinking" (L. M. Terman). In general, what is measured by intelligence tests is the ability to succeed in school-type tasks.

Intelligence quotient (IQ). A derived score, used originally in scoring the Stanford–Binet Intelligence Scale. A ratio IQ is computed by dividing the examinee's *mental age (MA)*, as determined from a score on an intelligence test, by his or her *chronological age (CA)* and multiplying the resulting quotient by 100. A deviation IQ is computed by multiplying the z score corresponding to a raw score on an intelligence test by the standard deviation of the deviation IQs and adding 100 to the product.

Intelligence test. A psychological test designed to measure an individual's aptitude for scholastic work or other kinds of activities involving verbal ability and problem solving.

Interest inventory. A test or checklist, such as the Strong Interest Inventory or the Kuder General Interest Survey, designed to assess individual preferences for certain activities and topics.

Interlocking items. Test items on which a response to one item is affected by or contingent on responses to other items on the test.

Internal consistency. The extent to which all items on a test measure the same variable or construct. The reliability of a test computed by the Spearman–Brown, Kuder–Richardson, or Cronbach–alpha formulas is a measure of the test's internal consistency.

Interrater (interscorer) reliability. Two scorers assign a numerical rating or score to a sample of people. Then the correlation between the two sets of numbers is computed.

Interval scale. A measurement scale on which equality of numerical differences implies equality of differences in the attribute or characteristic being measured. The scale of temperature (Celsius, Fahrenheit) and, presumably, standard score scales (z, T, etc.) are examples of interval scales.

Interview. A systematic procedure for obtaining information by asking questions and, in general, verbally interacting with a person (the interviewee).

Intraclass reliability. An index of agreement among the ratings assigned by a group of raters ("judges") to a characteristic or behavior of a person.

Introvert. Carl Jung's term for orientation toward the self; primarily concerned with one's own thoughts and feelings rather than with the external environment or other people; preference for solitary activities.

Inventory. A set of questions or statements to which the individual responds (e.g., by indicating agreement or disagreement), designed to provide a measure of personality interest, attitude, or behavior.

Ipsative measurement. Test item format (e.g., forced choice) in which the variables being measured are compared with each other so that a person's score on one variable is affected by his or her scores on other variables measured by the instrument.

Ischemia. Local and temporary deficiency of blood supply to a region of the brain, usually resulting in damage to the area.

Item. One of the units, questions, or tasks of which a psychometric instrument is composed.

Item analysis. A general term for procedures designed to assess the utility or validity of a set of test items.

Item bias. Extent to which an item measures different constructs in different ethnic, cultural, regional, or gender groups.

Item characteristic curve. A graph, used in item analysis, in which the proportion of examinees passing a specified item is plotted against total test scores.

Item difficulty index. An index of the easiness or difficulty of an item for a group of examinees. A convenient measure of the difficulty of an item is the percentage (p) of examinees who select the correct answer.

Item discrimination index. A measure of how effectively an item discriminates between examinees who score high on the test as a whole (or on some other criterion variable) and those who score low.

Item overlap. Extent to which two items measure the same variable and, consequently, the scores on the items are correlated.

Item-response (characteristic) curve. Graph showing the proportion of examinees who get a test item right, plotted against an internal (total test score) or external criterion of performance.

Item-response theory (IRT). Theory of test items in which item scores are expressed in terms of estimated scores on a latent ability continuum.

Item sampling. Procedure for selecting subsets of items from a total item pool; different samples of items are administered to different groups of examinees.

Job analysis. A general term for procedures used to determine the factors or tasks making up a job. A job analysis is usually considered a prerequisite to the construction of a test for predicting performance on a job.

Job-replica test. A test on which the examinee is required to perform a set of operations or tasks similar to those on an actual job. Also known as a *work sample test.*

Kuder–Richardson formulas. Formulas used to compute a measure of internal-consistency reliability from a single administration of a test having 0–1 scoring.

Language test. A test composed of verbal or numerical items, that is, items involving the use of language. (See *nonverbal test*)

Latent trait theory. Any one of several theories (e.g., item characteristic curve theory, Rasch model) and associated statistical procedures that relate item and test scores to estimated standing on some hypothetical latent ability trait or continuum; used in item analysis and test standardization.

Leaderless group discussion (LGD). Six or so individuals (e.g., candidates for an executive position) are observed while discussing an assigned problem to determine their effectiveness in working with the group and reaching a solution.

Learning disability. Difficulty in learning to read, write, spell, perform arithmetic, solve nonverbal problems or other academic skills by a person whose score on an intelligence test (IQ) is average or above.

Least stigmatizing label. Label or classification category that is considered to be the least socially stigmatizing and yet appropriate for the diagnosed condition.

Leniency error. Tendency to rate an individual higher on a positive characteristic and less severely on a negative characteristic than he or she actually should be rated.

Likert scale. Attitude scale in which respondents indicate their degree of agreement or disagreement with a particular proposition concerning some object, person, or situation.

Linear regression analysis. Procedure for determining the algebraic equation of the best-fitting line for predicting scores on a dependent variable from one or more independent variables.

Linking. Item-response-based methodology for equating two tests by transforming the item parameters of one form of the test to those of a second form of the test so that the corresponding parameters on the two tests will be on the same numerical scale.

Local norms. Percentile ranks, standard scores, or other norms corresponding to the raw test scores of a relatively small, local group of examinees.

Locus of control. J. B. Rotter's term for a cognitive–perceptual style characterized by the typical direction (internal or self versus external or other) from which individuals perceive themselves as being controlled.

Looking-glass theory. After C. H. Cooley, the idea that the self is formed as a result of the individual's perception of how others view her or his person and behavior.

Magnetic resonance imaging (MRI scan). Diagnostic procedure in which changes in the magnetic resonance of atoms in the brain are drawn by computer.

Man-to-man scale. Procedure in which ratings on a specific trait (e.g., leadership) are made by comparing each person to be rated with several other people whose standings on the trait have already been determined.

Mastery test. (See *criterion-referenced test*)

Matching item. A test item requiring examinees to indicate which of several options in one list is (are) the correct match(es) or answer(s) for each of the several options in another list.

Measurement. Procedures for determining (or indexing) the amount or quantity of some construct or entity; assignment of numbers to objects or events.

Median. Score point in a distribution of scores below and above which 50% of the scores fall.

Mediation. Dynamic assessment strategy in which the examiner interacts continuously with the examinee to increase the likelihood that a solution will be found to a presented problem.

Mental age (MA). A derived score on an intelligence test such as the Stanford–Binet. An examinee's mental age corresponds to the chronological age of a representative sample of children of the same chronological age whose average score on the test was equal to the examinee's score. (See *intelligence quotient*)

Mental age grade placement. An index of the grade level at which a person is functioning mentally.

Mentally gifted. A person who is significantly above average in intellectual functioning, variously defined as an IQ of 130 or 140 and above.

Mentally retarded. A person who is significantly below average in intellectual functioning, variously defined as an IQ of 70 or 75 and below.

Mesomorph. W. H. Sheldon's term for a person having an athletic physique; correlated with a somatotonic temperament (active, aggressive, energetic).

Mode. The most frequently occurring score in a group of scores.

Moderator variable. Demographic or personality variable (e.g., age, sex, cognitive style, compulsivity) affecting the correlation between two other variables (e.g., aptitude and achievement).

Multilevel test. A test designed to be appropriate for several age levels; a separate test is constructed for each level.

Multiple abstract variance analysis (MAVA). Statistical procedure, devised by R. B. Cattell, for determining the relative effects of heredity and environment on a particular personality characteristic.

Multiple aptitude battery. A battery of conormed tests designed to assess mental abilities.

Multiple-choice item. A test item consisting of a stem (statement, question, phrase, etc.) and several response options (usually three to five), only one of which is correct.

Multiple correlation coefficient (*R*). A measure of the overall degree of relationship, varying between –1.00 and +1.00, of several variables with a single criterion variable. The multiple correlation of a group of scholastic aptitude tests with school grades is typically around .60 to .70, a moderate degree of correlation.

Multiple cutoff. Selection strategy in which applicants are required to make at least specific minimum scores on several selection criteria to be accepted (employed, admitted, etc.).

Multiple-regression analysis. Statistical method for analyzing the contributions of two or more independent variables in predicting a dependent variable.

Multitrait–multimethod matrix. Matrix of correlation coefficients resulting from correlating measures of the same trait by the same method, different traits by the same method, the same trait by different methods, and different traits by different methods. The relative magnitudes of the four types of correlations are compared in evaluating the construct validity of a test.

National norms. Percentile ranks, standard scores, or other norms based on a national sample. (See *local norms; norms*)

Neuropsychological assessment. Measurement of cognitive, perceptual, and motor performance to determine the locus, extent, and effects of neurological damage and malfunction.

Neuropsychological disorder. A disorder of the nervous system accompanied by psychological symptoms.

Nominal scale. The lowest type of measurement, in which numbers are used merely as descriptors or names of things, rather than designating order or amount.

Nomination technique. Method of studying social structure and personality in which students, workers, or other groups of individuals are asked to indicate with which persons in the group they would like to do a certain thing or whom they feel possess(es) certain characteristics.

Nomothetic approach. Approach to personality and research in which the person is understood in relation to general principles or norms of behavior rather than their individual uniqueness. (See *idiographic approach*)

Nonverbal behavior. Any communicative behavior that does not involve making word sounds or signs. It includes movements of large (*macrokinesics*) and small (*microkinesics*) body parts, interpersonal distance or territoriality (*proximics*), tone and rate of voice sounds (*paralinguistics*), and communications imparted by culturally prescribed matters relating to time, dress, memberships, and the like (culturics).

Nonverbal test. A test that does not necessitate the use of spoken or written words, but requires the examinee to construct, manipulate, or respond to test materials in other nonverbal ways.

Normal curve equivalents (NCEs). Normalized standard scores having a mean of 50, a standard deviation of 21.06, and ranging from 1 to 99.

Normal distribution. A smooth, bell-shaped frequency distribution of scores, symmetric about the mean and described by an exact mathematical function. The test scores of a large group of examinees are frequently distributed approximately in this way.

Normalized standard scores. Scores obtained by transforming raw scores in such a way that the transformed scores are normally distributed with a mean of 0 and a standard deviation of 1 (or some linear function of these numbers).

Norm group. Sample of people on which a test is standardized.

Norm-referenced test. A test whose scores are interpreted with respect to norms obtained from a representative sample of examinees. (See *criterion-referenced test*)

Norms. A list of scores and the corresponding percentile ranks, standard scores, or other transformed scores of a group of people on whom a test has been standardized.

Objective test. A test scored by comparing an examinee's responses to a list of correct answers (a key) prepared beforehand, in contrast to a subjectively scored test. Examples of objective test items are multiple choice and true–false.

Oblique rotation. In a factor analysis, a rotation in which the factor axes are allowed to form acute or obtuse angles with each other. Consequently, the factors are correlated.

Observation method. Observing behavior in a controlled or uncontrolled situation and making a formal or informal record of the observations.

Occipital lobe. Area of the cerebral cortex lying at the back of the head; especially important in vision.

Odd–even reliability. The correlation between total scores on the odd-numbered and total scores on the even-numbered items of a test, corrected by the Spearman–Brown reliability formula. (See *Spearman–Brown formula*)

Omnibus test. A test consisting of a variety of items designed to measure different aspects of mental functioning. The Otis–Lennon School Ability Test and the Henmon–Nelson Test of Mental Ability are omnibus tests. (See *spiral omnibus test*)

Open-ended item. (See *constructed response item*)

Operation. In J. P. Guilford's structure-of-intellect model, one of five possible types of mental processes (cognitive, memory, divergent thinking, convergent thinking, evaluation). In J. Piaget's theory of cognitive development, an operation is any mental action

that is reversible (can be returned to its starting point) and integrated with other reversible mental actions.

Opinion. A verbalized judgment concerning a specific occurrence or situation. The meaning of *opinion* is similar to that of *attitude,* but the former term has the connotation of being more specific and based on more thought than the latter. In addition, a person is aware of his or her opinions, but not necessarily aware of his or her attitudes.

Opinion polling. Questioning a sample of a target population on their opinions concerning particular objects, issues, and events.

Oral test. A test on which the examinee provides oral answers to oral or written questions.

Ordinal scale. Type of measurement scale on which the numbers refer merely to the ranks of objects or events arranged in order of merit (e.g., numbers referring to order of finishing in a contest).

Orthogonal rotation. In factor analysis, a rotation that maintains the independence of factors; that is, the angles between factors are kept at 90 degrees and hence the factors are uncorrelated.

Out-of-level testing. Administering a test designed primarily for one age or grade level to examinees below or above that level.

Parallel forms. Two tests that are equivalent in the sense that they contain the same kinds of items of equal difficulty and are highly correlated. The scores made on one form of the test are very close to those made by the same persons on the other form.

Parallel forms reliability. An index of reliability determined by correlating the scores of individuals on parallel forms of a test.

Parietal lobe. Portion of the cerebral cortex located behind the central fissure and between the frontal and occipital lobes; contains neural structures for experiencing somesthetic sensations.

Parkinsonism. A progressive brain disorder resulting from damage to the basal ganglia and occurring most often in older adulthood. The symptoms are muscular tremors; spastic, rigid movements; propulsive gait; and a masklike, expressionless face. Also called *Parkinson's disease.*

Participant observation. A research technique, used primarily by cultural anthropologists, in which an observer attempts to minimize the intrusiveness of his or her person and observational activities by becoming part of the group being observed, for example, by dressing and acting like other members of the group.

Peaked test. A test designed to measure efficiently within a fairly narrow range of ability.

Percentile. The test score at or below which a specified percentage of scores falls.

Percentile band. A range of percentile ranks within which there is a specified probability that an examinee's true score on a test will fall.

Percentile norms. A list of raw scores and the corresponding percentages of the test standardization group whose scores fall below the given percentile.

Percentile rank. The percentage of scores falling below a given score in a frequency distribution or group of scores; the percentage corresponding to the given score.

Performance assessment. Type of assessment procedure that requires students to construct, create, or demonstrate something. In most cases, there are multiple ways of assessing performance and more than one acceptable response.

Performance test. A test on which the examinee is required to manipulate various physical objects; performance tests are contrasted with paper-and-pencil tests. Examples are the performance scale of the Wechsler Intelligence Scale and the Arthur Point Scale of Performance.

Perseveration. Persistent focus on and repetition of a stimulus even when it is no longer appropriate to do so.

Personality. The sum total of all the qualities, traits, and behaviors that characterizes a person and by which, together with his or her physical attributes, the person is perceived as an individual.

Personality assessment. Description and analysis of personality by means of various techniques, including observing, interviewing, and administering checklists, rating scales, personality inventories, and projective techniques.

Personality inventory. A self-report inventory or questionnaire consisting of statements concerning personal characteristics and behaviors. On a true–false inventory, the respondent indicates whether each item is self-descriptive; on a multiple-choice or forced-choice inventory, the respondent selects the words, phrases, or statements that are self-descriptive.

Personal orientation. Generalized personality disposition, such as gender role or self-actualization, that directs behavior in a variety of situations.

Phallometrics. The measurement of male erectile response as a scientific measure of men's sexual preferences.

Phrenology. Discredited theory and practice relating affective and cognitive characteristics to the configuration (bumps) of the skull.

Pilot test. A test administered to a representative sample of people to try out some aspects of the test or test items.

Pluralistic model. In the System of Multicultural Pluralistic Assessment (SOMPA), a combination made up of the Student Assessment Materials and the Parent Interview. A child's scores on the various measures are interpreted by comparing them with the scores of other children having a similar sociocultural background.

Point–biserial coefficient. Correlation coefficient computed between a dichotomous variable and a continuous variable; derived from the product–moment correlation coefficient.

Point scale. A test on which points (e.g., 0, 1, or 2) are assigned for each item, depending on the accuracy and completeness of the answer.

Portfolio. A collection of a student's performances or products over a period of time that may be subject to assessment.

Power test. A test with ample time limits so that all examinees have time to attempt all items. Many of the items are difficult, and they are often arranged in order from easiest to most difficult.

Predictive validity. Extent to which scores on a test are predictive of performance on some criterion measured at a later time; usually expressed as a correlation between the test (predictor variable) and the criterion variable.

Preoperational period. In J. Piaget's theory of cognitive development, the egocentric period of development (3 to 7 years) when the child acquires language and other symbolic representations.

Primacy effect. The tendency of raters to assign more weight to initial behaviors or performances than to subsequent behaviors of ratees.

Privileged communication. Confidential communication between a person and his or her lawyer, doctor, religious leader, or spouse. The information communicated is privileged against disclosure in court if the privilege is claimed by the person (client, patient, penitent, spouse).

Profile. A graphic representation of a person's score on a series of tests or subtests comprising a test composite or battery.

Prognostic test. A test used to predict a person's achievement in a particular subject, for example, a reading-readiness test.

Projective hypothesis (See *projective technique*)

Projective technique. A relatively unstructured personality assessment technique in which the person responds to materials such as inkblots, ambiguous pictures, incomplete sentences, and other materials by telling what he or she perceives, making up stories, or constructing and arranging sentences and objects. Theoretically, because the material is fairly unstructured, the structure imposed on it by the examinee represents a projection of his or her own personality characteristics (needs, conflicts, sources of anxiety, etc.).

Pseudodementia due to depression. Loss of cognitive function due to depression, rather than to organic (physiological) factors.

Psychometrics. Theory and research pertaining to the measurement of psychological (cognitive and affective) characteristics.

Psychomotor skills. Skills involving motoric activities, such as throwing, catching, inserting, and otherwise manipulating objects (e.g., athletic skills).

Pupillometrics. Procedure for measuring pupillary diameter as an indicator of pleasure or interest in a specific stimulus.

Q technique (Q-sort). Personality assessment procedure that centers on sorting decks of cards (*Q*-sorts) containing statements that may or may not be descriptive of the rater.

Quartile. A score in a frequency distribution below which either 25% (first quartile), 50% (second quartile), 75% (third quartile), or 100% (fourth quartile) of the total number of scores fall.

r. A symbol for the Pearson product–moment correlation coefficient.

Race norming. Basing test score norms only on a specific race or ethnic group, and evaluating the scores of applicants of that group only with respect to those scores.

Random sample. A sample of observations (e.g., test scores) drawn from a population in such a way that every member of the target population has an equal chance of being selected in the sample.

Range. A crude measure of the spread or variability of a group of scores computed by subtracting the lowest score from the highest score.

Ranking. Placing a group of individuals in order according to their judged standing on some characteris-

tic; placing a list of characteristics of an individual in order according to their salience or significance.

Rapport. A warm, friendly relationship between examiner and examinee.

Rasch model. One-parameter (item difficulty) model for scaling test items for purposes of item analysis and test standardization. The model is based on the assumption that indexes of guessing and item discrimination are negligible parameters. As with other latent trait models, the Rasch model relates examinees' performances on test items (percentage passing) to their estimated standings on a hypothetical latent ability trait or continuum.

Rating scale. A list of words or statements concerning traits or characteristics, sometimes in the form of a continuous line divided into sections corresponding to degrees of the characteristics, on which the rater indicates judgments of either his or her own behavior or characteristics or the behavior or characteristics of another person (ratee). The rater indicates how or to what degree the behavior or characteristic is possessed by the ratee.

Ratio IQ. An intelligence quotient obtained by dividing an examinee's mental age score on an intelligence test (such as the older Stanford–Binet) by his or her chronological age and multiplying the quotient by 100. (See *deviation IQ*)

Ratio scale. A scale of measurement, having a true zero, on which equal numerical ratios imply equal ratios of the attribute being measured. Psychological variables are typically not measured on ratio scales, but height, weight, energy, and many other physical variables are.

Raw score. An examinee's unconverted score on a test, computed as the number of items answered correctly or the number of correct answers minus a certain portion of the incorrect answers.

Readiness test. A test that measures the extent to which a person possesses the skills and knowledge necessary to learn a complex subject such as reading, mathematics, or spelling.

Realistic stage. Final stage in the development of vocational interests, usually occurring during late adolescence or early adulthood. At this stage the individual has a realistic notion about what particular occupations entail and the vocation he or she would like to pursue.

Rearrangement item. A test item on which examinees are required to rearrange or reorder the items into their correct sequence.

Regression equation. A linear equation for forecasting criterion scores from scores on one or more predictor variables; a procedure often used in selection programs or actuarial prediction and diagnosis.

Regression toward the mean. Tendency for test scores or other psychometric measures to be closer to the mean on retesting; the more extreme the original score is, the closer it will be to the mean on retesting.

Reliability. The extent to which a psychological assessment device measures anything consistently. A reliable instrument is relatively free from errors of measurement, so the scores obtained on the instrument are close in numerical value to the true scores of examinees.

Reliability coefficient. A numerical index, between .00 and 1.00, of the reliability of an assessment instrument. Methods for determining reliability include test–retest, parallel forms, and internal consistency.

Representative sample. A group of individuals whose characteristics are similar to those of the population of individuals for whom a test is intended.

Response sets (styles). Tendencies for individuals to respond in relatively fixed or stereotyped ways in situations where there are two or more response choices, such as on personality inventories. Tendencies to guess, to answer true (acquiescence), and to give socially desirable answers are some of the response sets that have been investigated.

RIASEC model. J. L. Holland's model of person–environment interest–personality types consisting of realistic, investigative, artistic, social, enterprising, and conventional themes.

Rubric. A procedure, scheme, or set of criteria according to which performance is assessed.

Scale. A system of graduated numbers, used in assigning measured values to selected characteristics of objects, events, or persons.

Scatter diagram. A cluster of points plotted from a set of X–Y values, in which X is the independent variable and Y the dependent variable.

Schema. In J. Piaget's theory of cognitive development, a mental structure (grasping, sucking, shaking, etc.) that is modified (accommodated) as a result of experience.

Scholastic aptitude test. Any test that predicts the ability of a person to learn the kinds of information and skills taught in school. The abilities measured by these tests (e.g., the Scholastic Aptitude Test) are similar to those measured by general intelligence tests.

Scoring formula. A formula used to compute raw scores on a test. Common scoring formulas are $S = R$ and $S = R - W/(k - 1)$, where S is the score, R is the number right, W is the number wrong, and k is the number of options per item.

Screening. A general term for any selection process, usually not very precise, by which some applicants are accepted and others are rejected.

Secure test. A test administered under conditions of tight security to make certain that only persons who are supposed to take the test actually take it and that copies of test materials are not removed from the examination room(s) by examinees.

Selection. The use of tests and other devices to select those applicants for an occupation or educational program who are most likely to succeed in that situation. Applicants who fall at or above the cutoff score on the test are selected (accepted); those who fall below cutoff are rejected.

Selection ratio. The proportion of applicants who are selected for a job or training (educational) program.

Self-concept. A person's evaluation of his or her ability to accomplish a particular task in a certain situation successfully.

Self-efficacy. A person's judgment concerning his or her ability to accomplish a particular task in a certain situation successfully.

Self-fulfilling prophecy. Tendency for a person's expectations and attitudes concerning future events or outcomes to affect their occurrence; the tendency for children to behave in ways in which parents or teachers expect them to behave.

Self-report inventory. A paper-and-pencil measure of personality traits or interests, comprised of a series of items that the respondent indicates as characteristic (true) or not characteristic (not true) of himself (herself).

Semantic differential. A rating scale for evaluating the connotative meanings of selected concepts. Each concept is rated on a 7-point, bipolar adjectival scale.

Semi-interquartile range (Q). A measure of the variability of a group of ordinal-scale scores, computed as half the difference between the first and third quartiles.

Sensorimotor stage. The first stage in J. Piaget's theory of cognitive development (0 to 2 years), during which the child learns to exercise simple reflexes and to coordinate various perceptions.

Sentence-completion test. A projective test of personality consisting of a series of incomplete sentences that the examinee is instructed to complete.

Sequential processing. Mental process in which a series of items is processed sequentially, in serial order. An example of a sequential task is attempting to recall a series of numbers. (See *simultaneous processing*)

Sequential testing. Testing procedure in which an examinee's answers to previous items determine which items will be presented next; also referred to as adaptive or tailored testing.

Short-answer item. Test item that requires the examinee to construct a short answer to fit into a blank or answer a question.

Simultaneous processing. Mental process in which several bits or pieces of information are synthesized or integrated simultaneously. (See *sequential processing*)

Situation(al) test. A performance test in which the person is placed in a realistic but contrived situation and directed to accomplish a specific task. Situation tests have been used to assess personality characteristics such as honesty and frustration tolerance.

Skewness. Degree of asymmetry in a frequency distribution. In a positively skewed distribution, there are more scores to the left of the mode (low scores); this is true when the test is too difficult for the examinees. In a negatively skewed distribution, there are more scores to the right of the mode (high scores); this is true when the test is too easy for the examinees.

Snellen chart. A chart containing letters of various sizes, designed to measure visual acuity at a distance.

Social desirability response set. Response set or style affecting scores on a psychological assessment instrument. Refers to the tendency for an examinee to answer in what he or she perceives as the more socially desirable direction, rather than answering in a manner that is truly characteristic or descriptive of him or her.

Sociogram. Diagram consisting of circles representing individuals in a group, with lines drawn indicating which people chose (accepted) each other and which people did not choose (rejected) each other. Terms used in referring to particular elements of a sociogram are *star, clique, isolate,* and *mutual admiration society.*

Sociometric technique. Method of determining and describing the pattern of acceptances and rejections in a group of people.

Somatotype. Classification of a body build (physique) in W. H Sheldon's three-component system (endomorphy, mesomorphy, ectomorphy).

Spearman–Brown prophecy formula. A general formula for estimating the reliability (r_{11}) of a test on which the number of items is increased by a factor of m. In the formula, $r_{mm} = mr_{11}/[1 + (m-1)]r_{11}$, r_{11} is the reliability of the original (unlengthened) test, and m is the factor by which it is lengthened.

Special children. Children having physical, psychological, cognitive, or social problems that make the fulfillment of their needs and potentials more difficult than they are for other children.

Specific determiner. Words such as all, always, never, and only, which indicate that a true–false item is probably false, or often, sometimes, and usually, which suggest that the item statement is true.

Specificity. The proportion of the total variance of a test that is due to factors specific to the test itself.

Specific learning disability. (See *learning disability*)

Speed(ed) test. A test consisting of a large number of fairly easy items but having a short time limit so that almost no one completes the test in the allotted time. Many tests of clerical, mechanical, and psychomotor ability are speeded.

Spiral omnibus test. A test consisting of a variety of items arranged in order of ascending difficulty. Items of a given type or content appear throughout the test, intermingled with other types of items of similar difficulty, in a spiral of increasing difficulty.

Split-half coefficient. An estimate of reliability determined by applying the Spearman–Brown formula for $m = 2$ to the correlation between two halves of the same test, such as the odd-numbered items and the even-numbered items.

Standard deviation. The square root of the variance; used as a measure of the dispersion or spread of a group of scores.

Standard error of estimate. Degree of error made in estimating a person's score on a criterion variable from his or her score on a predictor variable.

Standard error of measurement. An estimate of the standard deviation of the normal distribution of test scores that an examinee would theoretically obtain by taking a test an infinite number of times. If an examinee's obtained test score is X, then the chances are two out of three that he or she is one of a group of people whose true scores on the test fall within one standard error of measurement of X.

Standardization. Administering a carefully constructed test to a large, representative sample of people under standard conditions for the purpose of determining norms.

Standardization sample. Subset of a target population on which a test is standardized.

Standardized test. A test that has been carefully constructed by professionals and administered with standard directions and under standard conditions. The test has usually been administered to a representative sample of people for the purpose of obtaining norms.

Standard scores. A group of scores, such as z scores, T scores, or stanine scores, having a desired mean and standard deviation. Standard scores are computed by changing raw scores to z scores, multiplying the z scores by the desired standard deviation, and then adding the desired mean of the transformed scores to the product.

Stanine. A standard score scale consisting of the scores 1 through 9; stanine scores have a mean of 5 and a standard deviation of approximately 2.

Statistic. A number used to describe some characteristic of a sample of test scores, such as the arithmetic mean or standard deviation.

Stratified random sampling. A sampling procedure in which the population is divided into strata (e.g., men and women; Blacks and Whites, lower class, middle class, upper class), and samples are selected at random from the strata; sample sizes within strata are proportional to strata sizes.

Stress interview. Interviewing procedure in which the interviewer applies psychologically stressful techniques (critical and hostile questioning, frequent interruptions, prolonged silences, etc.) to break down the interviewee's defenses and or determine how the interviewee reacts under pressure.

Structured interview. Interviewing procedure in which the interviewee is asked a predetermined set of questions.

Sublimation. Diversion of the energy of a sexual or other biological impulse from its immediate goal to one of a higher social, moral, or esthetic nature or use.

Subtest. A portion or subgroup of items on a test (e.g., a group of items measuring the same function or items at the same age level or difficulty level).

Summated ratings (method of). Technique of attitude-scale construction devised by R. Likert. Raters check the numerical values on a continuum, with 3 to 7 (usually 5) categories corresponding to the degree of positivity or negativity of each of a large number of attitude statements concerned with the topic in question. Twenty or so statements are selected according to certain statistical criteria to comprise the final attitude scale.

Summative evaluation. Evaluation at the end of an instructional unit or course of study to provide a sum total or final product measure of achievement.

Survey test. As contrasted with a diagnostic test, an achievement test that focuses on the examinee's overall performance on the test.

T **scores.** Converted, normalized standard scores having a mean of 50 and a standard deviation of 10. Z scores are also standard scores with a mean of 50 and a standard deviation of 10, but in contrast to T scores they are not normalized.

Table of specifications. A two-way table prepared as an outline or skeletal framework of an achievement test. The behavioral objectives are the row headings, and the content (topical) objectives are the column headings of such a table.

Tailored test. (See *adaptive testing, sequential testing*)

Target behaviors. Specific, objectively defined behaviors observed and measured in behavioral assessments. Of particular interest are the effects on these behaviors of antecedent and consequent events.

Target population. The population of interest in standardizing a test or other assessment instrument; the norm group (sample) must be representative of the target population if valid interpretations of (norm-referenced) scores are to be made.

Taxonomy of educational objectives. A hierarchically arranged, mutually inclusive set of objectives for a lesson or achievement test.

Taxonomy of psychomotor behavior. A taxonomy of objectives for a lesson or test in the psychomotor domain.

Taylor–Russell tables. Tables for evaluating the validity of a test as a function of the information contributed by the test beyond the information contributed by chance.

Temporal lobe. Lobe of the brain located in the temporal region of the head. Plays a role in hearing, speech, and certain other higher-order neurological functions.

Teratogen. A substance (alcohol, drugs, etc.) that crosses the placental barrier between mother and fetus and produces a physical deformity in the fetus.

Test. Any device used to evaluate the behavior or performance of a person. Psychological tests are of many kinds—cognitive, affective, and psychomotor.

Test anxiety.   Anxiety in a testing situation.

Test bias.   Condition in which a test unfairly discriminates between two or more groups.

Test–retest reliability.   A method of assessing the reliability of a test by administering it to the same group of examinees on two different occasions and computing the correlation (coefficient of stability) between their scores on the two occasions.

Testwiseness.   Techniques, other than knowledge of the test material, employed by examinees to enhance their test scores.

Trade test.   Test of knowledge and skill in a particular trade; used for employee selection, placement, and licensing.

Trainable mentally retarded (TMR).   Children in the moderately retarded range of IQs (approximately 36 to 50), who usually cannot learn to read and write, but can perform unskilled tasks under supervision.

Transfer hypothesis (of ability differentiation).   G. A. Ferguson's hypothesis that the different abilities isolated by factor analysis are the results of overlearning and differential positive transfer in certain areas of learning.

True–false item.   Test item consisting of a statement that is either true or false.

True score.   The hypothetical score that is a measure of the examinee's true knowledge of the test material. In test theory, an examinee's true score on a test is the mean of the distribution of scores that would result if the examinee took the test an infinite number of times.

Unobtrusive observations.   Observations made without interfering with or otherwise influencing the behavior to be observed.

Validity.   The extent to which an assessment instrument measures what it was designed to measure. Validity can be assessed in several ways: by analysis of the instrument's content (*content validity*), by relating scores on the test to a criterion (*predictive validity* and *concurrent validity*), and by a more thorough study of the extent to which the test is a measure of a certain psychological construct (*construct validity*).

Validity coefficient.   The correlation between scores on a predictor variable and scores on a criterion variable.

Validity generalization.   The application of validity evidence to situations other than those in which the evidence was obtained.

Variability.   The degree of spread or deviation of a group of scores around their average value.

Variable.   In contrast to a *constant,* any quantity that can assume more than one state or numerical value.

Variance.   A measure of variability of test scores, computed as the sum of the squares of the deviations of raw scores from the arithmetic mean, divided by one less than the number of scores; the square of the standard deviation.

Vascular dementia.   The most common type of dementia in old age; due to cerebrovascular disease associated with hypertension and vascular damage to the brain.

Verbal ability.   Understanding words and their interrelationships in language; the ability to solve problems concerned with words.

Verbal test.   A test with verbal directions requiring oral or written word and/or number answers.

Visual analogue scale.   A psychometric device for measuring subjective experiences such as pain, anxiety, and cravings for certain substances. The patient points to or marks the point on a line corresponding to the intensity of his or her experience.

Visual neglect.   A neuropsychological disorder in which a person does not have awareness of a portion of their vision (but not due to blindness).

Wernicke's area.   Area in the left cerebral hemisphere concerned with the understanding of language. Patients with damage to Wernicke's area can hear words, but fail to understand their meanings. (See *Broca's area*)

Word-association test.   A projective test on which the examinee responds to each of several words presented by the examiner with the first word that comes to mind. Unusual responses or slow responding to certain words may be indicative of conflicts or other emotional problems associated with those words.

Work-sample test.   A test consisting of miniature replicas of the tasks employed in the job for which an applicant has applied. (*See job-replica test*)

z score.   Any one of a group of derived scores varying from – to +, computed from the formula $z =$ (raw score—mean)/standard deviation, for each raw score. In a normal distribution, over 99% of the cases lie between $z = -3.00$ and $z = +3.00$.

Zone of potential development.   The difference (distance) between a child's actual developmental level (his or her completed development as might be assessed by a standardized test) and his or her potential development (the degree of competence he or she can attain with assistance).

ANSWERS TO QUANTITATIVE QUESTIONS

CHAPTER 3

4d. Uncorrected score-number right-30.

Corrected score-rights-wrongs/3 = $30 - 16/3 = 25$.

If items are true–false, uncorrected score = number right = 30, and corrected score = rights – wrongs = 14.

CHAPTER 4

2b. Since $.27 \times 75 = 20.25$, there are 20 people in the upper group and 20 people in the lower group. Therefore, $p = (18 + 12)/40 = .75$ and $D - (18 - 12)/20 = .30$. The item is in the acceptable ranges of both p and D.

2c. $U = 30$, $L = 20$, $U_p = 20$, and $L_p = 10$, so $p = (20 + 10)/50 = .60$ and $D = 20/30 - 10/20 = .17$.

2d.

ITEM	1	2	3	4	5	6	7	8	9	10
p	.50	.45	.45	.55	.40	.75	.50	.50	.60	.40
D	.40	.30	.30	.50	.60	.30	.20	.20	.40	.60

Table 4.1 gives the optimum mean p value of a four-option multiple-choice item as .74. Taking ±.20 around this value, acceptable items should be in the p range of .54 to .94. The D value of acceptable items should be .30 or higher. According to these criteria, only items 4, 6, and 9 are acceptable. The remaining seven items should be revised or discarded.

6a. George's z-score on the arithmetic test is $z_a = (65 - 50)/10 = 1.50$; his z-score on the reading test is $z_r = (80 - 75)/15 = .33$. His Z-scores on the two tests are $Z_a = 10(1.5) + 50 = 65$ and $Z_r = 10(.3) + 50 = 53$. Therefore, George is slightly better in arithmetic than he is in reading.

6b.

% RANK	z	T	CEEB	STANINE	DEVIATION IQ
10	−1.28	37	372	2	81
20	−.84	42	416	3	87
30	−.52	45	448	4	92
40	−.25	48	475	4	96
50	.00	50	500	5	100
60	.25	52	525	6	104
70	.52	55	552	6	108
80	.84	58	584	7	113
90	1.28	63	628	8	119

6c.

SCORE INTERVAL	MIDPOINT	FREQUENCY	CUMULATIVE FREQUENCY BELOW MIDPOINT	PERCENTILE RANK	z	Z	z_n	Z
96–98	97	1	29.5	98.33	2.00	70	2.13	71
93–95	94	2	28	98.33	1.54	65	1.50	65
90–92	91	3	25.5	85.00	1.08	61	1.04	60
87–89	88	5	21.5	71.67	.63	56	.57	56
84–86	85	5	16.5	55.00	.17	52	.13	51
81–83	82	5	11.5	38.33	−.29	47	−.30	47
78–80	79	4	7	23.33	−.75	43	−.73	43
75–77	76	2	4	13.33	−1.21	38	−1.11	39
72–74	73	2	2	6.67	−1.66	33	−1.50	35
69–71	70	1	.5	1.67	−2.12	29	−2.13	29

CHAPTER 5

2b. $r_{oe} = .226$, $r_{11} = .369$, $KR_{20} = .610$, $KR_{21} = .580$.

4b. Substituting in formula 5.9, we have $m = .90\,(1 - .80)/[.80\,(1 - .90)\,] = .18/.08 = 2.25$. Multiplying n by m gives $40 \times 2.25 = 90$. Therefore, 50 more items of the same general type as those on the test must be added to the test to increase its reliability coefficient to .90.

5b. $S_{err} = 4.00$

95% confidence interval for $X = 40$ is 32.16–47.84.

95% confidence interval for $X = 50$ is 42.16–57.84.

95% confidence interval for $X = 60$ is 52.16–67.84.

8c. $s_{est} = s\sqrt{1 - r^2} = .5\sqrt{1 - .60^2} = .5(8) = .4$. The probability is .68 that the student's grade-point average will fall between 2.1 and 2.9 and .95 that it will fall between 1.72 and 3.28.

9b.

PREDICTOR VARIABLE	CRITERION VARIABLE (Y)					
	26–34	*35–41*	*42–48*	*49–55*	*56–62*	*63–70*
71–78			1(100)			1(50)
63–70				1(100)		2(67)
56–62			2(100)	2(67)	1(33)	1(17)
49–55		2(100)	1(67)	2(50)		1(17)
42–48		1(100)	1(80)	2(60)		1(20)
35–41		2(100)	1(50)	1(25)		
28–34	1(100)			1(67)	1(33)	
21–27	1(100)					

CHAPTER 6

4b. $IQ = 100(MA/CA) = 100(77/105) = 73.$

CHAPTER 7

8b. $h^2 = .65,$ implying that 65% of the variance in IQ scores is attributable to genetic factors.

CHAPTER 10

6c. The regression equation for predicting Y from X is $Y_{pred} = .44X + 28.34$ for the majority group and $Y_{pred} = .43X + 24.57$ for the minority group; the corresponding correlation coefficients are .52 and .47. The correlation coefficient suggests that the test may be a slightly more accurate predictor for the majority group than for the minority group, but not significantly so. Thus, it may be concluded that the test is not appreciably biased according to the traditional definition of fairness.

Assuming that 50% of the majority group and 25% of the minority group can perform the job, then $.50(30) = 15$ examinees in the majority group and $.25(20) = 5$ examinees in the minority group should be selected if the test is fair. If the cutoff score is set at $X = 52$, then 7 minority group members and 15 majority group members will be selected; if it is set at $X = 53$, then 5 minority and 13 majority group members will be selected. According to Thorndike's definition, the first cutoff score would slightly favor the minority group and the second would slightly disfavor the majority group.

Assuming that 40% of the entire group of 50 examinees is capable of performing the job, then $.40(30) = 12$ majority group members and $.40(20) = 8$ minority group members should be selected if the test is fair according to Cole's definition. Any cutoff score that yields a total number of selectees close to 20 will tend to favor the majority group according to this definition. Thus, using this procedure, the test is slightly biased toward the majority group.

Combining the scores of the majority and minority groups yields a correlation between X and Y of $r = .517$ and the regression equation $Y_{pred} = .46X + 25.639$. If the cutoff score is set at $X = 50$, the number of false-positive and false-negative errors in each group will be as follows:

	FALSE POSITIVES	FALSE NEGATIVES
Majority group	6 (20%)	6 (20%)
Minority group	5 (25%)	2 (10%)

These percentages are based on the total number of applicants in each group. The total percentage of errors is 5 points greater for the majority group than for the minority group, but the percentage of false positives is greater in the minority group and the percentage of false negatives is greater in the majority group. In this case, the question of bias is complex, depending on which type of error is considered more serious.

CHAPTER 11

5c. Yes. $S_{est} = 10\sqrt{2 - .90 - .85} = 5$, and $2 \times 5 = 10$ is equal to the difference between the two T scores.

CHAPTER 13

1b.

STATEMENT	SCALE VALUE (MEDIAN)	AMBIGUITY INDEX (Q)
D	8.96	1.14
N	5.19	1.22
X	2.50	1.01

1c.

	Attitude Statement						
RESPONDENT	*1*	*2*	*3*	*4*	*5*	*6*	TOTAL "+"
A	+	+	+	+	+	+	6
D	+	+	+	+	+	−	5
E	−	−	+	+	+	+	4
B	−	−	+	+	+	−	3
F	−	−	+	−	+	+	3
G	−	−	+	+	−	−	2
C	−	−	−	−	+	−	1
Total "+"	2	2	6	5	6	3	
Errors	0	0	0	2	2	2	

$R = 1 - 6/(7 \times 6) = .857$

The reproducibility coefficient is below .90 and hence does not provide evidence that the six statements form a true Guttman scale.

APPENDIX A

1c. Mode 88

2c. .5%, 1%, 2.5%, 5%, 50%, 95%, 97.5%, 99%, 99.5%

.00, .25, .52, .84, 1.28

4b $\overline{X} = 34.00$, $s_x = 6.58$

$\overline{Y} = 27.00$, $s_y = 11.03$

$r_{y \cdot x} = .54$, $Y_{pred} = .91X - 3.78$

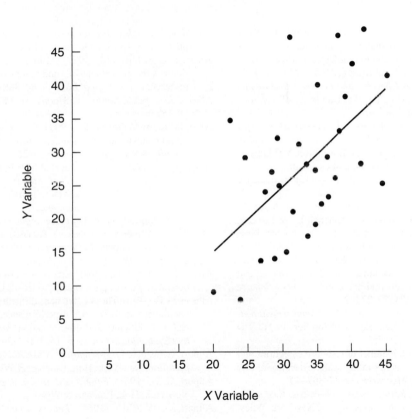

REFERENCES

Abrahams, N. M., Neumann, I., & Gilthens, W. H. (1971). Faking vocational interests: Simulated vs. real life motivation. *Personnel Psychology, 24,* 5–12.

Achenbach, T. M., & Edelbrock, C. (1983). *Manual of the Child Behavior Checklist and Revised Child Behavior Profile.* Burlington, VT: University of Vermont, Department of Psychiatry.

Achenbach, T. M., & Edelbrock, C. (1986). *Manual for the Teacher's Report Form and Teacher Version of the Child Behavior Profile.* Burlington, VT: University of Vermont, Department of Psychiatry.

Achenbach, T. M., & Edelbrock, C. (1987). *Manual for the Youth Self-Report and Profile.* Burlington, VT: University of Vermont, Department of Psychiatry.

Ackenbach, T., Krukowski, R., Dumenci, L., & Ivanova, M. (2005). Assessment of adult psychopathology: Meta-analysis and implications of cross-informant correlations. *Psychological Bulletin, 131,* 361–382.

Aiken, L. R. (1979). Attitudes toward mathematics and science in Iranian middle schools. *School Science and Mathematics, 79,* 229–234.

Aiken, L. R. (1983a). *The case for oral achievement testing.* ERIC Document Reproduction Service No. ED 222 578 & TM 820 755.

Aiken, L. R. (1983b). Number of response categories and statistics on a teacher rating scale. *Educational and Psychological Measurement, 43,* 397–401.

Aiken, L. R. (1996). *Rating scales & checklists: Evaluating behavior, personality, and attitudes.* New York: Wiley.

Aiken, L. R. (1997). *Questionnaires & inventories: Surveying opinions and assessing personality.* New York: Wiley.

Aiken, L. R. (1998). *Tests & examinations: Measuring abilities and performance.* New York: Wiley.

Aiken, L. R. (1999). *Human differences.* Mahwah, NJ: Erlbaum.

Aiken, L. R. (2000). Computer programs for facilitating objective grading. *Educational Research Quarterly, 24*(2), 55–61.

Airasian, P. W., & Terrasi, S. (1994). Test administration. In T. Husén & T. N. Postlethwaite (Eds.), *International encyclopedia of education* (2nd ed., Vol. 11, pp. 6311–6315). Tarrytown, NY: Elsevier.

Ajzen, I., & Fishbein, M. (1977). Attitude–behavior relations: A theoretical analysis and review of empirical research. *Psychological Bulletin, 84,* 888–918.

Albemarle Paper Company v. *Moody.* 10 FEP 11 1181 (1975).

Albright, L., & Malloy, T. E. (1999). Self-observation of social behavior and metaperception. *Journal of Personality & Social Psychology, 77,* 726–734.

Alderton, D. L. (1994). Mechanical ability. In R. J. Sternberg (Ed.), *Encyclopedia of human intelligence* (pp. 697–700). New York: Macmillan.

Alhberg, J., Tuck, J. R., & Allgulander, C. (1996). Pilot study of the adjunct utility of a computer-assisted Diagnostic Interview Schedule (C-DIS) in forensic psychiatric patients. *Bulletin of the American Academy of Psychiatry & the Law, 24,* 109–116.

Allard, G., & Faust, D. (2000). Errors in scoring objective personality tests. *Assessment, 7,* 119–129.

Allison, D. E. (1984). The effect of item-difficulty sequence, intelligence, and sex on test performance, reliability, and item difficulty and discrimination. *Measurement and Evaluation in Guidance, 16,* 211–217.

Allport, G. W. (1937). *Personality: A psychological interpretation.* New York: Holt, Rinehart & Winston.

Allport, G. W. (1961). *Pattern and growth in personality.* New York: Holt, Rinehart & Winston.

Allport, G. W. (Ed.). (1965). *Letters from Jenny.* New York: Harcourt Brace Jovanovich.

Allport, G. W., & Odbert, H. S. (1936). Trait-names. A psycholexical study. *Psychological Monographs, 47,* Bi, 211 161.

Allport, G. W., Vernon, P. E., & Lindzey, G. (1960). *Study of Values* (3rd ed.): *Manual.* Chicago: Riverside Publishing Co.

Altus, W. D. (1966). Birth order and its sequelae. *Science, 151,* 44–49.

Alwin, D. F., & Krosnick, J. A. (1991). The reliability of survey attitude measurement. *Sociological Methods & Research, 20,* 139–181.

American Association of Mental Retardation. (2002). *Mental retardation: Definition, classification, and systems of supports* (10th ed.). Washington, DC: Author.

American College. (1978). *Test wiseness: Test taking skills for adults.* New York: McGraw-Hill.

American Educational Research Association, American Psychological Association, & National Council on Measurement in Education. (1999). *Standards for educational and psychological testing.* Washington, DC: American Psychological Association.

American Law Institute. (1956). *Model penal code.* Tentative Draft Number 4.

American Psychiatric Association. (1994). *Diagnostic and statistical manual of mental disorders* (4th ed.). Washington, DC: Author.

American Psychological Association. (1992). Ethical principles of psychologists and code of conduct. *American Psychologist, 47,* 1597–1611.

American Psychiatric Association. (2001). *Diagnostic and statistical manual of mental disorders.* (4th ed., text rev.). Washington, DC: Author.

American Psychological Association. (2002). Ethical principles of psychologists and code of conduct. *American Psychologist, 57,* 1060–1073.

American Psychological Association, Committee on Professional Standards & Committee on Psychological Tests and Assessment. (1986). *Guidelines for computer-based tests and interpretations.* Washington, DC: American Psychological Association.

Ames, L. B. (1967). Predictive value of infant behavior examinations. In J. Hellmuth (Ed.), *Exceptional infant. Vol. 1: The normal infant* (pp. 207–239). Seattle: Straub & Hellmuth.

Ames, L. B. (1989). *Arnold Gesell—Themes of his work.* New York: Human Sciences Press.

Ames, L. B. Gillespie, B. S., Haines, J., & Ilg, F. L. (1979). *The Gesell Institute's child from one to six: Evaluating the behavior of the preschool child.* New York: Harper & Row.

Anastasi, A., & Urbina, S. (1997). *Psychological testing* (7th ed.). Upper Saddle River, NJ: Prentice Hall.

Andreasen, N. C. (1987). Creativity and mental illness: Prevalence rates in writers and their first-degree relatives. *American Journal of Psychiatry, 144,* 1288–1297.

Andrew, D. M., Paterson, D. G., & Longstaff, H. P. (1979). *Manual: Minnesota Clerical Test.* Cleveland, OH: Psychological Corporation.

Anrig, G. R. (1987). "Golden Rule": Second thoughts. *APA Monitor, 18*(8), 3.

APA task force releases final report on integrity testing (1991, May/June). *Psychological Science Agenda 4*(3), 1, 6. Washington, DC: American Psychological Association.

Armor, D. J. (2001). On family size and intelligence. *American Psychologist, 56,* 521–522.

Arthur, G. (1947). *Arthur point scale of performance tests.* Chicago, IL: Soetling.

Arvey, R. D. (1979). Unfair discrimination in the employment interview: Legal and psychological aspects. *Psychological Bulletin, 86,* 736–765.

Arvey, R. D., & Campion, J. E. (1982). The employment interview: A summary and review of recent research. *Personnel Psychology, 35,* 281–322.

Ash, P. (1995). Review of the Eating Disorder Inventory-2. *Twelfth Mental Measurements Yearbook,* 334–335.

Baker, E. L., O'Neil, H. F., & Linn, R. L. (1993). Policy and validity prospects for performance-based assessment. *American Psychologist, 48,* 1210–1218.

Baker, F. (2001). *The basics of item response theory* (2nd ed.). College Park, MD: University of Maryland, ERIC Clearinghouse on Assessment and Evaluation. Online ericae.net/irt/baker/software.htm.

Baller, W. R., Charles, D. C., & Miller, E. L. (1967). Midlife attainment of the mentally retarded: A longitudinal study. *Genetic Psychology Monographs, 75,* 235–329.

Baltes, P. B., & Schaie, K. W. (1974). The myth of the twilight years. *Psychology Today, 7*(10), 35–40.

Baltes, P. B., & Willis, S. L. (1982). In F. I. M. Craik & S. E. Trehub (Eds.), *Aging and cognitive processes* (pp. 353–389). New York: Plenum Press.

Bandura, A. (1977). *Social learning theory.* Englewood Cliffs, NJ: Prentice Hall.

Banks, S. (1990, May 3). Reprimands issued on test cheating. *Los Angeles Times,* p. B-3:1.

Bartels, M., Rietveld, M. J., Van Baal, G. C., & Boomsma, D. I. (2002). Genetic and environmental influences on the development of intelligence. *Behavior Genetics, 32,* 237–240.

Baumrind, D. (1993). The average expectable environment is not good enough: A response to Scarr. *Child Development, 64,* 1299–1317.

Bayley, N. (1993). *Bayley Scales of Infant Development* (2nd ed.). San Antonio, TX: Psychological Corporation.

Bayley, N., & Oden, M. M. (1955). The maintenance of intellectual ability in gifted adults. *Journal of Gerontology, 10,* 91–107.

Beck, A. T. (1990). *Beck Anxiety Inventory Manual.* San Antonio, TX: Psychological Corporation.

Beck, A. T. (1991). *Beck Scale for Suicide Ideation Manual.* San Antonio, TX: Psychological Corporation.

Beck, A. T., & Steer, R. A. (1993). *Beck Depression Inventory: Manual.* San Antonio, TX: Psychological Corporation.

Belcher, M. J. (1992). Review of the Wonderlic Personnel Test. *The Eleventh Mental Measurements Yearbook.* Lincoln: University of Nebraska Press.

Bell, A., & Zubek, J. (1960). The effect of age on the intellectual performance of mental defectives. *Journal of Gerontology, 15,* 285–295.

Bellak, L., & Abrams, D. M. (1997). *The T.A.T., C.A.T., and S.A.T. in clinical use.* (6th ed.). Boston: Allyn and Bacon.

Bellezza, F. S., & Bellezza, S. F. (1989). Detection of cheating on multiple-choice tests by using error-similarity analysis. *Teaching of Psychology, 16,* 151–155.

Bellezza, F. S., & Bellezza, S. F. (1995). Detection of copying on multiple-choice tests: An update. *Teaching of Psychology, 22,* 180–182.

Bem, D. J., & Allen, A. (1974). On predicting some of the people some of the time: The search for cross-situational consistencies in behavior. *Psychological Review, 81,* 506–520.

Bem, S. L. (1974). The measurement of psychological androgyny. *Journal of Consulting & Clinical Psychology, 42,* 165–172.

Benbow, C. P., & Lubinski, D. (1997). Intellectually-talented children: How can we best meet their needs? In N. Colangelo & G. Davis (Eds.), *Handbook of gifted education* (2nd ed., pp. 155–169). Boston: Allyn and Bacon.

Bender, L. (1938). A visual motor gestalt test and its clinical uses (Research Monograms No. 3). New York: American Orthopsychiatric Association.

Bender, W. N. (1995). *Learning disabilities: Characteristics, identification, and teaching strategies* (2nd ed.). Boston: Allyn and Bacon.

Benjamin, J., Ebstein, R. P., & Belmaker, R. H. (Eds.). (2002). Molecular genetics and human personality. Washington, DC: American Psychiatric Publishing.

Benjamin, L. T., Cavell, T. A., & Shallenberger, W. R. (1984). Staying with initial answers on objective tests: Is it a myth? *Teaching of Psychology, 11,* 133–141.

Bennett, G. K. (1994). *Manual: BMCT-Bennett Mechanical Comprehension Test* (2nd ed.). San Antonio, TX: Harcourt Assessment.

Bennett, G. K., Seashore, H. G., & Wesman, A. G. (1984). *Differential Aptitude Test: Technical supplement.* San Antonio, TX: Psychological Corporation.

Ben-Porath, Y. S., Shondrick, D. D., & Stafford, K. P. (1995). MMPI-2 and race in a forensic diagnostic sample. *Criminal Justice and Behavior, 22,* 19–32.

Bergstrom, B. A., & Lunz, M. E. (1999). CAT for certification and licensure. In F. Drasgow & J. B. Olson-Buchanan (Eds.), *Innovations in computerized assessment* (pp. 67–91). Mahwah, NJ: Erlbaum.

Berne, E. (1966). *Principles of group treatment.* New York: Oxford University Press.

Betsworth, D. G., Bouchard, T. J., Cooper, C. R., Grotevant, H. D., Hansen, J. C., Scarr, S., & Weinberg, R. A. (1994). Genetic and environmental influences on vocational interests assessed using adoptive and biological families and twins reared apart and together. *Journal of Vocational Behavior, 44,* 263–278.

Betz, N. E. (1992). Counseling uses of career self-efficacy theory. *Career Development Quarterly, 47*(1), 22–26.

Betz, N. E. (1994). Self-concept theory in career development and counseling. *Career Development Quarterly, 43,* 32–42.

Beutler, L. E., Clarkin, J. F., & Bongar, B. (2000). *Guidelines for the systematic treatment of the depressed patient.* New York: Oxford University Press.

Beutler, L. E., & Groth-Marnat, G. (2003). *Integrative assessment of adult personality.* New York: Guilford.

Beutler, L. E., Groth-Marnat, G., & Rosner, R. (2003). Introduction to integrative assessment of adult personality. In L. E. Beutler & G. Groth-Marnat (Eds.), *Integrative assessment of adult personality* (pp. 1–37). New York: Guilford.

Beutler, L. E., & Malik, M. L. (Eds.). (2002). *Rethinking the DSM: A psychological perspective.* Washington, DC: American Psychological Association.

Biemiller, L. (1986, January 8). Critics plan assault on admissions tests and other standard exams. *Chronicle of Higher Education,* pp. 1, 4.

Binion, R. (1976). *Hitler among the Germans.* New York: Elsevier.

Black, H. (1962). *They shall not pass.* New York: Morrow.

Blakley, B. R., Quinones, M. A., Crawford, M. S., & Jago, I. A. (1994). The validity of isometric strength tests. *Personnel Psychology, 47,* 247–274.

Bloom, B. S., & Krathwohl, D. R. (1956). *Taxonomy of educational objectives: Handbook I. The cognitive domain.* New York: David McKay.

Boake, C. (2002). From the Binett–Simon to the Wechsler–Bellevue: Tracing the history of intelligence testing. *Journal of Clinical & Experimental Neuropsychology, 24,* 383–405.

Bogardus, E. S. (1925). Measuring social distances. *Journal of Applied Sociology, 9,* 299–308.

Boring, E. G. (1923, June). Intelligence as the tests test it. *New Republic,* 35–37.

Bouchard, T. J., Jr., Lykken, D. T., McGue, M., Segal, N. L., & Tellegen, A. (1990). Sources of human psychological differences: The Minnesota Study of Twins Reared Apart. *Science, 250,* 223–228.

Bouchard, T. J., Jr., & McGue, M. (1981). Familial studies of intelligence: A review. *Science, 212,* 1055–1059.

Bouchard, T. J., Jr., et al. (1983, June). *Family resemblance for psychological interests.* Paper presented at meeting of International Congress on Twins Research, London.

Bowman, M. L. (1989). Testing individual differences in Ancient China. *American Psychologist, 44,* 576–578.

Boyle, G. J. (1995). Review of the Personality Assessment Inventory. *Twelfth Mental Measurements Yearbook,* 764–766.

Boyle, M. H., Offord, D. R., Racine, Y. A., Szatmari, P., Sanford, M., & Fleming, J. E. (1996). Interviews versus checklists: Adequacy for classifying childhood psychiatric disorder based on adolescent reports. *International Journal of Methods in Psychiatric Research, 6,* 309–319.

Boyle, M. H., Offord, D. R., Racine, Y. A., Szatmari, P., Sanford, M., & Fleming, J. E. (1997). Adequacy of interviews vs. checklists for classifying childhood psychiatric disorder based on parent reports. *Archives of General Psychiatry, 54,* 793–799.

Bracken, B. A., & McCallum, R. S. (1998). *Universal Nonverbal Intelligence Test.* Itasca, IL: Riverside.

Braithwaite, V. A., & Scott, W. A. (1991). Values. In J. P. Robinson, P. R. Shaver, & L. S. Wrightsman (Eds.), *Measures of personality and social psychological attitudes* (pp. 661–753). San Diego: Academic Press.

Brazelton, T. B. (1973). *Neonatal Behavioral Assessment Scale.* Philadelphia: Lippincott.

Brazelton, T. B. (1984). *Neonatal Behavioral Assessment Scale* (2nd ed.). Philadelphia: Lippincott.

Bredemeier, M. (1991). IQ test ban for blacks called unconstitutional. *California Association of School Psychologists Today,* Nov./Dec., 22–23.

Brennan, R. L. (2001). *Generalizability theory.* New York: Springer-Verlag.

Bricklin, B. (1984). *Bricklin Perceptual Scales.* Furlong, PA: Village.

Bridgman, C. S., & Hollenbeck, G. P. (1961). Effect of simulated applicant status on Kuder Form D occupational interest scores. *Journal of Applied Psychology, 45,* 237–239.

Brigham, C. C. (1923). *A study of American intelligence.* Princeton, NJ: Princeton University Press.

Brigham, C. C. (1930). Intelligence tests of immigrant groups. *Psychological Review, 37,* 158–165.

Brodie, F. M. (1983). *Richard Nixon: The shaping of his character.* Cambridge, MA: Harvard University Press.

Brody, N. (1985). The validity of tests of intelligence. In B. B. Wolman (Ed.), *Handbook of intelligence* (pp. 353–389). New York: Wiley.

Brody, N. (1992). *Intelligence* (2nd ed.). San Diego: Academic Press.

Bruvold, W. H. (1975). Judgmental bias in the rating of attitude statements. *Educational & Psychological Measurement, 45,* 605–611.

Bucholz, K. K., Marion, S. L., Shayka, J. J., Marcus, S. C., & Robins, L. N. (1996). A short computer interview for obtaining psychiatric diagnoses. *Psychiatric Services, 47,* 293–297.

Buck, J. N. (1992). *House–Tree–Person Projective Drawing Technique (H–T–P): Manual and interpretative guide* (revised by W. L. Warren). Los Angeles: Western Psychological Services.

Bukatman, B. A., Foy, J. L., & De Grazia, E. (1971). What is competency to stand trial? *American Journal of Psychiatry, 127,* 1225–1229.

Bureau of Labor Statistics (1996). *Occupational outlook handbook.* Washington, DC: Author.

Bureau of Labor Statistics (2000). *Occupational outlook handbook, 2000–2001.* Washington, DC: Superintendent of Documents.

Burket, G. R. (1973). Empirical criteria for distinguishing and validating aptitude and achievement measures. In D. R. Green (Ed.), *The aptitude–achievement distinction.* Monterey, CA: CTB/McGraw-Hill.

Burton, N. W., & Ramist, L. (2001). Predicting success in college: SAT studies of classes graduating since 1980, Research Report No. 2001 2. New York: College Entrance Examination Board.

Busse, E. W., & Maddox, G. (1985). *The Duke longitudinal studies of normal aging.* New York: Springer.

Butcher, J. N., Perry, J., & Hahn, J. (2004). Computers in clinical assessment: Historical developments, present status, and future challenges. *Journal of Clinical Psychology, 60*(3), 331–345.

Camara, W. J., Nathan, J. S., & Puente, A. E. (2000). Psychological test usage: Implications in professional psychology. *Professional Psychology: Research & Practice, 31,* 141–154.

Camara, W. J., & Schneider, D. L. (1994). Integrity tests: Facts and unresolved issues. *American Psychologist, 49,* 112–119.

Camilli, G., & Shepard, L. A. (1994). *Methods for identifying biased test items.* Newbury Park, CA: Sage.

Campbell, D. P. (1965). A cross-sectional and longitudinal study of scholastic abilities over twenty-five years. *Journal of Counseling Psychology, 12,* 55–61.

Campbell, D. P. (1971). *Handbook for the Strong Vocational Interest Blank.* Stanford, CA: Stanford University Press.

Campbell, D. P., & Fiske, D. W. (1959). Convergent and discriminant validation by the multitrait–multimethod matrix. *Psychological Bulletin, 56,* 81–105.

Campbell, D. P., & Hansen, J. C. (1981). *Manual for the Strong–Campbell Interest Inventory* (3rd ed.). Stanford, CA: Stanford University Press.

Campbell, F., & Ramey, C. T. (1994). Effects of early intervention on intellectual and academic achievement: A follow-up study of children from low-income families. *Child Development, 65,* 684–698.

Campion, M. A., Pursell, E. D., & Brown, B. K. (1988). Structured interviewing: Raising the psychometric properties of the employment interview. *Personnel Psychology, 41,* 25–42.

Cannell, J. J. (1988). Nationally normed elementary school testing in America's public schools: How all 50 states are testing above the national average (with commentaries). *Educational Measurement: Issues & Practice, 7*(2), 5–9.

Cannell, J. J. (1989). *How public educators cheat on achievement tests: The Lake Wogebon report.* Albuquerque, NM: Friends for Education.

Canter, A. (1983). *The Canter Background Interference Procedure for the Bender Gestalt Test.* Los Angeles: Western Psychological Services.

Carlson, J. F. (1998). Review of the Beck Depression Inventory. *Thirteenth Mental Measurements Yearbook,* 117–120.

Carroll, J. B. (1973). The aptitude–achievement distinction: The case of foreign language aptitude and proficiency. In D. R. Green (Ed.), *The aptitude–achievement distinction.* Monterey, CA: CTB/McGraw-Hill.

Carroll, J. B. (1993). *Human cognitive abilities: A survey of factor-analytic studies.* New York: Cambridge University Press.

Carson, A. D. (1998). Why has musical aptitude assessment fallen flat? And what can we do about it? *Journal of Career Assessment, 6,* 311–328.

Carver, R. P. (1974). Two dimensions of tests: Psychometric and edumetric. *American Psychologist, 29,* 512–518.

Castro, J. G., & Jordan, J. E. (1977). Facet theory attitude research. *Educational Researcher, 6,* 7–11.

Cattell, R. B. (1963). Theory of fluid and crystallized intelligence: A critical experiment. *Journal of Educational Psychology, 54,* 1–22.

Chaplin, W. F., & Goldberg, L. R. (1984). A failure to replicate the Ben and Allen study of individual differences in cross-situational consistency. *Journal of Personality and Social Psychology, 47,* 1074–1090.

Charles, D. C., & James, S. T. (1964). Stability of average intelligence. *Journal of Genetic Psychology, 105,* 105–111.

Chauncey, H., & Dobbin, J. E. (1963). *Testing: Its place in education today.* New York: Harper & Row.

Childs, A., & Klimoski, R. J. (1986). Successfully predicting career success: An application of the biographical inventory. *Journal of Applied Psychology, 71,* 3–8.

Chinn, P. C., Drew, C. J., & Logan, D. R. (1975). *Mental retardation: A life cycle approach.* St. Louis, MO: Mosby.

Christensen, H., Mackinnon, A., Jorm, A. F., Henderson, A. S., Scott, L. R., & Korten, S. E. (1994). Age differences and interindividual variation in cognition in community-dwelling elderly. *Psychology and Aging, 9,* 381–390.

Christenson, S. L. (1992). Review of the Child Behavior Checklist. *Eleventh Mental Measurements Yearbook,* 164–166.

Christiansen, K., & Knussman, R. (1987). Sex hormones and cognitive functioning in men. *Neuropsychobiology, 18,* 27–36.

Cizak, G. J. (1999). *Cheating on tests: How to do it, detect it, and prevent it.* Mahwah, NJ: Erlbaum.

Cocks, G., & Crosby, T. L. (Eds.). (1987). *Psycho/history: Readings in the method of psychology, psychoanalysis, and history.* New Haven, CT: Yale University Press.

Cohen, D. S., Colliver, J. A., Marcy, M. S., Fried, E. D., & Swartz, M. H. (1996). Psychometric properties of a standardized-patient checklist and rating-scale form used to assess interpersonal and communication skills. *Academic Medicine, 71* (Suppl 1), S87-S89.

Cole, N. S. (1973). Bias in selection. *Journal of Educational Measurement, 10,* 237–255.

Cole, N. S., & Moss, P. A. (1989). Bias in test use. In R. L. Linn (Ed.), *Educational measurement* (3rd ed., pp. 201–219). New York: Macmillan.

College Entrance Examination Board (1971). *Report of the Commission on Tests.* New York: Author.

Conners, C. K. (1973). Rating scales for use in drug studies with children. *Psychopharmacology Bulletin* [Special issue, Pharmacotherapy of children], 24–84.

Conners, C. K., & Barkley, R. A. (1985). Rating scales and checklists for child psychopharmacology. *Psychopharmacology Bulletin* [Special issue, Rating scales and assessment instruments for use in pediatric psychopharmacology research], *21,* 809–815.

Converse, P. E., Dotson, J. D., Hoag, W. J., & McGee III, W. H. (1980). *American social attitudes data sourcebook, 1947–78.* Cambridge, MA: Harvard University Press.

Cooley, H. H. (1922). *Human nature and the social order.* New York: Scribner.

Corcoran, K., & Fischer, J. (2000). *Measures for clinical practice* (3rd ed., Vols 1 & 2). New York: Free Press.

Costantino, G. (1978, Nov.). *Preliminary report on TEMAS: A new thematic apperception test to assess ego functions in ethnic minority children.* Paper presented at the Second American Conference on Fantasy and the Imaging Process, Chicago.

Costantino, G., Malgady, R., & Rogler, L. H. (1988). *Tell-Me-A-Story—TEMAS—Manual.* Los Angeles: Western Psychological Services.

Courts, P. L., & McInerney, K. H. (1993). *Assessment in higher education: Politics, pedagogy, and portfolios.* Westport, CT: Praeger.

Crites, J. O. (1969). Interests. In R. L. Ebel (Ed.), *Encyclopedia of educational research* (4th ed., pp. 678–685). New York: Macmillan.

Cronbach, L. J. (1970). *Essentials of psychological testing* (3rd ed.). New York: Harper & Row.

Cronbach, L. J., & Drenth, P. J. D. (Eds.). (1972). *Mental tests and cultural adaptation*. The Hague: Mouton.

Cronin, J., Daniels, N., Hurley, A., Kroch, A., & Webber, R. (1975). Race, class, and intelligence: A critical look at the IQ controversy. *International Journal of Mental Health, 3*(4), 46–132.

Dahlstrom, W. G., & Gynther, M. D. (1986). Previous MMPI research on black Americans. In W. G. Dahlstrom, D. Lachar, & L. E. Dahlstrom (Eds.), *MMPI patterns of American minorities*. Minneapolis: University of Minnesota Press.

D'Amato, R. C. (1995). Review of the Adult Personality Inventory. *Twelfth Mental Measurements Yearbook,* 52–54.

Darley, J. B., & Hagenath, T. (1955). *Voctional interest measurement*. Minneapolis: University of Minnesota Press.

Das, J. P., Naglieri, J. A., & Kirby, J. P. (1994). *Assessment of cognitive processes: The PASS theory of intelligence*. Boston: Allyn and Bacon.

Davidshofer, C. (1985). Review of Jackson Vocational Interest Survey. *Ninth Mental Measurements Yearbook,* 739–740.

Dawis, R. V. (2004). Job satisfaction. In J. Thomas (Ed.), *Comprehensive handbook of psychological assessment* (Vol. 4; pp. 470–481). Hoboken, NJ: Wiley.

Debra v. Turlington, 644 F.2d 397 (1981); 730F.2d 1406 (1984).

Denton, L. (1988, August). Board votes to oppose Golden Rule technique. *APA Monitor,* p. 7.

Derogatis, L. R. (1994). *SCL-90-R: Symptom Checklist 90 R: Administration, scoring, and procedures manual* (3rd ed.). Minneapolis, MN: National Computer Systems.

Diamond, E. E. (1979). Sex equality and measurement practices. *New Directions for Testing and Measurement, 3,* 61–78.

Diana v. State Board of Education, C-70 37 RFT (N.D. Cal 1970).

Diekhoff, G. M. (1984). True–false tests that measure and promote structured understanding. *Teaching of Psychology, 11,* 99–101.

Dignon, A. M. (1996). Acceptability of a computer-administered psychiatric interview. *Computers in Human Behavior, 12,* 177–191.

Dik, B. J., & Hansen, J. C. (2004). Development and validation of discriminant functions for the Strong Interest Inventory. *Journal of Vocational Behavior, 64,* 182–197.

Dipboye, R. L., Wooten, K., & Halverson, S. K. (2004). Behavioral and situational interviews. In J. C. Thomas (Ed.), *Comprehensive handbook of psychological assessment, Vol. 4, Industrial and organizational assessment* (pp. 297–318). Hoboken, NJ: Wiley.

Doebele, J. (1999, June/July). A common language: Community colleges become fluent in workforce development. *Community College Journal.*

Dolliver, R. H., Irvin, J. A., & Bigley, S. E. (1972). Twelve-year follow-up of the Strong Vocational Interest Blank. *Journal of Counseling Psychology, 19,* 212–217.

Donlon, T. F. (Ed.). (1984). *The College Board technical handbook for the Scholastic Aptitude and Achievement Tests*. New York: College Entrance Examination Board.

Donnay, D. A. C. (1997). E. K. Strong's legacy and beyond: 70 years of the Strong Interest Inventory. *Career Development Quarterly, 46,* 2–22.

Doppelt, J. E., & Wallace, W. L. (1955). Standardization of the Wechsler Adult Intelligence Scale for older persons. *Journal of Abnormal and Social Psychology, 51,* 312–330.

Dorr-Bremme, D. W., & Herman, J. L. (1986). *Assessing student achievement: A profile of classroom practices* (CSE Monograph 11). Los Angeles: University of California, Center for the Study of Evaluation.

Dowd, E. T. (1992). Review of the Beck Hopelessness Scale. *Eleventh Mental Measurements Yearbook,* 81–82.

Dowd, E. T. (1998). Review of the Beck Anxiety Inventory. *Thirteenth Mental Measurements Yearbook,* 97–98.

Doyle, K. O., Jr. (1974). Theory and practice of ability testing in Ancient Greece. *Journal of the History of the Behavioral Sciences, 10,* 202–212.

Drake, R. M. (1954). *Drake Musical Aptitude Tests*. Chicago: Science Research Associates.

Drakeley, R. J., Herriot, P., & Jones, A. (1988). Biographical data, training success, and turnover. *Journal of Occupational Psychology, 61,* 145–152.

DuBois, P. H. (1970). *The history of psychological testing*. Boston: Allyn and Bacon.

Dudek, B., & Makowska, Z. (1993). Psychometric characteristics of the Orientation to Life Questionnaire for measuring the sense of coherence. *Polish Psychological Bulletin, 24,* 309–318.

Dunnette, M. D. (1963). Critics of psychological tests: Basic assumptions; how good? *Psychology in the Schools, 1,* 63–69.

Dunnette, M. D., & Borman, W. C. (1979). Personnel selection and classification systems. *Annual Review of Psychology, 30,* 477–525.

Dusky v. United States, 362 U.S. 402. (Apr. 18, 1960).

Dykens, E. M., Hosdapp, R. M., & Leckman, J. F. (1994). *Behavior and development in fragile X syndrome.* Newbury Park, CA: Sage.

Ebel, R. L. (1979). *Essentials of educational measurement* (3rd ed.). Upper Saddle River, NJ: Prentice Hall.

Edelbrock, C. (1988). Informant reports. In E. S. Shapiro & T. R. Kratchowill (Eds.), *Behavioral assessment in schools: Conceptual foundations and practical applications* (pp. 351–383). New York: Guilford Press.

Edelbrock, C., & Achenbach, T. M. (1984). The teacher version of the Child Behavior Profile: 2. Boys aged 6–11. *Journal of Consulting & Clinical Psychology, 52,* 207–212.

Edens, J. F., Hart, S. D., Johnson, D. W., Johnson, J. K., & Iver, M. E. (2000). Use of the Personality Assessment Inventory to assess psychopathy in offender populations. *Psychological Assessment, 12,* 132–139.

Educational Testing Service. (1992). *What we can learn from performance assessment for the professions.* ETS Conference on Education and Assessment. Princeton, NJ: Author.

Edwards, A. L. (1954). *Manual—Edwards Personal Preference Schedule.* New York: Psychological Corporation.

Eisdorfer, C. (1963). The WAIS performance of the aged: A retest evaluation. *Journal of Gerontology, 18,* 169–172.

Ekman, P., & Friesen, W. V. (1978). *The Facial Action Coding System: A technique for the measurement of facial movement.* Palo Alto, CA: Consulting Psychologists Press.

Ekman, P., & Friesen, W. V. (1984). *Unmasking the face* (reprint ed.). Palo Alto, CA: Consulting Psychologists Press.

Elliot, C. D. (1990). *Differential Ability Scales (DAS) administration and scoring manual.* San Antonio, TX: Psychological Corporation.

Elliott, S. N., & Busse, R. T. (1992). Review of the Child Behavior Checklist. *Eleventh Mental Measurements Yearbook,* 166–169.

Elms, A. (1976). *Personality and politics.* San Diego: Harcourt Brace Jovanovich.

Embretson, S. E. (2000). *Item response theory for psychologists.* Mahwah, NJ: Erlbaum.

Erikson, E. H. (1969). *Gandhi's truth: On the origins of militant nonviolence.* New York: Norton.

Erikson, M. P. H. (1995). *Family centered assessment of young children at risk: The IDA readings.* Itasca, IL: Riverside Publishing.

Esquivel, G. B., & Lopez, E. (1988). Correlations among measures of cognitive ability, creativity, and academic achievement for gifted minority children. *Perceptual and Motor Skills, 67,* 395–398.

Exner, J. E. (2003). *The Rorschach: A comprehensive system. Vol. 1. Basic foundations* (4th ed.). Hoboken, NJ: Wiley.

Eysenck, H. J. (1965). The effects of psychotherapy. *International Journal of Psychiatry, 1,* 97–178.

Eysenck, H. J. (1971). *The IQ argument.* New York: Library Press.

Eysenck, H. J. (Ed.). (1981). *A model for personality.* New York: Springer.

Eysenck, H. J. (1984). Recent advances in the theory and measurement of intelligence. *Early Child Development and Care, 15,* 97–115.

Fabiano, E. (1989). *Index to tests used in educational dissertations.* Phoenix, AZ: Oryx Press.

Farrell, A. D. (1993). Computers and behavioral assessment: Current applications, future possibilities, and obstacles to routine use. *Behavioral Assessment, 13,* 159–170.

Feather, N. T. (1986). Value systems across cultures: Australia and China. *International Journal of Psychology, 21,* 697–715.

Feigelson, M. E., & Dwight, S. A. (2000). Can asking questions by computer improve the candidness of responding? A meta-analytic perspective. *Consulting Psychology Journal: Practice & Research, 52,* 248–255.

Feldman, D. H., & Goldsmith, L. T. (1991). *Nature's gambit: Child prodigies and the development of human potential.* New York: Teachers College Press.

Feldman, R. G., & White, R. F. (1992). Lead neurotoxicity and disorders of learning. *Journal of Child Neurology, 7,* 354–359.

Fernandez, E. (1998). Review of the Beck Hopelessness Scale. *Thirteenth Mental Measurements Yearbook,* 123–125.

Feuerstein, R., Feuerstein, R., & Gross, S. (1997). The Learning Potential Assessment Device. In D. P. Flanagan, J. L. Genshaft, & P. L. Harrison (Eds.), *Contemporary intellectual assessment: Theories, tests, and issues* (pp. 297–313). New York: Guilford Press.

Fish, L. J. (1941). *One hundred years of examinations in Boston.* Dedham, MA: Transcript Press.

Fishbein, M., & Ajzen, I. (1975). *Belief, attitude, intention, and behavior: An introduction to theory and research.* Reading, MA: Addison-Wesley.

Fisher, R. P., McCauley, M. R., & Geiselman, R. E. (1994). Improving eyewitness testimony with the cognitive interview. In D. Ross, J. D. Read, & M. Toglia (Eds.), *Adult eyewitness testimony: Current trends and developments* (pp. 245–269). New York: Cambridge University Press.

Flanagan, D., & Harrison, P. L. (Eds.). (2005). *Contemporary intellectual assessment: Theories, tests, and issues* (2nd ed.). New York: Guilford.

Flanagan, J. C. (1954). The critical incident technique. *Psychological Bulletin, 51,* 327–358.

Flanagan, J. C., Tiedeman, D. V., & Willis, M. G. (1973). *The career data book.* Palo Alto, CA: American Institutes for Research.

Fleishman, E. A. (1972). On the relation between abilities, learning, and human performance. *American Psychologist, 27,* 1017–1032.

Fleishman, E. A., & Reilly, M. E. (1995). *Handbook of human abilities: Definitions, measurements, and job task requirements.* Potomac, MD: Management Research Institute.

Flynn, J. R. (1987). Massive IQ gains in 14 nations: What IQ tests really measure. *Psychological Bulletin, 101,* 171–191.

Flynn, J. R. (2000). The hidden history of IQ and special education: Can the problems be solved? *Psychology, Public Policy, & Law, 6,* 191–198.

Forbey, J. D., Handel, R. W., & Ben-Porath, Y. S. (2000). A real-data simulation of computerized adaptive administration of the MMPI-A. *Computers in Human Behavior, 16,* 83–96.

Frank, L. K. (1939). Projective methods for the study of personality. *Journal of Psychology, 8,* 389–413.

Freud, S. (1905, reprinted 1959). Fragment of an analysis of a case of hysteria. In *Collected papers,* Vol 3. New York: Basic Books.

Freud, S., & Bullitt, W. C. (1967). *Thomas Woodrow Wilson.* Boston: Houghton Mifflin.

Frisby, C. L. (1999). Culture and test session behavior: Part II. *School Psychology Quarterly, 14,* 281–303.

Frueh, B. C., Smith, D. W., & Libet, J. M. (1996). Racial differences on psychological measures in combat veterans seeking treatment for PTSD. *Journal of Assessment, 66,* 41–53.

Funder, D. C., & Colvin, C. R. (1991). Some behaviors are more predictable than others. *The Score* (Newsletter of Division of the American Psychological Association), *13*(4), 3–4.

G. I. Forum et al. v. Texas Education Agency et al., U.S. District Court's ruling, see TM 031 923, 2000.

Galton, F. (1879). Psychometric experiments. *Brain, 2,* 149–162.

Garb, H. N. (1998). *Studying the clinician.* Washington, DC: American Psychological Association.

Garb, H. N. (1999). Call for a moratorium on the use of the Rorschach Inkblot Test in clinical and forensic settings. *Assessment, 6,* 313–317.

Garb, H. N. (2005). Clinical judgment and decision making. *Annual review of psychology.* Palo Alto, CA: Annual Reviews.

Gardner, H. (1983). *Frames of mind: The theory of multiple intelligences.* New York: Basic Books.

Gardner, H. (1997). Failing to act: Regrets of Terman's geniuses. *Journal of Creative Behavior, 31,* 120–124.

Gardner, H. (1999). Are there additional intelligences? The case for naturalistic, spiritual, and existential intelligences. In J. Kane (Ed.), *Education, information, and transformation* (pp. 111–131). Upper Saddle River, NJ: Prentice Hall.

Gardner, W., Lidz, C. W., Mulvey, E. P., & Shaw, E. C. (1996). Clinical versus actuarial predictions of violence in patients with mental illnesses. *Journal of Counseling & Clinical Psychology, 64,* 602–609.

Geiger, M. A. (1991a). Changing multiple-choice answers: Do students accurately perceive their performance? *Journal of Experimental Education, 59,* 250–257.

Geiger, M. A. (1991b). Changing multiple-choice answers: A validation and extension. *College Student Journal, 25,* 181–186.

Geiselman, R. E., Fisher, R. P., MacKinnon, D. P., & Holland, H. L. (1985). Eyewitness memory enhancement in the police interview: Cognitive retrieval mnemonics versus hypnosis. *Journal of Applied Psychology, 70,* 401–412.

Geisinger, K. F. (2000). Psychological testing at the end of the millennium: A brief historical review. *Professional Psychology: Research & Practice, 31,* 117–118.

Georgia State Conferences of Branches of NAACP v. State of Georgia. Eleventh Circuit Court of Appeals, No. 84–8771 (1985).

Gerow, J. R. (1980). Performance on achievement tests as a function of the order of item difficulty. *Teaching of Psychology, 7,* 93–94.

Gesell, A., & Amatruda, C. S. (1941). *Developmental diagnosis.* New York: Paul B. Hoeber.

Getzels, J. W., & Jackson, P. W. (1962). *Creativity and intelligence: Explorations with gifted students.* New York: Wiley.

Ghiselli, E. E. (1973). The validity of aptitude tests in personnel selection. *Personnel Psychology, 26,* 461–477.

Gifford, B. R., & O'Connor, M. C. (Eds.). (1992). *Changing assessments: Alternative views of aptitude, achievement, and instruction.* Boston: Kluwer.

Gill, K., & Keats, D. M. (1980). Elements of intellectual competence: Judgments by Australian and Malay university students. *Journal of Cross-Cultural Psychology, 11,* 233–243.

Glad, B. (1980). *Jimmy Carter: In search of the great White House.* New York: Norton.

Glass, G. V., & Hopkins, K. D. (1996). *Statistical methods in education and psychology* (3rd ed.). Boston: Allyn and Bacon.

Glick, P., Gottesman, D., & Joltan, J. (1989). The fault is not in the stars: Susceptibility of skeptics and believers in astrology to the Barnum effect. *Personality and Social Psychology Bulletin, 15,* 572–583.

Goddard, H. H. (1920). *Human efficiency and levels of intelligence.* Princeton, NJ: Princeton University Press.

Goertzel, M. G., Goertzel, V., & Goertzel, T. G. (1978). *Three hundred eminent personalities.* San Francisco: Jossey-Bass.

Goldberg, L. R. (1970). Man vs. model of man: A rationale, plus some evidence for a method of improving on clinical inferences. *Psychological Bulletin, 73,* 422–432.

Golden, C. J., Purisch, A. D., & Hammeke, T. A. (1985). *Luria-Nebraska Neuropsychological Battery: Forms I and II manual.* Los Angeles: Western Psychological Services.

Goldman, B. A., Mitchell, D. F., & Egelson, P. E. (Eds.). (1997). *Directory of unpublished experimental mental measures* (Vol. 7). Washington, DC: American Psychological Association.

Goldstein, A. M. (2003). *Handbook of psychology: Forensic psychology, Vol. 11.* Hoboken, NJ: Wiley.

Goodstadt, M. S., & Magid, S. (1977). When Thurstone and Likert agree: A confounding of methodologies. *Educational & Psychological Measurement, 37,* 811–818.

Gordon, R., & Peck, L. A. (1989). *The Custody Quotient.* Dallas, TX: Willington Institute.

Gottfredson, G. D., Holland, J. L., & Gottfredson, L. S. (1975). The relation of vocational aspirations and assessments to employment reality. *Journal of Vocational Behavior, 7,* 135–148.

Gottfredson, L. S. (1994). The science and politics of race-norming. *American Psychologist, 49,* 955–963.

Gottfredson, L. S., & Becker, H. J. (1981). A challenge to vocational psychology: How important are aspirations in determining male career development? *Journal of Vocational Behavior, 18,* 121–137.

Gough, H. G., & Bradley, P. (1996). *CPI manual* (3rd ed.). Palo Alto, CA: Consulting Psychologists Press.

Gould, S. J. (1981). *The mismeasure of man.* New York: Norton.

Granick, S., & Patterson, R. D. (1972). *Human aging, II: An eleven year follow-up biomedical and behavioral study.* Washington, DC: U.S. Government Printing Office.

Graves, M. (1948). *Design Judgment Test.* New York: Psychological Corporation.

Green, K. (1984). Effects of item characteristics on multiple-choice item difficulty. *Educational & Psychological Measurement, 44,* 551–561.

Green, K. E. (1991). Measurement theory. In K. E. Green (Ed.), *Educational testing: Issues and applications* (pp. 3–25). New York: Garland Publishing.

Greenbaum, P. E., Dedrick, R. F., & Lipien, L. (2004). (The child Behavior Checklist/4–18 (CBCL/4–18). In M. Hilsenroth & D. L. Segal (Eds.), *Comprehensive handbook of psychological assessment, Vol. 2, Personality assessment* (pp. 179–191). Hoboken, NJ: Wiley.

Greene, H. A., Jorgensen, A. N., & Gerberich, J. R. (1954). *Measurement and evaluation in secondary school* (2nd ed.). New York: David McKay.

Greenfield, P. M. (1998). The cultural evolution of IQ. In U. Neisser (Ed.), *Intelligence on the rise?* Washington, DC: American Psychological Association.

Gregory, R. J. (2004). *Psychological testing: History, principles, and applications.* Boston: Allyn & Bacon.

Griggs v. *Duke Power Company.* 401 U.S. 424, 3FEP175 (1971).

Gross, M. L. (1962). *The brain watchers.* New York: Random House.

Gross, M. L. (1965). Testimony before House Special Committee on Invasion of Privacy of the Committee on Government Operations. *American Psychologist, 20,* 958–960.

Grotevant, H. D., Scarr, S., & Weinberg, R. A. (1977). Patterns of interest similarity in adoptive and biological families. *Journal of Personality and Social Psychology, 35,* 667–676.

Groth-Marnat, G. (1999a). *Handbook of Psychological Assessment* (3rd ed. revised). New York: Wiley.

Groth-Marnat, G. (1999b). Financial efficacy of clinical assessment: Current status and a blueprint for future research. *Journal of Clinical Psychology, 55,* 813–824.

Groth-Marnat, G. (1999c). Current status and future directions of psychological assessment: Introduction. *Journal of Clinical Psychology, 55,* 781–786.

Groth-Marnat, G. (2000a). Visions of clinical assessment: Then, now, and a brief history of the future. *Journal of Clinical Psychology, 56,* 349–365.

Groth-Marnat, G. (2000b). *Neuropsychological assessment in clinical practice.* Hoboken, NJ: Wiley.

Groth-Marnat, G. (2001). The Wechsler intelligence scales. In A. S. Kaufman & N. L. Kaufman (Eds.), *Specific learning disabilities and difficulties in children and adolescents: Psychological assessment and evaluation.* New York: Cambridge University Press.

Groth-Marnat, G. (2003). *Handbook of psychological assessment* (4th ed.). Hoboken, NJ: Wiley.

Groth-Marnat, G. (in press a). Introduction to the Special Series on the psychological report. *Journal of Clinical Psychology.*

Groth-Marnat, G., Gallagher, R. E., Hale, R. B., & Kaplan, E. (2000). The Wechsler intelligence scales. In G. Groth-Marnat (Ed.), *Neuropsychological assessment in clinical practice.* Hoboken, NJ: Wiley.

Groth-Marnat, G., & Horvath, L. (in press). The psychological report: A review of current controversies. *Journal of Clinical Psychology*.

Groth-Marnat, G., & Roberts, L. (1998). Human figure drawings and House–Tree–Person drawings as indicators of self-esteem: A quantitative approach. *Journal of Clinical Psychology, 54,* 219–222.

Groth-Marnat, G., & Schumaker, J. F. (1989). Issues and guidelines in computer-based psychological testing. *American Journal of Orthopsychiatry, 59,* 257–263.

Grove, W. M., Zald, D. H., Lebow, B. S., Snitz, B. E., & Nelson, C. (2000). Clinical versus mechanical prediction: A meta-analysis. *Psychological Assessment, 12,* 19–30.

Guadalupe v. *Tempe Elementary School District,* Stipulation and Order (January 24, 1972).

Guilford, J. P. (1954). A factor analytic study across the domains of reasoning, creativity, and evaluation. I. Hypothesis and description of tests. *Reports from the Psychology Laboratory.* Los Angeles: University of Southern California.

Guilford, J. P. (1967). *The nature of human intelligence.* New York: McGraw-Hill.

Guilford, J. P. (1985). The structure-of-intellect model. In B. B. Wolman (Ed.), *Handbook of intelligence: Theories, measurements and applications.* New York: Wiley.

Guilford, J. P., & Zimmerman, W. S. (1956). Fourteen dimensions of temperament. *Psychological Monographs, 70*(10).

Guttman, L. (1944). A basis for scaling quantitative data. *American Sociological Review, 9,* 139–150.

Gynther, M. D. (1981). Is the MMPI an appropriate assessment device for blacks? *Journal of Black Psychology, 7,* 67–75.

Haak, R. A. (1990). Using the sentence completion to assess emotional disturbance. In C. R. Reynolds & R. W. Kamphaus (Eds.), *Handbook of psychological and educational assessment of children: Personality, behavior, and context* (pp. 147–167). New York: Guilford Press.

Hager, P. (1991, Oct. 29). Court bans psychological tests in hiring. *Los Angeles Times,* p. A-20.

Haladyna, T. M., & Downing, S. M. (1993). How many options is enough for a multiple-choice test item? *Educational & Psychological Measurement, 53,* 999–1010.

Hallahan, D. P., Kauffman, J. M., & Lloyd, J. W. (1996). *Introduction to learning disabilities.* Boston: Allyn and Bacon.

Halpern, D. F. (1997). Sex differences in intelligence: Implications for education. *American Psychologist, 52,* 1091–1101.

Halpern, D. F. (2003). *Sex differences in cognitive abilities* (3rd ed.). Mahwah, NJ: Erlbaum.

Hambleton, R. K. (1996). Advances in assessment models, methods, and practices. In D. C. Berliner & R. C. Calfee (Eds.), *Handbook of educational psychology* (pp. 899–925). New York: Macmillan Reference.

Hambleton, R. K., & Pitoniak, M. J. (2002). Testing and measurement: Advances in item response theory and selected testing practices. In H. Pashler & J. Wixted (Eds.), *Stevens' handbook of experimental psychology* (3rd ed., Vol. 4, pp. 517–561).

Hamersma, R. J., Paige, J., & Jordan, J. E. (1973). Construction of a Guttman facet designed cross-cultural attitude-behavior scale toward racial ethnic interaction. *Educational & Psychological Measurement, 33,* 565–576.

Hammer, E. G., & Kleiman, L. S. (1988). Getting to know you. *Personnel Administrator, 33*(5), 86–92.

Hammill, D. D., Brown, L., & Bryant, B. R. (1992). *A consumer's guide to tests in print* (2nd ed.). Austin, TX: pro.ed.

Hammill, D. D. (1999). *Detroit Tests of Learning Aptitude-4 (DTLA-4).* Austin, TX: PRO-ED.

Hammill, D. D., Pearson, N. A., & Wiederholt, J. L. (1996). *Comprehensive Test of Nonverbal Intelligence.* Austin, TX: Pro-Ed.

Hampson, E. (1990). Variations in sex-related cognitive abilities across the menstrual cycle. *Brain and Cognition, 14,* 26–43.

Hanes, K. R. (1998). Review of the Beck Scale for Suicide Ideation. *Thirteenth Mental Measurements Yearbook,* 125–126.

Hansen, J. C. (1984). The measurement of vocational interests: Issues and future directions. In R. B. Lent & S. D. Brown (Eds.), *Handbook of counseling psychology* (pp. 99–136). New York: Wiley.

Hansen, J. C. (1988). Changing interests of women: Myth or reality? *Applied Psychology: An International Review, 37*(2), 133–150.

Hansen, J. C., & Campbell, D. P. (1985). *Manual for the SVIB-SCII* (4th ed.). Stanford, CA: Stanford University Press.

Hansen, J. C., & Dik, B. (2004). Measures of career interests. In J. C. Thomas (Ed.), *Comprehensive handbook of psychological assessment,* Vol. 4 (pp. 166–191). Hoboken, NJ: Wiley.

Harasty, J., Double, K. L., Halliday, G. M., Kril, J. J., & McRitchie, D. A. (1997). Language-associated cortical regions are proportionally larger in the female brain. *Archives of Neurology, 54,* 171–176.

Harmon, L. W., Hansen, J. C., Borgen, F. H., & Hammer, A. L. (1994). *Strong Interest Inventory: Applications and technical guide.* Palo Alto, CA: Consulting Psychologists Press.

Harrell, T. W. (1992). Some history of the Army General Classification Test. *Journal of Applied Psychology, 77,* 875–878.

Harrell, T. W., & Harrell, M. S. (1945). Army General Classification Test scores for civilian occupations. *Educational & Psychological Measurement, 5,* 229–342.

Harris, G. T., & Rice, M. E. (1996). The science in phallometric measurement of male sexual interest. *Current Directions in Psychological Science, 5,* 156–160.

Harris, M. M., & Schaubroeck, J. (1988). A meta-analysis of self–supervisor, self–peer, and peer–supervisor ratings. *Personnel Psychology, 41,* 43–62.

Harris, R. (2002, March 7). *Anti-plagiarism strategies for research papers.* Available online at www.virtualsalt.com/antipla.htm.

Hartshorne, H., & May, M. A. (1928). *Studies in the nature of character. Vol. 1: Studies in deceit.* New York: Macmillan.

Hathaway, S. R., & McKinley, J. C. (1989). *MMPI-2.* Minneapolis: University of Minnesota Press.

Hattie, J. (1980). Should creativity tests be administered under test-like conditions? An empirical study of three alternative conditions. *Journal of Educational Psychology, 72,* 87–98.

Haynes, S. N., & Heiby, E. M. (2004). *Comprehensive handbook of psychological assessment: Vol. 3, Behavioral assessment.* Hoboken, NJ: Wiley.

Hays, J. R. (1997). Note on concurrent validity of the Personality Assessment Inventory in law enforcement. *Psychological Reports, 81,* 244–246.

Heaton, R. K., Chelune, G. J., & Talley, J. L. (1993). *Wisconsin Card Sorting Test. Manual revised and updated.* Odessa, FL: Psychological Assessment Resources.

Hebb, D. O. (1949). *The organization of behavior.* New York: Wiley.

Heilbrun, A. B., Jr. (1969). Parental identification and the patterning of vocational interests in college males and females. *Journal of Counseling Psychology, 16,* 342–347.

Henard, D. H. (2000). Item response theory. In L. G. Grimm & P. R. Harnold (Eds.), *Reading and understanding MORE multivariate statistics* (pp. 67–97). Washington, DC: American Psychological Association.

Henriksson, A. (2001). *Mangled Moments of Western Civilization from Today's "Brightest" College Kids.* New York: Workman.

Herman, J. L. (1994). Item writing techniques. In T. Husén & T. N. Postlethwaite (Eds.), *International encyclopedia of education* (2nd ed., Vol. 5, pp. 3061–3066). Tarrytown, NY: Elsevier.

Herrnstein, R. J., & Murray, C. (1994). *The bell curve.* New York: Free Press.

Hess, E. H. (1965). Attitude and pupil size. *Scientific American, 212,* 46–54.

Heubert, J. P., & Hauser, R. M. (Eds.). (1999). *High stakes: Testing for tracking, promotion and graduation.* Washington, DC: National Research Council, National Academy Press.

Hier, D. B., & Crowley, W. F., Jr. (1982). Spatial ability in androgen-deficient men. *New England Journal of Medicine, 306,* 1202–1205.

Hilsenroth, M. J. (2004). Overview, conceptual foundations, and empirical foundations. In M. J. Hilsenroth & D. L. Segal (Eds.), *Comprehensive handbook of psychological assessment, Vol. 2, Personality assessment* (pp. 283–296). Hoboken, NJ: Wiley.

Hirsch, N. D. M. (1926). A study of natio-racial mental differences. *Genetic Psychology Monographs, 1,* 231–406.

Hiskey, M. S. (1966). *Manual for the Hiskey-Nebraska Test of Learning Aptitude.* Lincoln, NE: Union College Press.

Hobson v. *Hansen,* 269 F. Suppl. 401 (D. D.C. 1967).

Hoffman, B. (1962). *The tyranny of testing,* New York: Crowell-Collier.

Hogan, J., & Quigley, A. (1994). Effects of preparing for physical ability tests. *Public Personnel Management, 23,* 85–104.

Hogan, T. (2003). *Psychological testing: A practical introduction.* Hoboken, Wiley.

Holland, J. L. (1985). *Making vocational choices: A theory of careers: A theory of vocational personalities and work environments* (2nd ed.). Upper Saddle River, NJ: Prentice Hall.

Holland, J. L. (1996). Exploring careers with a typology: What we have learned and some new directions. *American Psychologist, 51,* 397–406.

Holland, J. L. (1999). Why interest inventories are also personality inventories. In M. L. Savickas & A. R. Spokane (Eds.), *Vocational interests: Meaning, measurement, and counseling use* (pp. 87–101). Palo Alto, CA: Davies-Black Publishing/Consulting Psychologists Press.

Holmes, T. H., & Rahe, R. H. (1967). The Social Readjustment Scale. *Journal of Psychosomatic Research, 11,* 213–218.

Holt, A. (1974). *Handwriting in psychological interpretations.* Springfield, IL: Charles C Thomas.

Holt, R. R. (1970). Yet another look at clinical and statistical prediction: Or, is clinical psychology worthwhile? *American Psychologist, 25,* 337–349.

Holtzman, W. H. (1988). Beyond the Rorschach. *Journal of Personality Assessment, 52,* 578–609.

Horn, C. A., & Smith, L. F. (1945). The Horn Art Aptitude Inventory. *Journal of Applied Psychology, 29,* 350–355.

Horn, J. L., & Cattell, R. B. (1966). Refinement and test of the theory of fluid and crystallized intelligence. *Journal of Educational Psychology, 57,* 253–270.

Horn, J. L. (1982). The theory of fluid and crystallized intelligence in relation to concepts of cognitive psychology and aging in adulthood. In F. I. M. Craik & S. Trehub (Eds.), *Advances in the study of communication and affect: Volume 8: Aging and cognitive processes* (pp. 237–278). New York: Plenum.

Horn, J. L. (1983). The Texas Adoption Project: Adopted children and their intellectual resemblance to biological and adoptive parents. *Child Development, 54,* 268–275.

Horn, J. L., & Hofer, S. M. (1992). Major abilities and development in the adult period. In R. J. Sternberg & C. A. Berg (Eds.), *Intellectual development* (pp. 44–99). New York: Cambridge University Press.

Howard, R. W. (2001). Searching the real world for signs of rising population intelligence. *Personality & Individual Differences, 30,* 1039–1058.

Hughes, H. H., & Converse, H. D. (1962). Characteristics of the gifted: A case for a sequel to Terman's study. *Exceptional Children, 29,* 178–183.

Hughes, S. (1995). Review of Denver: II. In J. C. Conoley & J. C. Impara (Eds.), *Twelfth Mental Measurements Yearbook* (pp. 263–265). Lincoln: Buros Institute of Mental Measures of the University of Nebraska, Lincoln.

Hunsley, J., & Bailey, J. M. (2001). Whither the Rorschach? *Psychological Assessment, 13,* 472–485.

Imada, A. S. (1982). Social interaction, observation, and stereotypes as determinants of differentiation in peer ratings. *Organizational Behavior & Human Performance, 29,* 397–415.

Impara, J. C., & Plake, B. S. (Eds.). (1998). *Thirteenth Mental Measurements Yearbook.* Lincoln, NE: Buros Institute of Mental Measurements, University of Nebraska, Lincoln.

Innocenti, G. M. (1994). Some new trends in the study of the corpus callosum. *Behavioral and Brain Research, 64,* 1–8.

Ireton, H. (1992). *Child Development Inventory: Manual.* Minneapolis, MN: Behavior Science Systems.

Ireton, H. (1998). *Preschool Development Inventory: Manual.* Minneapolis: Behavior Science Systems.

Isaacs, M., & Chen, K. (1990). Presence/absence of an observer in a word association test. *Journal of Personality Assessment, 55,* 41–51.

Jackson, D. N. (1998). *Multidimensional Aptitude Battery-II manual.* Port Huron, MI: Sigman Assessment Systems.

Jackson, D. N. (2000). *Jackson Vocational Interest Survey manual.* Port Huron, MI: Sigman Assessment Systems.

Jackson, J. F. (1993). Human behavioral genetics, Scarr's theory, and her views on interventions: A critical review and commentary on their implications for African American children. *Child Development, 64,* 1318–1332.

Jackson, N. E. (1992). Precocious reading of English: Origins, structure, and predictive significance. In P. S. Klein & A. J. Tannenbaum (Eds.), *To be young and gifted* (pp. 171–203). Norwood, NJ: Ablex.

Jamison, K. R. (1993). *Touched with fire: Manic-depressive illness and the artistic temperament.* New York: Free Press.

Jancke, L., & Steinmetz, H. (1994). Interhemispheric-transfer time and corpus callosum size. *Neuroreport, 5,* 2385–2388.

Janos, P. M., & Robinson, N. M. (1985). Psychosocial development in intellectually gifted children. In F. D. Horowitz & M. O'Brien (Eds.), *The gifted and talented: Developmental perspectives* (pp. 149–195). Washington, DC: American Psychological Association.

Jeanneret, P. R., D'Egidio, E. L., & Hanson, M. A. (2004). Assessment and developmental opportunities using the Occupational Assessment Information Network (O*NET). In J. Thomas (Ed.), *Comprehensive handbook of psychological assessment,* Vol. 4 (pp. 192–202). Hoboken, NJ: Wiley.

Jensen, A. R. (1969). How much can we boost IQ and scholastic achievement? *Harvard Educational Review, 39,* 1–123.

Jensen, A. R. (1980). *Bias in mental testing.* New York: Free Press.

Jensen, A. R. (1981). *Straight talk about mental tests.* New York: Free Press.

Jessell, J. C., & Sullins, W. L. (1975). Effect of keyed response sequencing of multiple-choice items on performance and reliability. *Journal of Educational Measurement, 12,* 45–48.

Johnson, S. C., Pinkston, J. B., Bigler, E. D., & Blatter, D. D. (1996). Corpus callosum morphology in normal controls and traumatic brain injury: Sex differences, mechanisms of injury, and neuropsychological correlates. *Neuropsychology, 10,* 408–415.

Joncas, J., & Standig, L. (1998). How much do accurate instructions raise scores on timed tests? *Perceptual & Motor Skills, 86,* 1257–1258.

Jones, H. E., & Conrad, H. S. (1933). The growth and decline of intelligence: A study of a homogeneous group. *Genetic Psychology Monographs, 13,* 223–298.

Jung, C. G. (1910). The association method. *American Journal of Psychology, 21,* 219–269.

Kaiser, S., & Wehrle, T. (1992). Automated coding of facial behavior in human computer interactions with FACS. *Journal of Nonverbal Behavior, 16,* 67–84.

Kanaya, T., Scullin, M. H., & Ceci, S. J. (2003). The Flynn effect and U.S. policies: The impact of rising IQ scores on American society via mental retardation diagnoses. *American Psychologist, 58,* 778–790.

Kapes, J. T., Borman, C. A., & Frazier, N. (1989). An evaluation of the SIGI and DISCOVER microcomputer-based career guidance systems. *Measurement and Evaluation in Counseling and Development, 22,* 126–136.

Kapes, J. T., & Vansickle, T. R. (1992). Comparing paper–pencil and computer-based version of the Harrington–O'Shea Career Decision Making System. *Measurement and Evaluation in Counseling and Development, 25,* 5–13.

Kaplan, R. M., & Sacuzzo, D. P. (2001). *Psychololigical testing: Principles, applications, and issues* (5th ed.). Belmont, CA: Wadsworth.

Kaufman, A. S. (2001). Do low levels of lead produce IQ loss in children? A careful examination of the literature. *Archives of Clinical Neuropsychology, 16,* 303–341.

Kaufman, A. S., & Kaufman, N. L. (1983). *K-ABC administration and scoring manual.* Circle Pines, MN: American Guidance Service.

Kaufman, A. S., & Kaufman, N. L. (1990). *Manual for the Kaufman Brief Intelligence Test (K-BIT).* Circle Pines, MN: American Guidance Service.

Kaufman, A. S., & Kaufman, N. L. (1993). *Manual for the Kaufman Adolescent and Adult Intelligence Test (KAIT).* Circle Pines, MN: American Guidance Service.

Kaufman, A. S., & Kaufman, N. (Eds.). (2001). *Specific learning disabilities and difficulties in children and adolescents: Psychological assessment and evaluation.* New York: Cambridge University Press.

Kaufman, A. S., & Lichtenberger, E. (2002). *Assessing adolescent and adult intelligence.* Boston: Allyn and Bacon.

Kaufman, A. S., & Kaufman, N. L. (2004). *Kaufman Assessment Battery for Children, technical manual* (2nd ed.). Circle Pines, MN: American Guidance Service.

Kavan, M. G. (1995). Review of the Personality Assessment Inventory. *Twelfth Mental Measurements Yearbook,* 766–768.

Kazdin, A. E. (2003). *Research design in clinical psychology* (4th ed.). Boston: Allyn and Bacon.

Kearns, D. (1976). *Lyndon Johnson and the American dream.* New York: Wilson.

Keating, D. P. (Ed.). (1976). *Intellectual talent: Research and development.* Baltimore: Johns Hopkins University Press.

Kelly, G. A. (1955). *The psychology of personal constructs.* New York: Norton.

Kendall, P. C., & Norton-Ford, J. D. (1982). *Clinical psychology: Scientific and professional dimensions.* New York: Wiley.

Keyser, D. J., & Sweetland, R. C. (Eds.). (2003). *Test critiques* (Vol. 11). Austin, TX: pro.ed.

Kimura, D., & Hampson, E. (1993). Neural and hormonal mechanisms mediating sex differences in cognition. In P. A. Vernon (Ed.), *Biological approaches to the study of human intelligence* (pp. 375–397). Norwood, NJ: Ablex.

Kimura, D., & Hampson, E. (1994). Cognitive pattern in men and women is influenced by fluctuations in sex hormones. *Psychological Science, 3,* 57–61.

King, L. A., & King, D. W. (1993). *Sex-Role Egalitarianism Scale manual.* Port Huron, MI: Sigma Assessment Systems.

Kinicki, A. J., & Bannister, B. D. (1988). A test of the measurement assumptions underlying behaviorally anchored rating scales. *Educational & Psychological Measurement, 48,* 17–27.

Kirk, S. A., Gallagher, J. J., & Anastasiow, N. J. (1997). *Educating exceptional children* (8th ed.). New York: Houghton Mifflin.

Kleinbaum, D. G., Kupper, L. L., Muller, K. E., & Nizam, A. (1998). *Applied regression analysis and other multivariable methods* (3rd ed.). Pacific Grove, CA: Brooks/Cole.

Klimko, I. P. (1984). Item arrangement, cognitive entry characteristics, sex, and test anxiety as predictors of achievement examination performance. *Journal of Experimental Education, 52,* 214–219.

Klineberg, O. (1963). Negro–white differences in intelligence test performance. *American Psychologist, 18,* 198–203.

Knobloch, H., & Pasamanick, B. (Eds.) (1974). *Gesell and Amatruda's developmental diagnosis* (3rd ed.). New York: Harper & Row.

Knobloch, H., Stevens, F., & Malone, A. (1987). *Manual of developmental diagnosis: The administration and interpretation of the Revised Gesell and Amatruda Developmental and Neurological Examination.* Houston, TX: Developmental Evaluation Materials.

Kobak, A. A., Greist, J. H., Jefferson, J. W., & Katzelnick, D. J. (1996). Computer-administered clinical rating scales: A review. *Psychopharmacology, 127,* 291–301.

Kobak, K. A., Taylor, L. H., Dottl, S. L., Greist, J. H., Jefferson, J. W., Burroughs, D., Mantle, J. M., Katzelnick, D. J., Norton, R., Henk, H. J., & Serlin, R. C. (1997). A computer-administered telephone interview to identify mental disorders. *Journal of the American Medical Association, 278,* 905–910.

Kohlberg, L. (1969). Stage and sequence: The cognitive–developmental approach to socialization. In D. Goslin (Ed.), *Handbook of socialization: Theory and research*. Chicago: Rand McNally.

Kohlberg, L. (1974). The development of moral stages: Uses and abuses. *Proceedings of the 1973 Invitational Conference on Testing Problems* (pp. 1–8). Princeton, NJ: Educational Testing Service.

Kohlberg, L., & Elfenbeim, D. (1975). The development of moral judgments concerning capital punishment. *American Journal of Orthopsychiatry, 45,* 614–639.

Kohs, S. C. (1920). The block-design tests. *Journal of Experimental Psychology, 3,* 357–376.

Krathwohl, D. R., Bloom, B. S., & Masia, B. B. (1964). *Taxonomy of educational objectives: Handbook II, the affective domain.* New York: David McKay.

Kretschmer, E. (1925). *Physique and character.* New York: Harcourt Brace Jovanovich.

Kruger, J., Wirtz, D., & Miller, D. (2005). Counterfactual thinking and the first instinct fallacy. *Journal of Personality and Social Psychology, 88,* 898–905.

Kuder, G. F., & Richardson, M. W. (1937). The theory of estimation of test reliability. *Psychometrika, 2,* 151–160.

Kurtines, W., & Greif, E. B. (1994). The development of moral thought: Review and evaluation of Kohlberg's approach. In B. Puka (Ed.), *The great justice debate: Kohlberg criticism* (pp. 269–286). New York: Garland Publishing.

Lachar, D. (2004). The Personality Inventory for Children, second edition (PIC-2), Personality Inventory for Youth (PIY), and Student Behavior Survey (SBS). In M. J. Hilsenroth & D. L. Segal (Eds.), *Comprehensive handbook of psychological assessment, Vol. 2, Personality assessment* (pp. 192–212). Hoboken, NJ: Wiley.

Lacks, P. (1999). *Bender–Gestalt screening for brain dysfunction* (2nd ed.). Hoboken, NJ: Wiley.

Lah, M. I. (1989). Sentence completion tests. In C. S. Newmark (Ed.), *Major psychological assessment instruments* (Vol. 2, pp. 133–163). Boston: Allyn and Bacon.

Lancer, I., & Rim, Y. (1984). Intelligence, family size and sibling age spacing. *Personality & Individual Differences, 5,* 151–157.

Landauer, T. K. (1999). Latent semantic analysis: A theory of the psychology of language and mind. *Discourse Processes, 27,* 303–310.

Landers, S. (1989, Dec.). Test score controversy continues. *APA Monitor,* p. 10.

Langer, W. C. (1972). *The mind of Adolf Hitler.* New York: Basic Books.

Langevin, R. (1983). *Sexual strands: Understanding and treating sexual anomalies in men.* Hillsdale, NJ: Erlbaum.

Larry P. v. Riles, 495 F. Supp. 926(N. D. Cal. 1979), appeal docketed, No. 80-4027 (9th Cir., Jan. 17, 1980).

Lazar, I., & Darlington, R. (Eds.). (1982). Lasting effects of early education: A report from the Consortium for Longitudinal Studies. *Monographs of the Society for Research in Child Development, 47* (Serial No. 195), 2–3.

Leiter, R. G. (1979). *Leiter International Performance Scale: Instruction manual.* Chicago, IL: Stoelting.

Lee, E. S. (1951). Negro intelligence and selective migration: A Philadelphia test of the Klineberg hypothesis. *American Sociological Review, 16,* 227–233.

Lenke, J. M. (1988, April). Controversy fueled by district and state reports of achievement test results . . . "Lake Wobegon—or Not?" *The Score,* pp. 5, 13 (Newsletter of Division 5 of the American Psychological Association).

Lent, R. W., Lopez, F. G., & Bieschke, K. J. (1991). Mathematics self-efficacy: Sources and relation to science-based career choice. *Journal of Counseling Psychology, 4,* 424–430.

Leonard, C. M., Lombardino, L. J., Mercado, L. R., Browd, S. R., Breier, J. I., & Agee, O. F. (1996). Cerebral asymmetry and cognitive development in children: A magnetic resonance imaging study. *Psychological Science, 7,* 89–95.

Levine, M. (1976). The academic achievement test: Its historical context and social functions. *American Psychologist, 31,* 228–238.

Lewinsohn, P. M. (1965). Psychological correlates of overall quality of figure drawings. *Journal of Consulting Psychology, 29,* 504–512.

Lewis, M., & Jaskir, J. (1983). Infant intelligence and its relation to birth order and birth spacing. *Infant Behavior & Development, 6,* 117–120.

Lezak, M. D., Howieson, D. B., & Loring, D. W. (2004). *Neuropsychological assessment* (4th ed.). New York: Oxford University Press.

Lichtenberger, E. (in press). Computer utilization and clinical judgment in psychological assessment reports. *Journal of Clinical Psychology.*

Liddell, D. L., Halpin, G., & Halpin, W. G. (1992). The Measure of Moral Orientation: Measuring the ethics of care and justice. *Journal of College Student Development, 33,* 325–330.

Lieberman, M. A. (1965). Psychological correlates of impending death: Some preliminary observations. *Journal of Gerontology, 20,* 71–84.

Lieberman, M. A., & Coplan, A. S. (1969). Distance from death as a variable in the study of aging. *Developmental Psychology, 2,* 71–84.

Likert, R., & Quasha, W. H. (1995). *Revised Minnesota Paper Form Board Test: Manual* (2nd ed.). San Antonio, TX: Harcourt Assessment.

Lillienfeld, S. O., Alliger, G., & Mitchell, K. (1995). Why integrity testing remains controversial. *American Psychologist, 50,* 457–458.

Lindzey, G. (1965). Seer versus sign. *Journal of Experimental Research on Personality, 1,* 17–26.

Linn, R. L. (1992). Achievement testing. In M. C. Alkin (Ed.), *Encyclopedia of Educational Research* (6th ed., pp. 1–12). New York: Macmillan.

Lipsitt, P. D., Lelos, D., & McGarry, A. L. (1971). Competency for trial: A screening instrument. *American Journal of Psychiatry, 128,* 105–109.

Little, E. B. (1962). Overcorrection for guessing in multiple-choice test scoring. *Journal of Educational Research, 55,* 245–252.

Loehelin, J. C. (1989). Partitioning environmental and genetic contributions to behavioral development. *American Psychologist, 10,* 411–414.

Ludwig, A. M. (1995). *The price of greatness: Resolving the creativity and madness controversy.* New York: Guilford Press.

Lundeberg, M. A., & Fox, P. W. (1991). Do laboratory findings on test expectancy generalize to classroom outcomes? *Review of Educational Research, 61,* 94–106.

Luria, A. (1973). *The working brain.* New York: Basic Books.

Lykken, D. T., Bouchard, T. J., McGue, M., & Tellegen, A. (1993). Heritability of interests: A twin study. *Journal of Applied Psychology, 78,* 649–661.

Lynn, R. (1982). IQ in Japan and the United States shows a growing disparity. *Science, 297,* 222–223.

Lynn, R. (1987). The intelligence of the mongoloids: A psychometric, evolutionary and neurological theory. *Personality and Individual Differences, 8,* 813–844.

Lynn, R. (1998). In support of the nutrition theory. In U. Neisser (Ed.), *The rising curve: Long-term gains in IQ and related measures* (pp. 207–215). Washington, DC: American Psychological Association.

Machover, K. (1971). *Personality projection in the drawing of the human figure.* Springfield, IL: Charles C Thomas.

MacKinnon, D. W. (1962). The nature and nurture of creativity talent. *American Psychologist, 17,* 484–495.

MacPhee, D., Ramey, C. T., & Yeates, K. O. (1984). Home environment and early cognitive development: Implications for intervention. In A. W. Gottfried (Ed.), *Home environment and early cognitive development. Longitudinal research.* Orlando, FL: Academic.

MacRae, H. M., Vu, N. V., Graham, B., Word-Sims, M., Colliver, J. A., & Robbs, R. S. (1995). Comparing checklists and databases with physicians' ratings as measures of students' history and physical-examination skills. *Academic Medicine, 70,* 313–317.

Maddox, T. (Ed.). (2003). *Tests—fifth edition.* Austin, TX: pro.ed.

Madhere, S. (1993). The development and validation of the Current Life Orientation Scale. *Psychological Reports, 72,* 467–472.

Mantwill, M., Koehnken, G., & Aschermann, E. (1995). Effects of the cognitive interview on the recall of familiar and unfamiliar events. *Journal of Applied Psychology, 80,* 68–78.

Martin, E., & McDuffee, D. (1981). *A sourcebook of Harris national surveys: Repeated questions, 1963–76.* Chapel Hill: University of North Carolina, Institute for Research in Social Science.

Martindale, C. (1989). Personality, situation, and creativity. In J. A. Glover, R. R. Ronning, & C. R. Reynolds (Eds.), *Handbook of creativity* (pp. 211–232). New York: Plenum Press.

Martorell, R. (1998). Nutrition and the worldwide rise in IQ scores. In U. Neisser (Ed.), *The rising curve: Long-term gains in IQ and related measures* (pp. 183–206). Washington, DC: American Psychological Association.

Maslow, A. H. (1954). *Motivation and personality.* New York: Harper & Row.

Masters, J. R. (1974). Relationship between number of response categories and reliability of Likert-type questionnaires. *Journal of Educational Measurement, 11,* 49–53.

Matarazzo, J. D. (1980). Behavioral health and behavioral medicine: Frontiers for a new health psychology. *American Psychologist, 35,* 807–817.

Matarazzo, J. D. (1992). Psychological testing and assessment in the 21st century. *American Psychologist, 47,* 1007–1018.

Maurer, S. D., & Fay, C. (1988). Effect of situational interviews, conventional structured interviews, and training on interview rating agreement: An experimental analysis. *Personnel Psychology, 41,* 329–344.

May, R. B., & Thompson, J. M. (1989). Test expectancy and question answering in prose processing. *Applied Cognitive Psychology, 3,* 261–269.

Mazlish, B. (1973). *In search of Nixon.* Baltimore: Penguin.

McArthur, C., & Stevens, L. B. (1955). The validation of expressed interests as compared with inventoried interests: A fourteen-year follow-up. *Journal of Applied Psychology, 39,* 184–189.

McCall, R. B. (1979). The development of intellectual functioning in infancy and the prediction of later IQ. In J. D. Osofsky (Ed.), *Handbook of infant development* (pp. 707–741). New York: Wiley.

McCallum, S., Bracken, B., & Wasserman, J. (2001). *Essentials of nonverbal assessment.* Hoboken, NJ: Wiley.

McCarthy, D. (1972). *Manual for the McCarthy Scales of Children's Abilities.* New York: Psychological Corporation.

McClelland, D. (1973). Testing for competence rather than for intelligence. *American Psychologist, 28,* 1–14.

McDonald, R. P. (2000). A basis for multidimensional response theory. *Applied Psychological Measurement, 24,* 99–114.

McGarry, A. L., et al. (1973). *Competency to stand trial and mental illness.* Washington, DC: U.S. Government Printing Office.

McGue, M., Bouchard, T. J., Jr., Iacono, W. G., & Lykken, D. T. (1993). Behavioral genetics of cognitive ability: A life-span perspective. In R. Plomin & G. E. McClearn (Eds.), *Nature, nurture, and psychology* (pp. 59–76). Washington, DC: American Psychological Association.

McNemar, Q. (1942). *The revision of the Stanford–Binet scale.* Boston: Houghton Mifflin.

McNemar, Q. (1964). Lost: Our intelligence? Why? *American Psychologist, 19,* 871–882.

Mead, A. D., & Drasgow, F. (1992). *Effects of administration: A meta-analysis.* Unpublished manuscript, University of Illinois, Champaign.

Mednick, S. A. (1962). The associative basis of the creative process. *Psychological Review, 69,* 1220–1232.

Meehl, P. E. (1954). *Clinical versus statistical prediction.* Minneapolis: University of Minnesota Press.

Mehrabian, A., & Weiner, M. (1967). Decoding of inconsistent communication. *Journal of Personality and Social Psychology, 6,* 109–114.

Meier, N. C. (1942). *The Meier Art Tests. I. Art Judgment; Examiner's manual.* Iowa City, IA: Bureau of Educational Research, University of Iowa.

Meijer, R. R., & Nering, M. L. (1999). Computerized adaptive testing: Overview and introduction. *Applied Psychological Measurement, 23,* 223–237.

Meisels, S. J., & Fenichel, E. (Eds.). (1996). *New visions for the developmental assessment of infants and young children.* Itasca, IL: Riverside Publishing.

Messick, S. (1995). Validity of psychological assessment. *American Psychologist, 50,* 741–749.

Meyer, G. (2004). The reliability and validity of the Rorschach and Thematic Apperception Test (TAT) compared to other psychological and medical procedures: An analysis of systematically gathered evidence. In M. J. Hilsenroth & D. L. Segal (Eds.), *Comprehensive handbook of psychological assessment, Vol. 2, personality assessment* (pp. 315–342). Hoboken, NJ: Wiley.

Meyer, G., Hilsenroth, M. J., Baxter, D., Exner, J. E., Fowler, J. C., Piers, C. C., et al. (2002). An examination of interrater reliability for scoring the Rorschach Comprehensive System in eight data sets. *Journal of Personality Assessment, 78,* 219–274.

Michalski, R. L., & Schackelford, T. K. (2001). Methodology, birth order, intelligence, and personality. *American Psychologist, 56,* 520–524.

Miller, L. (1993). FirstSTEP: Screening Test for Evaluating Preschoolers Manual. San Antonio, TX: Psychological Corporation.

Miller, V. M. (1999). The opportunity of structure: Implications for career counseling. *Journal of Employment Counseling, 36,* 2–11.

Millon, T., & Meagher, S. E. (2004). The Millon Clinical Multiaxial Inventory-III. In M. J. Hilsenroth & D. L. Segal (Eds.). *Comprehensive handbook of psychological assessment, Vol. 2, personality assessment* (pp. 108–121). Hoboken, NJ: Wiley.

Millon, T., Millon, C., & Davis, R. (1997). *Manual for the MCMI-III* (2nd ed.). Minneapolis, MN: NCS Assessments.

Mills, C. N. (1999). Development and introduction of a computer adaptive Graduate Record Examinations General Test. In F. Drasgow & J. B. Olson-Buchanan (Eds.), *Innovations in computerized assessment* (pp. 117–135). Mahwah, NJ: Erlbaum.

Mischel, W. (1968). *Personality and assessment.* New York: Wiley.

Mischel, W. (1986). *Introduction to personality* (4th ed.). New York: Holt, Rinehart & Winston.

Moffatt, S. D., & Hampson, E. (1996). A curvilinear relationship between testosterone and spatial cognition in humans: Possible influence of hand preference. *Psychoneuroendocrinology, 21,* 323–337.

Molfese, V. J., DiLalla, L. F., & Bunce, D. (1997). Prediction of the intelligence test scores of 3- to 8-year-old children by home environment, socioeconomic status, and biomedical risks. *Merrill–Palmer Quarterly, 43,* 219–234.

Monahan, J., & Steadman, H. J. (2001). Violence risk assessment: A quarter century of research. In L. E. Frost & R. J. Bonnie (Eds.). *The evolution of mental health law* (pp. 195–211).

Moreland, K. L., Eyde, L. D., Robertson, G. J., Primoff, E. S., & Most, R. B. (1995). Assessment of test user qualifications: A research-based measurement procedure. *American Psychologist, 50,* 14–23.

Moretti, R. J., & Rossini, E. D. (2004). The Thematic Apperception Test (TAT). In M. J. Hilsenroth & D. L. Segal (Eds.), *Comprehensive handbook of psychological assessment, Vol. 2* (pp. 356–371). New York: Wiley.

Morey, L. C., & Boggs, C. D. (2004). Personality Assessment Inventory (PAI). In M. J. Hilsenroth & D. L Segal (Eds.). *Comprehensive handbook of psychological assessment, Vol. 2, personality assessment* (pp. 15–29). Hoboken, NJ: Wiley.

Murphy, K. R., & Davidshofer, C. O. (1994). *Psychological testing: Principles & applications* (3rd ed.). Upper Saddle River, NJ: Prentice Hall.

Murphy, L. L., & Plake, B. S., Impara, J. C., & Spies, R. A. (Eds.). (2002). *Tests in print VI.* Lincoln, NE: University of Nebraska Press.

Murray, B. (1998, August). The latest techno tool: Essay-grading computers. *APA Monitor, 29*(8), 43.

Murray, H. A. (and collaborators). (1938). *Explorations in personality.* New York: Oxford University Press.

Myart v. *Motorola,* 110 Cong. Record 5662–64 (1964).

Myers, I. B., & McCaulley, M. H. (1985). *Manual: A guide to the development and use of the Myers–Briggs Type Indicator.* Palo Alto, CA: Consulting Psychologists Press.

Nachmann, B. (1960). Childhood experiences and vocational choices in law, dentistry, and social work. *Journal of Counseling Psychology, 7,* 243–250.

Naglieri, J. A., & Das, J. P. (1997). *Das–Naglieri: Cognitive assessment system.* Itasca, IL: Riverside Publishing.

Naglieri, J. A., Drasgaw, F., Schmit, M., Handler, L., Prifitera, A., Margolis, A., & Valasquez, R. (2004). Psychological testing on the Internet: New problems, old issues. *American Psychologist, 59,* 150–162.

Naglieri, J. A., McNeish, T., & Bardos, A. (1991). *Draw-a-Person: Screening procedure for emotional disturbance.* Austin, TX: pro.ed.

Naglieri, J. A., & Pfeiffer, S. I. (1992). Performance of disruptive behavior disordered and normal samples on the Draw-a-Person: Screening procedure for emotional disturbance. *Psychological Assessment, 4,* 156–159.

Naglieri, J. A. (1999). *Essentials of CAS assessment.* Hoboken, NJ: Wiley.

National Center for Education Statistics. (1996, November). *Learning, curriculum, and achievement in international context.* Pittsburgh, PA: Superintendent of Documents.

National Center for Education Statistics. (1997, June). *Pursuing excellence: A study of U.S. fourth-grade mathematics and science achievement in international context.* Pittsburgh, PA: Superintendent of Documents.

National Center for Education Statistics. (1998, February). *Pursuing excellence: A study of U.S. twelfth-grade mathematics and science achievement in international context.* Washington, DC: Author.

National Center for Education Statistics. (2001). *Digest of education statistics 2000.* Washington, DC: U.S. Department of Education.

National Center for Health Statistics. (1999). Births, marriages, divorces, and deaths for 1998. *Monthly Vital Statistics Report, 47*(21). Hyattsville, MD: Author.

Neisser, U., Boodoo, G., Bouchard, T. J., Boykin, A. W., Brody, N., Ceci, S. J., et al. (1996). Intelligence: Knowns and unknowns. *American Psychologist, 51,* 77–101.

Nettler, G. (1959). Test burning in Texas. *American Psychologist, 14,* 682–683.

Nisbet, J. D. (1957). Intelligence and age: Retesting after twenty-four years' interval. *British Journal of Educational Psychology, 27,* 190–198.

Nowak, L. I., et al. (1996). Team testing increases performance. *Journal of Research for Business, 71,* 253–256.

Nunnally, J. C., & Bernstein, I. H. (1994). Psychometric theory (3rd ed.). New York: McGraw-Hill.

Oakland, T., & Hu, S. (1993). International perspectives on with children and youths. *Journal of School Psychology, 31,* 501–517.

O'Boyle, M. W., Alexander, J. E., & Benbow, C. P. (1991). Enhanced right hemisphere activation in the mathematically precocious: A preliminary EEG investigation. *Brain & Cognition, 17,* 138–153.

Ochse, R. (1991). The relation between creative genius and psychopathology: An historical perspective and a new explanation. *South African Journal of Psychology, 21,* 45–53.

Oden, M. H. (1968). The fulfillment of promise: 40-year follow-up of the Terman gifted group. *Genetic Psychology Monographs, 77,* 3–93.

Oliver, J. M., Cole, N. H., & Hollingsworth, H. (1991). Learning disabilities as functions of familial learning problems and developmental problems. *Exceptional Children, 57,* 427–440.

Ones, D. S., Viswesvaran, C., & Schmidt, F. L. (1995). Integrity tests: Overlooked facts, resolved issues, and remaining questions. *American Psychologist, 50,* 456–457.

Ortar, G. (1963). Is a verbal test cross-cultural? *Scripta Hierosolymitana* (Hebrew University, Jerusalem), *13,* 329–335.

Osgood, C. E., Suci, G. J., & Tannenbaum, P. H. (1957). *The measurement of meaning.* Urbana: University of Illinois Press.

Osipow, S. H. (1983). *Theories of career development* (3rd ed.). New York: Appleton-Century-Crofts.

Ostrom, T. M., Bond, C. F., Jr., Krosnick, J. A., & Sedikides, C. (1994). Attitude scales: How we measure the unmeasureable. In S. Shavitt & T. C. Brock (Eds.), *Persuasion: Psychological insights and perspectives* (pp. 15–42). Boston: Allyn and Bacon.

Owen, S. V. (1992). Review of the Beck Hopelessness Scale. *Eleventh Mental Measurements Yearbook*, 82–83.

Owens, W. A., Jr. (1953). Age and mental abilities: A longitudinal study. *Genetic Psychology Monographs, 48*, 3–54.

Owens, W. A., Jr. (1966). Age and mental abilities: A second adult follow-up. *Journal of Educational Psychology, 57*, 311–325.

Parker, K. C., Hanson, R. K., & Hunsley, J. (1988). MMPI, Rorschach, and WAIS: A meta-analytic comparison of reliability, stability, and validity. *Psychological Bulletin, 103*, 367–373.

(PASE) Parents in Action on Special Education v. *Joseph P. Hannon*, No. 74C 3586 (N. D. Ill. 1980).

Paterson, D. G., Elliott, R. M., Anderson, L. D., Tooks, H. A., & Heidbreder, E. (1930). *The Minnesota Mechanical Ability Tests*. Minneapolis: University of Minnesota Press.

Paul, A. M. (2004). *The cult of personality: How personality tests are leading us to miseducate our children, mismanage our companies, and misunderstand ourselves*. New York: Simon & Schuster.

Paul, G. L. (1966). *Insight vs. desensitization in psychotherapy*. Stanford, CA: Stanford University Press.

Payne, A. F. (1928). *Sentence completions*. New York: New York Guidance Clinic.

Pedersen, N. L., Plomin, R., Nesselroade, J. R., & McClearn, G. E. (1992). A quantitative genetic analysis of cognitive abilities during the second half of the life span. *Psychological Science, 3*, 346–353.

Peterson, G. W., Ryan-Jones, R. E., Sampson, J. P., Readon, R. C., et al. (1994). A comparison of the effectiveness of three computer-assisted career guidance systems: Discover, SIGI, and SIGI PLUS. *Computers in Human Behavior, 10*, 189–198.

Peterson, R. C., & Thurstone, L. L. (1933). *Motion pictures and the social attitudes of children*. New York: Macmillan.

Piaget, J. (1972). *The psychology of intelligence*. Totowa, NJ: Littlefield Adams.

Piotrowski, C. (2000). How popular is the Personality Assessment Inventory in practice and training? *Psychological Reports, 86*, 65–66.

Piotrowski, C., & Keller, J. W. (1992). Psychological testing in applied settings: A literature review from 1982–1992. *Journal of Training & Practice in Professional Psychology, 6*, 74–82.

Pithers, W. D., & Laws, D. R. (1995). Phallometric assessment. In B. K. Schwartz & H. R. Cellini (Eds.), *The sex offender: Corrections, treatment and legal practice* (pp. 12-1–12-18). Kingston, NJ: Civic Research Institute.

Pitner, R., & Patterson, D. G. (1917). *A scale of performance tests*. New York: Appleton.

Plake, B. S., Ansorge, C. J., Parker, C. S., & Lowry, S. R. (1982). Effects of item arrangement, knowledge of arrangement, test anxiety and sex on test performance. *Journal of Educational Measurement, 19*, 49–57.

Plake, B. S., Impara, J. C., & Spies, R. A. (Eds.). (2003). *The fifteenth mental measurements yearbook*. Lincoln: University of Nebraska Press.

Plomin, R. (1990). *Nature and nurture: An introduction to human behavior genetics*. Pacific Grove, CA: Brooks/Cole.

Plomin, R., & Foch, T. T. (1980). A twin study of objectively assessed personality in childhood. *Journal of Personality & Social Psychology, 39*, 680–688.

Porteus, S. D. (1915). Mental tests for the feeble-minded: A new series. *Journal of Psycho-Aesthetics, 19*, 200–213.

Powers, D. E. (1986). Relations of test item characteristics to test preparation/test practice effects: A quantitative summary. *Psychological Bulletin, 100*, 67–77.

Powers, D. E. (1993). Coaching for the SAT: A summary of the summaries and an update. *Educational Measurement: Issues & Practice, 12*(2), 24–30.

Powers, D. E., & Rock, D. A. (1999). Effects of coaching on SAT I: Reasoning Test scores. *Journal of Educational Measurement, 36*, 93–118.

Prediger, D. J., & Hanson, G. R. (1976). Holland's theory of careers applied to men and women: Analysis of implicit assumptions. *Journal of Vocational Behavior, 8*, 167–184.

Procter, M. (1993). Measuring attitudes. In N. Gilbert (Ed.), *Researching social life* (pp. 116–134). London: Sage.

Provence, S., Erikson, J., Vater, S., & Palmeri, S. (1995). *Infant-Toddler Developmental Assessment-Family centered assessment of young children at risk: The IDA readings*. Chicago: Riverside.

Quay, H C., & Peterson, D. R. (1983). *Interim manual for the Behavior Problem Checklist*. Unpublished manuscript, University of Miami.

Raju, N. S., Normand, J., & Burke, M. J. (1990). A new approach for utility analysis. *Journal of Applied Psychology, 75*, 3–12.

Ralston, C. A., Borgen, F. H., Rottinghaus, P. J., & Donnay, D. A. C. (2004). Specificity in interest measurement: Basic scales and major field of study. *Journal of Vocational Behavior, 65*, 203–216.

Ramey, C. T., Campbell, F. A., Burchinal, M., Skinner, M. L., Gardner, D. M., & Ramely, S. L. (2000). Persistent effects of early childhood education on high-risk children and their mothers. *Applied Developmental Science, 4*, 2–14.

Randahl, G. J. (1991). A typological analysis of the relations between measured vocational interests and abilities. *Journal of Vocational Behavior, 38,* 333–350.

Rapaport, D., Gill, M. M., & Schafer, R. (1968). *Diagnostic psychological testing* (rev. ed.). New York: International Universities Press.

Raudenbush, S. W. (1984). Magnitude of teacher expectancy effects on pupil IQ as a function of the credibility of expectancy induction: A synthesis of findings from experiments. *Journal of Educational Psychology, 76,* 85–97.

Reilly, R. R., & Chao, G. T. (1982). Validity and fairness of some alternative employee selection procedures. *Personnel Psychology, 35,* 1–62.

Reimanis, G., & Green, R. F. (1971). Imminence of death and intellectual decrement in the aging. *Developmental Psychology, 5,* 270–272.

Reise, S. P., & Henson, J. M. (2000). Computerization and adaptive administration of the NEO PI-R. *Assessment, 7,* 347–364.

Reitan, R. M., & Wolfson, D. (1993). *The Halstead–Reitan Neuropsychological Test Battery: Theory and clinical interpretation* (2nd ed.). Tucson, AZ: Neuropsychology Press.

Remmers, H. H. (1960). *Manual for the Purdue Master Attitude Scales.* Lafayette, IN: Purdue Research Foundation.

Reynolds, C. R., Chastain, R. L., Kaufman, A. S., & McLean, J. E. (1987). Demographic characteristics and IQ among adults: Analysis of the WAIS-R standardization sample as a function of the stratification variables. *Journal of School Psychology, 25,* 323–342.

Riegel, K. F., & Riegel, R. M. (1972). Development, drop, and death. *Developmental Psychology, 6,* 306–319.

Roback, H. (1968). Human figure drawings: Their utility in the clinical psychologist's armamentarium for personality assessment. *Psychological Bulletin, 70,* 1–19.

Roberts, G. E. (1994). *Interpretive handbook for the Roberts Apperception Test for Children.* Los Angeles, CA: Western Psychological Services.

Robinson, J. P., Shaver, P. R., & Wrightsman, L. S. (1991). *Measures of personality and social psychological attitudes.* New York: Academic Press.

Robinson, J. P., Shaver, P. R., & Wrightsman, L. S. (1999). *Measures of political attitudes. Measures of psychological attitudes* (Vol. 2). San Diego: Academic Press.

Robinson, N. M., Zigler, E., & Gallagher, J. J. (2000). Two tails of the normal curve: Similarities and differences in the study of mental retardation and giftedness. *American Psychologist, 55,* 1413–1424.

Rocklin, T. R., O'Donnell, A. M., & Holst, P. M. (1995). Effects and underlying mechanisms of self-adapted testing. *Journal of Educational Psychology, 87,* 103–116.

Rodgers, J. L., Cleveland, H. H, van den Oord, E., & Rowe, D. C. (2000). Resolving the debate over birth order, family size, and intelligence. *American Psychologist, 55,* 599–612.

Roe, A. (1956). *The psychology of occupations.* New York: Basic Books.

Roe, A., & Klos, D. (1969). Occupational classification. *Counseling Psychologist, 1,* 84–92.

Roe, A., & Siegelman, M. (1964). *The origin of interest.* Washington, DC: American Personnel and Guidance Association.

Rogers, C. R., & Dymond, R. F. (Eds.). (1954). *Psychotherapy and personality change.* Chicago: University of Chicago Press.

Rogers, R., Ustad, K. L., & Salekin, R. T. (1998). Convergent validity of the Personality Assessment Inventory: A study of emergency referrals in correctional setting. *Assessment, 5,* 3–12.

Rogers, W. T., & Harley, D. (1999). An empirical comparison of three- and four-choice items and tests: Susceptibility to testwiseness and internal consistency reliability. *Educational & Psychological Measurement, 59,* 234–247.

Rogers, W. T., & Yang, P. (1997). Test-wiseness: Its nature and application. *European Journal of Psychological Assessment, 12,* 247–259.

Roid, G. H. (2003). *Stanford–Binet Intelligence Scales, Fifth Edition.* Itasca, IL: Riverside.

Roid, G. H., & Miller, L. J. (1997). Leiter International Performance Scale-Revised: Examiner's manual. In G. H. Roid & L. J. Miller (Eds.), *Leiter International Performance Scale-Revised.* Wood Dale, IL: Stoelting.

Rokeach, M. (1968). *Beliefs, attitudes, and values: A theory or organization and change.* San Francisco: Jossey-Bass.

Rokeach, M. (1973). *The nature of human values.* New York: Free Press.

Rokeach, M. (1979). *Understanding human values.* Palo Alto, CA: Consulting Psychologists Press.

Romer, D., Hornik, R., Stanton, B., Black, M., Li, X., Ricardo, I., & Feigelman, S. (1997). "Talking" computers: A reliable and private method to conduct interviews on sensitive topics with children. *Journal of Sex Research, 34,* 3–9.

Rosenbaum, B. (1973). Attitude toward invasion of privacy in the personnel selection process and job applicant demographic and personality correlates. *Journal of Applied Psychology, 58,* 333–338.

Rosenman, R. H. (1986). Current and past history of Type A behavior pattern. In T. H Schmidt, T. M. Dembroski, & G. Blumchen (Eds.), *Biological and psychological factors in cardiovascular disease* (pp. 15–40). New York: Springer-Verlag.

Rosenthal, R., Hall, J. A., DiMatteo, M. R., Rogers, P. L., & Archer, D. (1979). *Sensitivity to nonverbal communication: The PONS test.* Baltimore: Johns Hopkins University Press.

Rosenthal, R., & Jacobson, L. (1968). *Pygmalion in the classroom.* New York: Holt, Rinehart & Winston.

Rosenzweig, S. (1978). *Aggressive behavior and the Rosenzweig Picture–Frustration Study.* New York: Praeger.

Ross, C. C., & Stanley, J. C. (1954). *Measurement in today's schools* (3rd ed.). Upper Saddle River, NJ: Prentice Hall.

Rothstein, H. R., Schmidt, F. L., Erwin, F. W., Owens, W. A., & Sparks, C. P. (1990). Biographical data in employment selection: Can validities be made generalizable? *Journal of Applied Psychology, 75,* 175–184.

Rotter, J. B. (1954). *Social learning and clinical psychology.* Upper Saddle River, NJ: Prentice Hall.

Rotter, J. B., Lah, M. I., & Rafferty, J. E. (1992). *Rotter Incomplete Sentences Blank manual.* San Antonio, TX: Psychological Corporation.

Rourke, B. P. (Ed.). (1989). *Nonverbal learning disabilities: The syndrome and the model.* New York: Guilford Press.

Rowley, G. L. (1974). Which examinees are most favoured by the use of multiple-choice tests? *Journal of Educational Measurement, 11,* 15–23.

Russell, M., & Karol, D. (1994). *The 16 PF Fifth Edition administrator's manual.* Champaign, IL: Institute for Personality and Ability Testing.

Sattler, J., & Dumont, R. (2004). *Assessment of children: WISC-IV and WPPSI-III supplement.* San Diego: Jerome Sattler Press.

Savitz, F. R. (1985). Effects of easy examination questions placed at the beginning of science multi-choice examinations. *Journal of Instructional Psychology, 12,* 6–10.

Scarr, S. (1992). Developmental theories for the 1990s: Development and individual differences. *Child Development, 63,* 1–19.

Scarr, S. (1993). Biological and cultural diversity: the legacy of Darwin for development. *Child Development, 64,* 1333–1353.

Scarr, S., & Weinberg, R. A. (1983). How people make their own environments: A theory of genotype–environment effects. *Child Development, 54,* 424–435.

Schaie, K. W. (1990). The optimization of cognitive functioning in old age: Prediction based on cohort-sequential and longitudinal data. In P. B. Baltes & M.

Baltes (Eds.), *Longitudinal research and the study of successful (optimal) aging* (pp. 94–117). Cambridge, UK: Cambridge University Press.

Schaie, K. W. (1994). The course of adult intellectual development. *American Psychologist, 49,* 304–313.

Schaie, K. W., & Hertzog, C. (1983). Fourteen-year cohort-sequential analyses of adult intellectual development. *Developmental Psychology, 19,* 531–543.

Schaie, K. W., & Willis, S. L. (1986). Can decline in adult cognitive functioning be reversed? *Developmental Psychology, 22,* 223–232.

Scheuneman, J. D., & Bleistein, C. A. (1989). A consumers' guide to statistics for identifying differential item functioning. *Applied Measurement in Education, 2,* 255–275.

Schinke, S. (1995). Review of the Eating Disorder Inventory-2. *Twelfth Mental Measurements Yearbook,* 335.

Schlaug, G., Jaencke, L., Huang, Y., Staiger, J. F., et al. (1995). Increased corpus callosum size in musicians. *Neuropsychologia, 33,* 1047–1055.

Schlaug, G., Jaencke, L., Huang, Y., & Steinmetz, H. (1995). In vivo evidence of structural brain asymmetry in musicians. *Science, 267*(5198), 699–701.

Schmidt, F. L., & Hunter, J. E. (2004). General mental ability in the world of work: Occupational attainment and job performance. *Journal of Personality and Social Psychology, 86,* 162–173.

Schmidt, F. L., Law, K., Hunter, J. E., Rothstein, H. R., Pearlman, K., & McDaniel, M. (1993). Refinements in validity generalization methods: Implications for the situational specificity hypothesis. *Journal of Applied Psychology, 78,* 3–12.

Schmidt, S. R. (1983). The effects of recall and recognition test expectancies on the retention of prose. *Memory and Cognition, 11,* 172–180.

Schneider, M. F. (1989). *Children's Apperceptive Storytelling Test.* Austin, TX: pro.ed.

Schneider, M. F., & Perney, J. (1990). Development of the Children's Apperceptive Story-telling Test. *Psychological Assessment: A Journal of Consulting & Clinical Psychology, 2,* 179–185.

Schoenfeldt, L. F., & Mendoza, J. L. (1994). Developing and using factorially derived biographical scales. In G. S. Stokes, M. D. Mumford, & W. A. Owens (Eds.), *Biodata handbook: Theory, research, and use of biographical information in selection and performance prediction* (pp. 147–169). Palo Alto, CA: Consulting Psychologists Press.

Schwab, D. P., & Packard, G. L. (1973). Response distortion on the Gordon Personal Inventory and the Gordon Personal Profile in the selection context: Some implications for predicting employee behavior. *Journal of Applied Psychology, 58,* 372–374.

Schwartz, S., & Wiedel, T. C.. (1981). Incremental validity of the MMPI in neurological decision-making. *Journal of Personality Assessment, 45,* 424–426.

Schweinhart, L., & Weikart, D. (1997). The High Scope preschool curricular comparison study through age 23. *Early Childhood Research Quarterly, 12,* 117–143.

Scribner, S., & Cole, M. (1973). Cognitive consequences of formal and informal schooling. *Science, 182,* 553–559.

Scully, J. A., Tosi, H., & Banning, K. (2000). Life event checklists: Revisiting the Social Readjustment Rating Scale after 30 years. *Educational & Psychological Measurement, 60,* 864–876.

Sears, R. R. (1977). Sources of life satisfactions of the Terman gifted men. *American Psychologist, 32,* 119–128.

Seashore, C. E. (1939). *Psychology of music.* New York: McGraw-Hill.

Segall, D. O., & Moreno, K. E. (1999). Development of the Computerized Adaptive Testing version of the Armed Services Vocational Aptitude Battery. In F. Drasgow & J. B. Olson-Buchanan (Eds.), *Innovations in computerized assessment* (pp. 35–65). Mahwah, NJ: Erlbaum.

Sellin, T., & Wolfgang, M. E. (1964). *The measurement of delinquency.* New York: Wiley.

Selltiz, C., Wrightsman, L. S., & Cook, S. W. (1976). *Research methods in social relations* (3rd ed.). New York: Holt, Rinehart & Winston.

Shaha, S. H. (1984). Matching test: Reduced anxiety and increased test effectiveness. *Educational & Psychological Measurement, 44,* 869–881.

Shaywitz, B. A., Shaywitz, S. E., Pugh, K. R., Constable, R. T., Skudlarski, P., Fulbright, R. K., Bronen, R. A., Fletcher, J. M., Shankweller, Katz, D. P., & Gore, J. C. (1995). Sex differences in the functional organization of the brain for language. *Nature, 373,* 607–609.

Sheldon, W. H., Stevens, S. S., & Tucker, W. B. (1940). *The varieties of human physique.* New York: Harper & Row.

Shogren, E. (1997, September 16). Debate over national school tests offers real-life lesson in politics. *Los Angeles Times,* p. A5.

Shurrager, H. C., & Shurrager, P. S. (1964). *Haptic Intelligence Scale for adult blind.* Chicago: Stoelting.

Siegelman, M., & Peck, R. F. (1960). Personality patterns related to occupational roles. *Genetic Psychology Monographs, 61,* 291–349.

Sigman, M., & Whaley, S. E. (1998). The role of nutrition in the development of intelligence. In U. Neisser (Ed.), *The rising curve: Long-term gains in IQ and related measures* (pp. 155–182). Washington, DC: American Psychological Association.

Silva, F., Martinez, A., Moro, M., & Ortet, G. (1996). Dimensions of interpersonal orientation: Description and construct validation of the Spanish assessment kit. *European Psychologist, 1,* 187–199.

Silverman, L. K. (1995). Highly gifted children. In J. Genschaft, M. Birely, & C. Hollinger (Eds.), *Serving gifted and talented students* (pp. 217–240). Austin, TX: pro.ed.

Simons, R., Goddard, R., & Patton, W. (2002). Hand-scoring error rates in psychological testing. *Assessment, 9,* 292–300.

Sinacore, J. M., Connell, K. J., Olthoff, A. J., Friedman, M. H., & Gecht, M. R. (1999). A method for measuring interrater agreement on checklists. *Evaluation & the Health Professions, 22,* 221–234.

Slack, W. V., & Porter, D. (1980). The Scholastic Aptitude Test: A critical appraisal. *Harvard Educational Review, 50,* 154–175.

Smith, D. (2003). What you need to know about the new code. *APA Monitor on Psychology, 34*(1), 62–65.

Smith, P. C., & Kendall, L. M. (1963). Retranslation of expectations: An approach to the construction of unambiguous anchors for rating scales. *Journal of Applied Psychology, 47,* 149–155.

Snyderman, M., & Rothman, S. (1987). Survey of expert opinion on intelligence and aptitude testing. *American Psychologist, 42,* 137–144.

Society for Industrial and Organizational Psychology, Inc. (2003). *Principles for the validation and use of personal selection procedures* (4th ed.). Bowling Green, OH: Author.

Sommers-Flanagan, J., & Sommers-Flanagan, R. (2003). *Clinical interviewing* (3rd ed.). Hoboken, NJ: Wiley.

Soroka v. *Dayton–Hudson Corp.* 91. L.A. Daily Journal D.A.R. 13204 (Cal. Ct. App. 1991).

Spearman, C. E. (1927). *The abilities of man.* London: Macmillan.

Speath, J. L. (1976). Characteristics of the work setting and the job as determinants of income. In W. H Sewell, R. M. Sauser, & D. L. Featherman (Eds.), *Schooling and achievement in American society.* New York: Academic Press.

Spielberger, C. D., & Reiser, E. C. (2004). Measuring anxiety, anger, depression, and curiosity as emotional states with the STAI, STAXI, and STPI. In M. J. Hilsenroth & D. L. Segal (Eds.), *Comprehensive handbook of psychological assessment, Vol. 2, personality assessment* (pp. 70–86). Hoboken, NJ: Wiley.

Stamoulis, D. T., & Hauenstein, N. M. A. (1993). Rater training and rating accuracy: Training for dimensional accuracy versus training for ratee differentiation. *Journal of Applied Psychology, 78,* 994–1003.

Stanford, G., & Oakland, T. (2000). Cognitive deficits underlying learning disabilities: Research perspectives from the United States. *School Psychology International, 21,* 306–321.

Stanley, J. C., Keating, D. P., & Fox, L. H. (Eds.). (1974). *Mathematical talent: Discovery, description, and development.* Baltimore: Johns Hopkins University Press.

Starch, D., & Elliott, E. C. (1913). Reliability of grading work in mathematics. *School Review, 21,* 254–259.

Steelman, L. C., & Doby, J. T. (1983). Family size and birth order as factors on the IQ performance of black and white children. *Sociology of Education, 56,* 101–109.

Steimel, R. J., & Suziedelis, A. (1963). Perceived parental influence and inventoried interests. *Journal of Counseling Psychology, 10,* 289–295.

Stell v. *Savannah–Chatham County Board of Education.* 210 F Supp. 667, 668 (S.D. Ga. 1963), rev'd 333 F.2d 55 (5th Cir. 1964), cert. denied, 379 U.S. 933 (1964).

Stephenson, W. (1953). *The study of behavior: Q-technique and its methodology.* Chicago: University of Chicago Press.

Sternberg, C. (1955). Personality trait patterns of college students majoring in different fields. *Psychological Monographs, 69,* No. 18 (Whole No. 403).

Sternberg, R. J. (1982). Thinking and learning skills: A view of intelligence. *Education Digest, 47,* 20–22.

Sternberg, R. J. (1986). *The triarchic mind: A new theory of human intelligence.* New York: Viking.

Sternberg, R. J. (1988). Mental self-government: A theory of intellectual styles and their development. *Human Development, 31,* 197–224.

Sternberg, R. J. (2003). A broad view of intelligence: The theory of successful intelligence. *Consulting Psychology Journal: Practice and Research, 55,* 139–154.

Stewart, J. R. (1998). Review of the Beck Scale for Suicide Ideation. *Thirteenth Mental Measurements Yearbook,* 126–127.

Stokes, G. S., & Cooper, L. A. (2004). Biodata. In J. C. Thomas (Ed.), *Comprehensive handbook of psychological assessment, Vol. 4, industrial and organizational assessment* (pp. 243–268). Hoboken, NJ: Wiley.

Stokes, G. S., Mumford, M. D., & Owens, W. A. (1994). *Biodata handbook: Theory, research, and use of biographical information in selection and performance prediction.* Palo Alto, CA: CPP Books.

Stott, D. H. (1983). Brain size and "intelligence." *British Journal of Developmental Psychology, 1,* 279–287.

Strong, E. K., Jr. (1955). *Vocational interests 18 years after college.* Minneapolis: University of Minnesota Press.

Sullivan, G. S., Mastropieri, M. A., & Scruggs, T. E. (1995). Reasoning and remembering: Coaching students with learning disabilities to think. *Journal of Special Education, 29,* 310–322.

Sulsky, L. M., & Day, D. V. (1994). Effects of frame-of-reference training on rater accuracy under alternative time and delays. *Journal of Applied Psychology, 79,* 515–543.

Sundberg, N. D. (1955). The acceptability of "fake" versus "bona fide" personality test interpretations. *Journal of Abnormal and Social Psychology, 50,* 145–147.

Sundberg, N. D. (1977). *Assessment of persons.* Upper Saddle River, NJ: Prentice Hall.

Super, D. E. (1973). The Work Values Inventory. In D. G. Zytowski (Ed.), *Contemporary approaches to interest measurement.* Minneapolis: University of Minnesota Press.

Super, D. E., & Bohn, M. J., Jr. (1970). *Occupational psychology.* Belmont, CA: Wadsworth.

Super, D. E., & Crites, J. O. (1962). *Appraising vocational fitness.* New York: Harper & Row.

Supple, A. J., Aquilino, W. S., & Wright, D. L. (1999). Collecting sensitive self-report data with laptop computers: Impact on the response tendencies of adolescents in a home interview. *Journal of Research on Adolescence, 9,* 467–488.

Swartz, J. D. (1992). The HIT and HIT 25: Comments and clarifications. *Journal of Personality Assessment, 58,* 432–433.

Swinton, S. S., & Powers, D. E. (1985). *The impact of self-study on GRE test performance* (Res. Rep. 85–12). Princeton, NJ: Educational Testing Service.

Tarasoff v. *Regents of University of California,* 17 Cal. 3d 425 (1983).

Taylor, H. C., & Russell, J. T. (1939). The relationship of validity coefficients to the practical effectiveness of tests in selection: Discussion and tables. *Journal of Applied Psychology, 23,* 565–578.

Taylor, J. A. (1953). A personality scale of manifest anxiety. *Journal of Abnormal and Social Psychology, 48,* 285–290.

Teeter, P. A. (1985). Review of Adjective Check List. *Ninth Mental Measurements Yearbook,* 50–52.

Terman, L. M., & Merrill, M. A. (1937). *Measuring intelligence.* Boston: Houghton Mifflin.

Terman, L. M., & Merrill, M. A. (1973). *Stanford–Binet Intelligence Scale: 1972 norms edition.* Boston: Houghton Mifflin.

Terman, L. M., & Oden, M. H. (1959). *The gifted group at midlife. Genetic studies of genius. V.* Stanford, CA: Stanford University Press.

Thissen, D., Nelson, L., Rosa, K., & McLeod, L. D. (2001). Item response theory for items scored in more than two categories. In D. Thissen & H. Wainer (Eds.), *Test scoring* (pp. 141–186). Mahwah, NJ: Erlbaum.

Thomas, G. E., Alexander, K. L., & Eckland, B. K. (1979). Access to higher education: The importance of race, sex, social class, and academic credentials. *School Review, 87,* 133–156.

Thomas, R. G. (1985). Review of Jackson Vocational Interest Survey. *Ninth Mental Measurements Yearbook,* 740–742.

Thompson, C. (1949). The Thompson modification of the Thematic Apperception Test. *Journal of Projective Techniques, 13,* 469–478.

Thoreson, C. E., & Mahoney, M. J. (1974). *Behavioral self-control.* New York: Holt, Rinehart & Winston.

Thorndike, E. L. (1912). The permanence of interests and their relation to abilities. *Popular Science Monthly, 81,* 449–456.

Thorndike, R. L. (1971). Concepts of culture-fairness. *Journal of Educational Measurement, 8,* 63–70.

Thorndike, R. L., Hagen, E. P., & Sattler, J. P. (1986). *The Stanford–Binet Intelligence Scale: Fourth Edition, Technical manual.* Chicago: Riverside Publishing Co.

Tinsley, H. E. A. (2000). The congruence myth: An analysis of the efficacy of the person–environment fit model. *Journal of Vocational Behavior, 56,* 147–179.

Tittle, C. K. (1984). Test bias. In T. N. Husén & T. Postlethwaite (Eds.), *International encyclopedia of education* (pp. 5199–5204). New York: Wiley.

Tokar, D. M., & Fischer, A. R. (1998). More of RIASEC and five-factor model of personality: Direct assessment of Prediger's (1982) and Hogan's (1983) dimensions. *Journal of Vocational Behavior, 56,* 246–255.

Tokar, D. M., & Swanson, J. L. (1995). Evaluation of the correspondence between Holland's vocational personality typology and the Five Factor model of personality. *Journal of Vocational Behavior, 46,* 89–108.

Tombari, M., & Borich, G. (1999). *Authentic assessment in the classroom: Applications and practice.* Upper Saddle River, NJ: Prentice Hall.

Torrance, E. P. (1988). The nature of creativity as manifest in its testing. In R. J. Sternberg (Ed.), *The nature of creativity: Contemporary psychological perspectives.* New York: Cambridge University Press.

Trull, T. J., Widiger, T. A., Useda, J. D., Holcomb, J., Doan, B.-T., Axelrod, S. R., Stern, B. L., & Gershuny, B. S. (1998). A structured interview for the assessment of the five-factor model of personality. *Psychological Assessment, 10,* 229–240.

Tuddenham, R. D., Blumenkrantz, J., & Wilkin, W. R. (1968). Age changes in AGCT: A longitudinal study of average adults. *Journal of Counseling & Clinical Psychology, 32,* 659–663.

Tulsky, D., Zhu, J., & Ledbetter, M. (1997). *WAIS-III, WMS-III technical manual.* San Antonio, TX: Psychological Corporation.

Turner, S. M., DeMers, S. T., Fox, H. R., & Reed, G. M. (2001). APA's guidelines for test user qualifications. *American Psychologist, 56,* 1099–1113.

Udai, P. (1995). Life-Orientation Inventory. In J. W. Pfeiffer (Ed.), *The 1995 annual: Vol. I, Training* (pp. 141–152). San Diego: Pfeiffer & Co.

Underwood, B., & Moore, B. S. (1981). Sources of behavioral consistency. *Journal of Personality and Social Psychology, 40,* 780–785.

United States v. *City of Buffalo,* 37 U.S. 628 (W.D.N.Y. 1985).

United States v. *Georgia Power Company,* 5 FEP 587 (1973).

U.S. Department of Defense. (September, 1995). *ASVAB 18/19 Counselor Manual: The ASVAB career exploration program.* North Chicago, IL: HQ USMEP-COM/MOP-TA.

U.S. Department of Defense. (December, 1999). *Technical manual for the ASVAB 18/19 career exploration program.* North Chicago, IL: HQ USMEPCOM.

U.S. Department of Education. (2001). *Twenty-third Annual Report to Congress on the Implementation of the Individuals with Disabilities Education Act.* Washington, DC: Author.

U.S. Department of Education, Office for Civil Rights. (July 22, 1997). *1994 elementary and secondary school civil rights compliance report: Projected values for the nation.* Unpublished table.

U.S. Department of Labor, Employment and Training Administration, U.S. Employment Service. (1991, 1993). *Dictionary of occupational titles, 4th ed.* Washington, DC: Author.

U.S. Equal Employment Opportunity Commission (1973, Aug. 23). *The uniform guidelines of employee selection procedures.* Discussion draft. Washington, DC: Author.

U.S. Equal Employment Opportunity Commission. (1994). *Enforcement guidance: Preemployment disability-related inquiries and medical examinations under the Americans with Disabilities Act* (Notice Number 915.002). Washington, DC: Author.

U.S. Equal Employment Opportunity Commission, Civil Service Commission, Department of Labor, and Department of Justice. (1978). *Uniform guidelines on employee selection procedures.* 29 C.F.R. 1607.

Utz, P., & Korben, D. (1976). The construct validity of the occupational themes on the Strong–Campbell Inventory. *Journal of Vocational Behavior, 9,* 31–42.

Vernon, P. E. (1960). *The structure of human abilities* (rev. ed.). London: Methuen.

Vernon, P. E. (1979). Intelligence testing and the nature/nurture debate, 1928–1978: What next? *British Journal of Educational Psychology, 49,* 1–14.

Vernon, P. E. (1985). Intelligence: Heredity–environment determinants. In T. Husén & T. N. Posthlethwaite (Eds.), *The international encyclopedia of education* (Vol. 5, pp. 2605–2611). New York: Wiley.

Vispoel, W. P. (1999). Creating computerized adaptive tests of music aptitude: Problems, solutions, and future directions. In F. Drasgow & J. B. Olson-Buchanan (Eds.), *Innovations in computerized assessment* (pp. 151–176). Mahwah, NJ: Erlbaum.

Voress, J. K., & Maddox, T. (1998). *Developmental Assessment of Young Children: Examiner's manual.* Austin, TX: PRO-ED.

Wagner, M. E., Schubert, H. J., & Schubert, D. S. (1985). Family size effects: A review. *Journal of Genetic Psychology, 146,* 65–78.

Wainer, H. (Ed.). (2000). *Computerized adaptive testing: A primer.* Mahwah, NJ: Erlbaum.

Wallach, M. A., & Kogan, N. (1965). *Modes of thinking in young children.* New York: Holt, Rinehart & Winston.

Waller, N. G. (1998a). Review of the Beck Anxiety Inventory. *Thirteenth Mental Measurements Yearbook,* 98–100.

Waller, N. G. (1998b). Review of the Beck Depression Inventory. *Thirteenth Mental Measurements Yearbook,* 120–121.

Waller, N. G., Lykken, D. T., & Tellegen, A. (1995). Occupational interests, leisure time interests, and personality: Three domains or one? Findings from the Minnesota Twin Registry. In D. J. Lubinski & R. V. Dawis (Eds.), *Assessing individual differences in human behavior: New concepts, methods, and findings* (pp. 233–259). Palo Alto, CA: Davies-Black Publishing/Consulting Psychologists Press.

Wallston, K. A., & Wallston, B. S. (1981). Health locus of control scales. In H. M. Lefcourt (Ed.), *Research with the locus of control construct* (Vol. 1, pp. 189–243). New York: Academic Press.

Wang, E. W., Rogers, R., Giles, C. L., Diamond, P. M., Herrington-Wang, L. E., & Taylor, E. R. (1997). A pilot study of the Personality Assessment Inventory (PAI) in corrections: Assessment of malingering, suicide risk, and aggression in male inmates. *Behavioral Sciences & the Law, 15,* 469–482.

Wards Cove Packing Company v. Antonio et al., 490, U.S. 642 (1989).

Warnath, G. F. (1975). Vocational theories: Direction to nowhere. *Personnel and Guidance Journal, 53,* 422–428.

Washington v. *Davis,* 426 U.S. 229, 12 FEP 1415 (1976).

Watkins, C. E., Jr., Campbell, V. L., & Nieberding, R. (1994). The practice of vocational assessment by counseling psychologists. *Counseling Psychologist, 22,* 115–128.

Watkins, C. E., Jr., Campbell, V. L., Nieberding, R., & Hallmark, R. (1995). Contemporary practice of psychological assessment by clinical psychologists. *Professional Psychology: Research and Practice, 26,* 54–60.

Watson v. *Fort Worth Bank and Trust,* 487 U.S. 977, 108 S. Ct. 277 (1988).

Webb, J. T., & Meckstroth, B. (1982). *Guiding the gifted child.* Columbus: Ohio Psychology Publishing Co.

Wechsler, D. (1939). *The measurement of male intelligence.* Baltimore: Williams & Wilkins.

Wechsler, D. (1955). *Manual for the Wechsler Adult Intelligence Scale.* New York: Psychological Corporation.

Wechsler, D. (1981). Manual for the Wechsler Adult Intelligence Scale—Revised. San Antonio, TX: Psychological Corporation.

Wechsler, D. (1997). *WAIS-III administration and scoring manual* (3rd ed.). San Antonio, TX: Psychological Corporation.

Wechsler, D. (2002). *WPPSI-III: Administration and scoring manual.* San Antonio, TX: Psychological Corporation.

Wechsler, D. (2003). *Wechsler Intelligence Scale for Children-Fourth Edition: Administration and scoring manual.* San Antonio, TX: Psychological Corporation.

Wechsler, D., Kaplan, E., Fein, D., Kramer, J., Morris, R., Delis, D., & Maerlender, A. (2004). *Wechsler Intelligence Scale for Children—Fourth Edition—Integrated.* San Antonio, TX: Psychological Corporation.

Weinberg, R. A. (1989). Intelligence and IQ: Landmark issues and great debates. *American Psychologist, 44,* 98–104.

Westen, D., & Rosenthal, R. (2003). Quantifying construct validity: Two simple measures. *Journal of Personality and Social Psychology, 84,* 608–618.

Weston, D. (1998). The scientific legacy of Sigmund Freud: Toward a psychodynamically informed psychological science. *Psychological Bulletin, 124,* 333–371.

Weston, D., & Weinberger, J. (2004). When clinical description becomes statistical prediction. *American Psychologist, 59,* 595–613.

Wewers, M. E., & Lowe, N. K. (1990). A critical review of visual analogue scales in the measurement of clinical phenomena. *Research in Nursing & Health, 13,* 227–236.

Wexley, K. N., & Klimoski, R. (1984). Performance appraisal: An update. In K. M. Rowland & G. R. Ferris (Eds.), *Research in personnel and human resources management* (Vol. 2, pp. 35–79). Greenwich, CT: JAI Press.

White, L. J. (1996). Review of the Personality Assessment Inventory: A new psychological test for clinical and forensic assessment. *Australian Psychologist, 31,* 38–40.

White, N., & Cunningham, W. R. (1988). Is terminal drop pervasive or specific? *Journal of Gerontology: Psychological Sciences, 43,* P141–P144.

Whyte, W. H., Jr. (1956). *The organization man.* Garden City, NY: Doubleday.

Wiederhold, B. K., & Wiederhold, M. D. (2005). *Virtual reality treatment for anxiety disorders.* Washington, DC: American Psychological Association.

Wiersma, U., & Latham, G. P. (1986). The practicality of behavioral observation scales, behavior expectation scales, and trait scales. *Personnel Psychology, 39,* 619–628.

Wiesner, W., & Cronshaw, S. (1988). A meta-analytic investigation of impact of interview format and the degree of structure on the validity of the employment interview. *Journal of Occupational Psychology, 67,* 189–205.

Wiggins, J. S., & Trapnell, P. D. (1997). Personality structure: The return of the big five. R Hogan, J. Johnson, & S. Briggs (Eds.), *Handbook of personality psychology* (pp. 737–766). San Diego: Academic Press.

Wiggins, N., & Kohen, E. S. (1971). Man versus model of man revisited: The forecasting of graduate school success. *Journal of Personality and Social Psychology, 19,* 100–106.

Wilbur, P. H. (1970). Positional response set among high school students on multiple-choice tests. *Journal of Educational Measurement, 7,* 161–163.

Wildman, R., et al. (1980). *The Georgia Court Competency Test: An attempt to develop a rapid, quantitative measure of fitness for trial.* Unpublished manuscript, Forensic Services Division, Center State Hospital, Milledgeville, GA.

Williams, W. M., & Ceci, S. J. (1997). Are Americans becoming more or less alike? Trends in race, class, and ability differences in intelligence. *American Psychologist, 52,* 1226–1235.

Willis, S. L. (1990). Introduction to the special section on cognitive training in later adulthood. *Developmental Psychology, 26,* 875–878.

Willson, V. L. (1982). Maximizing reliability in multiple-choice questions. *Educational & Psychological Measurement, 42,* 69–72.

Wilson, R. S. (1983). The Louisville Twin Study: Developmental synchronies in behavior. *Child Development, 54,* 298–316.

Winner, E. (1996). *Gifted children: Myths and realities.* New York: Basic Books.

Winner, E. (2000). The origins and ends of giftedness. *American Psychologist, 55,* 159–169.

Wissler, C. (1901). The correlation of mental and physical tests. *Psychological Review,* Monograph Supplement 3(6).

Witelson, S. F., Glezer, I. I., & Kigar, D. L. (1995). Women have greater density of neurons in posterior temporal cortex. *Journal of Neuroscience, 15,* 3418–3428.

Wober, M. (1974). Towards an understanding of the Uganda concept of intelligence. In J. W. Berry & P. R. Dasen (Eds.), *Culture and cognition: Readings in cross-cultural psychology.* London: Methuen.

Wolff, W. T., & Merrens, M. R. (1974). Behavioral assessment: A review of clinical methods. *Journal of Personality Assessment, 38,* 3–16.

Wolins, L., & Dickinson, T. T. (1973). Transformations to improve reliability and/or validity for affective scales. *Educational & Psychological Measurement, 33,* 711–713.

Wolk, R., & Wolk, R. (1971). *The Gerontological Apperception Test.* New York: Behavioral Publications.

Woodcock, R. W. (1998). Extending Gf–Gc theory into practice. In J. J. McArdle & R. W. Woodcock (Eds.), *Human cognitive abilities in theory and practice* (pp. 137–156). Mahwah, NJ: Erlbaum.

Woodcock, R. W., McGrew, K. S., & Mather, N. (2001). *Woodcock Johnson-III Test of Achievement.* Itasca, IL: Riverside Publishing.

World Health Organization. (1992). *International statistical classification of diseases and related health problems* (10th revision, ICD-10). Geneva: Author.

Wrightsman, L. S. (1994). *Adult personality development. Vol. 1. Theories and concepts.* Thousand Oaks, CA: Sage.

Yang, S.-Y., & Sternberg, R. J. (1997). Taiwanese Chinese people's conceptions of intelligence. *Intelligence, 25,* 21–36.

Yerkes, R. M. (Ed.). (1921). Psychological examining in the United States army. *Memoirs of the National Academy of Sciences,* Vol. 15.

Zarske, J. A. (1985). Review of Adjective Check List. *Ninth Mental Measurements Yearbook,* 52–53.

Zimbardo, P. G., Butler, L. D., & Wolfe, V. A. (2002). Teaching testing boosts test scores. *Journal of Experimental Education,* 71(2).

Zook, J. (1993). Two agencies start work on national test of college students' analytical skills. *Chronicle of Higher Education, 39*(29), A23.

Zuckerman, M., & Lubin, B. (1985). *Manual for the Multiple Affect Adjective Check List-Revised.* San Diego: EdITS.

Zytowski, D. G. (1976). Predictive validity of the Kuder Occupational Interest Survey: A 12- to 19-year follow-up. *Journal of Counseling Psychology, 23,* 221–233.

AUTHOR INDEX

Page numbers followed by an *n* are references to footnotes.

SUBJECT INDEX

Page numbers followed by an *n* are references to footnotes.

TEST INDEX